11/7/2018

DEAR RANDY,

WHAT A WONDERFUL VISIT AND PRESENTATION. YOUR CAREER HAS CHANGED SCIENCE AND HEALTH. THANK YOU FOR ALL.

George Corcoran

fabulous presentation
Certainly food for thought!

Wonderful to host you!
Cathy Lysack

A History of Wayne State University in Photographs

A History of Wayne State University in Photographs

Second Edition

EVELYN ASCHENBRENNER

WITH A FOREWORD BY M. ROY WILSON

Wayne State University Press
Detroit

ISBN 978-0-8143-4584-9 (jacketed cloth); ISBN 978-0-8143-4595-5 (e-book)

Library of Congress Cataloging Number: 2018941406

Wayne State University Press
Leonard N. Simons Building
4809 Woodward Avenue
Detroit, Michigan 48201–1309

Visit us online at wsupress.wayne.edu

For Thomas Featherstone, who helped with the first book, and has since passed.
Also to M. J. Murakawa, Wayne State photographer, who has since retired.

Contents

Foreword by President M. Roy Wilson

This year, 2018, is the 150th anniversary of Wayne State University's founding as the Detroit Medical College. It can be tempting to ask, "Why should we care?" Two thousand eighteen is just another year, and we continue to serve our mission and strive toward our vision of being a preeminent, public, urban research university. But anniversaries like this—our sesquicentennial—are special. Why? Because they give us something that is hard to get during the normal work week: perspective. The opportunity to pause, and place ourselves in a longer and larger context; to appreciate where we've come from, and the many who came before us; to assess where we stand today, and to envision a brighter future.

We are located in Midtown Detroit. In 1868, there was no such place. In *A Place of Light*, a history of Wayne State written to celebrate its centennial, a passage describes the time and place of our founding:

> that nearer at hand, beyond Canfield Street at the Harper Hospital grounds, something unusual was happening. A lumber-dray stood by the road; as they passed the last patch of woods and the hospital's northerly board fence, the rattle of hammers and zip of hand saws met their ears. . . . A few veterans from Harper's Soldiers' Home stood or sat watching. Otherwise, all was quiet, normal, almost rural. At the hitching-rail on Woodward, in front of the long picket fence, waited a

> couple of doctors' rigs. Neither the farmers nor anyone else could imagine they were witnessing an historic event—that here was the beginning of a medical school destined to endure for a century and become part of a state university.

I read this passage at my inauguration because it allows us to imagine our humble beginnings and understand our awesome responsibility, today, to build upon the legacy of the great men and women who forged this university over the past 150 years. Our founders call to us from the past, driving us to do better. We accept the challenge, even as we honor a history that includes achievements that have changed the world, improved health for millions, and opened wide the door of opportunity for thousands who went on to succeed in countless ways.

It was at Wayne State that the first open heart surgery was performed. It was at Wayne State that AZT was created, giving new hope to millions of AIDS patients. It was at Wayne State that the Braille system for mathematics was created; where the crash dummies were invented; where thousands of ideas, innovations, breakthroughs, cures, and advances that shaped and improved our lives were born. We honor the men and women who were pioneers for a better world, and are forever a part of our history, as we proudly celebrate our first 150 years in the heart of Detroit.

But our time is now, and now is an exciting time for Wayne State University.

- From our founding as the Detroit Medical College we have become a thriving university with thirteen schools and colleges serving more than twenty-seven thousand students.
- We began in Detroit and have *remained* in Detroit—a city that has seen the highest heights and the deepest depths, and now is reinventing the great American city.
- We continue to uphold our heritage as a university of opportunity and access, where students from a wide range of socioeconomic backgrounds and educational preparation have a chance to receive an excellent education.
- Our campus models our values of diversity and inclusion, and includes a tapestry of races, cultures, creeds, and views.
- We continue to make great strides in meeting the goals of our five-year strategic plan. Our enrollment continues to be strong as we welcome increasing numbers of new students every fall. Our overall six-year graduation rate continues to rise rapidly, and our African American graduation rate is more than double what it was just a few years ago. Our Pivotal Moments fund-raising campaign is on track to meet or exceed its $750 million goal. Our research programs are accelerating, with broad impact for the communities we serve.
- As I write, a new eight-hundred-bed facility to accommodate exploding demand for student housing is well under construction on Anthony Wayne Drive. Architects are envisioning plans for a new STEM Innovation Learning Center to restore an aging science building on our campus. The Mike Ilitch School of Business is scheduled to open its doors in 2018, extending our campus into the District Detroit while expanding our academic programs in the business of sports and entertainment. Our new "Warrior Strong" brand campaign is helping us tell our unique stories and unleash our common spirit.

Driving all of this is our mission: to create and advance knowledge, prepare a diverse student body to thrive, and positively impact local and global communities. The words are simple and direct, and may perhaps mask the passion behind our service to this mission. This is what we do. This is why we get up in the morning. This is why we chose our path, and this university, in this city. To ensure every student has an opportunity to succeed and make their unique mark on the world. To give every scholar the chance to be the next great pioneer in their chosen field. To continue to be an anchor institution in this city, rising to the challenges faced by urban centers around the world—from health disparities to clean water—and seizing the opportunities unique to our time and place.

We all have choices in our lives—where to live, what career to pursue, which causes to support or injustices to oppose. My choice to join Wayne State University is one for which I am profoundly grateful. I have the privilege to serve as president during this momentous era, but the greater privilege is to be part of a community that daily demonstrates a passion for learning and a compassion for others, whether students on campus or citizens on the street. A community that sees our cultural values—integrity, excellence, collaboration, innovation, diversity, and inclusion—as more than words on paper but ideals for which we constantly strive and that are keys to achieving our vision. A community that holds each other accountable and lends a helping hand to a stranger.

We owe a debt to our past, and we pay that debt as we honor the accomplishments of the past. We also owe a debt to the future: to people who are not yet born but will benefit from what we do today; people who will hold Wayne State's bicentennial in 2068 and look back at all we faced and all we accomplished; people who will write the history that we live today and benefit from the legacy we leave. We will not disappoint them.

But we cannot live in the future. Our greatest responsibility is to today. To the mission and people we serve, the vision that guides us, and the community we share. What we do in the present honors both the past and the future. This is our time. Our moment. Let us seize our opportunity with pride and determination.

Foreword by Bill McGraw

My first day at Wayne State University was October 1, 1969. I can pinpoint the date because I got off the crosstown bus from the East Side and picked up a *South End* in front of its office at Cass and Warren.

I'll never forget the cover story. It was a vivid exposé of a Detroit meat store by a summer employee, Wayne student Gary Reder. The headline was a crude play on words, and the text was surrounded by photos of sausage links. "I saw greedy, pitiful men making their livings by cheating the poor, taking their money and giving them, in return, rotten garbage in plastic bags," wrote Reder.

Before sitting down for my first class, my consciousness had been raised by this report of an insidious "machine," as Reder called it, that poisoned and exploited inner-city residents. Reading the student newspaper that morning turned out to be the first of many encounters—intellectual and otherwise—I would experience over the next forty years of contact with Wayne State.

WSU is where I worked my first full-time job, ate my first bagel, met my first communist, rented my first apartment, received my first parking ticket, found my first dead body, and got my first chance to see Iggy and the Stooges. It is also where I first heard someone get passionate about the green light at the end of the dock in *The Great Gatsby*, where I was asked to think about what it means to be an American, where I came to understand the meticulous planning involved in the murder of six million people, and where I heard professors and students raise the issue of an urban university:

Is it a place to seek knowledge, a place that mass-produces middle managers, or both?

Mine is only one of hundreds of thousands of personal histories going back to the founding of Wayne in the nineteenth century. Imagine the range of stories that exist concerning WSU and the quest for enlightenment, the search for a parking space, and the never-ending struggle with a bureaucracy that can be as clunky in the twenty-first century as it was in the twentieth.

When I was eighteen and walking down Cass for the first time, Wayne State looked like a sort of Emerald City for young people, nestled in the middle of the big, buzzing city. The sidewalks were jammed, and the campus was both funky and fantastic, with a skyline that included one building that looked like a wedding cake, another like upside-down toy blocks, and yet another like an IBM punch card. Surrounding them were old brick homes, World War I–era apartments, and the remarkable 1890s high school called Old Main.

I came to love Wayne's Cass Avenue neighbor, the Detroit Public Library, but it was quickly apparent that the campus was also a borderland where the academic world bumped up against beaten-down neighborhoods filled with struggling people. That was especially true to the south in the once-crowded Cass Corridor, where junkies, prostitutes, and burning buildings offered a vivid counterpoint to classroom readings and discussions.

Looming to the north were the opulent Fisher Building, its glowing orange tower a symbol of Detroit's golden age four decades earlier, and the mighty stone fortress that was headquarters to General Motors, the most powerful corporation in the world.

No matter where you came from in metro Detroit, the Wayne State neighborhood didn't seem like your neighborhood. The campus has always been an exception to the region's social segregation, and on any visit over the past forty years you've been likely to encounter people speaking Arabic, Chinese, and Spanish; people wearing African clothes; young men in yarmulkes; retired people taking classes; and single moms who bring their children to school with them.

From my first day to the present day, classes were filled with students who were different from me in age and background. By the end of my freshman year I had met a Finnish grad student who wore an elaborate costume in a New Orleans Mardi Gras parade, a Jewish dope dealer from Miami, a member of the Parking Lot Yippies, a black Detroiter who worshiped—and kind of looked like—Jimi Hendrix, a half-mad street poet who roamed the campus hawking his poems, third-generation Irish kids from St. Mary's of Redford parish in northwest Detroit, and an Iranian who once asked me to explain Groundhog Day. He never got it.

Then there were the professors. Once inside the classroom, I was rarely disappointed, and I was frequently amazed. Prominent in my memory are three teachers who are long gone from WSU: a nerdy and passionate social science instructor named Marty Slobin, who got first-year students to think about the people who rule America; David Riddle, a truck driver-turned-PhD who spiced his modern American history lectures with videos of *The Honeymooners* and tapes of blues and jazz; and Chris Johnson, a French history prof with a long reading list who crammed his lectures with big ideas on subjects ranging from prisons to art.

Wayne also served as my learning lab in a different way. In 1972, I began working as a parking security guard, whose one duty was repairing the wooden gate arms broken off by the cars of frustrated students. It was my first real job, and it introduced me to the adult world of drinking blackberry brandy with your morning coffee, goofing off, and stealing quarters, which is one of the reasons Wayne eventually shifted to a cashless system for its structures and lots.

We were supervised by Public Safety, the former name of the WSU Police, and that association gave me a rare civilian's glimpse into law and order in inner-city Detroit. I saw the cops dealing with a rape victim, entering an apartment building after reports of gunfire, and transporting a student who had gone into labor.

One night I came upon a dusty Mustang that had been sitting for thirty days inside the parking structure at Cass and Palmer. In the driver's seat was the body of a male student. He had committed suicide by swallowing a bottle of prescription pills and had fallen into eternal sleep listening to radio station CKLW, the leading pop-music station of the era, whose sensational newscasts would include news of his death.

Those memories sprang to mind, of course, in preparing this foreword. I went to campus one day to research old editions of *South End* and spent a pleasant morning amid the visiting scholars and document boxes at the Walter Reuther Library. Then I walked through the malls to my car, which was parked near Old Main.

I stopped in the campus bookstore. In the lobby, a sad-looking man asked for money. "No disrespect," he said, "but I haven't eaten in two days."

Detroit is an increasingly troubled town, but Wayne State soldiers on, a bulwark of stability. It now has high-rise dorms, lush landscaping, and a new name for the football team. GM has moved, and it fights for survival. The Cass Corridor is called Midtown and is filled with renovated buildings.

When I stepped off the crosstown bus in October 1969, I had no idea that I would remain so attached to Wayne State. The university is far from perfect, but it remains a tremendously appealing place where the ivory tower meets the real world. Forty years later, I still feel energized every time I find myself around Cass and Warren.

Preface and Acknowledgments

A few months before graduating from Wayne State University, I became interested in Wayne State's history. I had been writing articles for the *South End* that required historical research, but all my trips to the Reuther Library failed to turn up a single recent book about Wayne. I did find the extremely well-researched book *A Place of Light* by Leslie Hanawalt, but it had been published during the university's centennial year, 1968.

My curiosity was piqued. When I looked around the campus, I saw former homes mixed in with modern university buildings and wondered how the campus had evolved. The past thirty years have been pivotal ones for Detroit—what had happened to Wayne State during that time? And most importantly, I wanted to know how a proudly working-class city had nurtured a research university.

This book has been years in the making. My first memories of Wayne predate my years as a student there. I remember being very young and accompanying my mom as she worked on her dissertation at Wayne State. One time in particular, I recall going to the Engineering Library and looking for four-leaf clovers with my brother in the grass along Warren Avenue.

Years later, one of the first things I did before beginning work on this book was to buy *A Place of Light*. As it was out of print, I had to purchase a used copy. When I opened it, I found the previous owner had pressed a four-leaf clover between the pages of the book.

This new edition of the book is dedicated, first and foremost, to two people. Without the late Thomas Featherstone's encouragement, support, and vast knowledge of the Reuther Library's collections, this book would not have been possible. Also, I would like to thank Mary Jane Murakawa, retired photographer for Wayne State University. Her extensive knowledge of the campus and its buildings was invaluable for both editions of the book.

For this edition of the book, I would like to thank Dave Whitman, of the Smith Group, for his help in locating images; and Derek Veerkamp, of Corvias, for his assistance in locating renderings.

There are a number of people who made the first edition of the book possible. First, I would like to thank Mike Smith, then director of the Walter Reuther Library, for his constant support of this project, especially in its initial stages; and Kathryn Wildfong, at Wayne State University Press, for her commitment to and faith in this project.

I would also like to thank Brecque Keith, then university archivist at the Reuther Library, for her enthusiasm and assistance regarding all things Wayne State; and Elizabeth Clemens and Mary Wallace, staff at the Reuther, for their assistance.

In addition, I would like to thank Dawn Eurich and David Poremba, of the Burton Historical Collection at the Detroit Public Library, for helping me locate photographs for this book; Leni Sinclair, for contributing photographs from her personal collection; Cara Cherry, from Yamasaki Associates; Charlotte Massey, photo technology specialist at the *Detroit News*; Ted Grevstad-Nordbrock, of the Michigan State Historic Preservation Office; historian Charles K. Hyde, for reviewing the captions and offering suggestions, and for his advice and enthusiasm regarding this project; and the staff at Studio One, Design Plus, and Ghafari Associates.

Finally, I would like to thank my parents, Tom Erwood and Lisa Anneberg.

Any mistakes or omissions that may be found in this book are my responsibility alone.

A History of Wayne State University in Photographs

INTRODUCTION

A BRIEF HISTORY OF WAYNE STATE UNIVERSITY

Charles K. Hyde

Foundations, 1868–1934

The university in Midtown Detroit, Michigan—variously known as Wayne State University or Wayne State or simply Wayne—has a complex history, one that evolved from the multiple strands of its ancestry. The institution achieved state-university status in April 1956 by means of Public Act 183; and in 1959, by means of a statewide referendum vote, it achieved the same constitutional status as both the University of Michigan and Michigan State University. Since then, it has remained one of three major institutions of higher education in Michigan and the only one distinctly urban in location and character. Wayne State University's origins, however, extend much further back in time.

What is now Wayne State University began as Wayne University, the creation of which began in 1927. Its birth, both remarkable and difficult, was the result of hard work by visionaries within the Detroit school system combined with the cooperation of faculty at various city colleges. In spite of these positive forces, the process was nevertheless delayed by political bickering. Frank Cody, superintendent of Detroit public schools from 1919 to 1942, was the key visionary. He had little formal training and no college degree, but he had advanced from village schoolteacher to superintendent of Detroit schools. Cody firmly believed that municipal colleges could provide quality higher education to working-class students. To this end, in mid-1927, Superintendent Cody decided to unite the various city colleges into a single entity. Funding for the institution would come entirely from the Detroit Board of Education, which already funded the separate city colleges through property taxes.

Cody hired Wilford L. Coffey as dean of the College of the City of Detroit in February 1928 to coordinate the consolidation. Coffey's career had included teaching in outstate school districts and serving in various positions with Michigan's Department of Public Instruction in Lansing from 1915 through 1927. In September 1930, Coffey and Cody took the first step in the consolidation by placing the Detroit Teachers College (DTC) under the jurisdiction of the dean of the College of the City of Detroit. Shortly thereafter, however, under pressure from DTC faculty, the Board of Education reestablished autonomy for the Detroit Teachers College, naming Waldo Lessinger acting dean in March 1931 and permanent dean six months later. This action marked the beginning of a two-year war between Coffey and Lessinger over the DTC's autonomy. Faculty at the DTC feared that they would face cuts in their enrollments and budget, interference in hiring, and the loss of control over their curriculum if they lost their status as an independent college. Cody feared that a large, independent DTC would dominate the municipal university that he planned to create. The strong personal ambitions of both Coffey and Lessinger also played a role in this dispute.

The feud between Dean Coffey and Dean Lessinger reached a fever pitch in early 1933. Superintendent Cody ultimately concluded that his dream of consolidating all of the municipally supported colleges could not be fulfilled as long as the public controversy raged over the autonomy of the Teachers College. In Cody's view, Coffey had become a major stumbling block in the project, and Cody withdrew his support from his former ally. As a result, Coffey resigned in May 1933. Coffey's departure freed Cody to advance his plans, which now included an independent College of Education.

Faculty members within the College of the City of Detroit (known informally as City College) were also instrumental in the consolidation process. During a series of meetings that began in September 1932, they produced a set of Articles of Cooperation articulating and specifying faculty governance and administrative structures for the new colleges. On April 12, 1933, the faculty formally adopted these articles, which would later become the Constitution of the College of Liberal Arts. The Articles of Cooperation protected faculty rights and privileges by defining the relationship between faculty, academic departments, deans, the superintendent of the Detroit public schools, and the Detroit Board of Education.

In August 1933, the Detroit Board of Education formally united the schools and colleges of medicine, pharmacy, liberal arts, education, and engineering, and called the new entity a university. The oldest component of this new amalgamation, the School of Medicine, had been founded in 1868 as the Detroit Medical College. Acknowledging these roots, Wayne State University's official seal uses 1868 as the birth date of the university. Superintendent Cody was named president of the university, and Deputy Superintendent Charles L. Spain became executive vice president and the operating head.

The next task involved choosing a permanent and distinctive name for the new university. Because the University of Detroit already existed, the Detroit Board of Education ruled out names containing the word *Detroit* in order to avoid confusion. The board considered the name Great Lakes University, until dissenting students argued that cheerleaders would have to yell, "Stick with G-L-U." Other possibilities included Cadillac University, Lewis Cass University, University of the Straits, Mackenzie University, Memorial University, and Wolverine University. Finally, Frank Cody proposed naming the university after General "Mad" Anthony Wayne, and on January 23, 1934, the Board of Education agreed. Anthony Wayne's victory over a large force of Native Americans at the Battle of Fallen Timbers near Toledo, Ohio, in August 1794 led to the British surrender of Fort Detroit to Wayne's troops some two years later. Wayne County, Michigan, which includes Detroit, was named after General Wayne.

The colleges and schools brought together in 1933 to form Wayne University had their own unique histories. The medical school was the oldest unit among them: five doctors had founded the Detroit Medical College in 1868 as a for-profit private enterprise. After a rival institution, the Michigan College of Medicine, began operating in Detroit in 1879, the two colleges competed for the same body of students, and both struggled to survive. In 1885 they merged as the Detroit College of Medicine (DCM) and in 1891 expanded by developing programs to train veterinarians, dentists, and pharmacists.

The DCM lost its American Medical Association (AMA) accreditation in January 1913 because the college had not required its students to have two years of premedical studies before enrolling and because the DCM did not have six full-time salaried faculty members, as new AMA rules required. To upgrade the college and regain its accreditation, the stockholders sold it to a well-heeled group of doctors and alumni led by Dr. Burt R. Shurly. They renamed it the Detroit College of Medicine and Surgery and within a year regained its accreditation from the AMA.

The college, however, continued to struggle because of falling enrollments and internal conflict. The faculty consisted of graduates of both the Detroit College of Medicine and its archrival, the University of Michigan. Further, a new college structure isolated most faculty from the dean. As a result, many alumni became alienated from the college and stopped making contributions. Subsequent operating deficits forced the Detroit Board of Education to take control in February 1918 to save the college. They ran the college successfully as a public institution, and eventually it became a cornerstone of Wayne University.

What is now the College of Education at Wayne State University began as the Detroit Normal Training School. In 1881, Superintendent John M. B. Sill established the normal school to train teachers for the Detroit public school system. Initially, the normal school was open only to unmarried women, reflecting the hiring practices of the school system at large. Married women were not admitted to the normal school until 1917, and only then because the Detroit public school system had agreed to allow them to begin teaching in 1918. Beginning in 1918, the Detroit school system also permitted men to teach, and thus they were also allowed to enroll in the normal school. The school offered a two-year curriculum until 1920, when it became a four-year college with a new name, the Detroit Teachers College. The Teachers College, which would play a key role in the struggle that led to the formation of Wayne University, was housed in the Wales C. Martindale Training School on West Grand Boulevard from 1914 until 1930, when it moved to the old Central High School (the Main Building).

Central High School was the third major component of Wayne University, evolving first into Detroit Junior College and later into the College of the City of Detroit. The Board of Education designed Central High School, which opened in 1896, as an elite secondary school that would serve the upper-middle-class families of Midtown Detroit. The Board of Education had lost Central High School's eminent principal Frederick Bliss in 1899 and had named a political hack as his replacement. During the late 1800s, the board had become highly politicized and had begun replacing professional administrators with political appointees, mostly friends and relatives of board members. When Bliss discovered that he and several other competent administrators were slated to be fired, he quit to become the principal of a private high school.

After five years of mismanagement, board leaders realized the repercussions of such hiring practices and were delighted in 1904 to hire as principal a man named David Mackenzie (1860–1926), who would prove well qualified to lead Central's students and faculty into a bright future. Mackenzie was born in Detroit's Corktown to Scottish parents. He earned a bachelor's and a master's degree from the University of Michigan and then served as superintendent of schools in both Flint and Muskegon, Michigan, before becoming principal of Central, where he served until his death.

Beginning in the fall of 1913, at the request of Dr. Shurly at the Detroit College of Medicine, Mackenzie began to offer a one-year college-level premedical program at Central High School. When enrollment jumped to ninety-six students in the fall of 1916, Mackenzie met with the Detroit Board of Education to propose expanding the program to two years and defining it as a junior college course of study. As a result, in 1917, the state legislature granted the Board of Education the power to establish the Detroit Junior College, the first of its kind in Michigan. David Mackenzie became dean of the new college, an extension of his duties as principal of the high school. In addition to the premedical program, the Detroit Junior College offered a two-year liberal arts and sciences program and adult education courses. Enrollments in the fall of 1917 jumped to 300, and crowding at Central High School became an issue as the junior college students competed with the high school students for space.

Demand for college-level courses continued to increase, and in April 1923 the Michigan legislature transformed the Detroit Junior College into the College of the City of Detroit, a four-year institution. By the fall of 1923, the Central High School building housed 2,800 students during the day and an additional 1,100 in the evening. To relieve overcrowding, the Board of Education built a new high school at Roosevelt Field, some three miles to the northwest. When the new Central High School opened in January 1926, the Board of Education granted the College of the City of Detroit exclusive use of the old building. With the departure of the high school students, Central High School became known as the Main Building until 1950, when it was officially renamed Old Main. Total enrollments in the College of the City of Detroit rose steadily, jumping from 1,905 in 1923 to 6,552 in 1933, the year before Wayne University was created.

At its inception in 1934, Wayne University also included Colleges of Pharmacy and Engineering, while the Law School and the School of Business Administration would enter the fold later during the 1930s. The College of Pharmacy originated at Cass Technical High School as a group of short courses created to prepare students for the state pharmacy exams. In June 1924, the Detroit Board of Education established a College of Pharmacy, part of the College of the City of Detroit, which remained at Cass

Tech for a year before moving to the Central High School building, where it was housed until 1935.

The Department of Engineering began operating within the College of the City of Detroit in 1929 under the direction of chemistry professor Arthur R. Carr. When the department became the College of Engineering in the new Wayne University, it offered degree programs in chemical, mechanical, electrical, civil, and aeronautical engineering.

What would become the Law School at Wayne University began as the Detroit City Law School, established in June 1927 by the Detroit Board of Education at the urging of local attorneys and judges. After years of enduring overcrowded offices and an inadequate law library in the Main Building, the Law School moved to the half-empty Detroit School of Commerce a mile and a half to the south. When the Detroit City Law School received accreditation from the American Bar Association in 1937, it officially joined Wayne University.

The School of Business Administration evolved more slowly than the Law School. Although the College of the City of Detroit offered courses in accounting and advertising beginning in the late 1920s, it did not establish a separate department of business administration until 1938, and the School of Business Administration did not officially come into existence until 1946.

Depression, War, and Postwar Growing Pains, 1934–59

Wayne University's enrollment skyrocketed in the 1930s, and as a result, overcrowded facilities became the defining feature of the young institution. The university offered Depression-era Detroiters the opportunity to earn a college degree at a much lower cost than a residential college at a time when students had few resources. Total enrollment of day and night students for the fall semester increased from 6,552 in 1933 to 11,394 in 1937 and then remained at roughly 12,000 from 1938 through 1941. With the military draft and wartime jobs drawing off Wayne's student population, enrollment fell to a low of 7,236 in the fall of 1943.

Space for classrooms, faculty offices, laboratories, and libraries was at a premium throughout this period. The Main Building could comfortably and safely hold only about 2,500 students at once. In 1934, Wayne University extensively remodeled the Main Building and in 1937 added a three-story wing along Warren Avenue, providing twenty-five new classrooms. To satisfy its seemingly insatiable appetite for space, Wayne University also began buying or leasing buildings, mostly private homes, within walking distance of the Main Building. By the end of 1937, the university owned or rented fifteen additional buildings.

In December 1936, Superintendent Frank Cody established an eighteen-member "blue-ribbon" Citizens' Committee to study the housing needs of Wayne University and to make recommendations for long-term development. In mid-February 1937, the group issued a report recommending that the Board of Education leave Wayne University at the Main Building and that it acquire by eminent domain the three blocks north of Warren Avenue and west of Cass Avenue for campus expansion. The Board of Education distributed sixty thousand copies of the report to build public support. The recommendations of the Citizens' Committee would ultimately define the core of the future campus.

The purchase of the three blocks identified for campus expansion was slowed, however, by a lack of funds, wartime conditions, and lengthy legal proceedings. Property owners on the first block north of Warren fought the city's attempts to condemn their homes until the end of April 1942, when a jury awarded them what they felt was appropriate compensation. The condemnation and purchase of the second block, extending from Putnam Street to Merrick Street, began in 1943 and was completed in 1944. It was not until June 1945 that a jury decision finally awarded the third block to the university. Meanwhile, Wayne continued to rent or buy available houses at reasonable prices. By March 1943, the university rented or owned thirty-one properties in addition to the Main Building.

Wayne University's acquisition of property could not, however, keep up with the surge in enrollment after World War II. The university's prodigious postwar growth was in part driven by the Servicemen's Readjustment Act, more generally known as the G.I. Bill of Rights, passed by Congress in June 1944. Under this law, the federal government paid the direct college expenses (tuition, fees, and books) of former servicemen and servicewomen, as well as providing a generous monthly subsistence allowance. Wayne's fall enrollments jumped from 9,941 students in 1945 to 15,041 in 1946. After increasing again to 17,358 in 1947, enrollment leveled off at roughly 18,000 during the period from 1948 to 1955.

Despite their numbers, veterans never made up a majority of Wayne's student body. They reached their peak share of enrollment (47.3 percent) in the spring term of 1947. The remainder of the student body consisted largely of working-class residents of southeast Michigan, primarily from Detroit and Wayne County. Wayne University was no longer exclusively a city college but had begun admitting students from all over Michigan.

By the time the war ended, it had become apparent that the Detroit Board of Education would no longer be able to fully fund Wayne University and its growing army of students. Starting in 1945, the state legislature took over part of Wayne's operating budget, with Wayne County providing additional financial support.

The end of World War II marked the beginning of an era of greater independence for the growing university. The first two presidents of Wayne, Frank Cody (1933–42) and Warren E. Bow (1942–45), had been superintendents of the Detroit public schools and thereby closely associated with the Detroit Board of Education. The first university president without ties to the Board was David Dodds Henry. In 1935, he came to Wayne as a professor of English. From 1939 to 1945, he served as executive vice president of the university, and following Warren Bow's death in 1945, he became president. His presidency marked a major step toward Wayne University's independence from the Detroit Board of Education. His appointment was a recognition that Wayne University was drawing students and funding from sources beyond Detroit and that its growing size and complexity required university-based leaders.

The sudden increase in enrollment after the war resulted in an endemic shortage of classrooms, office space, laboratories, and library facilities at Wayne that lasted well into the 1950s. During this period, overcrowding reached legendary proportions: students were forced to eat their lunches on the staircases in the Main Building due to the lack of cafeteria space. Wayne University's leaders, especially Arthur Neef, dean of the Law School, were resourceful in finding solutions to overcrowding, although temporary and imperfect ones. At Neef's urging, the Board of Education bought the Webster Hall Hotel at Cass Avenue and Putnam Street in April 1946, converting the upper floors into student housing and the lower floors into a student center. The hotel-turned-dormitory was called the Student Center Building (or, popularly, Webster Hall) until 1961, when it was renamed David Mackenzie Hall.

Neef also arranged for more than 1,100 first-year students in the College of Liberal Arts to attend classes in leased space at Northern High School on Woodward Avenue, several miles north of the main campus, during the 1946–47 academic year. Wayne University also made use of dozens of war surplus "temporary buildings," including Quonset huts, which provided one hundred classrooms and additional offices. Some of these temporary structures remained in use until 1959.

The Michigan legislature funded the first two new buildings constructed exclusively for Wayne University: State Hall, which opened in fall 1948, and Science Hall, which opened a year later. Both buildings were placed well back from the streets on the main campus that ran east-west—Warren, Putnam, and Merrick—to preserve the existing houses on those streets for Wayne's use. Neither State Hall nor Science Hall provided faculty office space, which was not a priority at the time—Wayne needed classrooms and laboratories. A fourth floor with offices was part of the 1957 State Hall addition that extended along Cass Avenue.

As funding became available, the Board of Education pushed for additional buildings. The completion of the Engineering Building (1952), Kresge Science Library (1953), General Library (1953), the Music (1955) and Art buildings (1956)—part of the Community Arts complex—established the core campus. Except for Science Hall, which was designed by the architect Ralph Calder, a single architect, Suren Pilafian, designed all the early buildings. The buildings of the core campus—including the Community Arts Auditorium complex (1959), which contains Alumni House and the president's apartment—share a similar modern appearance. Pilafian served as the chief architectural planner for Wayne University and the Cultural Center, a collection of Detroit's cultural institutions immediately east of Wayne University, which includes the Detroit Public Library, the Detroit Institute of the Arts, the Detroit Historical Museum, and, more recently, the Detroit Science Center and the Museum of African American History.

Wayne University's enrollment stabilized in the mid-1950s, but declining enrollment of veterans and rising operating costs created a constant financial squeeze. The university's budget increased from $10 million for the 1950–51 academic year to $16.5 million for 1955–56, but in the latter year, the Board of Education provided only $8.3 million in operating funds and $1.8 million in capital funds. The need for additional facilities remained critical, but the Board of Education lacked the necessary resources to pay for campus expansion. In 1953, Detroit's voters approved a millage, or property tax, that would support Wayne University through 1959, but the Board of Education would have to face another millage election in 1958 to continue taxpayer support.

With an eye toward a permanent, stable source of funding, Clarence B. Hilberry, president of Wayne University between 1952 and 1965, and Provost Arthur Neef proposed that Wayne become a state university, a designation that would mean funding would come principally from the state. Hilberry and Neef met with Michigan governor G. Mennen Williams in December 1954 and persuaded him to appoint a nonpartisan panel of citizens to study the issue of state control. The resulting thirty-nine-member committee was dubbed the Study Commission on State Support for Wayne University. Alexander Ruthven, president emeritus of the University of Michigan, served as chair. The Ruthven Commission completed its work in December 1955, when it unanimously recommended that Wayne become a state university. The commission proposed a three-year transition period during which the Board of Education would continue its financial support and the state would gradually increase its contribution.

In March and April 1956, the state legislature approved Public Act 183, which granted state-university status to Wayne University, known from that time forward as Wayne State University. Governor Williams signed the bill in late April, near the site of his birthplace on Merrick Avenue, at the center of Wayne's campus. During the three fiscal years ending in 1959, the Board of Education allocated $31.5 million for Wayne University. Additionally, the state provided $3.2 million the first year, $6.5 million the second year, and $9.7 million in 1958–59, effectively giving the university nearly $20 million in funding during the transition.

As a result of this increased funding, the late 1950s saw a second burst of campus construction: the State Hall addition (1957); the Community Arts Auditorium complex (1959); the McGregor Memorial Conference Center (1958), a Minoru Yamasaki design; the Richard Cohn Memorial Building (1959); the Life Science Building (1960); and the College of Education Building, also a distinctive Yamasaki design (1960). Yamasaki (1912–86) also designed the Meyer and Anna Prentis Building and the Helen L. DeRoy Auditorium, both completed in 1964. Yamasaki based his architectural practice in Detroit from 1945 until his death and is best known as the designer of the World Trade Center (1976) in New York City.

Growth and Turmoil, 1960–75

In the mid-1950s, President Clarence Hilberry and Provost Arthur Neef created a university planning office to project Wayne State University's future need for facilities. That office predicted that Wayne's full-time equated enrollment would more than double between 1957 and 1966—from 13,824 to 28,372—and then reach 46,302 in 1973. In order to adequately serve a student body of that size, the planning office warned that the university would have to add 350 classrooms, each capable of holding thirty students.

To help develop a rational strategy for the future growth of the campus, the Board of Governors hired architect Minoru Yamasaki in February 1957 to develop a campus plan. Yamasaki completed his master plan in April 1958, which envisioned a compact urban campus with all streets closed to traffic, buildings limited to four stories, and little open green space. Wayne State carried out only minor aspects of Yamasaki's plan, mainly due to objections to his high-density layout of the campus.

Between 1956 and 1959, the Wayne campus continued to expand to accommodate growing numbers of students, faculty, and staff. During this period, the university purchased 155 properties for a total price of $6 million. In a brief spending spree during the first part of 1961, the university purchased the First Church of Christ, Scientist—which was renamed the Hilberry Theatre—for $225,000 and the Chatsworth Apartments, with the Chatsworth Annex, for $900,000. The Chatsworth Apartments provided housing for students, faculty, and staff, as did the half dozen small apartment houses Wayne purchased between 1959 and 1961 on Merrick Street between Second and Third avenues. In an innovative experiment, the university also arranged for married Wayne State students to occupy an entire high-rise tower in the nearby Jeffries Housing Project from January 1960 until the fall of 1966, when an unfortunate increase in crime against Wayne State students ended the experiment. The dormitory space in the Student

Center Building (Webster Hall) was converted in 1960 to offices for university faculty and administration.

By the early 1960s, the university owned most of the area bounded by the Ford and Lodge expressways, Hancock Street, and Cass Avenue. From June 1961 until the end of 1965, Wayne spent only $256,633 to purchase additional properties, choosing to allocate resources instead for construction of new campus buildings. Yamasaki's 1958 recommendation, to close Second Avenue between Warren and Palmer to vehicular traffic, finally came to pass in 1964, when the city widened Third Avenue (renamed Anthony Wayne Drive in 1967) into a two-way boulevard from Forest to Palmer. This adjustment eliminated automobile traffic from the center of the campus and helped create the atmosphere of a typical college campus.

Construction of new buildings on university property continued into the mid-1960s. The Helen Newberry Joy Residence for Women, built to house nursing students, opened in 1963. The Prentis Building and the Helen L. DeRoy Auditorium opened in 1964. Other substantial academic buildings constructed during this period include the Physics Research Building (1965), Shapero Hall of Pharmacy (1965), and the Law School Building (1966). Wayne State University also completed the first of its many parking structures during the mid-1960s, signature buildings that proclaimed the university's status as a commuter college. The Palmer parking ramp, appropriately named Parking Structure #1, opened for business in 1966.

The physical expansion of the campus before 1960 assumed that Wayne would remain a commuter college, with few students living on campus. Wayne provided little student or faculty housing, no athletic or recreation facilities, and little residential parking. The vision of the future university changed as a result of Section 112 of the Federal Housing Act of 1959, which encouraged cities and universities to participate in urban renewal by providing federal funding for approved projects. Under the act, cities and universities were required to pay only one-third of the cost toward such things as land acquisition and the demolition and clearing of existing buildings, with federal grants paying the remaining two-thirds of the cost of the project. Detroit's director of city planning, Charles A. Blessing, proposed a joint City of Detroit–Wayne State University project in which the city would be named as the grant recipient with the university paying part of the cost required by the Housing Act. In January 1960, Blessing urged President Hilberry to establish a joint city-university planning committee to set in motion the plans for "University City."

University City proposed to renew a total of 302 acres of the city and double the size of the central campus from 90 to 180 acres. The land bounded by the Lodge Freeway on the east, Canfield Street on the south, Trumbull Street on the west, and the Ford Expressway on the north would be used for student housing and recreational facilities. The area between Trumbull and Twelfth Street to the west would include new private housing. University City also called for new public elementary and high schools south of Forest Avenue near the Lodge Freeway. The project as planned would proceed in five stages.

In reality, the University City project moved forward at a glacial pace, largely because three entities—Wayne State University, the City of Detroit, and the federal government—had to coordinate and approve each stage of the plan. The City of Detroit initially requested federal funds for the project in January 1961, but three years passed before the three entities signed a contract—and then for Phase I only. The City of Detroit then took until December 1966, nearly three more years, to acquire the Phase I properties and transfer them to Wayne State.

Starting in late 1965, Wayne State also faced sustained and militant opposition to Phase I of University City from a variety of Detroit political leaders and community groups. Previously, Wayne's expansion into the surrounding neighborhoods had been aided by a combination of court-ordered property condemnations and voluntary sales by owners. While some property owners complained about the prices they received, no widespread, organized opposition to Wayne's expansion had emerged. During the implementation of Phase I of the University City plan, the university's luck changed drastically. Residents of the communities immediately to the west and south of the campus, the area that would be affected by Phase I, viewed representatives of the university as arrogant, insensitive, and racist. The university's relations with its neighbors reached a low point during the presidency of William Rea Keast (1965–71) and improved only marginally during the administration of George E. Gullen Jr. (1971–78).

Specifically, critics of University City argued that the Phase I area was not, as the university portrayed it, a slum full of substandard housing but merely a neighborhood whose residents happened to be predominantly African American. They also argued that the plan did not provide those displaced by Phase I with comparable housing. University officials struggled to justify Wayne State's taking this land and displacing thousands of residents to build athletic fields and recreational facilities.

The most effective opposition to University City came from the West Central Organization (WCO), a grassroots coalition of churches, block clubs, and school groups, founded in June 1965 by social activist clergy. The WCO challenged the practices of the Federal Urban Renewal Administration, part of the Department of Housing and Urban Development (HUD) created by President Lyndon Johnson on September 9, 1965. They publicly confronted Wayne State University, the Detroit Common Council, and Mayor Jerome Cavanagh over the rationale and fairness of the urban renewal plans. They demanded that Phase I include low-income housing for those displaced. Their opposition, however, did not stop Wayne State from completing Phase I as planned. The Frederick C. Matthaei Physical Education and Recreation Building opened in 1967, with a handball and squash court added a year later. The football stadium, with bleachers, practice fields, a baseball diamond, outdoor track, and tennis courts, opened in 1968.

While the WCO could not stop Phase I of University City, they and other community activists modified and ultimately killed University City Phase II, which targeted the lands between Warren Avenue and Canfield Street from Trumbull Street to Woodward Avenue. Wayne State would have used most of this land for faculty housing and academic buildings. However, the Detroit Common Council, fueled by public sentiment, reexamined Phase II and in July 1966 approved a revised plan that significantly reduced the size of the project. The Common Council again revised Phase II in October 1967, but the City of Detroit and HUD did not sign a contract for Phase II until June 1969.

The WCO continued to protest Phase II but was itself nearly destroyed in late 1966 when the Citizens' Sponsor Committee, a consortium of local churches financially supporting the WCO, sharply cut its support. The WCO's paid staff was forced to resign, and the organization nearly disappeared. A new community action group, People Concerned About Urban Renewal (PCAUR), emerged in September 1969 and demanded an immediate stop to all work on Phase II of University City.

Wayne State's urban renewal plans were also the subject of highly critical stories in the *Detroit Free Press*, and state senator Coleman A. Young, who represented the Detroit area, held hearings in May 1970 to consider complaints about the Wayne State project. As a result, in an interview published in the *Free Press* in January 1971, George E. Gullen Jr., Wayne State vice president for university relations, announced that the university would not take any additional land for campus expansion. By the mid-1970s, Wayne State had abandoned even its scaled-down plans for University City Phase II, but the damage had already been done to the university's reputation in the neighborhoods adjacent to campus and in the wider Detroit community.

Restricted to the core campus area, the building program nevertheless continued into the late 1960s and early 1970s. In addition to the various athletic facilities completed in 1968 and 1969, Wayne opened two major academic buildings around the same time: University Center (the new student center) in 1969 and the Chemistry Building/Science Library complex in 1970. That year also saw the completion of the Speech and Languages Building (renamed Alex Manoogian Hall in 1975) and the General Lectures Building. Campus construction continued with the Law Library (1971) and Parking Structure #2 (1972). The Walter P. Reuther Library opened in 1975, along with the University Bookstore. With proposed University City lands unavailable for student housing, Wayne State instead built—on existing university property—the Helen L. DeRoy Apartments (1974) on Anthony Wayne Drive and the Forest Apartments (1976) on Forest Street. The DeRoy Apartments housed graduate students, while the Forest Apartments housed undergraduates.

While Detroit residents were protesting University City during the late 1960s and early 1970s, Wayne State students, much like students attending other American universities, became involved in various strains of activism, particularly Vietnam War protests. In mid-October 1965, Wayne State held a student debate on the Vietnam War and the draft, but it was cut short by fights between students. The Detroit riots of July 1967, which reached the edge of campus, also affected the university. Classes were canceled for three days, but more important, the riots increased community resistance to the university's urban renewal projects.

Wayne students participated in major peace marches and demonstrations on Woodward Avenue on October 15, 1967, and in Washington, D.C., on October 21, 1967. Another major antiwar protest on campus followed in October 1969, with teach-ins and other protests that continued into 1970. President William Keast, often under pressure from the Board of Governors to suppress demonstrations, generally upheld students' rights to demonstrate peacefully. Student radicals gained control of the student newspaper, the *Daily Collegian*, in 1967, renamed it the *South End*, and used it to promote their militant, anticapitalist agenda. Two years later, President Keast cut off funding to the *South End* and fired its editor.

Keast's successor, George E. Gullen Jr., served as president from 1971 until 1978. During his presidency, Wayne State faced severe budgetary problems as Michigan suffered a recession between 1973 and 1976 due to the energy crisis and the state economy's dependence upon automobile manufacturing. Additionally, Gullen had to put out the smoldering fires left by the university's urban renewal program and continuing antiwar protests. Gullen also courted controversy by deciding to eliminate Monteith College.

The college began in 1958 as an experimental program in interdisciplinary education, funded by a Ford Foundation grant of $700,000. Named after the Reverend John Monteith (1788–1868), an early Detroit educator and cofounder of the University of Michigan, the new college was to create the ethos of a small liberal arts college within the framework of a large, comprehensive urban university. The Monteith curriculum featured a series of team-taught course sequences in natural sciences, social sciences, and humanistic disciplines. The small classes at Monteith were taught by Wayne State University faculty. Any student admitted to Wayne State could attend Monteith on a first-come, first-served basis. Students completed the college's highly structured program in general education and finished the remainder of their undergraduate work fulfilling the requirements of a traditional major or professional program from other colleges in the university.

Monteith College was the birthplace of the innovative Chicano-Boricua Studies Program (1971) and the Weekend College Program (1974), among others. In October 1975, the Curriculum and Instruction Committee of the University Council recommended that the university phase out Monteith College, emphasizing that the decision was based on economics rather than an adverse academic evaluation of Monteith. President Gullen strongly supported this recommendation, and the university's Board of Governors voted in December 1975 to eliminate Monteith. Gullen's action touched off a wave of protests from former and current Monteith students and faculty, who argued that this drastic action would bring very little in savings to the university. Nevertheless, the Board of Governors upheld its decision but extended the phase-out period until 1981, allowing current Monteith students time to complete their degrees and faculty to transfer to other colleges within the university.

Crises and Revitalization, 1975–Present

Given the severe financial pressures on the university during the late 1970s—the latter part of George Gullen's administration—and continuing into the early 1980s, it is not surprising that Wayne State opened no new buildings on the main campus between 1976 and 1987. The campus nevertheless expanded considerably during this period. Through dozens of real estate purchases, Wayne bought nearly all the property bounded by Woodward, Warren, Cass, and Willis between 1977 and 1989.

Wayne State also acquired the properties and programs of the Merrill-Palmer Institute in 1981. Founded in 1920, this internationally renowned educational institute had pioneered the study of early childhood development. Merrill-Palmer had experienced operating deficits starting in 1965, but the generosity of patron Eleanor Clay Ford had kept the ship afloat. After her death in 1976, Merrill-Palmer used its endowment to operate, but by 1980 those funds had evaporated. Wayne State loaned the struggling institute $330,000 in March 1980 and in September increased the amount to $1.1 million. On July 1, 1981, Wayne State University officially took over the Merrill-Palmer Institute's assets, including its real estate on the north side of Ferry Street between Woodward Avenue and John R Avenue.

Throughout its history of physical expansion, Wayne State had routinely demolished older buildings on campus to make way for the new, with little objection from the public. In 1973, for example, President Gullen endorsed plans—later scrapped—to demolish Old Main and replace it with a new classroom building once funds were available. Remarkably, these plans evoked no protest from alumni or current students. This lack of concern, especially for such a grand and historically significant structure, reflected a widespread view of buildings as disposable. However, Gullen's plan in 1975 to demolish David Mackenzie House (1895) to make way for a sewer that would serve the planned Forest Apartments spurred the creation of a student-led historic preservation movement.

The student activists adopted the name "Preservation Wayne" in fall 1976, and by March 1977 they had launched a public counterattack against Gullen's plans to raze the Mackenzie House (not to be confused with Mackenzie Hall). Allen Wallace, William Colburn, and other student members of Preservation Wayne made several appeals to Wayne State's Board of Governors, urging it to reconsider this decision. At a meeting held in early July 1977, the Board of Governors gave the Mackenzie House a one-year reprieve, a defeat for President Gullen near the end of his presidency. A year later, the Board of Governors officially endorsed the preservation of the Mackenzie House, and in early 1979 Preservation Wayne received a $60,000 federal grant for restoration work.

In the years that followed, the university's administration generally ignored Preservation Wayne's objections to tearing down more than a dozen campus buildings. Demolition sometimes occurred during Christmas vacation, often under the cover of secrecy. Preservation Wayne managed to have nine campus buildings placed on the National Register of Historic Places in 1984 and 1985, but Wayne State subsequently demolished three of them (the Santa Fe Apartments, Mackenzie Hall, and the Thomas S. Sprague House). Still, this small student organization forced Wayne State's administration at least to consider preservation as an alternative.

The presidents of Wayne State University entertained several interesting "dreams and schemes" that are worth recalling. During his presidency (1978–82), World War II veteran and historian Thomas N. Bonner championed two proposals intended to garner national attention for the university. The first was an effort to buy Olympia Arena, the aging sports venue that had served as the home of the Detroit Red Wings from its opening in 1927 until December 1979, when the Red Wings played their last game in the "Red Brick Barn" before moving to the new Joe Louis Arena on Detroit's riverfront. President Bonner saw Olympia as the key element in establishing Wayne State as a national power in intercollegiate hockey and basketball. Moreover, the university could use Olympia for other varsity and intramural sports, concerts, commencements, and other events that would allow Wayne to break even. Bonner's administration produced several feasibility studies in July 1979. It concluded that the plan would be economically viable only if donors contributed about $2 million to renovate the building and provided an annual operating subsidy of $200,000. Unsurprisingly, discussions about acquiring Olympia ended abruptly in mid-December 1979.

President Bonner also sponsored a plan to build a replica of William Shakespeare's second Globe Theatre on Detroit's riverfront. The effort began in May 1979, when Wayne State held the International Symposium for the Reconstruction of the Globe Playhouse. In February 1981, Mayor Coleman Young designated city-owned land on the Detroit River as the site for the theater. Wayne State hired the architectural firm of Schervish, Vogel, Merz to complete preliminary studies of the site. By spring 1981, the Bonner administration concluded that construction would require Wayne State to raise about $17 million in private funds but that the university was unlikely to raise more than half that amount. Then came the shocking revelation that fund-raising was already under way in Europe and elsewhere to rebuild the first Globe Theatre on its original site in London. On the heels of this news, the project quietly died in the early months of President David Adamany's administration (1982–97).

Adamany's presidency was often controversial, as he clashed with faculty and staff over a variety of issues. His relationship with the faculty and staff union, affiliated with the American Association of University Professors (AAUP), was a hostile and confrontational one. The AAUP had won certification as the bargaining agent for Wayne State's faculty and staff in June 1972. However, President Adamany opposed the very idea of labor unions representing university faculty members. He did not want labor agreements hampering his efforts to reform the university. Negotiations for the first contract under the Adamany administration took nearly two years. The AAUP called a one-day strike in September 1986 and a bitter two-week walkout in September 1988. The willingness of a large number of faculty to put the semester in jeopardy demonstrated the resolve of the union to President Adamany. Gradually, his resistance to the AAUP waned but did not fade completely. The AAUP needed only a two-day walkout in September 1990 to secure a new contract, no strike at all in September 1992, and only a brief walkout, lasting less than forty-eight hours, in September 1994. The relationship between a substantial part of Wayne State's faculty and President Adamany was bitter and acrimonious for most of his term in office.

Perhaps Adamany's most divisive academic reform was moving the science departments out of the College of Liberal Arts in 1992 and creating a new College of Science. Adamany claimed he did so because the College of Liberal Arts was too large and unmanageable. It was widely believed at the time, however, that he created a separate College of Science to divert more resources to the science departments, which he favored, and to thereby weaken the political power of the Liberal Arts faculty.

Wayne State nevertheless also experienced many positive changes during the Adamany administration. He established the College of Urban, Labor and Metropolitan Affairs (CULMA) in 1985, a move that would allow the university to better carry out its urban mission. Wayne State's goal in launching CULMA was a practical one: to create programs that would serve the needs of governmental entities, nonprofit organizations, and private enterprise in the metropolitan Detroit area. CULMA's contributions included scholarly work generated by the Center for Urban Studies and the Department of Geography and Urban Planning; programs to train local labor union officials and small business owners; and the creation of demographic, economic, and social statistics for metropolitan Detroit. Adamany also supported the creation of a separate Africana Studies Department in the College of Liberal Arts in 1989. He devoted attention and resources to repairing and rehabilitating many neglected campus classroom and office buildings, part of a campus beautification program.

During Adamany's tenure—and following a long hiatus in building construction, a reflection of the state's budgetary problems—new campus facilities began to appear. As the state economy began to improve in the mid-1980s, Wayne State secured additional funding for campus projects. In 1987, Wayne State upgraded and enlarged the College of Engineering's inadequate facilities with the completion of a $14.3 million addition. Parking Structure #5 also opened that same year. The Faculty/Administration Building, costing $12.8 million, opened in April 1990, as a replacement facility for Mackenzie Hall (formerly the Student Center Building/Webster Hall), which was subsequently demolished on February 17, 1991, by implosion. In late 1990, Wayne completed its School of Business Administration Annex by rehabilitating and upgrading the historic William Rands House (1913) to provide office space for the business school. The Biological Sciences Building, costing $20.6 million, opened in 1991, as did the Leonard Woodcock Wing of the Walter P. Reuther Library.

President Adamany announced the largest capital-spending program in university history ($84.2 million) in 1993. Many new facilities, completed since 1995, have replaced cramped or inadequate quarters for administrators, academic programs, and students. The Academic/Administration Building at Cass Avenue and Palmer Street, completed in 1995, replaced substandard buildings that housed several administrative departments. The University Tower Apartments opened on Cass in 1995 as well, the first new student housing built in twenty years. The Manufacturing Engineering Building was completed in 1996, followed by the David Adamany Undergraduate Library in 1997. A major addition to the Law School facilities (2000) and the Eugene Applebaum College of Pharmacy and Health Sciences Building (2002) on Mack Avenue were the last major academic buildings built during this period.

Although the David Adamany administration and the Irvin Reid administration (1997–2008) that followed demolished several historic houses on campus, Wayne State selectively rehabilitated and restored several historic campus buildings. Wayne started three projects in 1994: a two-year rehabilitation and modernization of Old Main; the refurbishment of St. Andrew's Memorial Episcopal Church (1902), which Wayne had purchased in 1989; and the renovation of the Fisher Wallpaper and Paint Building at 4809 Woodward for the Wayne State University Press. This Albert Kahn–designed building (1914) originally served as a service center and office for the Goodrich Rubber Company. In 1999, Wayne State also converted the historic Max Jacob House (1915), which had housed the Art History Department for many years, into a home for the president.

Irvin Reid's administration (1997–2008) focused resources on making the Wayne State campus less a commuter campus and more a residential campus. Accordingly, the Mort Harris Recreation and Fitness Center opened in 2000, followed by new dormitories, North Residence Hall (2002) and South Residence Hall (2003). Two adjoining buildings on the north side of Warren Avenue near Woodward opened in 2002: the University Bookstore and the Welcome Center. The Welcome Center finally achieved a long-delayed goal of Wayne State University presidents since Clarence Hilberry: to have a "Window on Woodward" that would increase the university's visibility and emphasize its connection to the City of Detroit. Wayne State's most recent foray into providing additional housing near campus was completed in June 2008: the 130-unit South University Village apartment complex on Woodward Avenue between Canfield Street and Forest Avenue.

President Reid significantly restructured the colleges within Wayne State University. He convinced Wayne's Board of Governors to disband the College of Urban, Labor and Metropolitan Affairs, which had been created by President Adamany in 1985. Reid argued that CULMA had no clear direction or focus and that Wayne State would relocate the existing programs in other parts of the university, while eliminating the administrative costs associated with a separate college. As a result, the college closed in 2005. President Reid also reunited the College of Liberal Arts and the College of Science, which President Adamany had torn asunder in 1992. Combining the two colleges meant eliminating one dean's office, a considerable savings to Wayne State.

President Reid's most innovative initiative was the development of the research and technology park and new-business incubator dubbed TechTown, which is located in a mix of old and new buildings between the main campus and the New Center neighborhood to the north. Begun in 1998 as a partnership between Wayne State University and General Motors, the venture is now funded by the State of Michigan, the City of Detroit, and various foundations. TechTown has quickly become an entrepreneurial village offering space and services for tech and neighborhood businesses, with satellite offices across the city.

With President Reid's support, the Wayne State Honors program, offered since 1986, grew to 1,300 students by 2008, when the Board of Governors created the Irvin D. Reid Honors College. Reid stepped down as president effective August 1, 2008, following ten years of service. He subsequently assumed the position of Applebaum Chair of Community Engagement, continuing to promote Wayne State's active involvement with the community it serves.

In 2008, Jay Noren became Wayne State's tenth president. Dr. Noren maintained the university's commitment to the larger community by addressing, through academics and community programs, the issues central to Detroit and to Michigan: economic transformation, educational revitalization, health care, transportation, and citizen involvement in improving the community. President Noren collaborated with School of Medicine leaders to strengthen the university's relationship with the Detroit Medical Center, Henry Ford Health System, and other partners. During his tenure, the university also opened the Marvin I. Danto Engineering Development Center.

Allan Gilmour assumed the presidency of Wayne State University in 2011. Under his leadership, Wayne State's reputation as a premier research university continued to grow. The National Institutes of Health awarded a second ten-year contract to Wayne State's Perinatology Research Branch, and construction began on the Integrative Biosciences Center. And looking to the future of WSU's sports teams, the Athletics Department opened a new multipurpose facility.

On August 1, 2013, Dr. M. Roy Wilson became the twelfth president of Wayne State. Since assuming leadership, President Wilson has realigned the university's numerous research divisions to emphasize team science and cluster hiring of scientists. This effort was reflected in the organization of the science teams in the $90 million IBio multidisciplinary research facility, which opened in 2015. He also developed a strategy to steer underrepresented students toward science careers. As part of this effort, in 2015 he formed a coalition of Detroit-based universities and colleges to launch the NIH-funded Building Infrastructure Leading to Diversity (BUILD) Program at the university.

Enhancing the student experience has been a priority for President Wilson. Beautification efforts on campus include the $26.5 million renovation of the Student Center Building and the redesigned green space surrounding Fountain Court. And as part of the revitalization of Midtown Detroit, the university is planning to expand on-campus student housing to meet the growing demand.

In an effort to increase the diversity of Wayne State's campus, President Wilson created the Office of Multicultural Student Engagement to, among other things, promote awareness initiatives that encourage academic success for underrepresented minorities and historically marginalized students.

Thanks to the leadership of its presidents and the engagement of faculty, students, and staff, the university maintains a dynamic relationship with the surrounding community. This relationship is manifest in the physical campus, which reflects Wayne State's history in Detroit and the farsighted vision of leaders such as David Henry, Clarence Hilberry, and Arthur Neef. Located at the convergence of Detroit's major expressways, the Wayne State campus is just next door to the institutions of the Detroit Cultural Center. The university is clearly part of the city and remains linked to it both physically and programmatically.

As a result of careful planning, the WSU campus offers an attractive island of calm in the midst of the urban bustle of Midtown. Wayne State's leaders and planners could have settled for an expedient clumping of high-rise structures, packed tightly together, but instead they chose to provide pedestrian malls and plentiful green spaces. They might have opted for standardized, look-alike designs but instead engaged the services of more than twenty noted architects. The result is a campus that in many ways represents the strongest attributes of both the university and its students: a campus in some respects practical and down-to-earth but at the same time various in its often delightful blend of heterogeneous styles and tastes.

Now, in the early twenty-first century, Wayne State University's physical campus, its academic programs, and its student body reflect the unique history of this institution. Developed as the City of Detroit's public university and intended to serve the educational needs of residents of Detroit and Wayne County, Wayne State has always had a student body made up largely of commuters. As it has from the beginning, the university makes higher education accessible to students who might not otherwise have such an opportunity. The university now also attracts residential undergraduates from all over southeast Michigan, a population that has substantially increased in recent years. In addition, Wayne State offers an impressive array of top-notch graduate and professional programs that attract students nationally and internationally. Looking toward the future, Wayne State University is poised to continue its notable record of service to Detroit, to Michigan, and to the wider world.

For Further Reading

The only full-length history of Wayne State University is Leslie L. Hanawalt, *A Place of Light: The History of Wayne State University* (Detroit: Wayne State University Press, 1968). Personal insights into Wayne State University from the early 1950s are offered by twenty-two faculty and staff members in Henry V. Bohm and Paul J. Pentacost, *Reminiscences of Wayne: Memoirs of Some Faculty and Staff Members of Wayne State University* (Ann Arbor, MI: Cushing-Malloy, 1999), available at the Purdy/Kresge Library at Wayne State University and at the Detroit Public Library. The relationship between the Detroit public school system and Wayne State University and its predecessor colleges is considered at some length in Jeffrey Mirel, *The Rise and Fall of an Urban School System: Detroit,*

1907–1981, 2nd ed. (Ann Arbor: University of Michigan Press, 1999). For the history of the campus and its buildings, see Charles K. Hyde, "The Physical Development History of the Campus of Wayne State University, Detroit, Michigan," September 1993, Walter P. Reuther Library, Archives of Labor and Urban Affairs, Wayne State University. The reader who wants more detailed sources for Wayne State's history should consult the extensive bibliographies found in the Hanawalt book and the Hyde report. The latter includes an appendix containing detailed information on all major buildings erected on the Wayne State campus from 1948 to 1991.

CHAPTER I

BEGINNINGS

THE MEDICAL COLLEGE, 1868–1913

At its heart, Wayne State University is a gathering of colleges united for a shared purpose. Unlike Michigan's other large universities, Wayne State did not have an official founding. Instead, it evolved over time as several different colleges merged to form one large university. The beginnings of Wayne State University's College of Medicine, the university's oldest college, can be traced back to the Civil War and the opening of Harper Hospital in 1864 to accommodate soldiers and veterans. In 1865, with wounded soldiers still recuperating, five hospital doctors campaigned for the establishment of a medical college. This group of young doctors had acquired knowledge from their battlefield experiences that they wanted to disseminate. More importantly, they wanted the self-improvement that teaching and studying would provide. Their campaign resulted in the founding of the Detroit Medical College, the seed of Wayne State University.

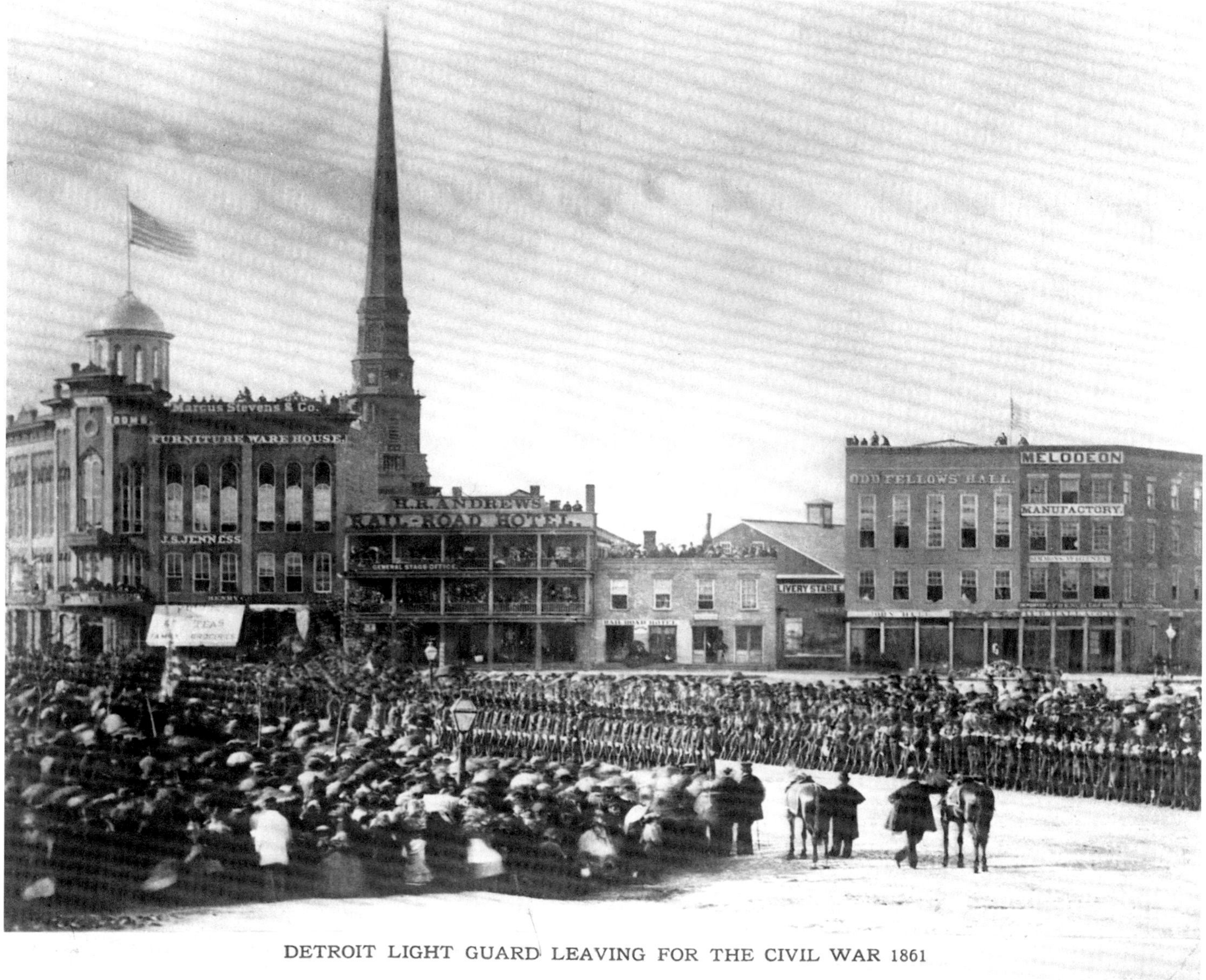

Campus Martius, May 11, 1861. During the Civil War, almost six thousand soldiers from Detroit fought on the front lines. In this photograph, a number of soldiers stand in formation at Campus Martius (which means "military ground") before leaving for the battlefields. Several influential Detroiters, including George Duffield, whose son Samuel was one of the founders of the Detroit Medical College, gave speeches that day. The spire of the First Presbyterian Church is visible left of center. (Walter P. Reuther Library, Archives of Labor and Urban Affairs, Wayne State University.)

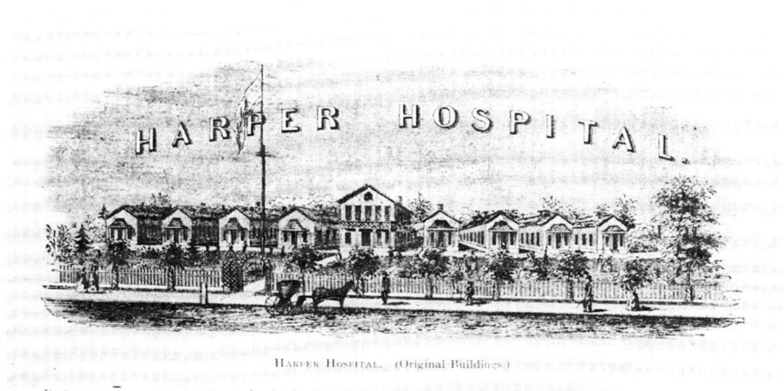

Harper Hospital, original buildings, about 1864. Although there were hospitals located near the Civil War battlefields, wounded soldiers were often moved home, based on the belief that they would recover faster in their hometowns, near family and friends. As early as 1859, Walter Harper, a wealthy, eccentric man, donated land specifically for use as a hospital, yet no hospital was built. Mounting war casualties created the impetus to speed the process along. The trustees of the Harper Hospital Association provided the funds for the buildings. On October 12, 1864, Harper Hospital opened its doors. The buildings pictured here were located on Woodward Avenue near present-day Alexandrine. (Walter P. Reuther Library, Archives of Labor and Urban Affairs, Wayne State University.)

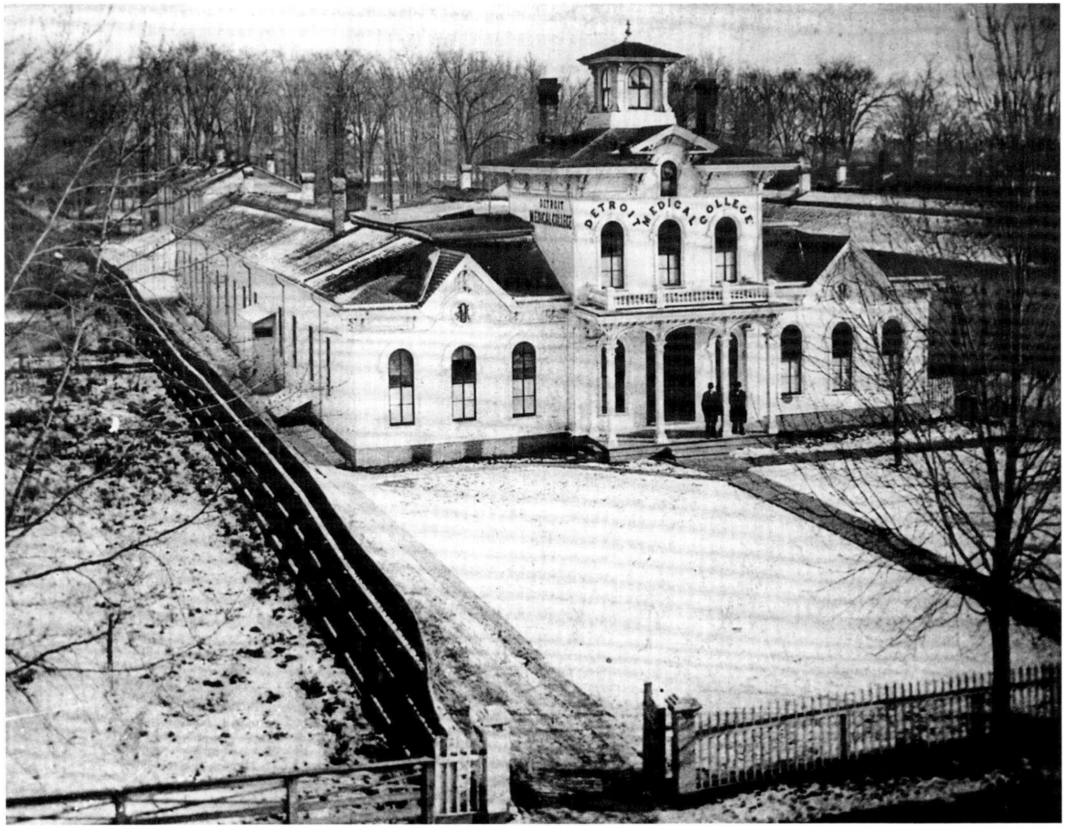

Detroit Medical College, original buildings, 1868. In April 1868, five doctors leased the northwest corner of Harper Hospital and founded the Detroit Medical College. The buildings of the college were located four blocks from the last stop on the Woodward line of horse-drawn streetcars. The first term began on Tuesday, November 3, 1868, when Professor Samuel Duffield delivered a lecture to forty-eight students. Since the Medical College is the original kernel of what would become, over the next century, Wayne State University, 1868 is cited as the birth date for the university. (Walter P. Reuther Library, Archives of Labor and Urban Affairs, Wayne State University.)

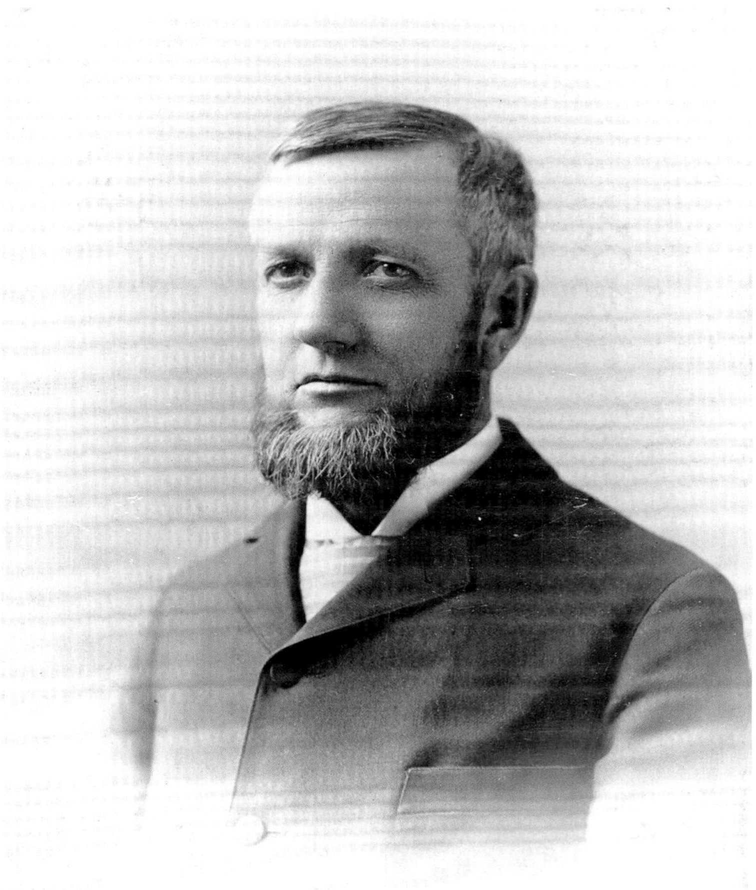

Professor Theodore A. McGraw, MD, Detroit Medical College. McGraw was the son of a wealthy Detroit merchant who had migrated from New York forty years earlier. He was one of five doctors—along with Samuel P. Duffield, David O. Farrand, George P. Andrews, and Edward W. Jenks—who founded the Detroit Medical College. A surgeon, he served as the faculty president during the 1880s. He continued to teach at the college until 1913, when he retired at the age of seventy-four. (Walter P. Reuther Library, Archives of Labor and Urban Affairs, Wayne State University.)

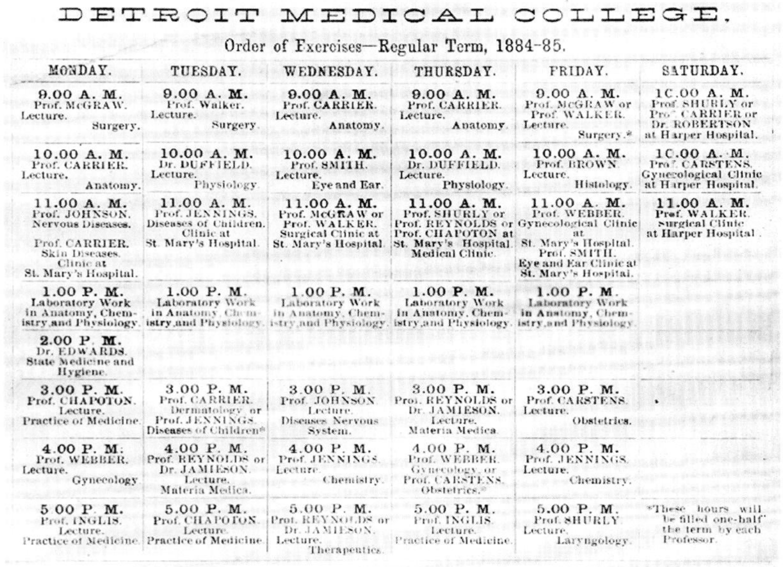

DETROIT MEDICAL COLLEGE.

Order of Exercises—Regular Term, 1884-85.

MONDAY.	TUESDAY.	WEDNESDAY.	THURSDAY.	FRIDAY.	SATURDAY.
9.00 A. M. Prof. McGRAW. Lecture. Surgery.	9.00 A. M. Prof. Walker. Lecture. Surgery.	9.00 A. M. Prof. CARRIER. Lecture. Anatomy.	9.00 A. M. Prof. CARRIER. Lecture. Anatomy.	9.00 A. M. Prof. McGRAW or Prof. WALKER. Lecture. Surgery.*	10.00 A. M. Prof. SHURLY or Prof. CARRIER or Dr. ROBERTSON at Harper Hospital.
10.00 A. M. Prof. CARRIER. Lecture. Anatomy.	10.00 A. M. Dr. DUFFIELD. Lecture. Physiology.	10.00 A. M. Prof. SMITH. Lecture. Eye and Ear.	10.00 A. M. Dr. DUFFIELD. Lecture. Physiology.	10.00 A. M. Prof. BROWN. Lecture. Histology.	10.00 A. M. Prof. CARSTENS. Gynecological Clinic at Harper Hospital.
11.00 A. M. Prof. JOHNSON. Nervous Diseases. Prof. CARRIER. Skin Diseases. Clinic at St. Mary's Hospital.	11.00 A. M. Prof. JENNINGS. Diseases of Children. Clinic at St. Mary's Hospital.	11.00 A. M. Prof. McGRAW or Prof. WALKER. Surgical Clinic at St. Mary's Hospital.	11.00 A. M. Prof. SHURLY or Prof. REYNOLDS or Prof. CHAPOTON at St. Mary's Hospital. Medical Clinic.	11.00 A. M. Prof. WEBBER. Gynecological Clinic at St. Mary's Hospital. Prof. SMITH. Eye and Ear Clinic at St. Mary's Hospital.	11.00 A. M. Prof. WALKER. Surgical Clinic at Harper Hospital.
1.00 P. M. Laboratory Work in Anatomy, Chemistry, and Physiology.	1.00 P. M. Laboratory Work in Anatomy, Chemistry, and Physiology.	1.00 P. M. Laboratory Work in Anatomy, Chemistry, and Physiology.	1.00 P. M. Laboratory Work in Anatomy, Chemistry, and Physiology.	1.00 P. M. Laboratory Work in Anatomy, Chemistry, and Physiology.	
2.00 P. M. Dr. EDWARDS. State Medicine and Hygiene.					
3.00 P. M. Prof. CHAPOTON. Lecture. Practice of Medicine.	3.00 P. M. Prof. CARRIER. Dermatology or Prof. JENNINGS. Diseases of Children*	3.00 P. M. Prof. JOHNSON Lecture. Diseases Nervous System.	3.00 P. M. Prof. REYNOLDS or Dr. JAMIESON. Lecture. Materia Medica.	3.00 P. M. Prof. CARSTENS. Lecture. Obstetrics.	
4.00 P. M. Prof. WEBBER. Lecture. Gynecology.	4.00 P. M. Prof. REYNOLDS or Dr. JAMIESON. Lecture. Materia Medica.	4.00 P. M. Prof. JENNINGS. Lecture. Chemistry.	4.00 P. M. Prof. WEBBER. Gynecology, or Prof. CARSTENS. Obstetrics.*	4.00 P. M. Prof. JENNINGS. Lecture. Chemistry.	
5.00 P. M. Prof. INGLIS. Lecture. Practice of Medicine.	5.00 P. M. Prof. CHAPOTON. Lecture. Practice of Medicine.	5.00 P. M. Prof. REYNOLDS or Dr. JAMIESON. Lecture. Therapeutics.	5.00 P. M. Prof. INGLIS. Lecture. Practice of Medicine.	5.00 P. M. Prof. SHURLY. Lecture. Laryngology.	*These hours will be filled one-half the term by each Professor.

Detroit Medical College class schedule, 1884–85. (Walter P. Reuther Library, Archives of Labor and Urban Affairs, Wayne State University.)

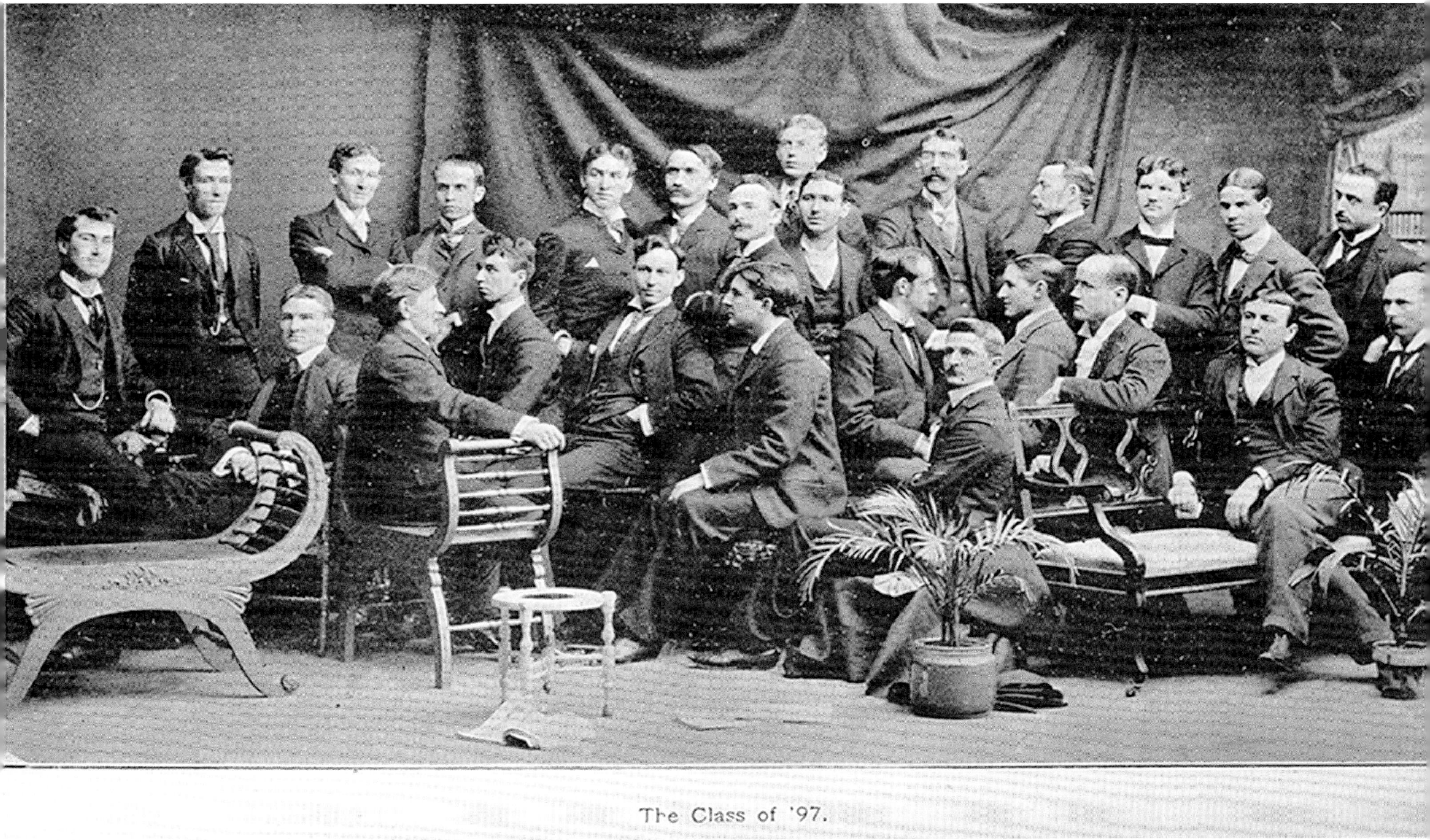

Medical students, 1897. The students of this graduating class removed their derbies before posing for the photographer. In its early years, the medical school drew students not just from Detroit but from across Michigan, Ohio, and Ontario. (Walter P. Reuther Library, Archives of Labor and Urban Affairs, Wayne State University.)

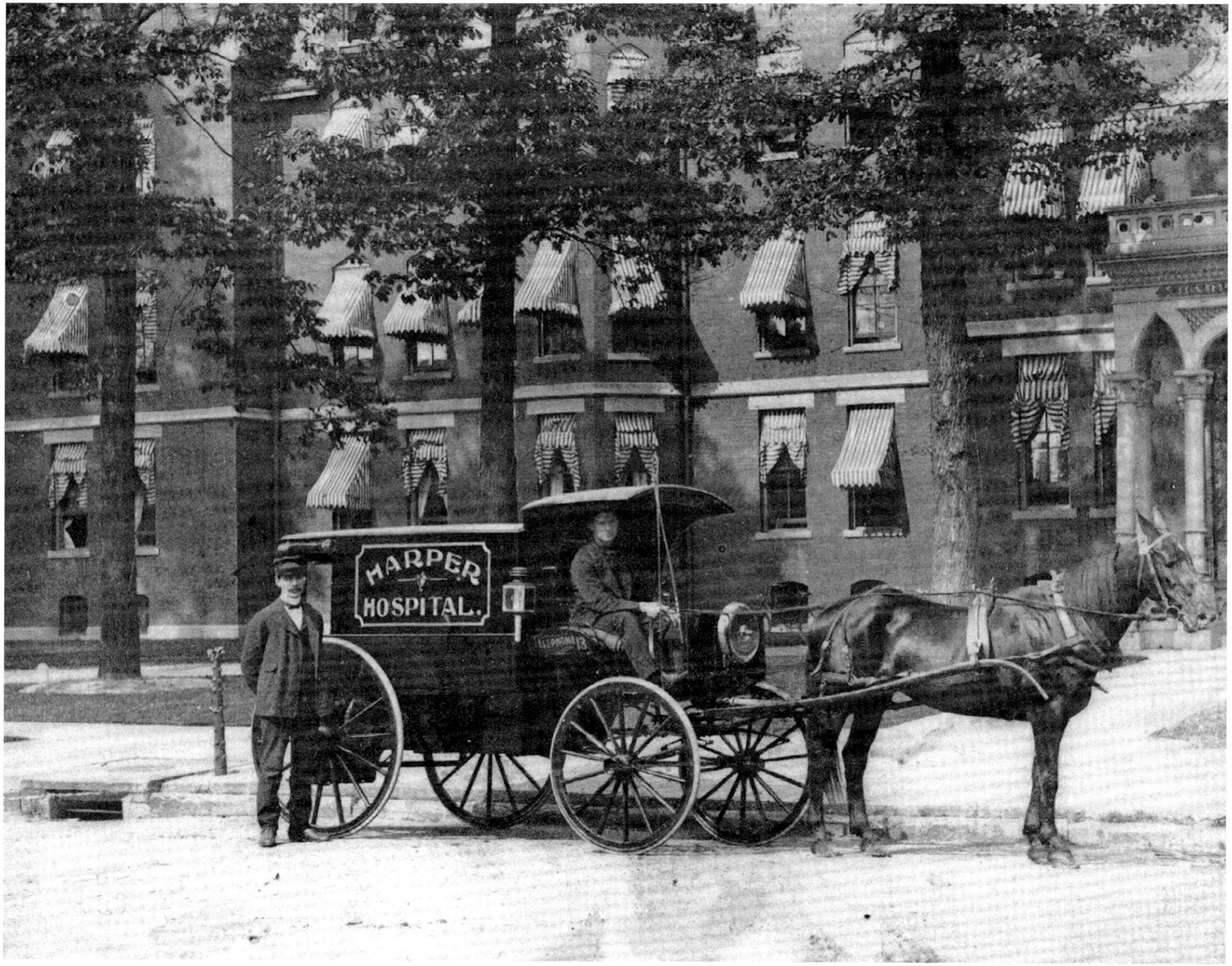

Harper Hospital horse-drawn ambulance, 1880s. Horse-drawn buggies first supplied Detroit with ambulance service on January 1, 1866. Both the Detroit Medical College and its rival, the Michigan College of Medicine, maintained horse-drawn ambulances until the 1880s. Students from both colleges boasted that their horses could cross Woodward Avenue in three jumps. The colleges dropped ambulance services after they merged in 1885, since they no longer needed to compete with one another. (Walter P. Reuther Library, Archives of Labor and Urban Affairs, Wayne State University.)

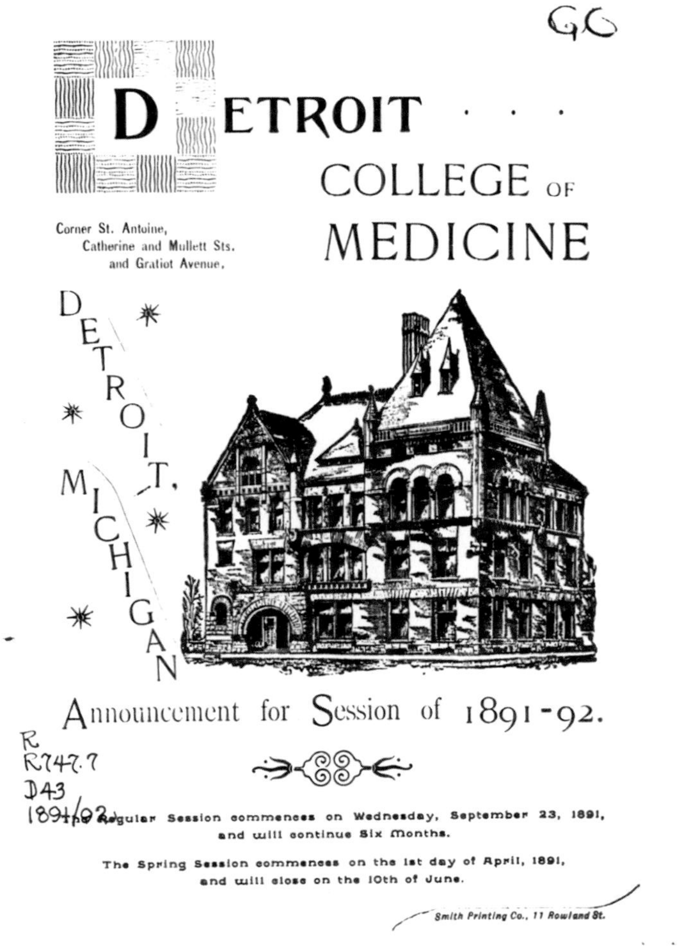

DETROIT . . .

COLLEGE OF MEDICINE

Corner St. Antoine,
Catherine and Mullett Sts.
and Gratiot Avenue,

DETROIT, MICHIGAN

Announcement for Session of 1891-92.

The Regular Session commences on Wednesday, September 23, 1891, and will continue Six Months.

The Spring Session commences on the 1st day of April, 1891, and will close on the 10th of June.

Smith Printing Co., 11 Rowland St.

Detroit College of Medicine leaflet, 1891. After a prosperous start, the Detroit Medical College experienced financial difficulties when a rival school, the Michigan College of Medicine, opened in Detroit in 1879 and drew away students and professors. Six years later, in 1885, the two colleges merged to form the Detroit College of Medicine. After the merger, the faculty oversaw the construction of a new building on Mullett Street. The building, completed in 1889, was the first Detroit building ever built exclusively as a college. The building shown on the leaflet, which was demolished in 1960, was located near present-day Greektown. (Walter P. Reuther Library, Archives of Labor and Urban Affairs, Wayne State University.)

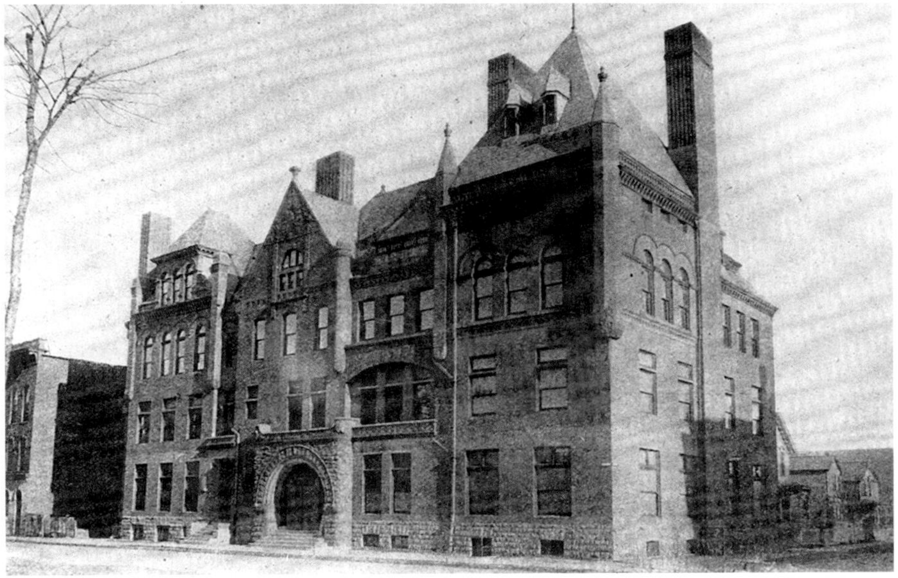

Detroit College of Medicine, Mullett Street, about 1894. While the exact date for this photograph is unknown, it was taken sometime after 1892, after the addition of a wing for the Department of Dental Surgery. The addition can be seen on the left side of the building. The medical school is indicated by the stone archway, with laboratories located on the right. The new addition is a symbol of the golden age of the Detroit College of Medicine that occurred between 1885 and 1903. This period was marked by a growing student body, skilled faculty, and important hospital connections. Faculty were added to keep pace with increased enrollments, and funding increased as a result of the additional tuition revenue and laboratory fees. (Walter P. Reuther Library, Archives of Labor and Urban Affairs, Wayne State University.)

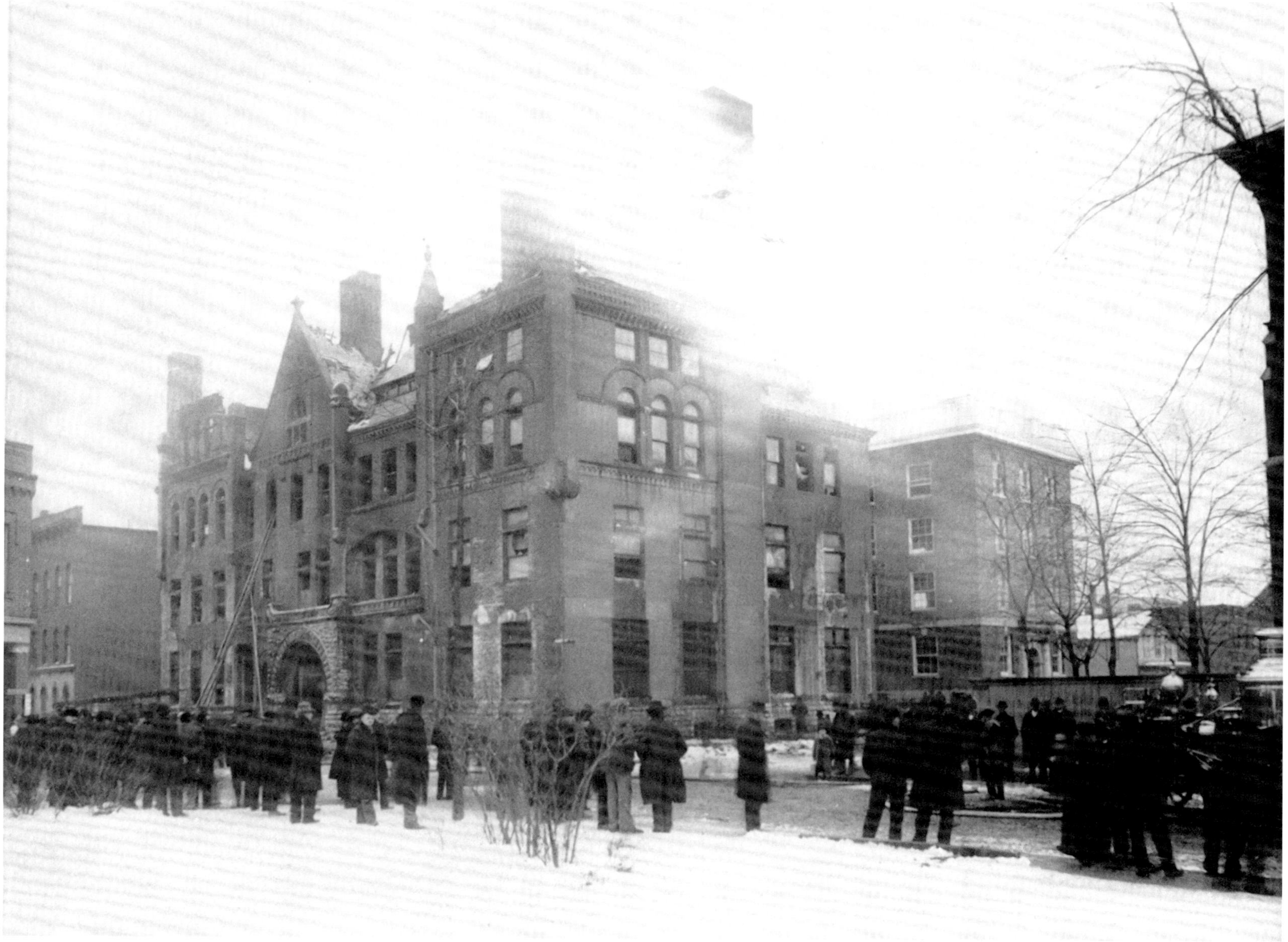

Medical school fire, December 17, 1896. After fire damaged the Detroit College of Medicine, the college was rebuilt, but the tall, pointed roofs were replaced by a more rectangular style. The Medical College occupied this building until 1954. (Walter P. Reuther Library, Archives of Labor and Urban Affairs, Wayne State University.)

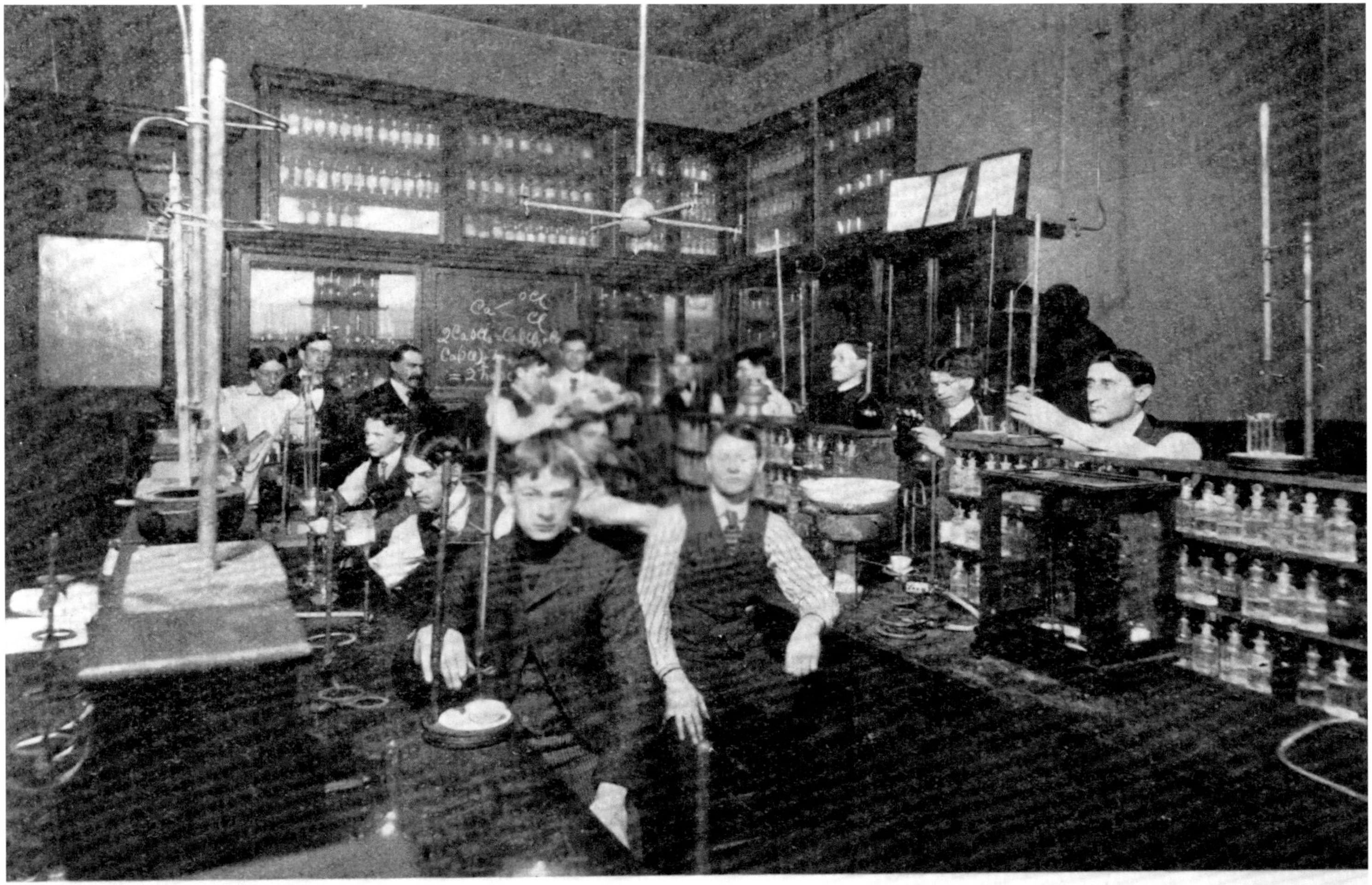

Photo by Spellman.

CHEMICAL LABORATORY.
(Pharmacy Department.)

Chemical lab, about 1900. The pharmacy students pausing in their experiments were typical of other medical students of this era: generally, they were not from wealthy families, and many of them had supported themselves by working in other fields before entering medical school. The pharmacy department was a short-lived unit of the medical school, operating from 1891 to 1905. (This department is unrelated to the present-day College of Pharmacy.) (Walter P. Reuther Library, Archives of Labor and Urban Affairs, Wayne State University.)

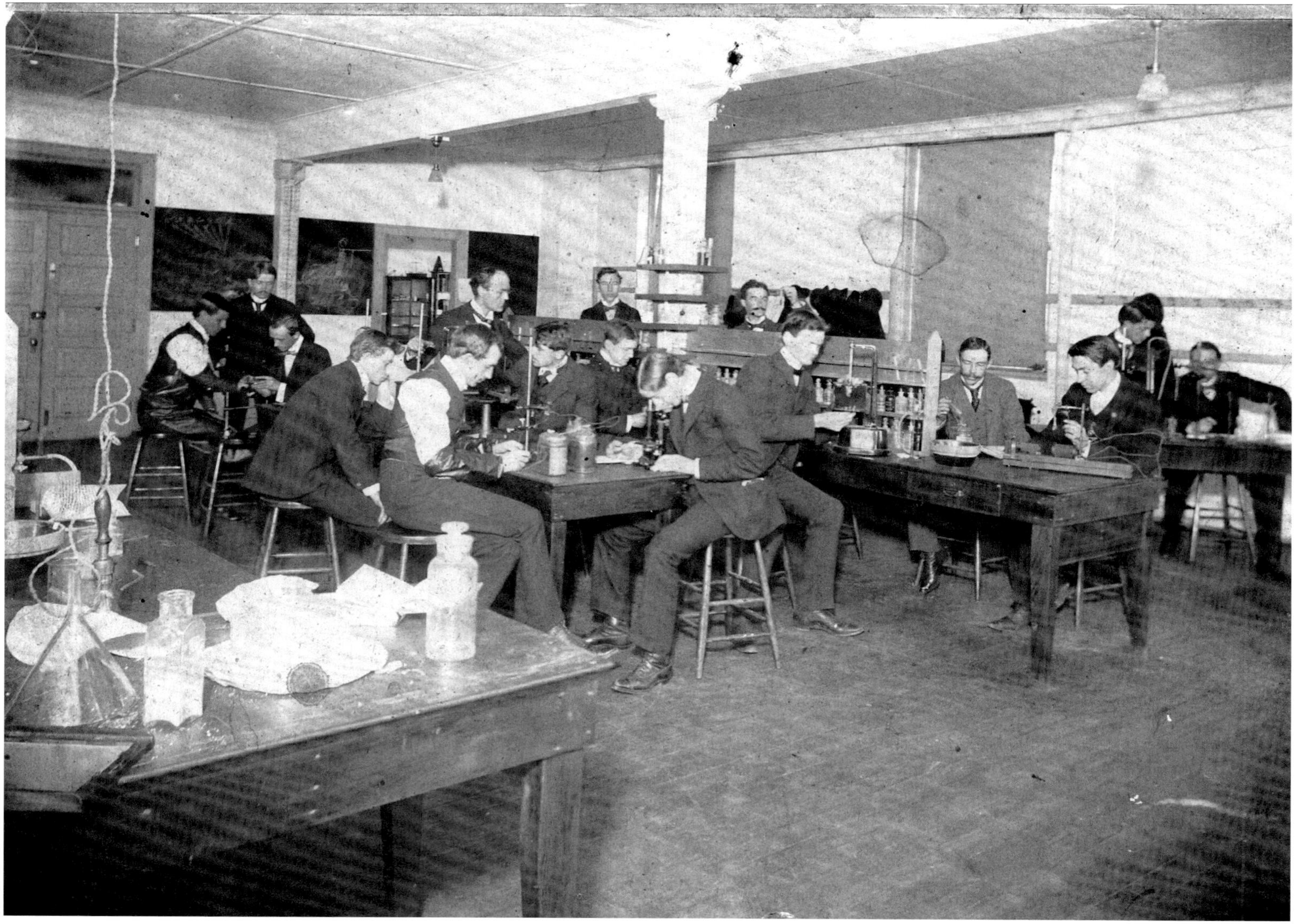

Physiology class, about 1900. The Medical College building was remodeled in 1880, after which more special-purpose rooms were available to students, including this laboratory. The mustached professor standing near the doors at the far left of the photo is Dr. Burt R. Shurly, a lecturer in physiology and an alumnus of the Detroit College of Medicine. Shurly would play an important role in the college's future. The balding professor standing left of center is Dr. Augustus Ives, professor of physiology. Both men taught at the college until the 1920s. (Walter P. Reuther Library, Archives of Labor and Urban Affairs, Wayne State University.)

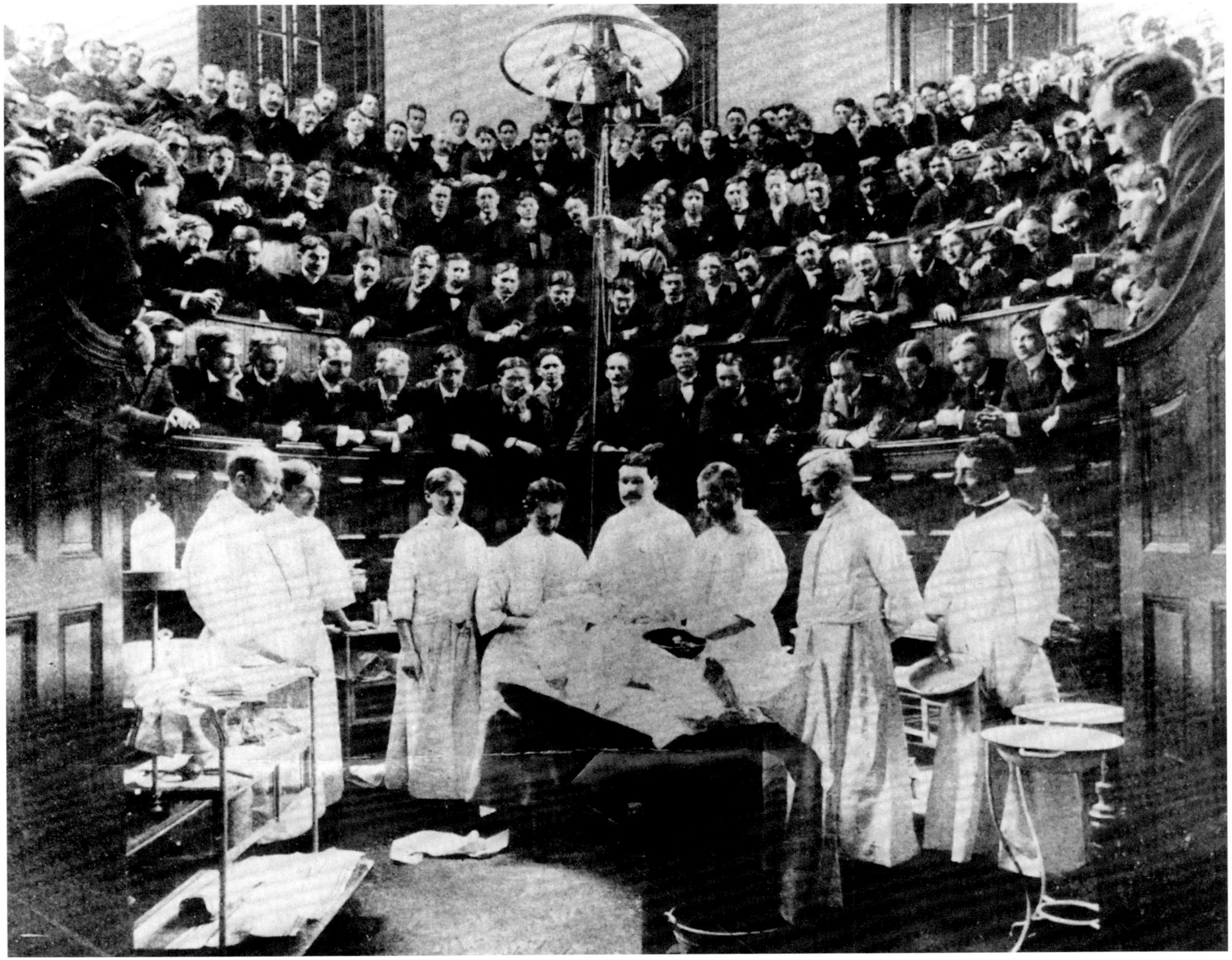

Amphitheater at St. Mary's Hospital, 1900s. The Medical College had an ongoing relationship with St. Mary's, along with several other teaching hospitals in Detroit. The amphitheater-style classroom gave all the medical students a clear view of the procedure being performed by college doctors. The doctor third from the right in this photo, who is performing the surgery, is Henry O. Walker, a surgeon who was popular with students. To his right, with his hands behind his back, is Dr. Theodore McGraw, a founding member of the Detroit Medical College. At the far left of the photo, with the beard, is Dr. Frank B. Walker. (Walter P. Reuther Library, Archives of Labor and Urban Affairs, Wayne State University.)

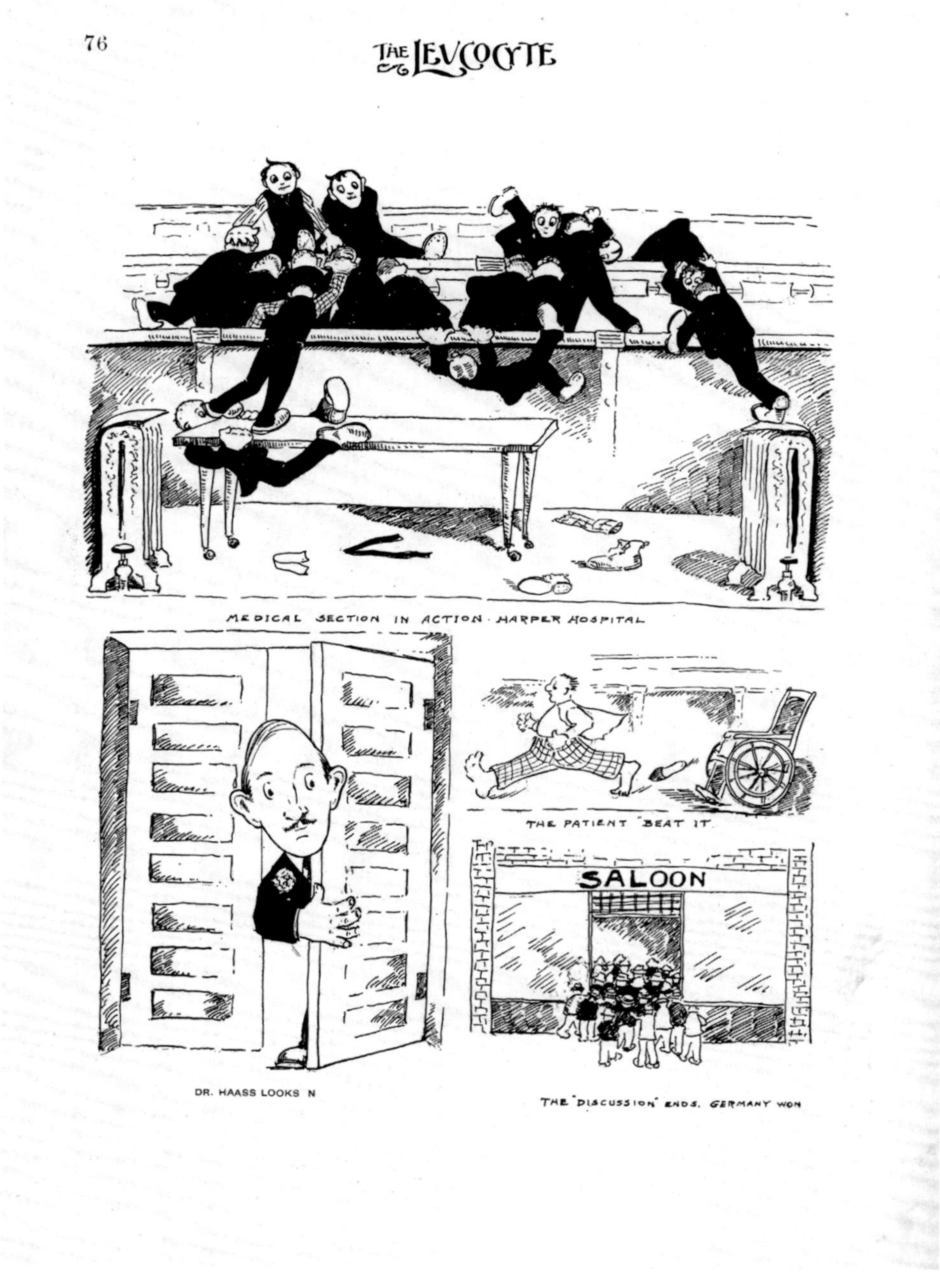

Cartoon from *The Leucocyte*, December 1914. The cartoon—from the magazine published by Detroit College of Medicine students—depicts an amphitheater similar to the one seen in the previous photograph. According to *The Leucocyte*, the cartoon was inspired by an incident at Harper Hospital that "caused a fracas." Upperclassmen usually sat at the front of the amphitheater, since those seats afforded the best view of the operation below, but as pictured, a scuffle ensued after underclassmen took the seats usually reserved for seniors. (Walter P. Reuther Library, Archives of Labor and Urban Affairs, Wayne State University.)

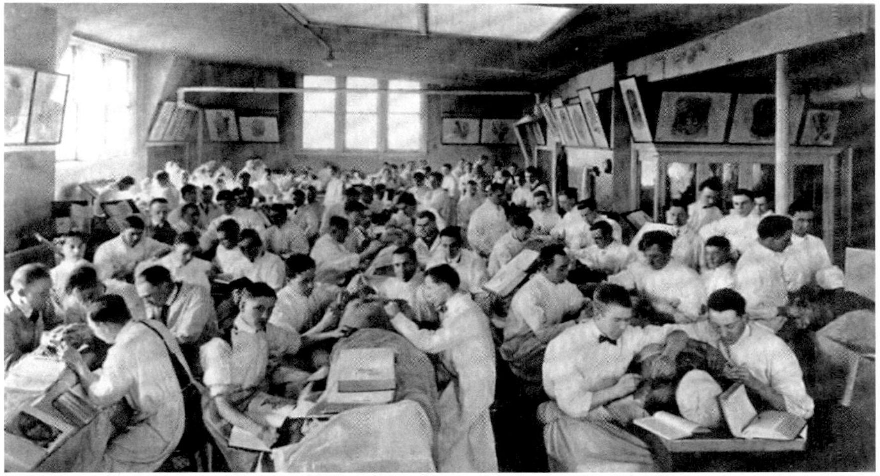

Dissecting room and anatomical laboratory, 1914. (Walter P. Reuther Library, Archives of Labor and Urban Affairs, Wayne State University.)

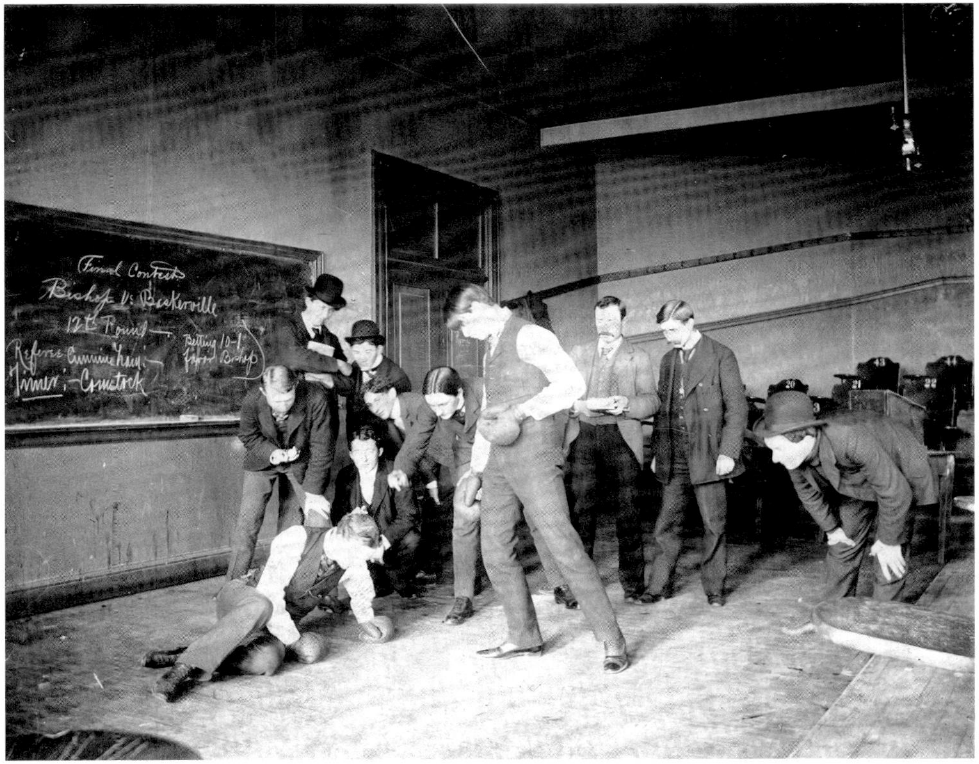

Class rush, Detroit College of Medicine, 1890s. The young man on the losing end of this boxing match is most likely a first-year student taking part in a type of hazing that began in the 1890s and pitted upperclassmen against freshmen in "brawls" like this one. Such methods of initiation lasted until 1914, when they were replaced by organized class contests held on Belle Isle. These competitions between medical school students were similar to the class rush games enjoyed later by College of the City of Detroit students. The chalkboard reads, in part: "Final Contest/ Bishop V. Baskerville/12th Round." (Walter P. Reuther Library, Archives of Labor and Urban Affairs, Wayne State University.)

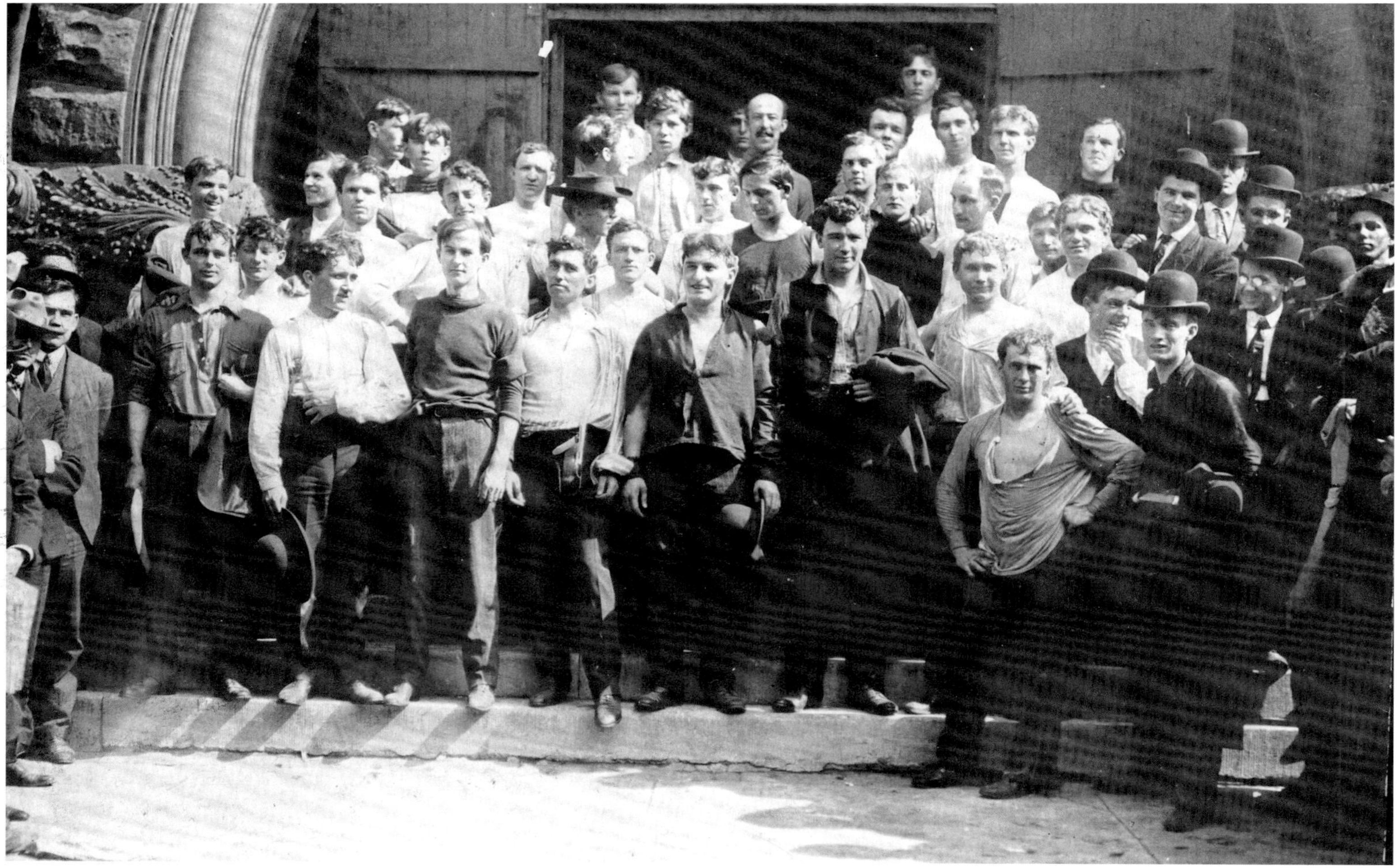

After a class rush, 1910. The clothes and hair of these medical students aren't disheveled because of difficult final exams but because of initiation activities. The students here are gathered in front of the medical school building on Mullett Street. (Walter P. Reuther Library, Archives of Labor and Urban Affairs, Wayne State University.)

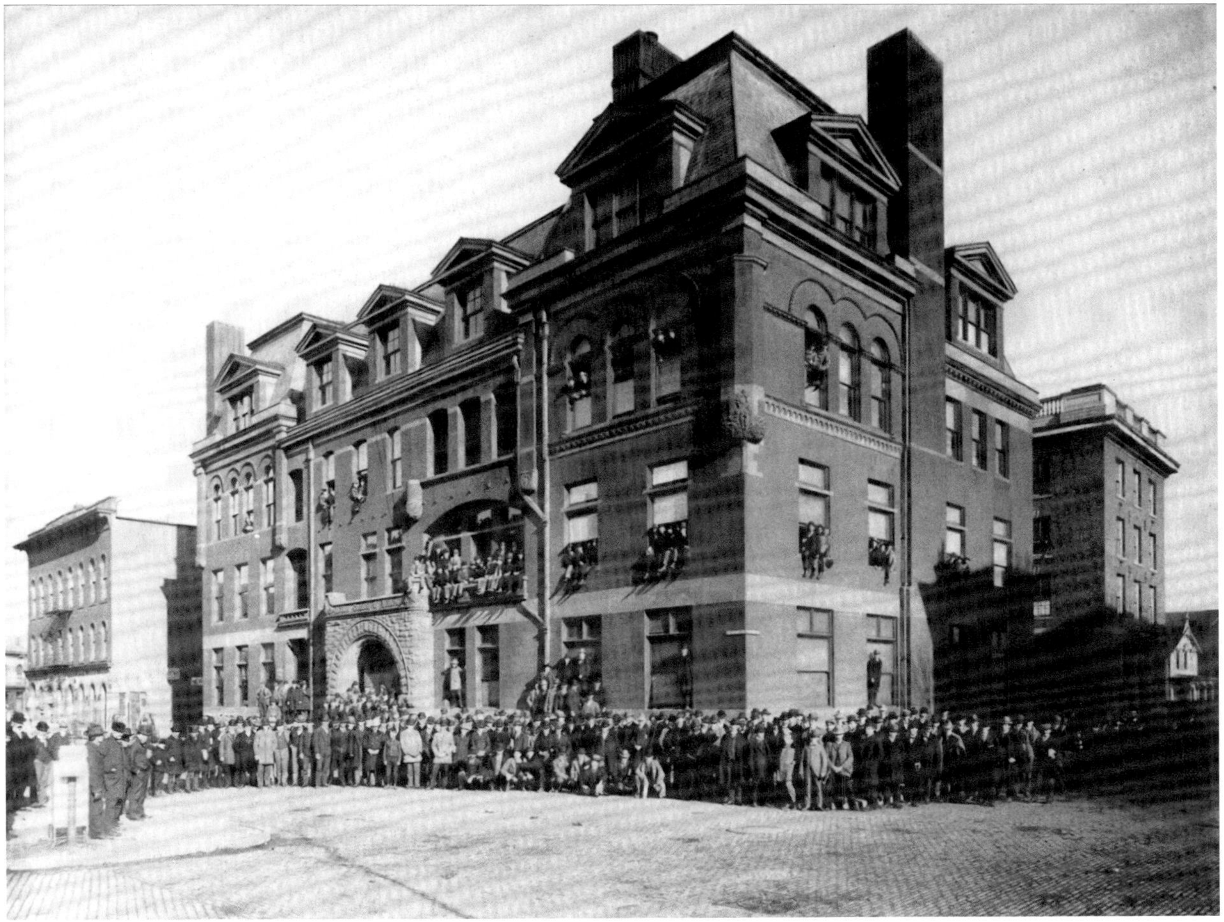

Detroit College of Medicine and Surgery, Mullett Street, April 1, 1913. After problems with finances and morale, the private college closed. Following refinancing and a reorganization of leadership, the college was reopened as the nonprofit Detroit College of Medicine and Surgery. There was no interruption of college classes. The students leaning out of the windows and the crowd of people on the sidewalk are gathered to celebrate the reopening of the college. (Walter P. Reuther Library, Archives of Labor and Urban Affairs, Wayne State University.)

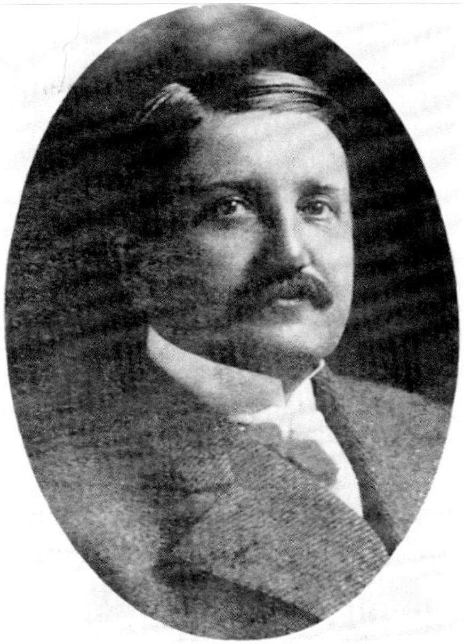

Dean Burt R. Shurly, around 1900. During the reorganization of the medical school, the American Medical Association required the college to offer a premedical course. Dr. Burt R. Shurly, a dean at the Detroit College of Medicine, arranged with the principal of Central High School, David Mackenzie, to enroll twenty-five students in a junior college course to be held at the high school during the fall of 1913. After this point, Central High became the college's chief source of first-year medical students, and the premedical classes evolved into the Detroit Junior College, the predecessor to Wayne State University. (Walter P. Reuther Library, Archives of Labor and Urban Affairs, Wayne State University.)

CHAPTER 2

THE COLLEGE AT CASS AND WARREN, 1913–32

Before Wayne State University and Old Main, there were the Detroit Junior College and Central High School. Wayne State's current College of Liberal Arts and Sciences grew out of premedical classes taught for the Detroit College of Medicine and Surgery, first held as junior college classes at Central High in 1913. Two years later, in 1915, the North Central Association of Colleges and Secondary Schools formally approved the college classes at Central, which meant that credit from these classes could be transferred to other colleges, as their credit status was fixed.

Central High School principal David Mackenzie worked with Detroit public schools superintendent Charles Chadsey and Dean Walter MacCraken of the Medical College to expand the selection of classes into a larger program. In 1917, the Detroit Junior College was born, when the Michigan legislature authorized the two-year course.

The junior college, similar to today's community college, attracted a variety of students, few of them traditional: young and old, employed (both full- and part-time) and unemployed, students working on a degree and students simply studying a subject. For Detroit's working and middle classes, the college offered affordable tuition and a convenient location—students could remain at home while they worked on their degrees. By the end of the 1920s, a new Central High School had been built, and what had been Central High School housed several separate colleges.

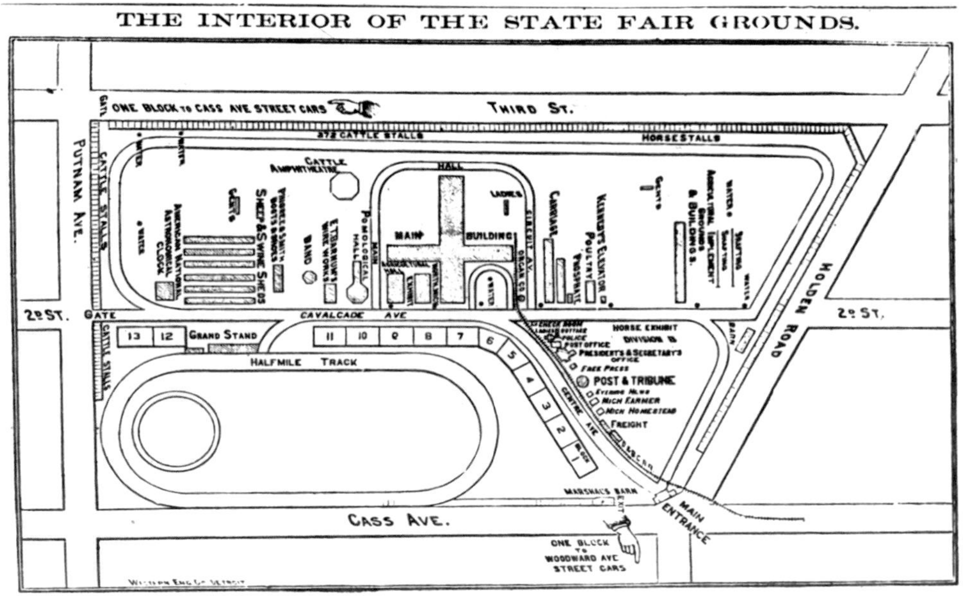

Map of the Michigan State Fair Grounds, 1879. In its early years, the Michigan State Fair was held in a number of different cities as well as in different locations in Detroit. In 1879, the fair was located at Cass Avenue and Putnam Street, near the future home of Wayne State's central campus. The cattle stalls on Putnam Street, at the left side of the map, occupy the site where State Hall now stands. Since the area has changed considerably, the map does not show Kirby, Ferry, or Palmer Street, and Holden Road now begins farther north of the campus. Note the hand symbols indicating streetcar routes on Cass and Woodward avenues. (Walter P. Reuther Library, Archives of Labor and Urban Affairs, Wayne State University.)

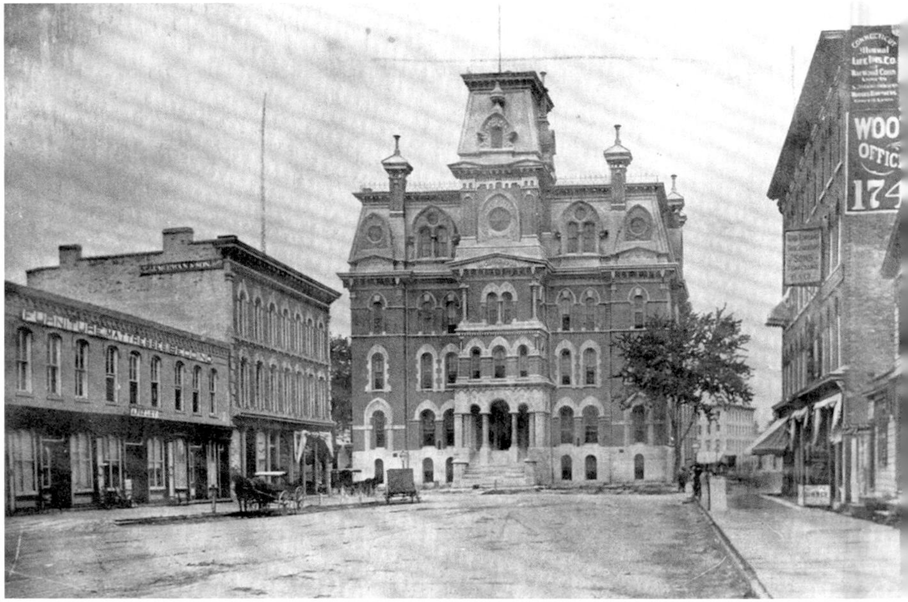

Capitol High School on Griswold Street at Gratiot Avenue, late 1870s. The building at the center of the photograph originally served as Michigan's state capitol, until Lansing became the capital city in 1847. After 1847, the building became Detroit's Capitol High School. It was remodeled extensively in the Second Empire style in 1875, when a brick facade was added. Beginning in 1881, the building housed the newly founded Detroit Normal Training School—predecessor to Wayne State's College of Education. The normal school was one result of a national movement demanding more education and training for teachers. "Normal" referred to a standardized system of training. Normal school students attended classes in this building until 1888, when the program moved to Russell School. (Walter P. Reuther Library, Archives of Labor and Urban Affairs, Wayne State University.)

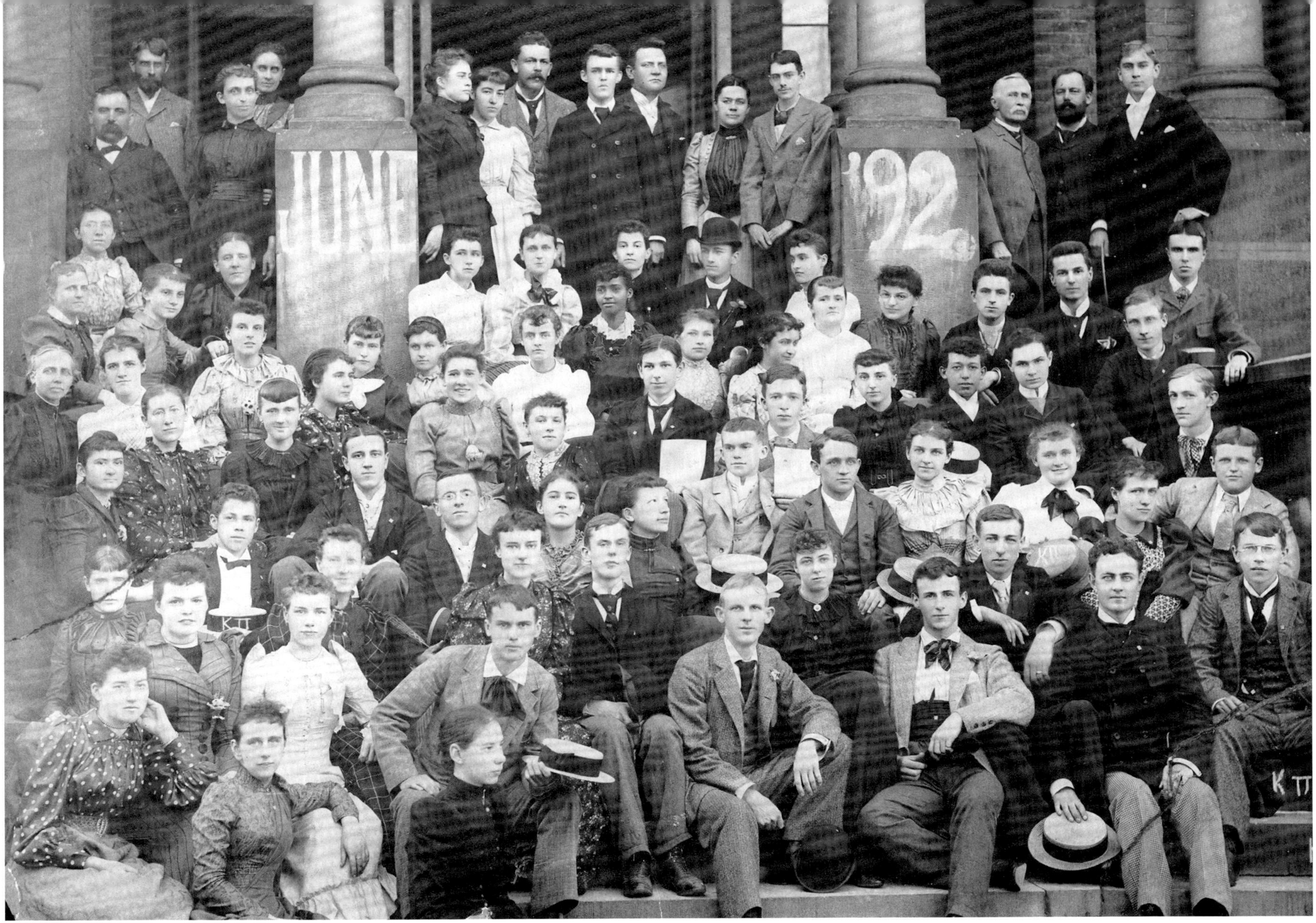

Capitol High School class of 1892. This photograph captures an image of the last class to graduate from Capitol High School, as the building was destroyed by fire in January 1893. After the fire, Central High School was constructed at Cass and Warren avenues to provide another school for Detroit secondary students. Wayne State's first classes would be held years later at Central High. (Walter P. Reuther Library, Archives of Labor and Urban Affairs, Wayne State University.)

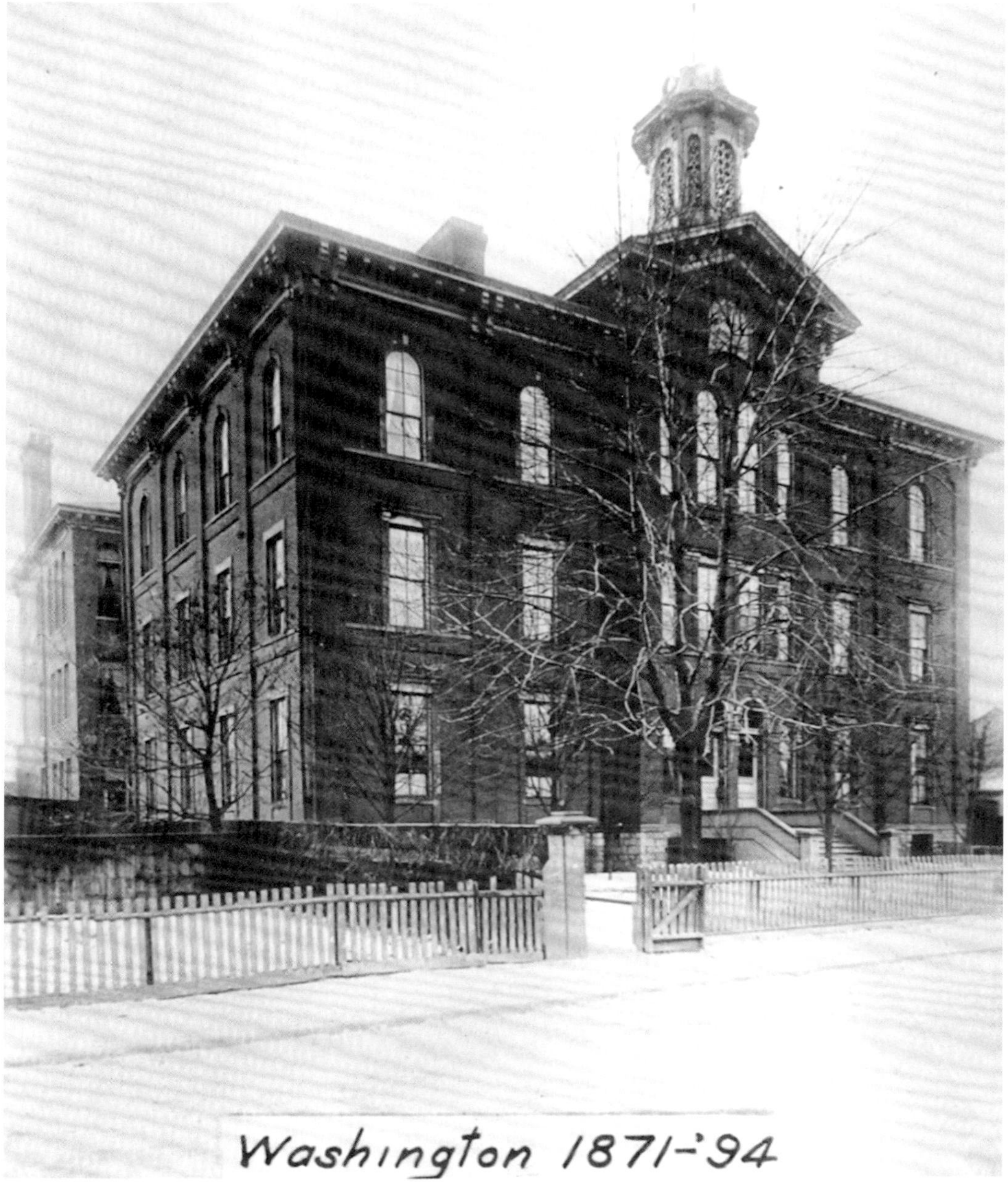

"Washington Normal," Beaubien Street and St. Harriet Avenue, 1890s. The Detroit Normal Training School finally found a long-term home in February 1895, when it moved from Miami School at 1354 Broadway into a six-room addition at Washington School, then located on Beaubien Street at St. Harriet Avenue (now Madison Avenue). The addition was nicknamed Washington Normal and was home to the training school for the next two decades. (Walter P. Reuther Library, Archives of Labor and Urban Affairs, Wayne State University.)

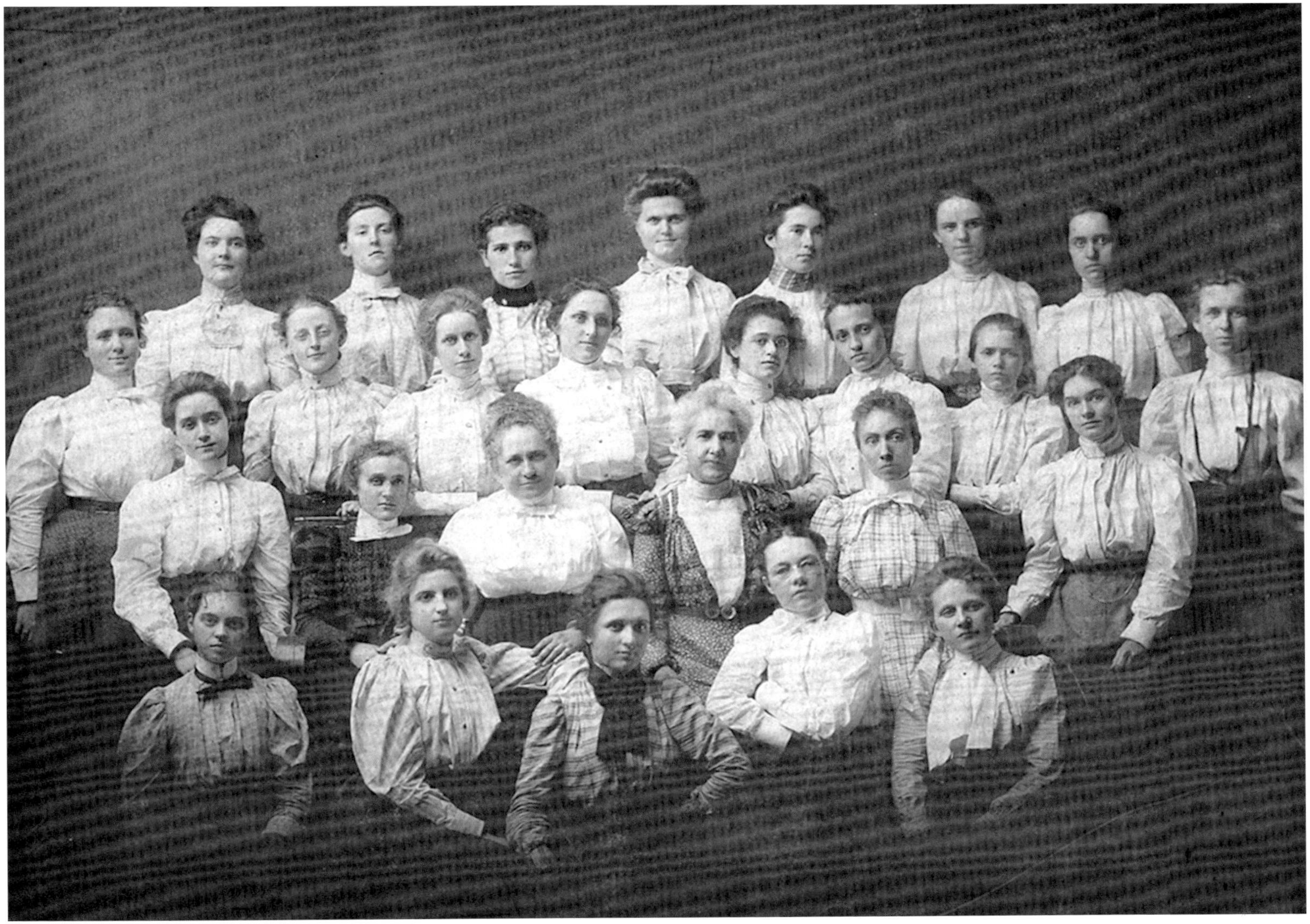

Detroit Normal Training School, class of 1899. Harriet Scott, in the second row, third from the right, served on the staff of the normal school for seventeen years and worked both as a teacher and as principal of the school. A sign of the times, married women were not admitted to train as teachers at the normal school until 1917. In fact, married women were not employed as teachers in the Detroit public schools until 1918. (Walter P. Reuther Library, Archives of Labor and Urban Affairs, Wayne State University.)

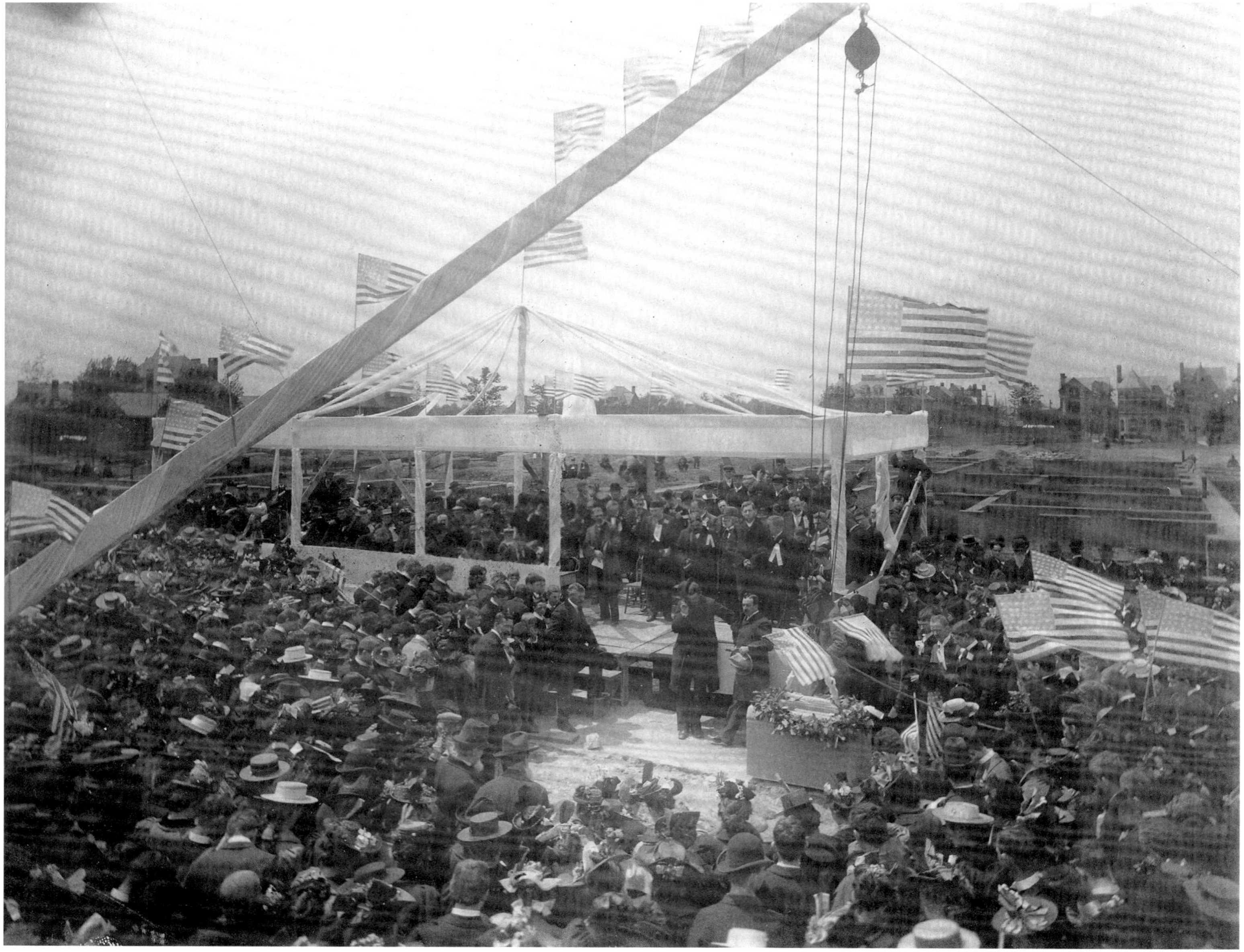

Central High School, cornerstone-laying ceremony, May 13, 1895. This is the earliest photograph of the building known today as Old Main. Detroit mayor Hazen Pingree, a well-known champion of social reform, and Dr. John E. Clark, president of the Board of Education, gave speeches to commemorate the laying of the cornerstone for the city's new high school. The houses visible in the distance on the right stand on Second Avenue. (Courtesy of the Burton Historical Collection, Detroit Public Library.)

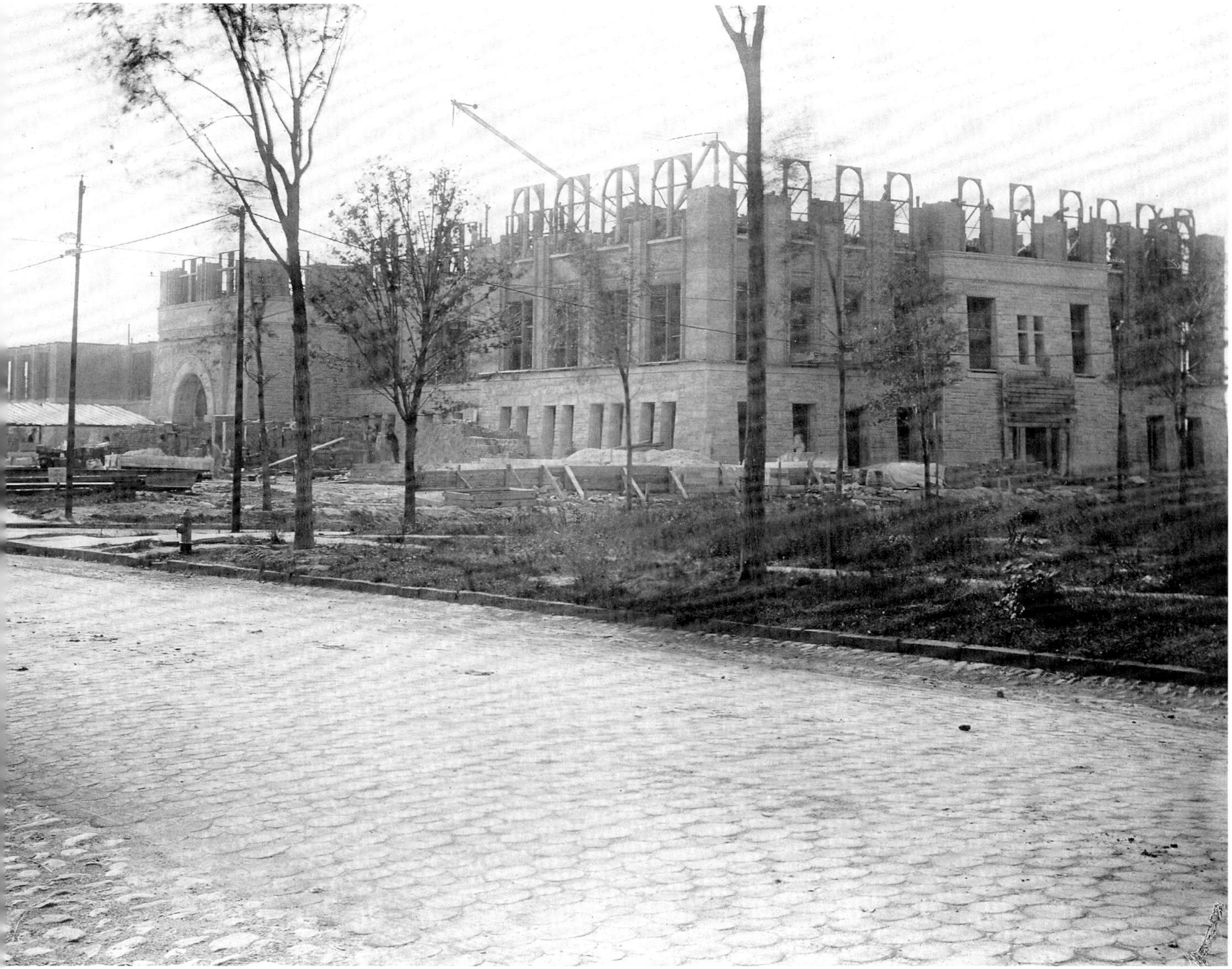

Construction of Central High School on Cass Avenue, as seen looking south, 1895. The school's front entrance is located at the far left of the photograph and is marked by an archway. The street running in front of the building is Cass Avenue, which is paved with cut logs. (Courtesy of the Burton Historical Collection, Detroit Public Library.)

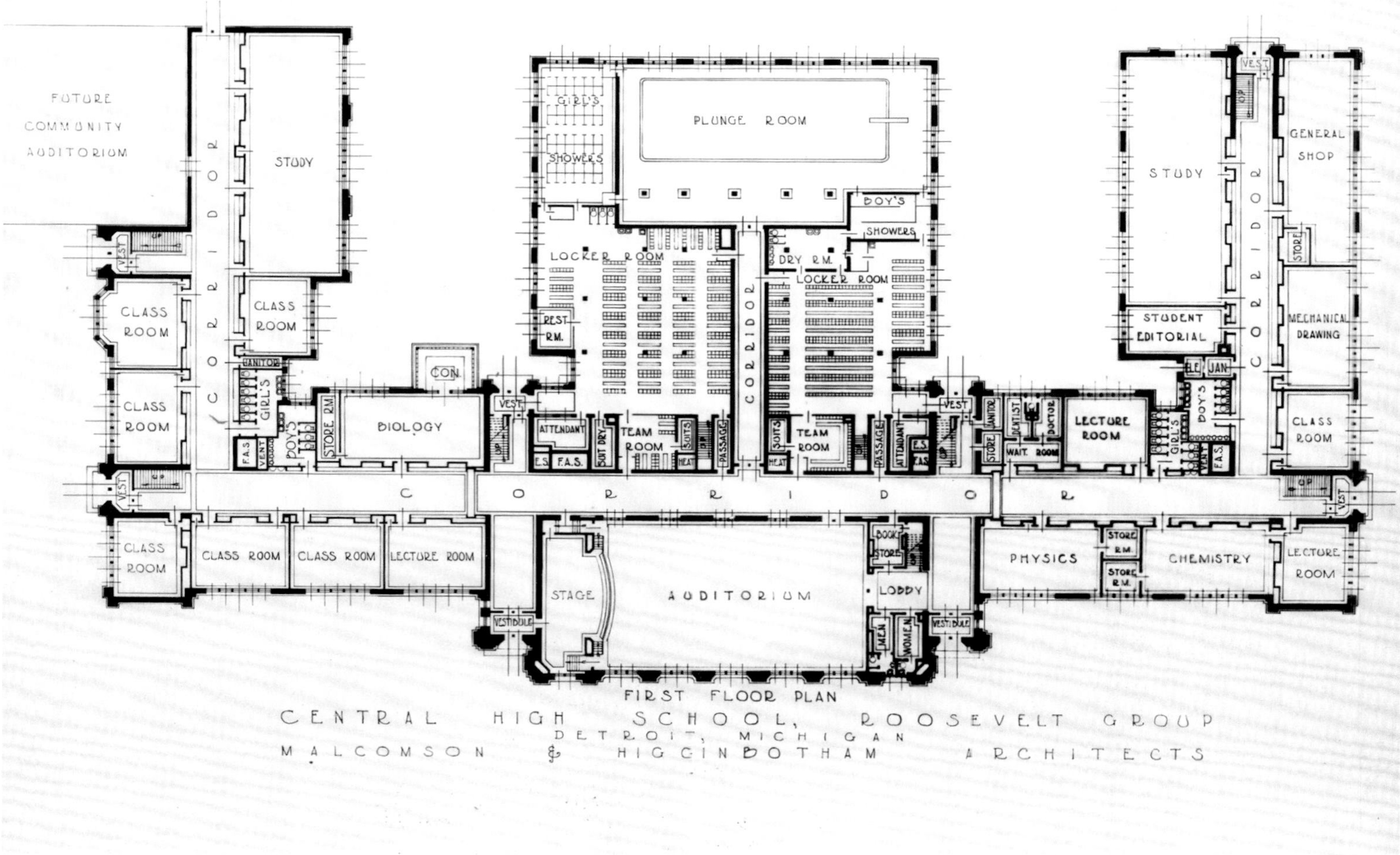

Floor plan for Central High School. (Courtesy of the Burton Historical Collection, Detroit Public Library.)

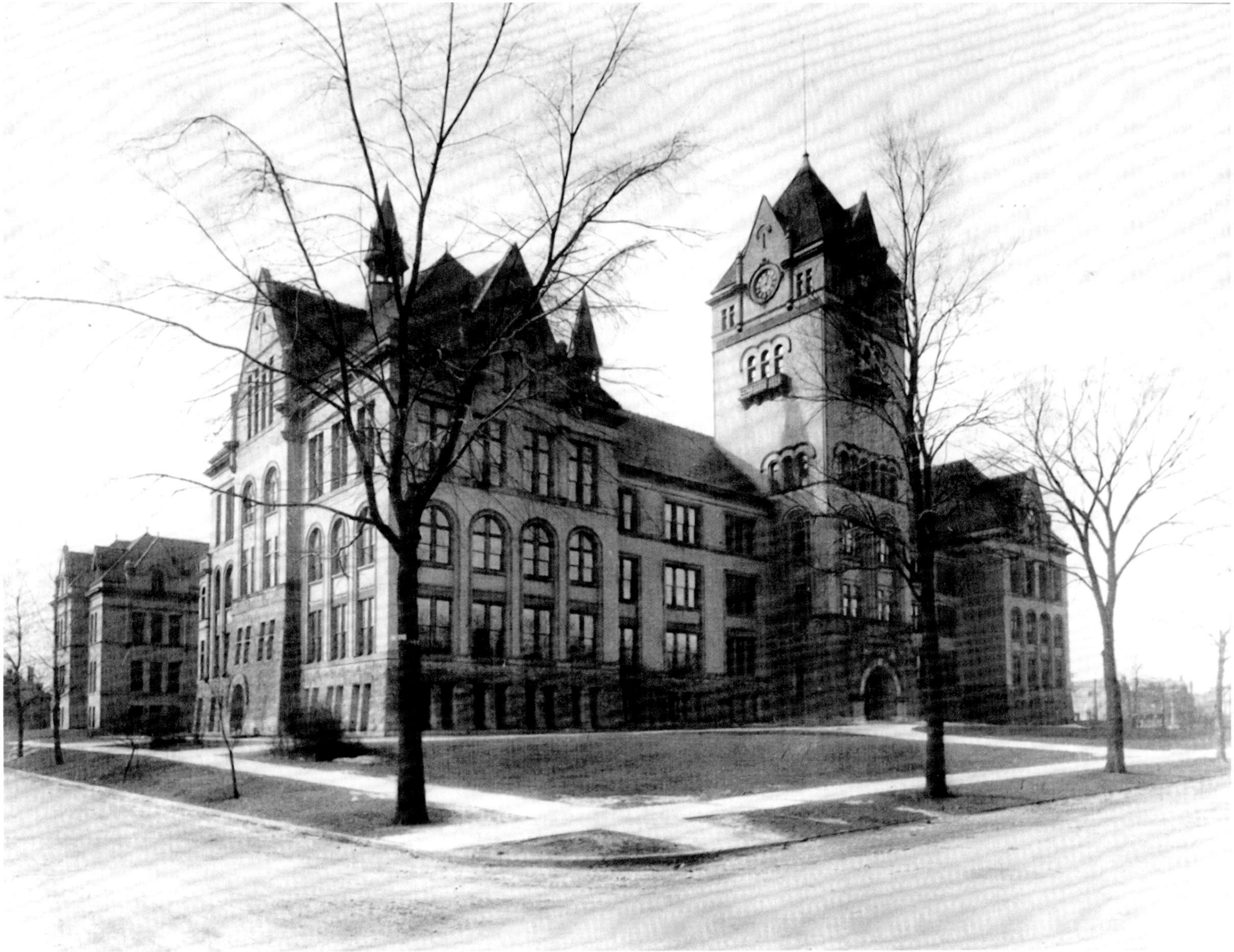

Central High School, 4841 Cass Avenue at Hancock Street, as seen looking northwest, 1897. This photograph shows the completed high school. Over the years, it would serve as home to a junior college, a municipal college, and, finally, a university. High school and college students shared this building for thirty years. (Walter P. Reuther Library, Archives of Labor and Urban Affairs, Wayne State University.)

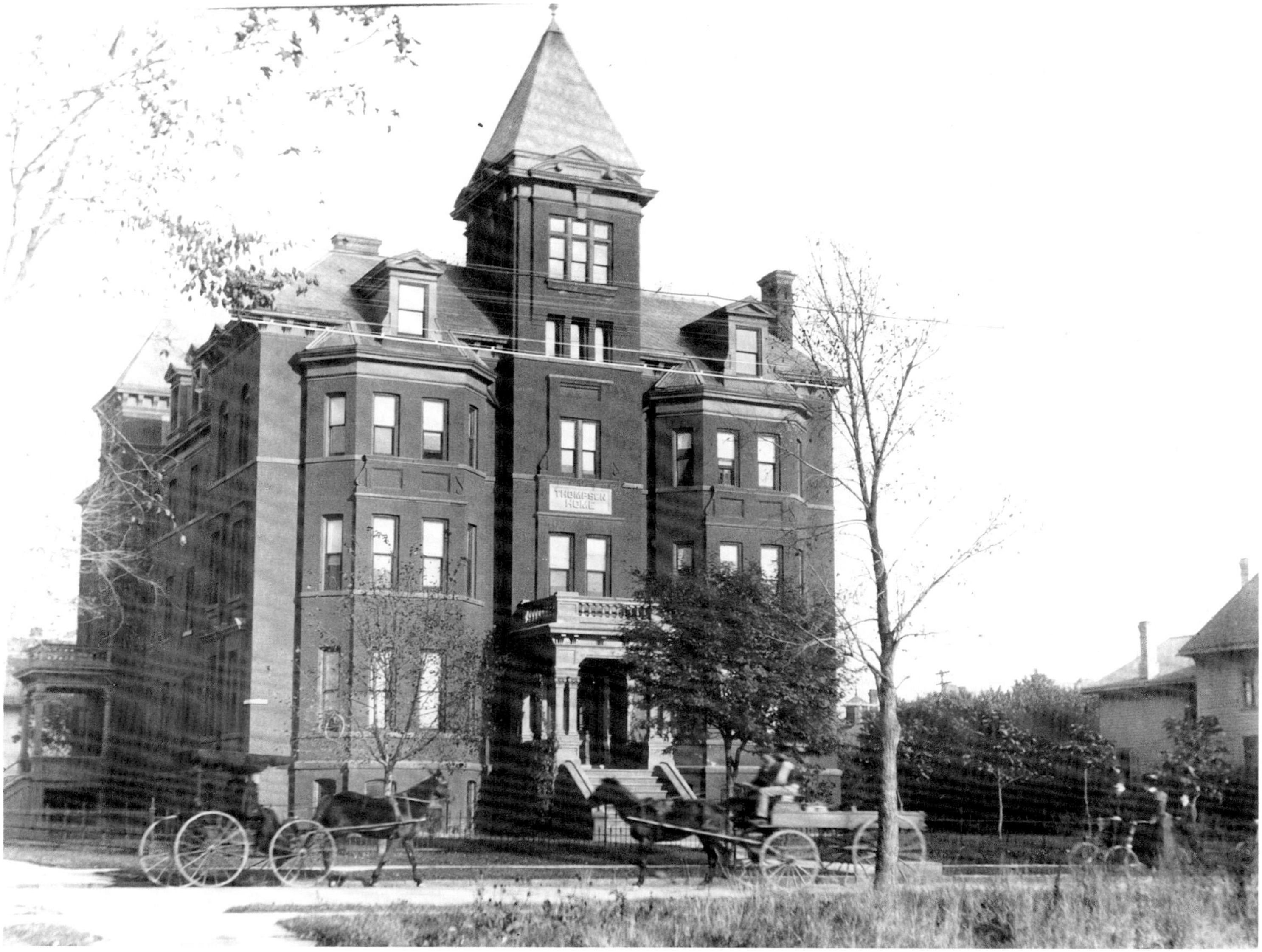

Thompson Home, 4756 Cass Avenue at Hancock Street, 1890s. Horse-drawn carriages drive down the street where many years later students would be trying to parallel park. Named for wealthy businessman David Thompson, this four-story Victorian house was built in 1884. It was originally used as a home for elderly women and was run by Thompson's wife, Mary. The building was purchased by Wayne State University in 1978 and was initially used as a faculty club. From 1990 to 2017, it housed the university's School of Social Work. Currently, it's used as student housing for the College of Fine, Performing and Communication Arts. (Courtesy of the Michigan State Historic Preservation Office.)

Looking south on Cass Avenue, 1899. This area, just north of Central High School, was owned by Cass Farms. Since the high school was two miles from downtown, the area around it remained mostly undeveloped until the 1890s. The tents are set up for the Christian Endeavor Convention. Central High is visible in the background, just left of center, with a flag flying from its spire. (Walter P. Reuther Library, Archives of Labor and Urban Affairs, Wayne State University.)

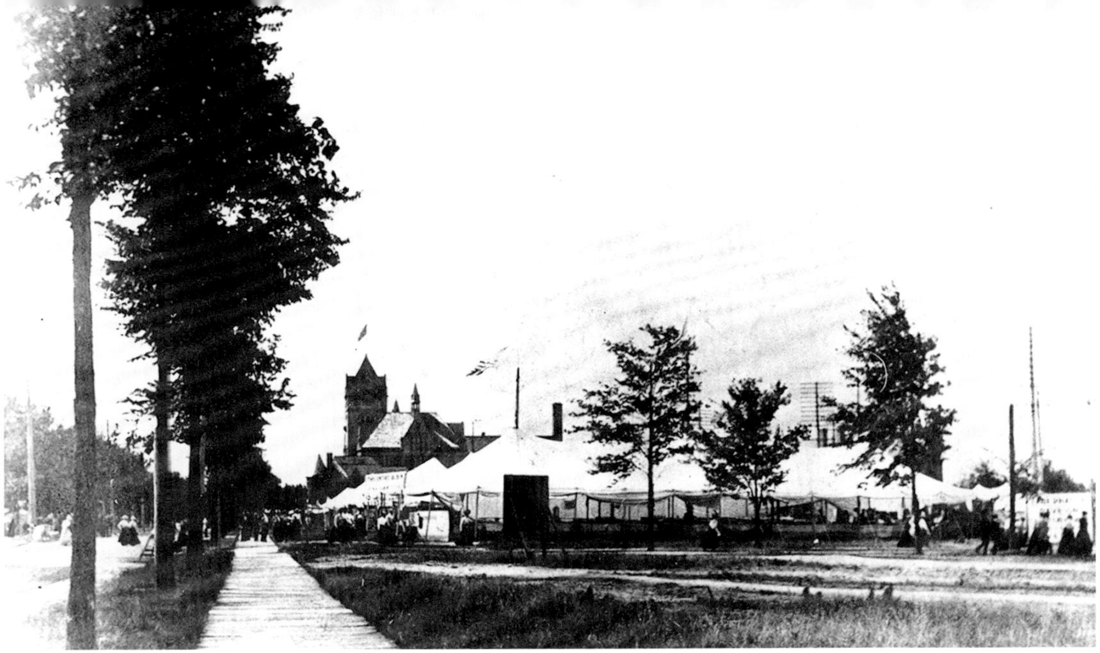

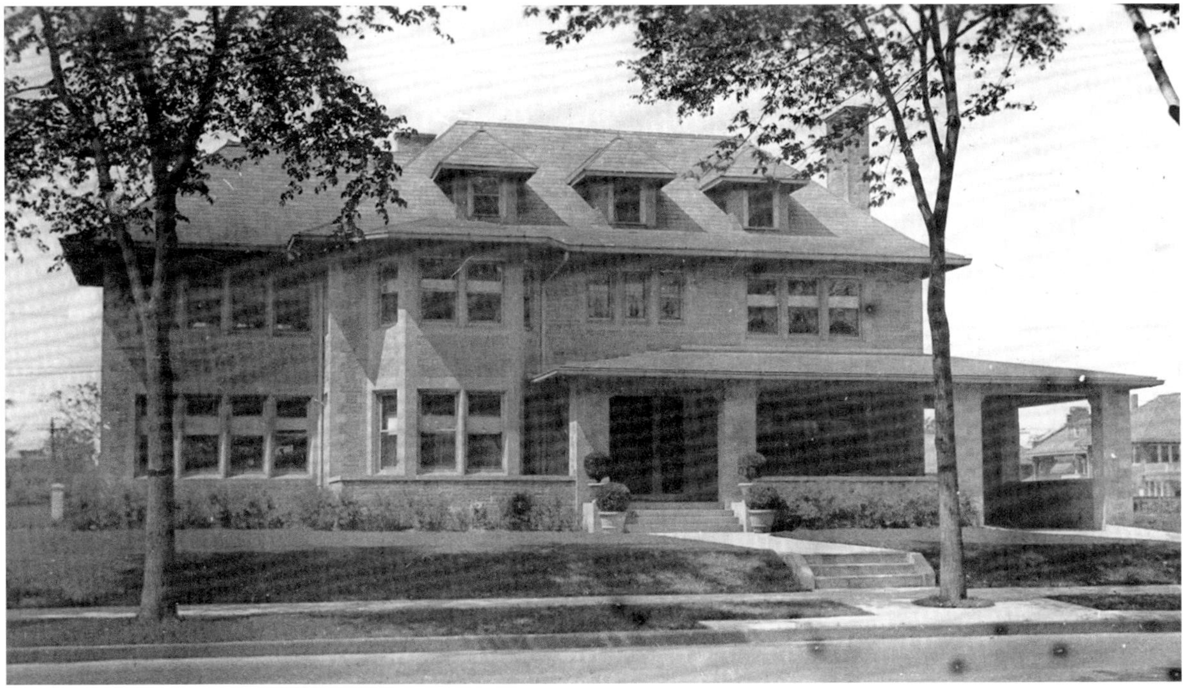

William C. Rands House, 5229 Cass Avenue, 1914. Between 1904 and 1920, a number of houses, including the Rands House, were built in the neighborhood near Central High School for Detroit's growing upper-middle class. The Rands House still stands on campus and is currently used by Wayne State as an annex for the School of Business Administration. (Courtesy of the Burton Historical Collection, Detroit Public Library.)

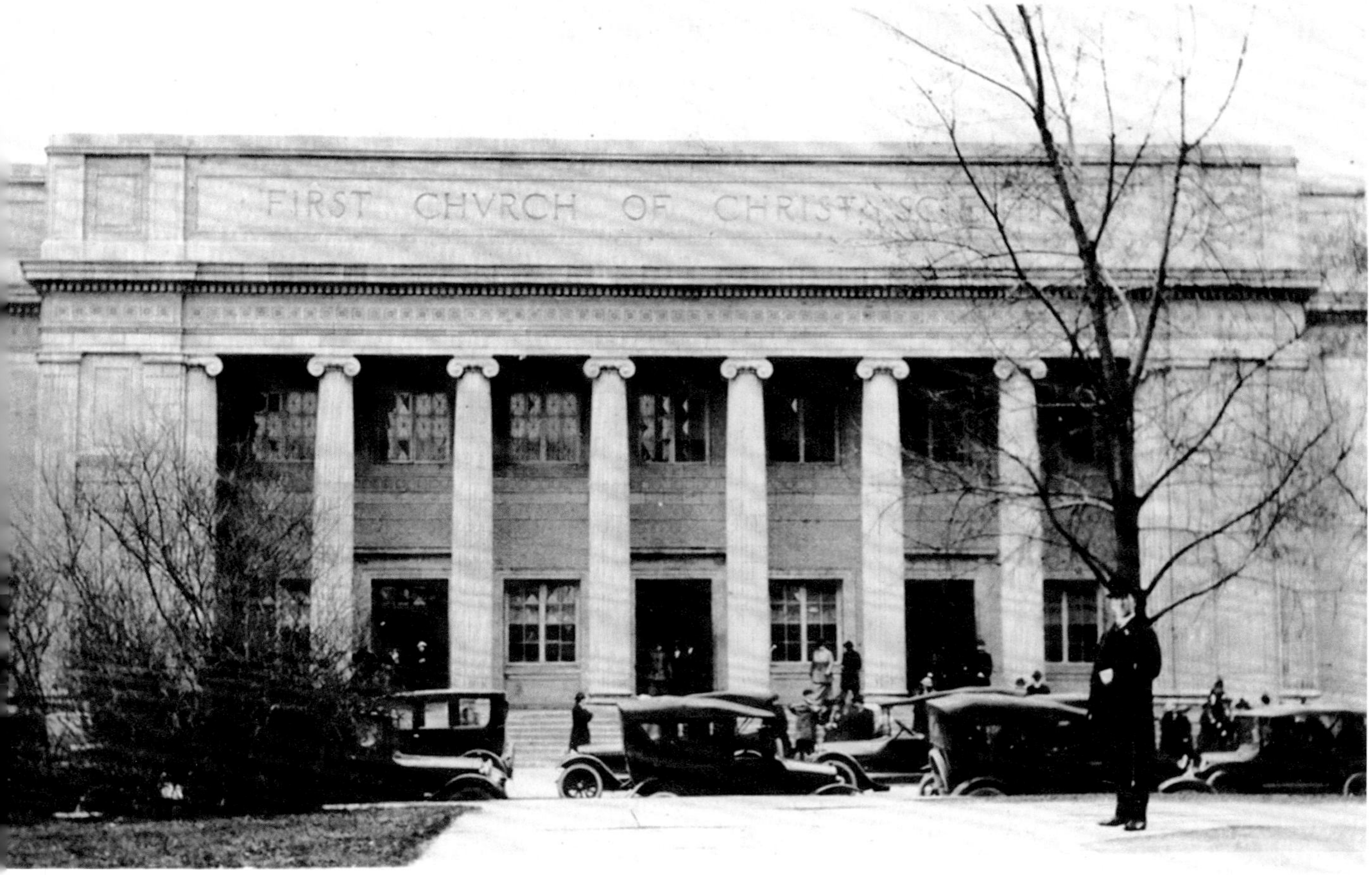

First Church of Christ, Scientist, 4743 Cass Avenue at Hancock Street, about 1917. This church first opened on March 4, 1917, and was used by the Detroit chapter of the First Church of Christ, Scientist. The church eventually did not need such a large structure, and it was purchased by Wayne State in 1961. The university converted the building into the Hilberry Theatre, and currently it is used for graduate performances by Wayne's theater department. (Walter P. Reuther Library, Archives of Labor and Urban Affairs, Wayne State University.)

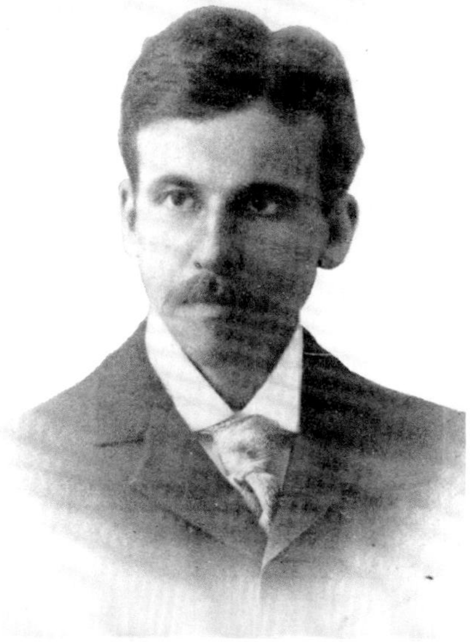

David Mackenzie, 1904. A Detroit native, David Mackenzie was appointed principal of Central High School in 1904. Mackenzie played a pivotal role in establishing the school that would later become Wayne State University, and he is therefore considered the intellectual founder of the university. Under Mackenzie's leadership, the college classes held at Central High School became the core of the Detroit Junior College, of which Mackenzie served as the first dean. Mackenzie championed the junior college because it catered to working-class students, students unable to leave their hometown to attend college. The Detroit Junior College would eventually become the College of the City of Detroit and, finally, the College of Liberal Arts at Wayne University. (Walter P. Reuther Library, Archives of Labor and Urban Affairs, Wayne State University.)

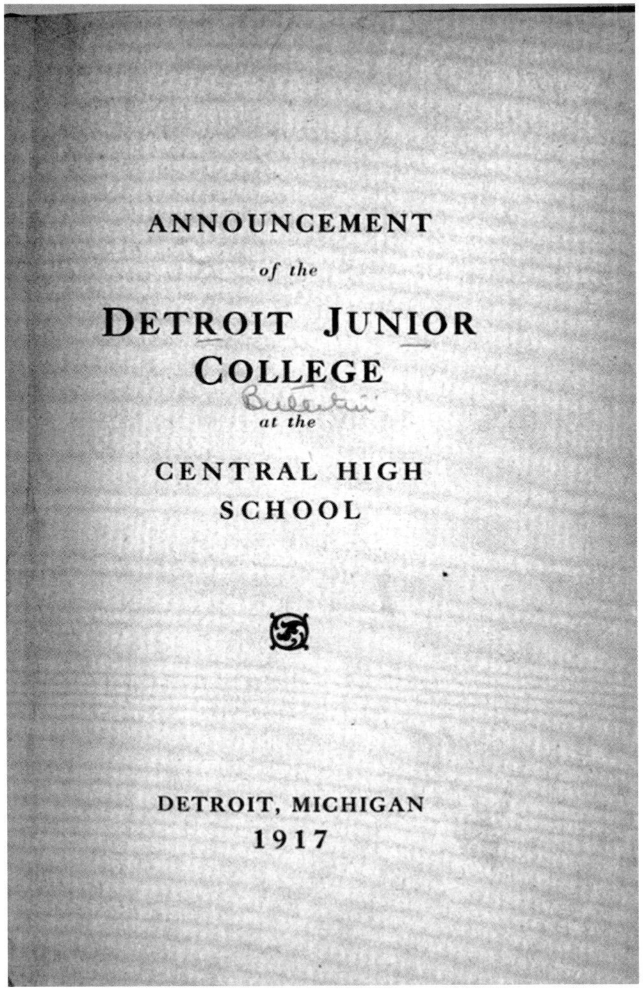
ANNOUNCEMENT
of the
DETROIT JUNIOR
COLLEGE
at the
CENTRAL HIGH
SCHOOL

DETROIT, MICHIGAN
1917

Detroit Junior College bulletin, 1917. This image shows the first schedule of classes issued by Dean David Mackenzie for the Detroit Junior College, one of Wayne State's antecedents. Wayne State University evolved from programs housed at Central High School. The Detroit Junior College was similar to today's community college. (Walter P. Reuther Library, Archives of Labor and Urban Affairs, Wayne State University.)

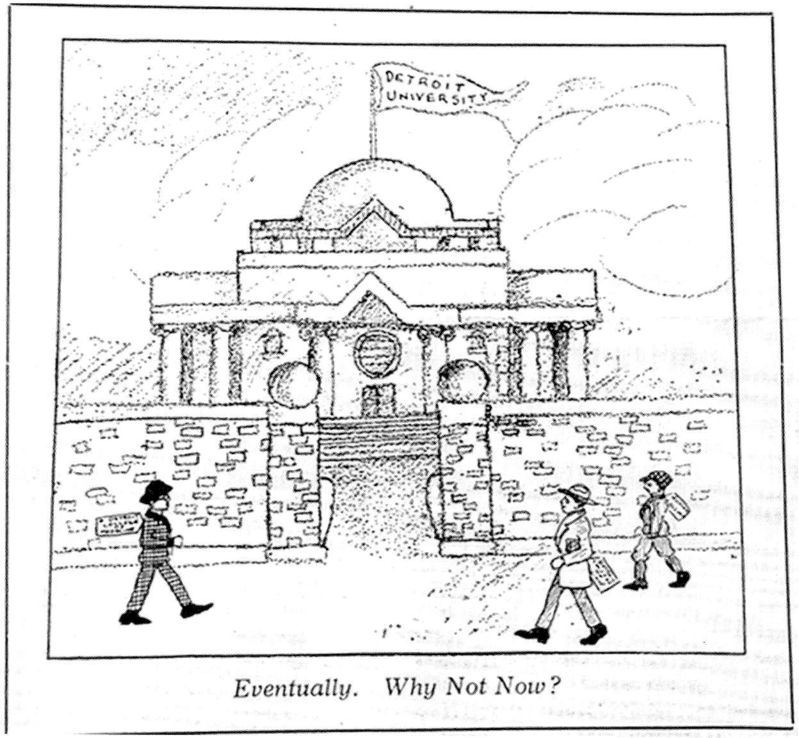

Cartoon, *The Collegian*, April 25, 1918. *The Collegian*, the student newspaper for Detroit Junior College, was first published semimonthly in 1918. This cartoon appeared alongside one of the many articles written in support of upgrading the college to a four-year institution. The change, if successful, would be crucial to the school's status, because it could then grant degrees. The students, from left to right, are labeled "Detroit College of Medicine," "Detroit School of Law," and "Junior College." Note the differences in dress between the college graduates and the junior college graduate. (Walter P. Reuther Library, Archives of Labor and Urban Affairs, Wayne State University.)

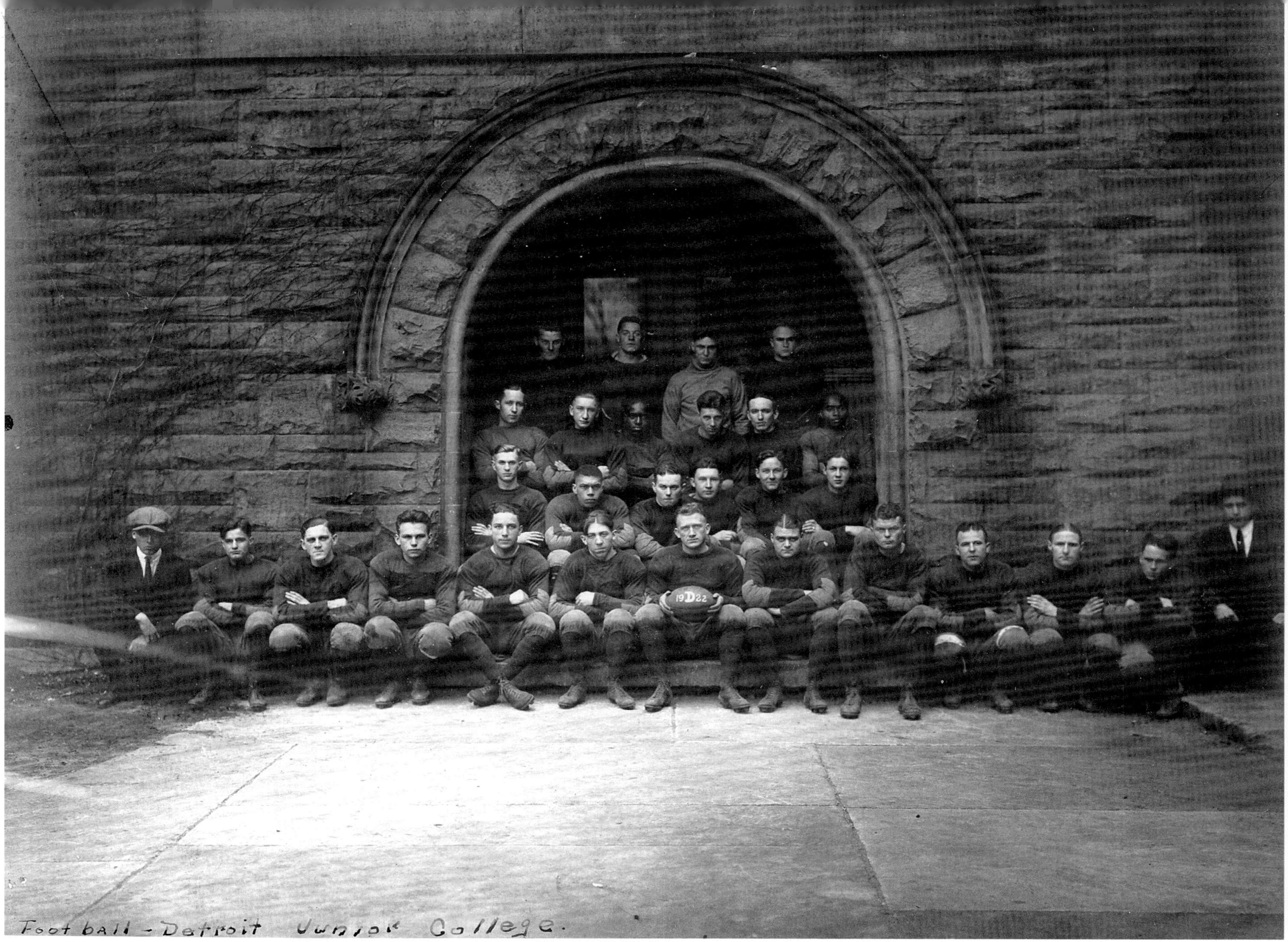
19D22
Football - Detroit Junior College.

Detroit Junior College football team, Central High School, 1922. Although student organizations were curtailed during World War I, by the time the second semester had begun at Detroit Junior College in 1918, individual students had already organized after-school groups, including a football team. The student council was organized in 1917 and adopted Old Gold and Kelly Green as the school's colors, needed for its basketball team, which played its first games under Coach David Holmes in the winter of 1917–18. The football team, which included members of the Student Army Training Corps, played its first game in the fall of 1918. (Courtesy of the Burton Historical Collection, Detroit Public Library.)

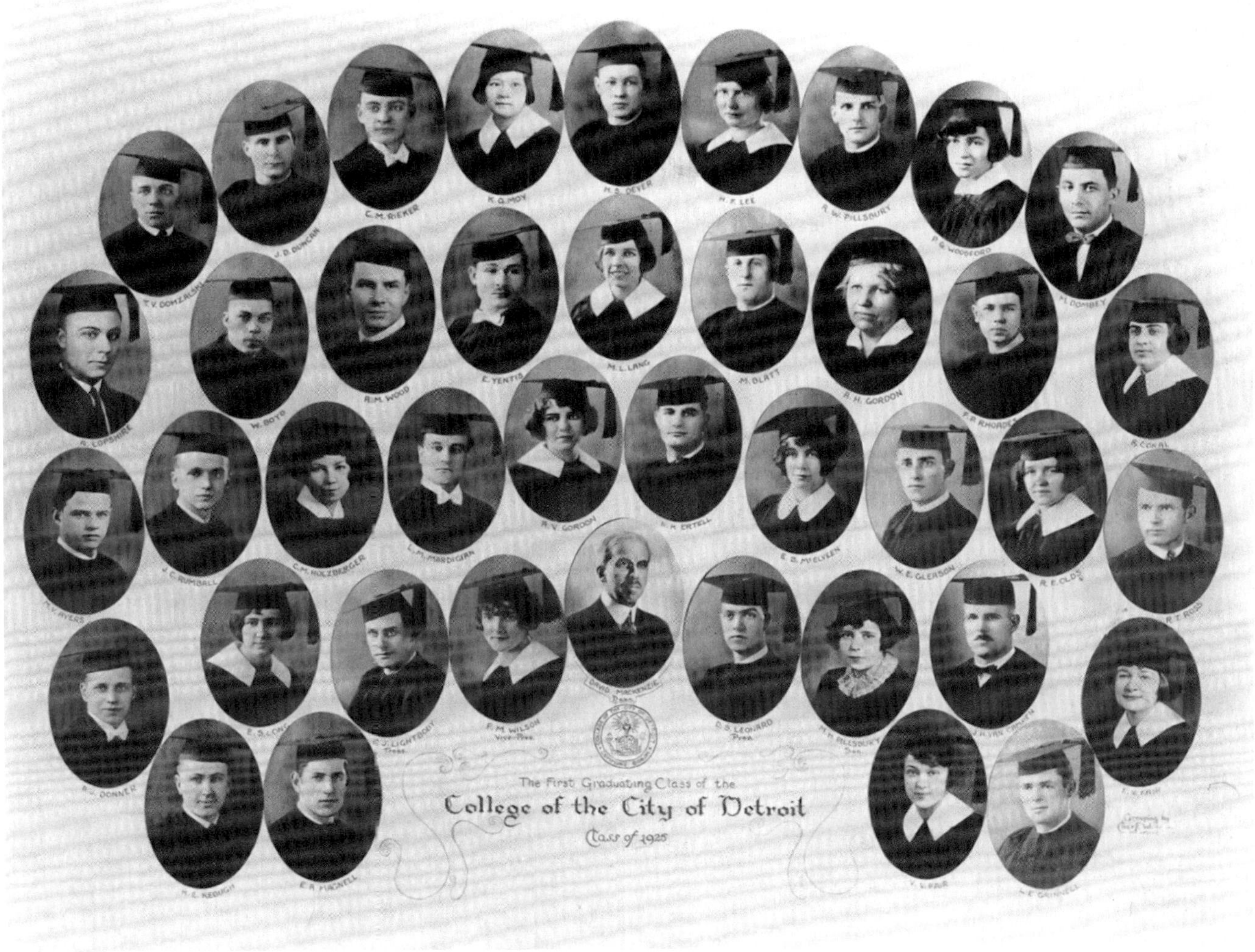

The first graduates of the College of the City of Detroit, 1925. In 1923, the Detroit Junior College became a four-year, degree-granting institution and was renamed the College of the City of Detroit. Two years later, City College, as students called it, held its first commencement exercise. David Mackenzie, dean of the college, awarded the degrees: forty-nine bachelor of arts degrees, eight bachelor of science degrees, and five pharmaceutical chemist degrees. The graduation ceremony celebrated not just the students' diplomas but seven years of hard work—by Dr. Andrew P. Biddle, president of the Detroit Board of Education; Walter MacCraken, dean of the College of Medicine; Frank Cody, superintendent of the Detroit public schools; and, especially, Dean David Mackenzie—to upgrade the school into a college. (Walter P. Reuther Library, Archives of Labor and Urban Affairs, Wayne State University.)

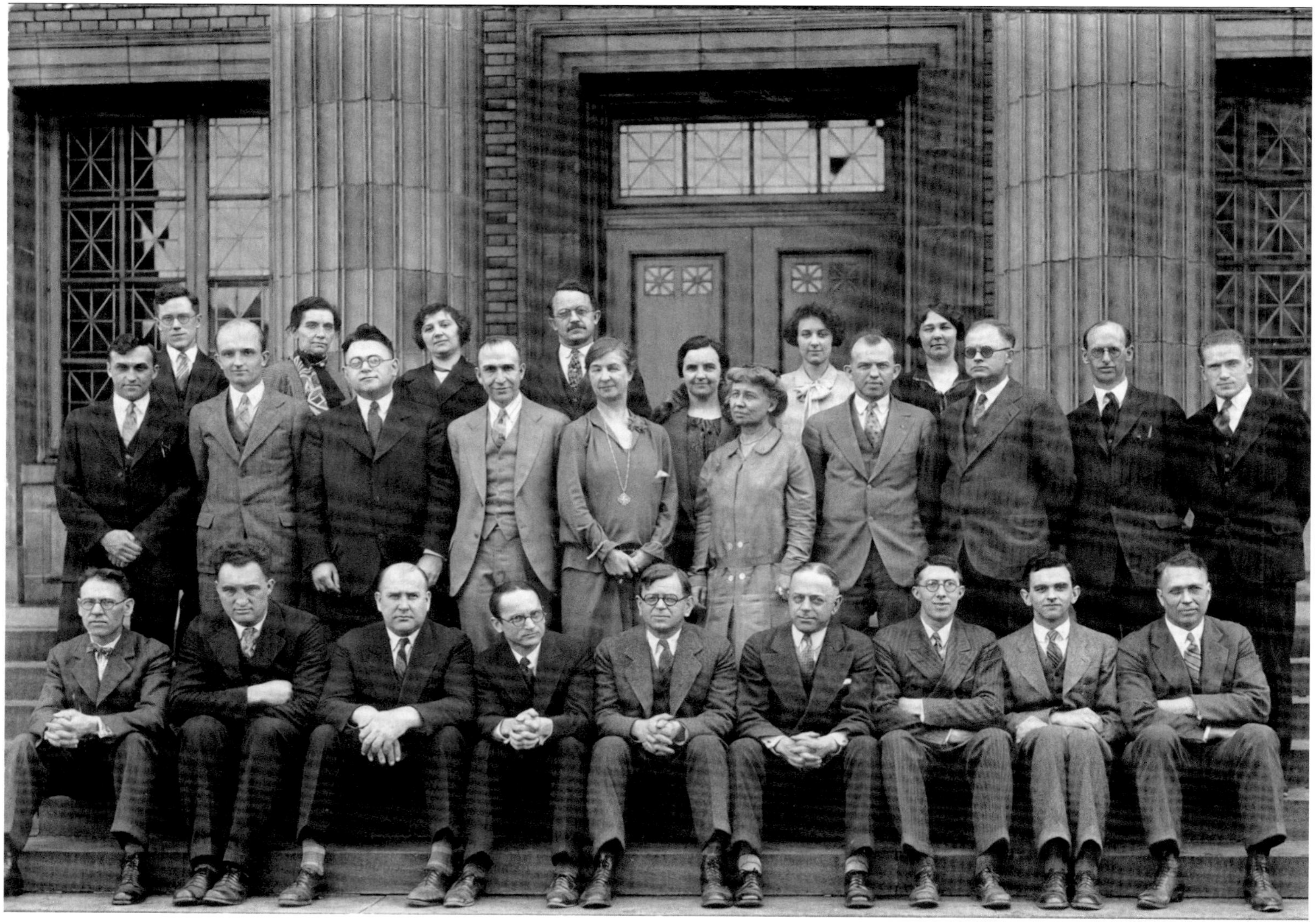

College of the City of Detroit faculty, September 1926. Shown here are some of City College's professors during the last year that high school classes were taught in the Central High School building. After 1926, only college classes were taught in the school, which was thereafter called the Main Building. High school students were relocated to the new Central High School building at Tuxedo Street and Linwood Avenue on Roosevelt Field. (Walter P. Reuther Library, Archives of Labor and Urban Affairs, Wayne State University.)

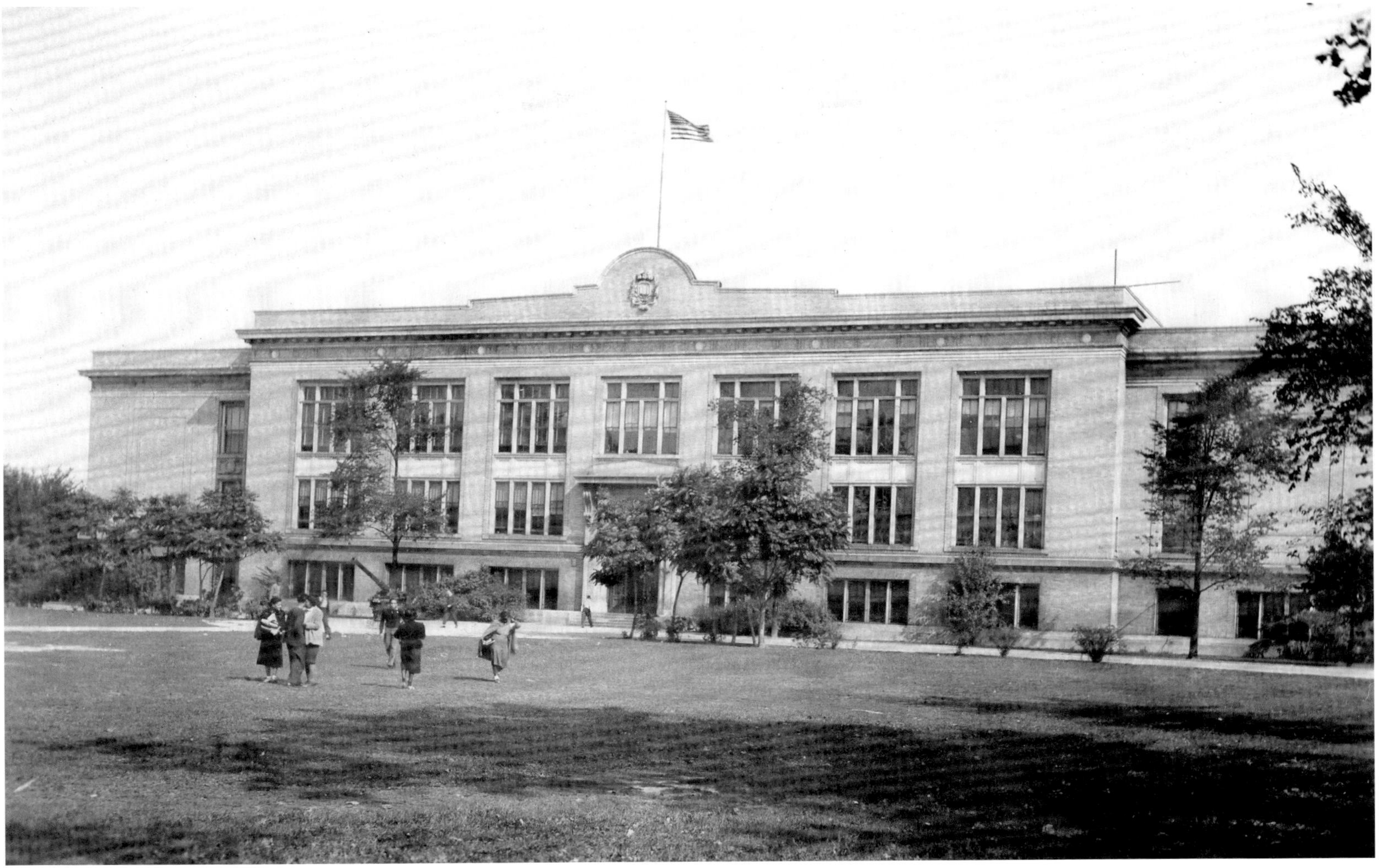

Northwestern High School on West Grand Boulevard. In January 1914, the Detroit Normal Training School moved from Washington School to the newly built Northwestern High School, and the program was officially named the Wales G. Martindale Normal Training School. In 1920, the normal school became a four-year college and was renamed the Detroit Teachers College. In 1930, the Teachers College moved into the Main Building, where it would become Wayne University's College of Education in 1933. (Courtesy of the Burton Historical Collection, Detroit Public Library.)

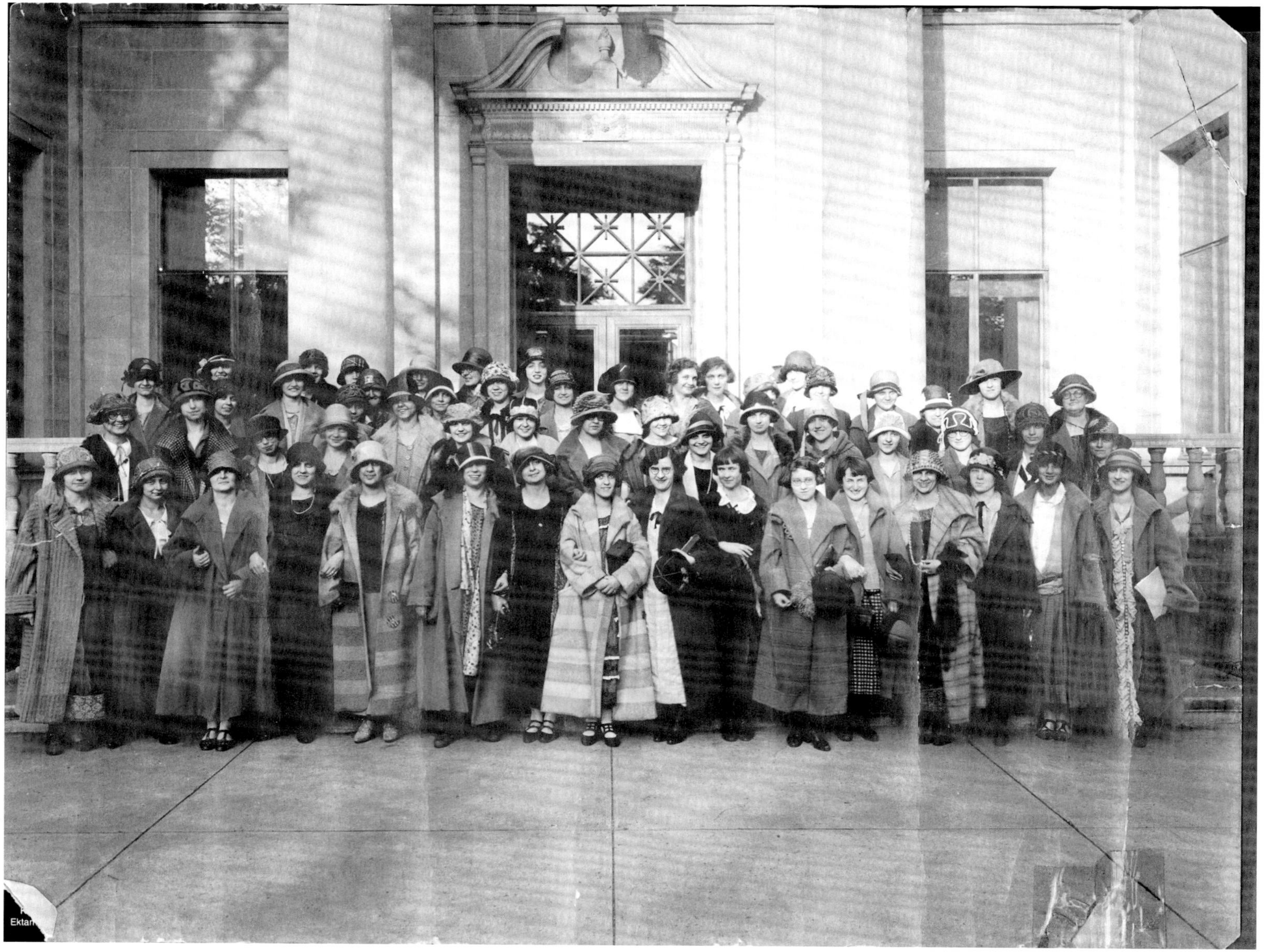

Graduating class, Detroit Teachers College, June 1924. In their cloche hats and shawl-collared coats typical of the era, the graduating class of the Detroit Teachers College of 1924 celebrate their accomplishments at the headquarters of the Women's Benefit Association in Port Huron, Michigan. (Courtesy of the Burton Historical Collection, Detroit Public Library.)

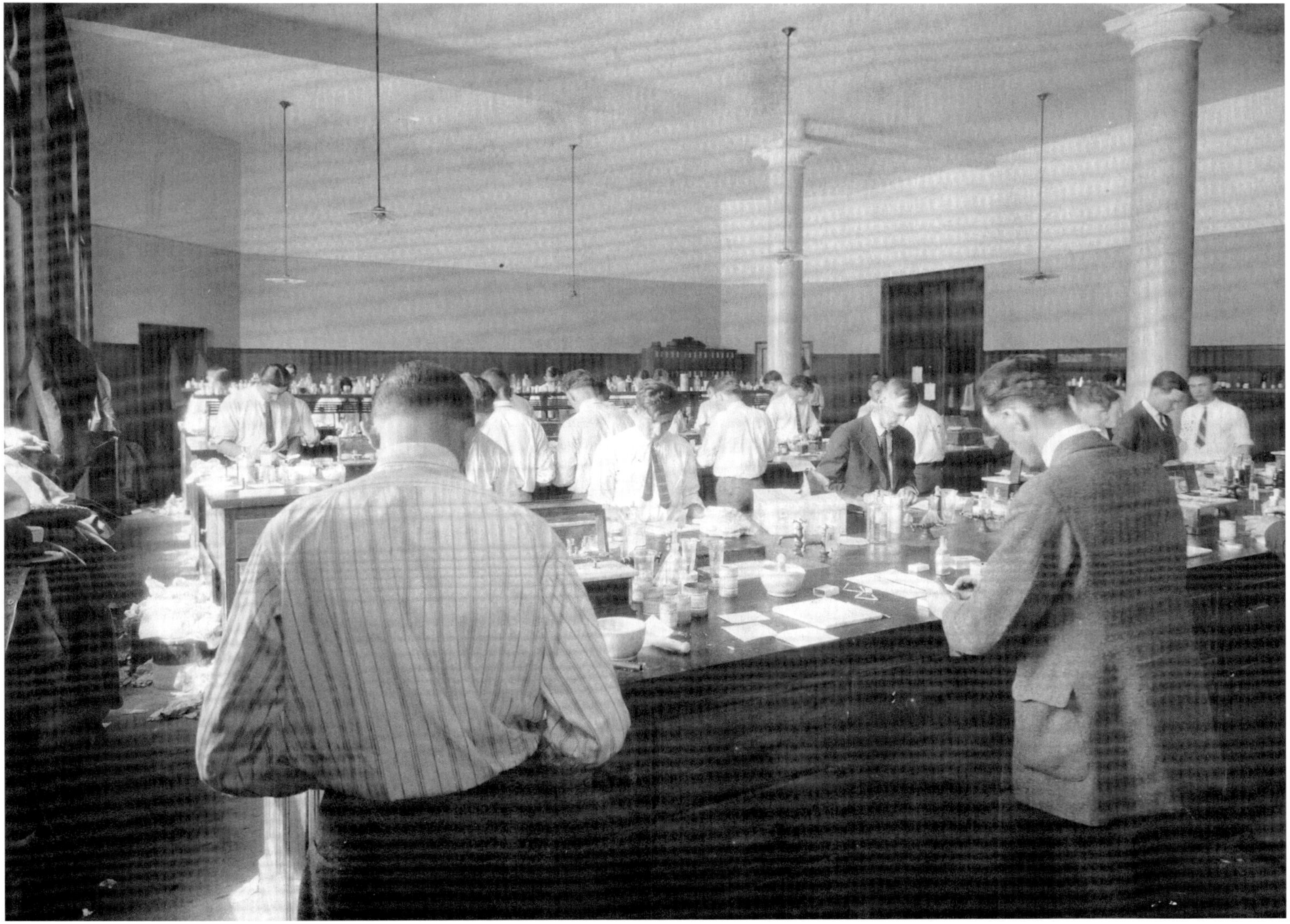

Pharmacy lab, 1920s. When the Detroit Junior College became a four-year school, the Detroit Retail Druggists' Association requested that the Board of Education also create a college of pharmacy. The field of medicine was becoming professionalized, and the group wanted similar professional status for pharmacists. The Board of Education subsequently created the College of Pharmacy, and in 1925, the College of the City of Detroit granted its first pharmacy degree. The following year the pharmacy school was moved from Cass Technical High School to the Main Building. (Walter P. Reuther Library, Archives of Labor and Urban Affairs, Wayne State University.)

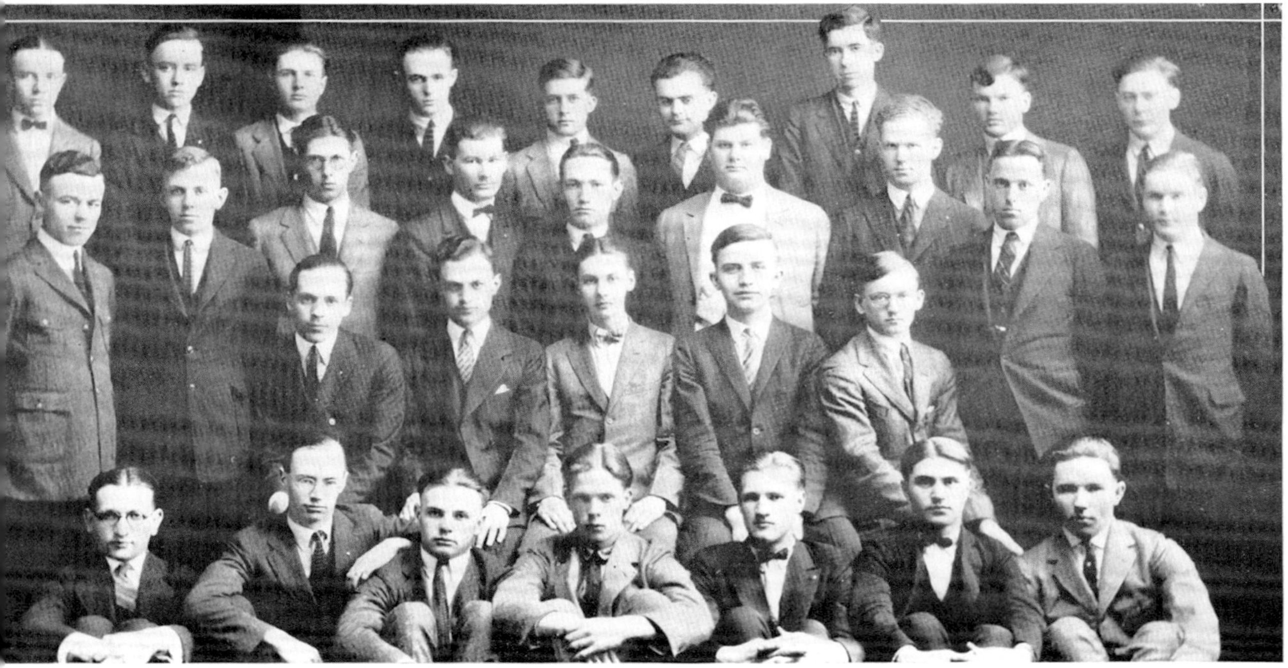

College of the City of Detroit Engineering Society, 1924. In 1917, a group of Detroit Junior College engineering students formed the Engineering Society, and two years later, they started their own publication, *Buzz-Saw*. Even after City College was established in 1923, the school did not offer a four-year engineering degree, so City College engineering students were forced—as their junior college equivalents had been—to go to the University of Michigan to finish their degrees. In 1927, the Detroit Board of Education was granted the authority by Michigan's legislature to award professional engineering degrees. A year later, four City College students received their degrees, including Elinor M. Batie, the first female engineer to graduate from the college. (Walter P. Reuther Library, Archives of Labor and Urban Affairs, Wayne State University.)

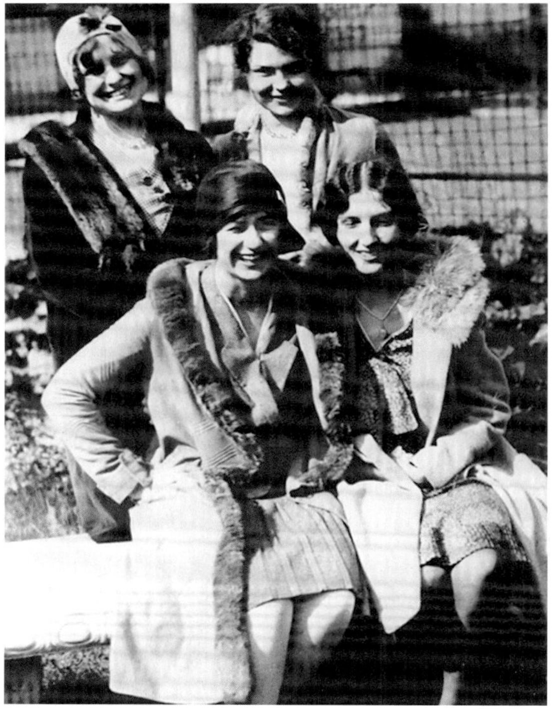

College of the City of Detroit students, 1928. As in the rest of the country, fur-trimmed coats and bobbed haircuts were the height of fashion in Detroit in the late 1920s. (Walter P. Reuther Library, Archives of Labor and Urban Affairs, Wayne State University.)

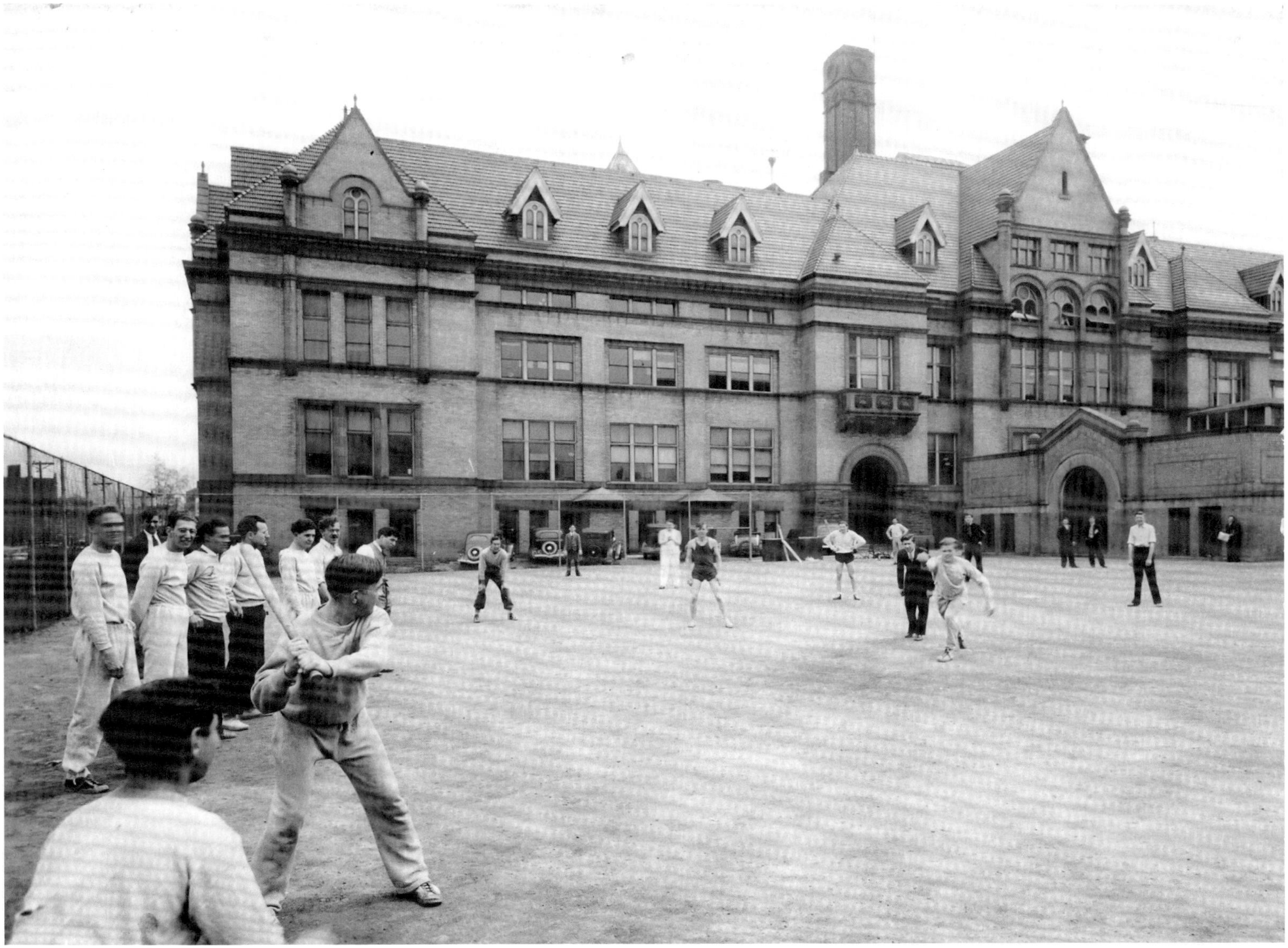

Softball game behind the Main Building, 1930s. Sports teams at Wayne State didn't have convenient or permanent practice fields for many years. Teams practiced in various athletic fields and facilities around Detroit—or in the yard behind the Main Building's powerhouse, an area roughly one-third the size of a football field. School sports teams did not attract many players, since many City College students worked to support themselves while attending classes. Most students were too busy to participate in athletics or attend the games. (Walter P. Reuther Library, Archives of Labor and Urban Affairs, Wayne State University.)

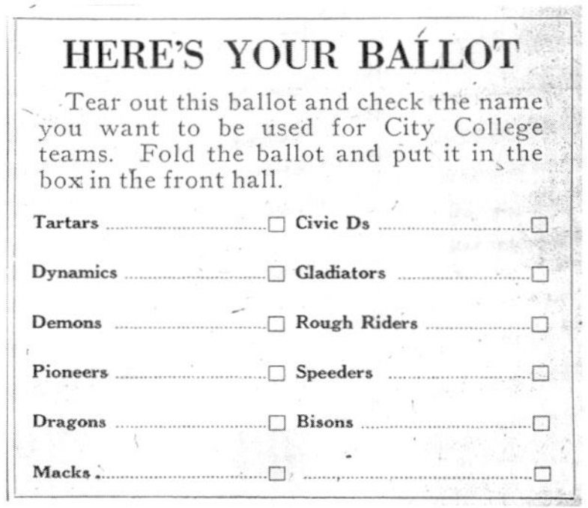

HERE'S YOUR BALLOT

Tear out this ballot and check the name you want to be used for City College teams. Fold the ballot and put it in the box in the front hall.

Tartars	☐	Civic Ds	☐
Dynamics	☐	Gladiators	☐
Demons	☐	Rough Riders	☐
Pioneers	☐	Speeders	☐
Dragons	☐	Bisons	☐
Macks	☐		☐

Tartar ballot, *The Collegian*, 1927. Students were asked to vote for an official team name to replace nicknames like "Munies" and "Munics," which were short for "municipal." When students chose "Tartars," after a Mongolian tribe, they could not have anticipated the endless stream of corny jokes that would arise from the nickname. Wayne State University sports teams were known as the Tartars for seventy-two years, until they became the Warriors in 1999. (Walter P. Reuther Library, Archives of Labor and Urban Affairs, Wayne State University.)

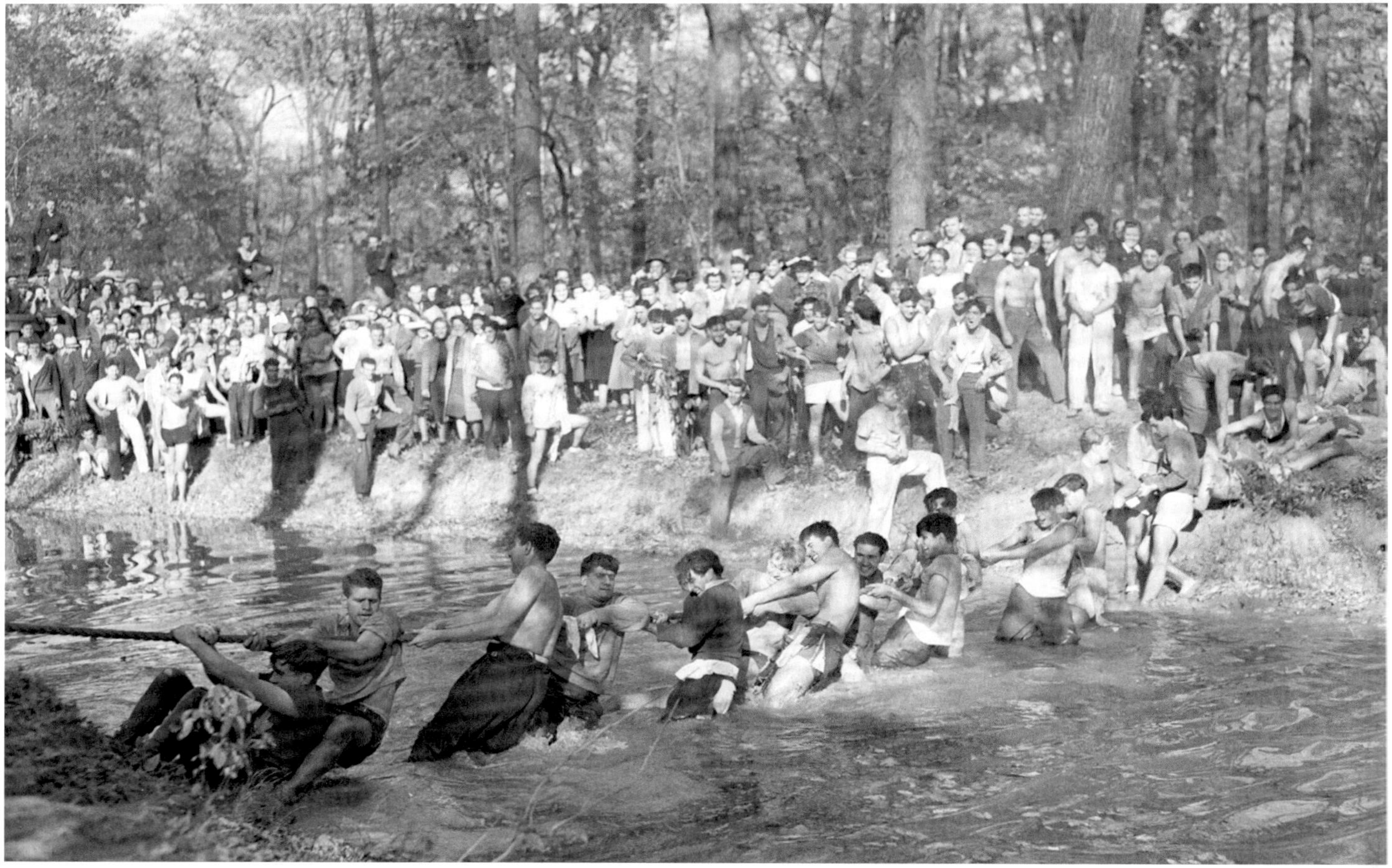

College of the City of Detroit class rush, Belle Isle, 1939. Call it freshman initiation, class rivalry, or just plain old hazing, this interclass competition took place at Belle Isle each fall during the 1920s and 1930s. Members of the freshman and sophomore classes competed against one another in games like tug-of-war and capture the flag. (Walter P. Reuther Library, Archives of Labor and Urban Affairs, Wayne State University.)

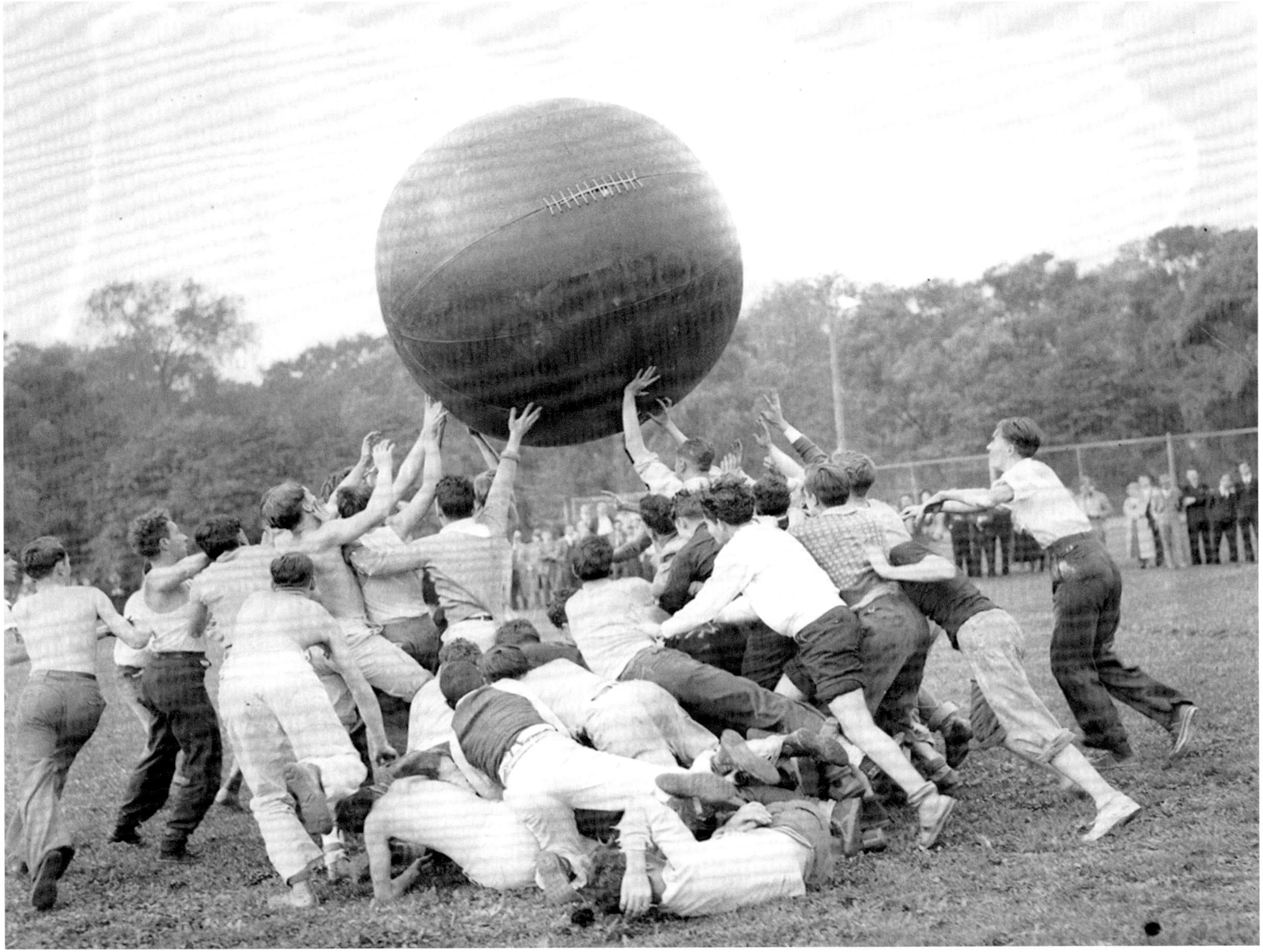

College of the City of Detroit class rush, Belle Isle, late 1920s. In this photograph, students are seen playing pushball. The object of the game is for the members of two teams to attempt to roll (or throw or carry) the ball over the other team's goal line. Pushball, like other class rush games, was used by upperclassmen as a vehicle for hazing City College freshmen. (Walter P. Reuther Library, Archives of Labor and Urban Affairs, Wayne State University.)

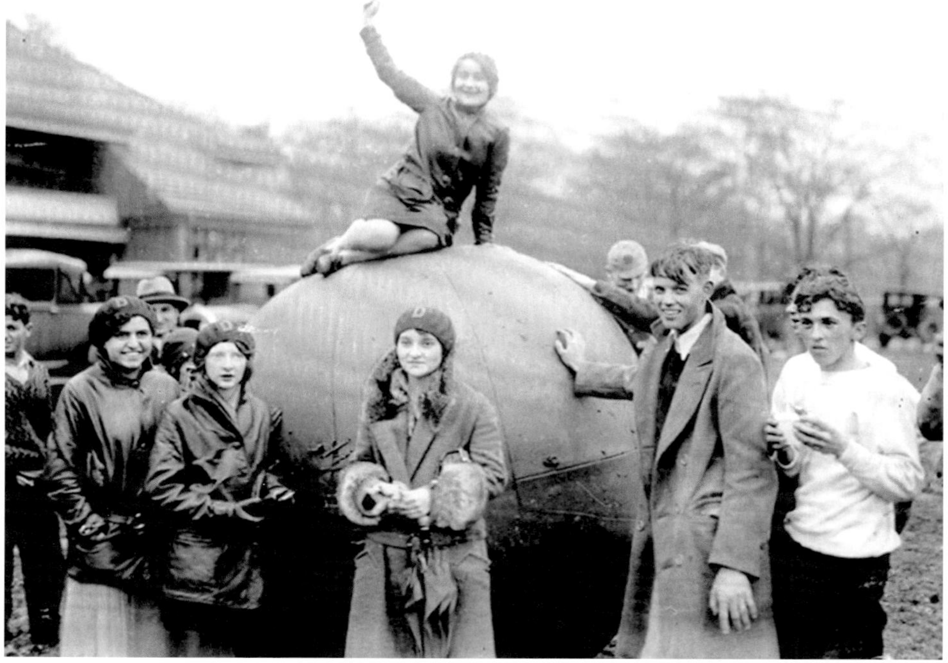

College of the City of Detroit class rush, Belle Isle, 1929. Here, a student sits atop the pushball. While class rush games were popular in the 1920s and 1930s, attitudes toward the roughhousing changed over the years. "Playful Skull Bashing," an article that appeared in the 1936 yearbook, derided the class games as "crude." In 1938, Joseph Selden, the dean of students, worked with the student council to bring the games under control. By the 1950s, hazing was a thing of the past. (Walter P. Reuther Library, Archives of Labor and Urban Affairs, Wayne State University.)

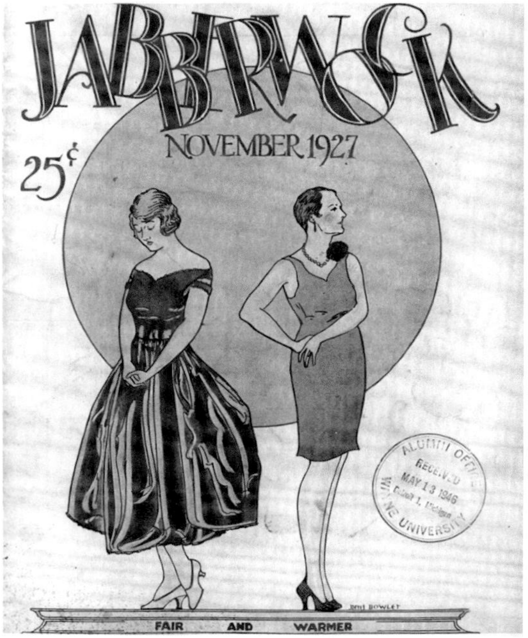

Jabberwock cover, 1927. *Jabberwock*, a monthly humor magazine, was one of many publications written by Wayne students. Other student publications from this period include the *Normalite*, a monthly paper written by students of the Teachers College; *Buzz-Saw* (later the *Wayne Engineer*), published by engineering students; the *Wayne Pharmic*, created by pharmacy students; and the student yearbook, *The Griffin*. (Walter P. Reuther Library, Archives of Labor and Urban Affairs, Wayne State University.)

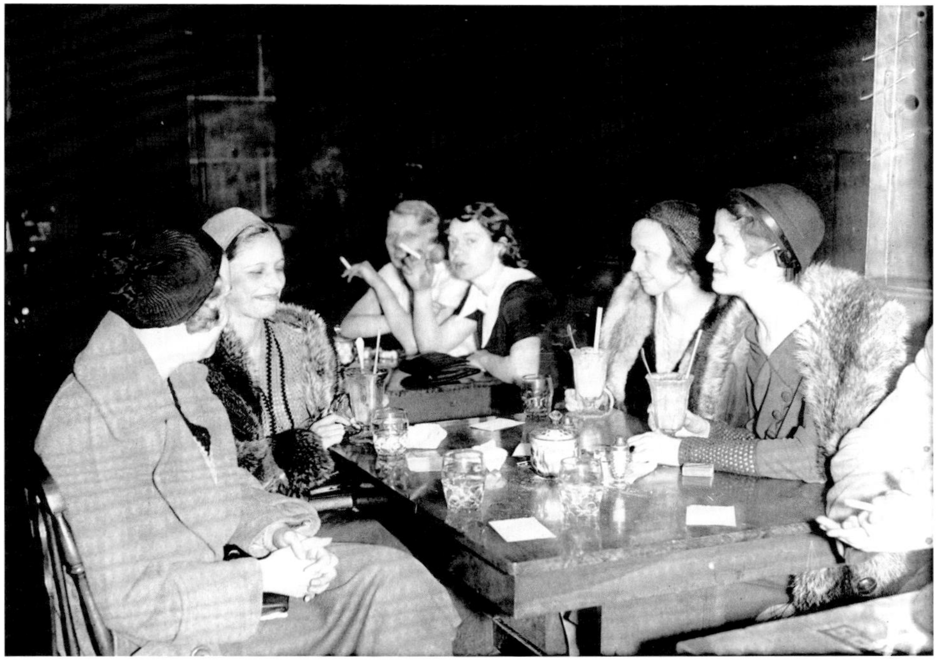

City College students, 1932. Students relax at a local restaurant. (Walter P. Reuther Library, Archives of Labor and Urban Affairs, Wayne State University.)

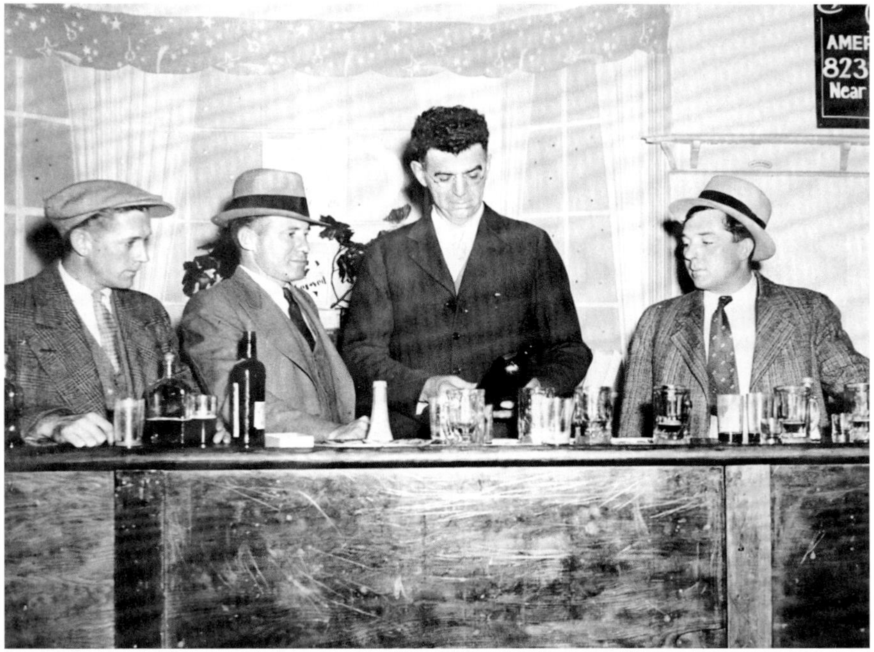

Detroit police officers after a raid on a speakeasy, November 1932. Police officers examine what's behind the bar at Club Oasis. The club, located near City College, was a popular student hangout during Prohibition (1920–33). In the western and midwestern United States, such speakeasies were called "blind pigs," after the tradition of exhibiting strange animals at speakeasies. (Walter P. Reuther Library, Archives of Labor and Urban Affairs, Wayne State University.)

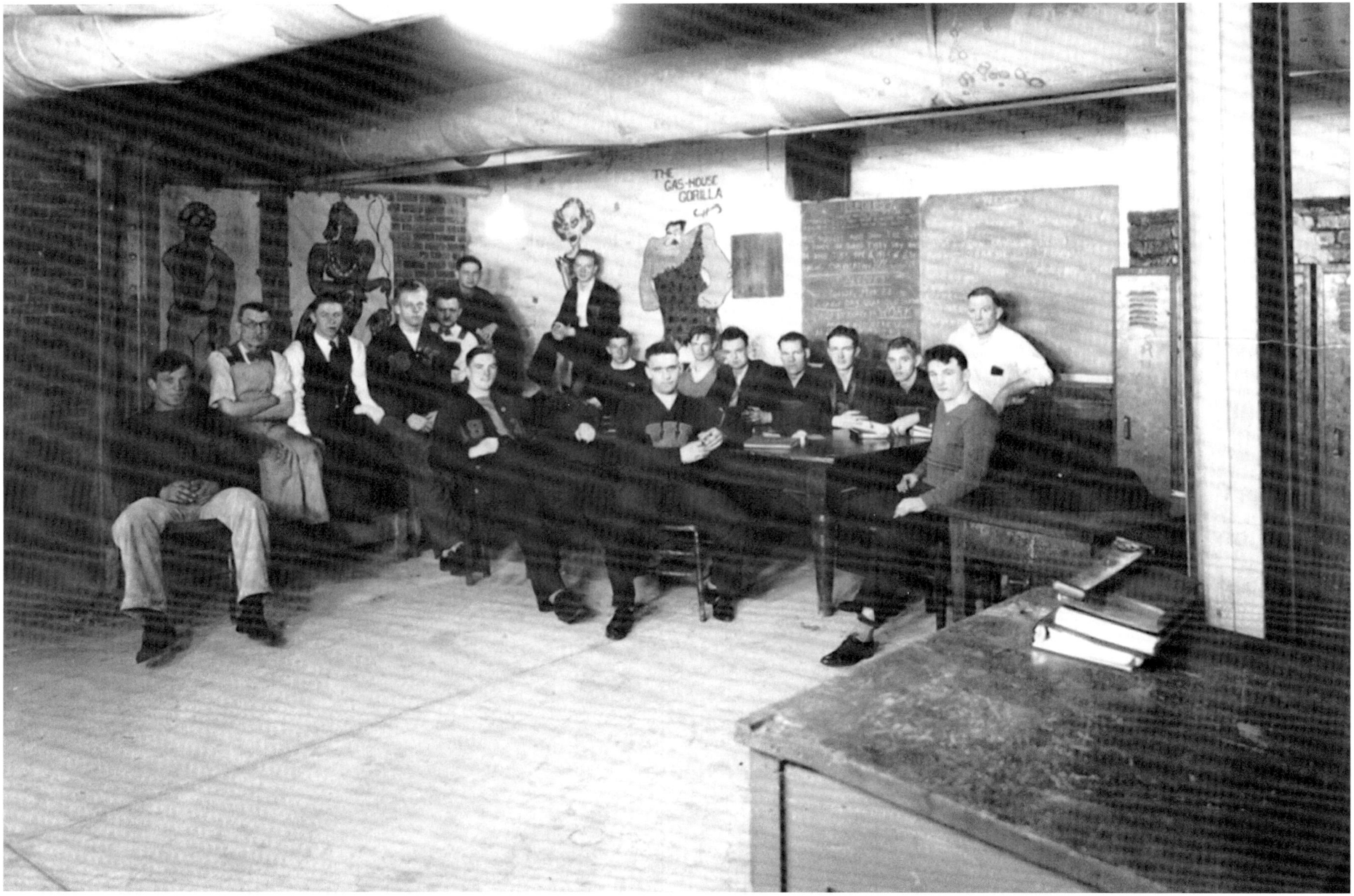

Gas House Gang members, 1935. Most Wayne football players joined the Gas House Gang, a group that resembled a fraternity. Founded in 1922, the club's meeting place was an old boiler room in the basement of the Main Building. (Walter P. Reuther Library, Archives of Labor and Urban Affairs, Wayne State University.)

Belcrest Apartment Hotel, 5440 Cass Avenue, 1928. Although not owned by Wayne State, the Belcrest has become part of the university landscape. Once one of Detroit's elegant hotels, the Belcrest is said to have hosted such stars as Cary Grant. During the 1950s, the Belcrest would serve as both a hotel and a residential apartment. The Belcrest and the Chatsworth Apartments, purchased by Wayne State in 1960, appear on the National Register of Historic Places and continue to operate as apartment buildings. The union that represents Wayne's professors, the American Association of University Professors, once had its offices in the Belcrest. (Walter P. Reuther Library, Archives of Labor and Urban Affairs, Wayne State University.)

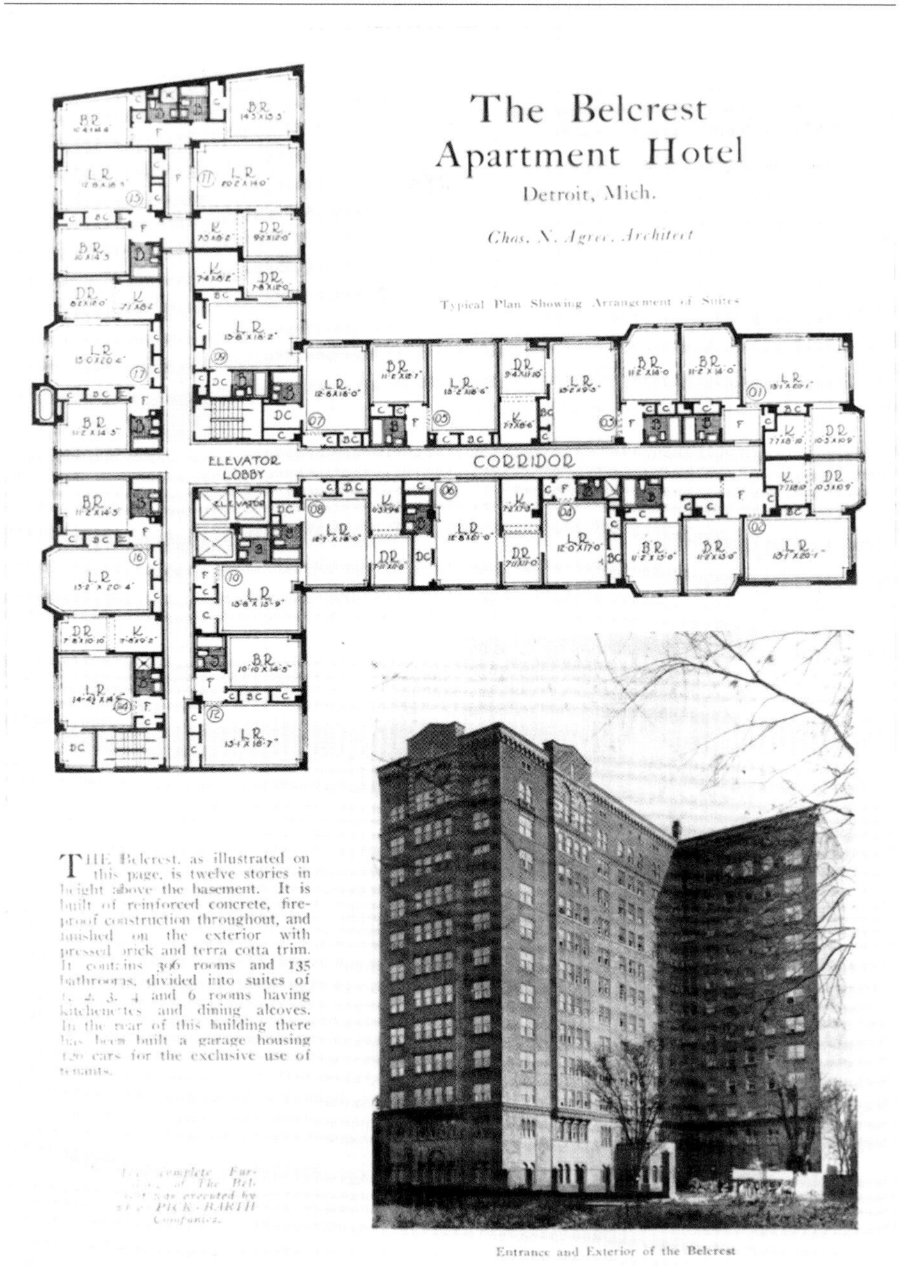

The Belcrest
Apartment Hotel
Detroit, Mich.

Chas. N. Agree, Architect

Typical Plan Showing Arrangement of Suites

THE Belcrest, as illustrated on this page, is twelve stories in height above the basement. It is built of reinforced concrete, fireproof construction throughout, and finished on the exterior with pressed brick and terra cotta trim. It contains 306 rooms and 135 bathrooms, divided into suites of 1, 2, 3, 4 and 6 rooms having kitchenettes and dining alcoves. In the rear of this building there has been built a garage housing 120 cars for the exclusive use of tenants.

The complete Furnishing of The Belcrest was executed by the PICK-BARTH Companies.

Entrance and Exterior of the Belcrest

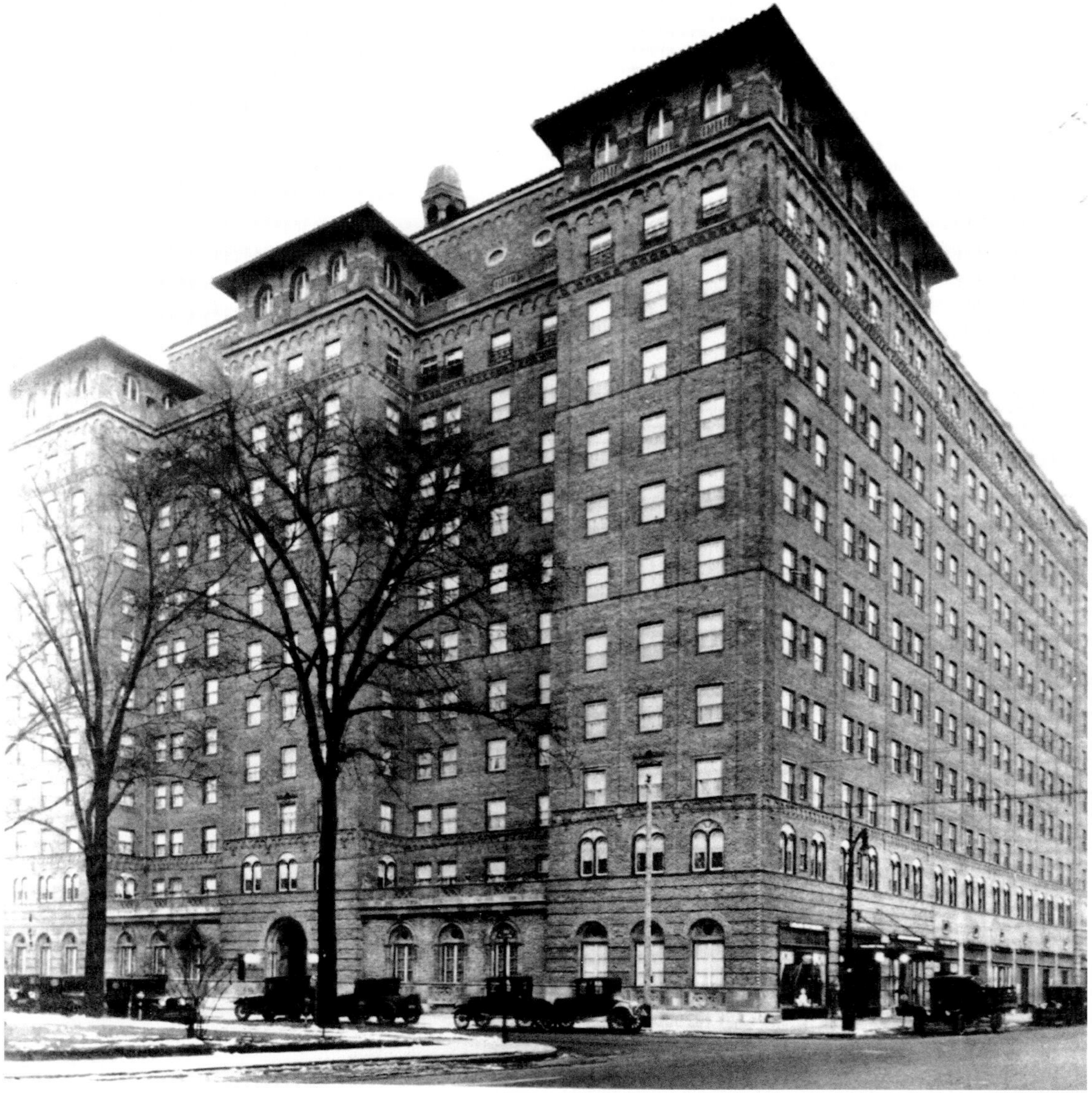

Webster Hall Hotel, 5050 Cass Avenue at Putnam Street, 1928. Built in 1924, the building was originally called the Webster Hall Hotel and catered exclusively to men (the hotel was named after Clyde I. Webster, a Detroit judge). Articles from *The Collegian* published during the 1930s indicate that fraternities used rooms in Webster Hall as meeting spaces and the swimming team used the pool for practice. The university purchased the hotel in 1946, converted it into Wayne's first student center and dormitory, and renamed it the Student Center Building, although it was still known popularly as Webster Hall. In 1961, the building was renamed Mackenzie Hall, after university founder David Mackenzie. (Walter P. Reuther Library, Archives of Labor and Urban Affairs, Wayne State University.)

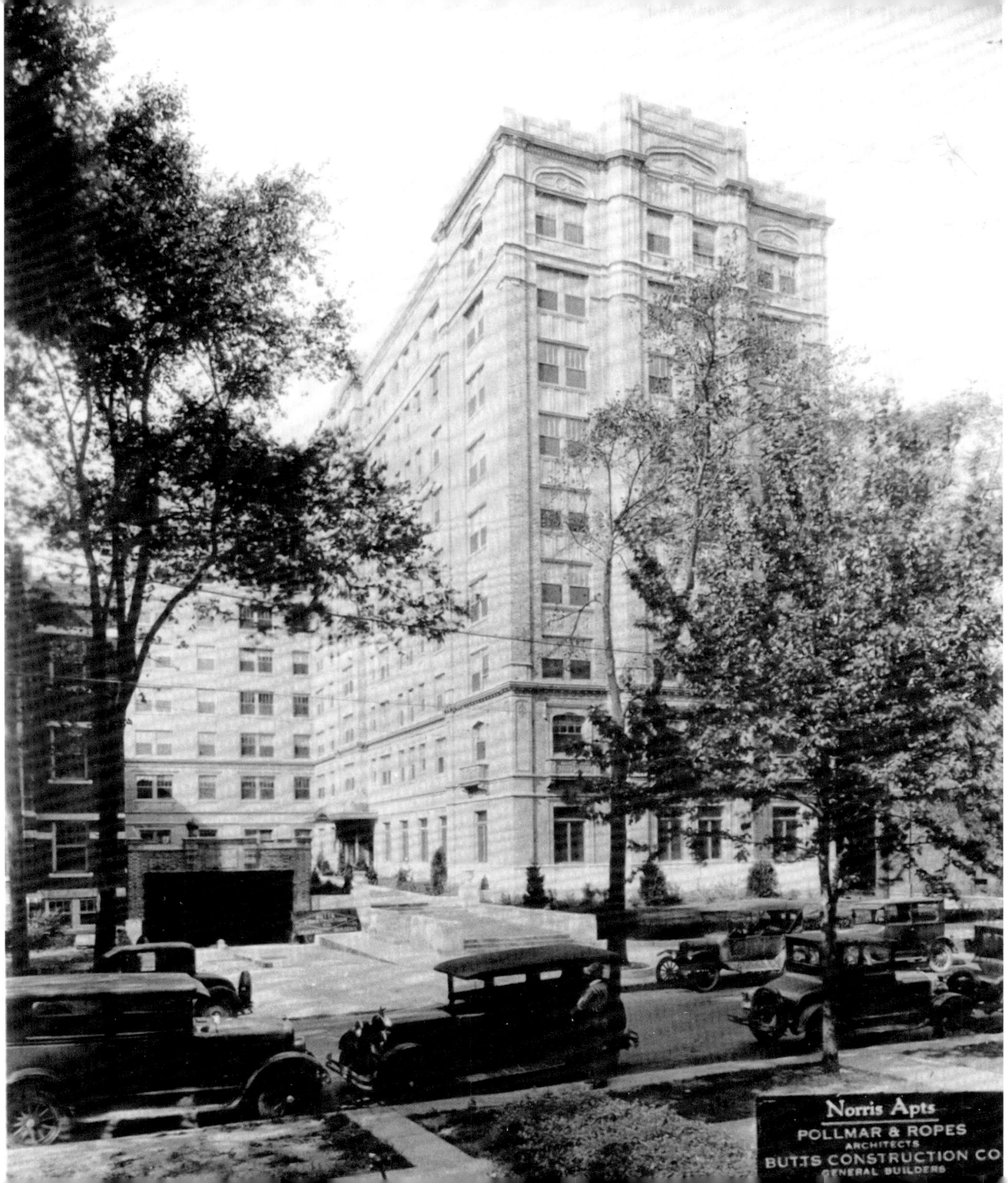

Chatsworth Tower, 630 Merrick, 1928. Described as "swank" in a 1951 *Collegian* news article, this apartment building was built in 1928. The Chatsworth, along with Webster Hall and the Belcrest, helped keep the character of the neighborhood around the Main Building of City College from becoming too commercial. Many homes in the area were being converted into rental properties, and more apartment houses rather than single-family homes were being built. Furthermore, the New Center neighborhood north of the campus was being developed as another automotive center, with numerous automobile dealerships and repair facilities. The Chatsworth Annex, the addition to the left of the tower, was demolished in the summer of 2005. (Walter P. Reuther Library, Archives of Labor and Urban Affairs, Wayne State University.)

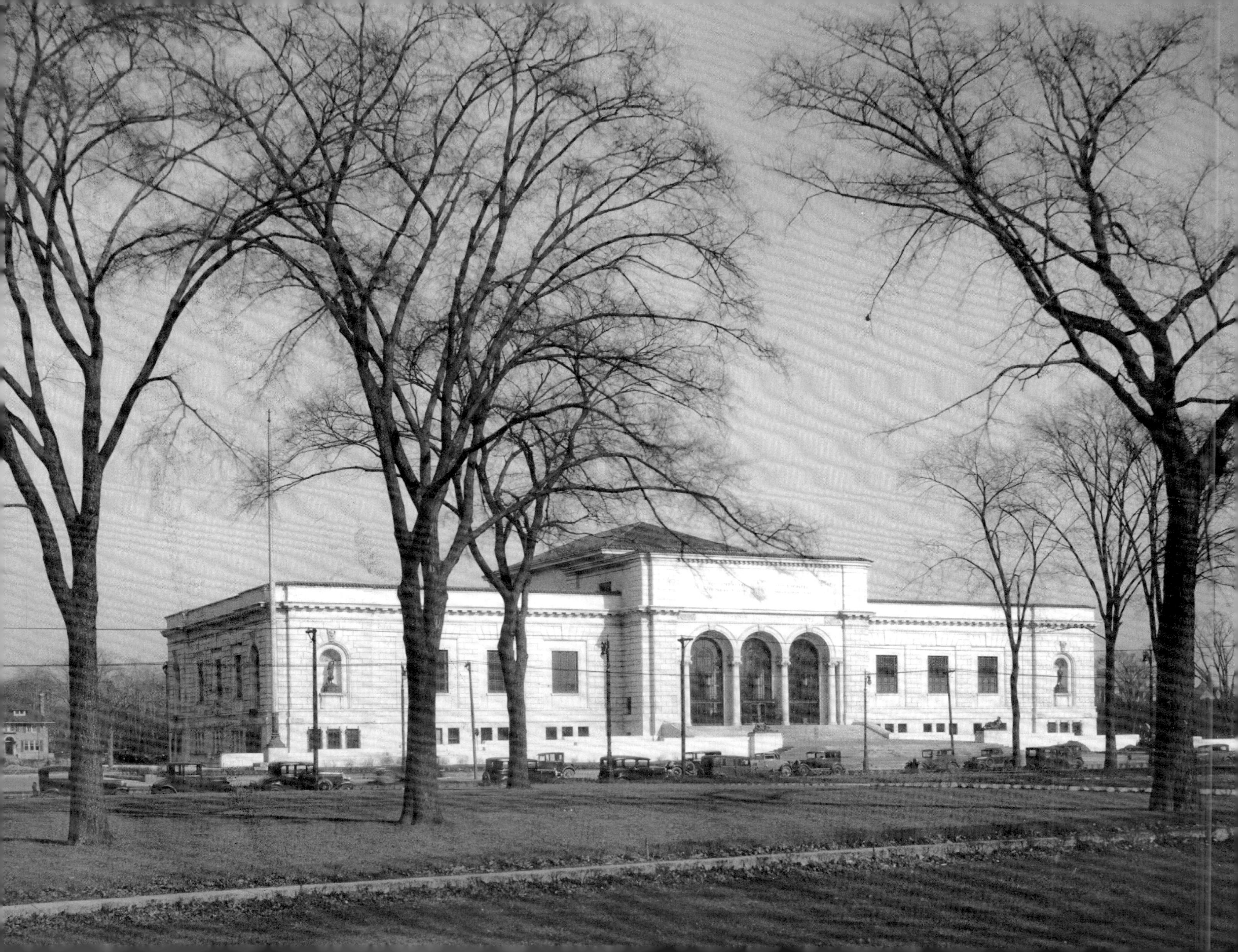

Detroit Institute of Arts, 5200 Woodward Avenue, as seen looking east, 1930. Complementing the public library in the city's new Cultural Center was the Detroit Institute of Arts (DIA). Ground was broken in 1922, and the museum was completed in 1927. The city's Cultural Center would grow to include the Detroit Historical Museum, Science Center, and the Charles H. Wright Museum of African American History. (Courtesy of the Burton Historical Collection, Detroit Public Library.)

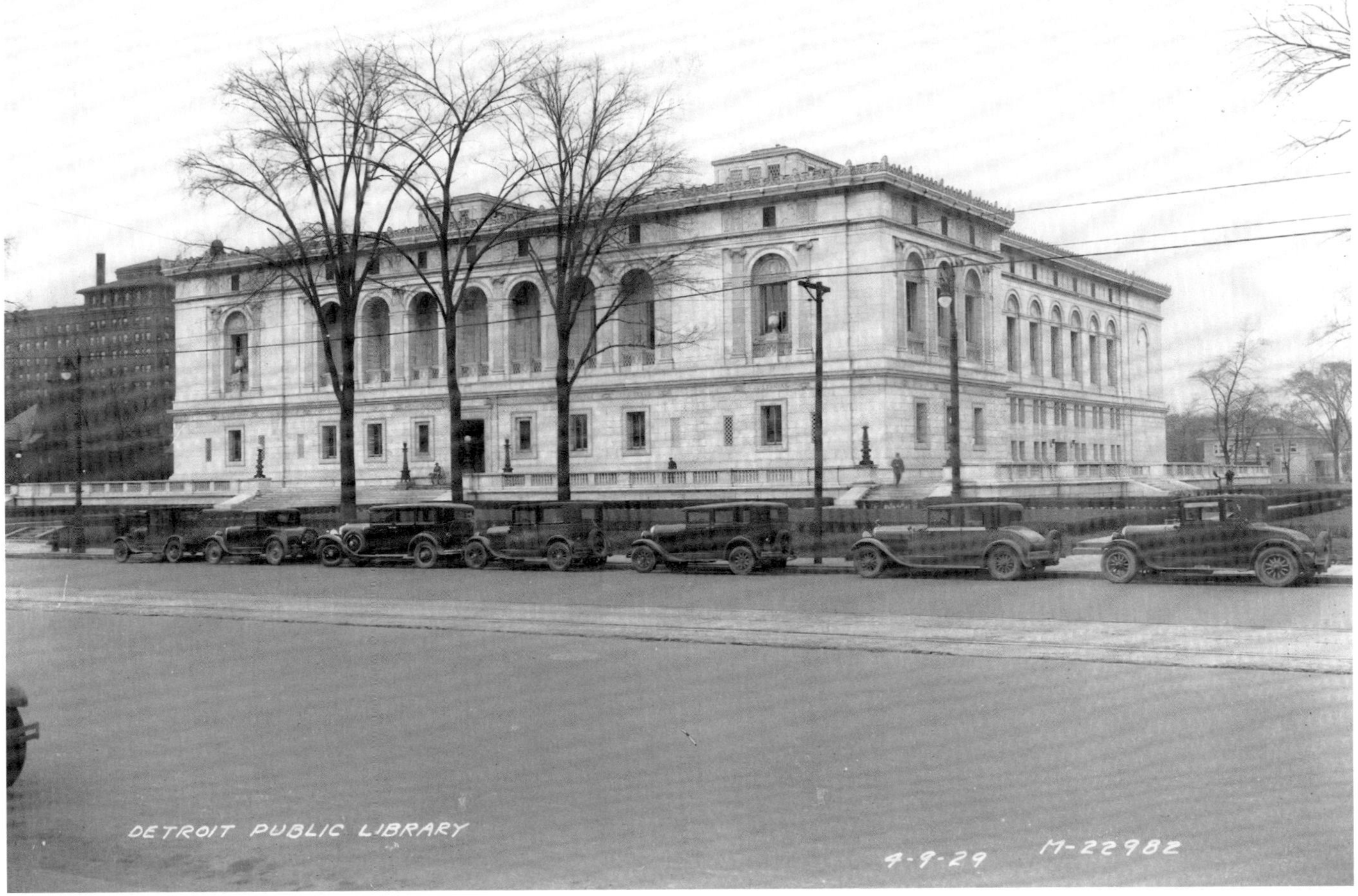

Detroit Public Library, Main Branch, 5201 Woodward Avenue, as seen looking west, 1929. Detroit's population grew tremendously between 1910 and 1930, and planning began for a library that would serve a growing public need. The Detroit Public Library's main branch was completed in 1921. The library was part of an area city planners had designated as a museum district—a place away from the business district downtown—where the city's cultural amenities could be grouped. The library and art museum were built across the street from one another as cornerstones of what planners called Detroit's Cultural Center. The Webster Hall Hotel can be seen in the distance on the left. (Courtesy of the Burton Historical Collection, Detroit Public Library.)

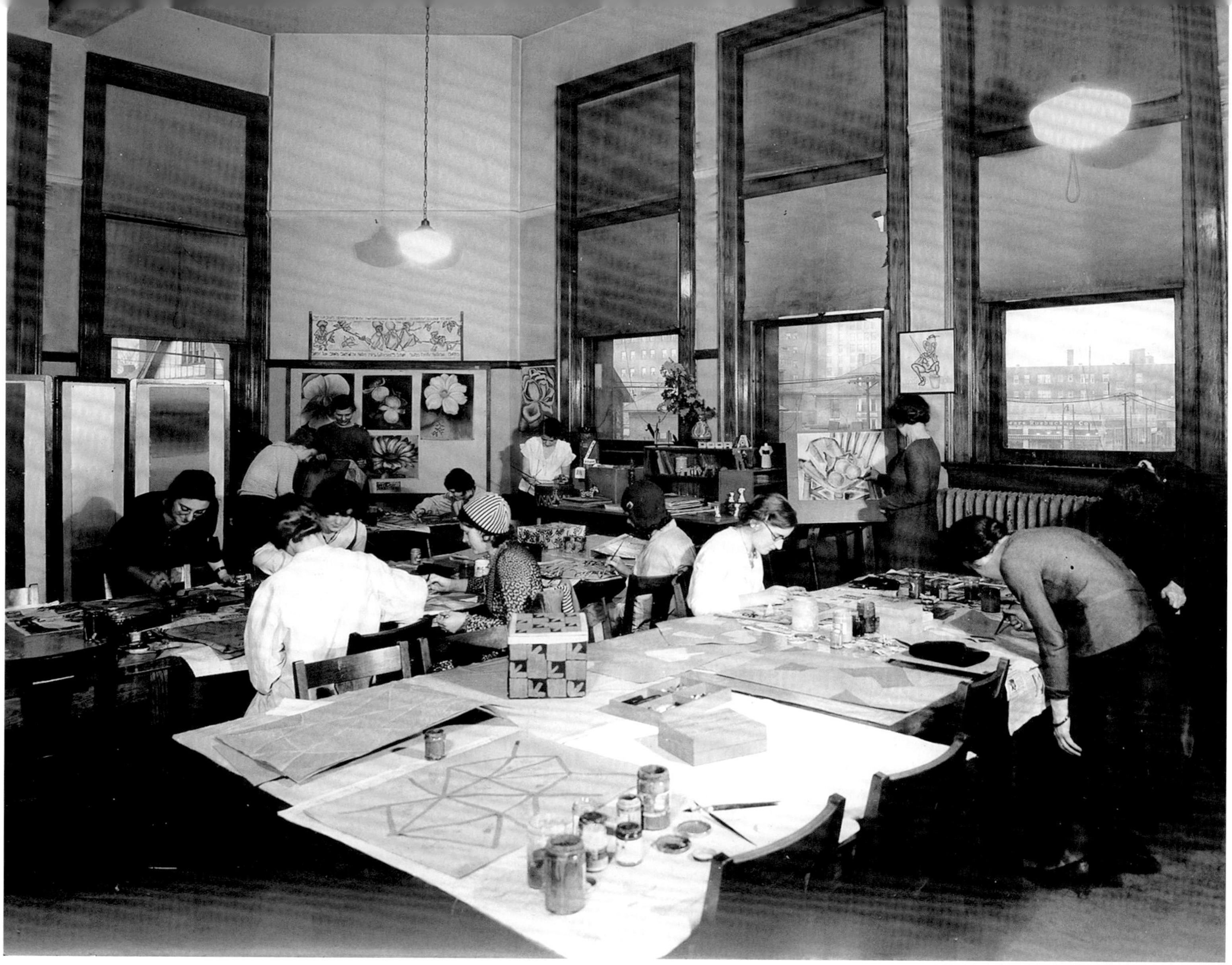

Art class in the Main Building, 1931. City College art students are seen at work in a Main Building classroom that serves as a studio. The Sears, Roebuck and Company building can be seen through the window on the far right. While the neighborhood around it was changing, so was the college. After the high school relocated in 1926, the college had room to expand. More subjects were given department status, and more separate degrees, such as engineering, were offered. (Walter P. Reuther Library, Archives of Labor and Urban Affairs, Wayne State University.)

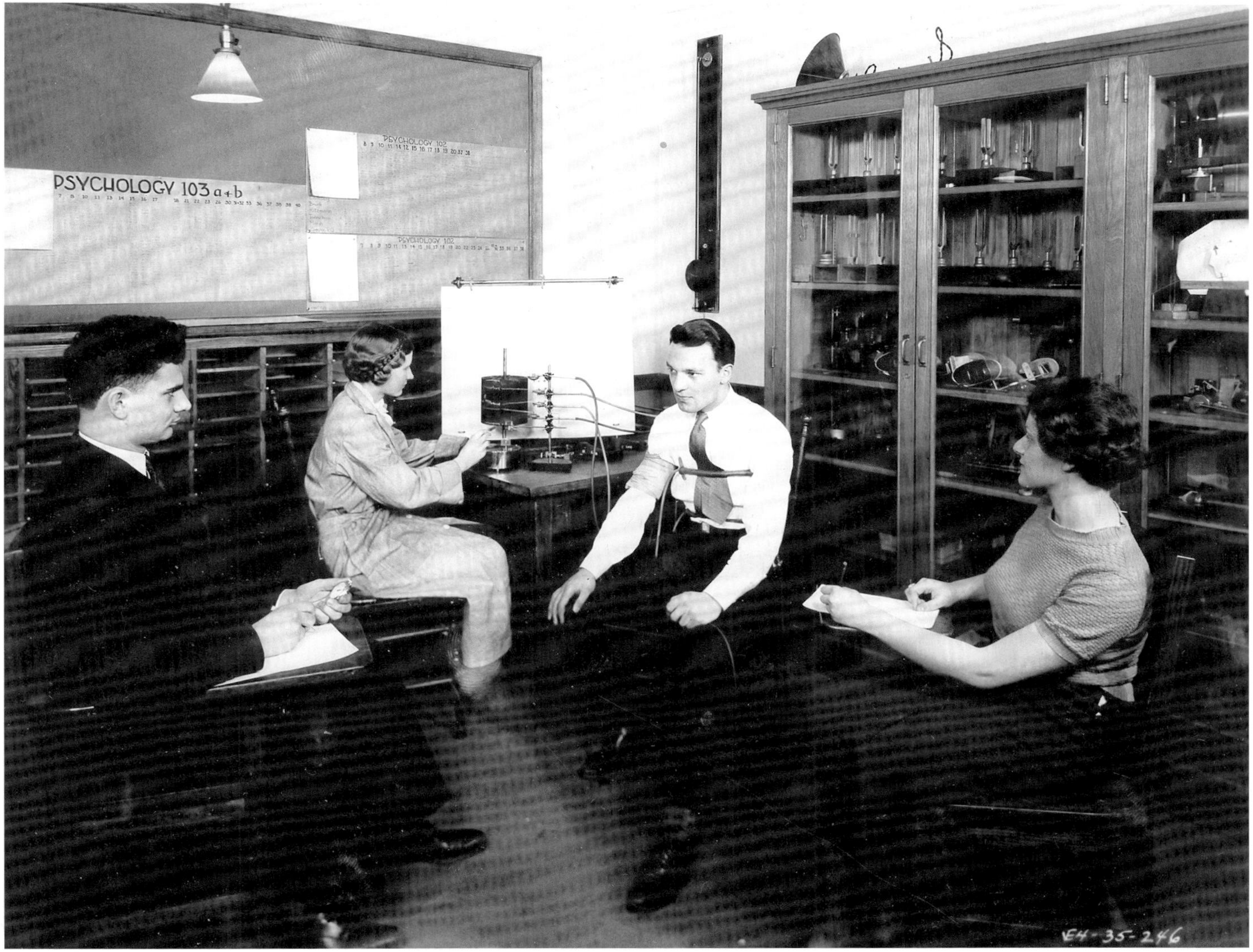

Psychology class in the Main Building, 1936. Students measure a fellow student's respiratory rate and pulse, possibly as an experiment for a lie detector test. His heart rate is displayed on the monitor. (Walter P. Reuther Library, Archives of Labor and Urban Affairs, Wayne State University.)

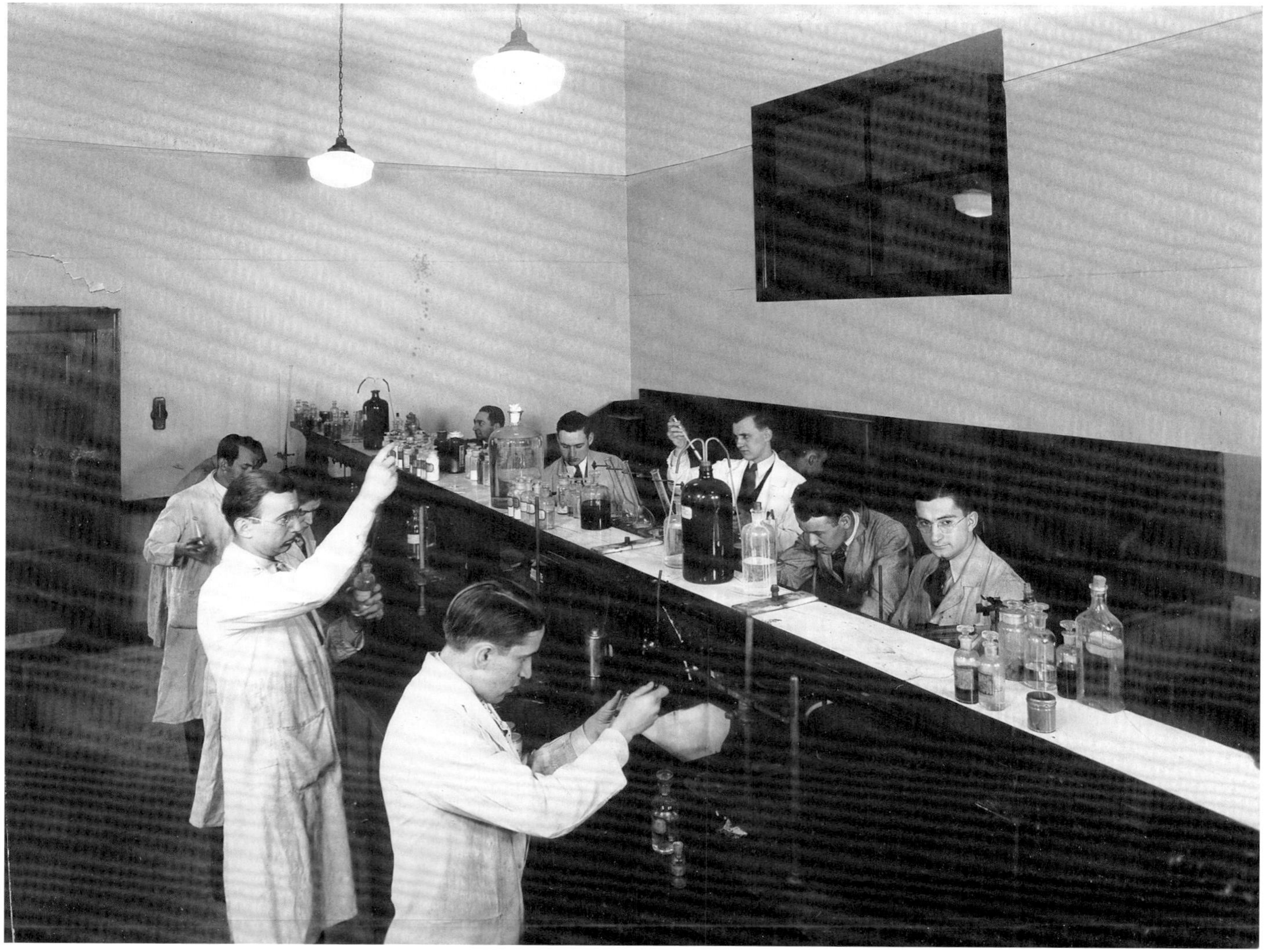

Pharmacy laboratory in the Main Building, 1936. By the beginning of the 1930s, the Main Building would house several separate colleges: the Detroit City Law School, the College of Pharmacy, the Detroit Teachers College, and City College. The schools had different but complementary goals. City College provided affordable higher education, while schools like the Detroit City Law School and the Detroit Teachers College aimed to provide increased training and respect for their professions. (Walter P. Reuther Library, Archives of Labor and Urban Affairs, Wayne State University.)

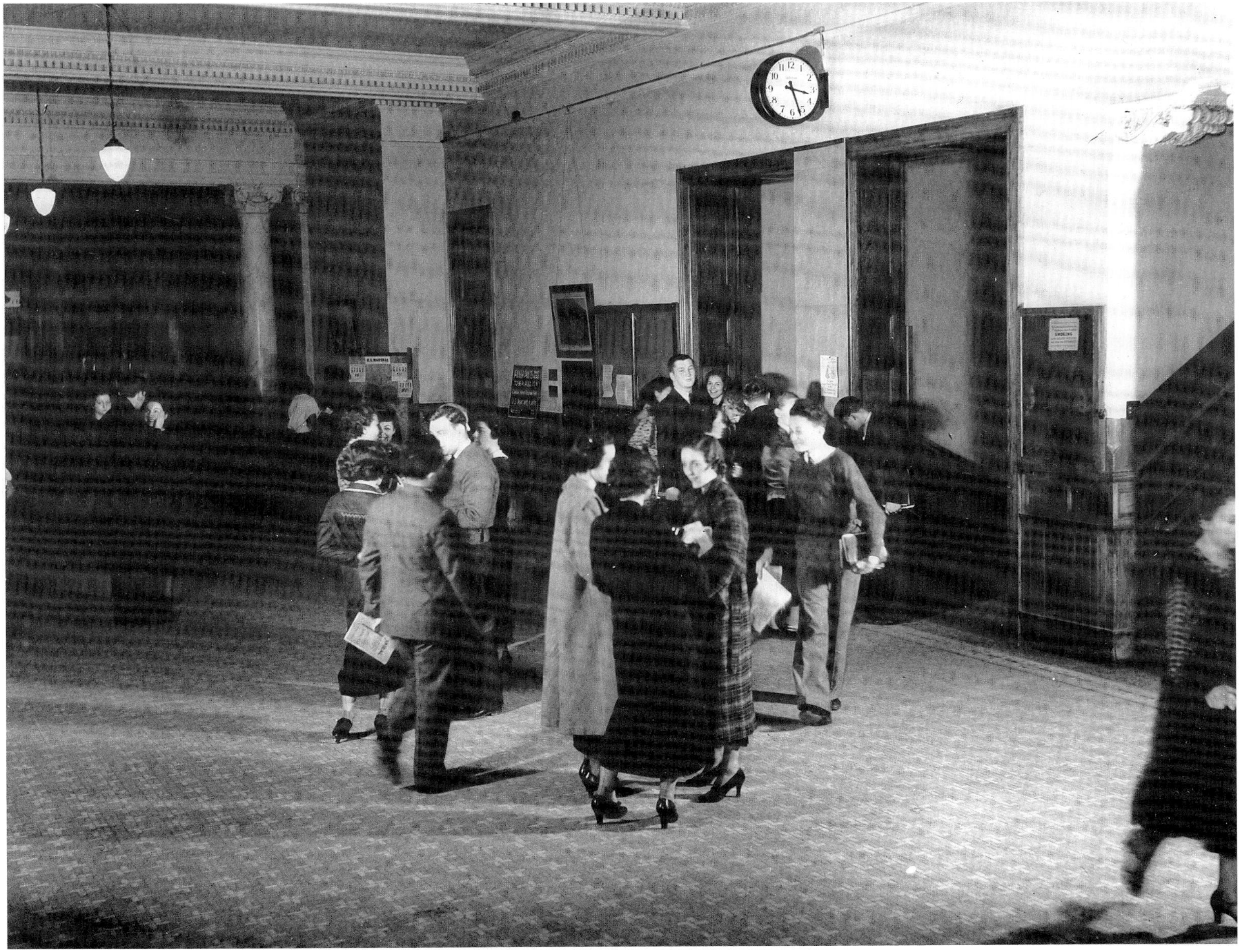

Interior of the Main Building, 1936. Like many of today's Wayne State graduates, most City College students were the first in their families to attend college. The college fulfilled a need for Detroit's growing working- and middle-class population: affordable higher education close to home. (Walter P. Reuther Library, Archives of Labor and Urban Affairs, Wayne State University.)

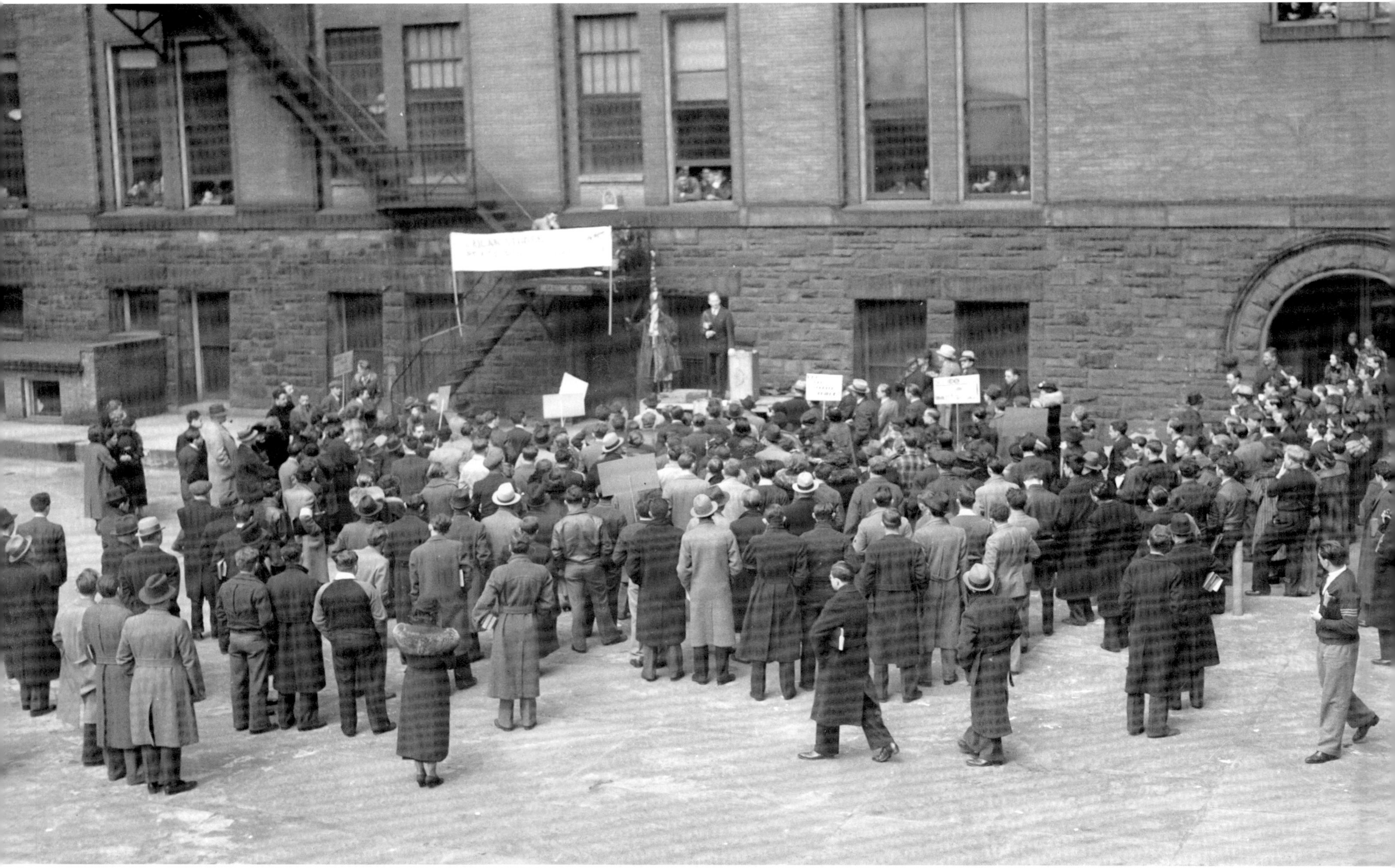

Peace strike behind the Main Building, April 22, 1936. Several hundred Wayne students walked out of their classes to take an oath not to support the government in any war. Part of a nationwide movement, this peace strike was organized by some seventeen student groups. The banner on the steps reads, in part, "Peace Before Profit." (Walter P. Reuther Library, Archives of Labor and Urban Affairs, Wayne State University.)

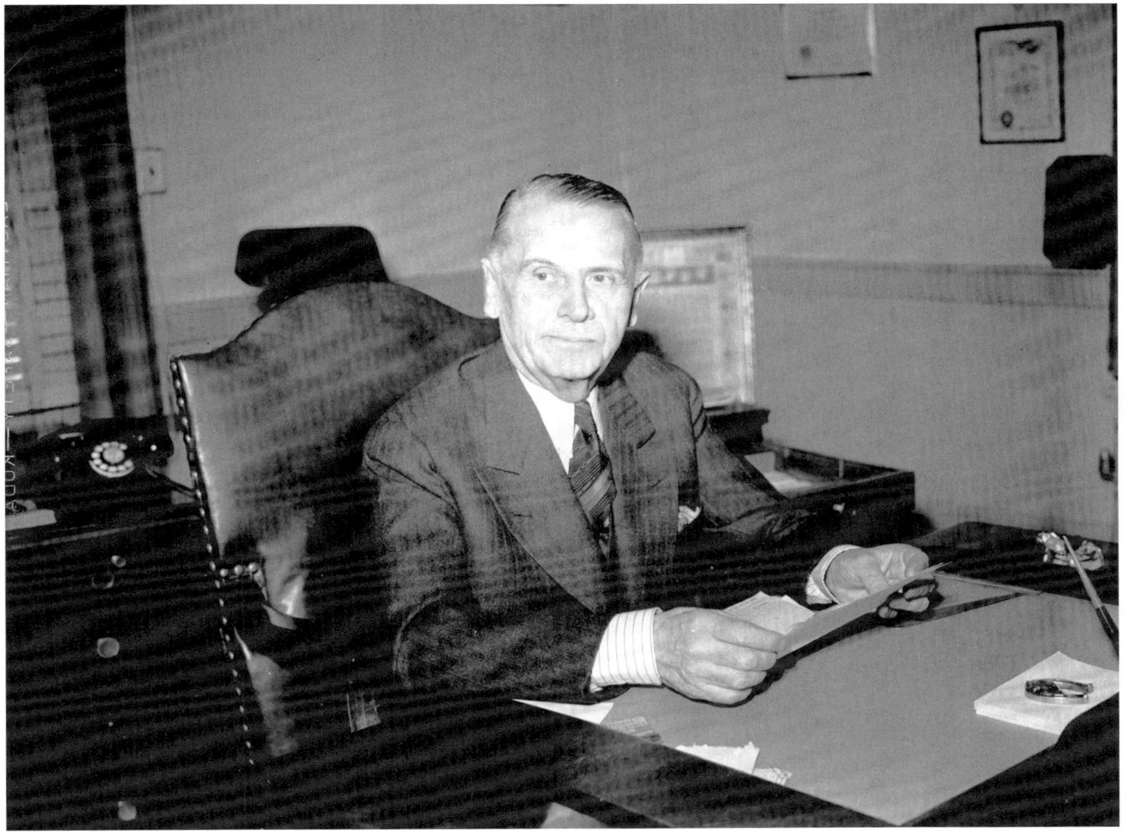

Frank Cody, superintendent of the Detroit public schools. Frank Cody was instrumental in the creation of Wayne University. After David Mackenzie died in 1926, Cody took the initiative in bringing the various colleges housed in the Main Building together as a university. By mid-1927, Cody and the Board of Education had organized a council of deans from the different colleges: law, pharmacy, education, and liberal arts. One result was a joint commencement that took place in 1929. While largely symbolic and ceremonial, it showed that the different colleges could work together. During the early 1930s, Cody provided the colleges with the tools needed to achieve university status: leadership, finances, and public recognition. (Walter P. Reuther Library, Archives of Labor and Urban Affairs, Wayne State University.)

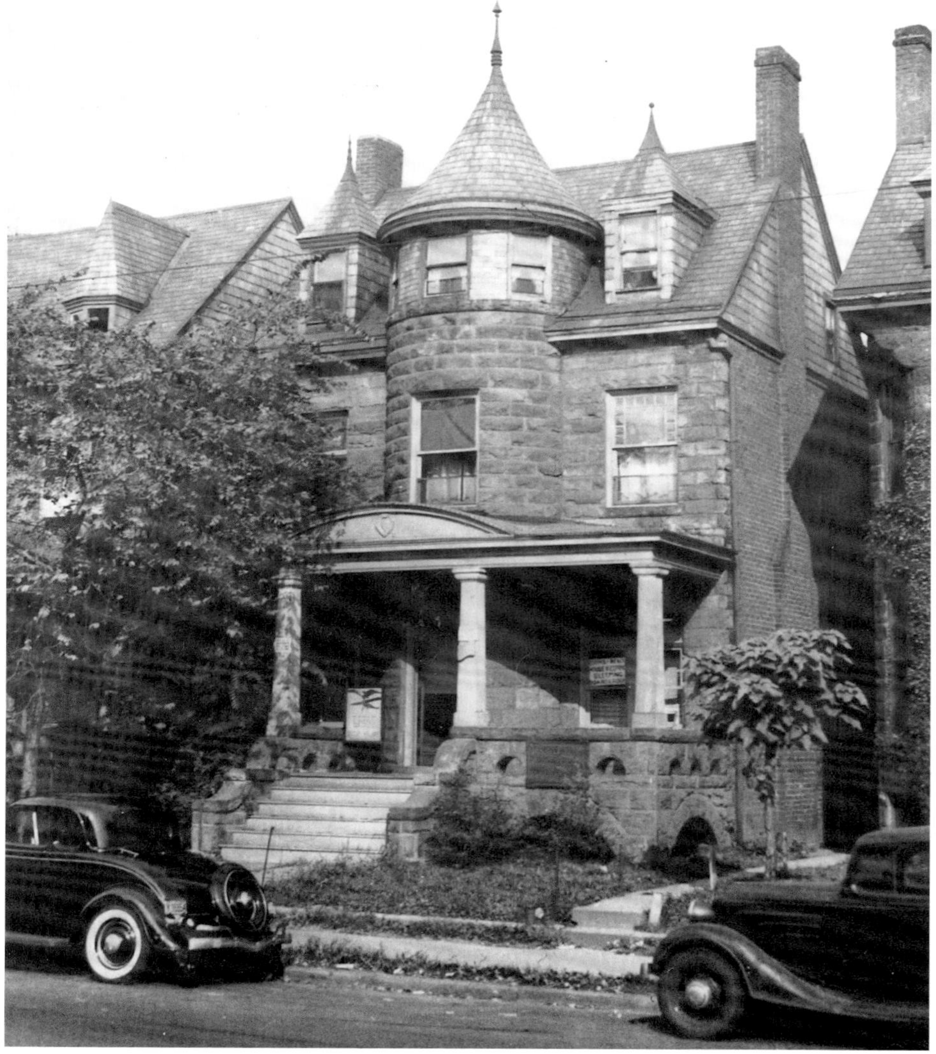

Lindbergh House, 1120 W. Forest, 1930s. This house was purchased by the Lindbergh family in 1898, and Charles Lindbergh was born here on February 4, 1902. After his successful flight across the Atlantic in 1927, a bronze plaque was placed on the front of the house. Despite its claim to fame, the house was used as a rental property for twenty-eight years. In 1961, Wayne State University's pharmacy fraternity Kappa Psi purchased the building. It was razed in 1973. (Walter P. Reuther Library, Archives of Labor and Urban Affairs, Wayne State University.)

The Main Building, as seen looking southwest, early 1930s. This photo of the old Central High School building, by this time renamed the Main Building, was taken before 1937, before the addition of a wing that closed off the grass courtyard along Warren, which runs along the bottom right of the photo. This addition was just one of several ways the administration altered the Main Building to accommodate the rising number of students. The nameplate over the arched doorway on the Cass Avenue side of the building, left of center in this photo, reads, "The College of the City of Detroit." The houses visible at the bottom right of the photo stand on the future site of Science Hall. (Walter P. Reuther Library, Archives of Labor and Urban Affairs, Wayne State University.)

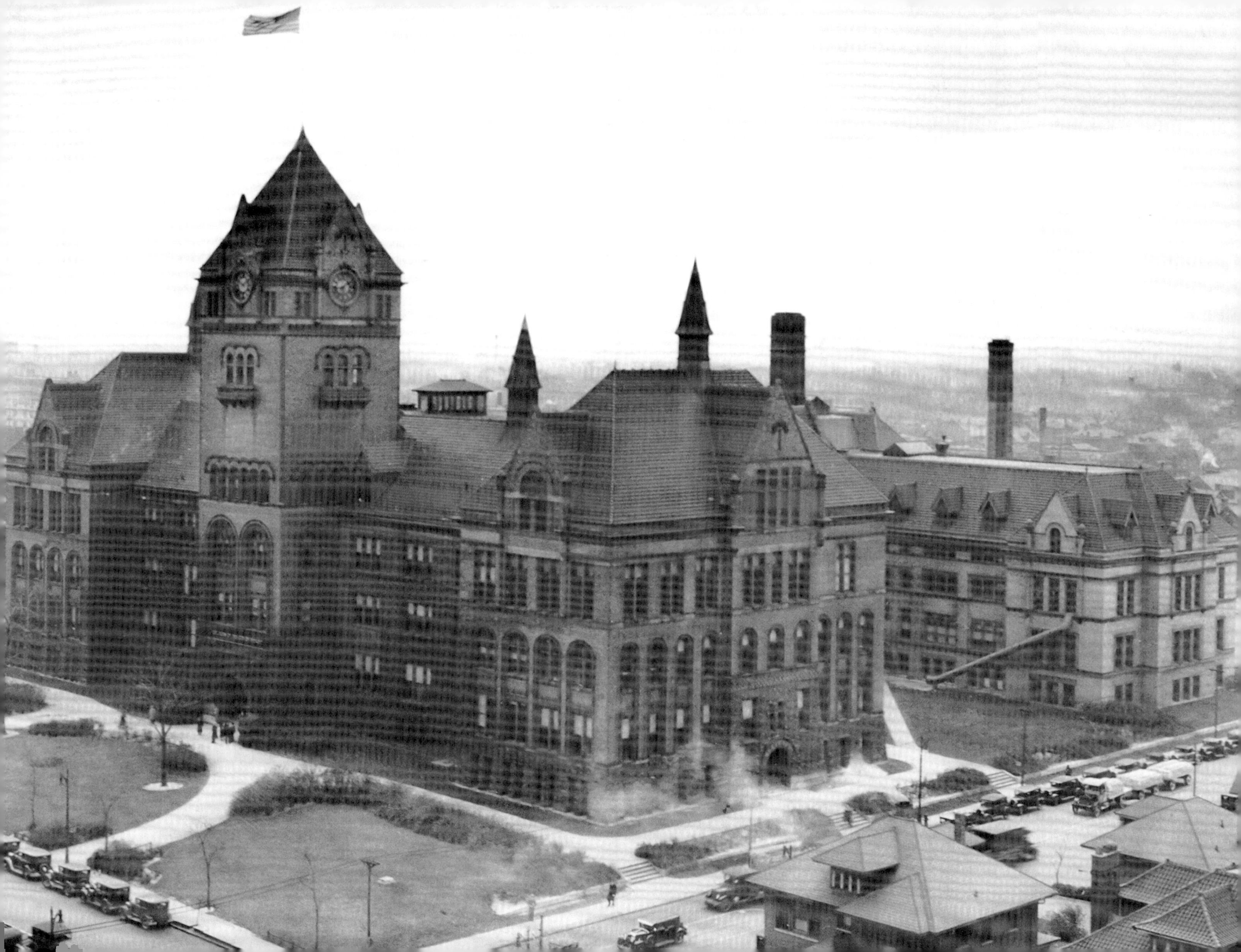

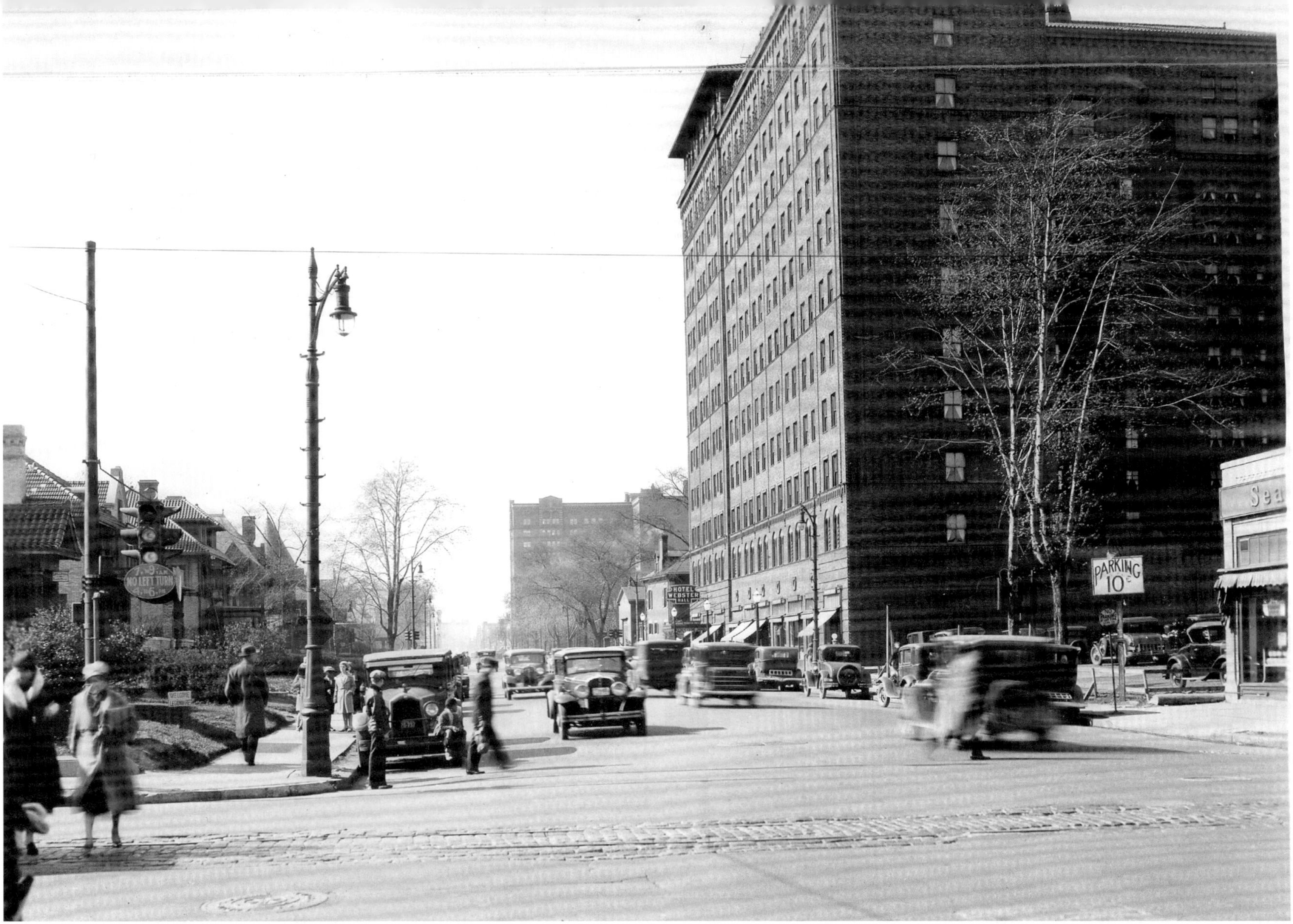

Cass and Warren avenues, looking north up Cass, 1930s. The Webster Hall Hotel appears on the right, and the Belcrest Apartments are visible in the distance, at the center of the photo. Science Hall would eventually be built just behind the houses that line the west side of Cass. Note the streetcar lines that run along Warren, which brought students from all over the city to campus. Like other municipal colleges, City College was a "streetcar college." Most students didn't drive. Public transportation from their homes was reliable and took them directly to campus; the crosstown junction on Warren was one of the city's most heavily trafficked streetcar thoroughfares. (Courtesy of the Burton Historical Collection, Detroit Public Library.)

CHAPTER 3

A YOUNG UNIVERSITY, 1933–49

Wayne State University came of age during the Great Depression. Since 1927, the Detroit Board of Education had worked to combine the various colleges it funded, and economic pressure helped bring that work to fruition. In 1933, for the sake of fiscal efficiency, the Board of Education merged five individual colleges—liberal arts, education, pharmacy, engineering, and medicine and a graduate school—into one university. Like other city-supported colleges, Wayne University grew rapidly during the Depression. Unable to find employment, many young Detroiters pursued higher education as a means to improve their prospects. Unless they minimized expenses by living at home, which Wayne allowed them to do, few of these students could afford the expense of a college degree.

During the university's early years, no city money was available to construct new buildings due to economic depression, and the onset of World War II meant that the university would not receive any outside funding for new construction. As the need for more space increased with enrollment, the university began renting houses near the Main Building, and plans were made to expand the campus into the surrounding neighborhoods. In the late 1940s, Wayne University students finally saw the first new buildings constructed on campus.

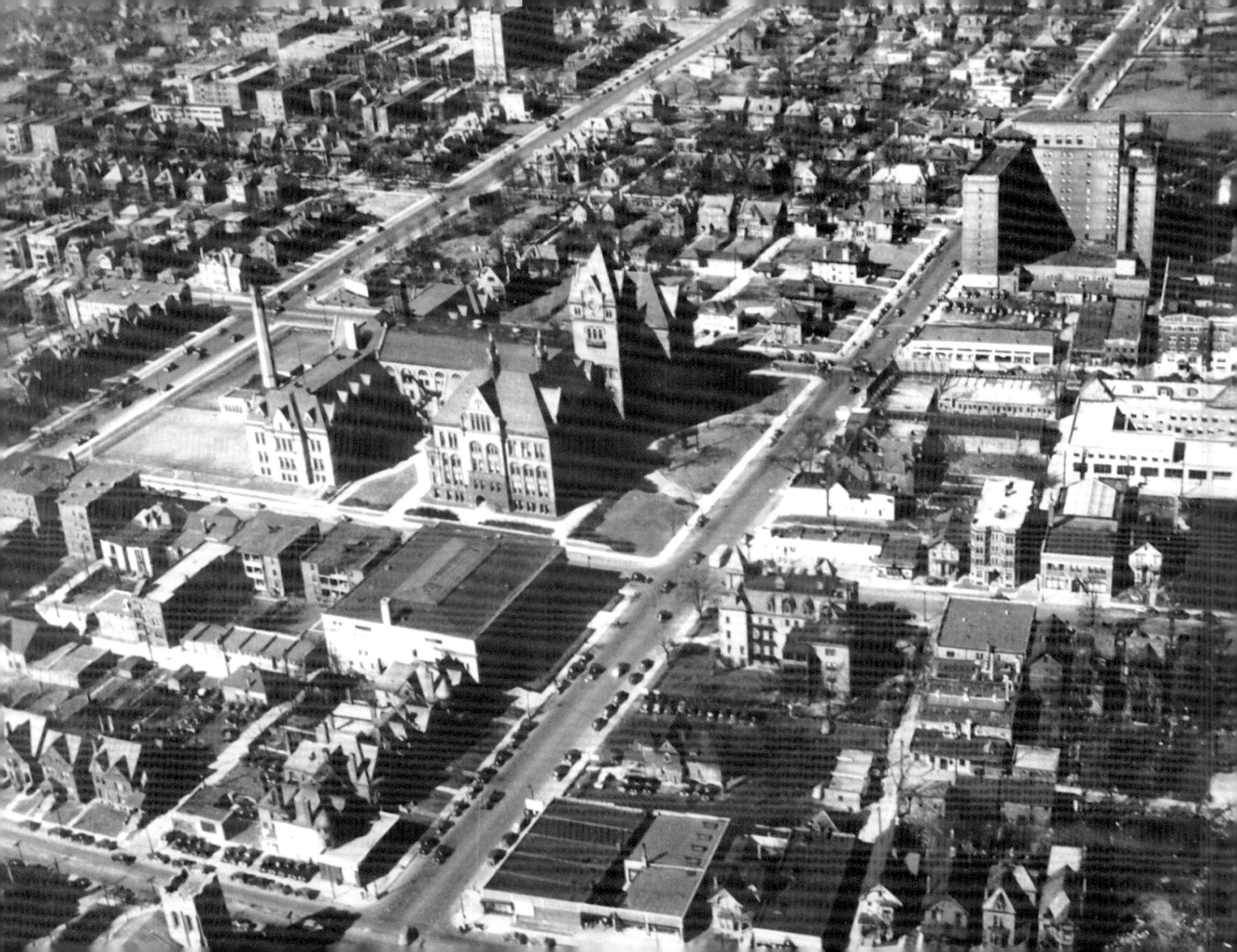

Aerial view, looking northwest, early 1930s. This photograph was taken before the campus expanded into the neighborhood around the Main Building—visible in the center of the photo. The houses northwest of the Main Building mark the area where Wayne State University's campus is located today. The Thompson Home is visible kitty-corner to the Main Building to the east. The Webster Hall Hotel is the tall, U-shaped building near the upper right corner. The front of the Main Building, marked by the semicircular sidewalk, faces Cass Avenue. (Walter P. Reuther Library, Archives of Labor and Urban Affairs, Wayne State University.)

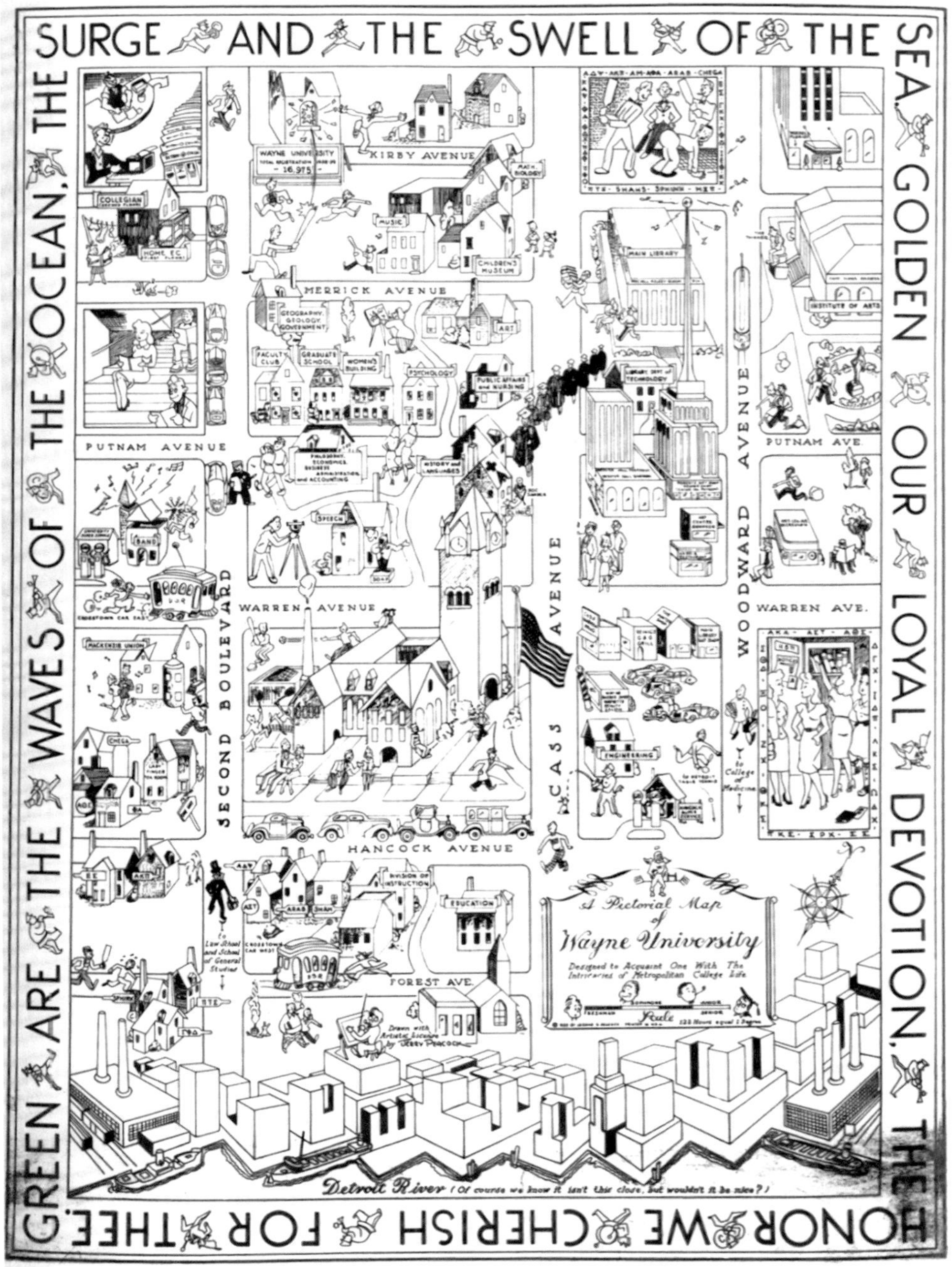

Cartoon map of the campus, 1939. This detailed rendering of Wayne's campus appeared in the 1942 yearbook, called *The Bluebook*. Note how the cartoon houses are labeled: for classes, such as psychology and art, or for student groups, such as fraternities and the Mackenzie Union. There is even a line of students in caps and gowns lined up across Cass Avenue. Commencement exercises were held at various locations in Detroit, including the Detroit Institute of Arts. (Walter P. Reuther Library, Archives of Labor and Urban Affairs, Wayne State University.)

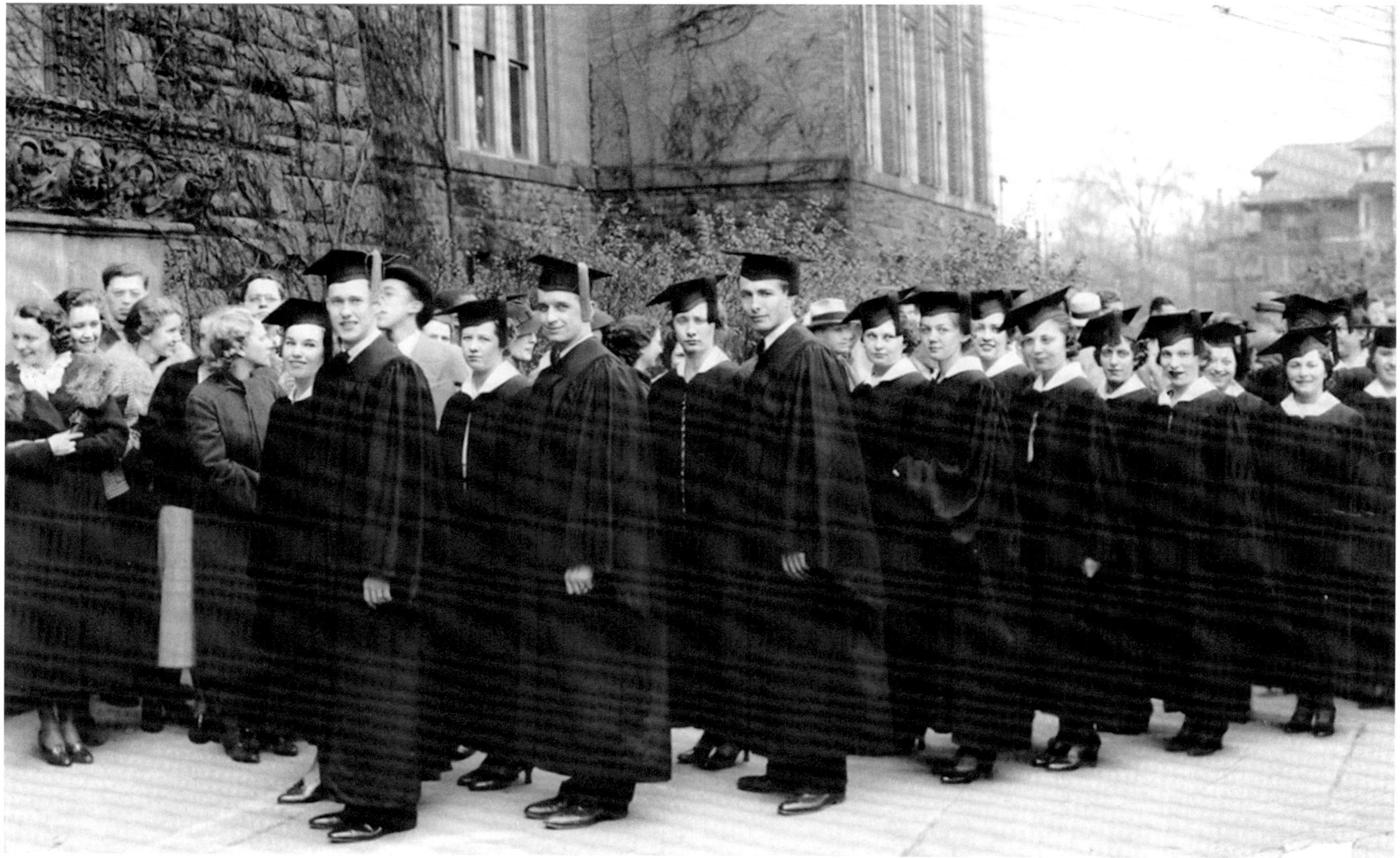

Commencement in front of the Main Building, 1935. One of the first graduating classes of the newly consolidated Wayne University. (Walter P. Reuther Library, Archives of Labor and Urban Affairs, Wayne State University.)

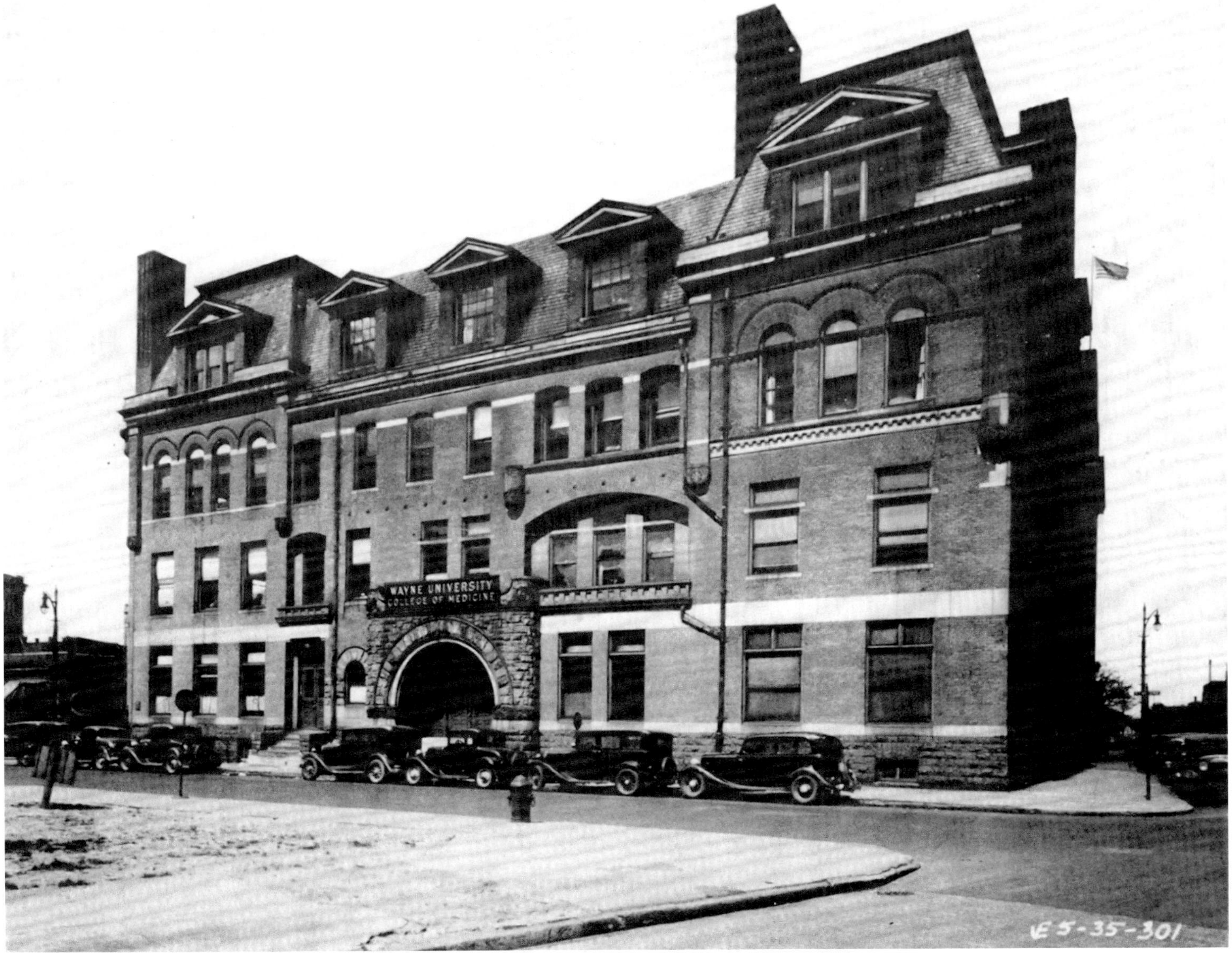

The College of Medicine, Wayne University, Mullett Street, 1935. The College of Medicine was one of the original six colleges that had united to create Wayne University in 1933. Medical classes were held in this building until 1954, when a new medical science building replaced it. (Walter P. Reuther Library, Archives of Labor and Urban Affairs, Wayne State University.)

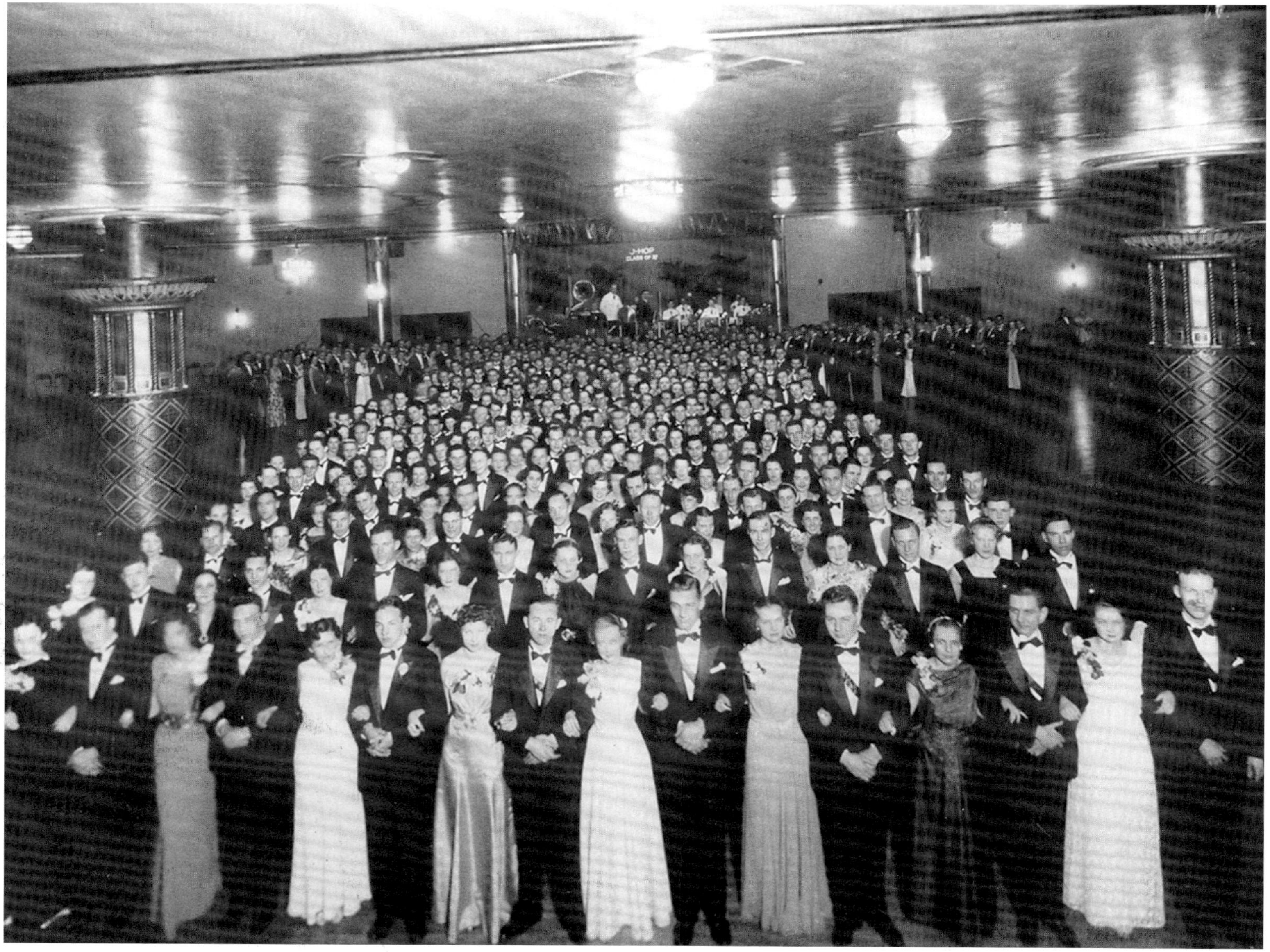

J-Hop dance, Detroit Masonic Temple, 1937. Wayne students, wearing tuxedos and evening gowns, are lined up for the grand march, the highlight of the Junior Hop, or J-Hop, a formal dance sponsored by the junior class and held at the Masonic Temple during the 1930s. Formal dances faded from popularity after World War II because they were a great expense to students and because, by the early 1960s, students preferred activities such as attending concerts, including performances by folk musicians. (Walter P. Reuther Library, Archives of Labor and Urban Affairs, Wayne State University.)

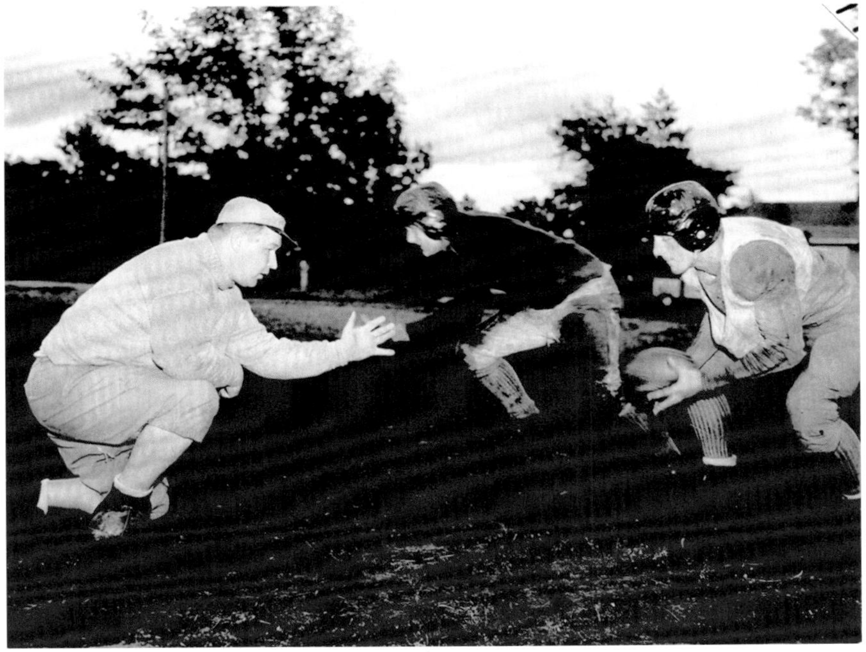

Football coach Joe Gembis with students, 1937. Formerly a noted kicker for the University of Michigan, Joe Gembis was a popular Wayne University football coach from 1932 until 1946. Football, like other sports at Wayne, was hampered by the lack of permanent playing facilities. (Walter P. Reuther Library, Archives of Labor and Urban Affairs, Wayne State University.)

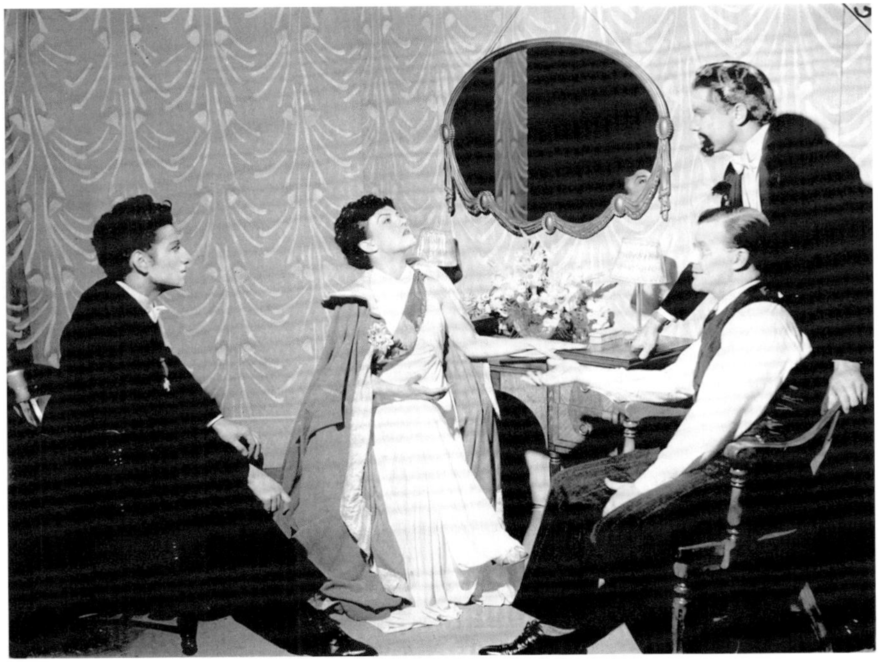

Theater rehearsal, 1939. Students rehearse for a play that would be performed in the auditorium of the Main Building. Founded in 1929, Wayne's theater department was celebrating its tenth anniversary. To commemorate the event, theater students would perform Eugene O'Neill's *Beyond the Horizon*, which had been the first play produced by the department. Admission to the show cost thirty cents. (Walter P. Reuther Library, Archives of Labor and Urban Affairs, Wayne State University.)

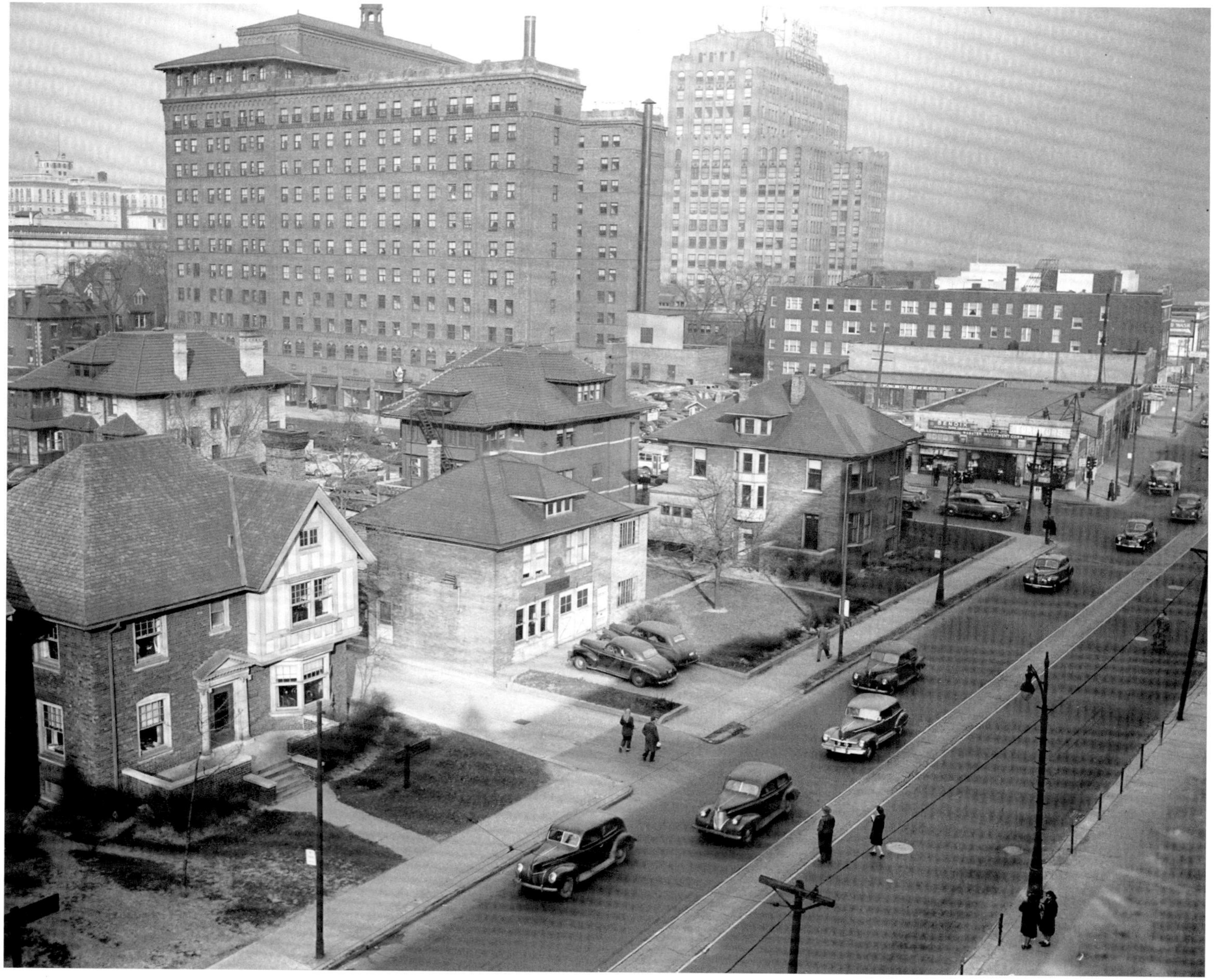

Warren Avenue near Cass Avenue, looking northeast, 1946. A view of the campus before the construction boom that followed World War II. The houses that line Warren would eventually be demolished to clear space for Science Hall. The Student Center Building (Webster Hall) is the tall building in the center left of the photo, and the Maccabees Building can be seen beyond it, center right. (Walter P. Reuther Library, Archives of Labor and Urban Affairs, Wayne State University.)

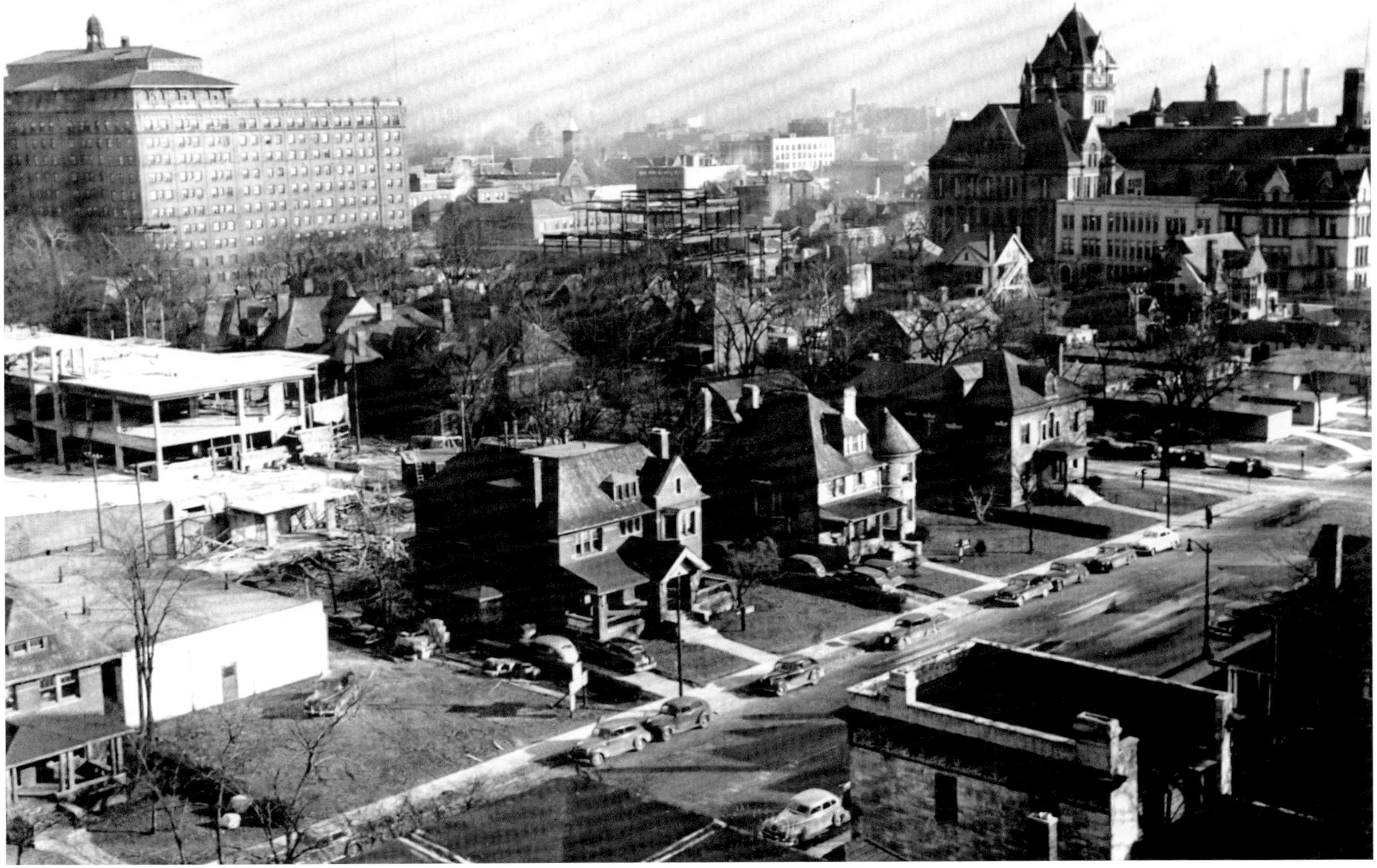

Second Avenue, looking southeast, 1947. This photograph shows the area that would become the center of Wayne State's campus. The Linsell House, the farthest house on the right, is one of the few remaining houses still standing on Wayne's campus. The Student Center Building (Webster Hall) is the tall building on the left, and the Main Building is on the right. Under construction, State Hall is taking shape on the far left of the image, and in the center of the picture, the skeleton of Science Hall rises between the Main Building and Webster Hall. (Walter P. Reuther Library, Archives of Labor and Urban Affairs, Wayne State University.)

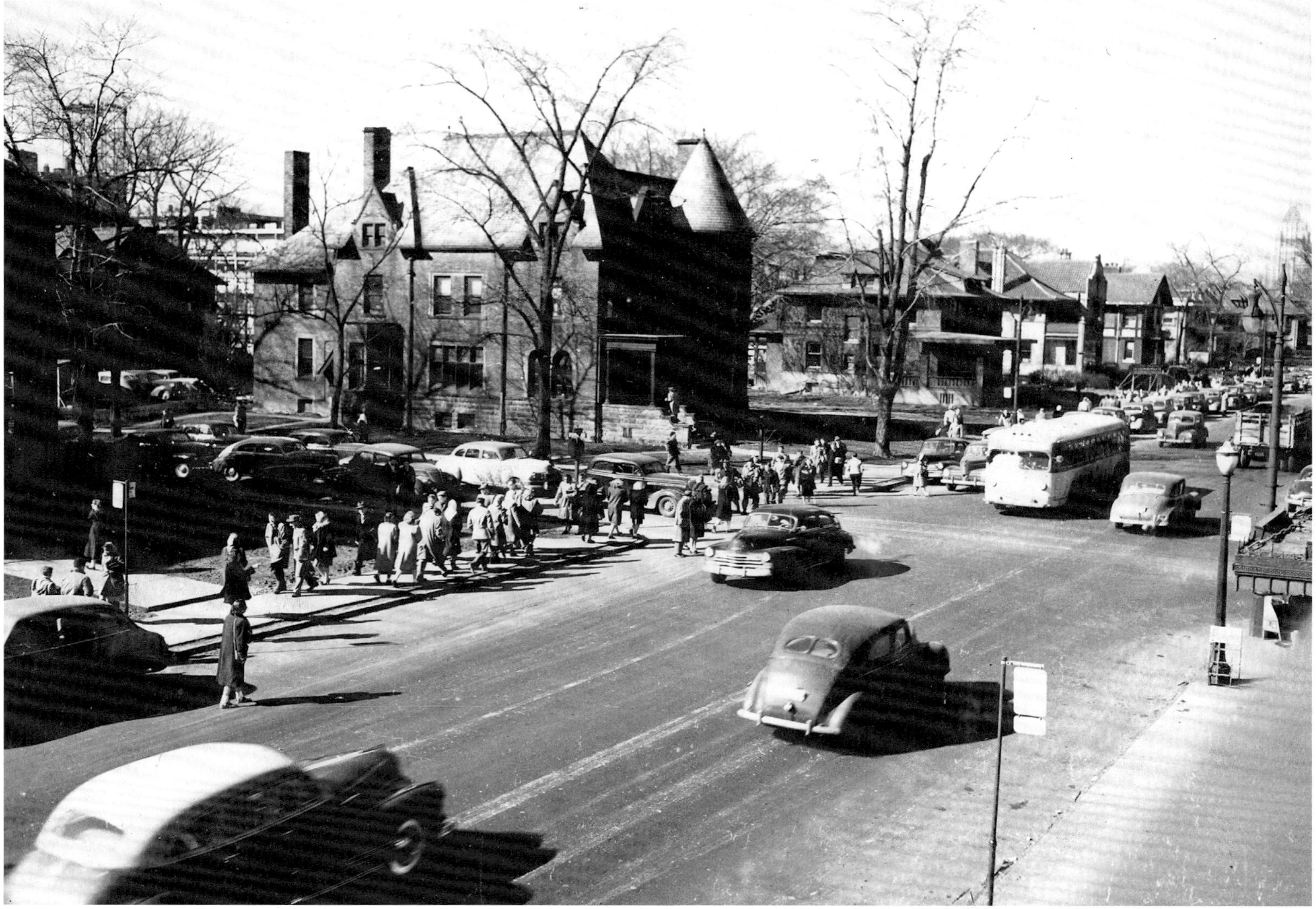

Cass Avenue at Putnam Street, facing northwest, 1948. Wayne students and professors on their way to classes, many of which at the time were held in former homes. Since the 1940s marked the first time that classes were held outside of the Main Building, time had to be allowed for walking between classes. State Hall is barely visible on the left, beyond the chimneys of the building in the center of the photo. (Walter P. Reuther Library, Archives of Labor and Urban Affairs, Wayne State University.)

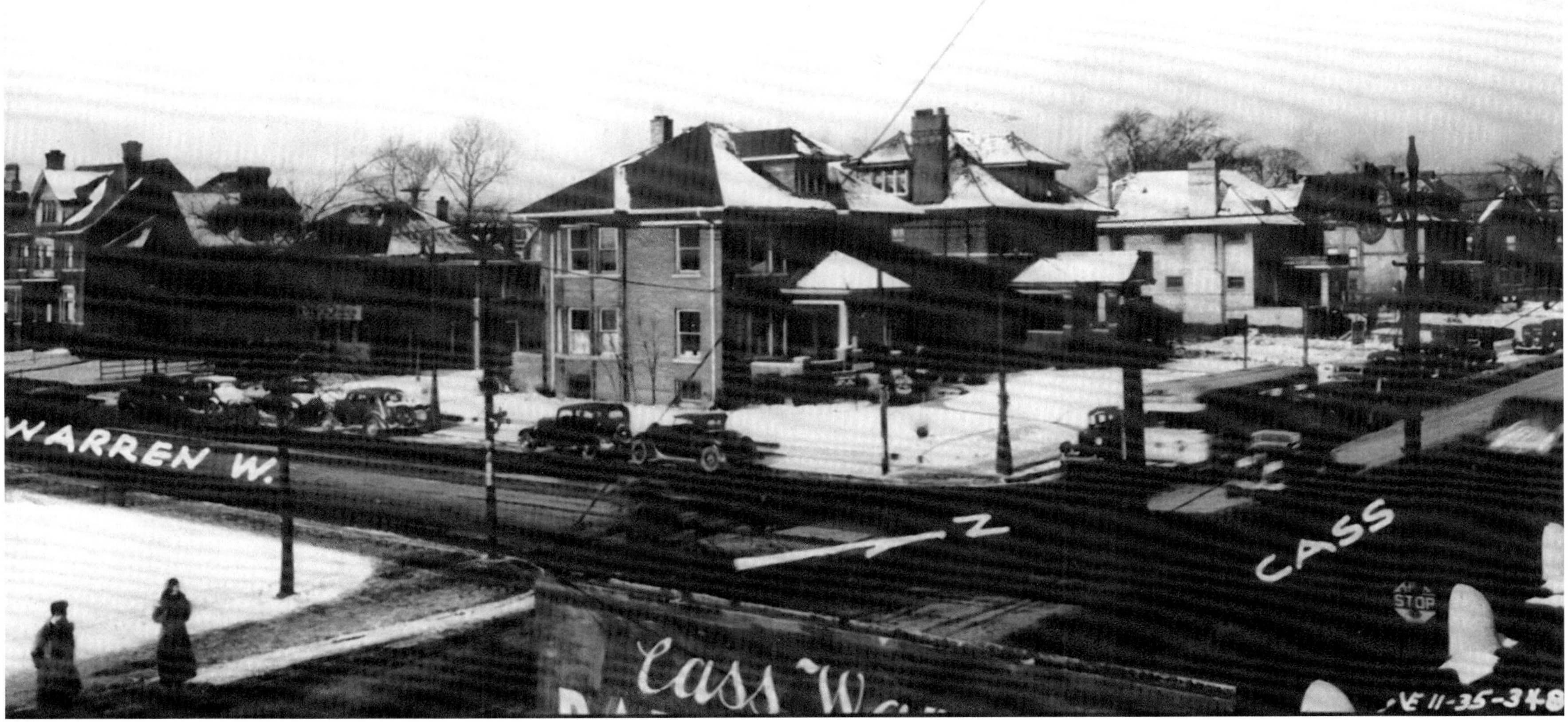

Cass and Warren avenues, facing northwest, 1935. The following three photos show the gradual evolution of the neighborhood around the Main Building into a college campus. Pictured here is the corner of Cass and Warren before the university constructed any new buildings. (Walter P. Reuther Library, Archives of Labor and Urban Affairs, Wayne State University.)

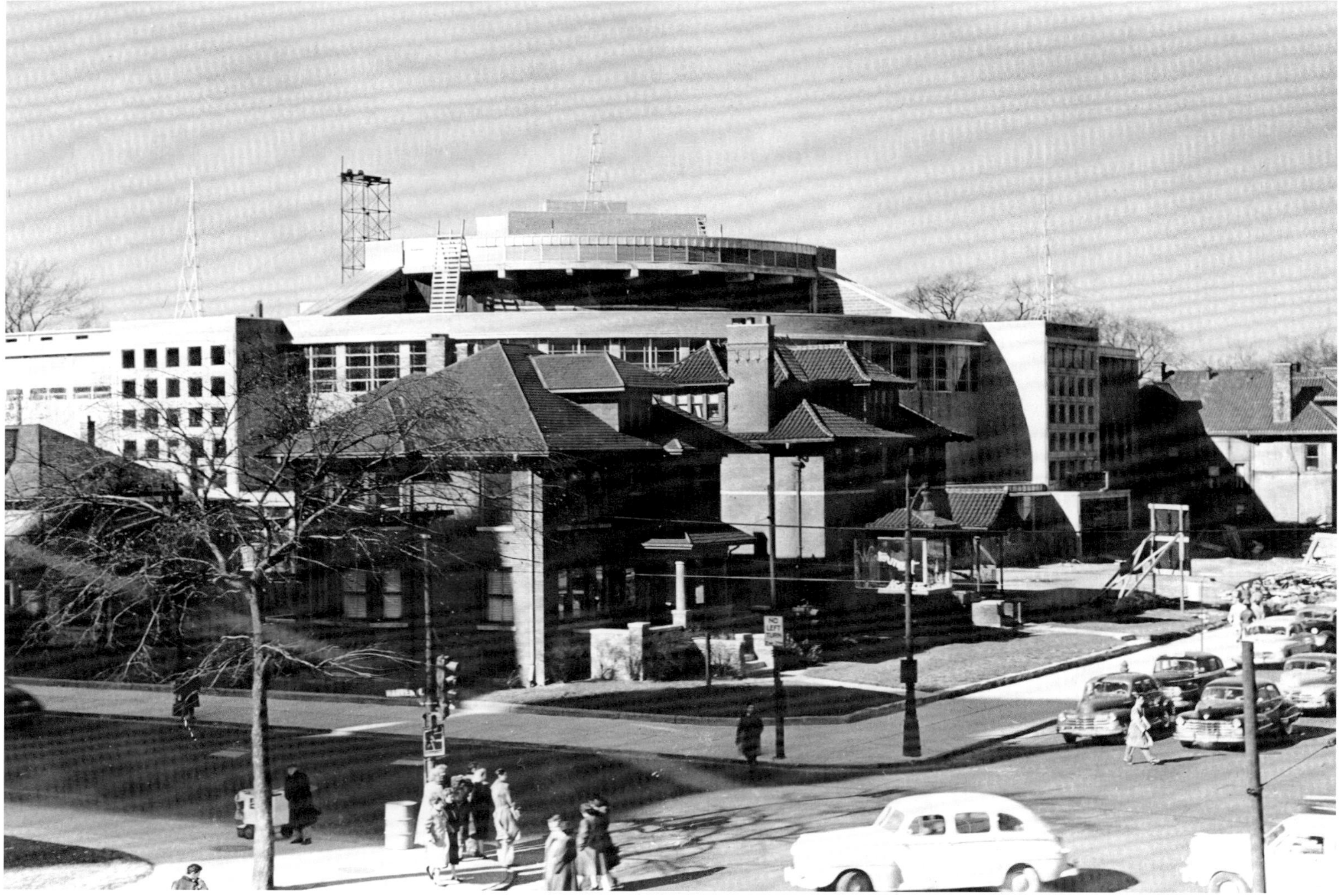

Cass and Warren avenues, facing northwest, 1949. The same corner, fourteen years later. Directly behind the houses stands Science Hall, completed in 1949. The houses on Cass and Warren were still needed for offices and classrooms, but new buildings were constructed very close to them. Along with State Hall, Science Hall was one of the first new buildings constructed after World War II. (Walter P. Reuther Library, Archives of Labor and Urban Affairs, Wayne State University.)

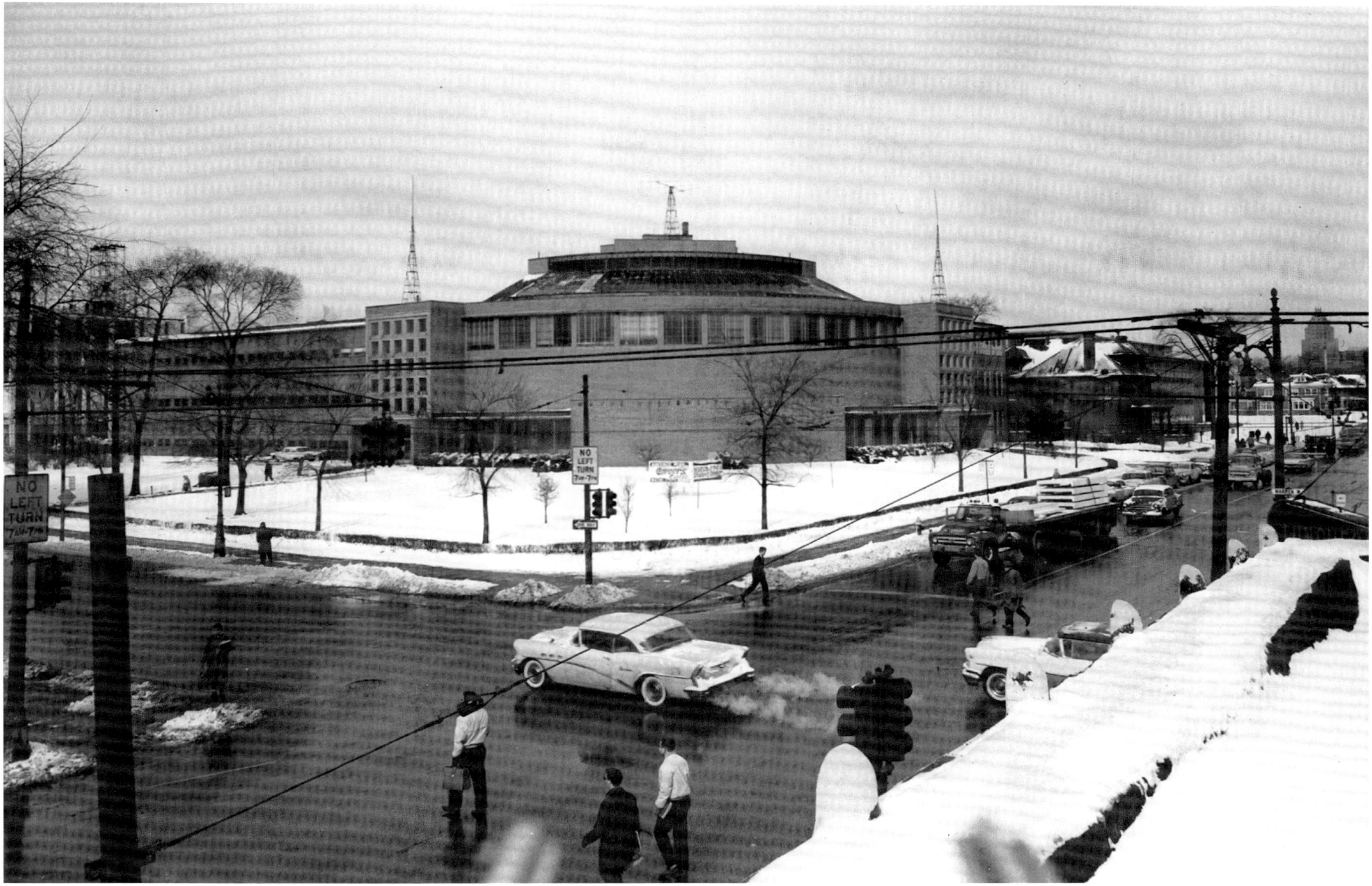

Cass and Warren avenues, facing northwest, 1960. The corner as recent Wayne State University students will recognize it—without the old houses. As the university grew, it demolished old buildings when it no longer needed the space they provided. The houses in front of Science Hall were razed in 1949. While the process was a gradual one, the results were dramatic—what had still seemed like a neighborhood suddenly became a college campus. Note the wide lawn in front of Science Hall, as this picture was taken prior to the widening of Warren Avenue in the 1970s. (Walter P. Reuther Library, Archives of Labor and Urban Affairs, Wayne State University.)

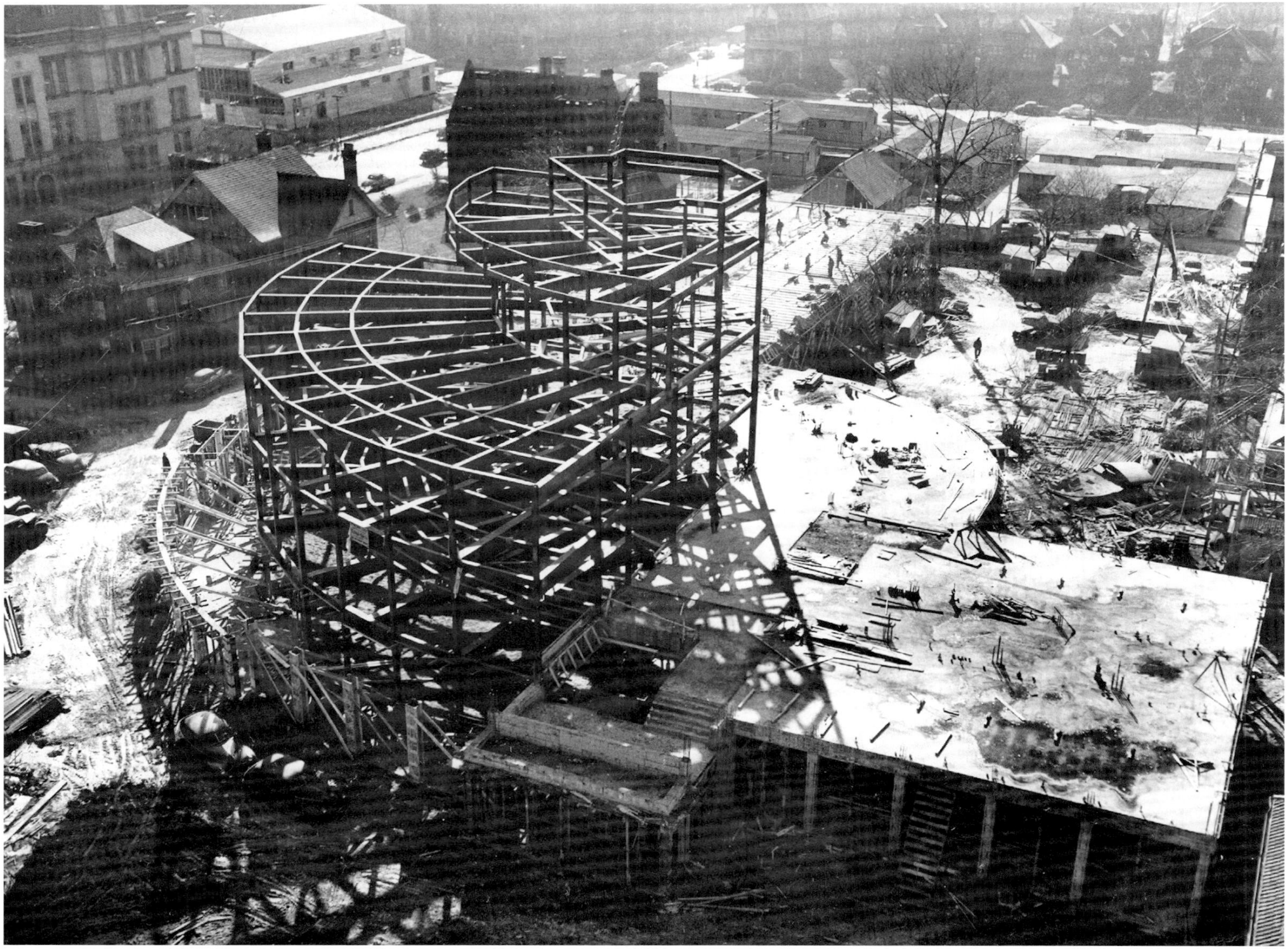

Science Hall construction at 5045 Cass Avenue, as seen looking west, late 1940s. Science Hall was the first new building constructed for Wayne students. The corner of the Main Building can be seen in the upper left-hand corner. Second Avenue, its row of houses still intact, runs across the top right of the picture. (Walter P. Reuther Library, Archives of Labor and Urban Affairs, Wayne State University.)

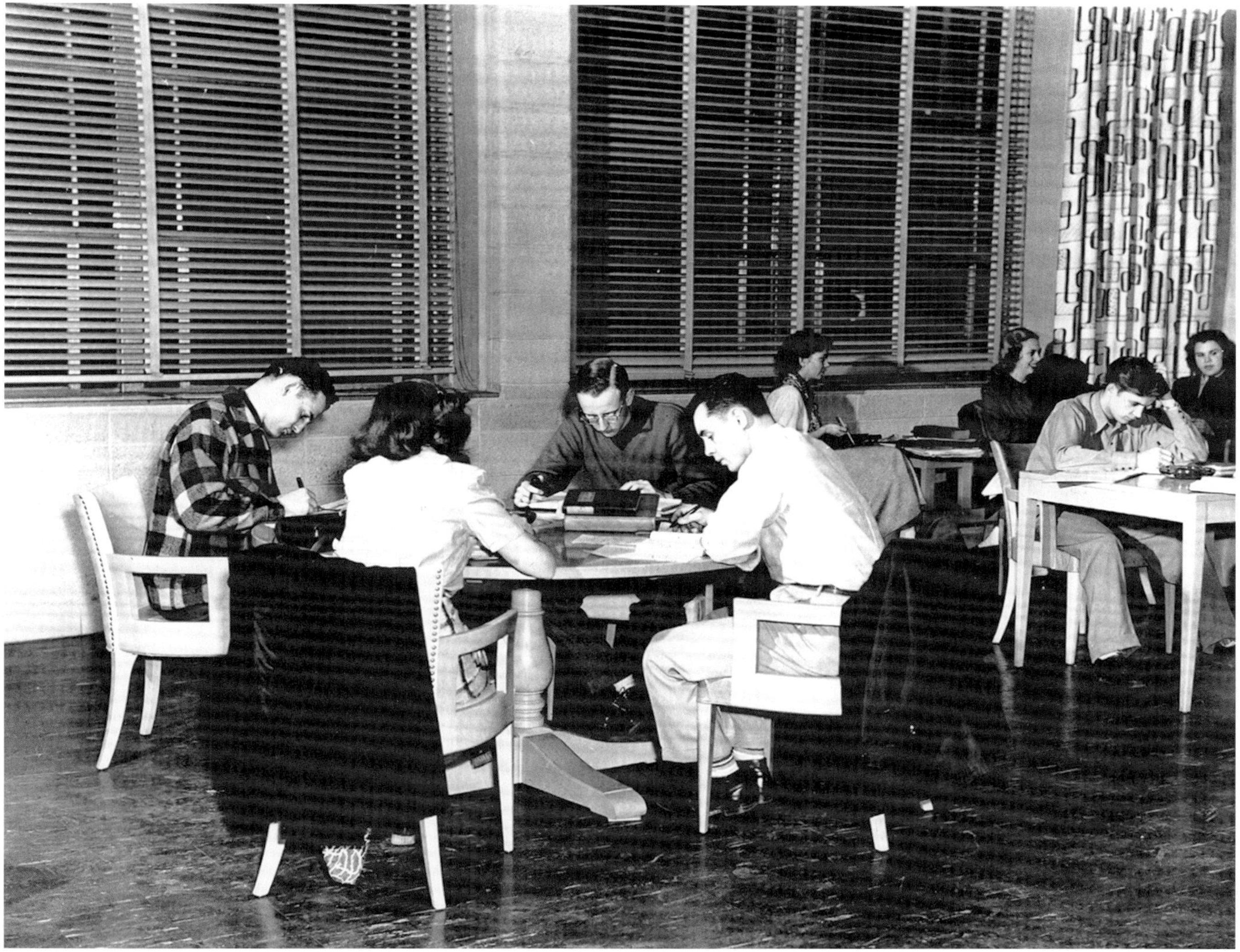

Science Hall lounge, undated. (Walter P. Reuther Library, Archives of Labor and Urban Affairs, Wayne State University.)

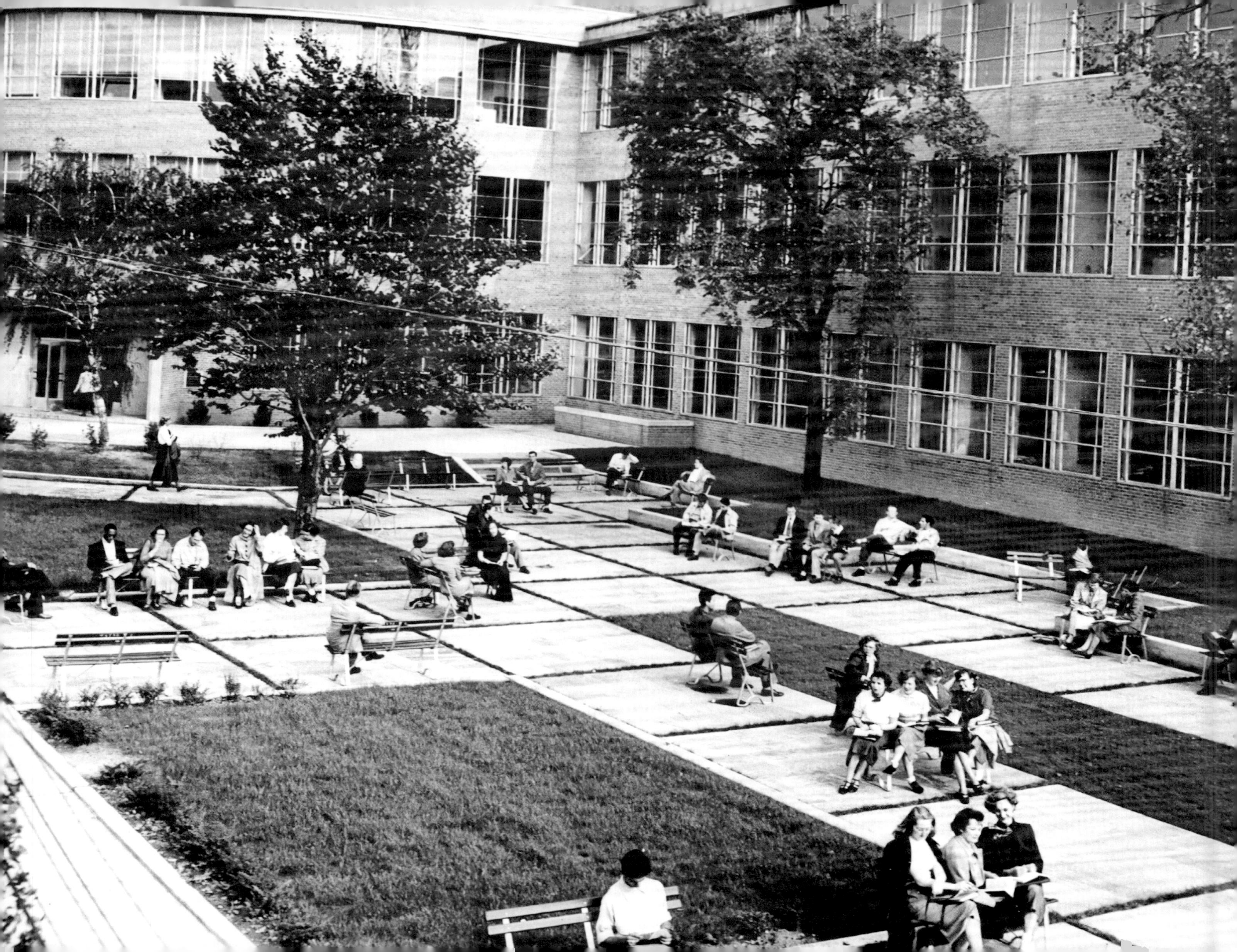

Courtyard behind Science Hall, 1950s. The courtyard between State Hall and Science Hall, a restful stop for students and professors between classes. The Chemistry Building and Science Library, constructed in 1970, would swallow up most of this space, but a smaller area with benches would be preserved between the Chemistry Building and State Hall. However, an addition to the Chemistry Building in 2005 would reduce this space further to a walkway. (Walter P. Reuther Library, Archives of Labor and Urban Affairs, Wayne State University.)

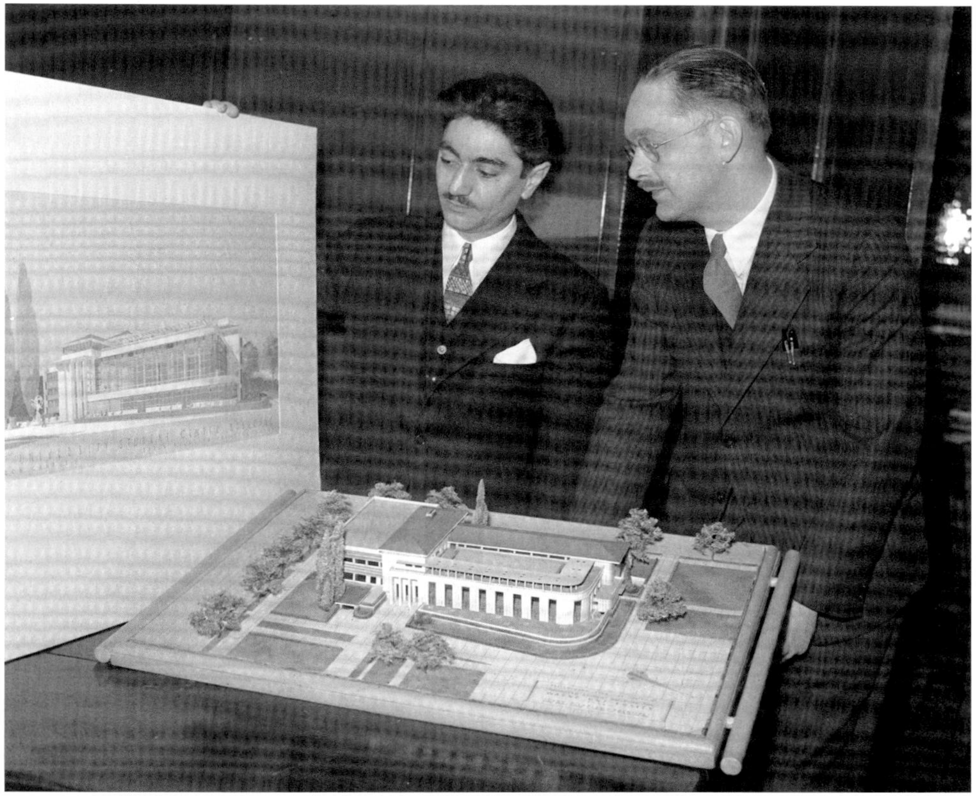

Designing a campus, 1943. Once Wayne University had acquired all of the property it wanted along Cass Avenue—from Putnam Street, to Kirby Street, to Ferry Street—university officials wanted to design a more traditional campus. The Board of Education awarded architect Suren Pilafian a contract to design a master plan for the university. Pilafian, on the left, is pictured with university president Dr. David D. Henry. The drawing and model show the University Student Center Building, which was never built. In addition to the master plan, Pilafian designed State Hall, the Engineering Building, the Purdy/Kresge Library, and the Community Arts Center. (Walter P. Reuther Library, Archives of Labor and Urban Affairs, Wayne State University.)

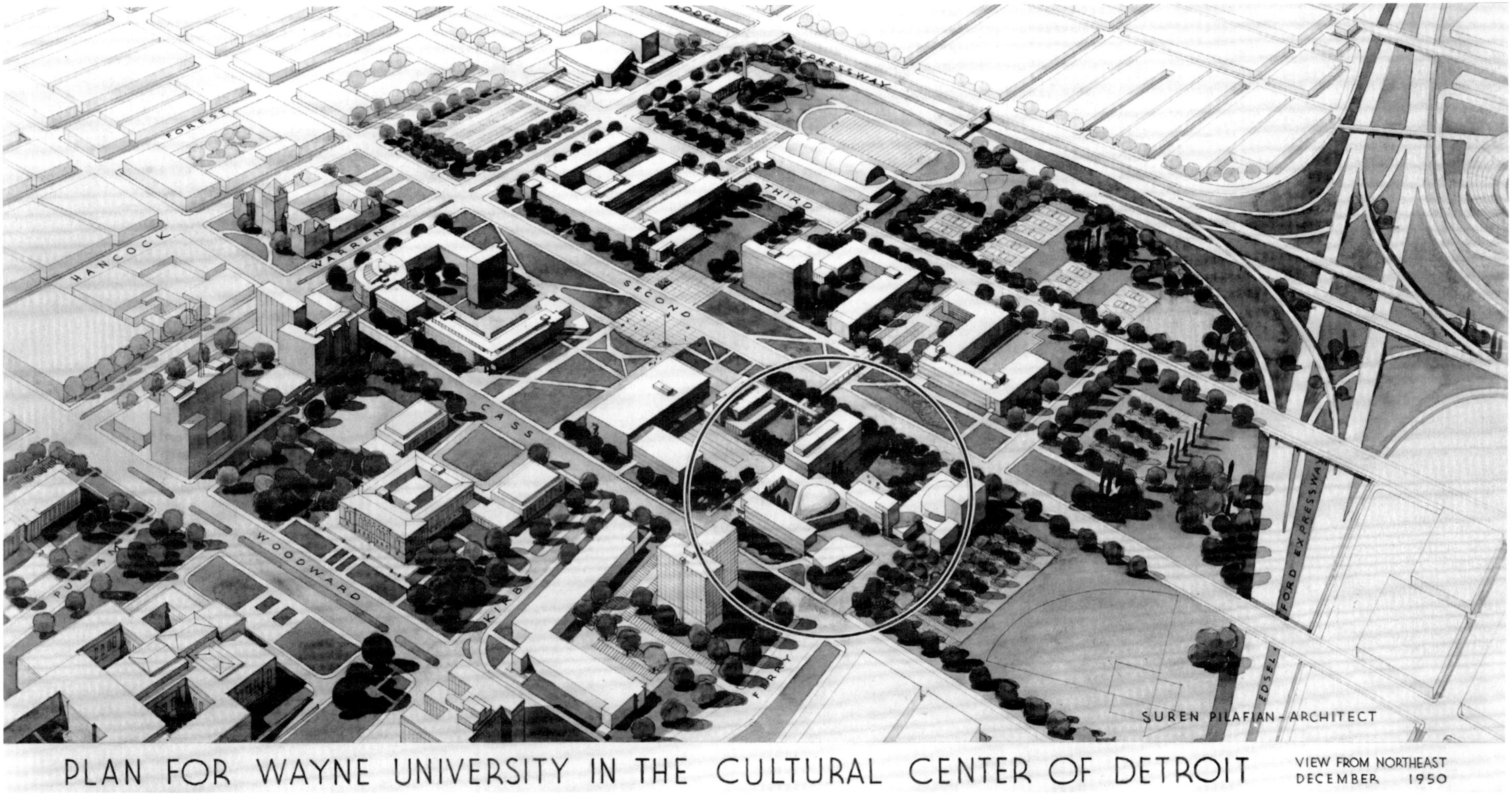

Master plan for Wayne University's campus, aerial view, 1950. The third of four campus plans designed by Pilafian, it shows the future Community Arts Center in the circled area and includes the Engineering Building and the General Library. While none of the master plans were fully implemented, elements of them were incorporated over the years. (Walter P. Reuther Library, Archives of Labor and Urban Affairs, Wayne State University.)

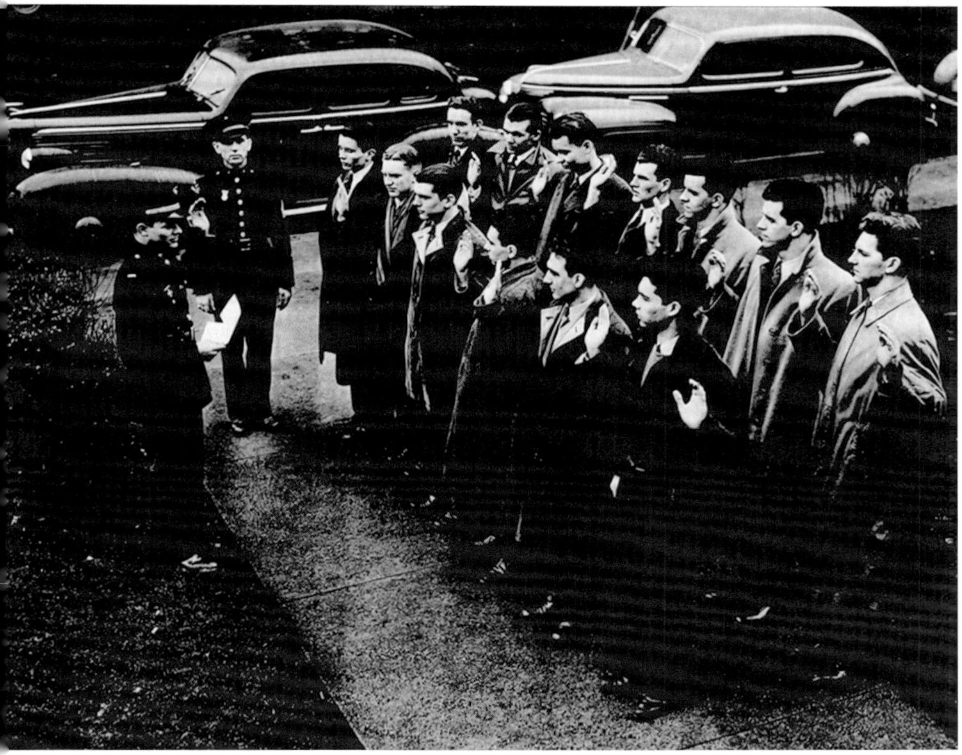

Students enlisting in the Marines, 1942. (Walter P. Reuther Library, Archives of Labor and Urban Affairs, Wayne State University.)

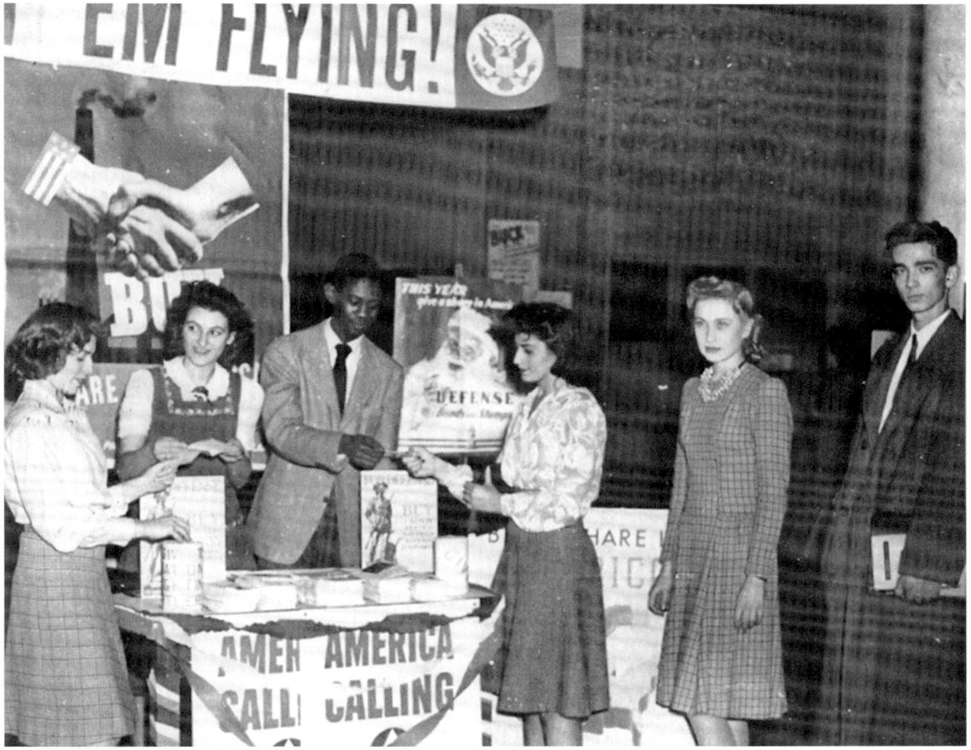

World War II activities, early 1940s. During the war, students organized salvage drives and blood banks; the speech department performed plays on the air; and home economics classes planted victory gardens and produced knitted goods. Here, Wayne students put together a display promoting activities in which students might participate to help the war effort. (Walter P. Reuther Library, Archives of Labor and Urban Affairs, Wayne State University.)

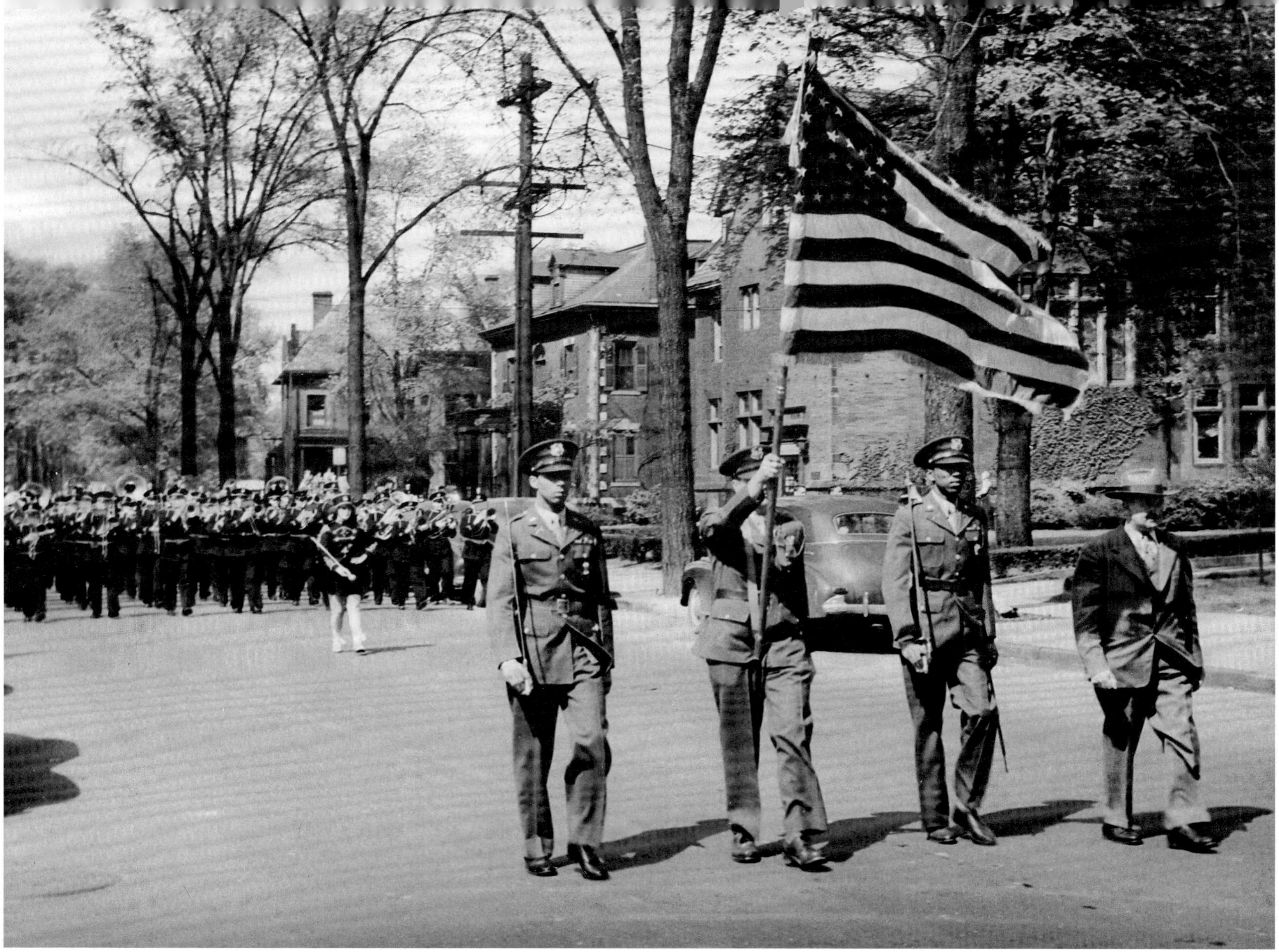

Reserve Officer Training Corps (ROTC) student parade, late 1940s. Students from the ROTC unit at Wayne march through the neighborhood around Old Main. The ROTC Air Force and Army units began training at Wayne in June 1947. In 1951, the units were housed in Wayne's Armory on Third Avenue. Budget constraints and plans to demolish the armory building to accommodate the widening of Second Avenue caused the ROTC units to disband in 1961. (Walter P. Reuther Library, Archives of Labor and Urban Affairs, Wayne State University.)

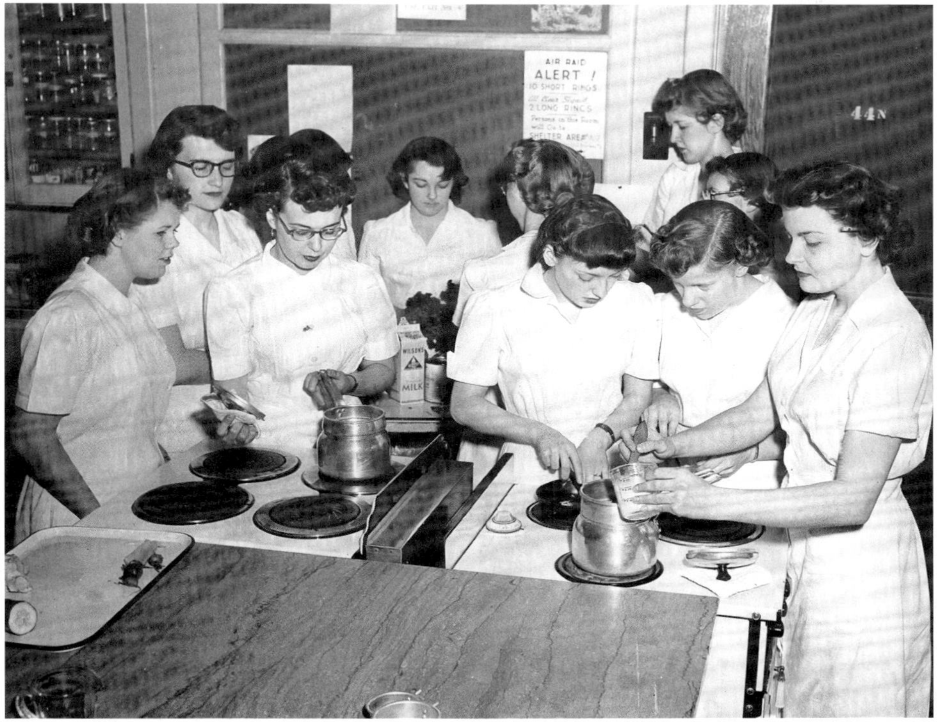

Home economics class, undated. Home economics was still offered as a program of study at Wayne in the 1940s. Note the air-raid alert sign on the bulletin board in the background. Air-raid drills were discontinued in the fall of 1944. To conform with brownout requirements, the light in the Main Building's clock tower was also periodically turned off during the early 1940s. (Walter P. Reuther Library, Archives of Labor and Urban Affairs, Wayne State University.)

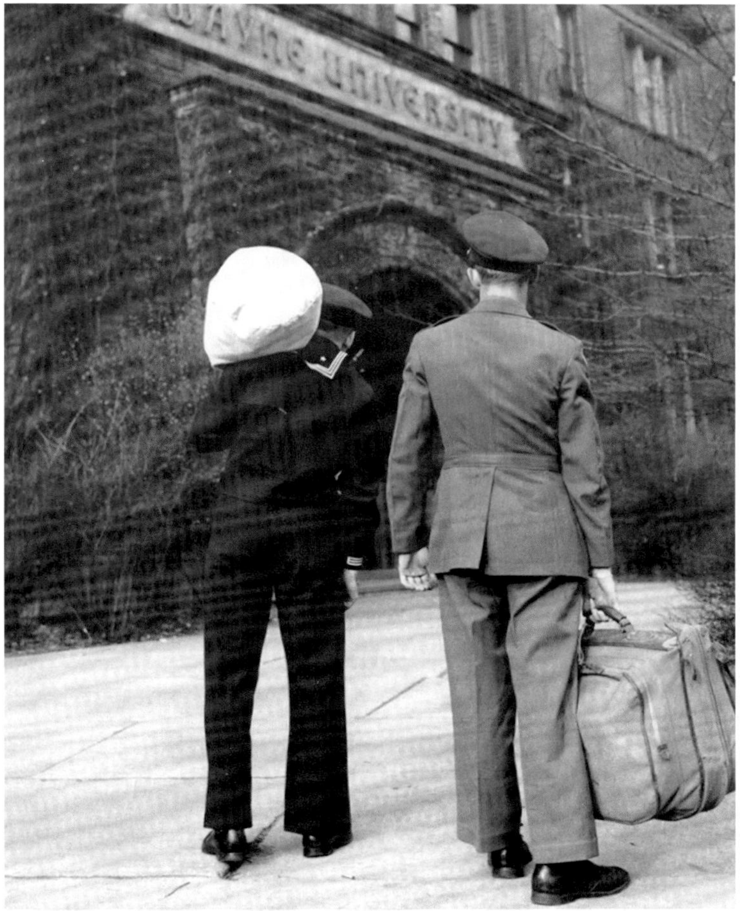

Veterans in front of the Main Building, late 1940s. (Walter P. Reuther Library, Archives of Labor and Urban Affairs, Wayne State University.)

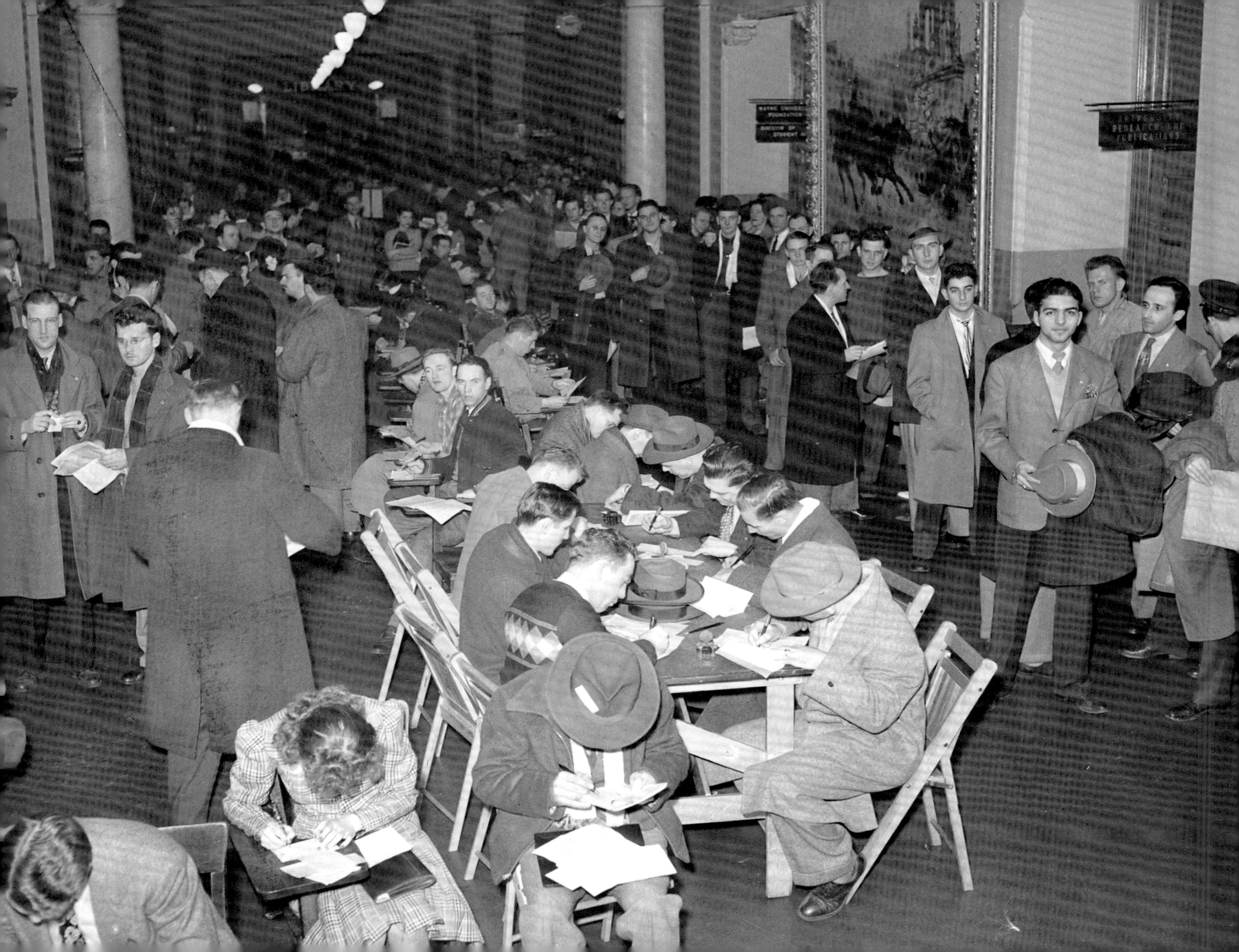

Veterans registering for classes, Main Building, 1946. Financial support provided as a result of the G.I. Bill helped thousands of returning veterans enroll at Wayne. Enrollment jumped about 35 percent after World War II: there were 9,941 students enrolled at Wayne in the fall of 1945; by fall of 1946, that number had increased to 15,041. (Walter P. Reuther Library, Archives of Labor and Urban Affairs, Wayne State University.)

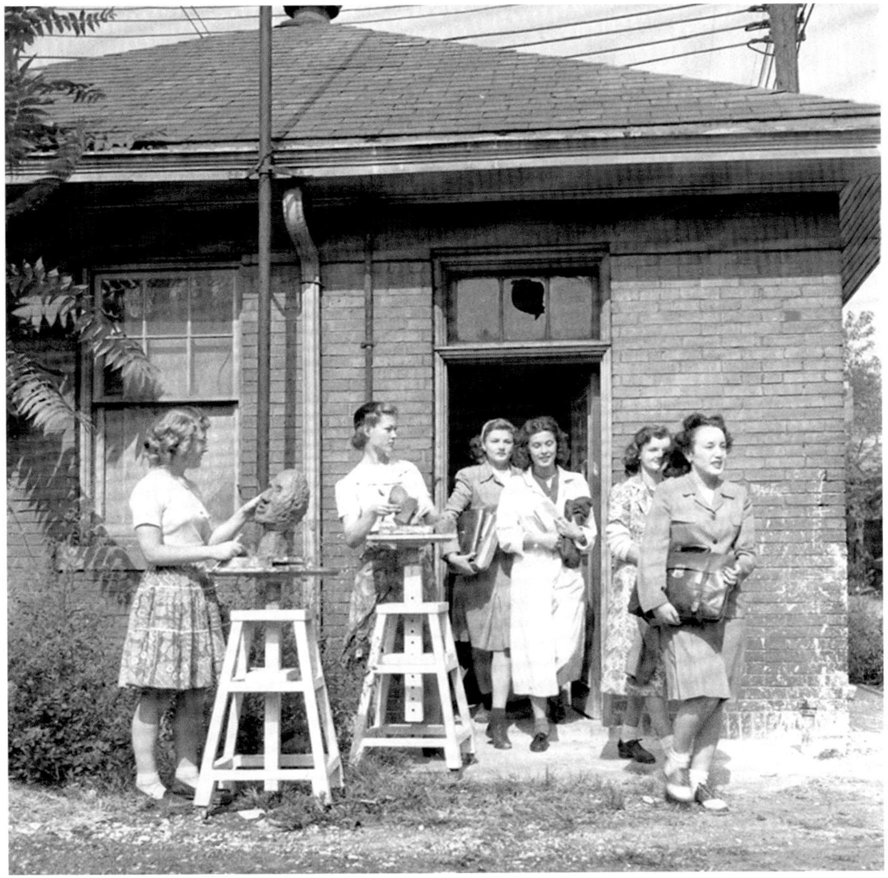

Sculpting class in a garage, 1944. The large influx of students after the war caused Wayne's master campus plans to be set aside. The immediate need for class space won out, and Pilafian's elaborate designs were put on hold indefinitely. Classes were held in rented houses around the Main Building—even in garages and attics. (Walter P. Reuther Library, Archives of Labor and Urban Affairs, Wayne State University.)

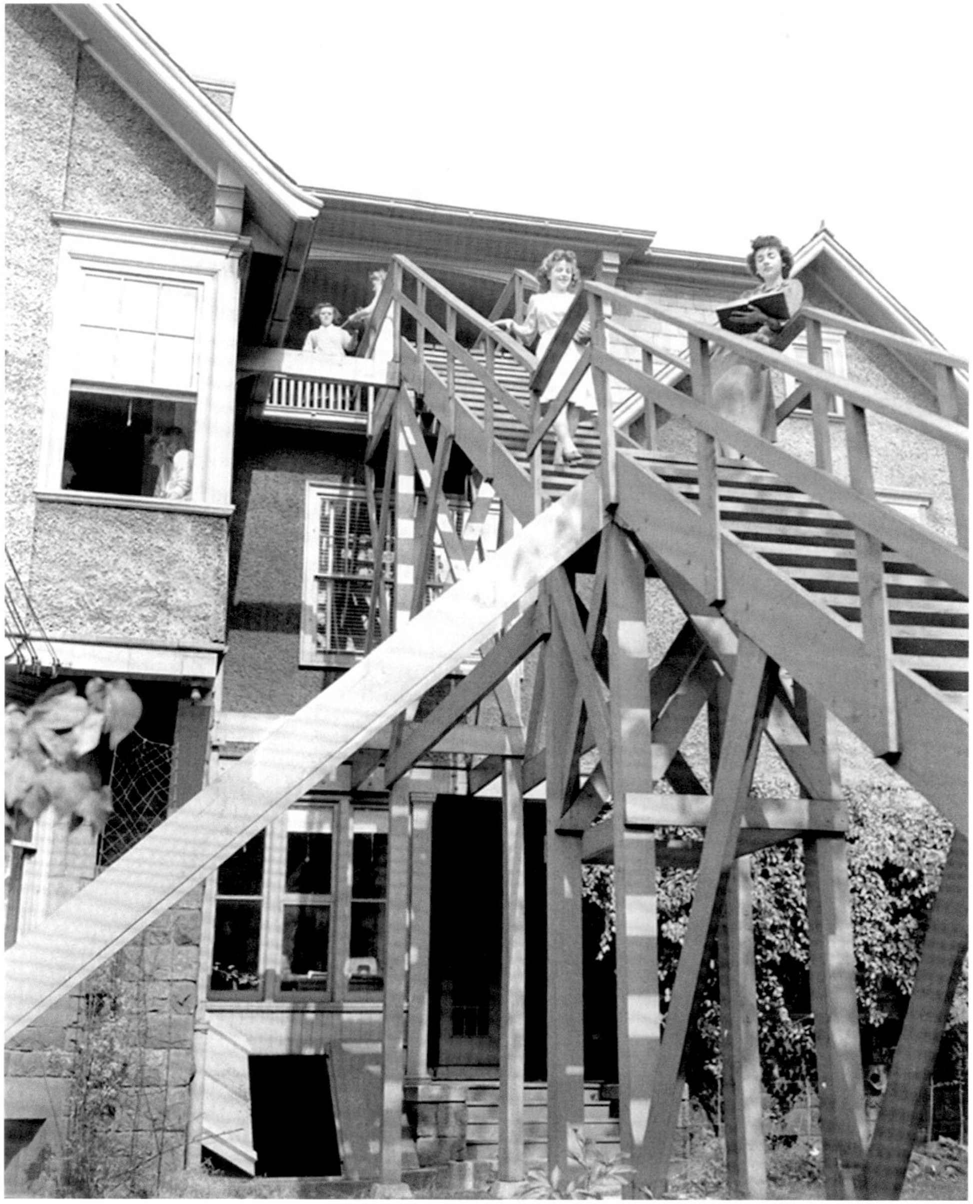

Attic classes, 1944. While classroom space was urgently needed, the old houses pressed into service had their share of problems. Not designed for classes, the houses were expensive to remodel and maintain, especially those with old furnaces. (Walter P. Reuther Library, Archives of Labor and Urban Affairs, Wayne State University.)

Temporary classrooms at Second and Warren avenues, as seen looking southeast, 1947. These war-surplus barracks were set up at Warren and Second to accommodate the flood of returning war veterans who enrolled at Wayne. Purchased by Provost Arthur Neef, the nineteen temporary classrooms stood roughly where the Life Science Building is located today. The Main Building is visible behind the barracks. (Walter P. Reuther Library, Archives of Labor and Urban Affairs, Wayne State University.)

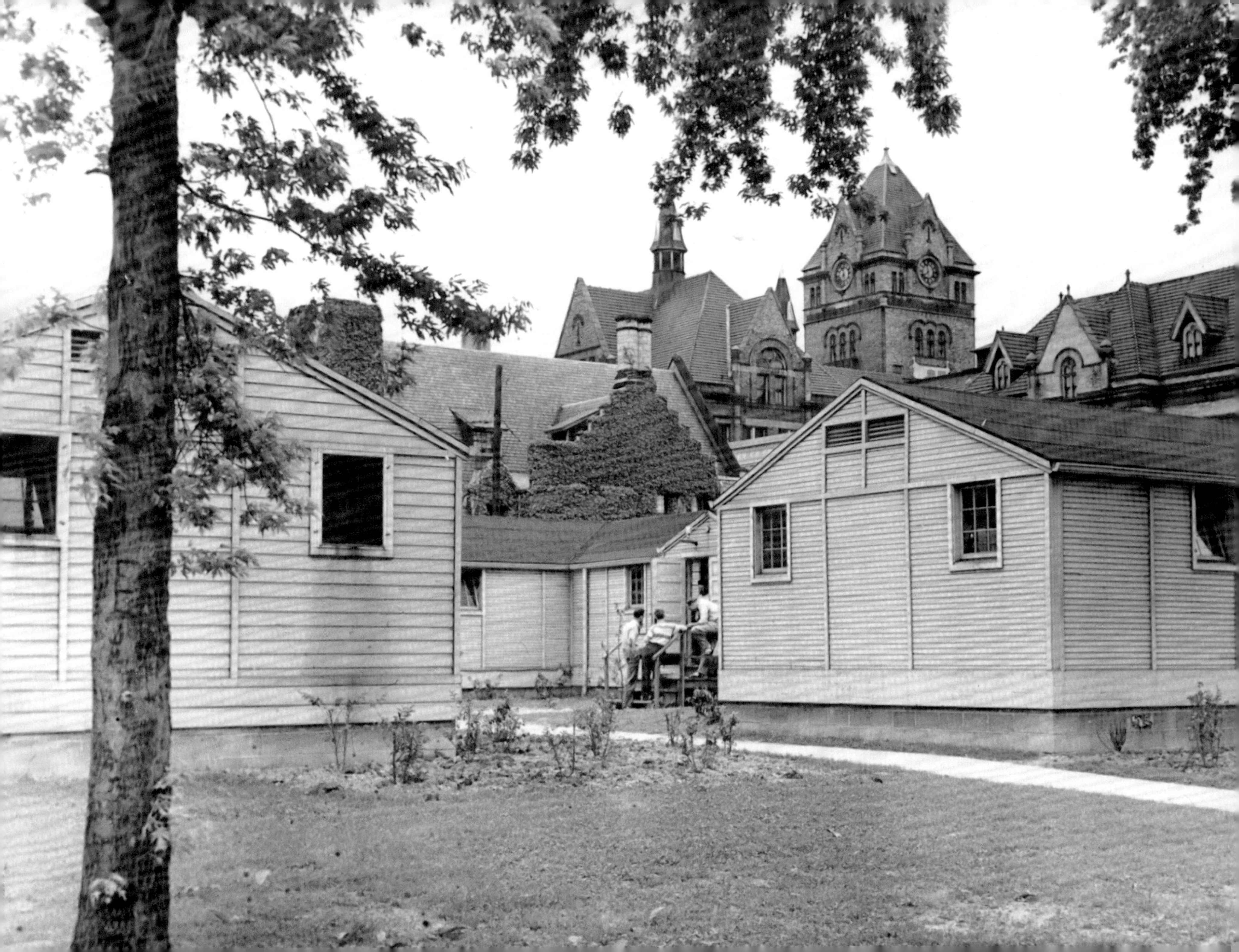

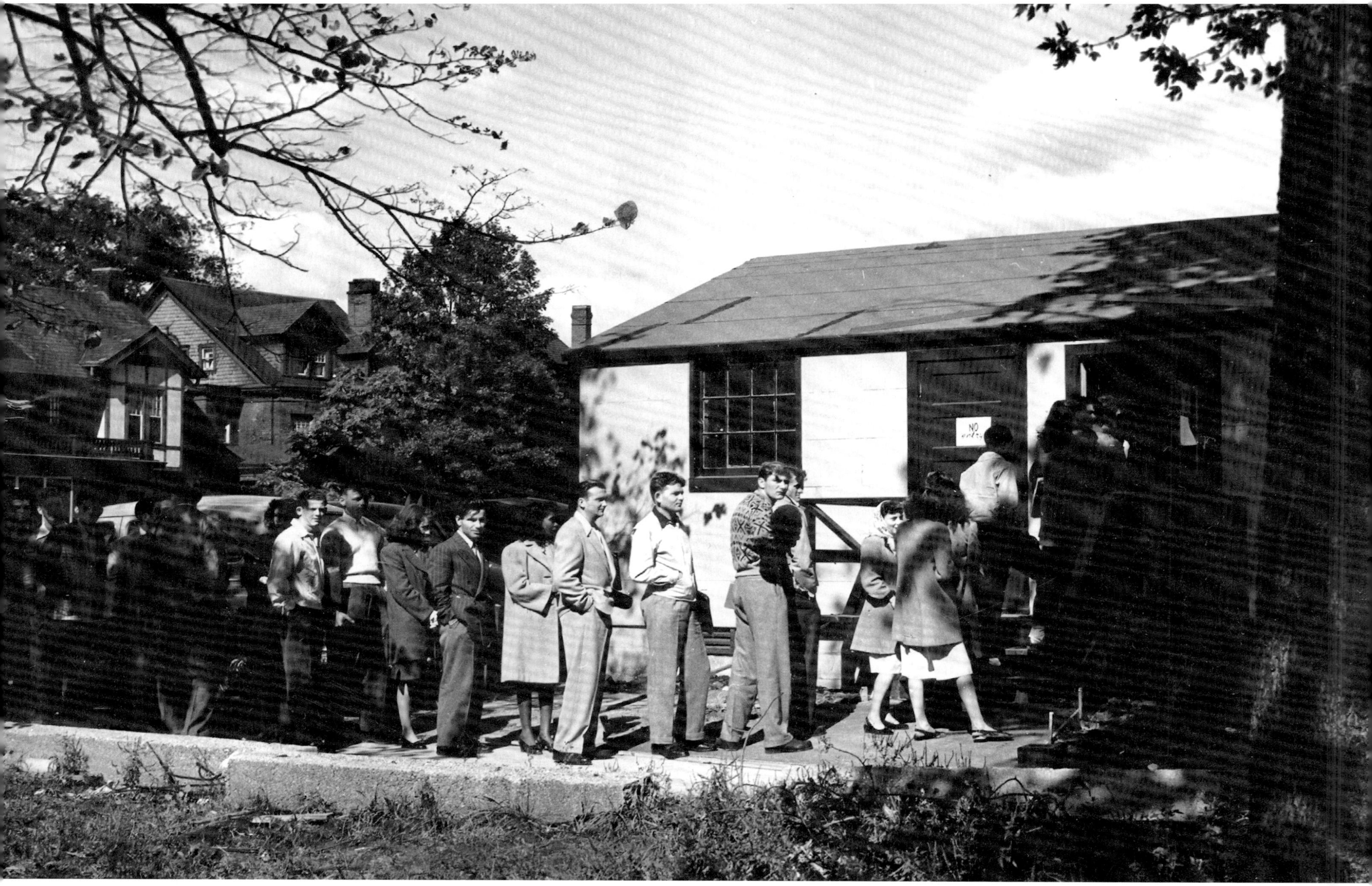
NO

Students lining up outside temporary classrooms, late 1940s. The nineteen barracks were assigned letters of the alphabet and grouped into a "Warren Quadrangle" and a "Kirby Quadrangle." (Walter P. Reuther Library, Archives of Labor and Urban Affairs, Wayne State University.)

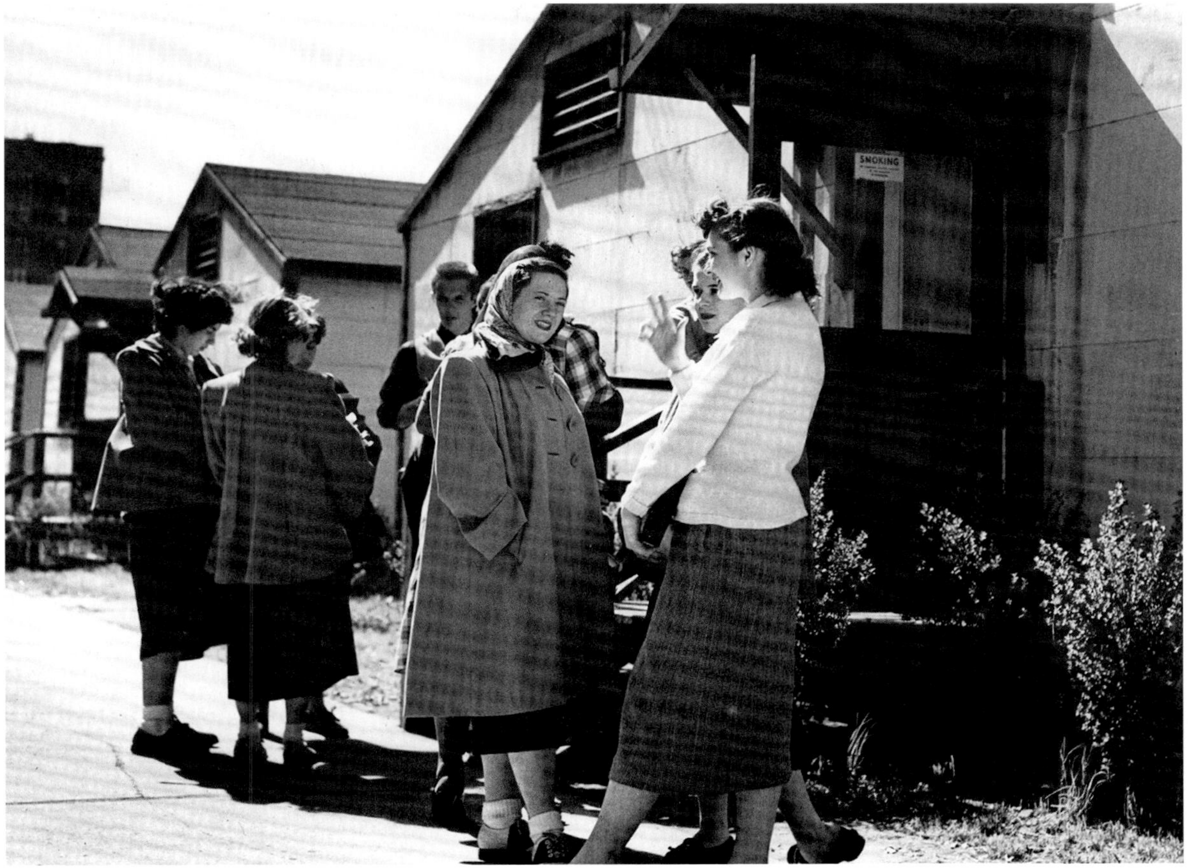

Students waiting outside a classroom, late 1940s. (Walter P. Reuther Library, Archives of Labor and Urban Affairs, Wayne State University.)

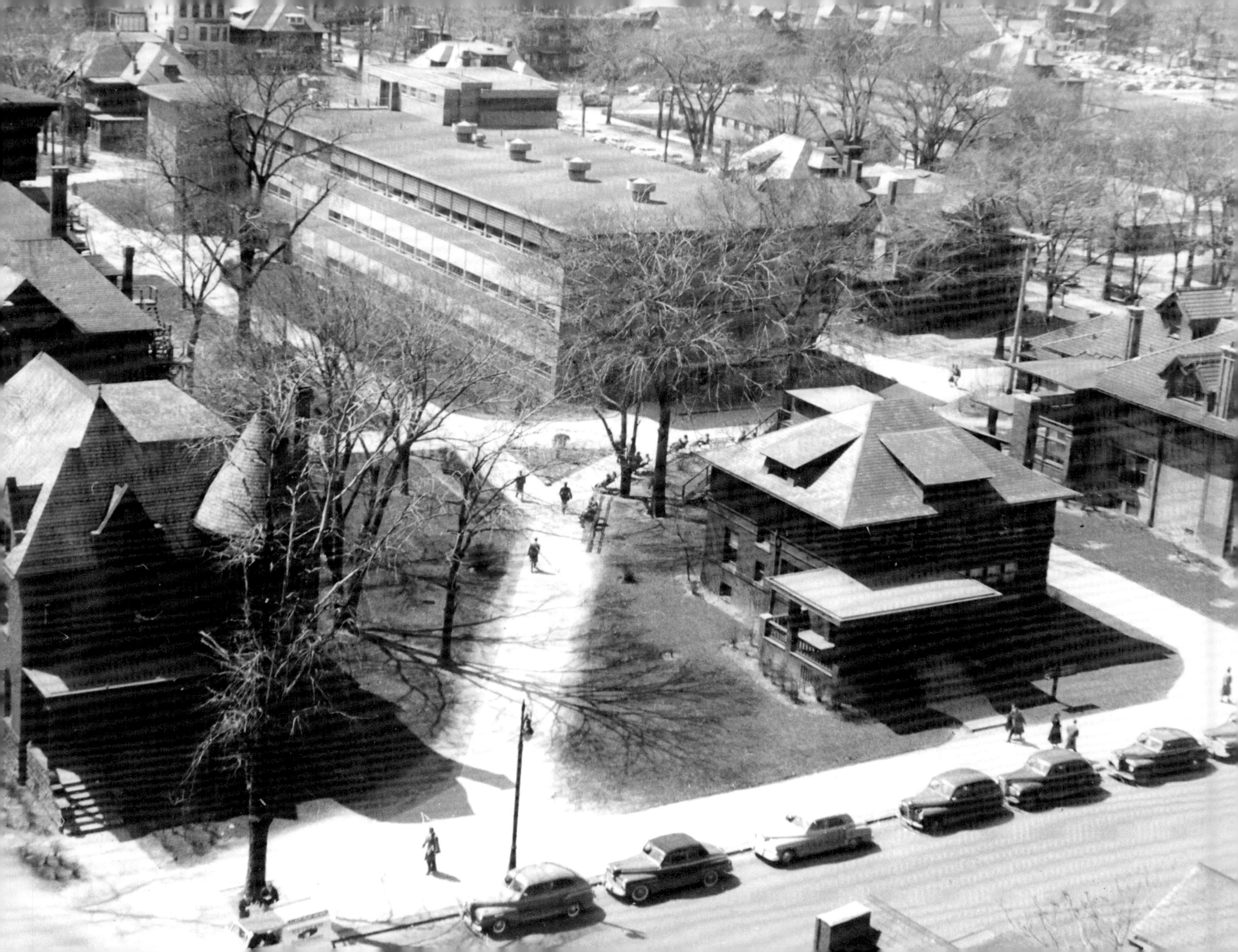

State Hall before the Cass Avenue wing was added in 1957, 5143 Cass Avenue at Putnam Street, looking northwest, 1951. Cass Avenue is in the foreground. (Courtesy of the Burton Historical Collection, Detroit Public Library.)

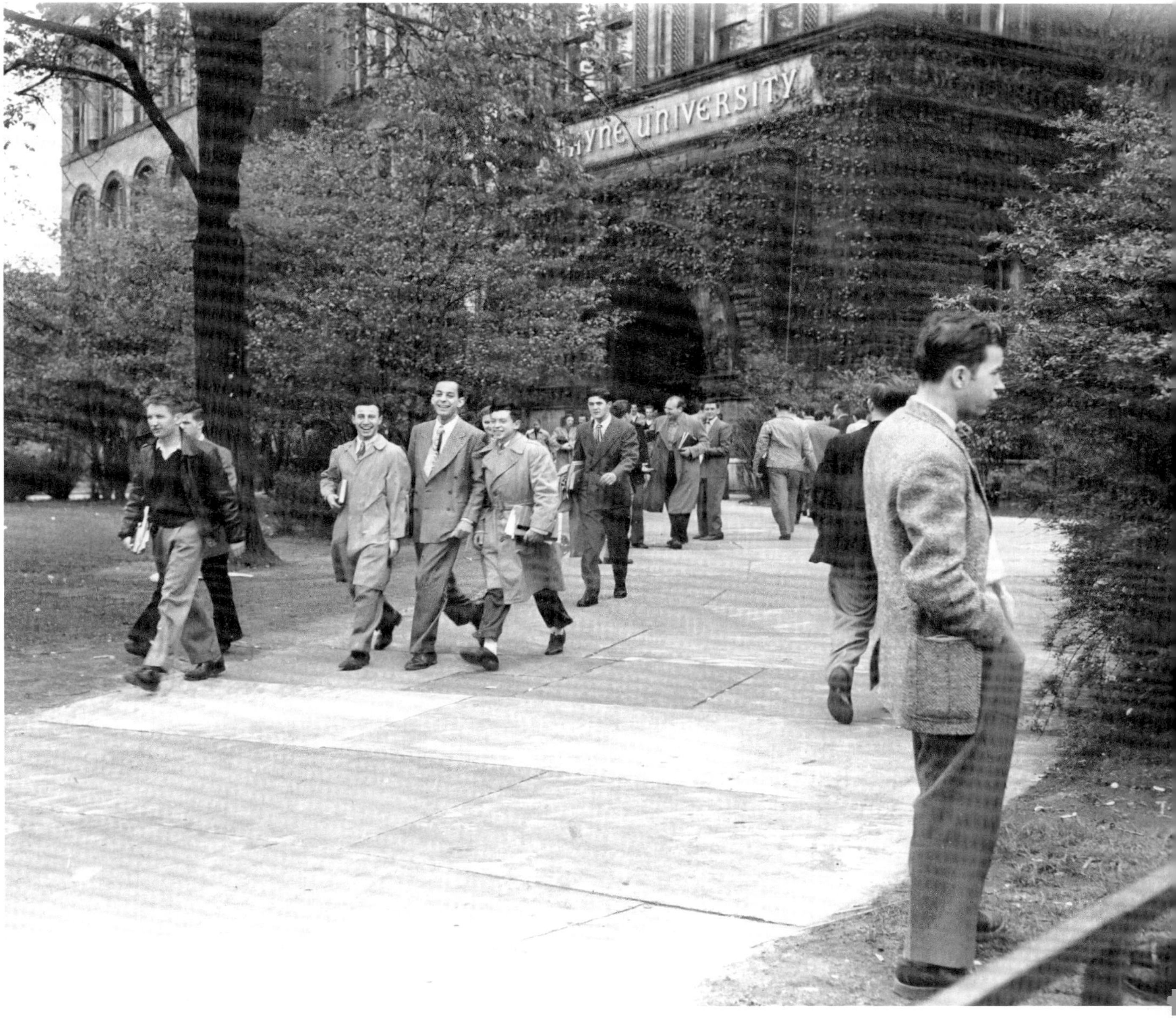

Students leaving Old Main, undated. The Main Building was officially renamed Old Main in 1950. The old Central High School building where Wayne's classes were first held had from the beginning been the cornerstone of the campus. (Walter P. Reuther Library, Archives of Labor and Urban Affairs, Wayne State University.)

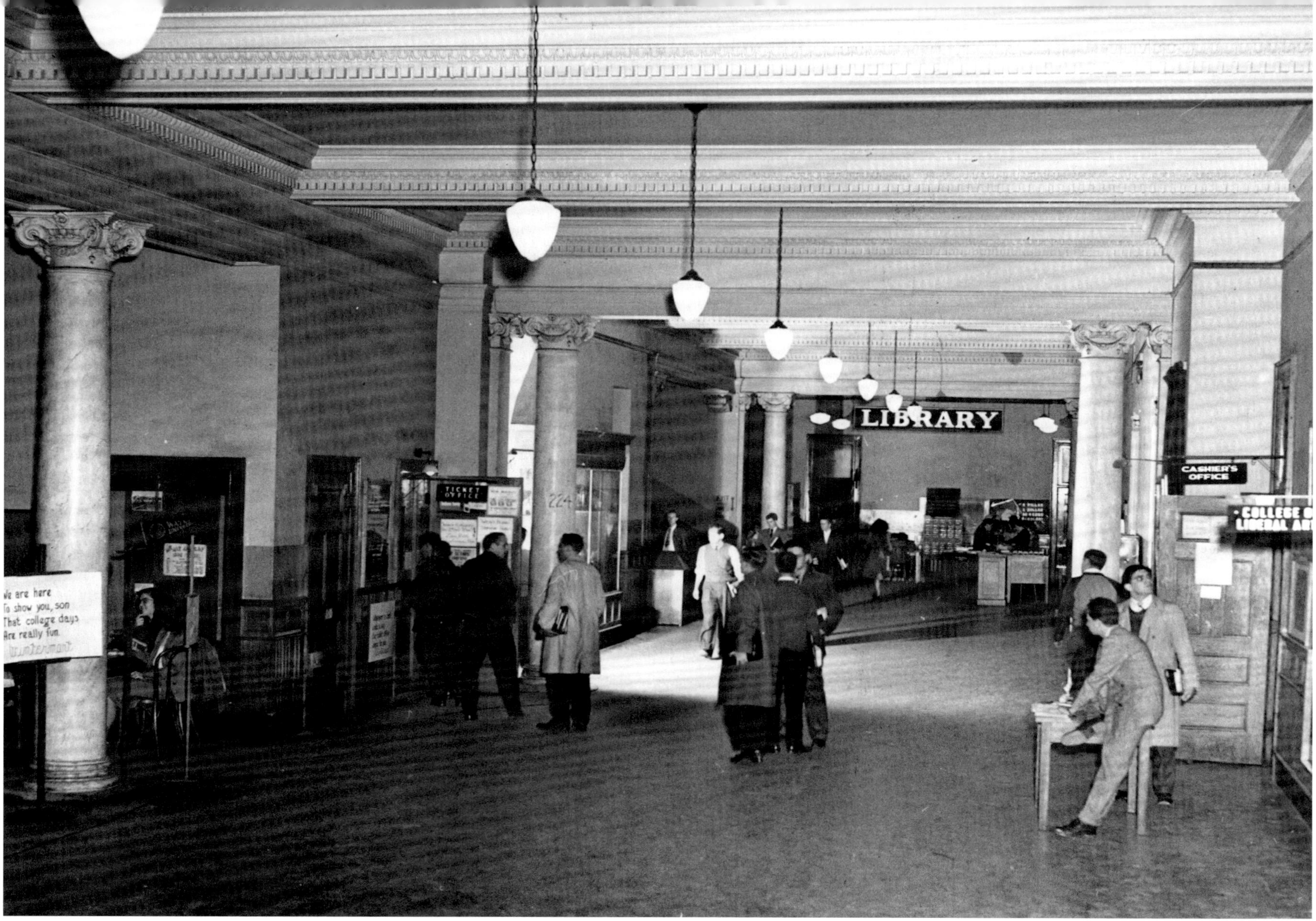

Interior of Old Main, early 1950s. Note the sign on the left, which reads: "We are here / To show you, son / That college days / Are really fun." It is a poster for Wintermart, a carnival held annually on Wayne's campus from the late 1930s through the 1950s to raise money for the construction of the War Memorial Mall. The mall, when it was officially dedicated in 1956, would take up all of the space between the General Library and State Hall, extending from Second Avenue all the way to Cass Avenue. It was intended as a memorial to Wayne University's war dead. In 1964, Prentis Hall and the Helen L. DeRoy Auditorium were built over the mall. (Walter P. Reuther Library, Archives of Labor and Urban Affairs, Wayne State University.)

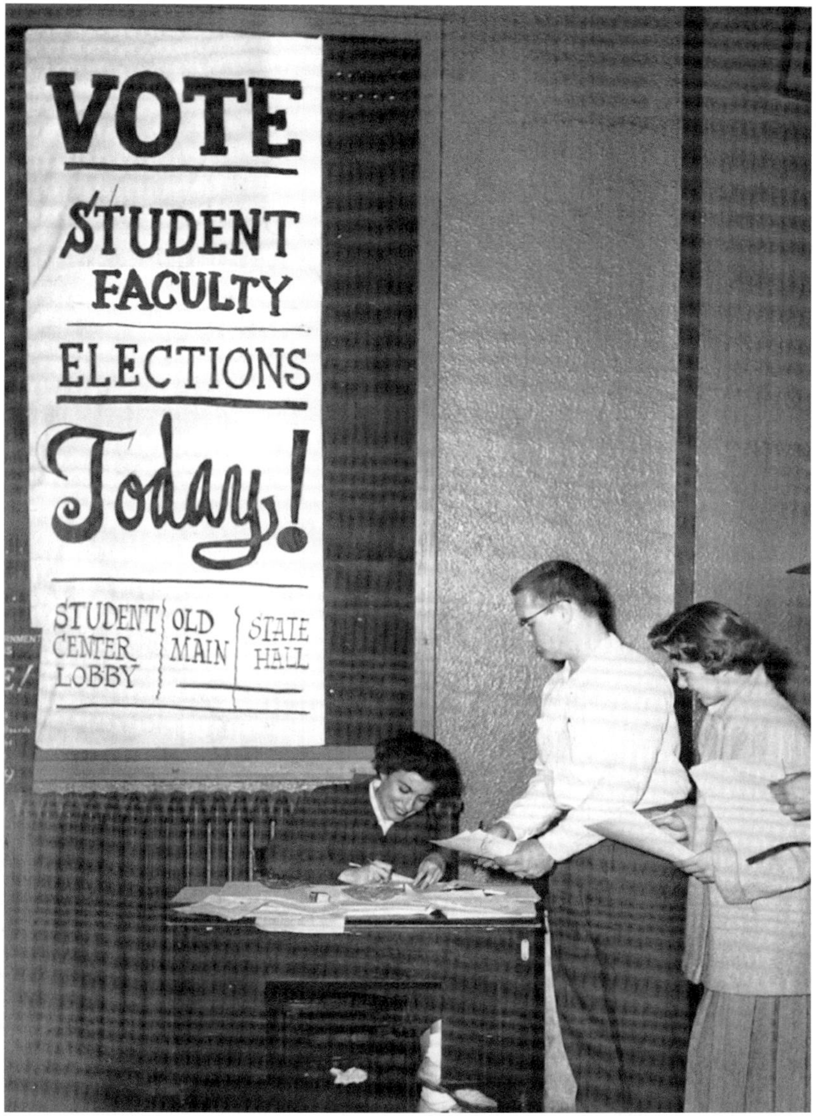

Student Council elections, undated. Formed in 1918 to oversee student groups and activities on campus, the Student Council has held elections regularly ever since. (Walter P. Reuther Library, Archives of Labor and Urban Affairs, Wayne State University.)

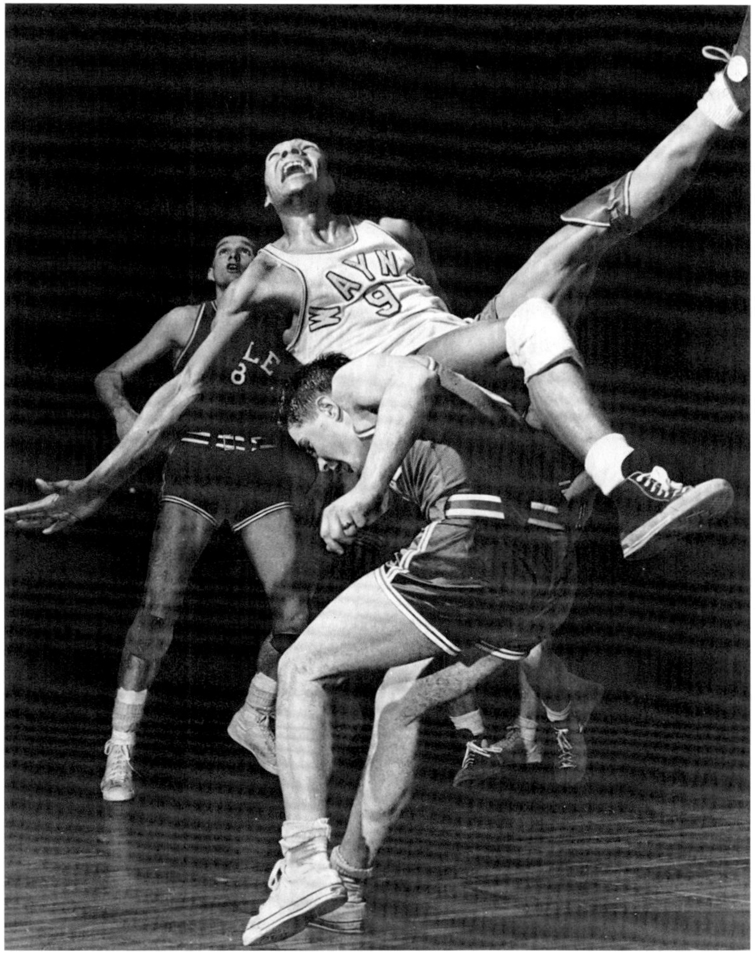

Basketball game, Wayne versus Yale, 1948. Like Wayne football players, Wayne basketball players practiced in a variety of locations: the Naval Armory, the Light Guard Armory, Olympia Stadium, the new Central High School, and Mackenzie High School. (Walter P. Reuther Library, Archives of Labor and Urban Affairs, Wayne State University.)

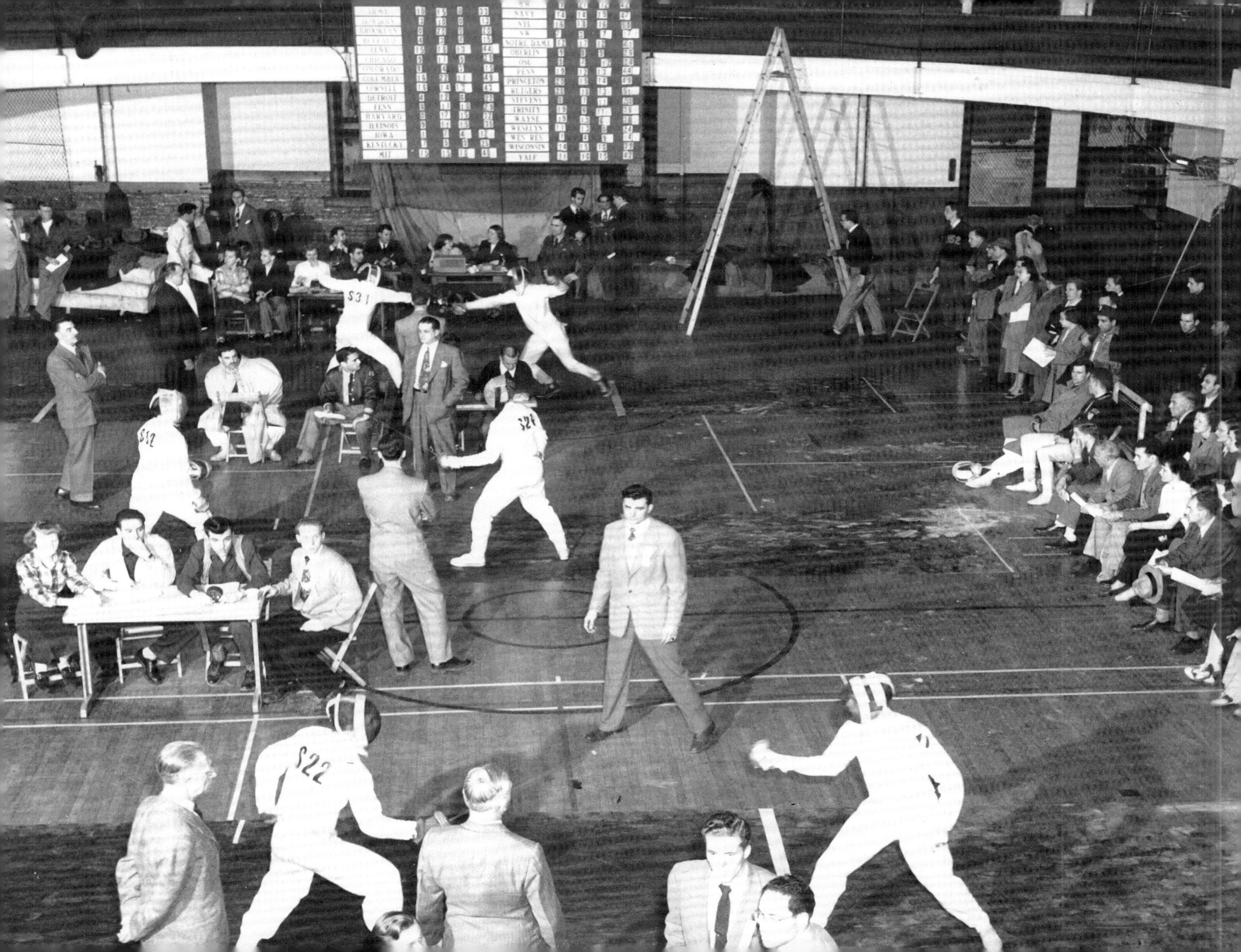
ARMY
BOWDOIN
BROOKLYN
BUFFALO
CCNY
CHICAGO
COLORADO
COLUMBIA
CORNELL
DETROIT
FENN
HARVARD
ILLINOIS
IOWA
KENTUCKY
MIT
NAVY
NYU
NW
NOTRE DAME
OBERLIN
OSU
PENN
PRINCETON
RUTGERS
STEVENS
TRINITY
WAYNE
WESLEYN
WES RES
WISCONSIN
YALE
S31
S32
S24
S22

Fencing practice, 1950s. After the first match, held in 1934, fencing became one of Wayne's most notable and enduring sports. The Wayne fencing team was started by Bela de Tuson, a fencer and former saber champion from Hungary. The team was regularly included in the top tier of the National Collegiate Athletic Association, and in 1961 it ranked among the top four fencing teams in the nation. (Walter P. Reuther Library, Archives of Labor and Urban Affairs, Wayne State University.)

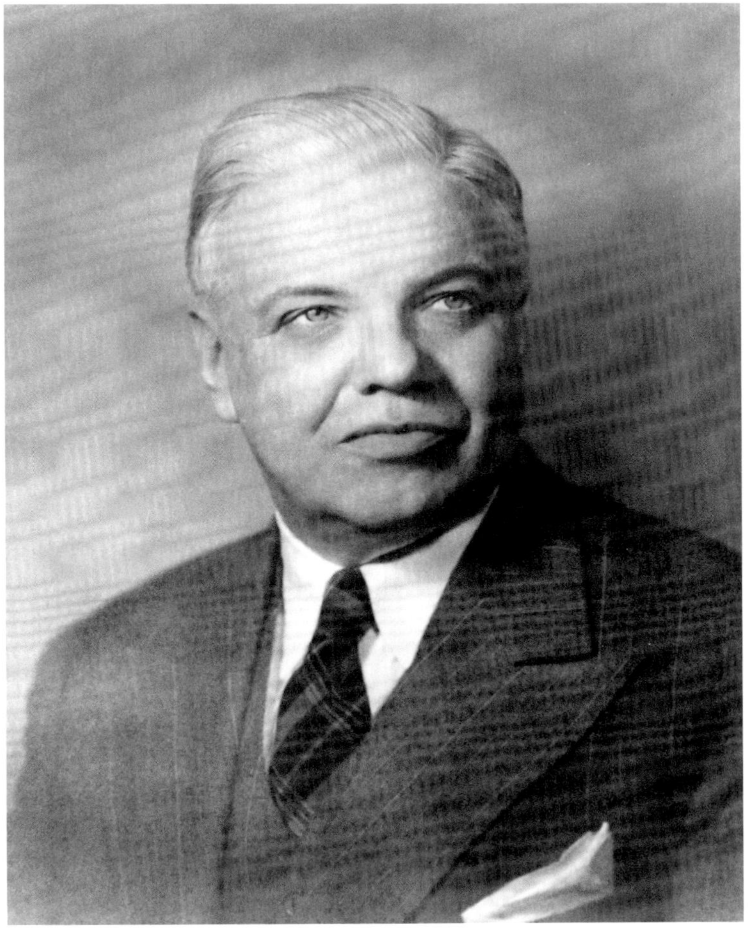

Warren E. Bow, superintendent of the Detroit public schools, early 1940s. Bow succeeded Frank Cody as president of Wayne University. He served from 1942 until 1945. (Walter P. Reuther Library, Archives of Labor and Urban Affairs, Wayne State University.)

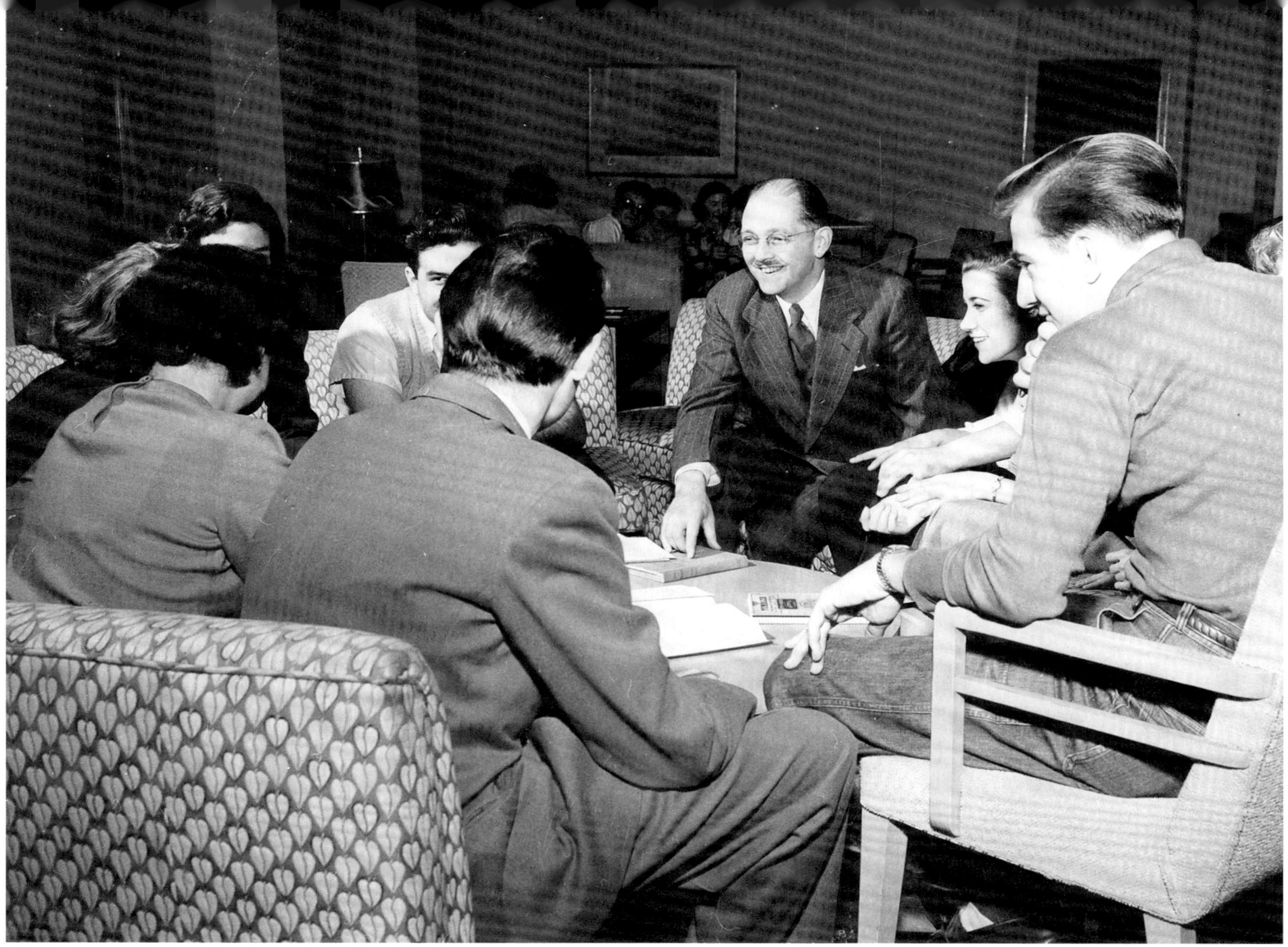

President David D. Henry (center) meeting with student group leaders. The end of the war coincided with the appointment of David D. Henry, Wayne's first full-time university president. Previously, the superintendent of Detroit public schools had also acted as president of Wayne University. Henry was also the first Wayne president to be drawn from higher education rather than the Detroit public school administration. During Henry's tenure (1945–52), the university began its first serious building program, one aimed at providing the college with the space it needed and making Wayne a much more visible and influential presence in the city. (Walter P. Reuther Library, Archives of Labor and Urban Affairs, Wayne State University.)

Cass Avenue at Putnam Street, 1949. The man in the hat, waiting with the students at the bus stop, is David D. Henry, president of the university. Henry liked to tour the campus while he was in office. Science Hall is seen on the right, Old Main at the center of the photo. A home still stands in front of Science Hall. (Walter P. Reuther Library, Archives of Labor and Urban Affairs, Wayne State University.)

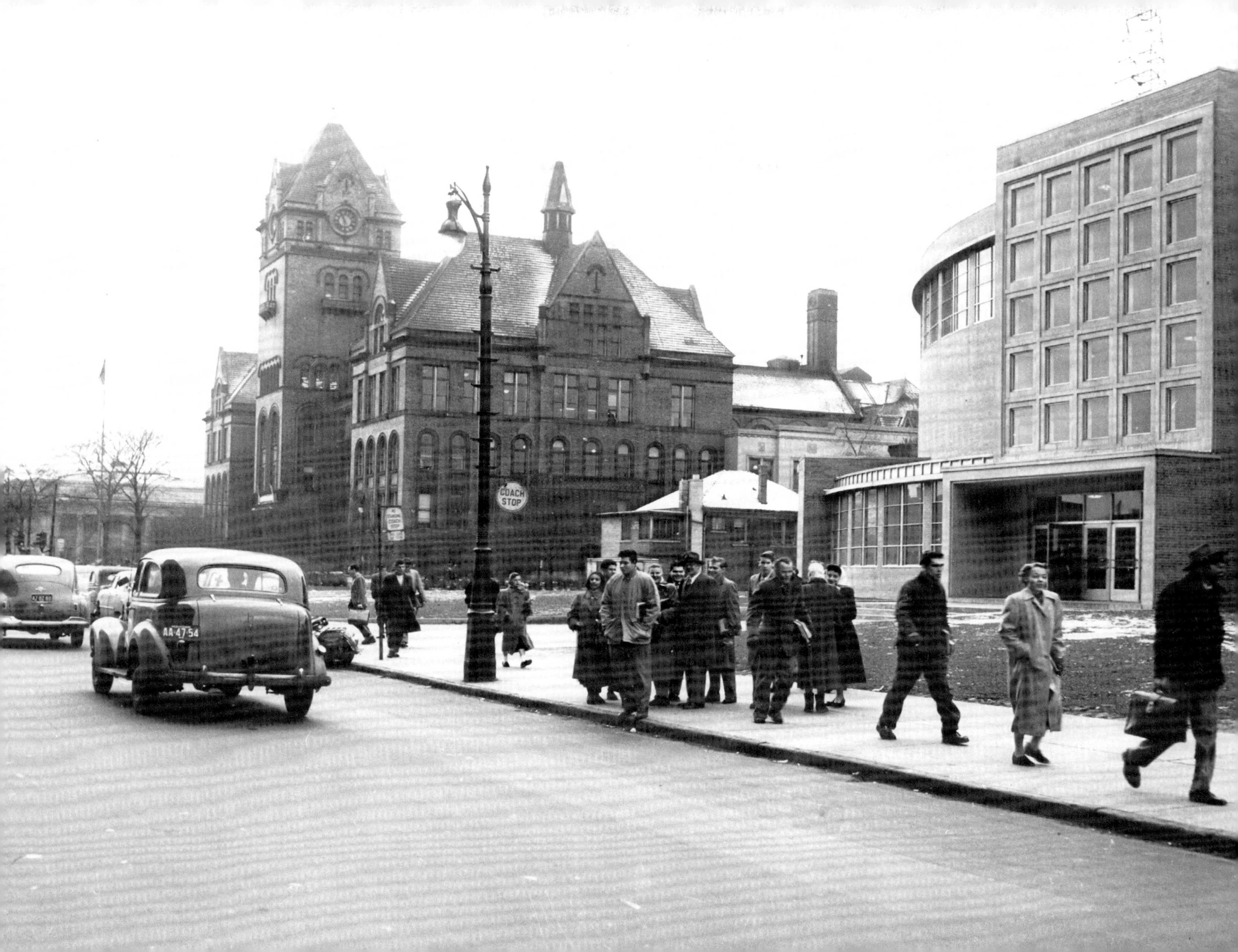
COACH
STOP
AA-47-54

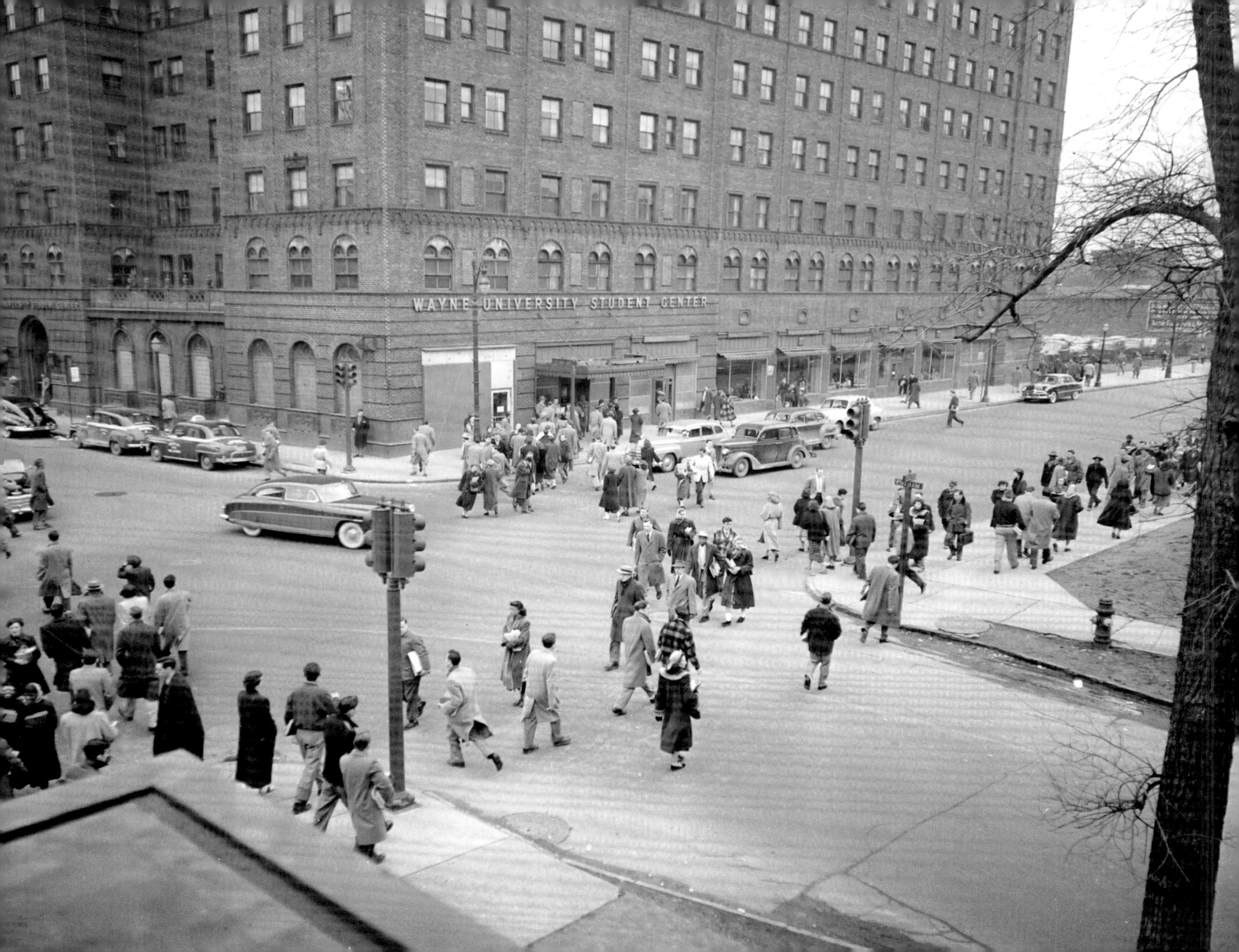
WAYNE UNIVERSITY STUDENT CENTER

The Student Center Building (Webster Hall) at Cass Avenue and Putnam Street, 1950. In 1946, the university purchased the Webster Hall Hotel and converted it into the Student Center Building, Wayne's first dormitory. In addition to dormitory rooms for students, the Student Center offered study lounges, student activity offices, and cafeterias. While it did not conform to the lofty plans that Suren Pilafian had designed, students welcomed the space that Webster Hall provided, and the former hotel became the center of Wayne's student life. The section of Putnam Street seen in the lower right-hand corner of the photo would later be closed to traffic. (Walter P. Reuther Library, Archives of Labor and Urban Affairs, Wayne State University.)

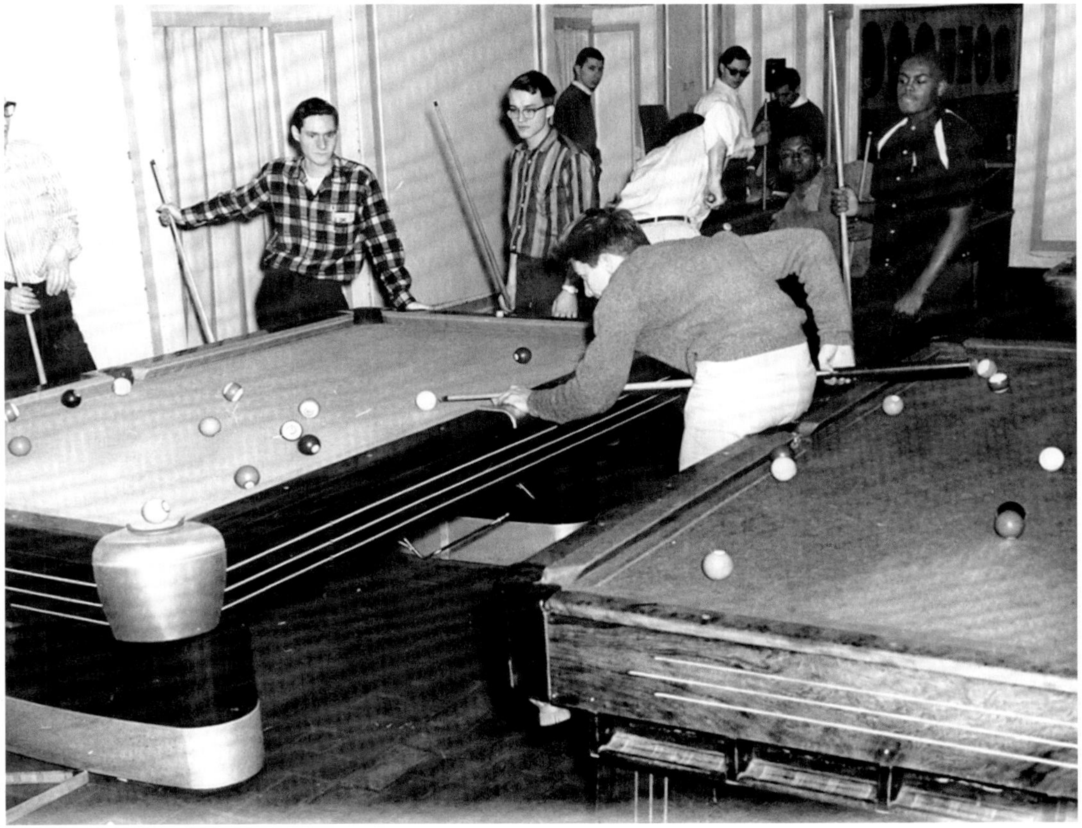

Students playing pool, Student Center Building (Webster Hall), undated. In addition to study spaces, Webster Hall offered places for students to relax, such as a pool hall. (Walter P. Reuther Library, Archives of Labor and Urban Affairs, Wayne State University.)

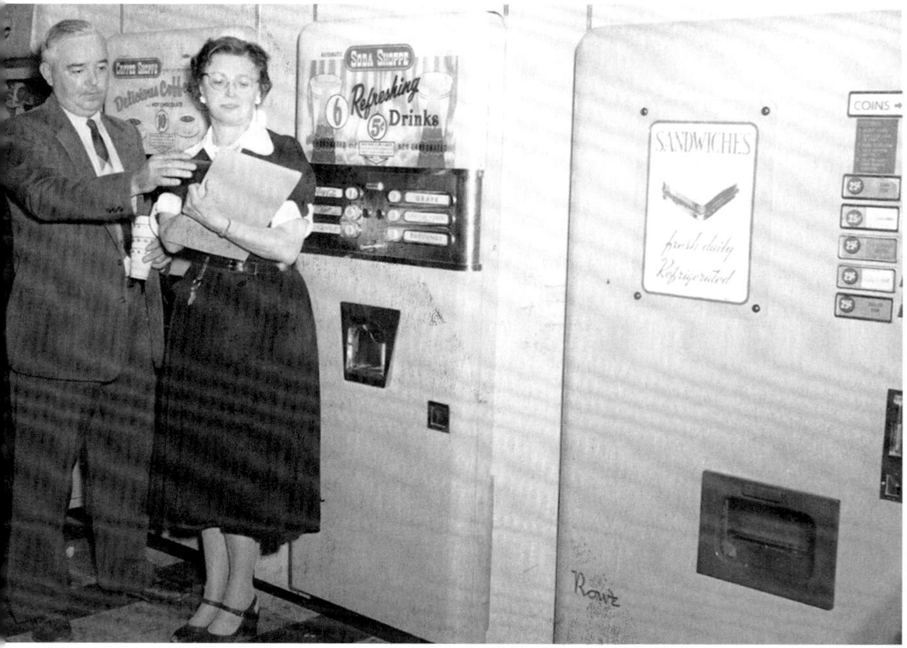

Interior of the Student Center Building (Webster Hall), 1950s. Webster Hall included amenities like a cafeteria and vending machines. (Walter P. Reuther Library, Archives of Labor and Urban Affairs, Wayne State University.)

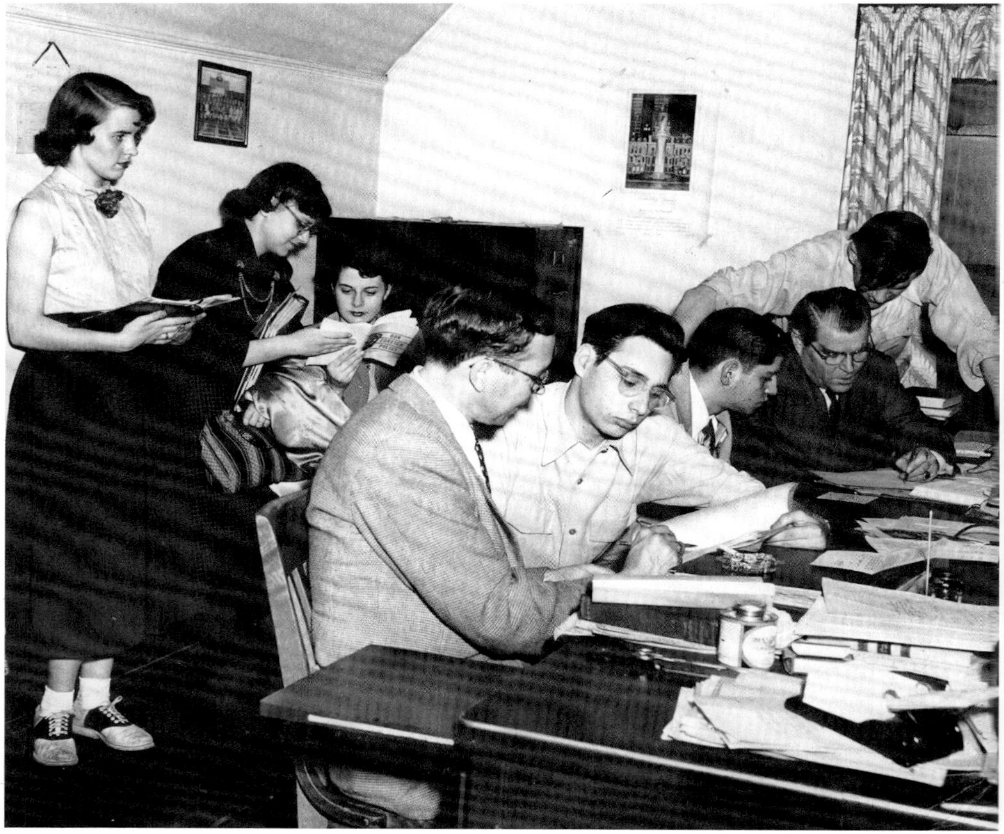

Speech class, 1950s. Old houses were used as classrooms through the late 1950s. Speech, once part of the English curriculum, became a separate department in 1933. (Walter P. Reuther Library, Archives of Labor and Urban Affairs, Wayne State University.)

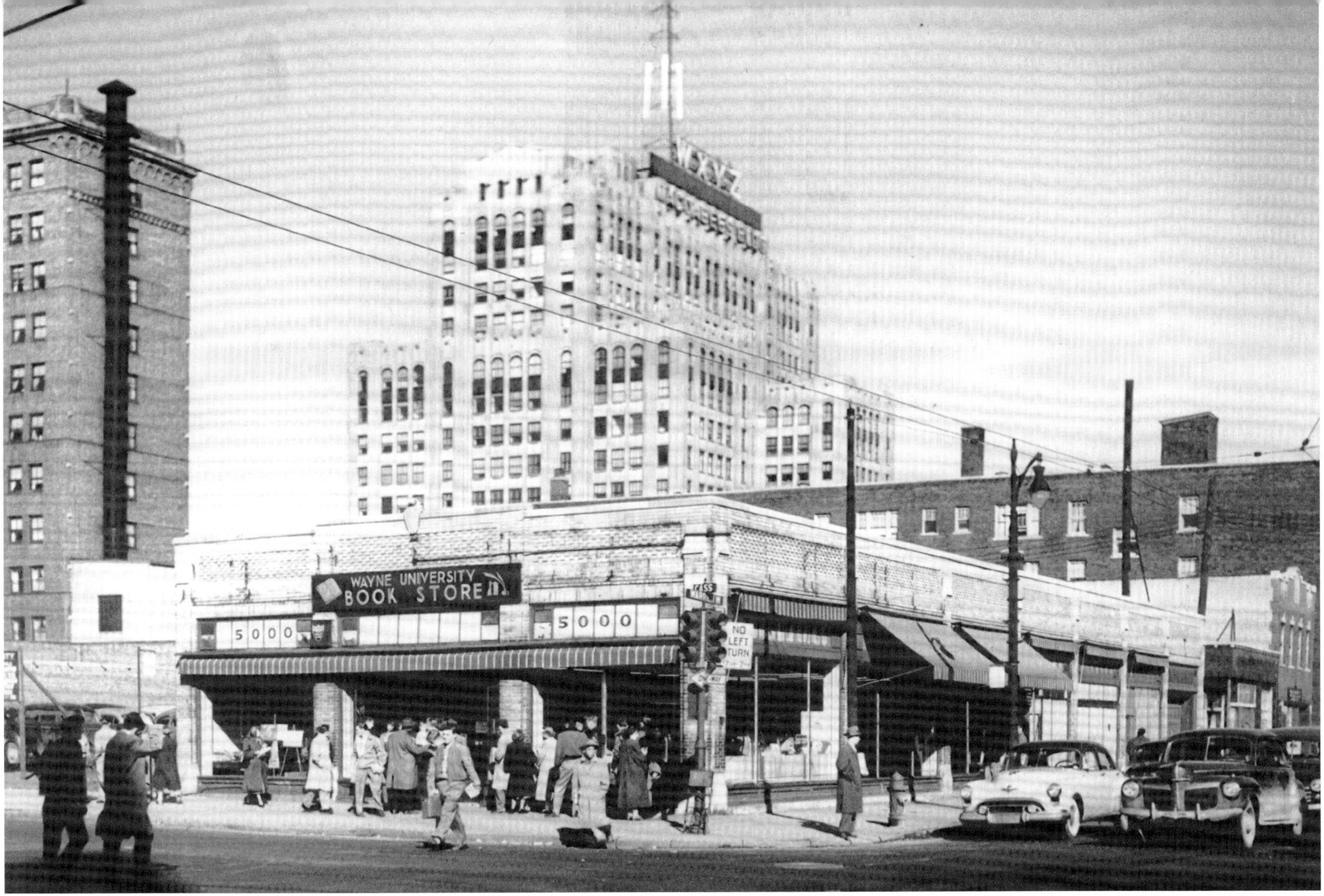

Wayne University Bookstore, 5000 Cass Avenue, as seen looking northeast, early 1950s. Over the years, this corner of Cass and Warren avenues has twice been the site of Wayne's bookstore. In 2002, a new bookstore was constructed on this corner, where it continues to operate today. The Student Center Building (Webster Hall) is just visible along the left side of the photo. The Maccabees Building looms behind the bookstore, its WXYZ sign visible on the roof. WXYZ-TV was the second television station to broadcast in Michigan. An ABC affiliate, the station was located in the Maccabees Building until 1959. (Walter P. Reuther Library, Archives of Labor and Urban Affairs, Wayne State University.)

CHAPTER 4

ESTABLISHING AN IDENTITY, 1950–64

Wayne State University's most dramatic physical change took place in the decade after World War II. In 1950, Old Main and homes in the surrounding neighborhood supplied Wayne with class and office space. This arrangement changed dramatically as rows of old houses and temporary war-surplus barracks were torn down to make way for new classroom buildings. Until this point, Wayne had been a campus in flux, but by 1965, most of the old houses were gone, replaced by modern college buildings, and Wayne had become a traditional college campus.

While Wayne State University's physical campus was evolving, so was the City of Detroit. The construction of interstate highways in the city center altered the landscape and changed how Wayne State University students came to class. By the 1960s, the university had changed from a streetcar college to a commuter college.

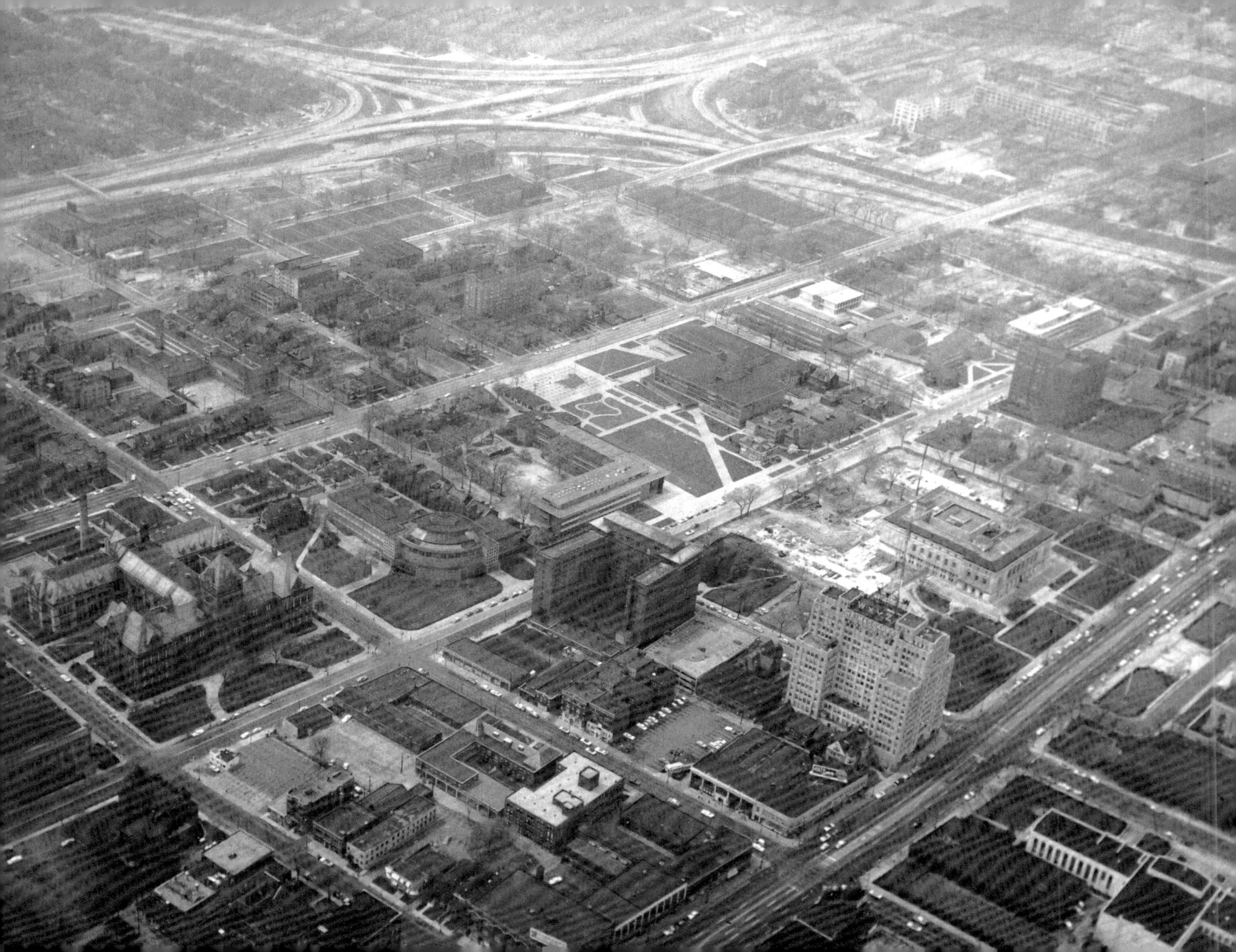

Aerial view of campus, looking northwest, 1959. This aerial view shows the development of the first three blocks of Wayne's campus: Putnam Street, Merrick Street, and Kirby Street, along Cass Avenue in the center of the photo. The U-shaped building near the center is the Student Center Building (Webster Hall). Old Main is visible to the left of the Student Center and across Cass, and the Detroit Public Library can be seen on the right. Running parallel to Cass Avenue are Second Avenue, slanting left to right toward the upper right corner of the photo, and Woodward Avenue in the bottom right corner. In 1959, Second Avenue is still open to traffic, and the area west of Second has not yet been developed by the university. The I-94 and Lodge interchange is visible in the upper part of the photo. Those freeways became operational in 1950 and 1953, respectively. (Walter P. Reuther Library, Archives of Labor and Urban Affairs, Wayne State University.)

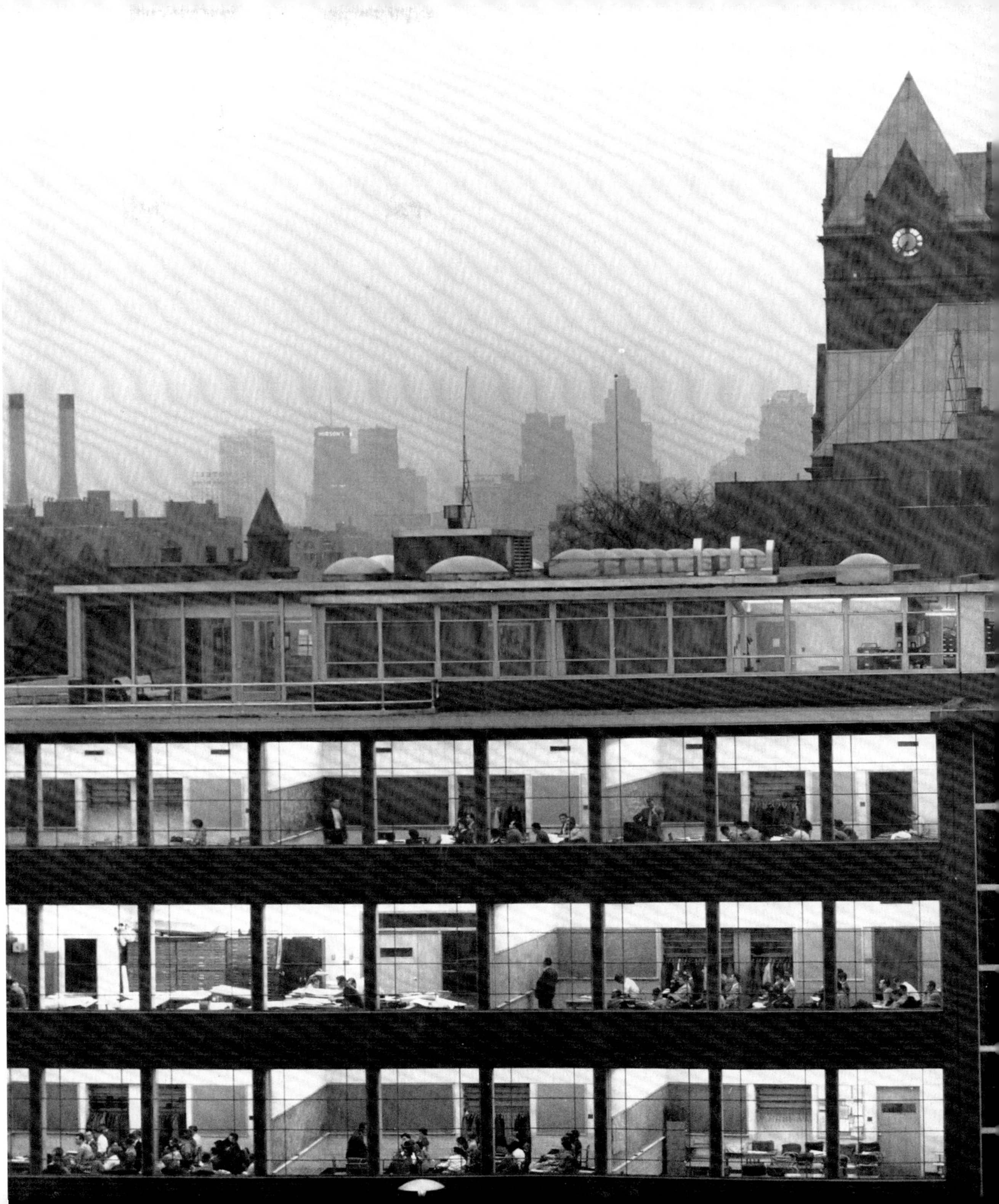

Night classes, 1958. Wayne State has a history of catering to nontraditional students. Since many Wayne students work or have other responsibilities that limit their ability to attend classes during the day, it is necessary for many classes to be held at night. Pictured here are evening classes in State Hall. The Detroit skyline is visible in the background. (Walter P. Reuther Library, Archives of Labor and Urban Affairs, Wayne State University.)

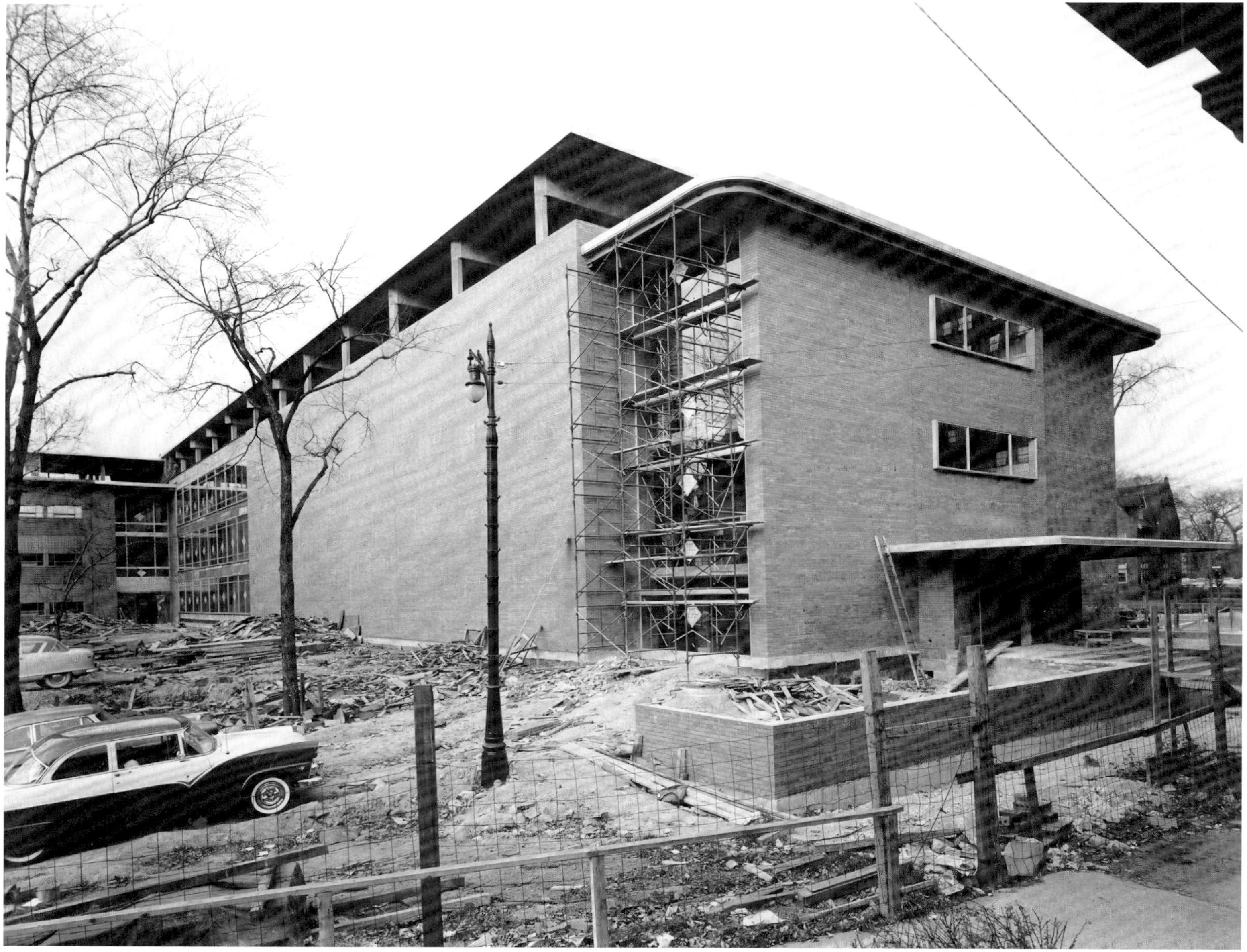

State Hall construction, about 1957. A major addition to State Hall, a wing that extends along Cass Avenue, was completed in 1957. (Walter P. Reuther Library, Archives of Labor and Urban Affairs, Wayne State University.)

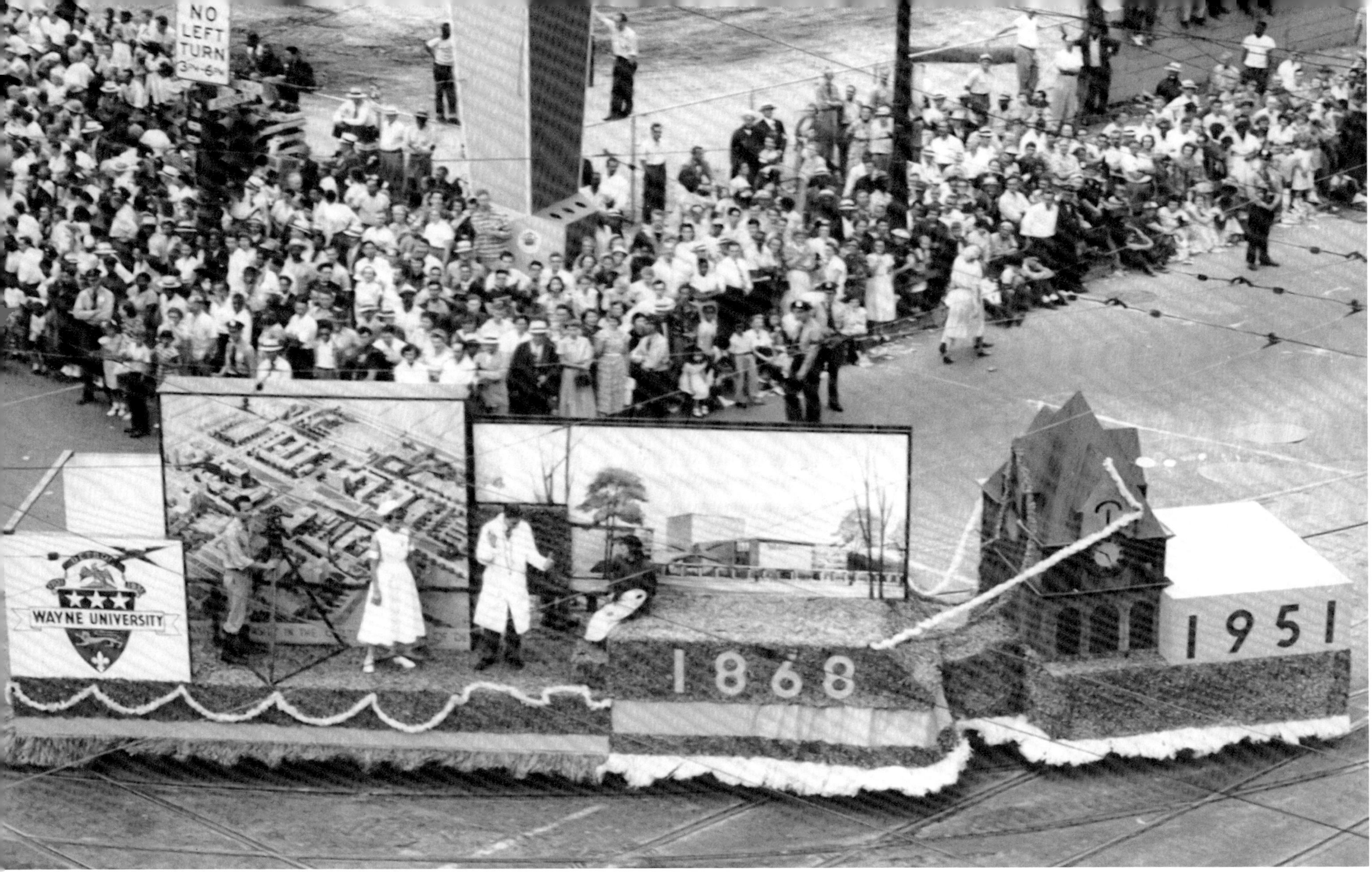

Float in the parade celebrating Detroit's 250th birthday, 1951. Detroiters celebrated the 250th anniversary of their city's founding. The float, featuring a miniature model of Old Main, was designed and produced by Wayne students. To mark the occasion, a Capital Gifts Committee chaired by Frederick C. Matthaei presented Detroit with two birthday presents: Cobo Hall and Wayne's Community Arts Center. (Walter P. Reuther Library, Archives of Labor and Urban Affairs, Wayne State University.)

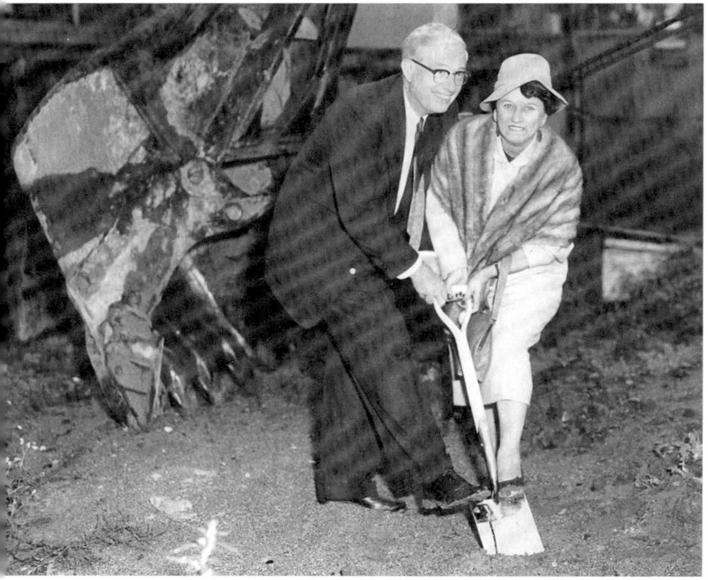

President Clarence Hilberry, groundbreaking for the Community Arts Auditorium, 1957. Dr. Hilberry and Ruth Stevens, representatives of the city's Capital Gifts Committee, are shown breaking ground for the final unit in the Community Arts Center. Hilberry would see Wayne through its largest physical expansion and help the college establish itself as a modern university. (Walter P. Reuther Library, Archives of Labor and Urban Affairs, Wayne State University.)

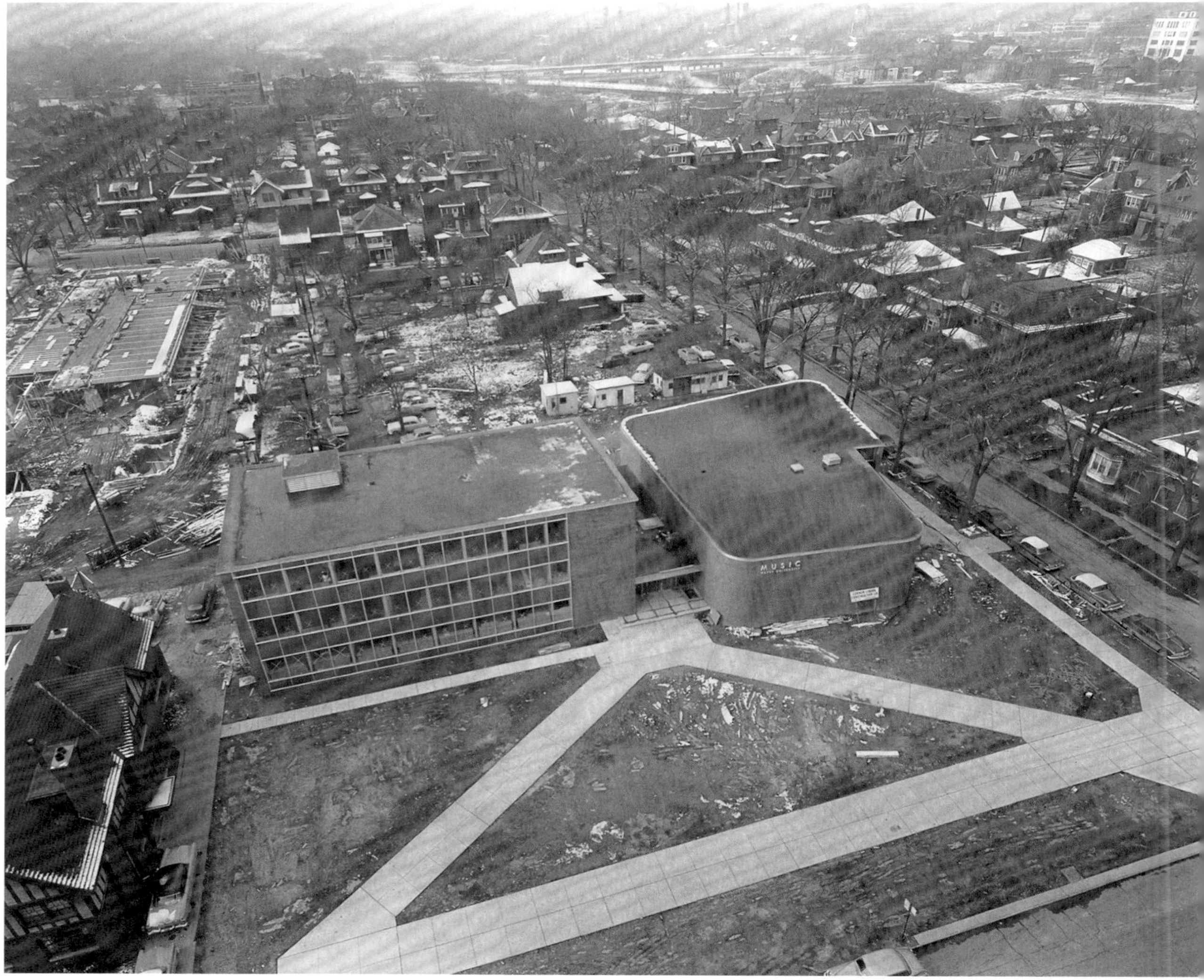

Community Arts Center, as seen looking west, December 1954. Construction on Wayne's Community Arts Center began in 1953. The center would consist of five buildings: the Music Building, the Art Building, the McGregor Memorial Conference Center, the Alumni House, and an auditorium with an exhibition area. The Music Building, shown in the foreground, was completed in 1955. The Art Building, upper left, is still under construction. The Herman Strasburg House, in the bottom left corner, currently serves as Wayne's music annex, having been incorporated into the Community Arts complex. Cars are parked along Ferry Street on the right. I-94 is also visible along the top of the photo. (Walter P. Reuther Library, Archives of Labor and Urban Affairs, Wayne State University.)

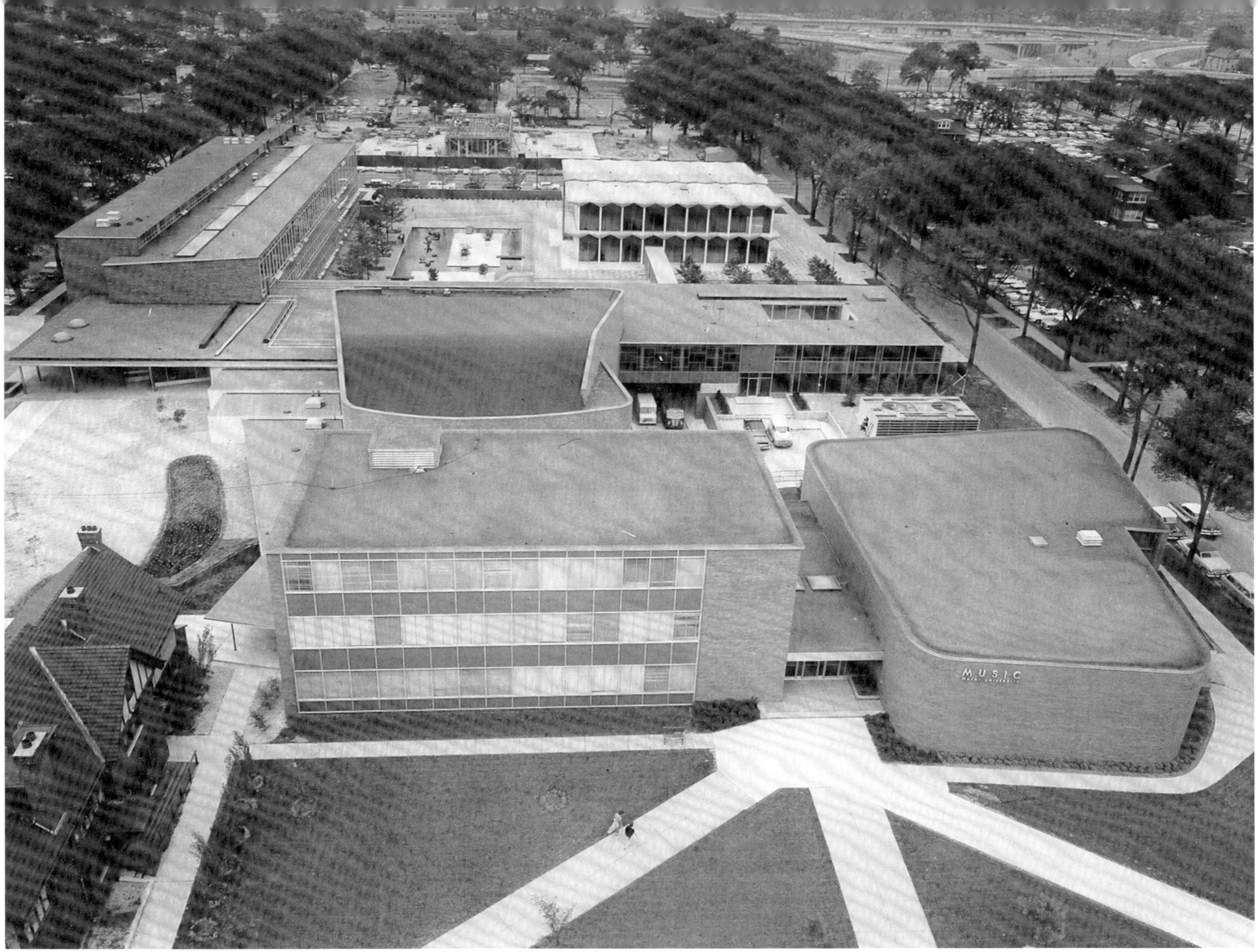

Community Arts Center, as seen looking west, 1959. Shown here is the completed Community Arts Center. The Music Building, which takes up most of the foreground of the photo, consists of two structures—the main building in the foreground and the exhibit area behind it to the left. The Alumni House is located behind the Music Building to the right, in the center of the photo. The Art Building, completed in 1956, is located along the upper left side of the photo, behind the Music Building and exhibit area. The Art Building faces the McGregor Memorial Conference Center, the white building near the top center of the photo. The Strasburg House is visible in the lower left-hand corner of the photo. (Walter P. Reuther Library, Archives of Labor and Urban Affairs, Wayne State University.)

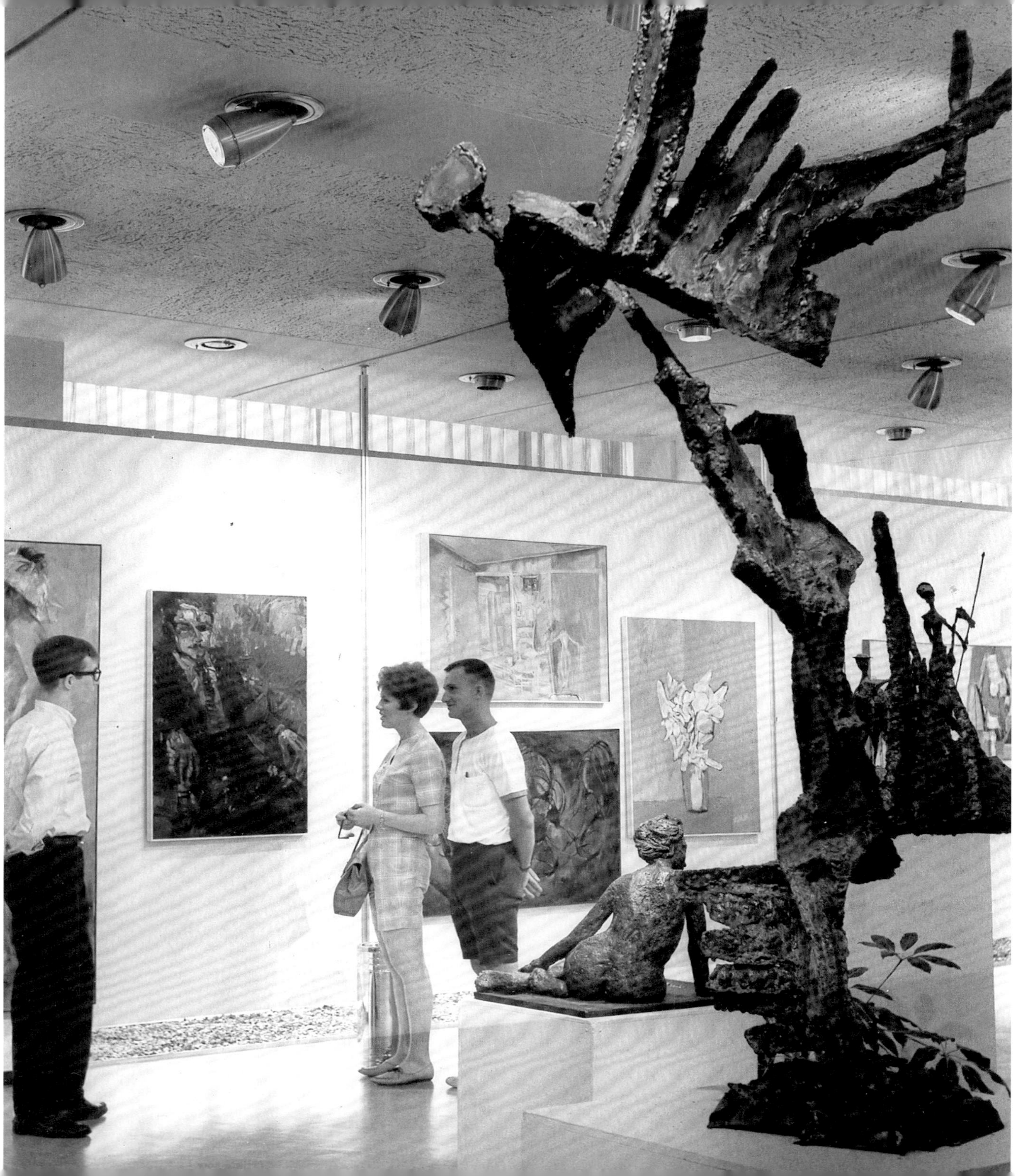

Exhibition of student artwork, Community Arts Building, 1950s. (Walter P. Reuther Library, Archives of Labor and Urban Affairs, Wayne State University.)

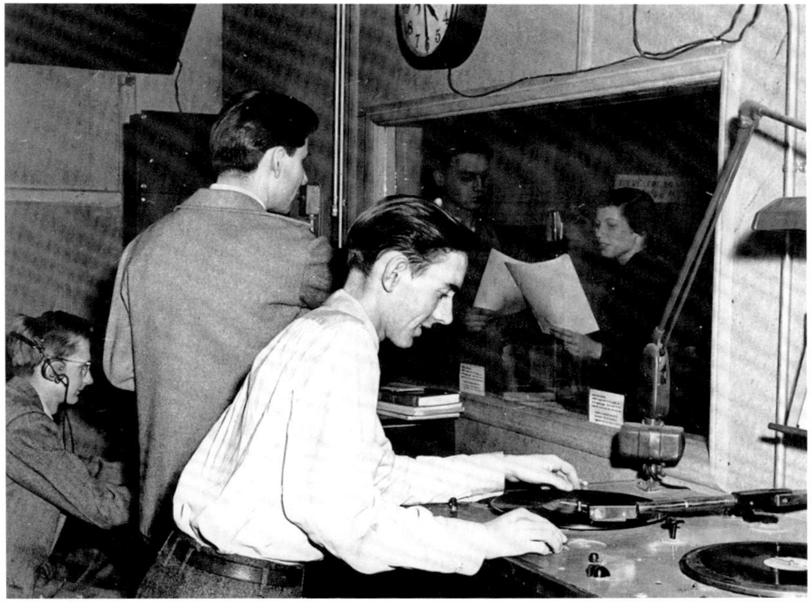

Students working in the studio of WDET, 1950s. Founded in 1949 by the United Auto Workers (UAW), WDET-FM was given to Wayne University in 1952. The public radio station had a very limited budget in its early years and depended on Wayne students and faculty members to work as volunteers in its studio. The station broadcast classical music, as well as lectures by notable writers, politicians, and scholars. On the air for less than fifty hours a week in the 1950s, WDET would grow to become an award-winning National Public Radio affiliate. It continues on the air today and is still supported and operated by the university. (Walter P. Reuther Library, Archives of Labor and Urban Affairs, Wayne State University.)

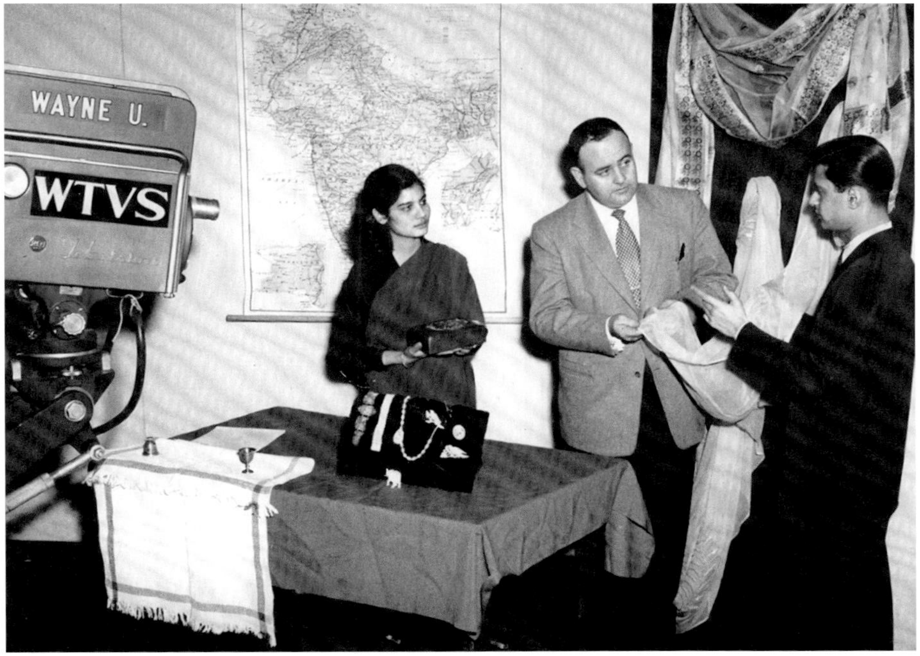

Rehearsal of a television show for WTVS, 1955. Wayne University students Saeeda Khan, left, and Khizer Haiat, from Pakistan, rehearse a discussion with host George E. Steiner of *Today's Student* in a studio in Old Main. Public broadcasting had its roots in educational systems, and in 1953 Wayne University joined with fourteen other educational bodies to form the Detroit Educational Foundation, which would oversee Channel 56, Detroit's voice in public television. The auditorium in Old Main was remodeled as one of WTVS's three studios. When WTVS first began broadcasting, Wayne was on the air thirty to forty-five hours a month. In the 1960s, WTVS obtained their own studios, separate from the university. (Walter P. Reuther Library, Archives of Labor and Urban Affairs, Wayne State University.)

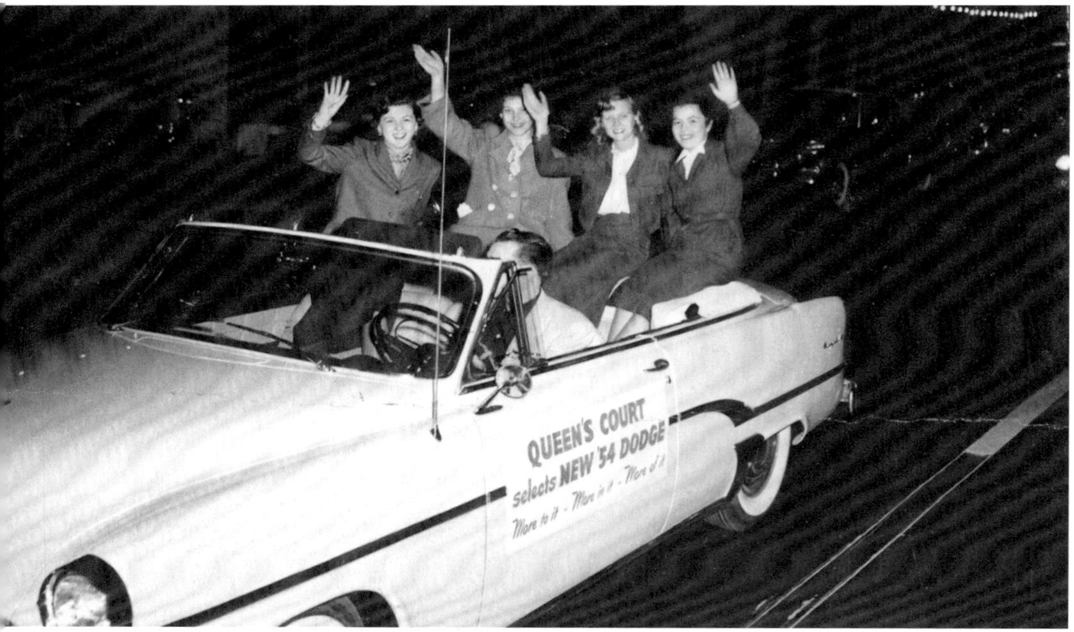

Homecoming court, 1953. Although Wayne has never overemphasized athletics, students celebrated their Homecoming game with a parade and court elections. (Walter P. Reuther Library, Archives of Labor and Urban Affairs, Wayne State University.)

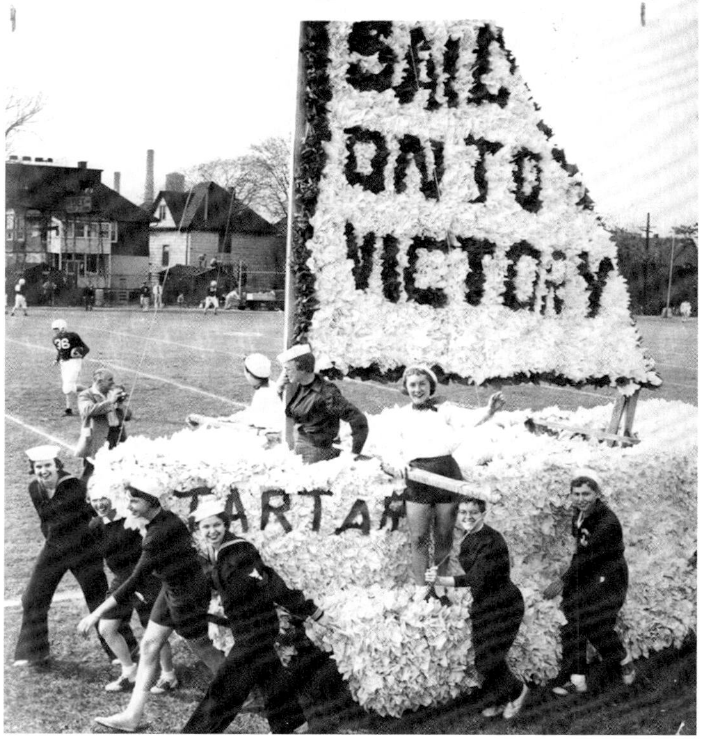

Homecoming float, 1956. The first Homecoming at Wayne was celebrated in 1935. However, the Homecoming parade was held only sporadically, until it disappeared completely in the early 1950s. Wayne State's minimal campus housing prevented a large number of students from living on campus, and as metro Detroit's population spread out during the 1950s, students increasingly viewed the university as a commuter college. As a result, interest in student activities on campus declined, especially after Wayne State began focusing on graduate and professional programs in the late 1960s and 1970s. (Walter P. Reuther Library, Archives of Labor and Urban Affairs, Wayne State University.)

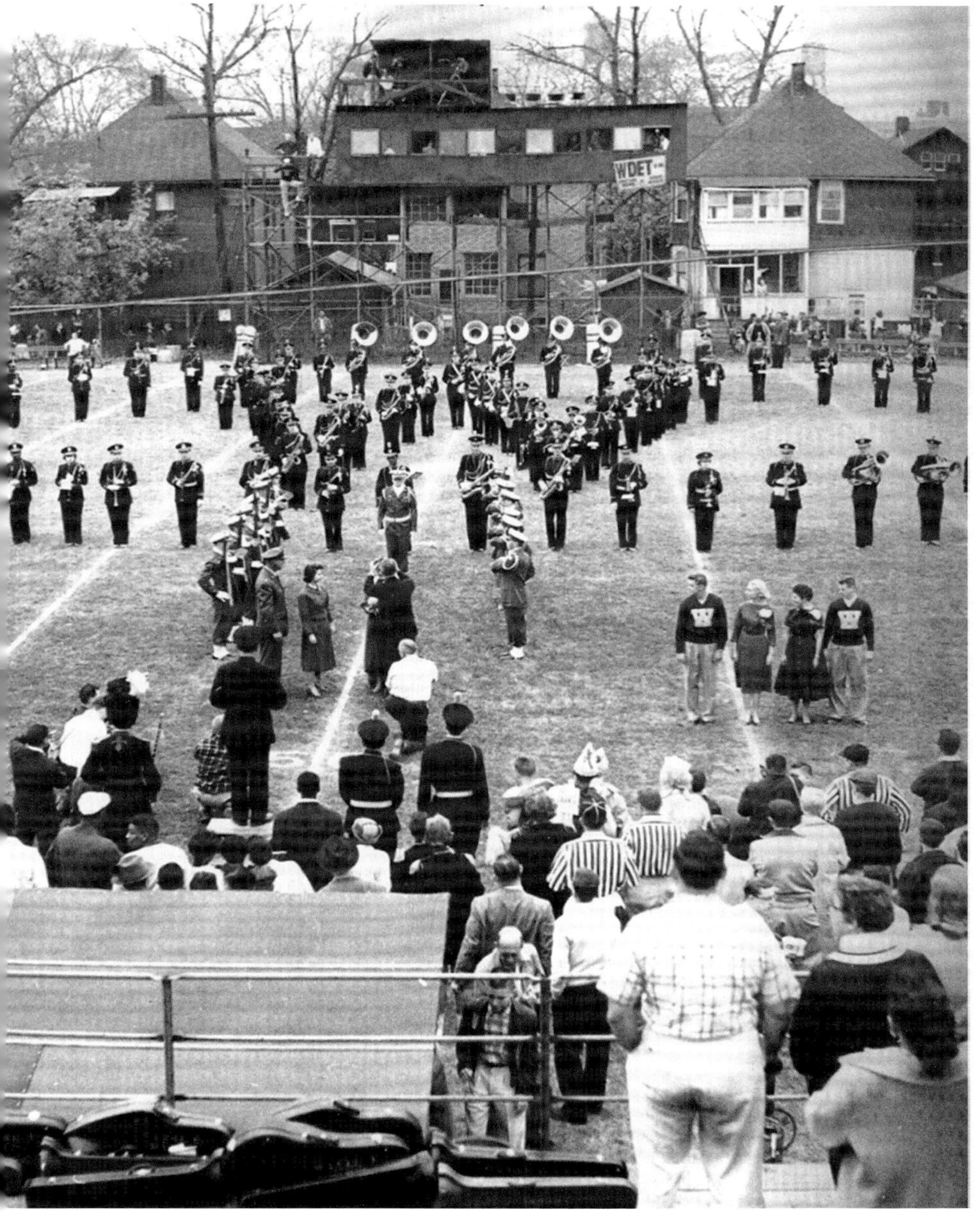

Marching band, Homecoming, 1956. (Walter P. Reuther Library, Archives of Labor and Urban Affairs, Wayne State University.)

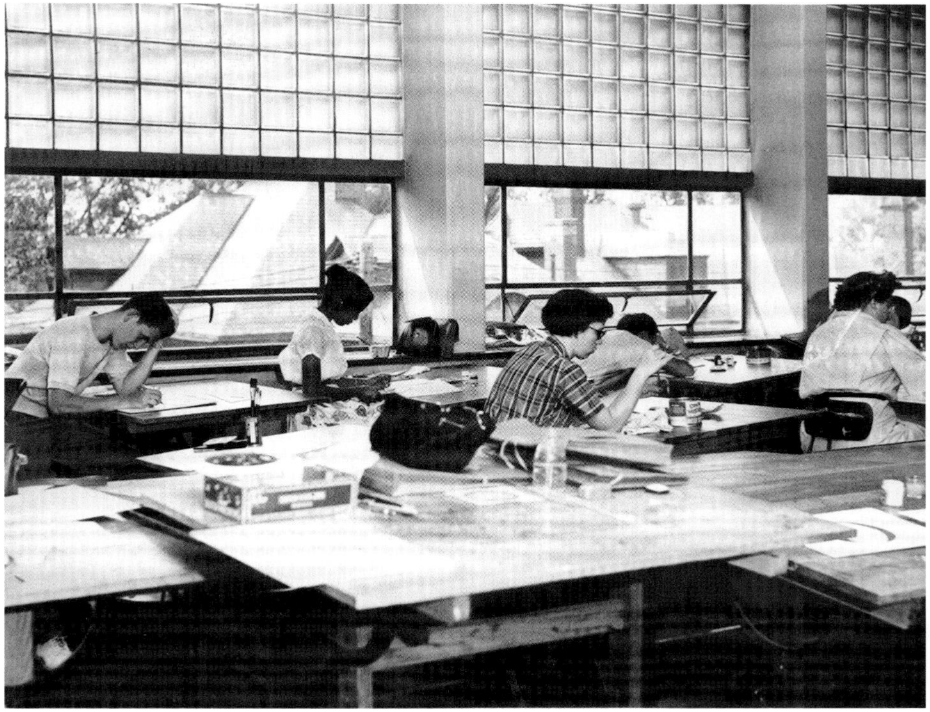

State Hall classroom, mid-1950s. As the neighborhood evolved into a campus, new buildings were constructed in close proximity to old houses. This view from State Hall shows a classroom overlooking the roofs of several homes. (Walter P. Reuther Library, Archives of Labor and Urban Affairs, Wayne State University.)

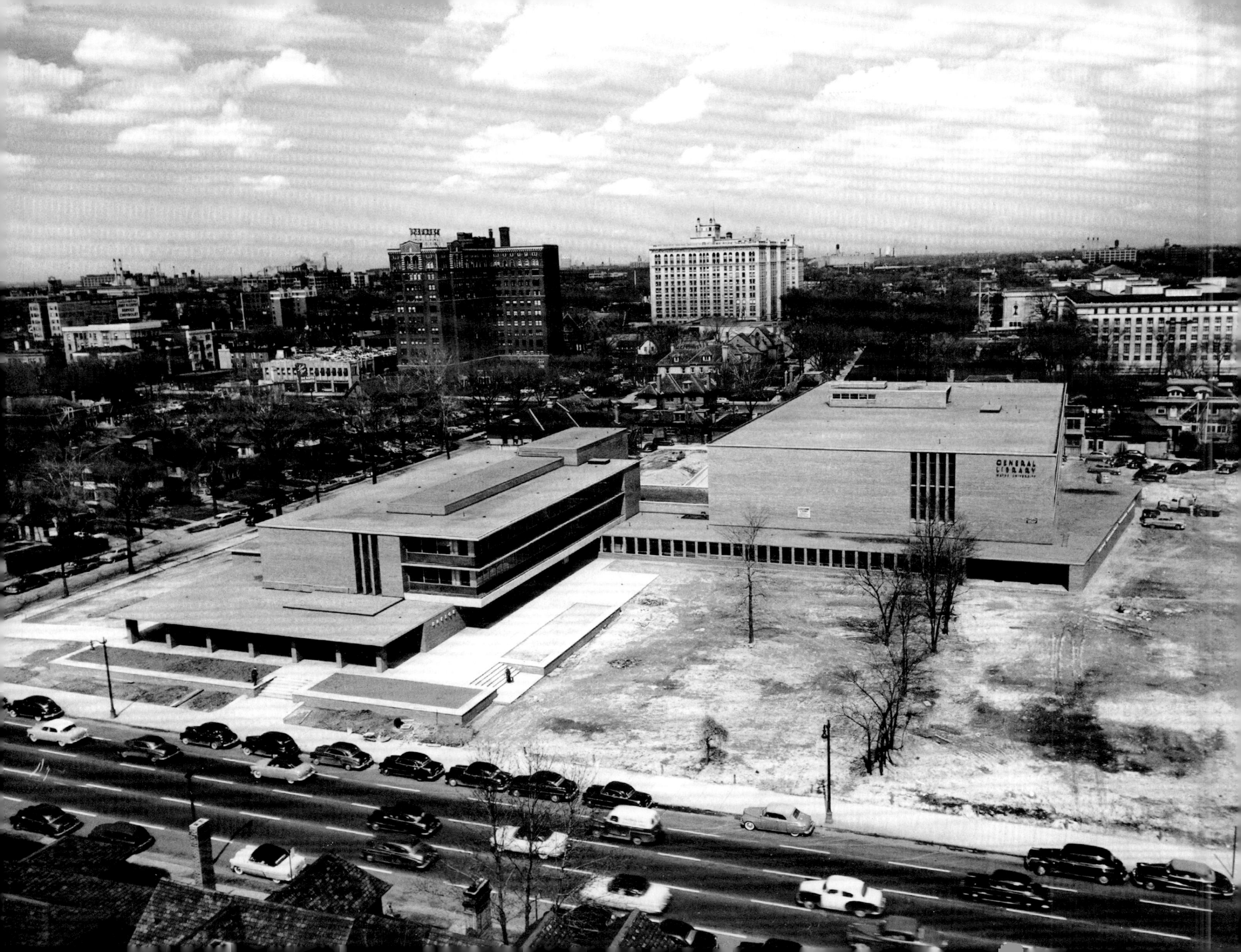
GENERAL
LIBRARY

General Library, 5244 Second Avenue, western facade, 1953. Before this library was built, Wayne's library was housed on three separate floors of Old Main. The first permanent library was designed by architect Suren Pilafian and consisted of two buildings—the General Library and the Kresge Science Library—connected by a hallway. The two tall buildings behind the library in the center of the photograph are the Belcrest on the left and the Park Shelton Apartments on the right. The Detroit Public Library's main branch is the white building at the far right in the photo. Second Avenue runs along the bottom of the photograph. (Walter P. Reuther Library, Archives of Labor and Urban Affairs, Wayne State University.)

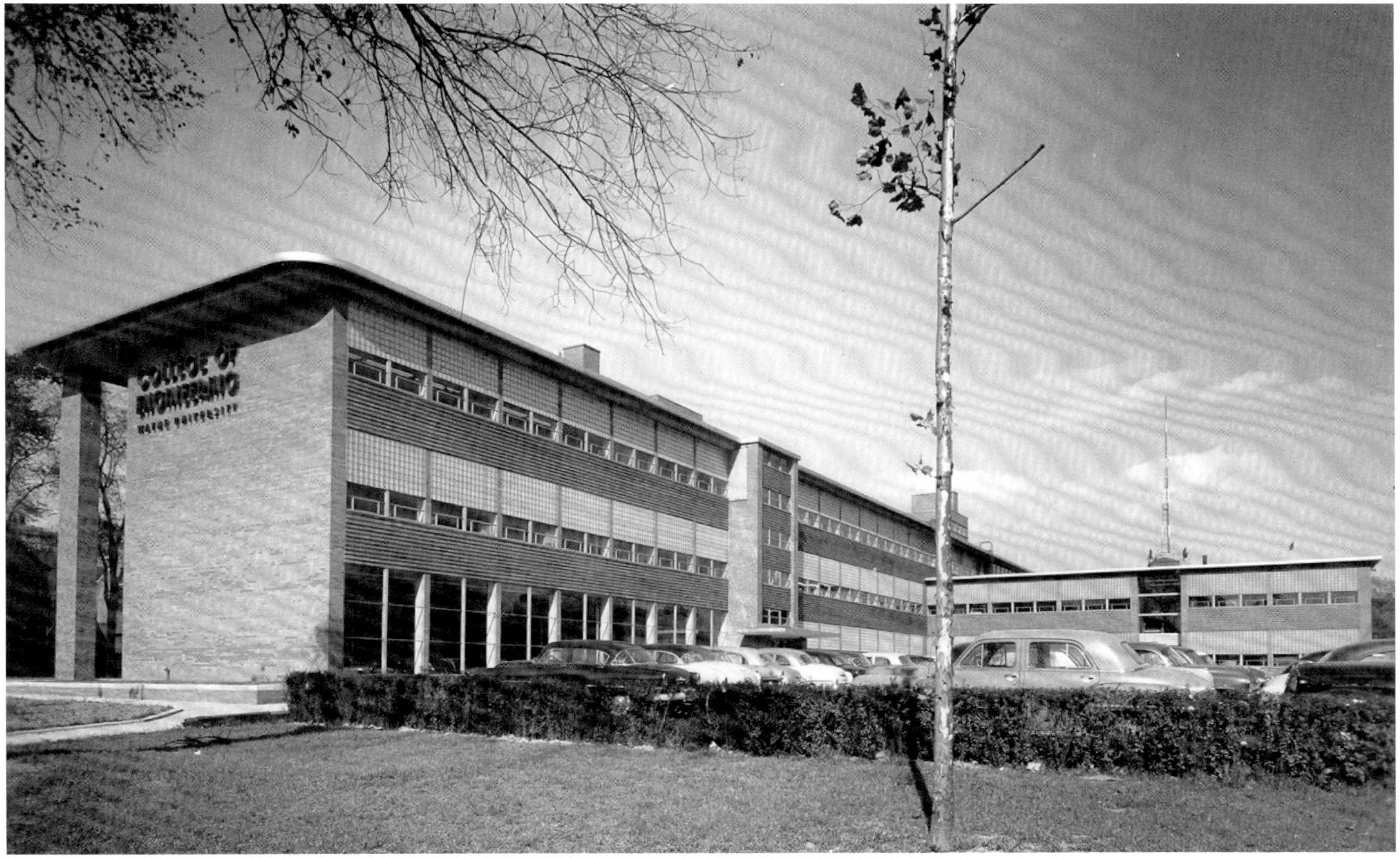

College of Engineering at Warren and Third avenues, looking northeast, 1953. This was the first of many buildings constructed for professional education at Wayne. Different programs needed their own facilities: art classes needed studio and exhibition space, science classes required laboratories. Individual colleges were gradually moved out of Old Main and into their own buildings. In addition to engineering, separate buildings were constructed for the colleges of pharmacy, nursing, and education. (Walter P. Reuther Library, Archives of Labor and Urban Affairs, Wayne State University.)

Airplane used by Wayne University's Department of Aeronautical Engineering, 1952. This Stearman-Boeing Trainer biplane was used by engineering students for flight experiments in the Flying Laboratory. The university obtained the plane from the Navy in 1948, and it was housed at the Detroit City Airport. (Walter P. Reuther Library, Archives of Labor and Urban Affairs, Wayne State University.)

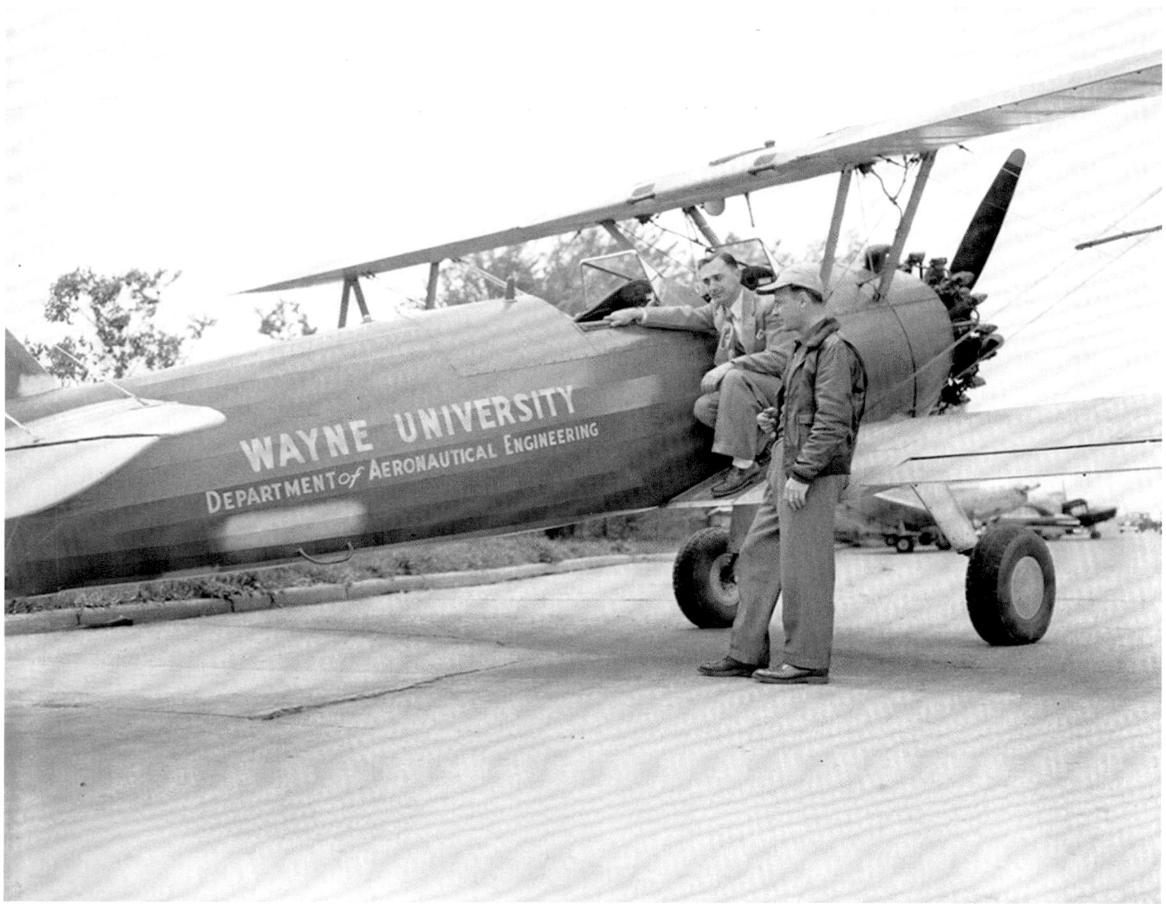

Bonstelle Theatre, 3424 Woodward, 1959. This building, designed by renowned architect Albert Kahn and completed in 1902, was originally a synagogue, the Temple Beth El, one of the oldest houses of Jewish worship in Detroit. In the 1920s, as the Bonstelle Playhouse, it was made famous by Jessie Bonstelle and her theater group. Wayne University rented the building for its theater department beginning in 1951 and purchased it in 1956. For a short time it was known as the Wayne University Theatre, before being renamed the Bonstelle Theatre. The theater offered a large stage, good acoustics, and the first permanent space for the university theater department. Prior to Wayne's purchase of the Bonstelle, Wayne thespians were forced to use makeshift spaces for rehearsal and performance, including rented spaces in churches and a garage on Putnam Street. (Walter P. Reuther Library, Archives of Labor and Urban Affairs, Wayne State University.)

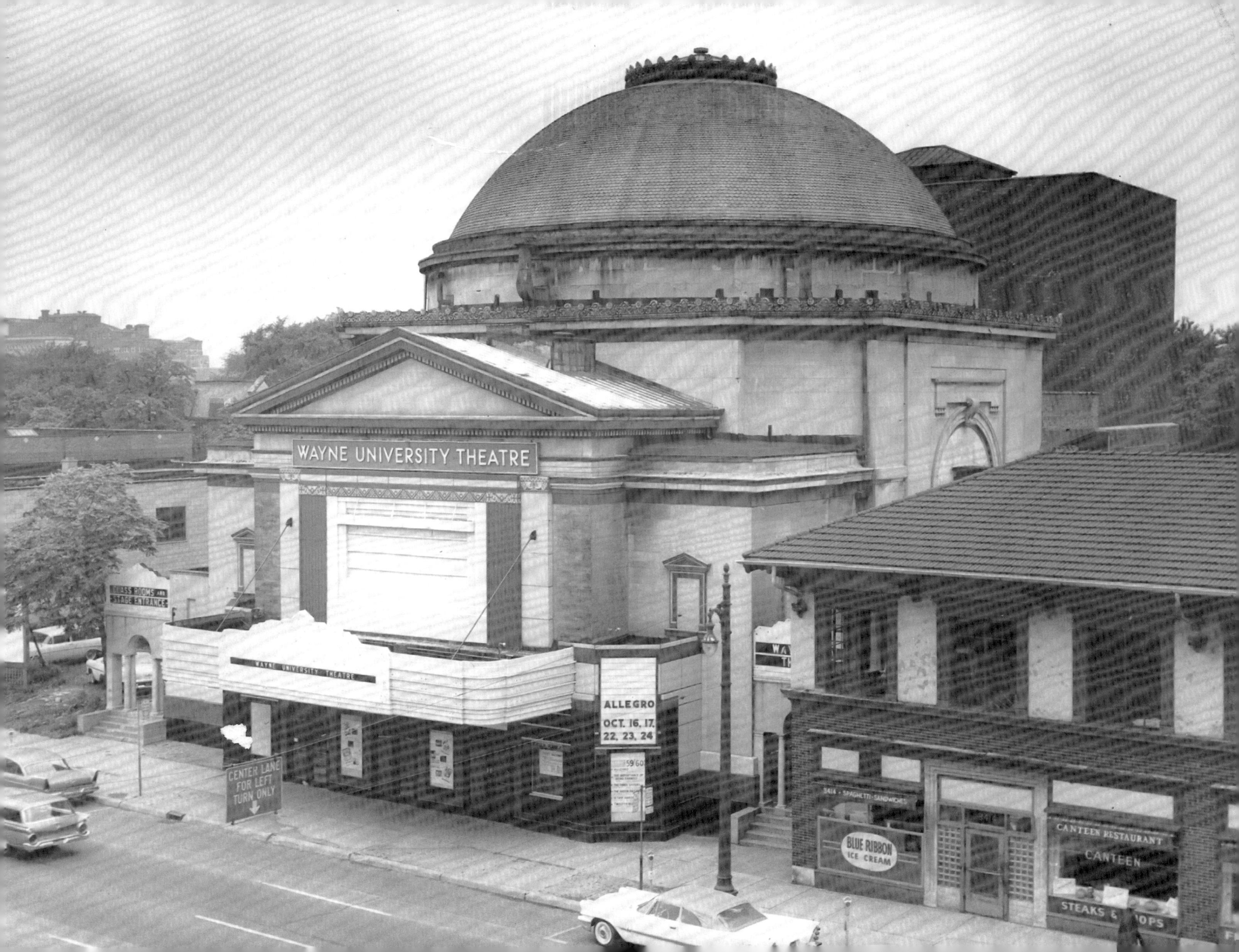
WAYNE UNIVERSITY THEATRE
STAGE ENTRANCE
WAYNE UNIVERSITY THEATRE
ALLEGRO
OCT. 16, 17.
22, 23, 24
CENTER LANE
FOR LEFT
TURN ONLY
BLUE RIBBON
ICE CREAM
CANTEEN RESTAURANT
CANTEEN

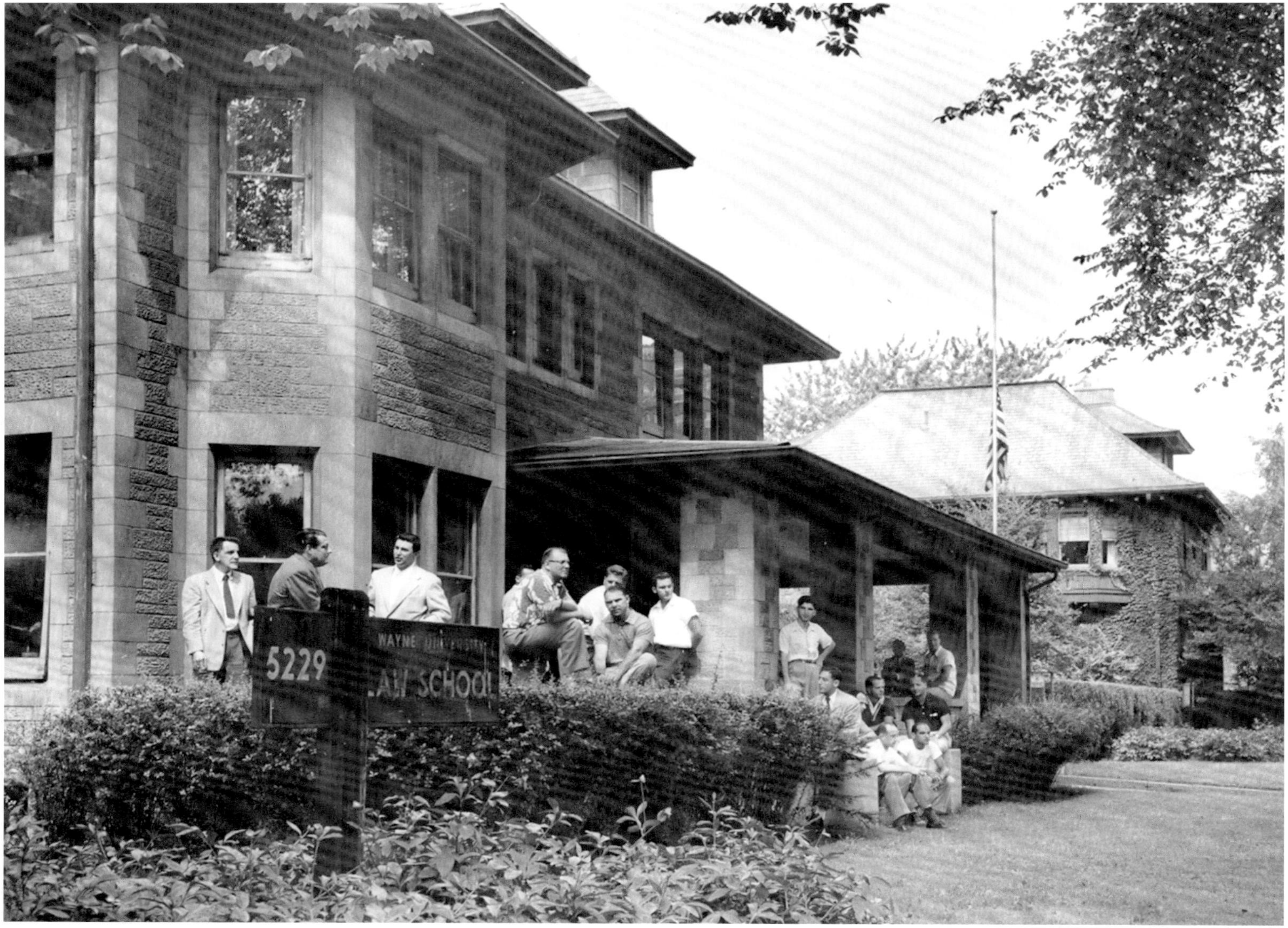

The Law School, 5229 Cass Avenue, 1956. Before funds for new buildings became available, classes were held in old homes. In this photograph, a group of aspiring lawyers sits on the steps of the Law School, which operated out of the William C. Rands House. Law had become a college at Wayne in 1937, when the school was accredited by the American Bar Association. Previously, since the founding of the Detroit City Law School in 1927, evening law classes had been held at Old Main. The William C. Rands House still stands on Wayne's campus and is currently used by the business school as an annex. (Walter P. Reuther Library, Archives of Labor and Urban Affairs, Wayne State University.)

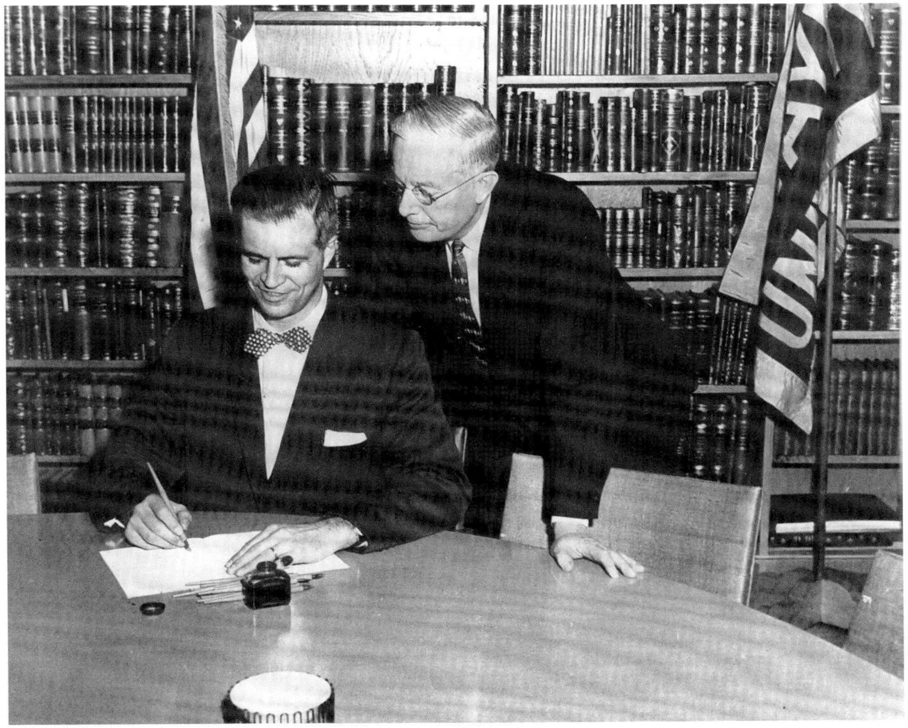

Clarence Hilberry and G. Mennen Williams signing Public Act 183, April 22, 1956. During Wayne's first twenty years as a university, it was funded by the Detroit Board of Education. Facing financial difficulties in the early 1950s, Wayne president Clarence Hilberry and the Board of Education sought funding from the state. Michigan's governor, G. Mennen Williams, supported the idea and helped promote it in Lansing. After the bill designating Wayne University as a state university passed both the Michigan House and Senate, Governor Williams signed Public Act 183 on April 22, 1956, and Wayne State University came into being. (Walter P. Reuther Library, Archives of Labor and Urban Affairs, Wayne State University.)

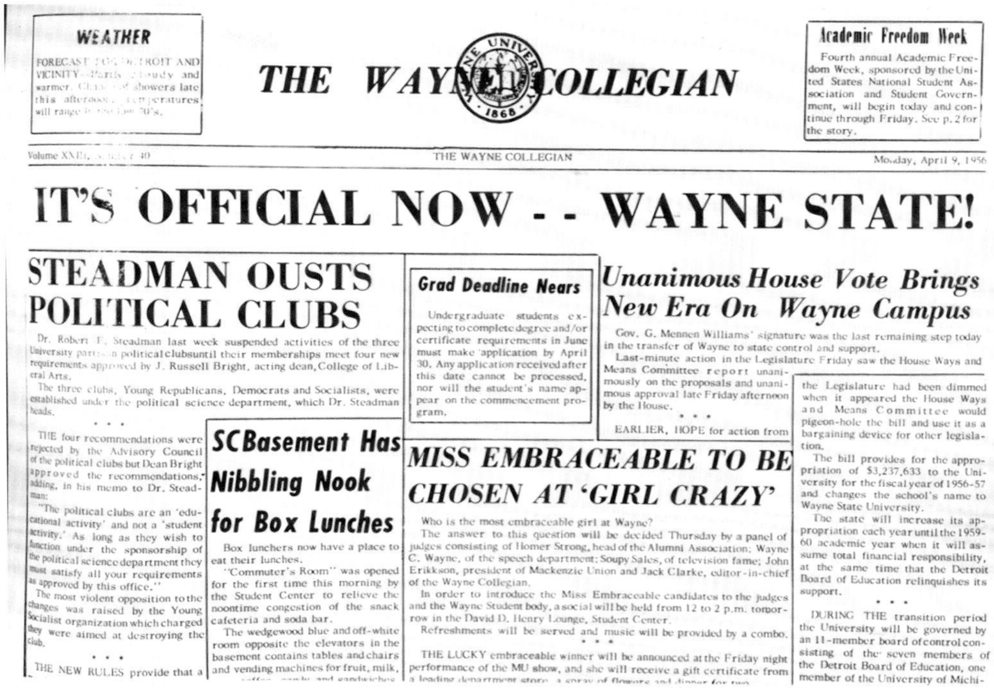

WEATHER

FORECAST FOR DETROIT AND VICINITY—Partly cloudy and warmer. Chance of showers late this afternoon. Temperatures will range in the low 70's.

THE WAYNE COLLEGIAN

Academic Freedom Week

Fourth annual Academic Freedom Week, sponsored by the United States National Student Association and Student Government, will begin today and continue through Friday. See p. 2 for the story.

Volume XXIII, Number 40 — THE WAYNE COLLEGIAN — Monday, April 9, 1956

IT'S OFFICIAL NOW - - WAYNE STATE!

STEADMAN OUSTS POLITICAL CLUBS

Dr. Robert F. Steadman last week suspended activities of the three University partisan political clubs until their memberships meet four new requirements approved by J. Russell Bright, acting dean, College of Liberal Arts.

The three clubs, Young Republicans, Democrats and Socialists, were established under the political science department, which Dr. Steadman heads.

* * *

THE four recommendations were rejected by the Advisory Council of the political clubs but Dean Bright approved the recommendations, adding, in his memo to Dr. Steadman:

"The political clubs are an 'educational activity' and not a 'student activity.' As long as they wish to function under the sponsorship of the political science department they must satisfy all your requirements as approved by this office."

The most violent opposition to the changes was raised by the Young Socialist organization which charged they were aimed at destroying the club.

* * *

THE NEW RULES provide that a

Grad Deadline Nears

Undergraduate students expecting to complete degree and/or certificate requirements in June must make application by April 30. Any application received after this date cannot be processed, nor will the student's name appear on the commencement program.

SCBasement Has Nibbling Nook for Box Lunches

Box lunchers now have a place to eat their lunches.

"Commuter's Room" was opened for the first time this morning by the Student Center to relieve the noontime congestion of the snack cafeteria and soda bar.

The wedgewood blue and off-white room opposite the elevators in the basement contains tables and chairs and vending machines for fruit, milk, coffee, candy and sandwiches

Unanimous House Vote Brings New Era On Wayne Campus

Gov. G. Mennen Williams' signature was the last remaining step today in the transfer of Wayne to state control and support.

Last-minute action in the Legislature Friday saw the House Ways and Means Committee report unanimously on the proposals and unanimous approval late Friday afternoon by the House.

* * *

EARLIER, HOPE for action from the Legislature had been dimmed when it appeared the House Ways and Means Committee would pigeon-hole the bill and use it as a bargaining device for other legislation.

The bill provides for the appropriation of $3,237,633 to the University for the fiscal year of 1956-57 and changes the school's name to Wayne State University.

The state will increase its appropriation each year until the 1959-60 academic year when it will assume total financial responsibility, at the same time that the Detroit Board of Education relinquishes its support.

* * *

DURING THE transition period the University will be governed by an 11-member board of control consisting of the seven members of the Detroit Board of Education, one member of the University of Michi-

MISS EMBRACEABLE TO BE CHOSEN AT 'GIRL CRAZY'

Who is the most embraceable girl at Wayne?

The answer to this question will be decided Thursday by a panel of judges consisting of Homer Strong, head of the Alumni Association; Wayne C. Wayne, of the speech department; Soupy Sales, of television fame; John Erikkson, president of Mackenzie Union and Jack Clarke, editor-in-chief of the Wayne Collegian.

In order to introduce the Miss Embraceable candidates to the judges and the Wayne Student body, a social will be held from 12 to 2 p.m. tomorrow in the David D. Henry Lounge, Student Center.

Refreshments will be served and music will be provided by a combo.

* * *

THE LUCKY embraceable winner will be announced at the Friday night performance of the MU show, and she will receive a gift certificate from a leading department store, a spray of flowers and dinner for two

The *Wayne Collegian*, 1956. The student newspaper announces the transition from Wayne University to Wayne State University. More than just a name change, this event marked the beginning of public control and support for the university. From this date on, the affairs of Wayne State would be directed by a Board of Governors elected by the citizens of Michigan. (Walter P. Reuther Library, Archives of Labor and Urban Affairs, Wayne State University.)

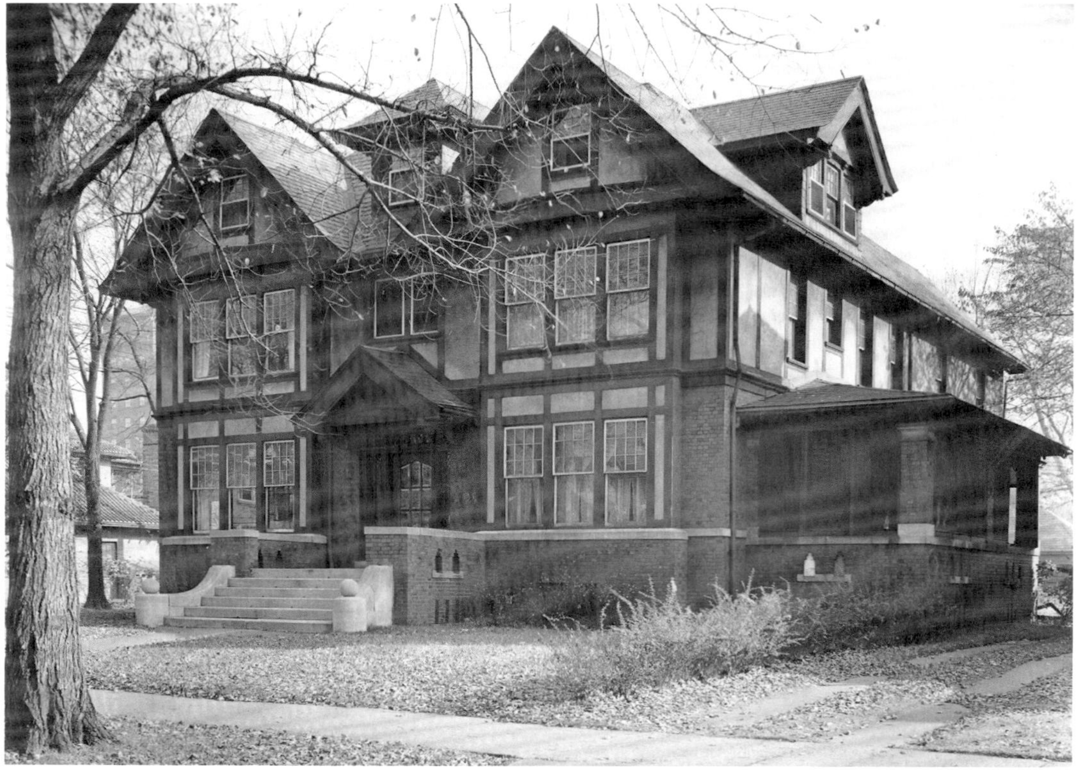

Williams House, 441 Merrick, 1943. Michigan governor G. Mennen Williams was born in this house on February 23, 1911. Once part of the affluent neighborhood around Central High School, after the Williams family moved to Grosse Pointe in 1924, the residence in turn housed the Detroit Historical Museum and Wayne's School of Social Work. Before the house was torn down in 1956, Williams requested the marble fireplace and mantel, along with the mahogany trim of the living room. Today, the Helen L. DeRoy Auditorium stands on this site. (Walter P. Reuther Library, Archives of Labor and Urban Affairs, Wayne State University.)

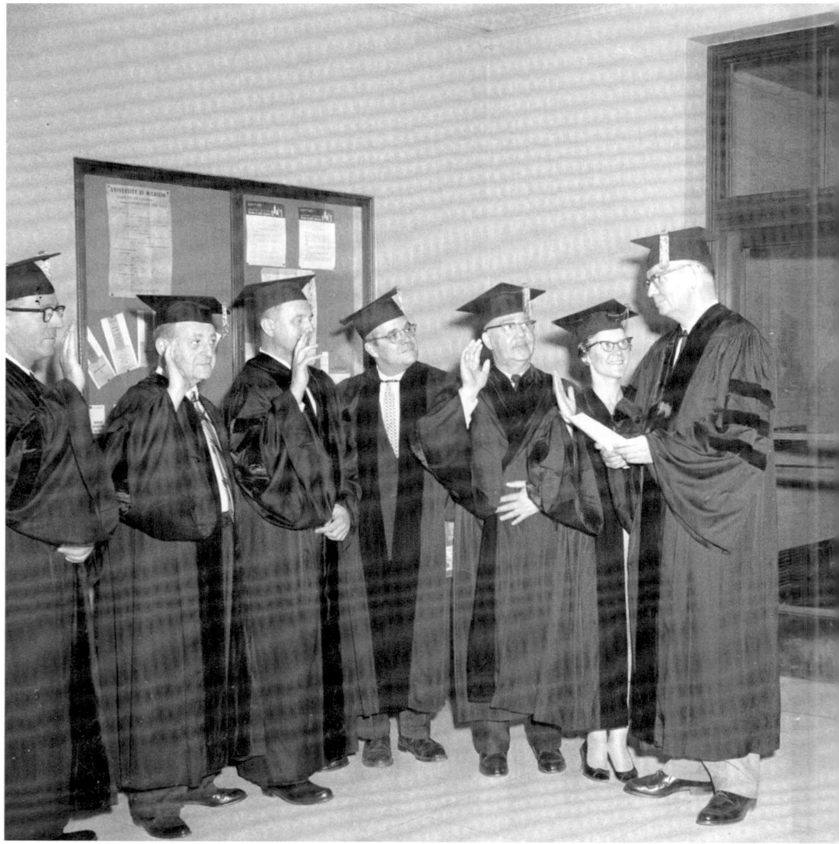

First Board of Governors sworn in, May 19, 1959. After Wayne became a state university, there was a three-year transitional period during which Wayne's governing body, the Board of Education, relinquished its power to the Board of Governors. Wayne State's first governors were elected in 1959. In this photograph, James M. Hare swears in, from right to left: Jean McKee, Dr. Dewitt T. Burton, Clair A. White, Dr. Michael Ference Jr., Benjamin D. Burdick, and Leonard Woodcock. (Walter P. Reuther Library, Archives of Labor and Urban Affairs, Wayne State University.)

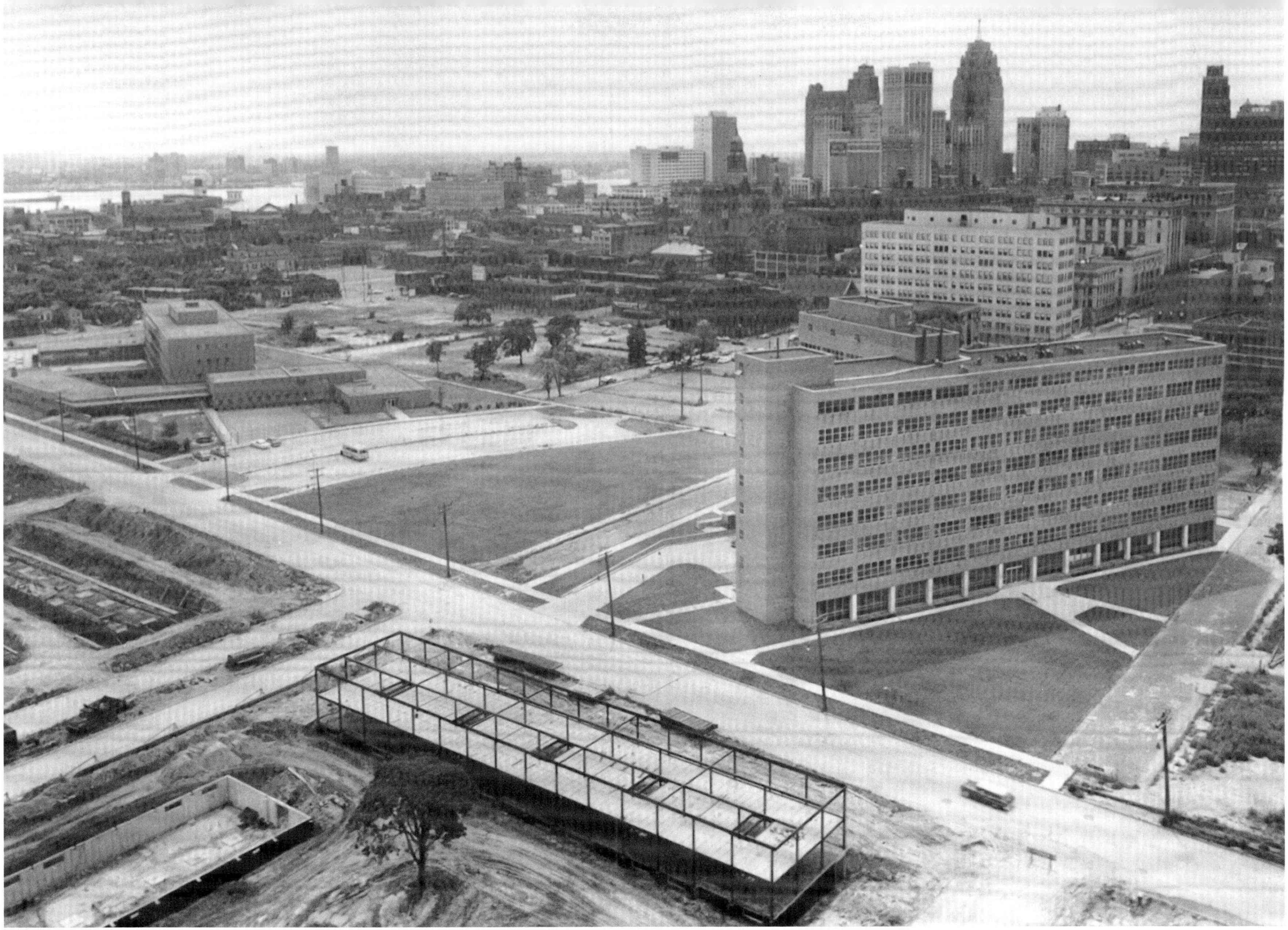

Medical Science Building, 1401 Rivard Street, northeastern facade, 1958. The first educational high-rise building in Detroit, this structure replaced the old Medical College buildings on Mullett Street. The Detroit skyline and the Detroit River are visible in the background. This picture was taken before the Chrysler Freeway (I-75) opened to traffic in 1963. (Walter P. Reuther Library, Archives of Labor and Urban Affairs, Wayne State University.)

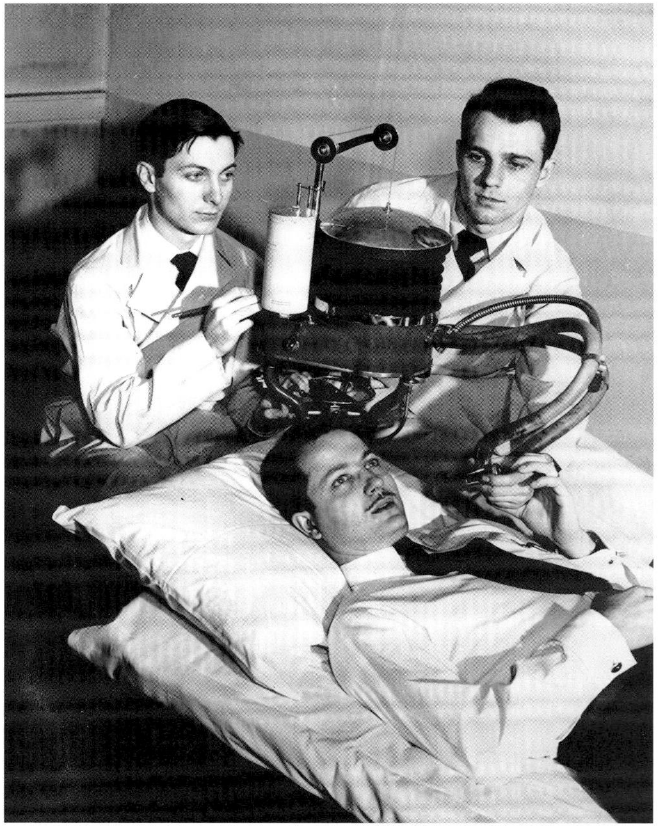

Medical school students, 1950s. Three College of Medicine students are calculating a fellow student's basal metabolic rate by measuring his oxygen consumption. (Walter P. Reuther Library, Archives of Labor and Urban Affairs, Wayne State University.)

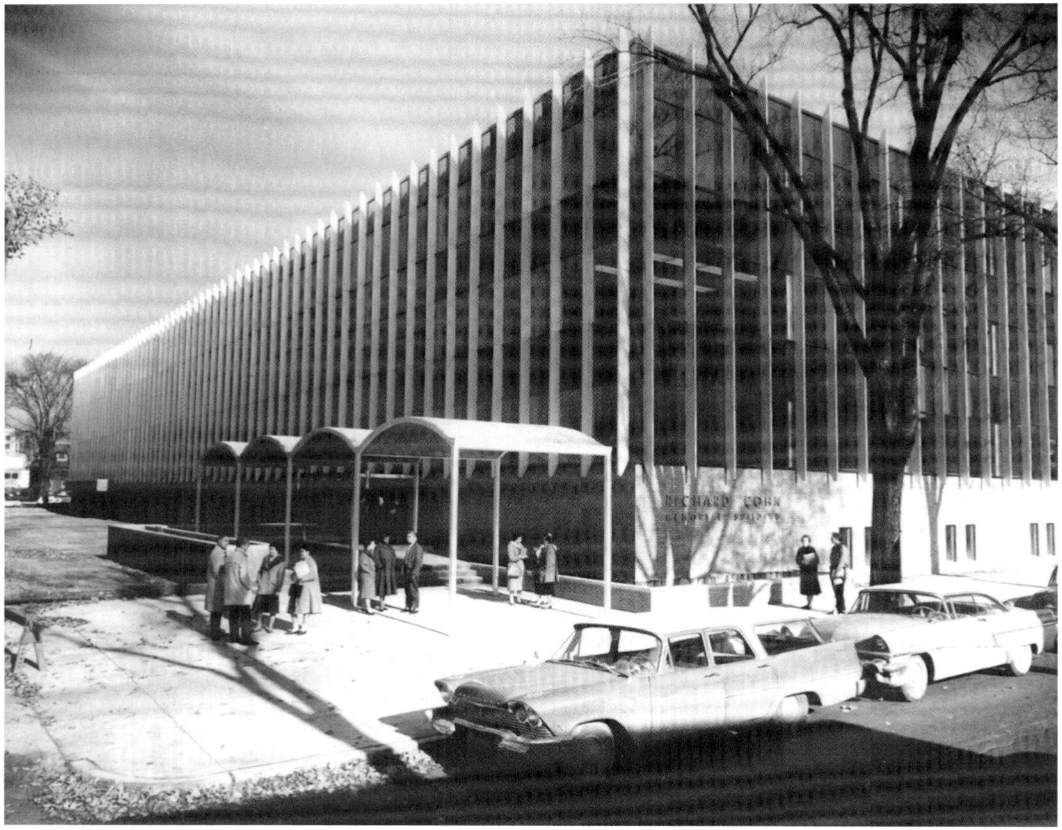

The Richard Cohn Building, 5557 Cass Avenue at Palmer Street, 1959. Nursing classes were held in the Cohn Building. The nursing department had been established at City College in 1930, and it became a college in 1945. Like Wayne's other professional schools—social work and business administration, for example—the College of Nursing was created because of professional demand. (Walter P. Reuther Library, Archives of Labor and Urban Affairs, Wayne State University.)

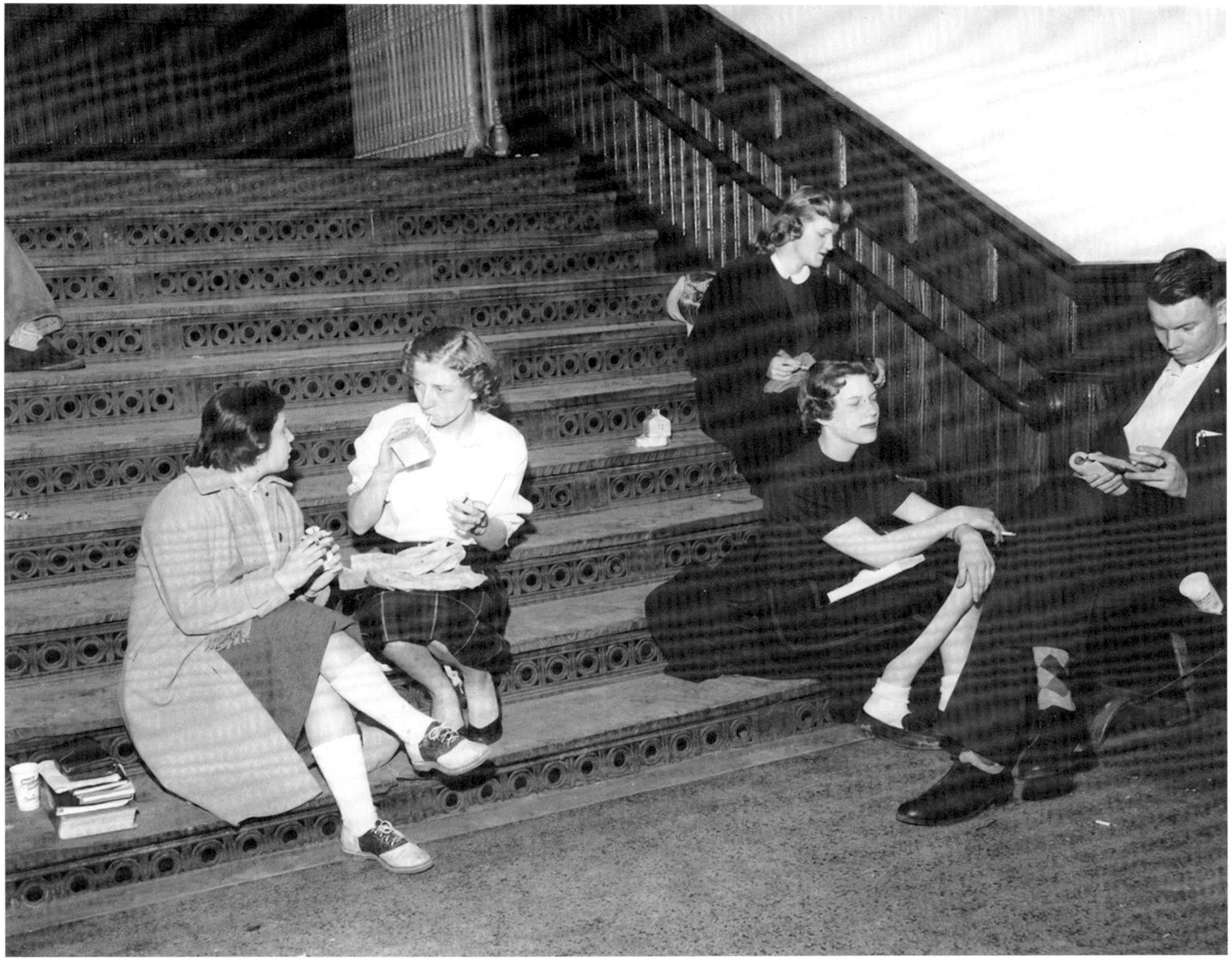

Students eating lunch on Old Main's staircase, 1957. These students decided to brown bag their lunch, forgoing a trip to Midge's Grill, a hamburger joint located on Cass Avenue, just across the street from Old Main. While buildings were being constructed around campus, space remained in high demand. Not only were classrooms at Wayne crowded, but study spaces and places to eat were hard to come by. (Walter P. Reuther Library, Archives of Labor and Urban Affairs, Wayne State University.)

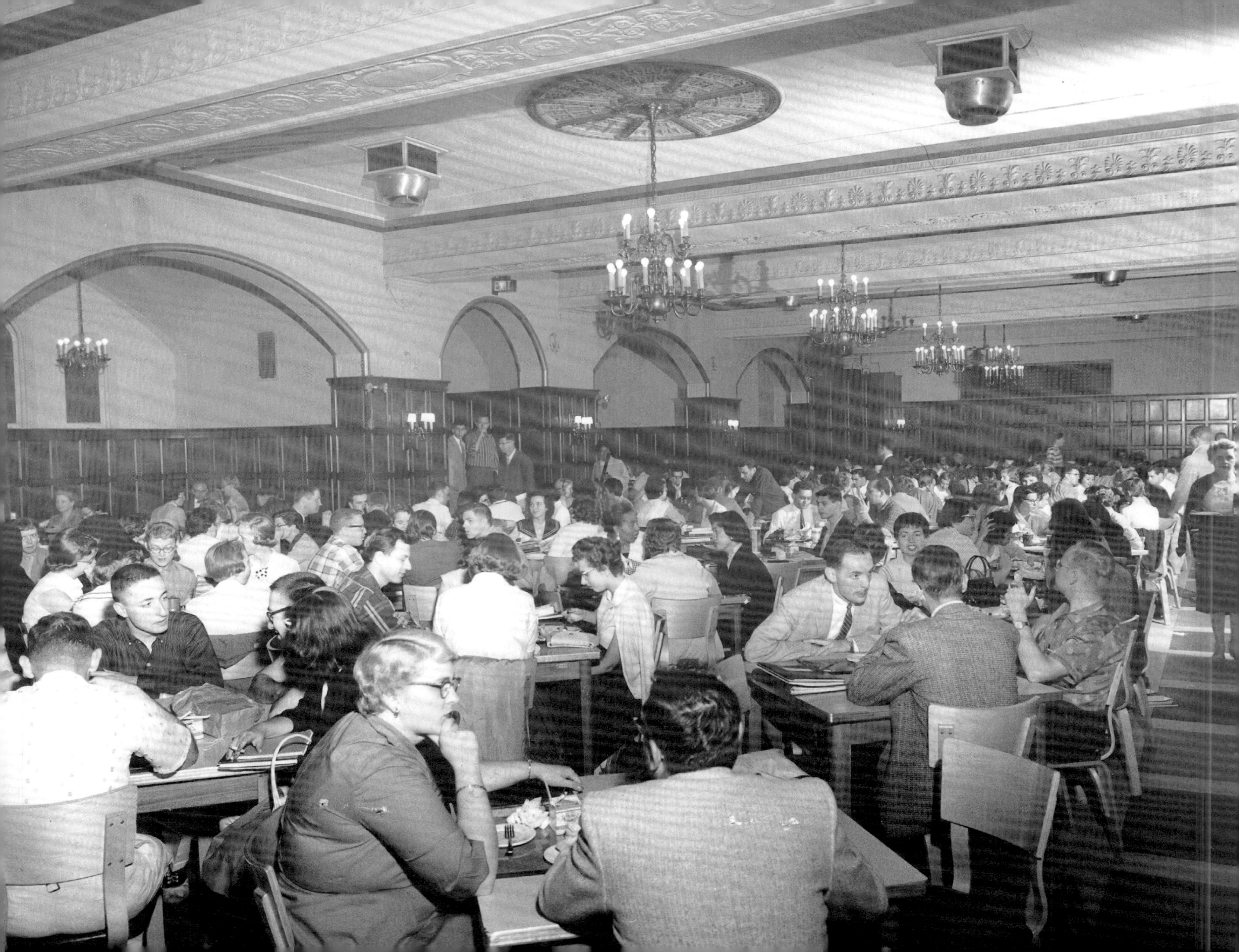
EXIT

Cafeteria at the Student Center Building (Webster Hall), 1958. The cafeteria in Wayne State's Student Center opened in 1949. (Walter P. Reuther Library, Archives of Labor and Urban Affairs, Wayne State University.)

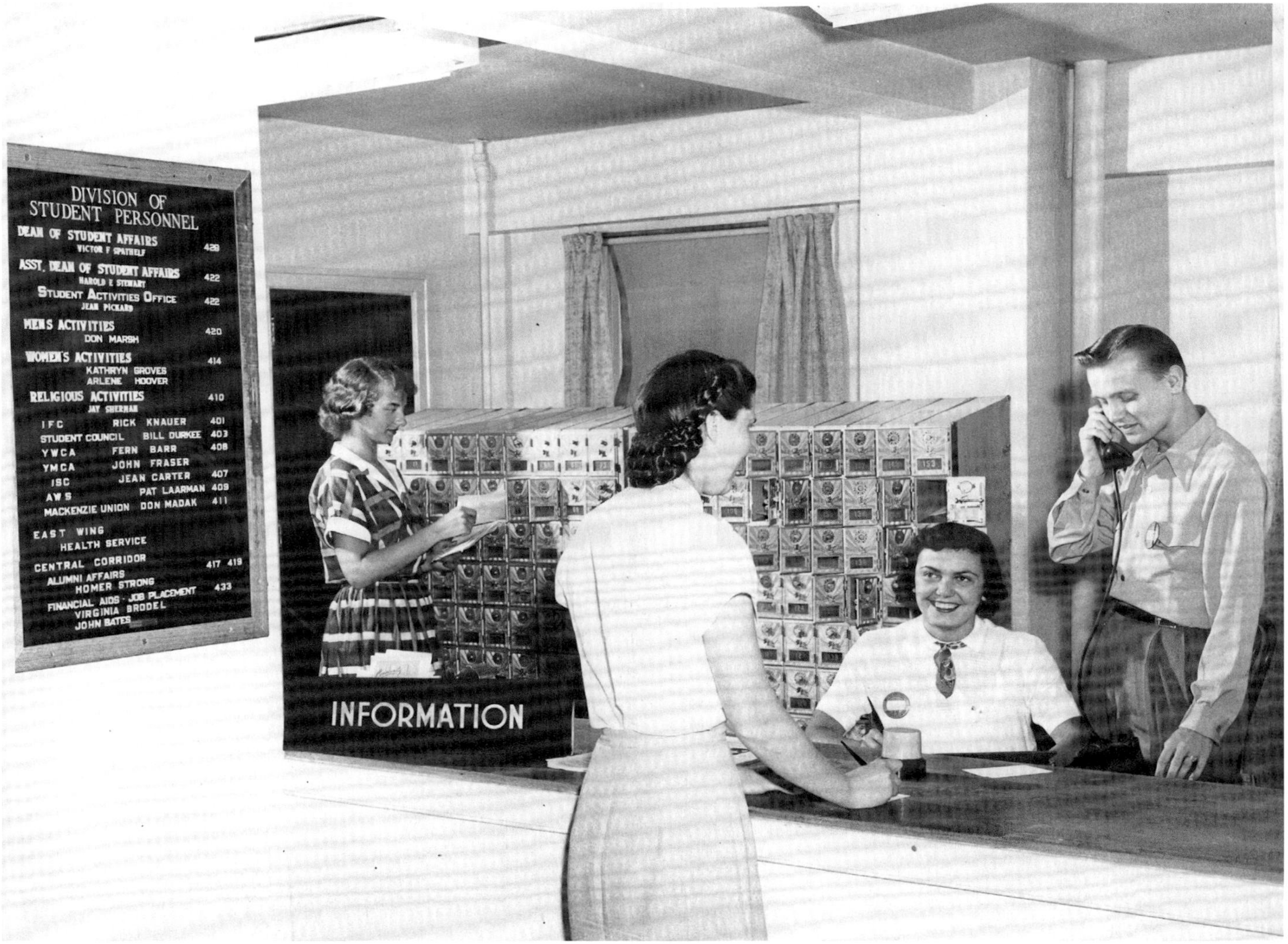

Office of the Dean of Student Affairs, the Student Center Building (Webster Hall), 1950s. In addition to meeting rooms, study spaces, and a cafeteria, administration offices were housed in the Student Center Building. (Walter P. Reuther Library, Archives of Labor and Urban Affairs, Wayne State University.)

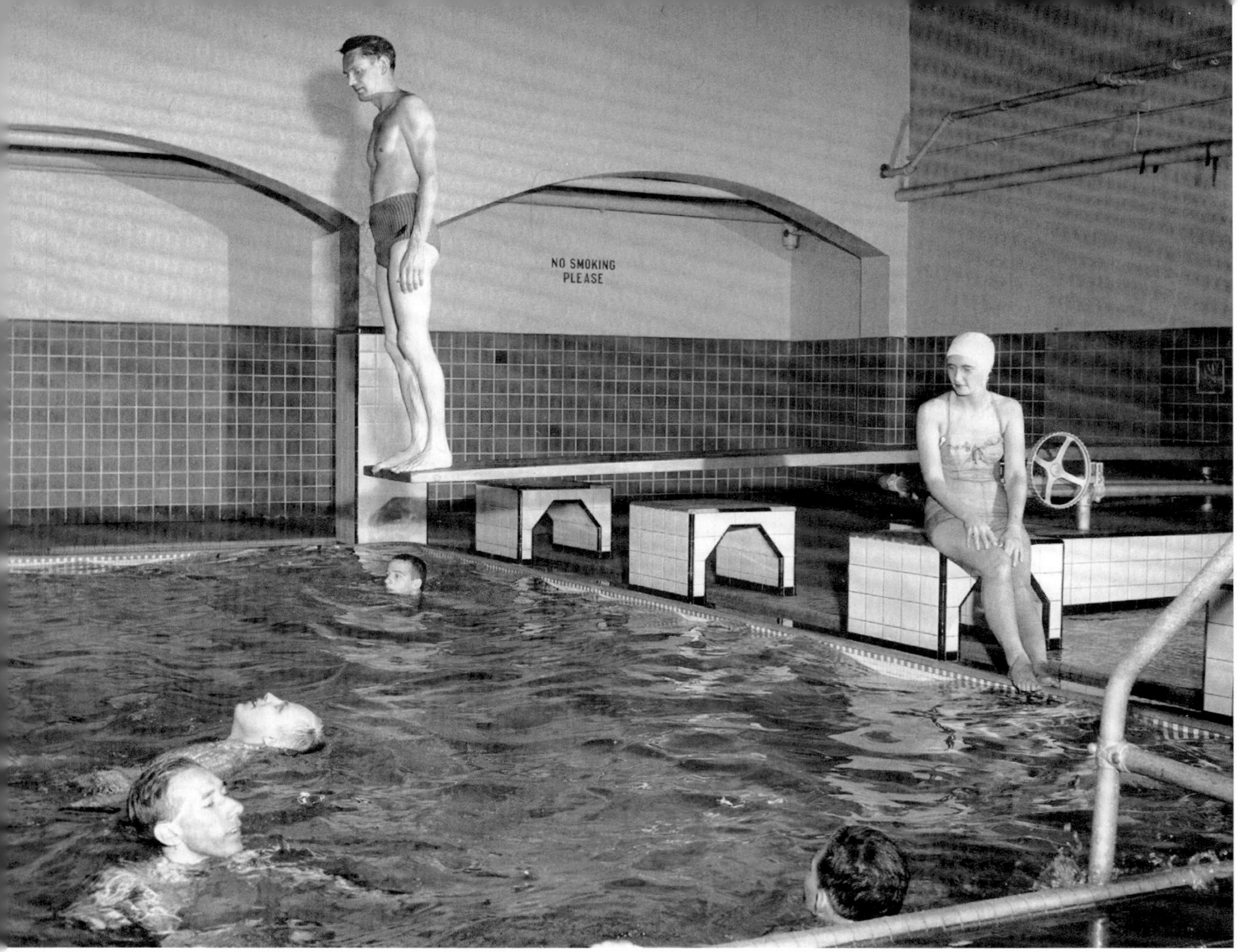

Swimming pool at the Student Center Building (Webster Hall), June 1958. The former hotel's swimming pool was used for recreation as well as by Wayne State's swimming team. (Walter P. Reuther Library, Archives of Labor and Urban Affairs, Wayne State University.)

Dorm room, Student Center Building (Webster Hall), 1958. The Student Center Building housed Wayne's first dormitory. As the veteran population declined and Detroit's housing shortage decreased, however, so did demand for dorms. The dormitory floors in Webster Hall were gradually given over to office space and finally disappeared in 1961, when the president and his staff moved into the tenth and eleventh floors of what would from that point on be called Mackenzie Hall. (Walter P. Reuther Library, Archives of Labor and Urban Affairs, Wayne State University.)

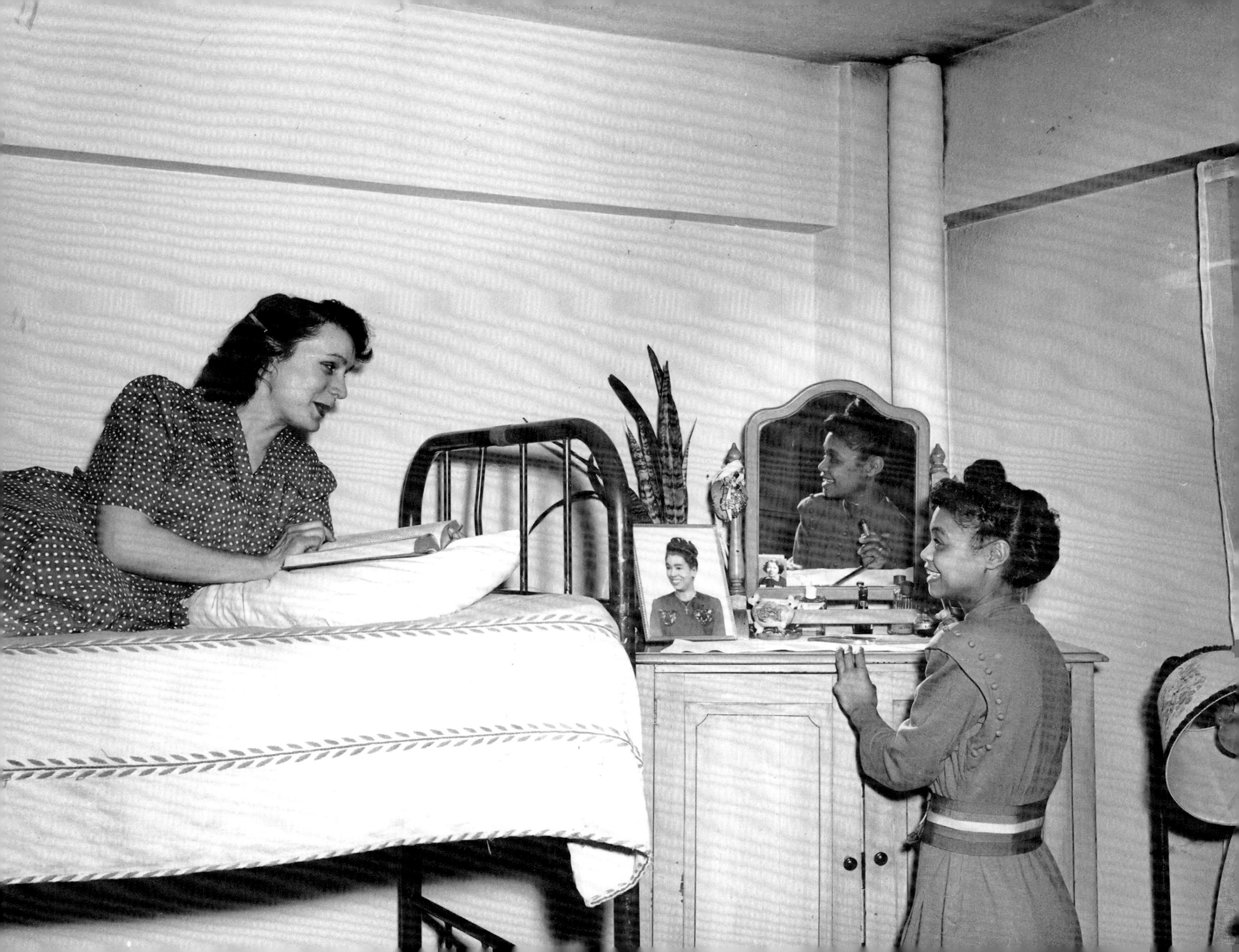

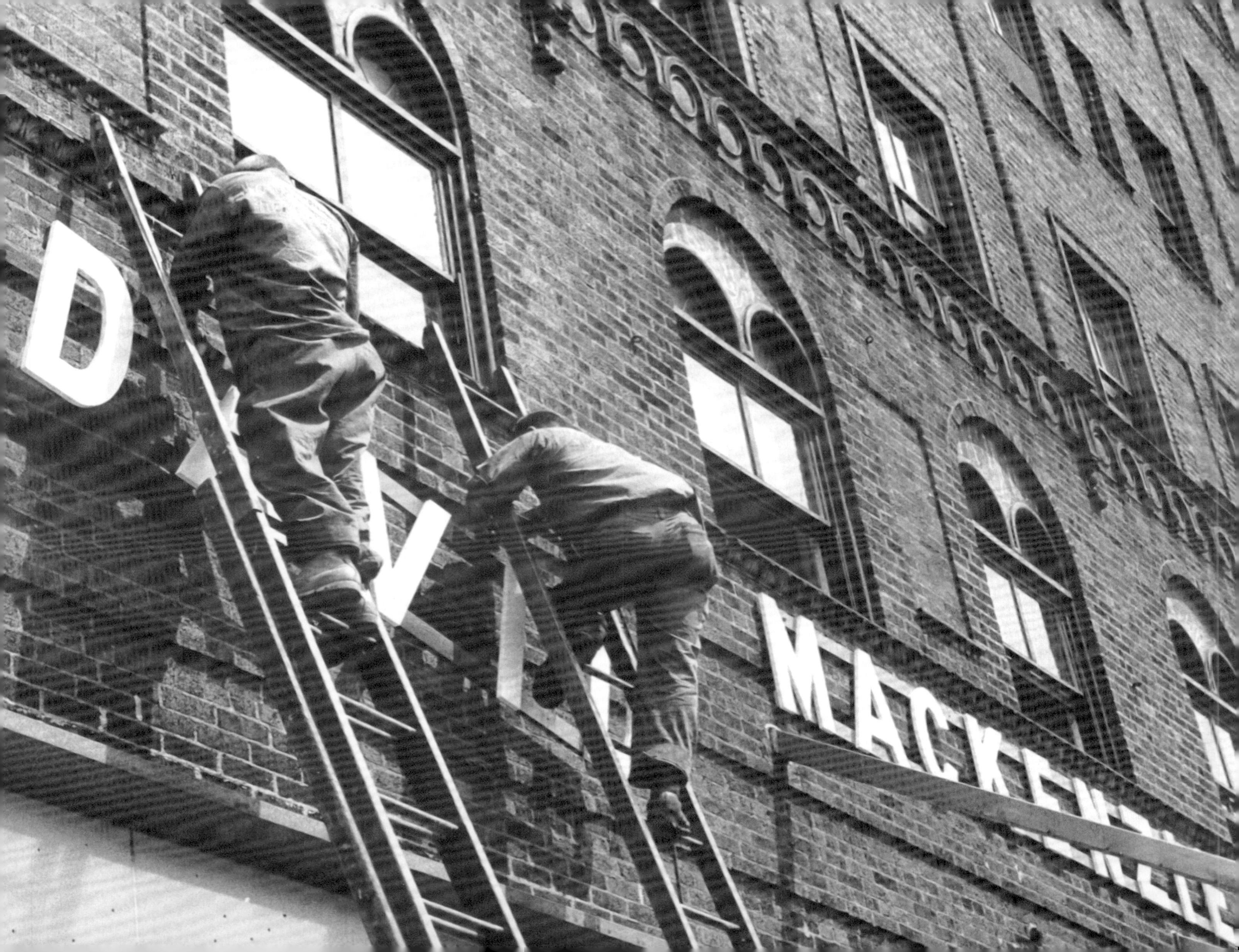

Mackenzie Hall sign, 1961. The Student Center Building (Webster Hall) was renamed Mackenzie Hall by the Board of Governors at its July 1961 meeting. Mackenzie Hall remained the center of student life and activities until the construction of the new student center, University Center, on Wayne State's main campus in 1969. (Walter P. Reuther Library, Archives of Labor and Urban Affairs, Wayne State University.)

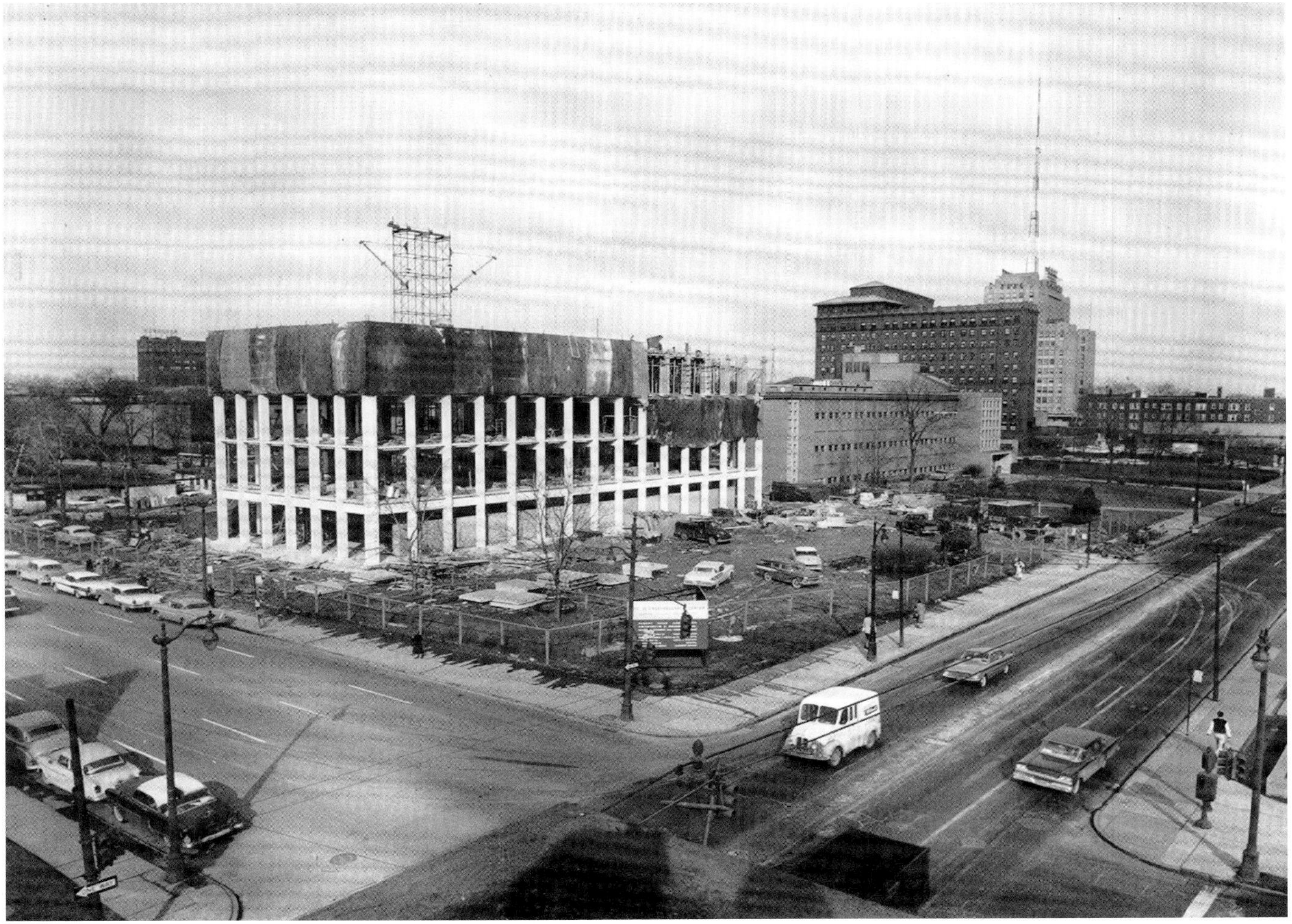

Construction of the Life Science Building, 5000 Second at Warren, northern and eastern facades, 1959. The Life Science Building replaced the last of the temporary war-surplus barracks on Wayne State's campus. The building was completed in 1960, the same year as the Education Building. Mackenzie Hall is the tall building on the right, with the Maccabees Building farther back in the distance. (Walter P. Reuther Library, Archives of Labor and Urban Affairs, Wayne State University.)

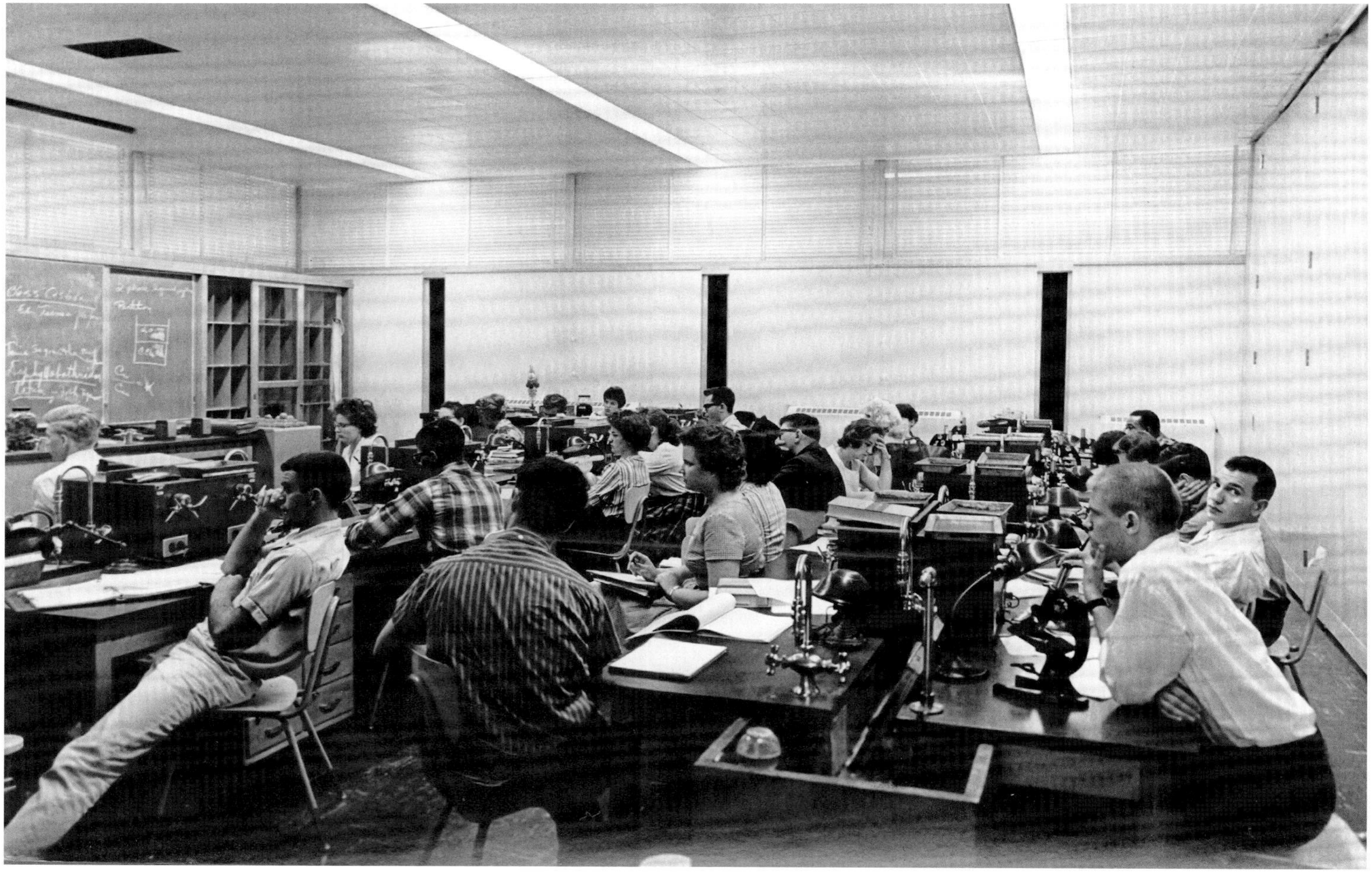

Teaching laboratory in the Life Science Building, 1961. (Walter P. Reuther Library, Archives of Labor and Urban Affairs, Wayne State University.)

Looking west from the center of campus, 1962. Merrick is the tree-lined street on the left side of the photo. The tall building at the center of the photo is the Chatsworth Tower Apartments. Today, the Student Center stands on the corner, directly in front of Chatsworth Tower. (Walter P. Reuther Library, Archives of Labor and Urban Affairs, Wayne State University.)

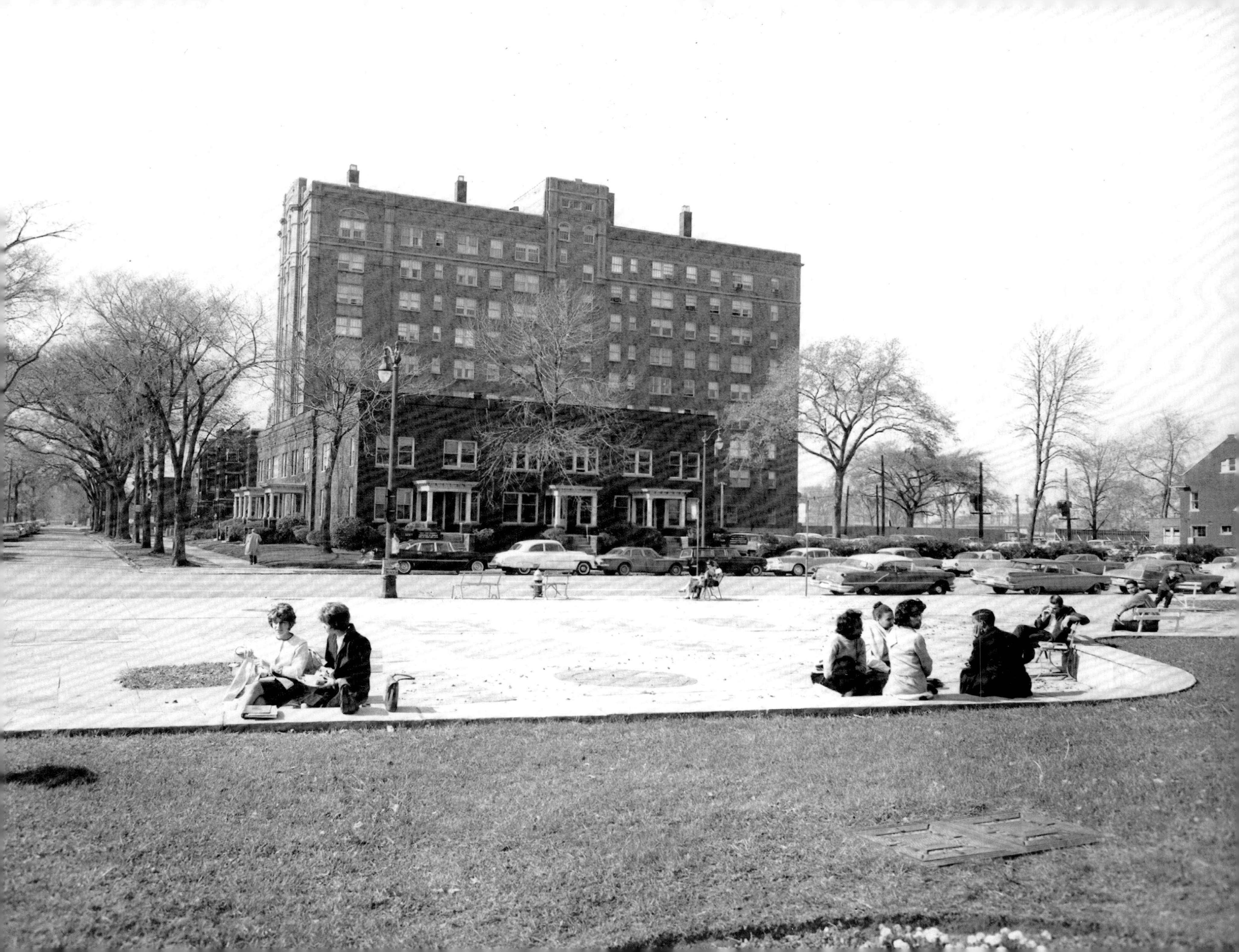

Corner of Second Avenue and Merrick Street, early 1960s. A campus crisscrossed with streets had its advantages. The ice cream truck is idling approximately where Gullen and Williams malls are located today, near the fountain in the center of Wayne's campus. (Walter P. Reuther Library, Archives of Labor and Urban Affairs, Wayne State University.)

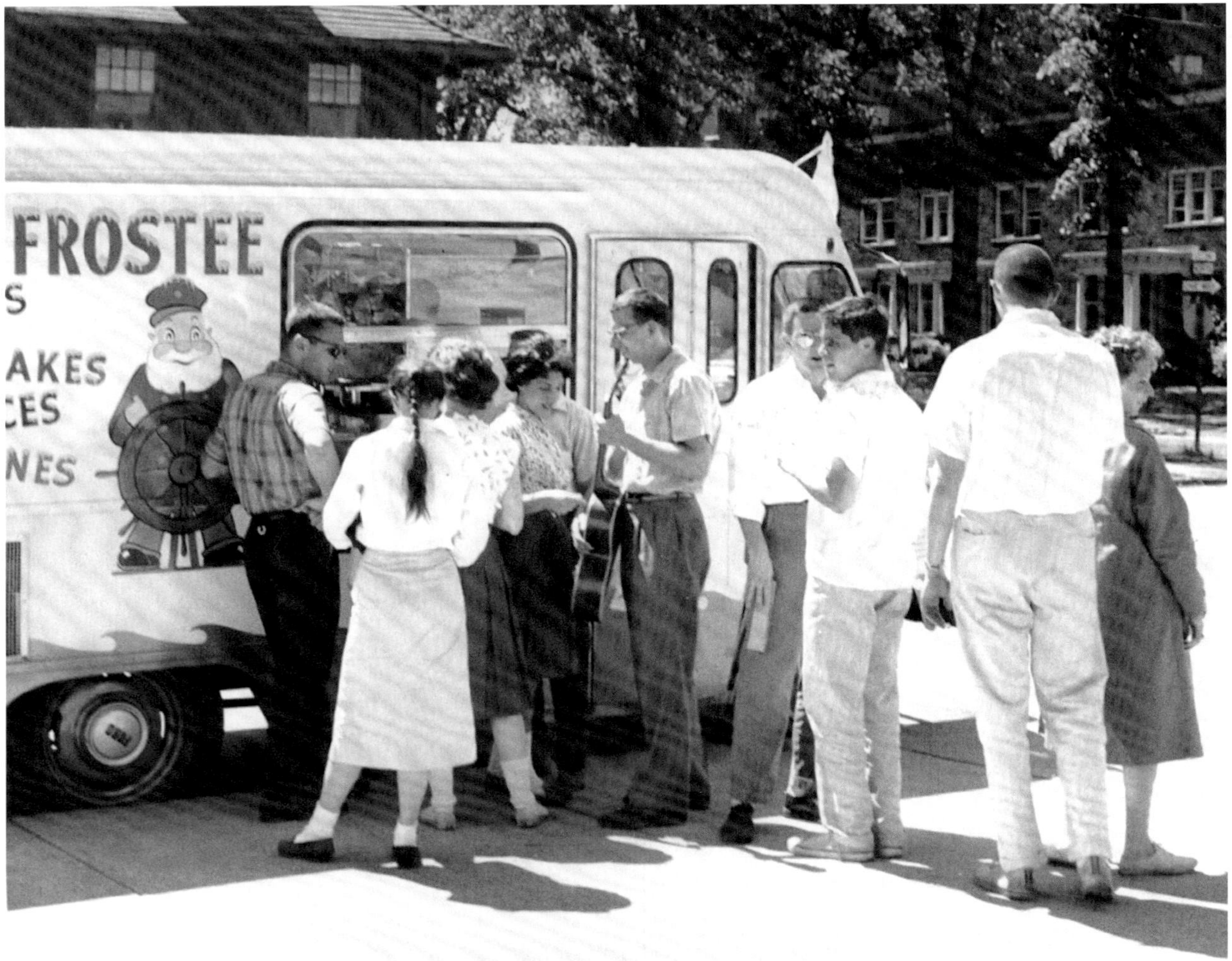

State Hall at Cass Avenue and Putnam Street, as seen looking east, early 1960s. The houses pictured here were torn down in 1962 for major additions to the Detroit Public Library, which is located a block down, on Woodward Avenue. (Walter P. Reuther Library, Archives of Labor and Urban Affairs, Wayne State University.)

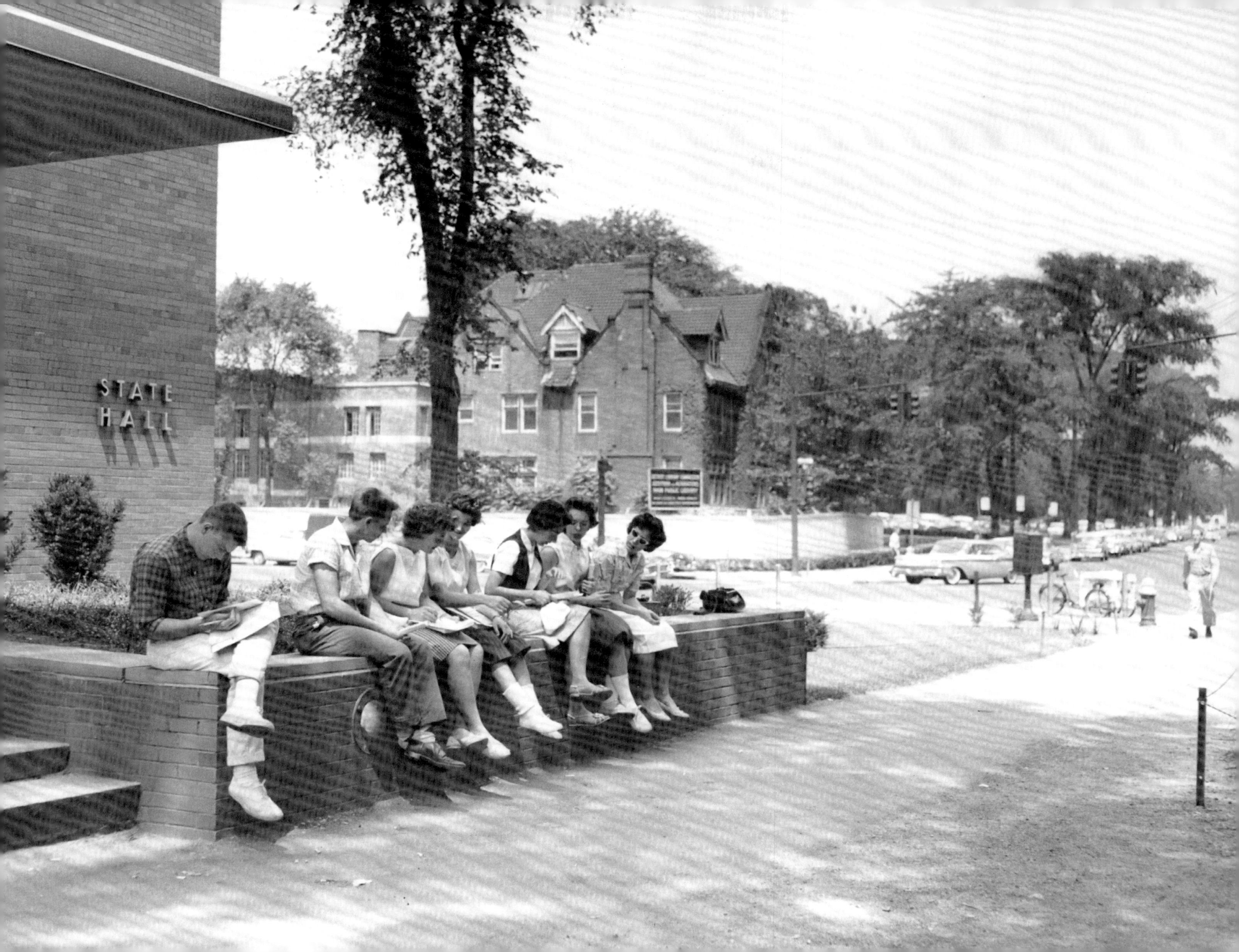
STATE
HALL

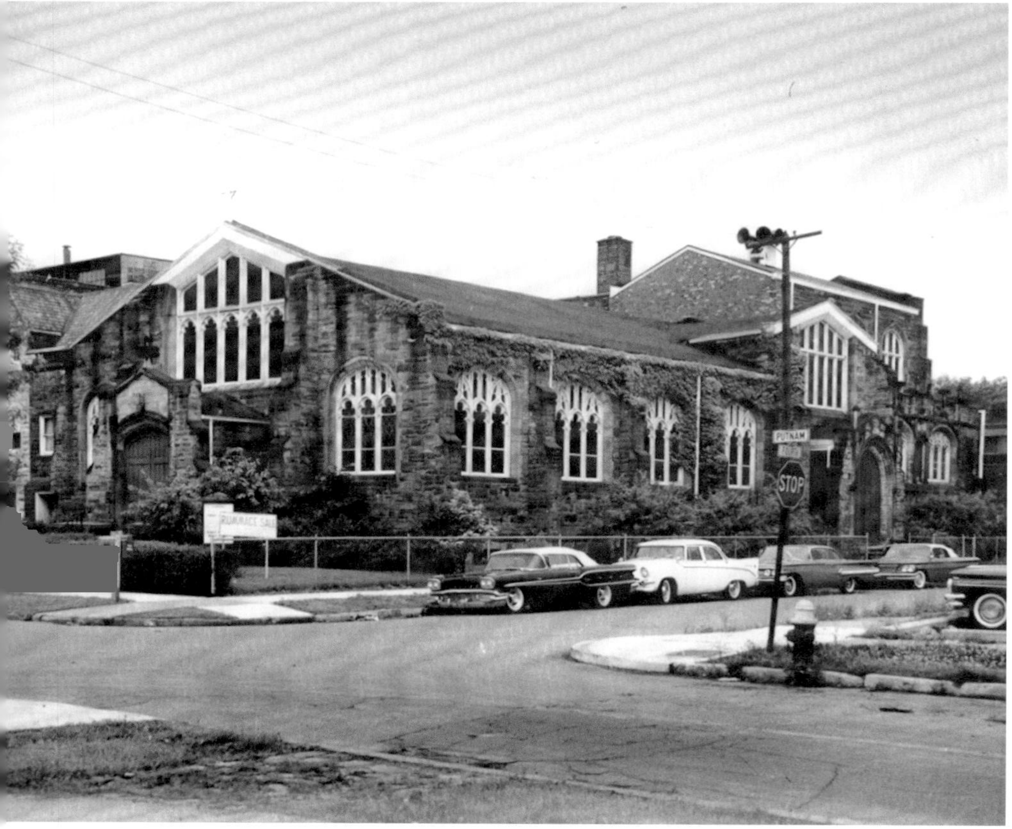

St. Andrew's Memorial Episcopal Church at Fourth and Putnam, 1961. Built in 1902, this church was the only neighborhood building left after construction of the John C. Lodge Freeway. Featuring windows that honor former Wayne State presidents Clarence Hilberry and Joseph Dodge, the church was privately owned until 1989, when it was purchased by the university. (Walter P. Reuther Library, Archives of Labor and Urban Affairs, Wayne State University.)

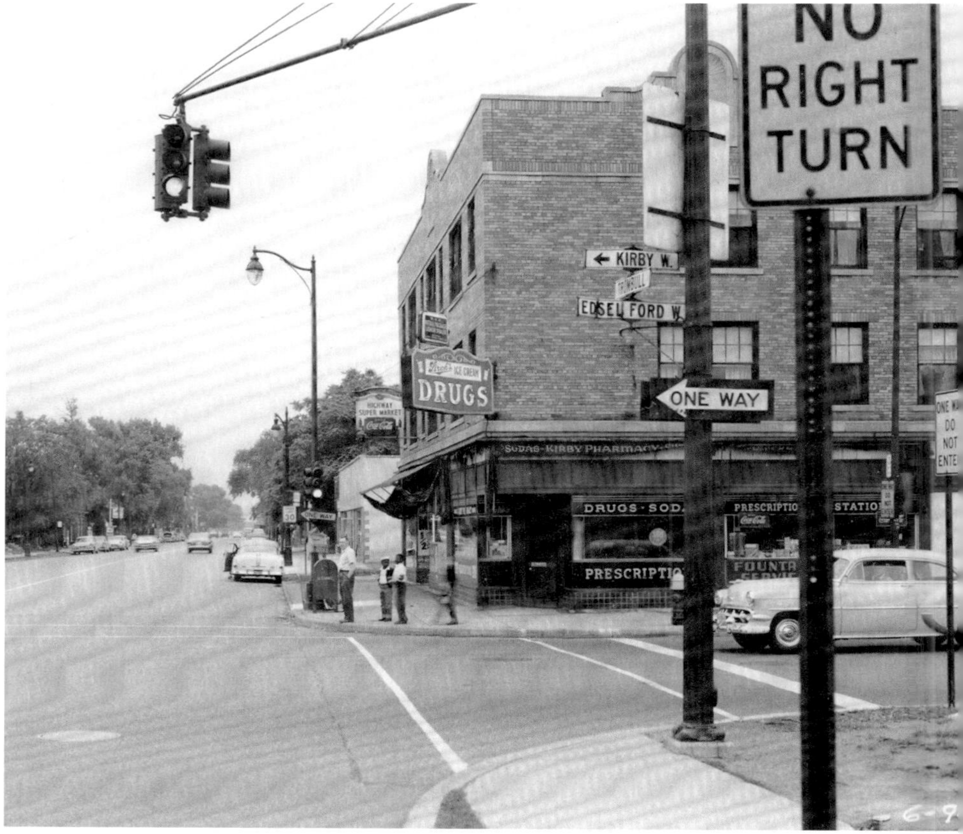

Kirby Street at the Edsel Ford Freeway service drive, looking south down Trumbull Street, 1958. A corner of the Woodbridge neighborhood, across from the area where the Matthaei Center would eventually be built. Students who commute to Wayne State University via west I-94 may recognize the drug store and soda fountain that served Stroh's ice cream. The building is still standing. (Courtesy of the Burton Historical Collection, Detroit Public Library.)

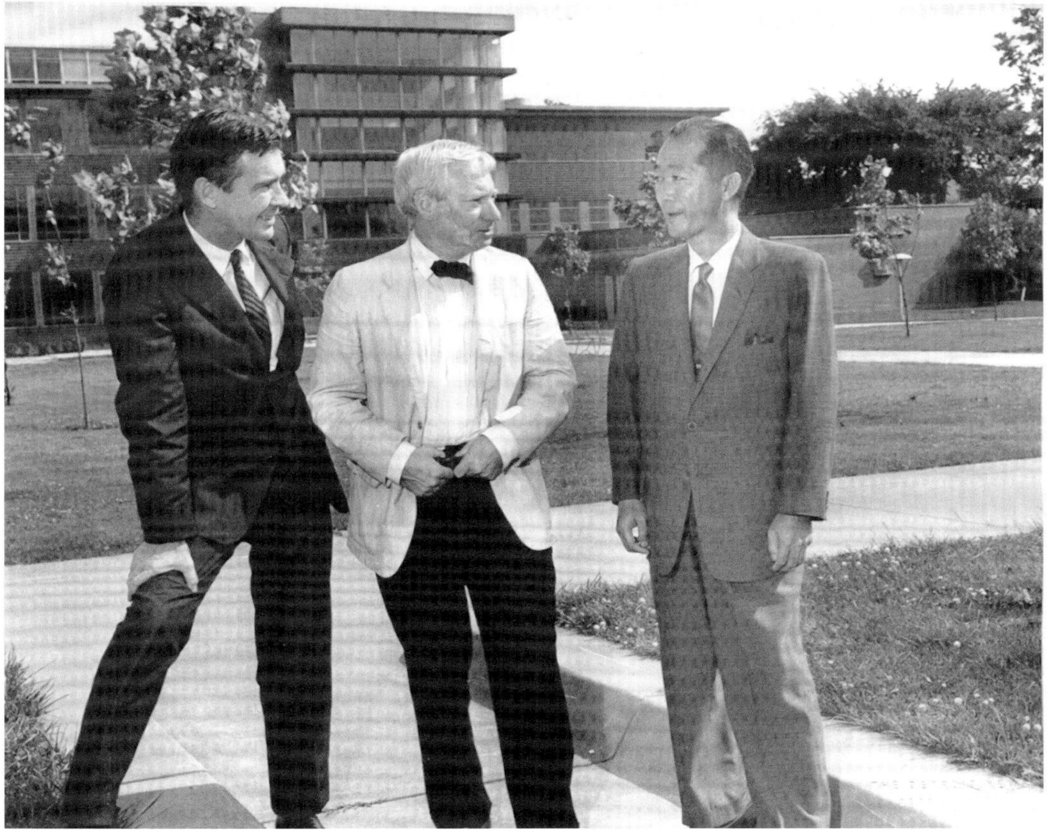

Campus architects, 1961. Pictured from right to left are Minoru Yamasaki, Louis I. Kahn, and Edward L. Barnes. Barnes designed the Helen Newberry Joy Residence for Women, and Kahn designed the Life Science Building. More significantly, Yamasaki's master plan for the campus became the basis for Wayne's major construction projects in the 1960s, and it was his firm that designed a substantial number of campus buildings in the early part of that decade. State Hall provides the backdrop for this photo. (Walter P. Reuther Library, Archives of Labor and Urban Affairs, Wayne State University.)

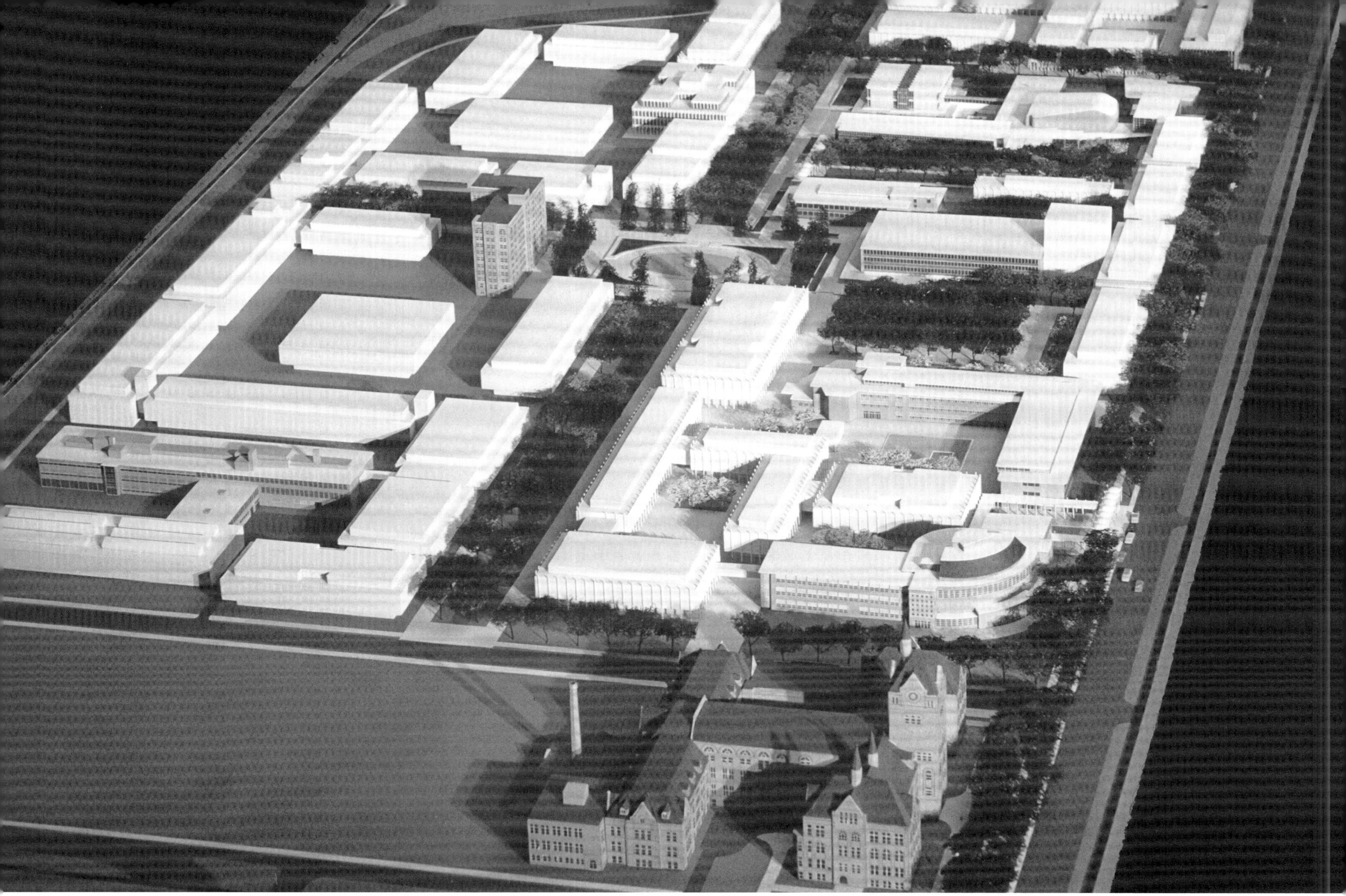

Campus plan, Minoru Yamasaki, undated. As is evident in this model, one of Yamasaki's proposals was to create a "superblock," a traditional campus with no through streets. Yamasaki's firm designed a substantial number of Wayne's buildings in the 1950s and 1960s, including the McGregor Memorial Conference Center (1958), the Education Building (1960), the Prentis Building (1964), and the DeRoy Auditorium (1964). (Courtesy of Yamasaki Associates, Inc.)

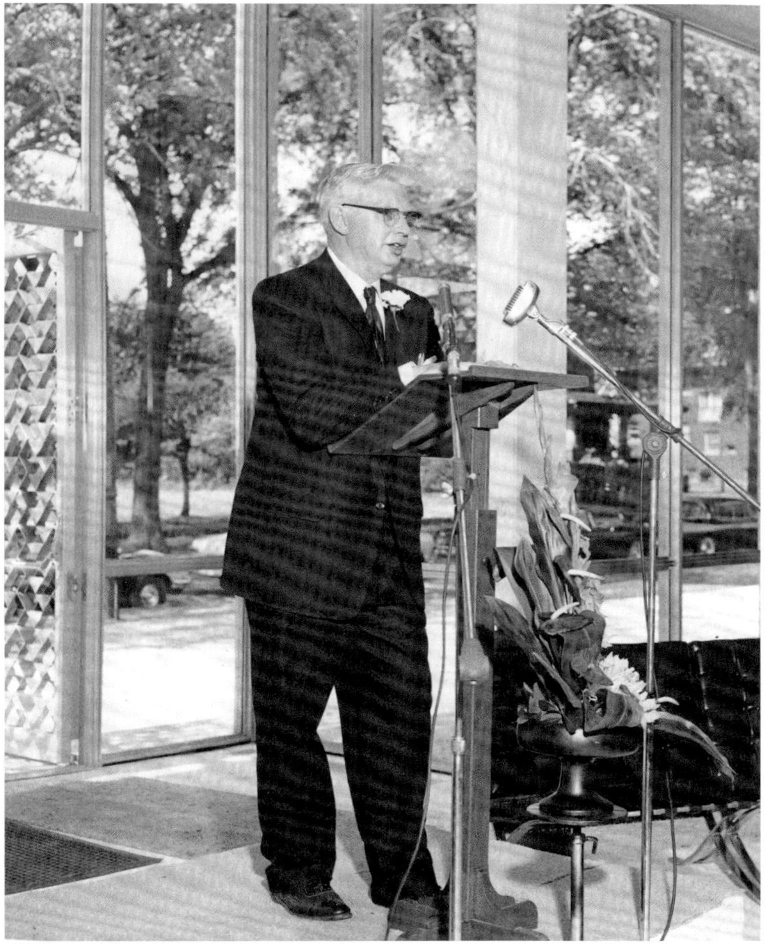

Dean of the Law School Arthur Neef at the dedication ceremony for the McGregor Memorial Conference Center, 1958. Neef made an important, lasting impact on the development of the Wayne State University campus, and he worked for Wayne for more than thirty years. He was named dean of the Law School in 1937 and held that post until 1966. While dean, he also served as provost under presidents David D. Henry and Clarence Hilberry, and briefly served as secretary to the Board of Governors in the late 1950s. When Neef retired in 1969, the Law Library was named in his honor. (Walter P. Reuther Library, Archives of Labor and Urban Affairs, Wayne State University.)

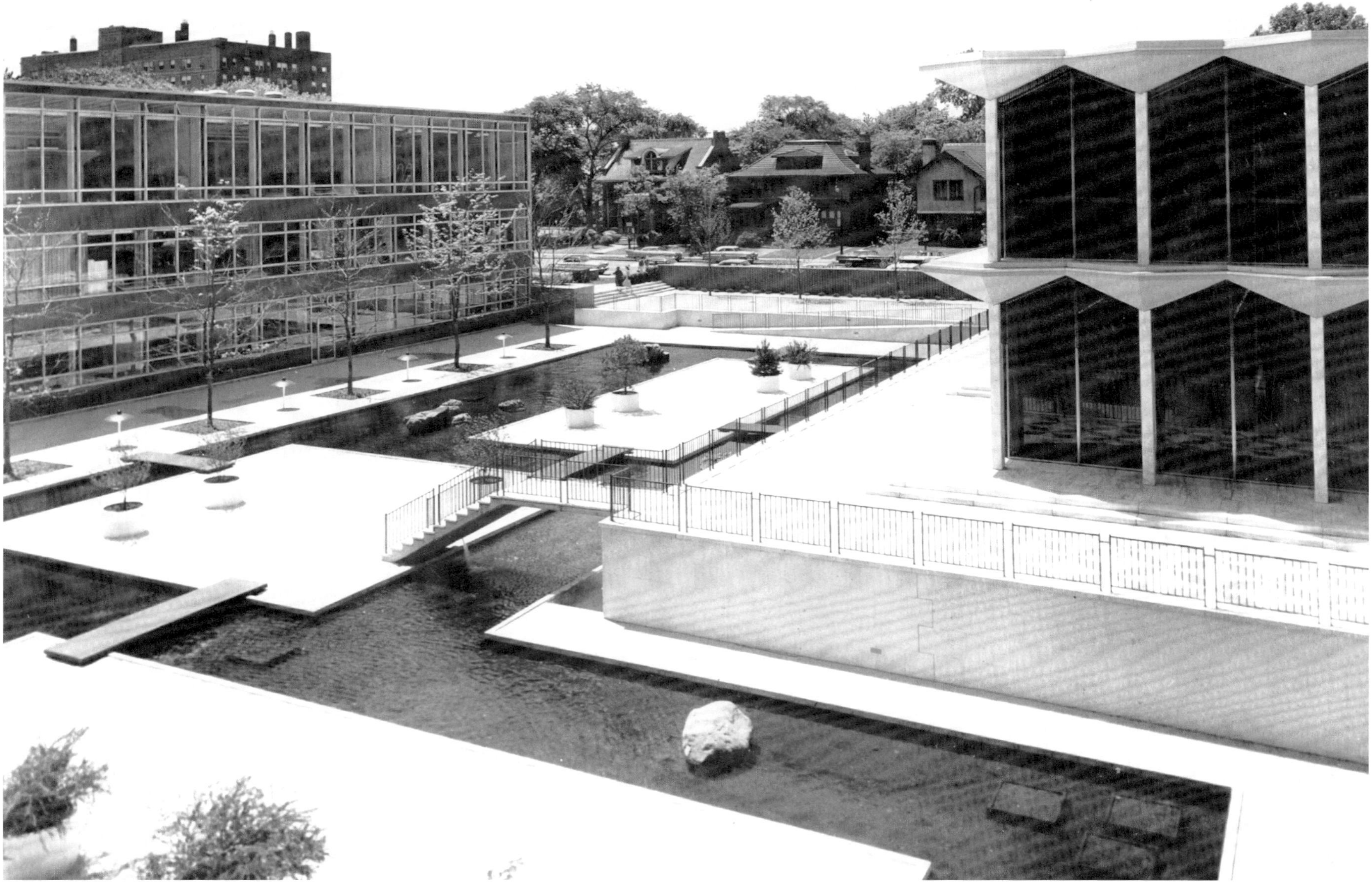

McGregor Memorial Conference Center, as seen looking west, late 1950s. Designed by renowned architect Minoru Yamasaki, McGregor was Wayne State's first building designed with luxury as well as utility in mind. Considered one of Detroit's architectural treasures, the two-story building is surrounded by a reflecting pool. Chatsworth is the tall building in the distance on the left, peeking over the Community Arts Building. The houses in the center of the photo are on Second Avenue. (Walter P. Reuther Library, Archives of Labor and Urban Affairs, Wayne State University.)

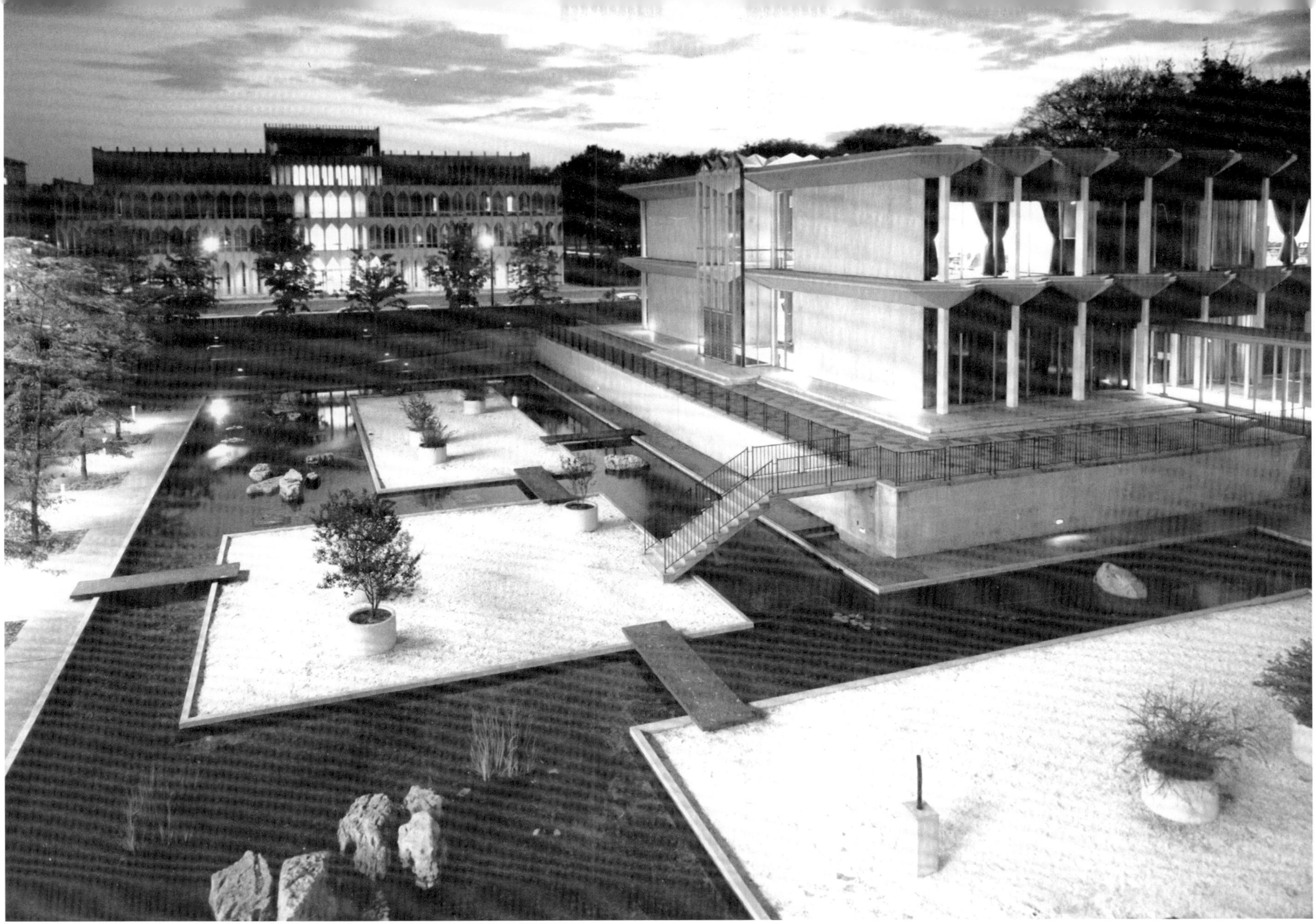

McGregor at night, as seen looking west, 1962. A more comprehensive view of McGregor's reflecting pool. The houses on Second Avenue were razed to make way for the Education Building, left of center in the photo, which was also designed by Yamasaki. (Walter P. Reuther Library, Archives of Labor and Urban Affairs, Wayne State University.)

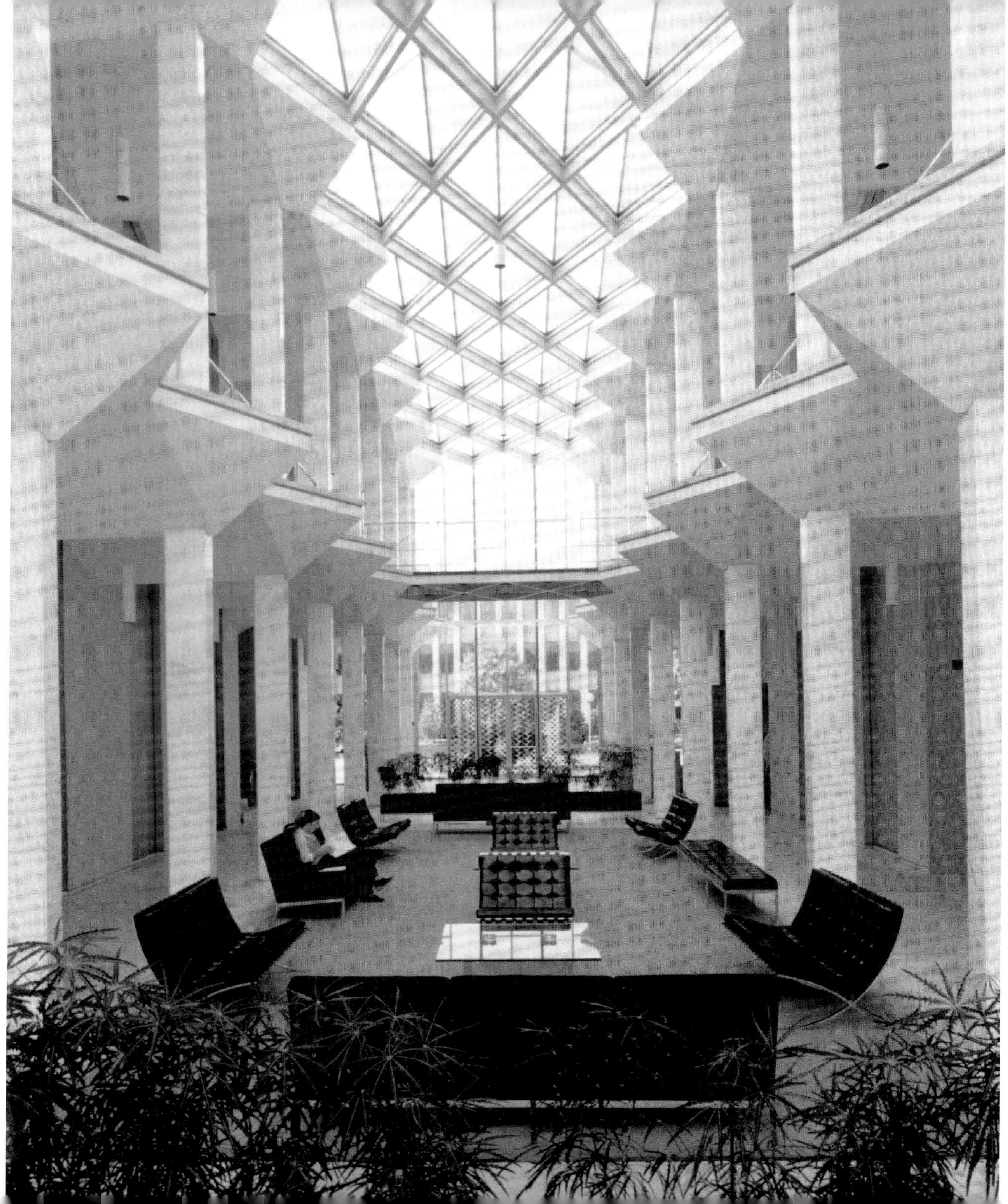

Interior of McGregor. (Courtesy of Yamasaki Associates, Inc.)

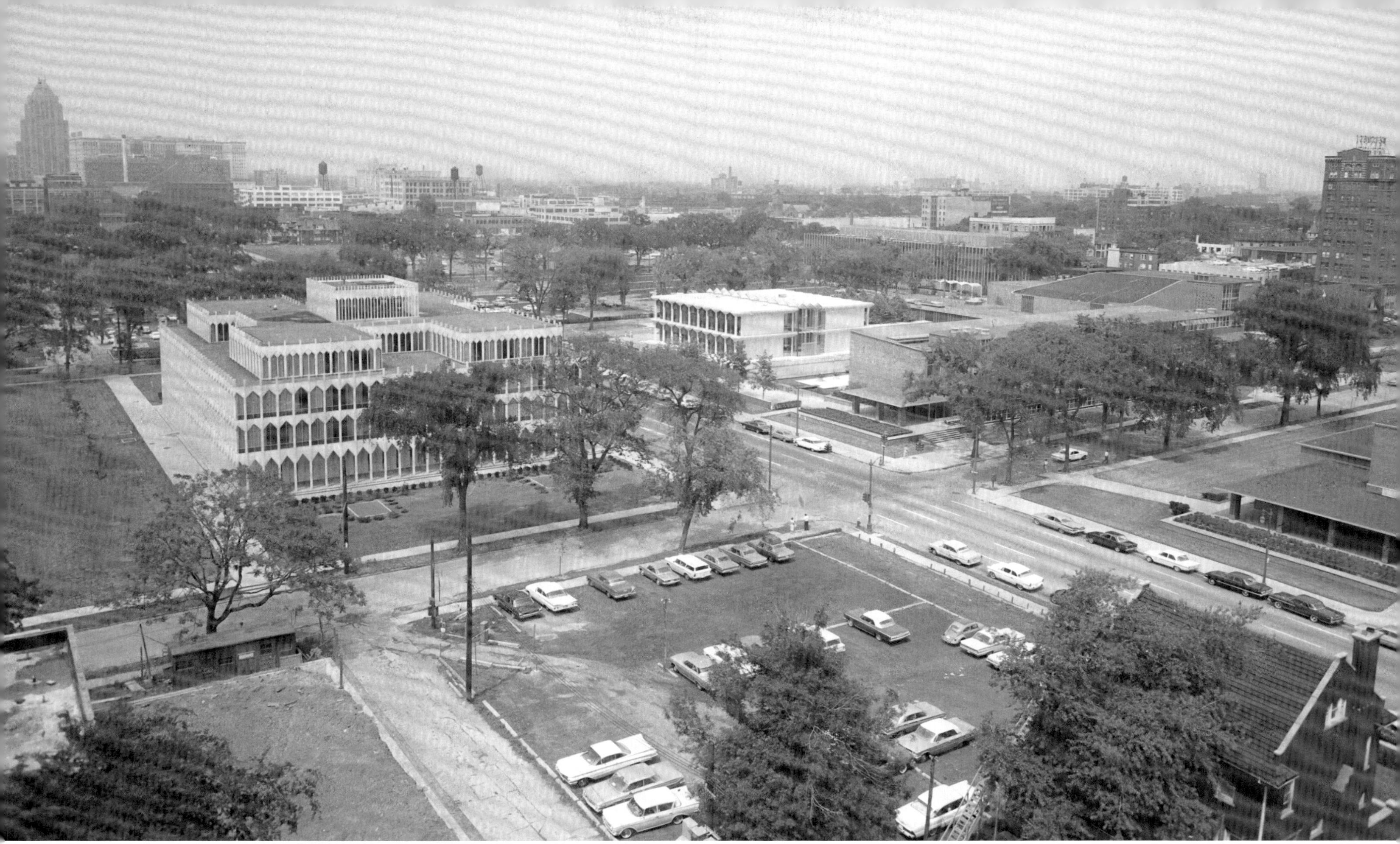

View of the campus, looking northeast, 1963. Taken before Second Avenue was closed to traffic, this picture shows the developing campus. The Education Building is the large white building on the left, the college's first permanent home after moving from building to building since 1881. Across Second Avenue is the McGregor Center, with the adjacent Community Arts Center crouched behind the row of trees. The Belcrest is the tall apartment building on the far right. The Fisher Building, a focal point of the New Center neighborhood directly north of the Wayne State campus, rises tall in the distance on the far left of the image. (Walter P. Reuther Library, Archives of Labor and Urban Affairs, Wayne State University.)

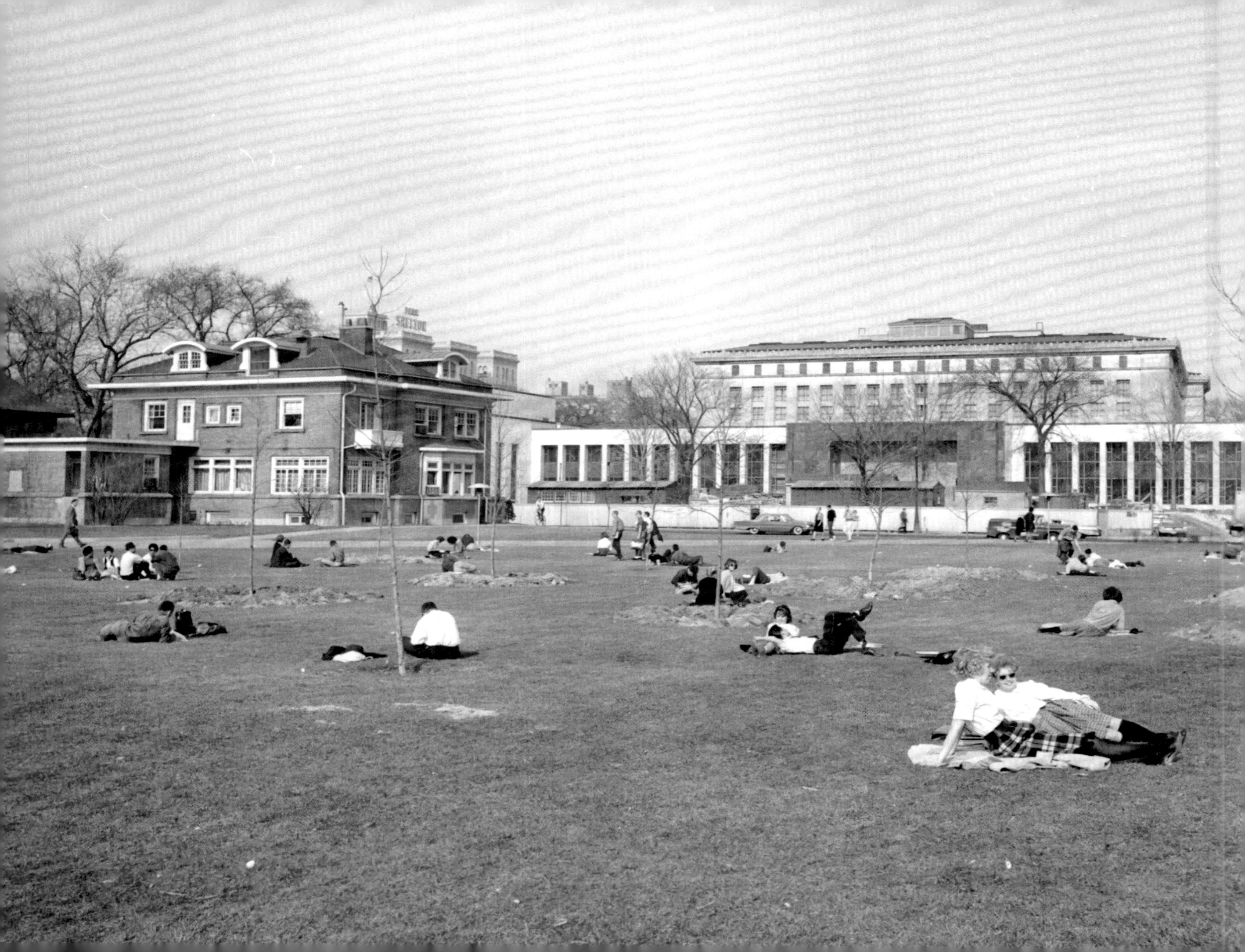

Center of Wayne State's campus, looking east, 1963. Students enjoy an autumn day on the lawn before this area was developed. The Detroit Public Library is the large building in the background. The former residence on the left is the William C. Rands House. The DeRoy Auditorium and the Prentis Building, both designed by Yamasaki, would be constructed on this space. (Walter P. Reuther Library, Archives of Labor and Urban Affairs, Wayne State University.)

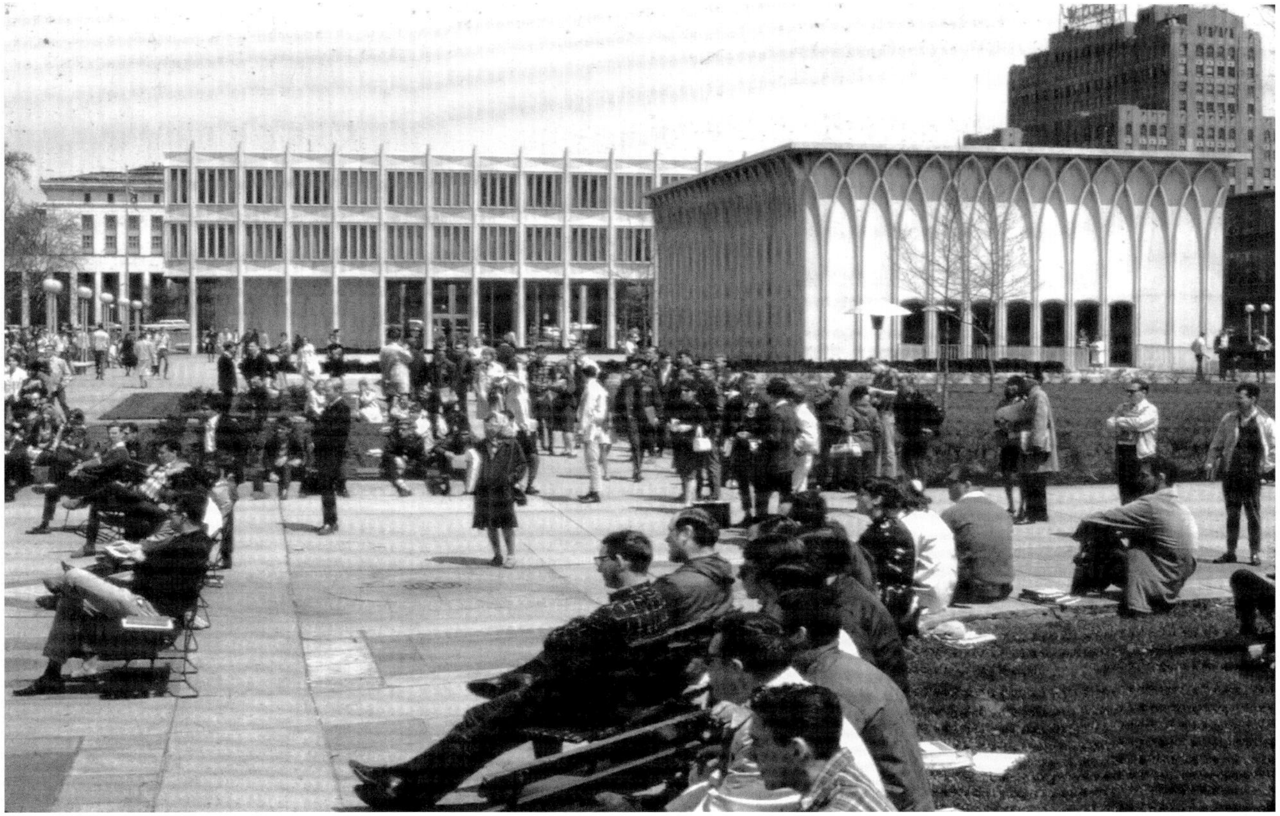

Center of Wayne State's campus, as seen looking east, about 1965. The Helen L. DeRoy Auditorium is in the foreground on the right; it houses two large auditoriums for lecture classes. The building's distinctive moat is not visible in this picture. Behind DeRoy and facing Cass Avenue is the Meyer and Anna Prentis Building, home to the School of Business Administration. A corner of the Detroit Public Library can be seen on the far left, behind the Prentis Building, and the Maccabees Building rises into the upper right corner. (Walter P. Reuther Library, Archives of Labor and Urban Affairs, Wayne State University.)

CHAPTER 5

CHANGE AND PRESERVATION, 1965–79

Many American college campuses were hotbeds of political activism in the late 1960s, and locally, student demonstrations combined with an increasingly radical student newspaper brought new challenges to Wayne State University during this period. Another challenge faced by the university was public opposition to its construction projects. In the mid-1960s, Wayne continued its expansion by having nearby lots and houses condemned through an urban renewal program that drew strong criticism from Detroit residents. In the late 1970s, the planned demolition of old houses that had been used as part of the campus since Wayne's founding was challenged for the first time by neighborhood groups and a student-run historic preservation group called Preservation Wayne.

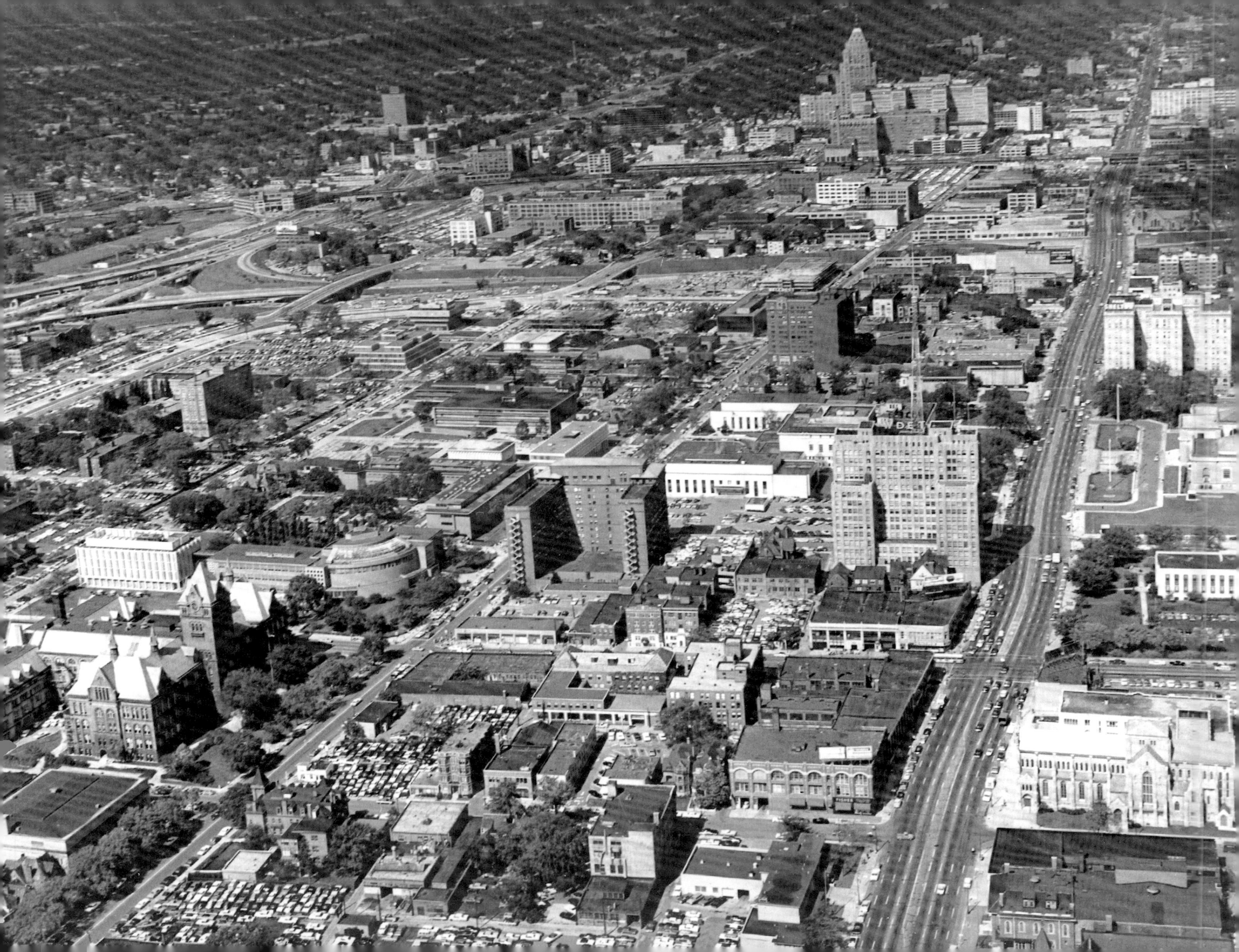

Aerial view of campus, looking northwest, 1965. In contrast to the earlier aerial views, here, few houses can be seen in the blocks adjacent to Old Main, pictured in the lower left corner. Instead, parking lots and campus buildings are visible. Wayne State's growth has turned most of the neighborhood into a campus. All of the Detroit Cultural Center, including the Detroit Public Library and the Detroit Institute of Arts, can be seen in this view. Woodward is the broad street running north-south along the right side of the photo. The Fisher Building appears in the distance, right of center, and the tall, dark Belcrest Apartments can be seen southeast of the Fisher Building, just above the center of the image. The first of Wayne State's many parking structures, Parking Structure #1 on Palmer, can just be made out north of the Belcrest. (Walter P. Reuther Library, Archives of Labor and Urban Affairs, Wayne State University.)

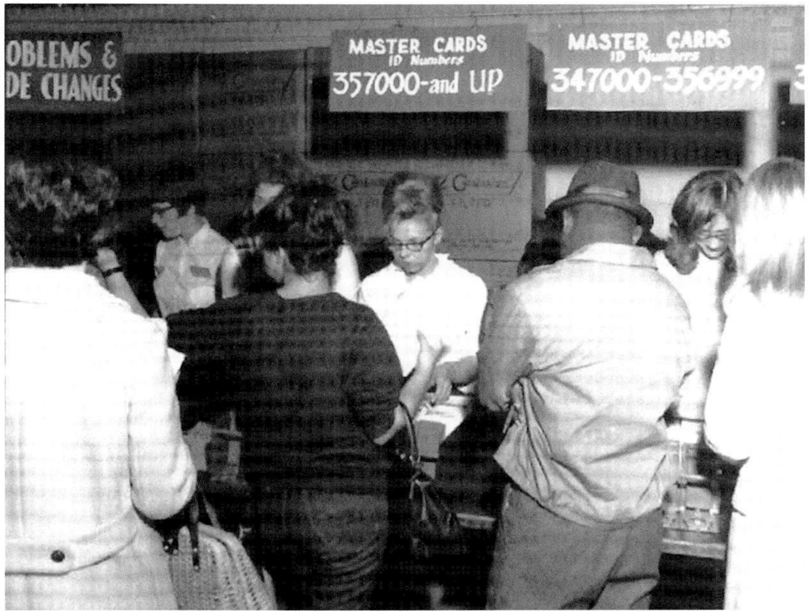

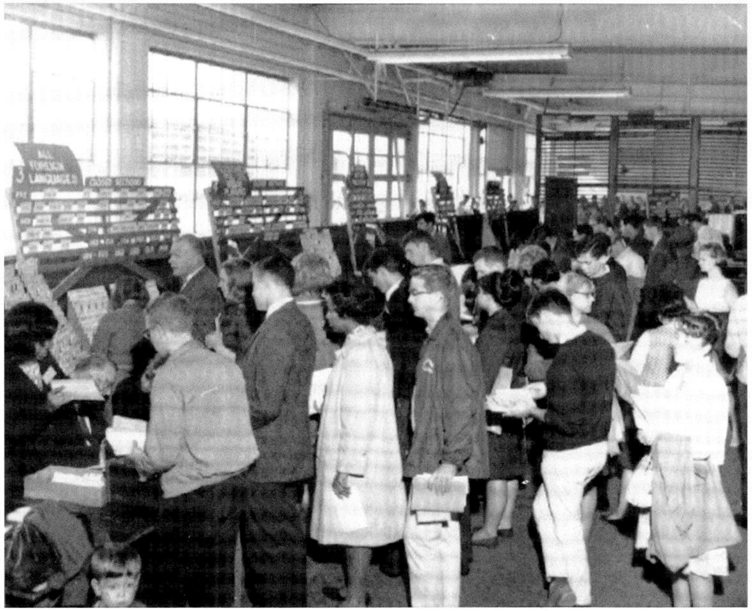

Registration, Administrative Services Building, 1960s. Proof of the old punch-card system for registration. Before telephone or online registration, Wayne State University students lined up to choose classes on registration day. (In the second picture, a child accompanying a Wayne State student can be seen in the lower left foreground.) Throughout the 1960s, the average age of Wayne State students rose, as the administration focused less on undergraduate programs and more on graduate and professional studies. During the 1970s, Wayne State president George Gullen's administration continued this focus. (Walter P. Reuther Library, Archives of Labor and Urban Affairs, Wayne State University.)

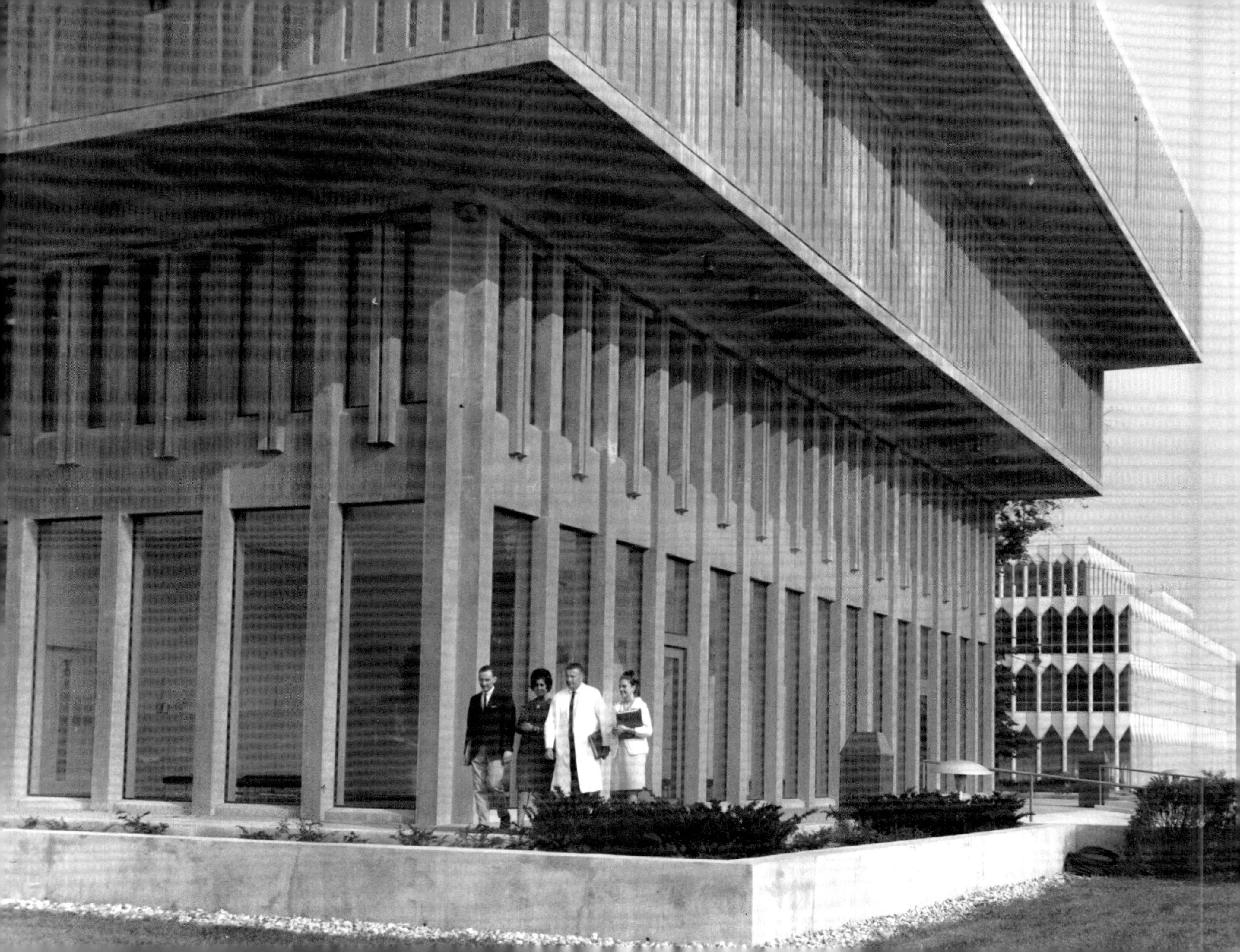

Shapero Hall, 5501 Second Avenue Mall, northern and western facades, 1965. During its early years, the College of Pharmacy was relocated three times before this building became its home in 1965 for the next decade. Behind Shapero Hall, a corner of the Education Building can be seen on the far right. Shapero Hall housed the College of Pharmacy until 1975, when pharmacy programs were gradually moved to the Medical Science Building at 1400 Chrysler, just off of I-75. In 1985, Shapero Hall was renamed the Natural Science Building, and the College of Pharmacy's new home was renamed Shapero Hall. (Walter P. Reuther Library, Archives of Labor and Urban Affairs, Wayne State University.)

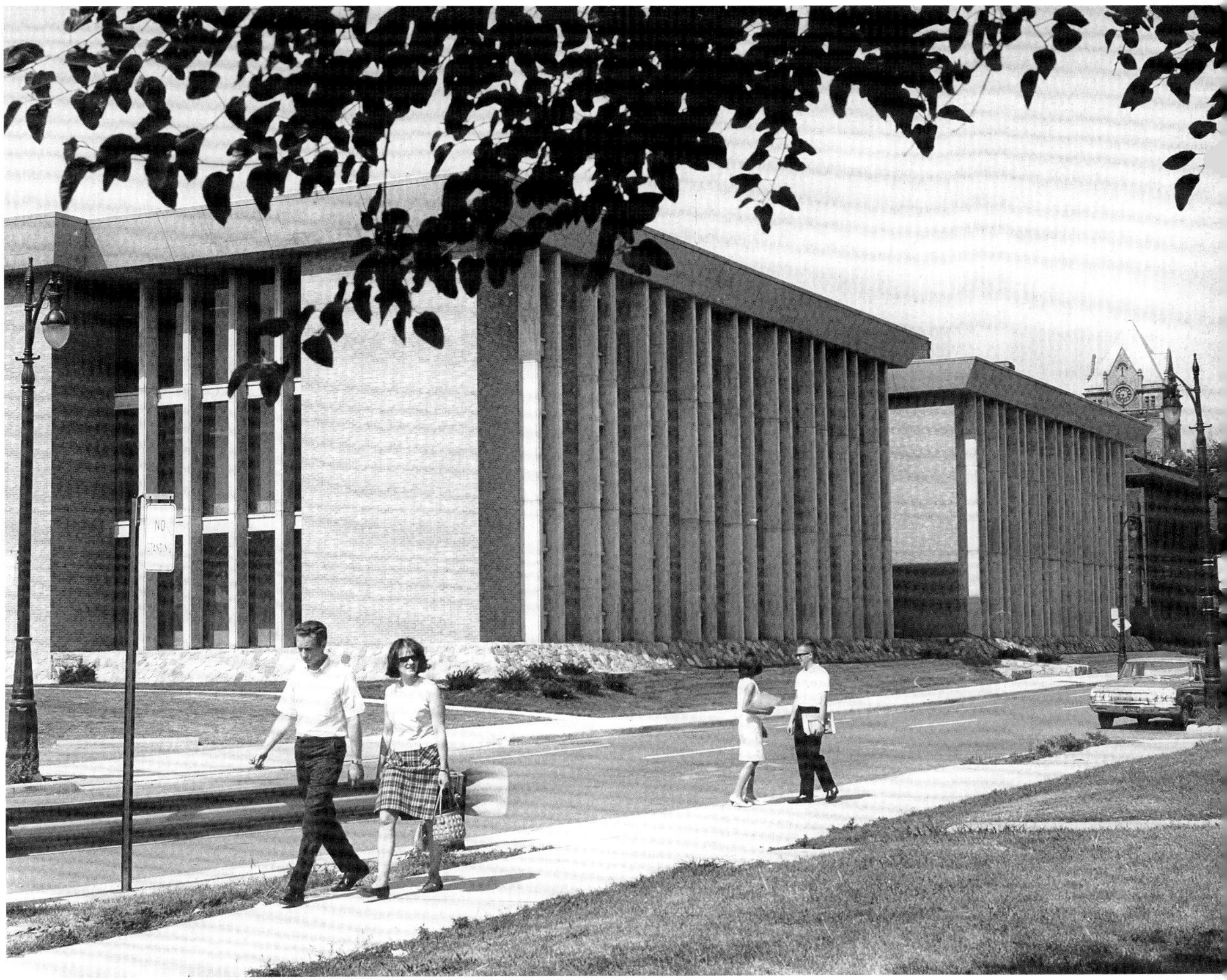

Physics Research Building, 666 West Hancock Street at Third Avenue, as seen facing northeast, 1965. The Physics Research Building was constructed in 1965, the same year as Shapero Hall. Old Main's clock tower can be seen in the distance on the far right. (Walter P. Reuther Library, Archives of Labor and Urban Affairs, Wayne State University.)

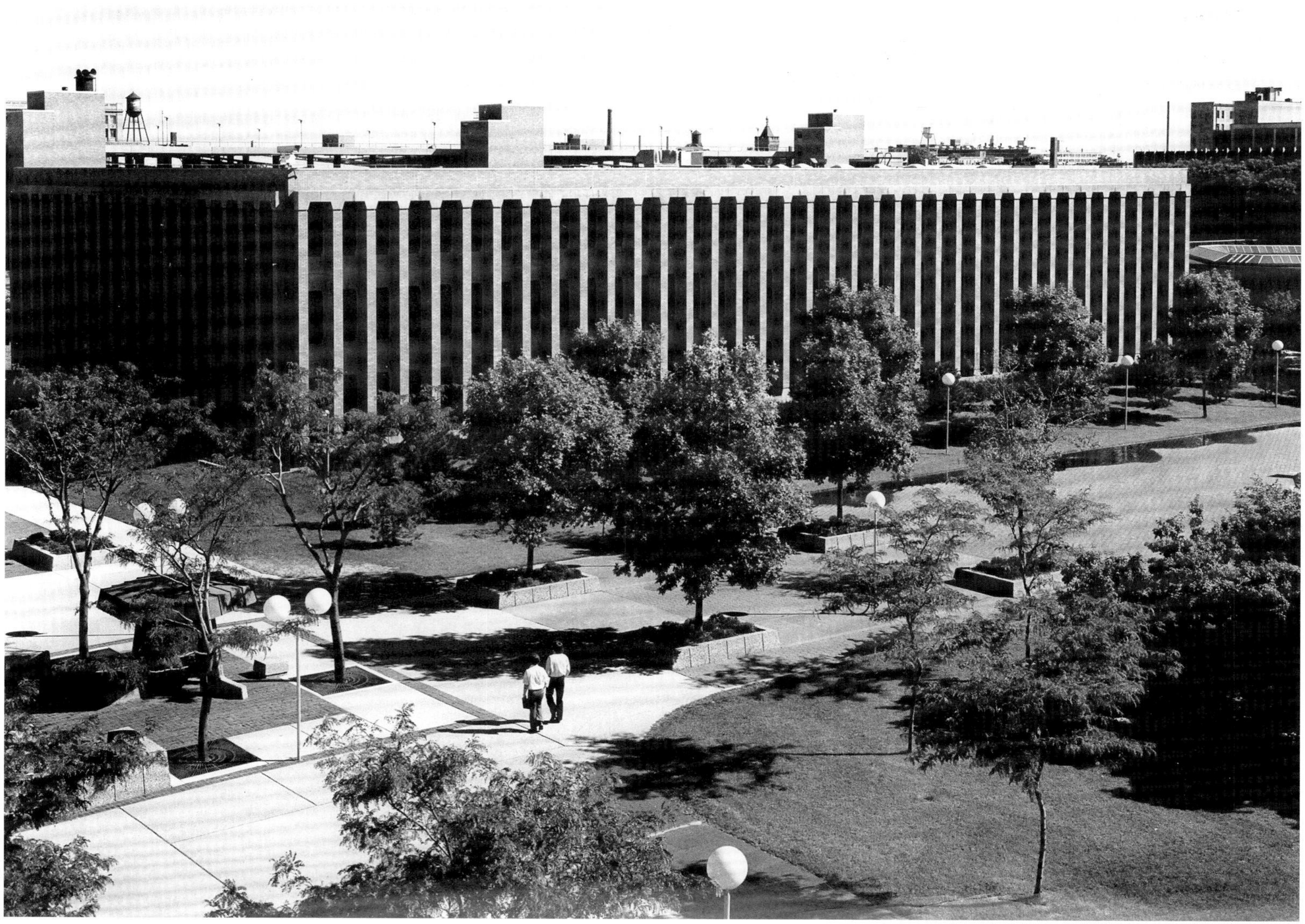

Law Library on Ferry Mall, northern and eastern facades, 1978. Aspiring lawyers welcomed the completion of this building. Before it was constructed, the law library was housed in the General Library (later Purdy/Kresge Library), and law classes were held in an old home. Completed in 1966, the Law Library included seminar rooms, a moot court, and a student lounge. A second building, connected to it by an arcade, housed lecture halls. (Walter P. Reuther Library, Archives of Labor and Urban Affairs, Wayne State University.)

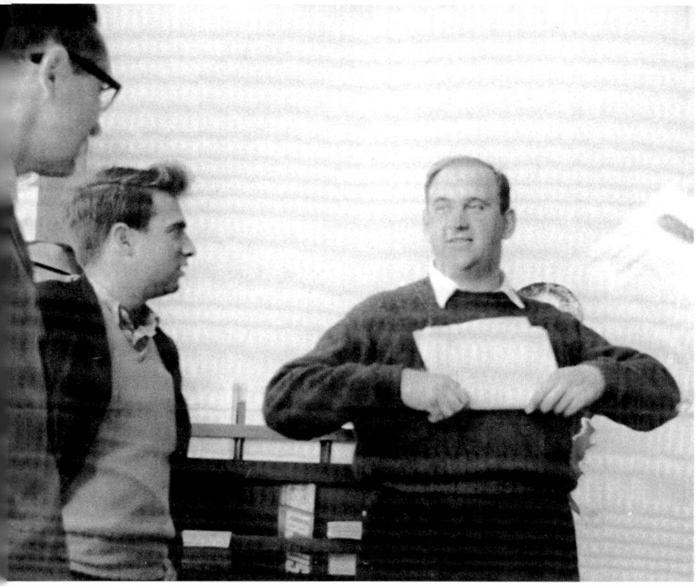

Monteith faculty, 1964. On the right is Otto Feinstein, long-serving professor at Wayne State who taught in Monteith College. Founded in 1958, the experimental college aimed to provide the experience of a small liberal arts college within a large urban university. Students at Monteith were active in the counterculture of the 1960s, and these students helped found the Detroit Artists' Workshop, a group of artists, musicians, and writers that celebrated its fortieth anniversary in 2005. In 1975, faced with declining revenues, President George Gullen's administration voted to phase out Monteith. (Courtesy of Leni Sinclair.)

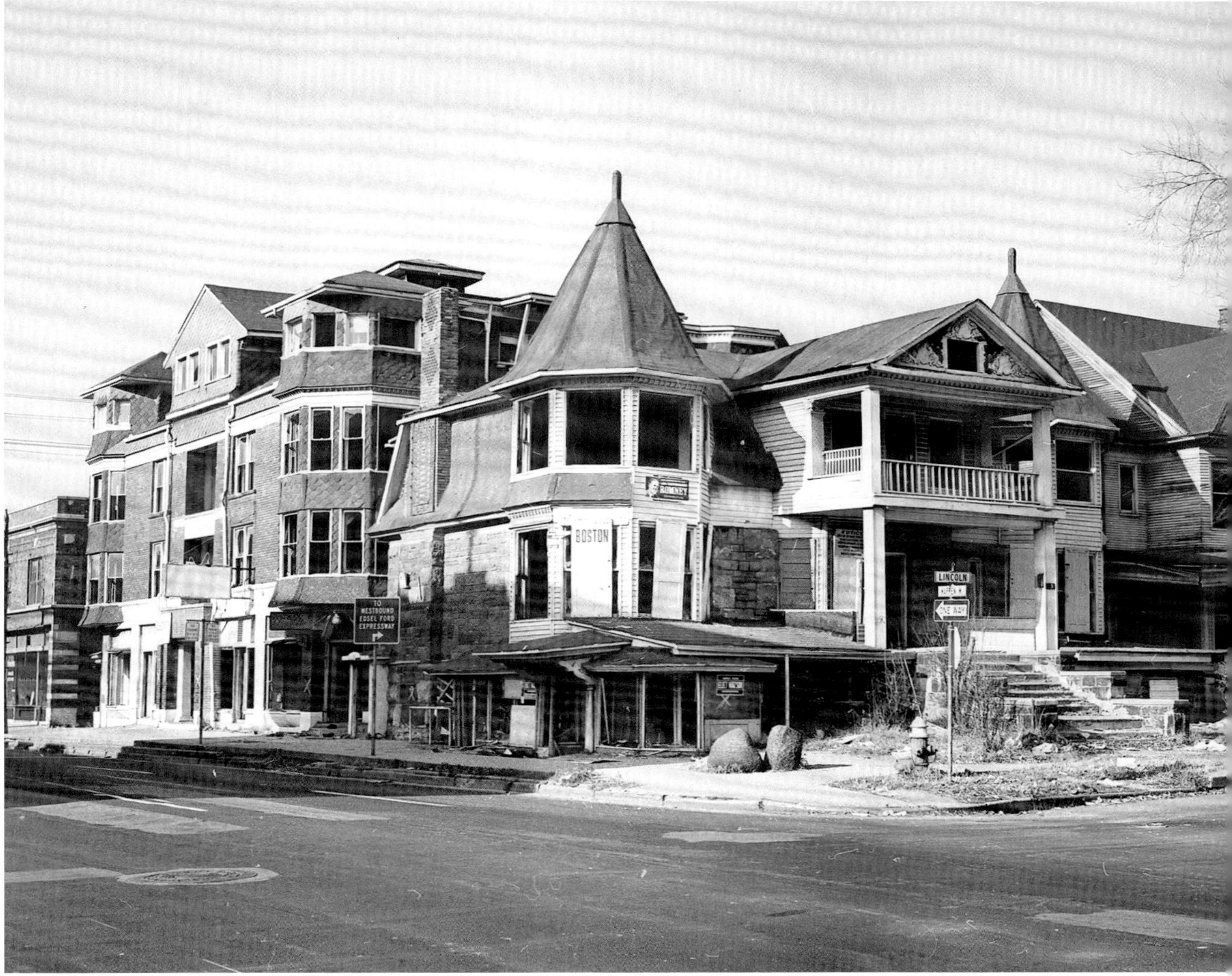

University City area, 1964. The intersection of West Warren Avenue and Lincoln Street, pictured here, was to be included in Phase II of the university's urban renewal project, University City. The project, however, was never completed. Empty storefronts dot Warren Avenue, and a George Romney gubernatorial campaign poster is tacked to the front of an abandoned house. (Walter P. Reuther Library, Archives of Labor and Urban Affairs, Wayne State University.)

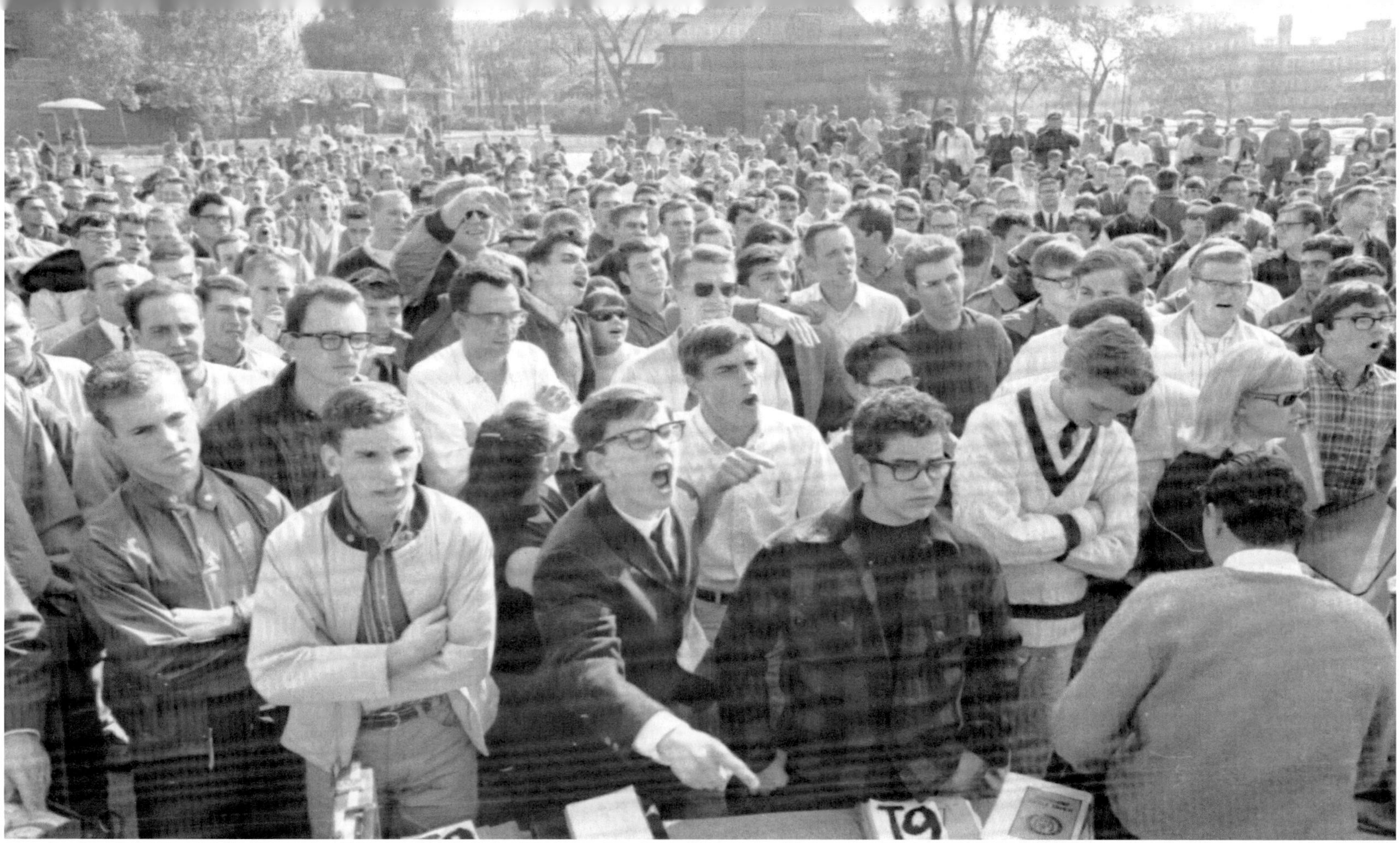

Vietnam War debate on Wayne State University's campus, October 15, 1965. To protest the Vietnam War, a student group, the Wayne Committee to End the War in Vietnam, scheduled two days of discussions on alternatives to the draft. However, the teach-in turned into a shouting match when members of the university's Republican Club and antiwar speakers challenged one another to a debate. The first of many antiwar activities on campus, the Vietnam War and draft debate attracted about six hundred students, almost all of them men. Due to fights that broke out among the students, the speeches ended two hours earlier than planned. The man in the suit, near the front, is likely a member of the Republican Club. State Hall is behind the students, on the far left of the photo. (Walter P. Reuther Library, Archives of Labor and Urban Affairs, Wayne State University.)

Detroit riots, July 1967. In the early morning hours of Sunday, July 23, 1967, a routine raid by Detroit police officers on an after-hours club in an African American neighborhood ignited a riot that would last nearly a week and leave forty-three dead. The 1967 riots would become synonymous with racial divisions in Detroit. Pictured here are members of the Detroit police and National Guard entering the riot area on Twelfth Street. The National Guard was called in to help quell the destruction caused by looting, arson, and rioting. The Guard mobilized at the Central High School grounds, where a command post had been set up. (Walter P. Reuther Library, Archives of Labor and Urban Affairs, Wayne State University.)

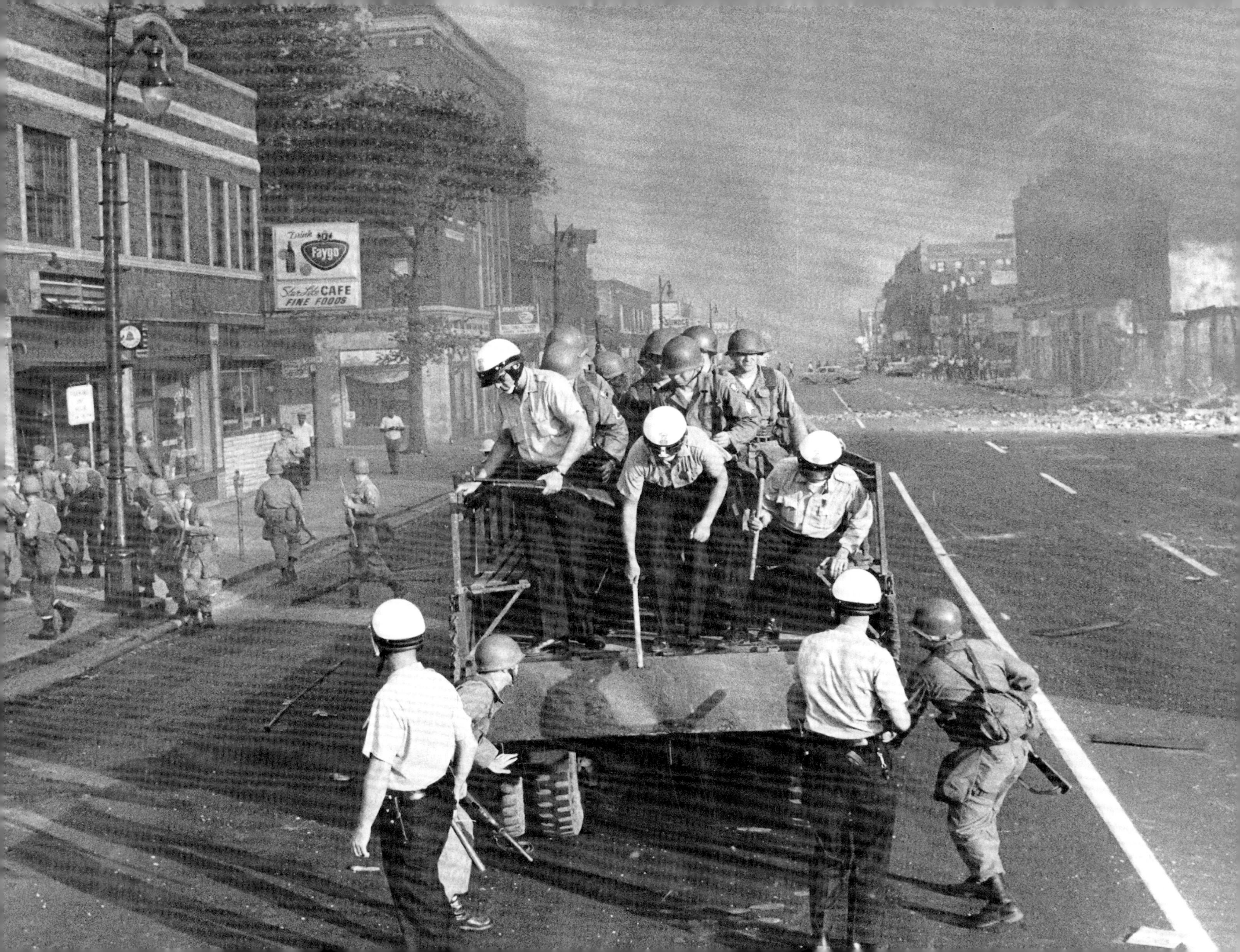
Drink
Faygo
CAFE
FINE FOODS

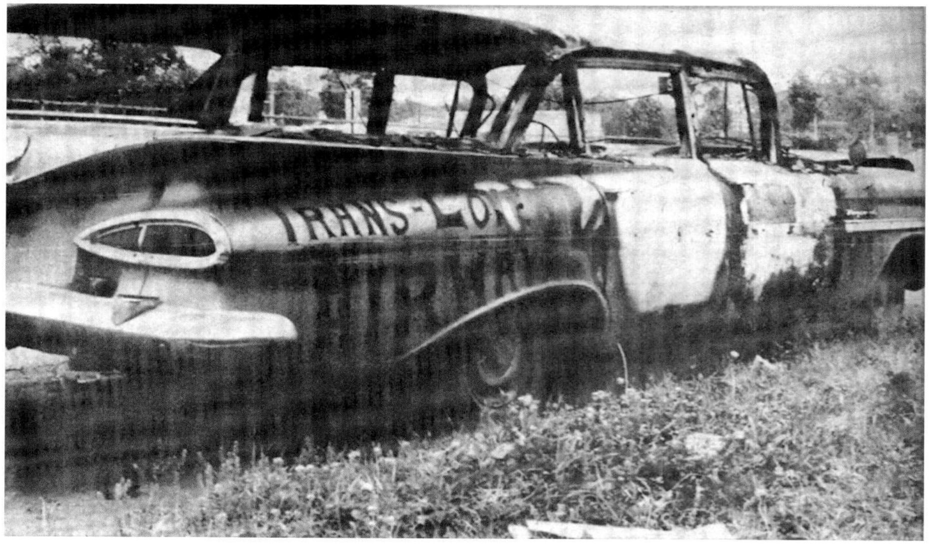

Burned car near campus, July 1967. Twelve fires were reported in the campus area, most of them burning cars. (Walter P. Reuther Library, Archives of Labor and Urban Affairs, Wayne State University.)

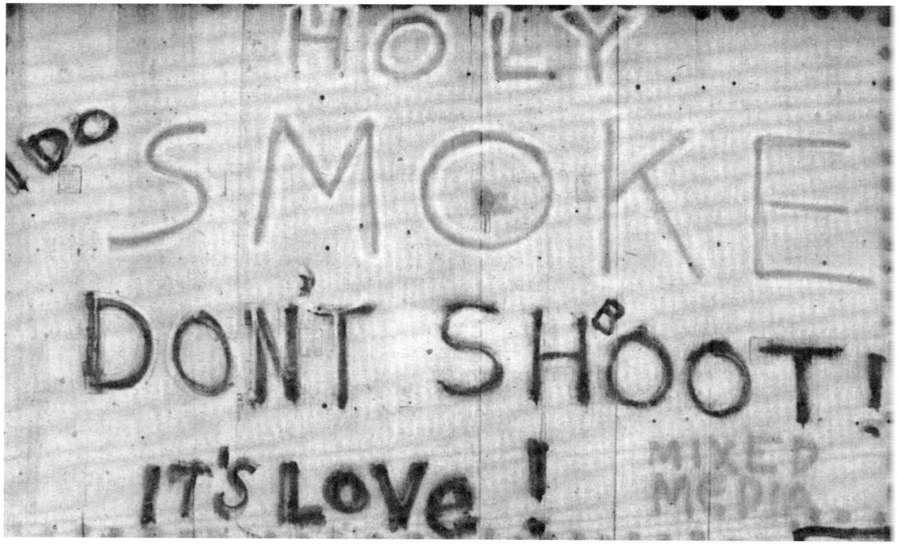

Boarded front of the Mixed Media Bookstore, 5704 Cass Avenue at Palmer Street, July 1967. (Walter P. Reuther Library, Archives of Labor and Urban Affairs, Wayne State University.)

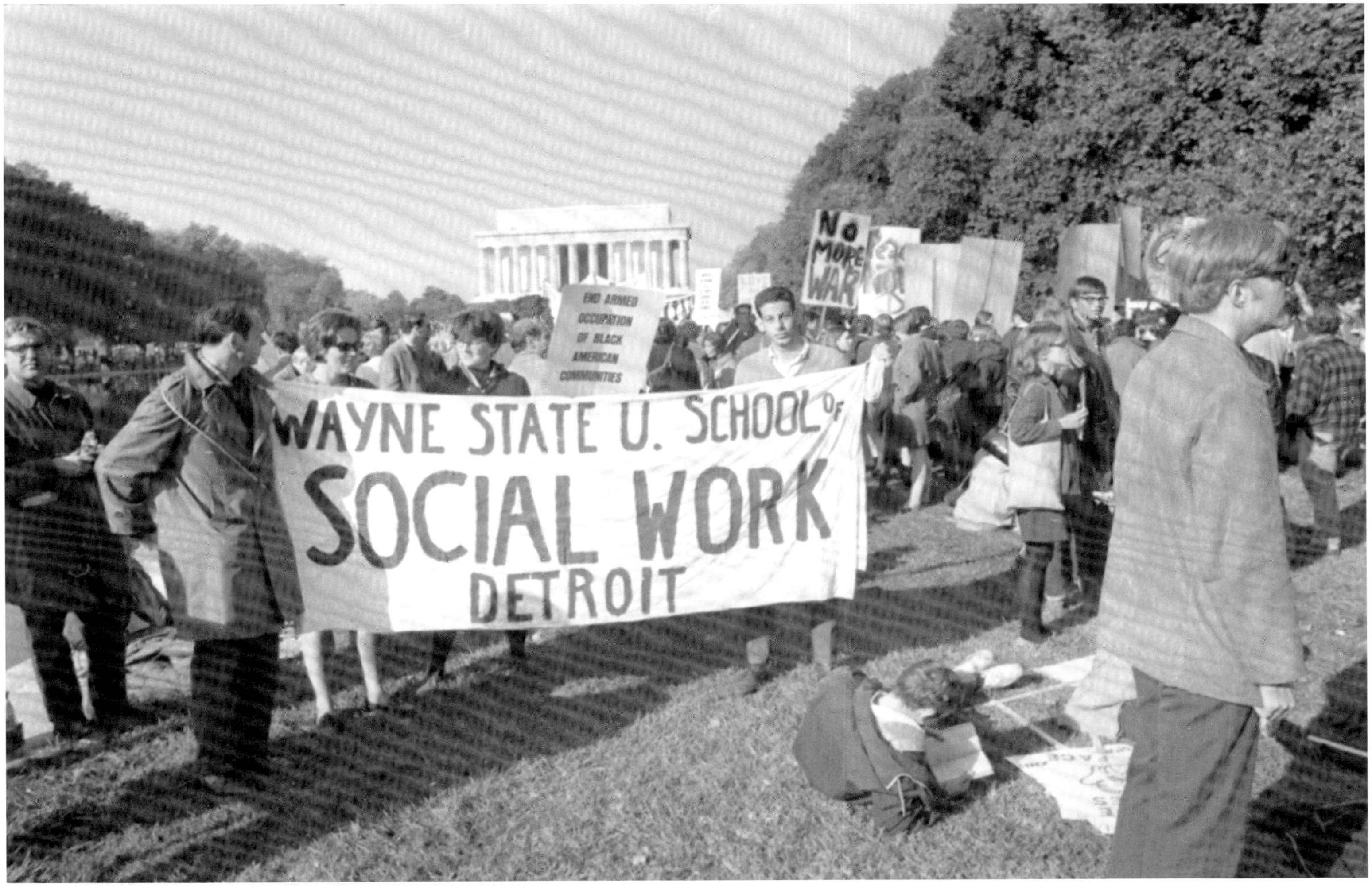

Peace demonstration, Washington, D.C., October 21, 1967. Like other college students across the country, during the late 1960s and into the 1970s, Wayne State University students were active in marches and demonstrations that advocated peace and civil rights. In this photograph, students from Wayne State's School of Social Work march at the Lincoln Memorial in Washington, D.C. (Walter P. Reuther Library, Archives of Labor and Urban Affairs, Wayne State University.)

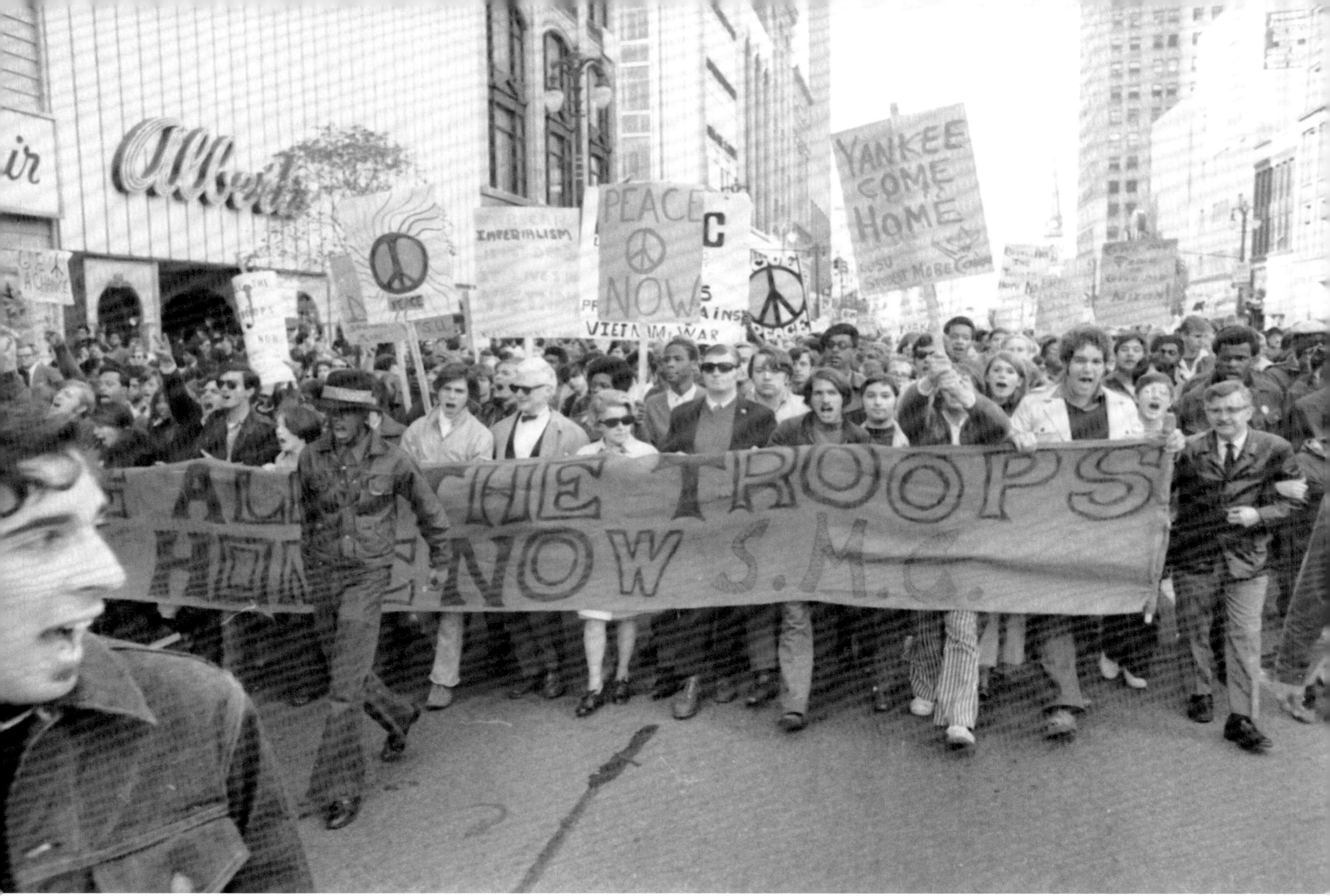
YANKEE COME HOME
PEACE NOW
IMPERIALISM
VIETNAM WAR
PEACE
THE TROOPS
NOW S.M.C.

Peace demonstration on Woodward, October 15, 1969. (Walter P. Reuther Library, Archives of Labor and Urban Affairs, Wayne State University.)

Peace demonstration on Woodward Avenue near downtown, October 15, 1969. This photograph, taken on Moratorium Day, shows one of many peace marches that included Wayne State students—and in this case, Wayne State's president. The white-haired man wearing sunglasses and a bowtie and marching just behind the banner is the university president. (Walter P. Reuther Library, Archives of Labor and Urban Affairs, Wayne State University.)

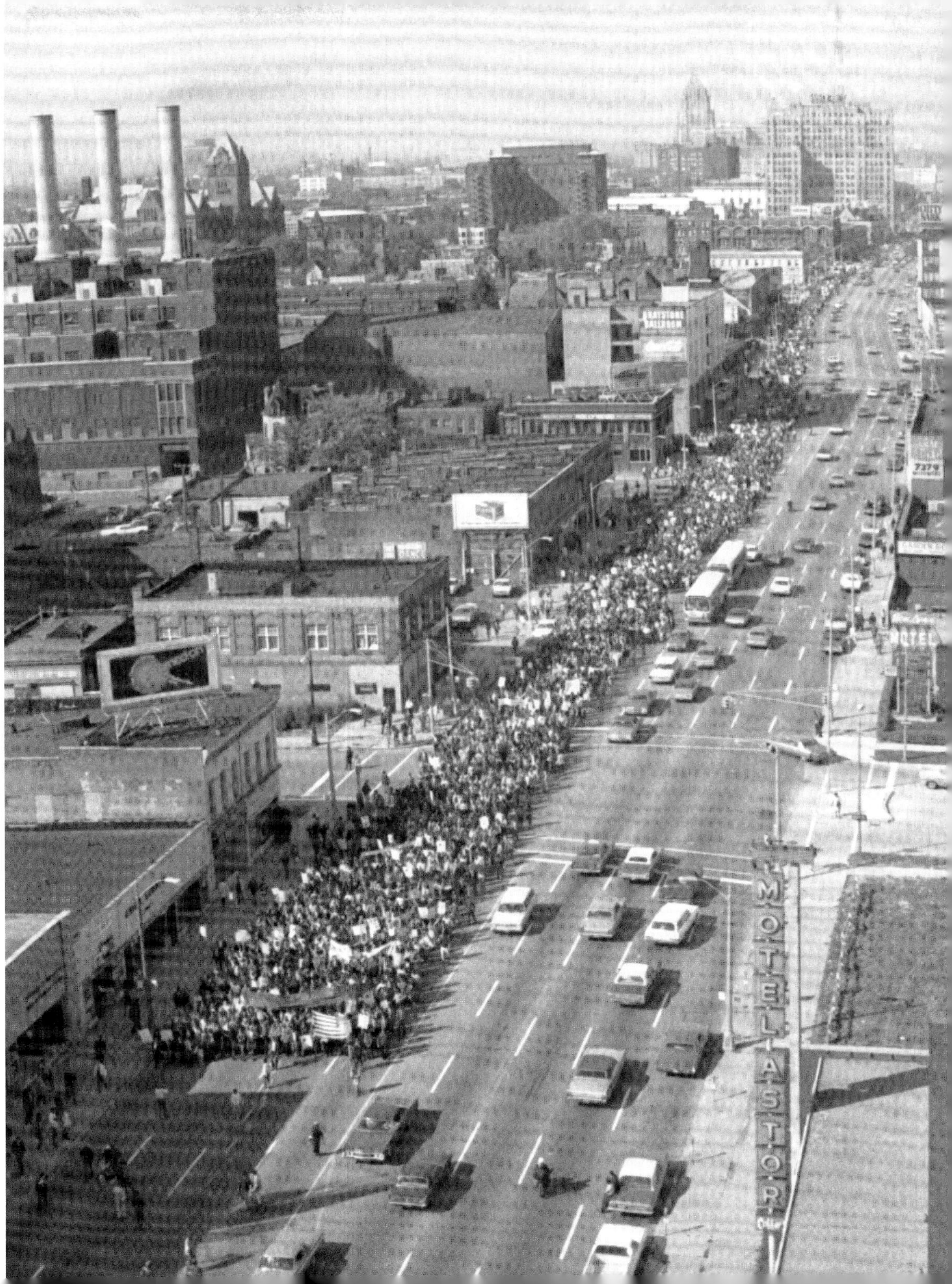

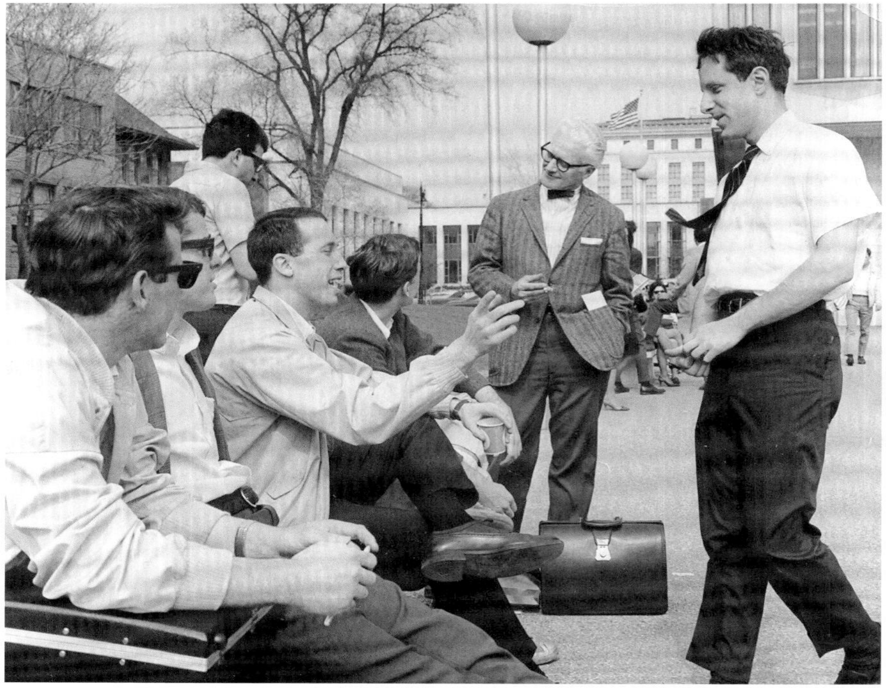

President Keast with students, outside the General Library, 1960s. President William Rea Keast, the man in the suit and bowtie, was largely responsible for holding Wayne State University together during the tumultuous late 1960s. He came under mounting pressure to clamp down on campus demonstrations and to closely regulate the *South End*, the student newspaper that was becoming increasingly radical. He is remembered for advocating moderation and for his ability to relate to students. (Walter P. Reuther Library, Archives of Labor and Urban Affairs, Wayne State University.)

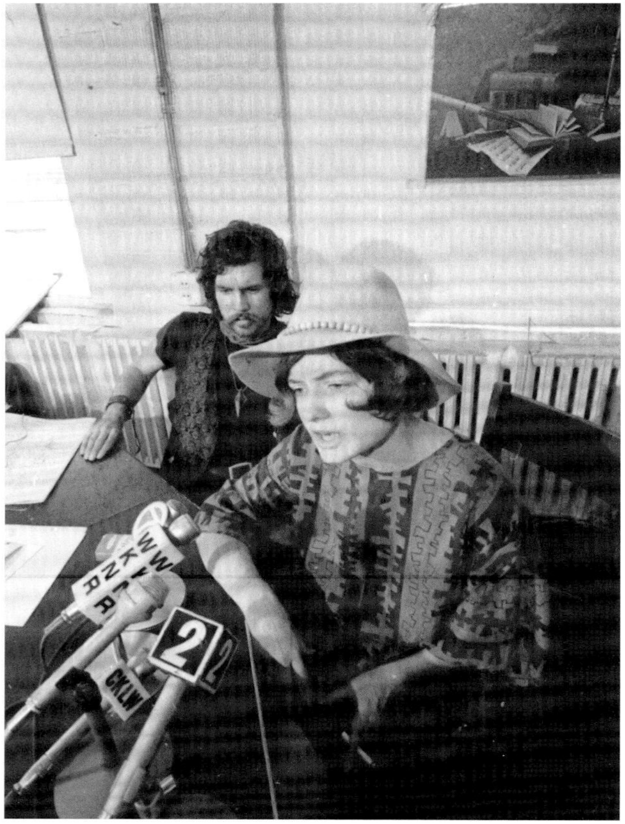

Editors of the *South End* speaking to reporters, July 11, 1969. In September 1967, a group of Wayne State University students changed the name of the student newspaper from the *Daily Collegian* to the *South End* and radically altered the paper's look and content, focusing coverage on antiwar protests, civil rights, and the drug culture. Pictured is Cheryl McCall, editor of the paper, speaking after Wayne State University president Keast temporarily suspended publication of the *South End*. Sitting next to McCall is Art Johnston, who had been the first editor of the revamped paper. The name, the *South End*, referred to the location of the student newspaper offices—near the Cass Corridor—in relation to the administrative offices on the north end of campus. The new title of the paper also expressed solidarity with the residents of the Cass Corridor as opposed to those of the wealthier New Center area and General Motors to the north. (Walter P. Reuther Library, Archives of Labor and Urban Affairs, Wayne State University.)

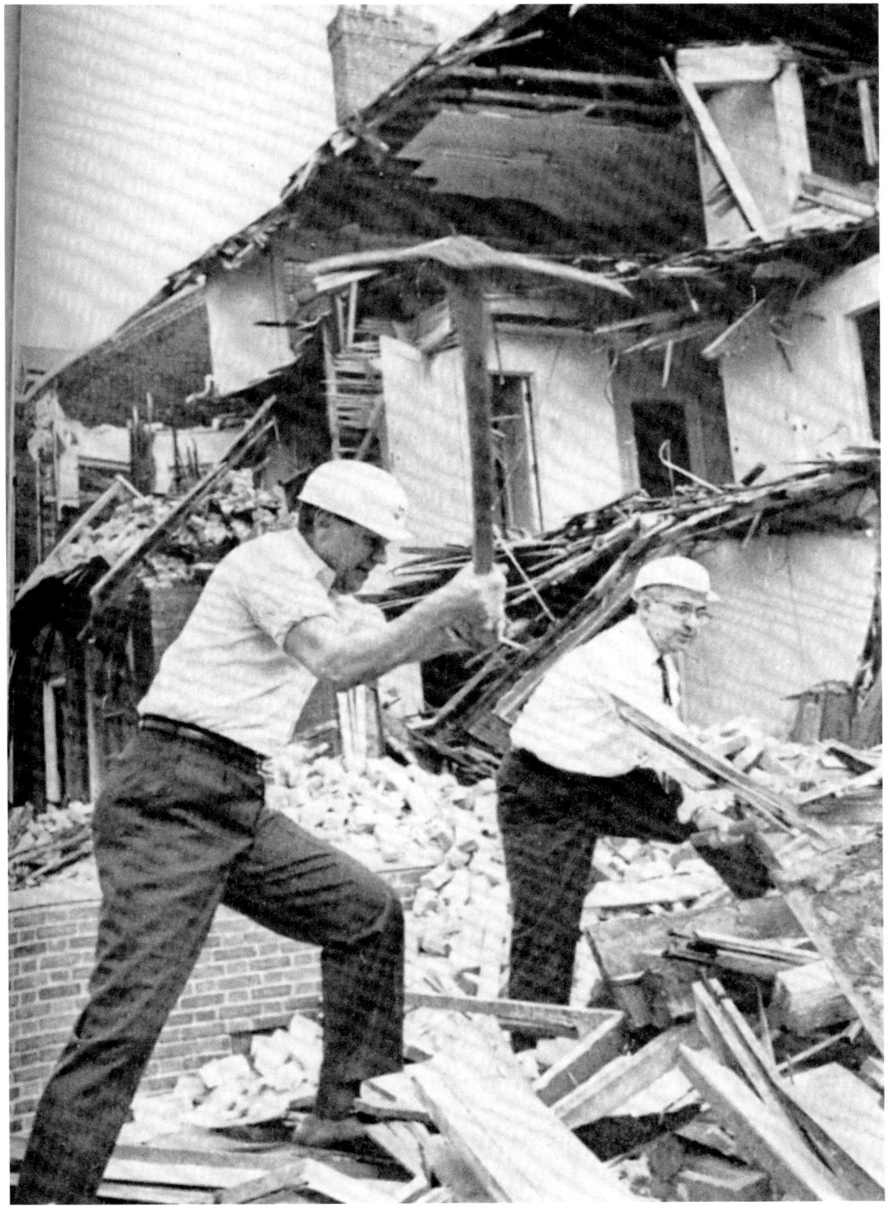

Faculty members knocking down houses, May 10, 1967. Motivated by the promise of new office space, chemistry professor Calvin Stevens, left, and department vice chairman, David Boltz, help clear room for construction of the Chemistry Building and the Science Library (later renamed the Science and Engineering Library). During the next decade, however, public attitudes toward the demolition of old houses on campus would change drastically. (Walter P. Reuther Library, Archives of Labor and Urban Affairs, Wayne State University.)

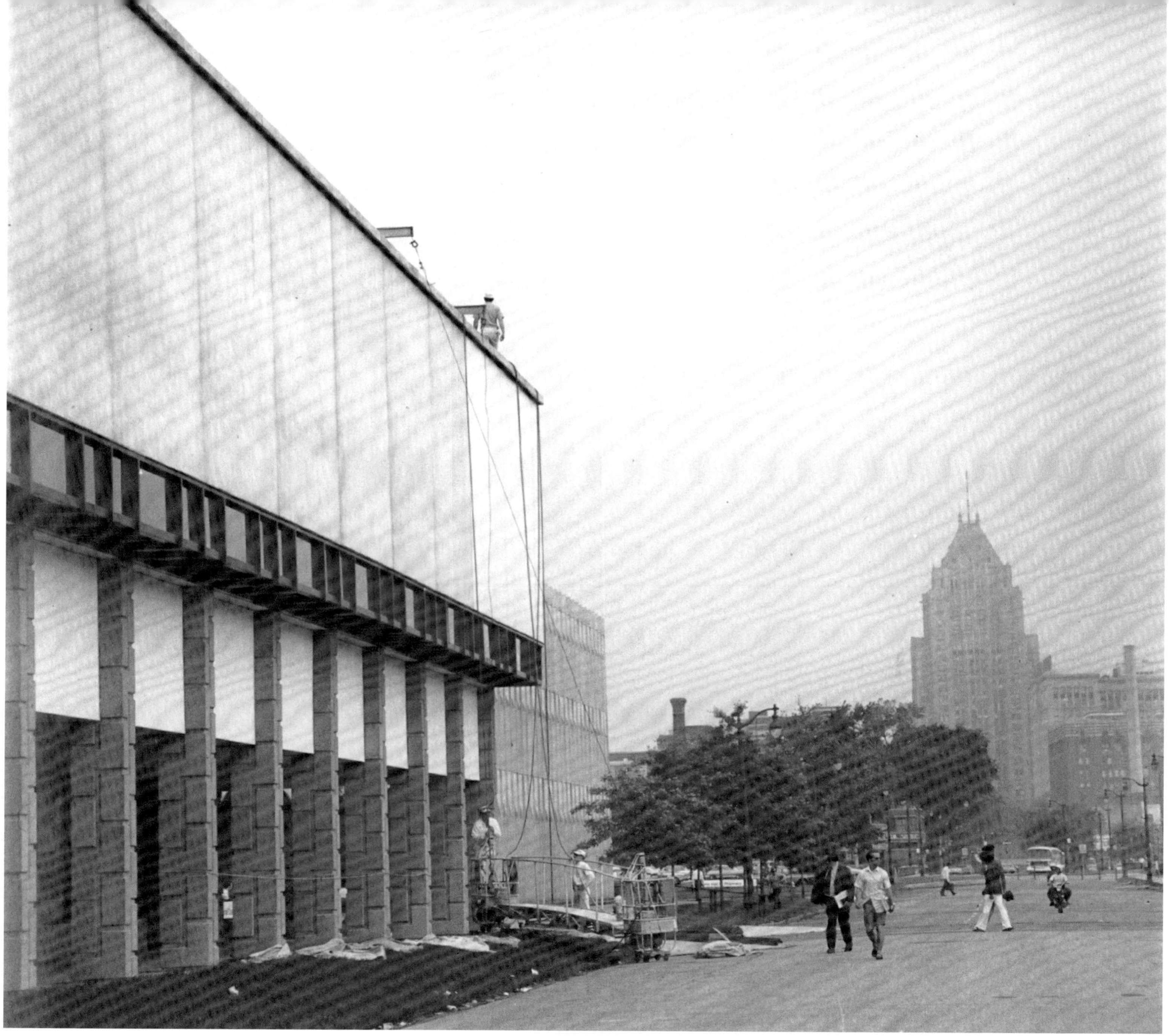

Construction of University Center, 5221 Second Avenue Mall, late 1960s. Originally named University Center, the building became known as the Student Center in 1974. Like Mackenzie Hall, University Center provided space for student organizations, food service, and the Grosberg Religious Center. After 1969, Mackenzie housed primarily administrative and faculty services. Completed in 1969, University Center was built on Second Avenue between Merrick and Kirby streets. The Fisher Building can be seen in the distance. Apparent in this photograph is one of the more striking changes made to the area: in 1964, Second Avenue north of Warren was partially closed, and in 1966, it was completely closed to traffic. Today, it is a spacious walkway named Gullen Mall. (Walter P. Reuther Library, Archives of Labor and Urban Affairs, Wayne State University.)

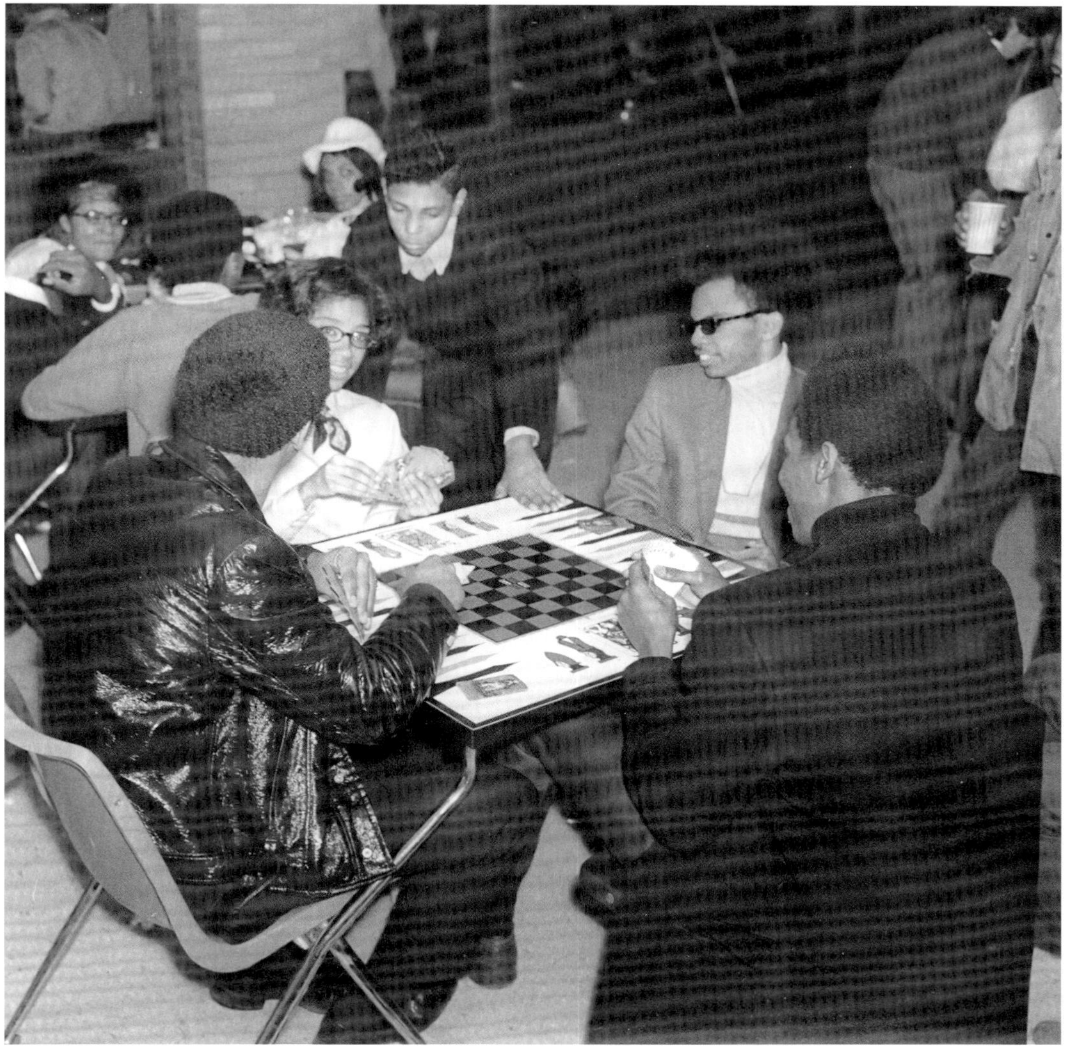

Students playing cards in University Center, 1970. Like Mackenzie Hall, University Center (the Student Center) quickly became a hangout for students. This building also benefited from being located in the center of campus, a short walk from class for all Wayne State students. (Walter P. Reuther Library, Archives of Labor and Urban Affairs, Wayne State University.)

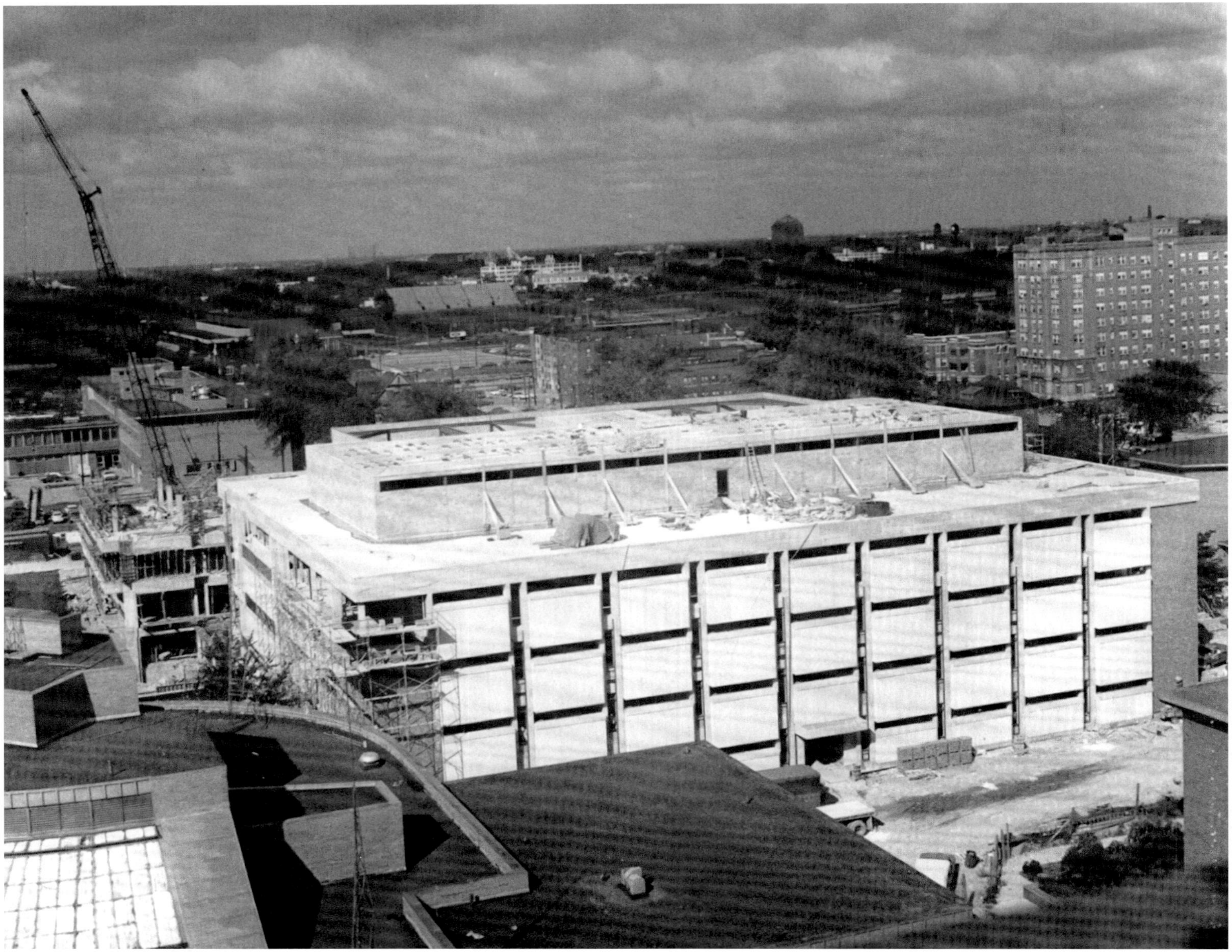

Chemistry Building under construction, eastern facade, 5101 Cass, 1968. This picture looks over the roof of Science Hall, lower left, at the Chemistry Building. The Science Library, behind the Chemistry Building and marked by the crane, is also under construction. Chatsworth Tower Apartments can be seen in the distance at the right. The Chemistry Building was completed in January 1970. (Walter P. Reuther Library, Archives of Labor and Urban Affairs, Wayne State University.)

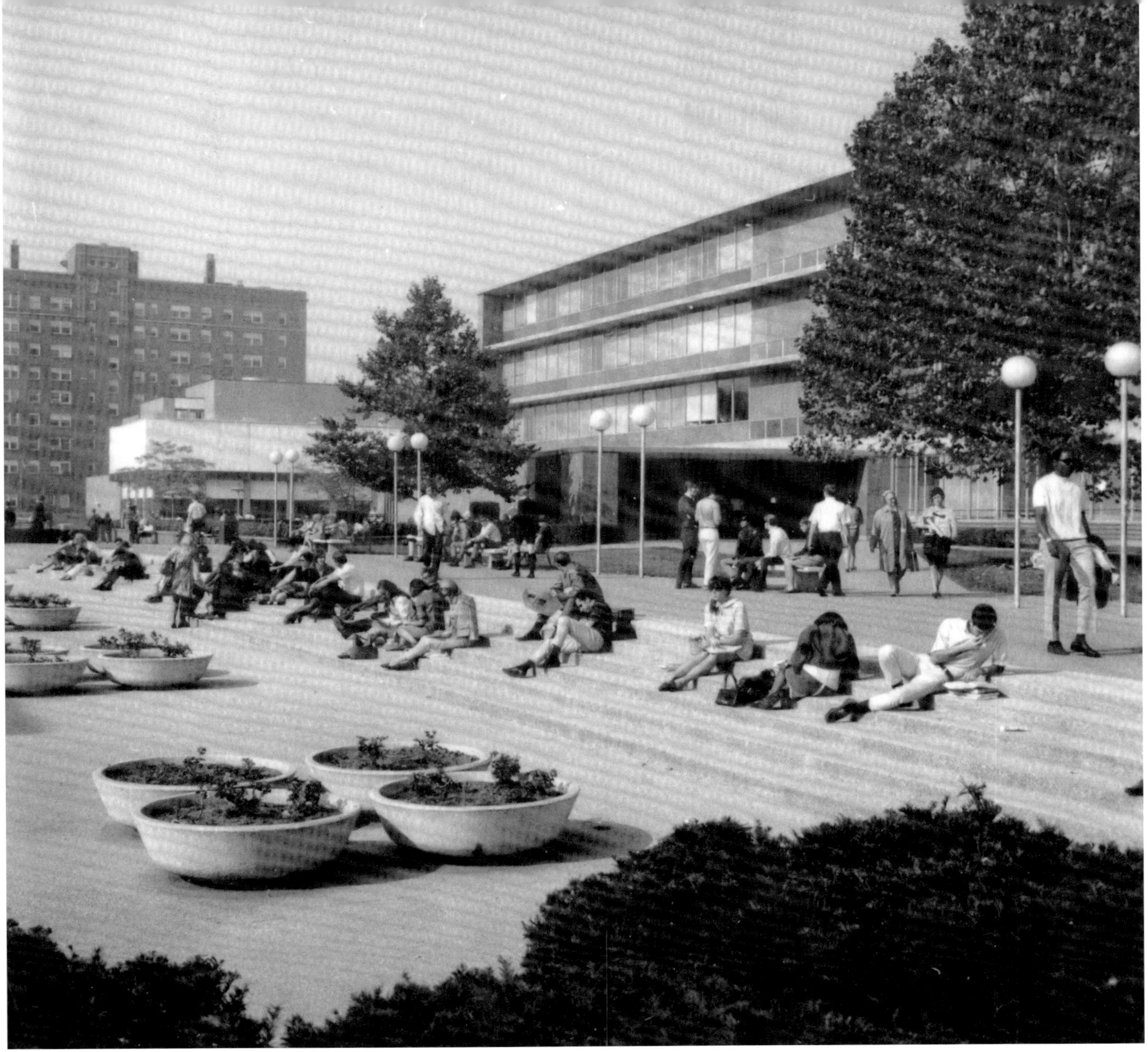

Students studying on DeRoy Auditorium's steps, as seen looking northwest, 1968. The General Library can be seen behind the students. University Center (the Student Center), with the Chatsworth Tower behind it, is on the left. The General Library was renamed the G. Flint Purdy Library in 1972. Purdy, the head librarian in 1936, played an essential role in ensuring that the library was constructed. The Purdy Library would later become the graduate library. As Wayne State focused less on undergraduate and more on graduate and professional enrollment, the rising numbers of masters and doctoral students warranted a library that catered to their needs. (Walter P. Reuther Library, Archives of Labor and Urban Affairs, Wayne State University.)

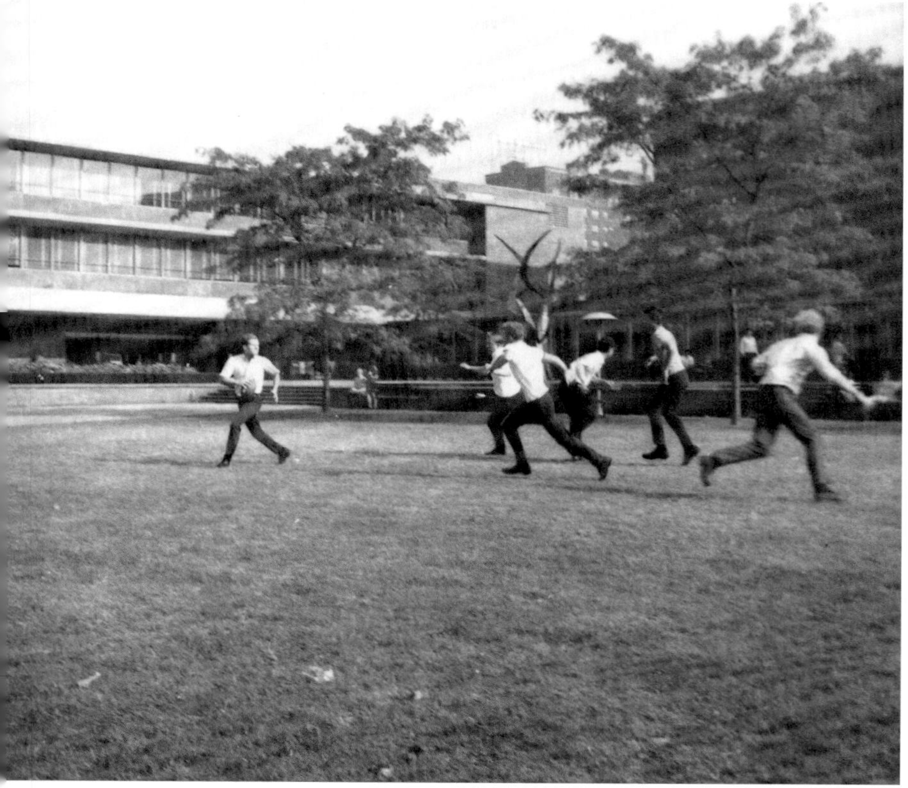

Students playing football, 1968. These students are playing on the lawn in front of the General and Kresge libraries, where today the Fitness Center is located. The Belcrest, obscured by a tree, can be seen in the background on the right. *The Wings of Learning*, a statue designed by G. Alden Smith of Wayne State's art department, rises in front of the libraries, beyond the football players. (Walter P. Reuther Library, Archives of Labor and Urban Affairs, Wayne State University.)

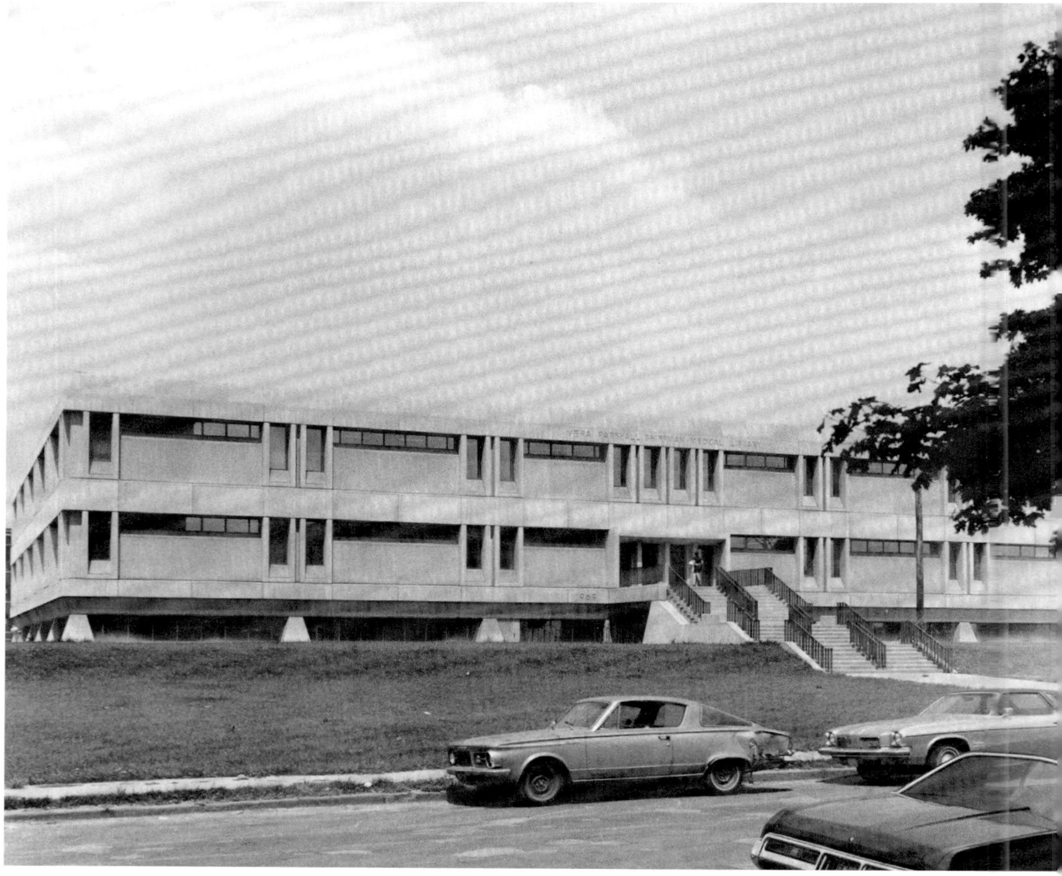

The Medical Library, 4325 Brush Street at Canfield Street, 1973. Officially named the Vera Parshall Shiffman Medical Library, it was the second of two new university buildings located in the group of hospitals known as the Detroit Medical Center. The first, the Helen Vera Prentis Lande Medical Research Building, had been completed in 1965. (Walter P. Reuther Library, Archives of Labor and Urban Affairs, Wayne State University.)

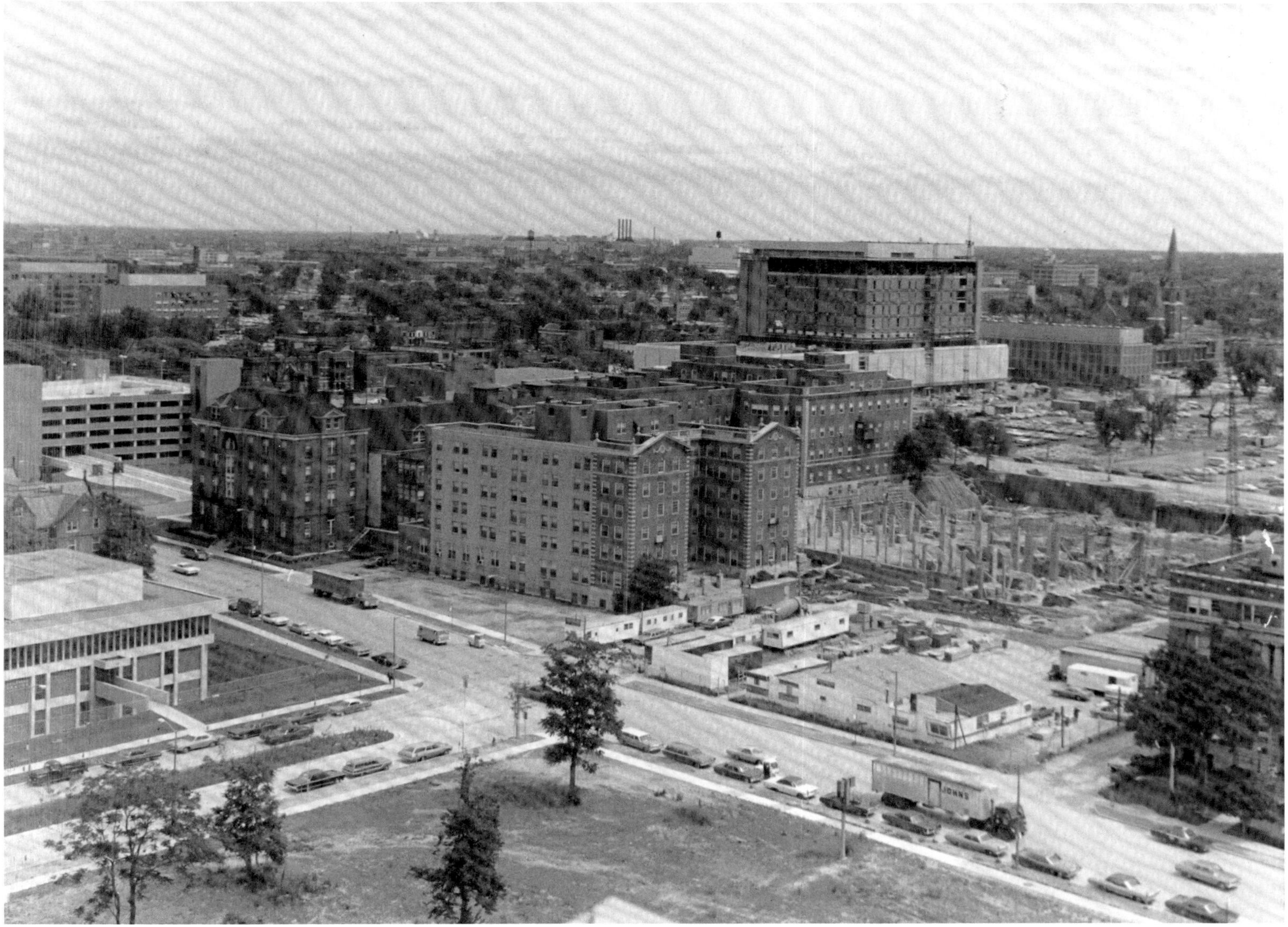

The Detroit Medical Center, as seen looking northeast, about 1971. Harper Hospital is the horseshoe-shaped building at the center of the photo. The Webber Wings of the hospital are under construction. The Gordon H. Scott Hall of Basic Medical Sciences is the tall building in the background, right of center. Scott Hall, located just three blocks away from the original site of the Detroit Medical College and built more than one hundred years later, houses the departments of anatomy, psychology, pharmacology, biochemistry, microbiology, and pathology. The Medical Research Building is the smaller building to the right of Scott Hall. (Walter P. Reuther Library, Archives of Labor and Urban Affairs, Wayne State University.)

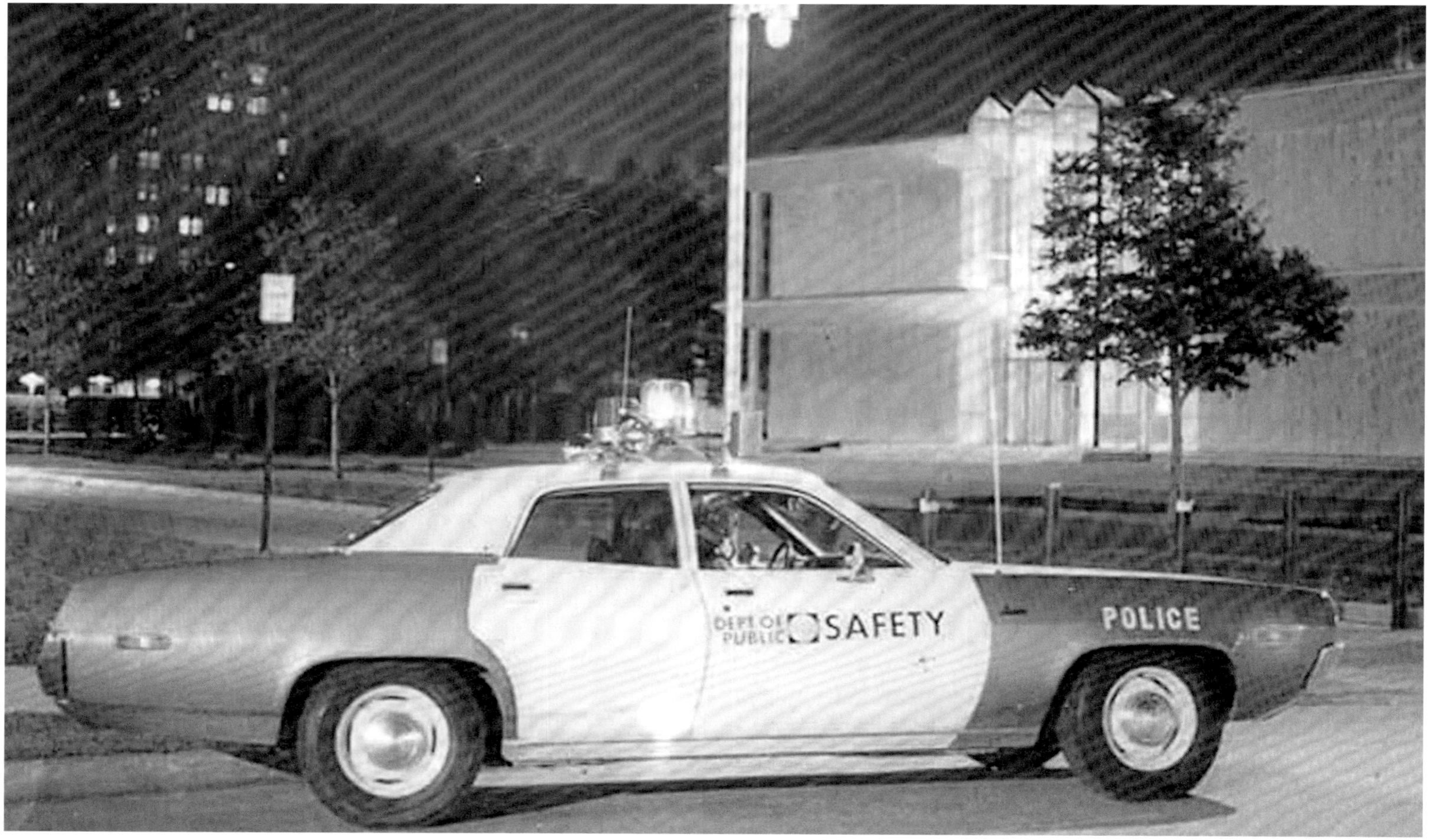

Members of the Wayne State University police force patrolling the campus at night, 1970s. In 1966, Wayne State established its own Department of Public Safety, staffed by deputized and armed police officers. Prior to that time, campus security was entrusted to seventeen unarmed watchmen with no police authority. A rising crime rate, coupled with pressure from students and faculty members, convinced the administration to organize a professional police force. Directly behind the squad car there is a light and telephone, part of the Blue Light Phone System, a network that connected directly to the Department of Public Safety. The lighted building just beyond the car is the McGregor Memorial Conference Center. On the left, the lighted windows of the Belcrest Apartments can be seen in the distance. (Courtesy of the Wayne State University Police Department.)

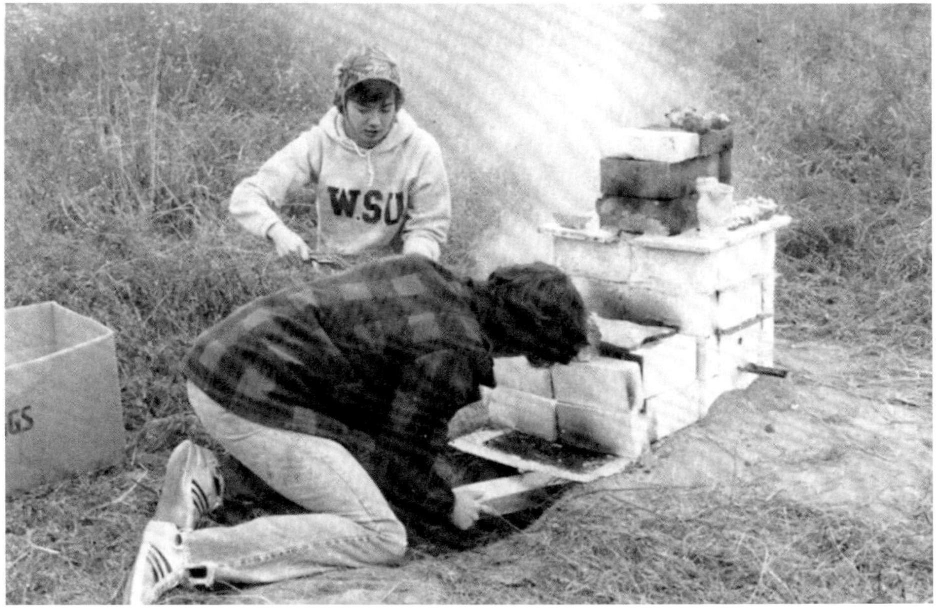

Art students firing ceramic pottery, 1973. (Walter P. Reuther Library, Archives of Labor and Urban Affairs, Wayne State University.)

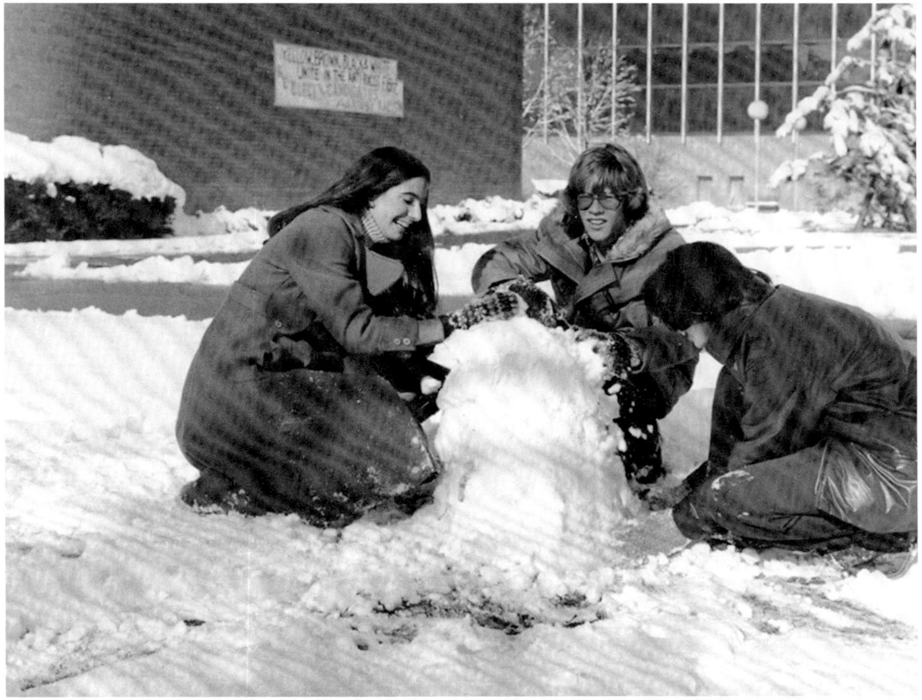

Students making a snowman, 1974. The sign on the building behind them, State Hall, reads: "Yellow, Brown, Black & White / Unite in the Anti-Racist Fight / Elect Candidates Against Racism." (Walter P. Reuther Library, Archives of Labor and Urban Affairs, Wayne State University.)

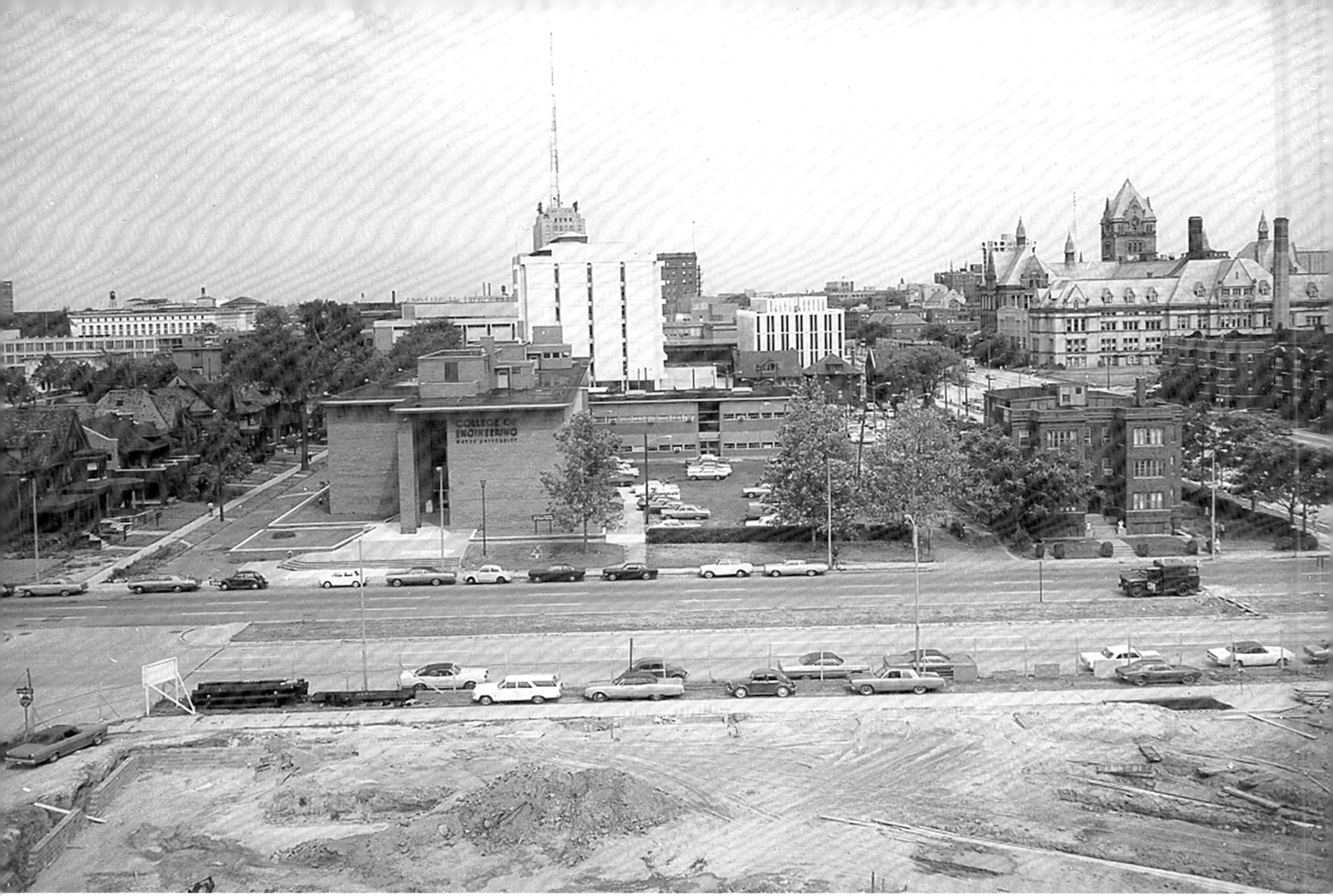
COLLEGE OF
ENGINEERING

College of Engineering, as seen looking east, 1970. This photograph was taken seventeen years before the major addition to the Engineering Building was completed. The white Chemistry Building rises behind the Engineering Building, at the center of the photograph, while Anthony Wayne Drive runs horizontally across the bottom of the photograph. The section of Third Avenue that runs past Wayne State University's campus was renamed Anthony Wayne Drive in 1968, honoring the general for whom Wayne County and Wayne State University are named. The row of houses on the far left stand on Merrick Street (now Williams Mall). Old Main can be seen on the far right. (Walter P. Reuther Library, Archives of Labor and Urban Affairs, Wayne State University.)

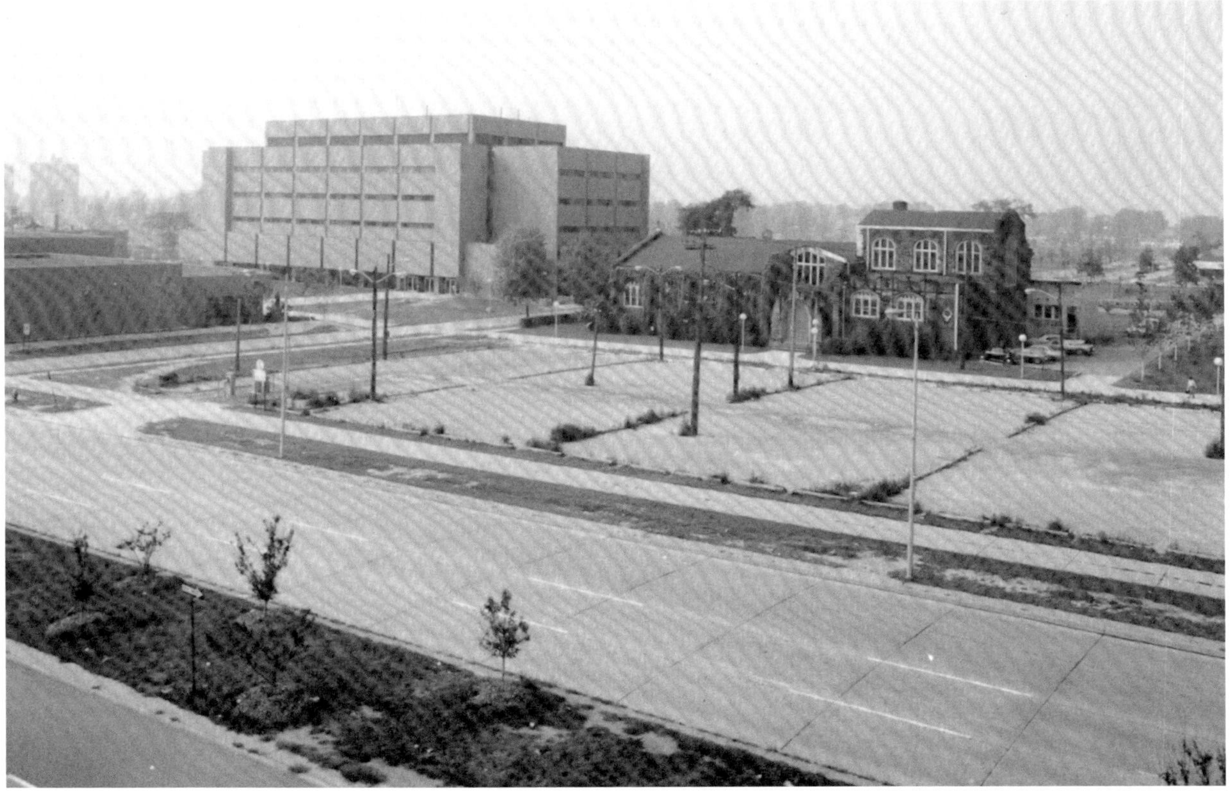

Speech and Languages Building, 906 W. Warren, as seen looking west, 1973. Anthony Wayne Drive is pictured in the foreground. The dark building with the white window frames on the right is a former church, St. Andrew's Hall. The taller, pale building left of center is the Speech and Languages Building, and the dark, low building on the far left is the General Lectures Building. The Speech and Languages Building was renamed Alex Manoogian Hall in 1975. (Walter P. Reuther Library, Archives of Labor and Urban Affairs, Wayne State University.)

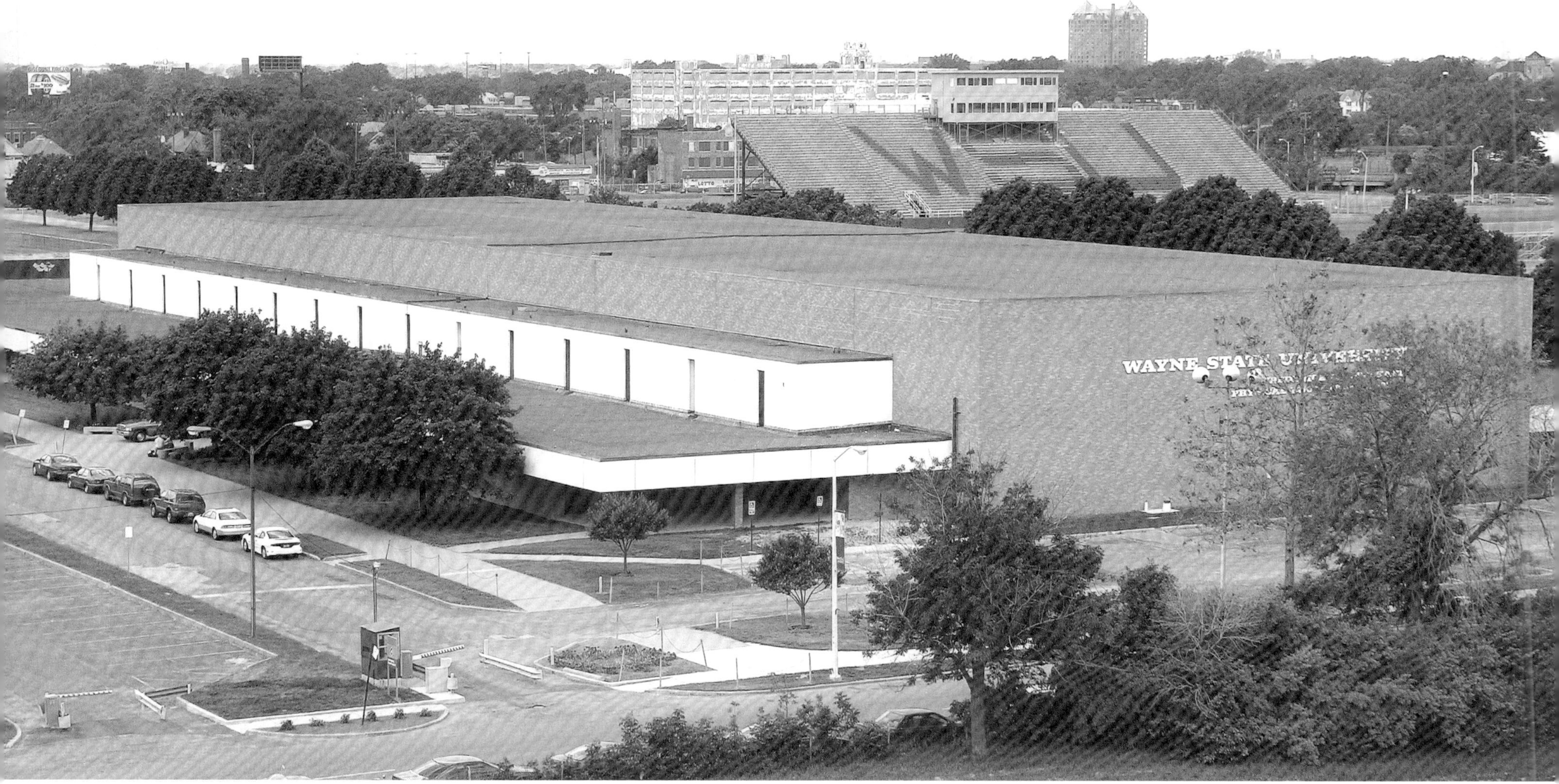

The Frederick C. Matthaei Physical Education Center, 5101 John Lodge Freeway at Warren Avenue, as seen looking west, undated. After years of practicing on different fields and stadiums across the city, Wayne State's athletes finally got a permanent sports facility in 1967. The physical education complex included three gyms, two swimming pools, a baseball diamond, tennis courts, practice fields, and a football stadium. Built between the Lodge and Ford expressways, it was part of Phase I of the controversial University City urban renewal project. The building was named for Frederick Matthaei, who had headed the Capital Gifts Committee that helped finance Cobo Hall and Wayne State's Community Arts Center. (Courtesy of Wayne State University Photographic Services.)

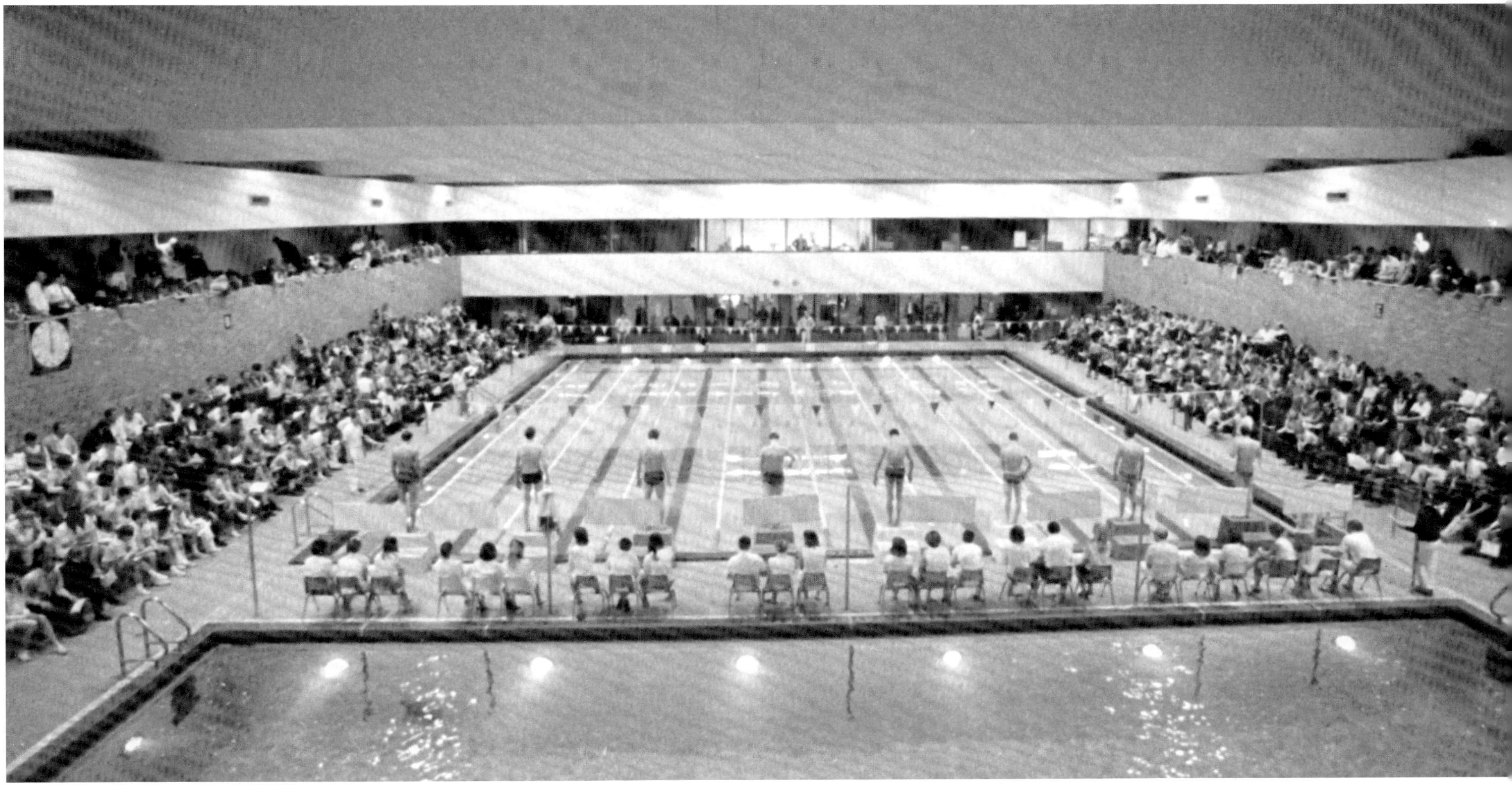

Athletic swimming pool in Matthaei Center, February 1969. Much grander than the Webster Hall swimming pool, the pool at the Matthaei Center allowed Wayne to host events such as the Michigan Invitational Championship. Swimmers wait on the diving blocks as a large crowd watches. Several years later, in 1974, athletics at Wayne State would get a boost when the university joined the Great Lakes Intercollegiate Conference. (Walter P. Reuther Library, Archives of Labor and Urban Affairs, Wayne State University.)

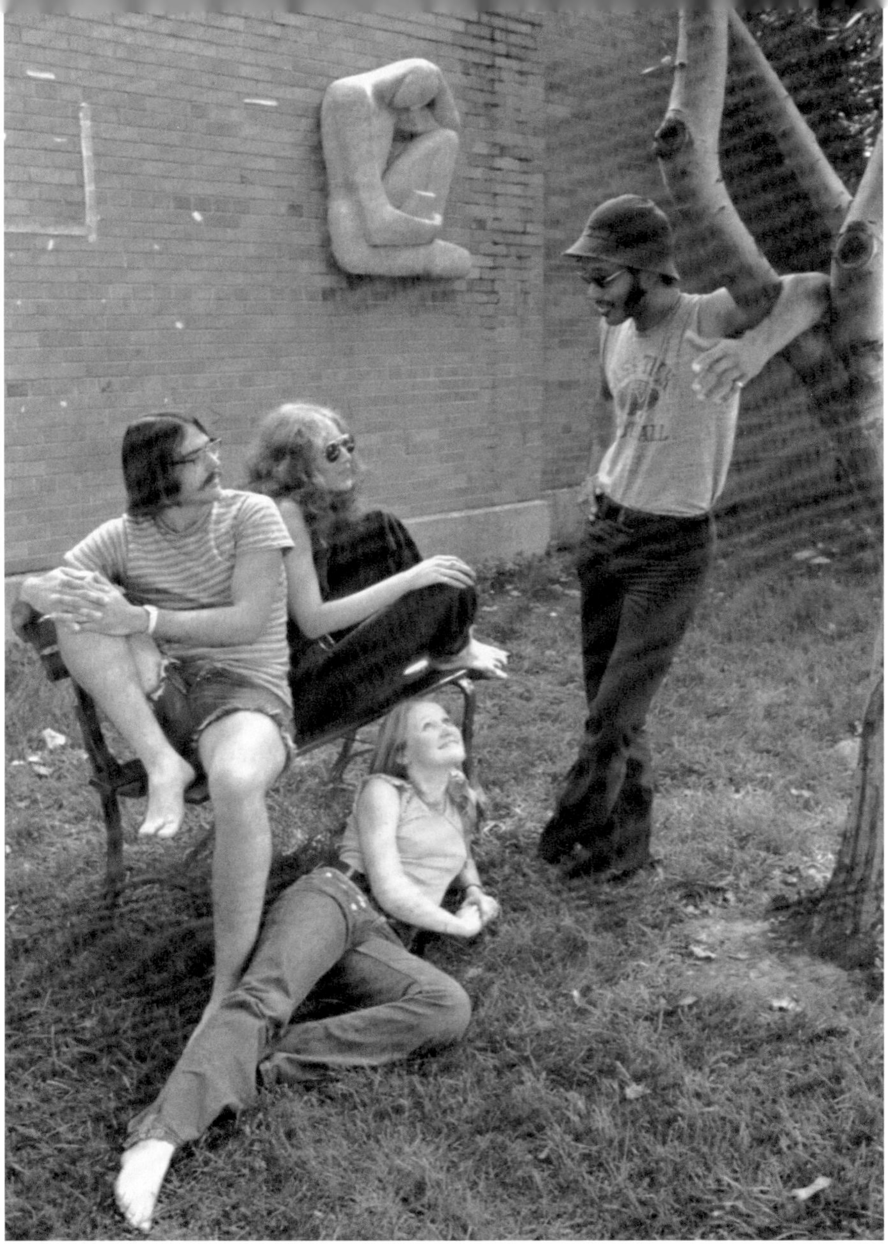

Students outside State Hall, 1970s. The statue on the building behind the students was designed by G. Alden Smith, a member of the university's art department, and was mounted when the building was dedicated in 1949. (Walter P. Reuther Library, Archives of Labor and Urban Affairs, Wayne State University.)

David Mackenzie House as the Campus Treasure Shop, 4735 Cass, 1977. Built in 1895, this house was designed by the same architect who designed Old Main. More significantly for Wayne State history, it was home to David Mackenzie, who first organized college classes at Old Main when it was Central High School. Mackenzie and his wife, Esther, lived in the house from 1906 until his death in 1926. His wife continued to live there until 1935, and the house was used successively as the University's Women's Building, offices for the College of Education, and finally as a resale shop. In response to Wayne State's plan to demolish the Mackenzie House in 1975, a student group called Preservation Wayne (now Preservation Detroit) successfully halted its demolition and subsequently went on to stop the demolition of a number of other buildings on campus. Today, Preservation Detroit has its offices in the Mackenzie House. (Walter P. Reuther Library, Archives of Labor and Urban Affairs, Wayne State University.)

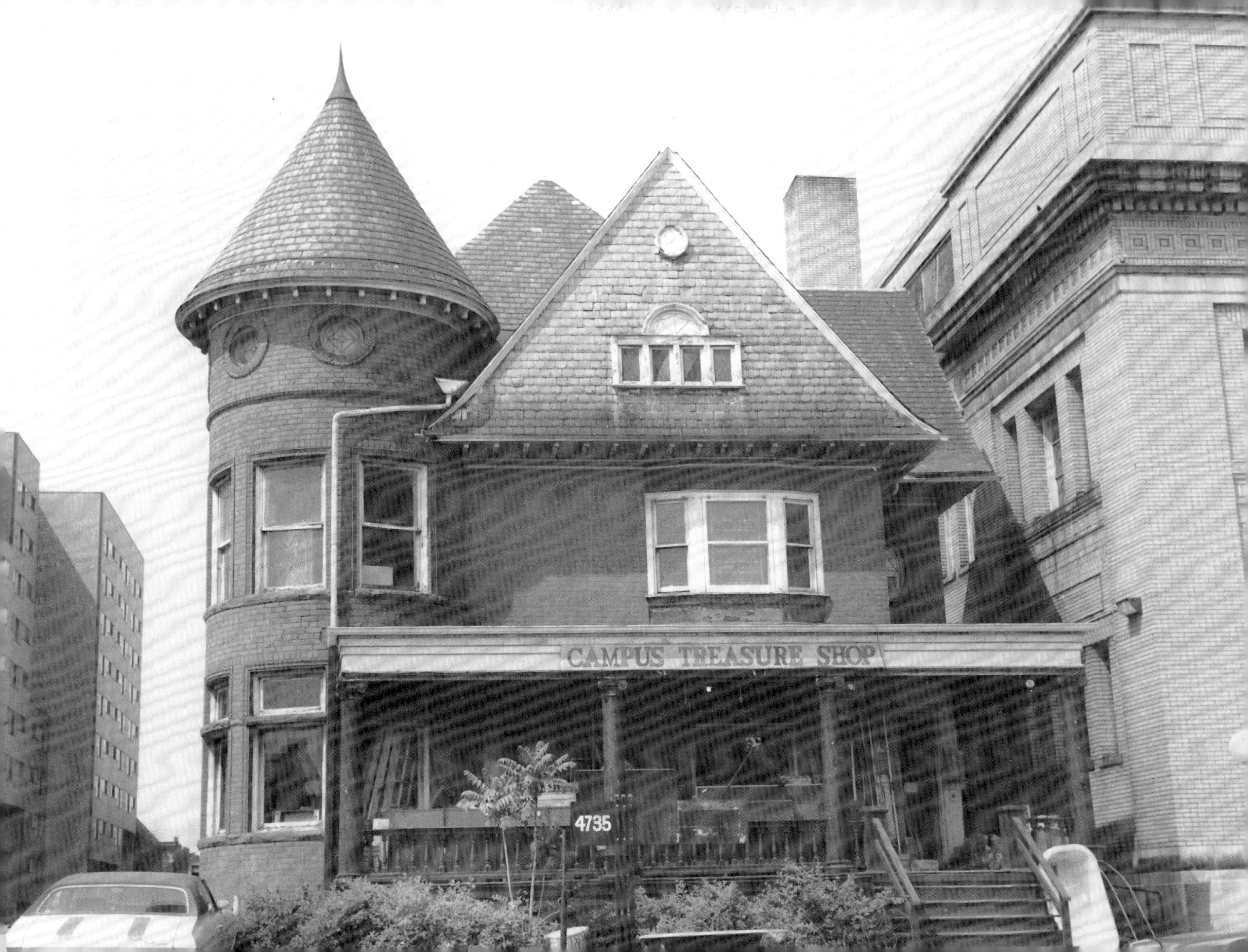
CAMPUS TREASURE SHOP
4735

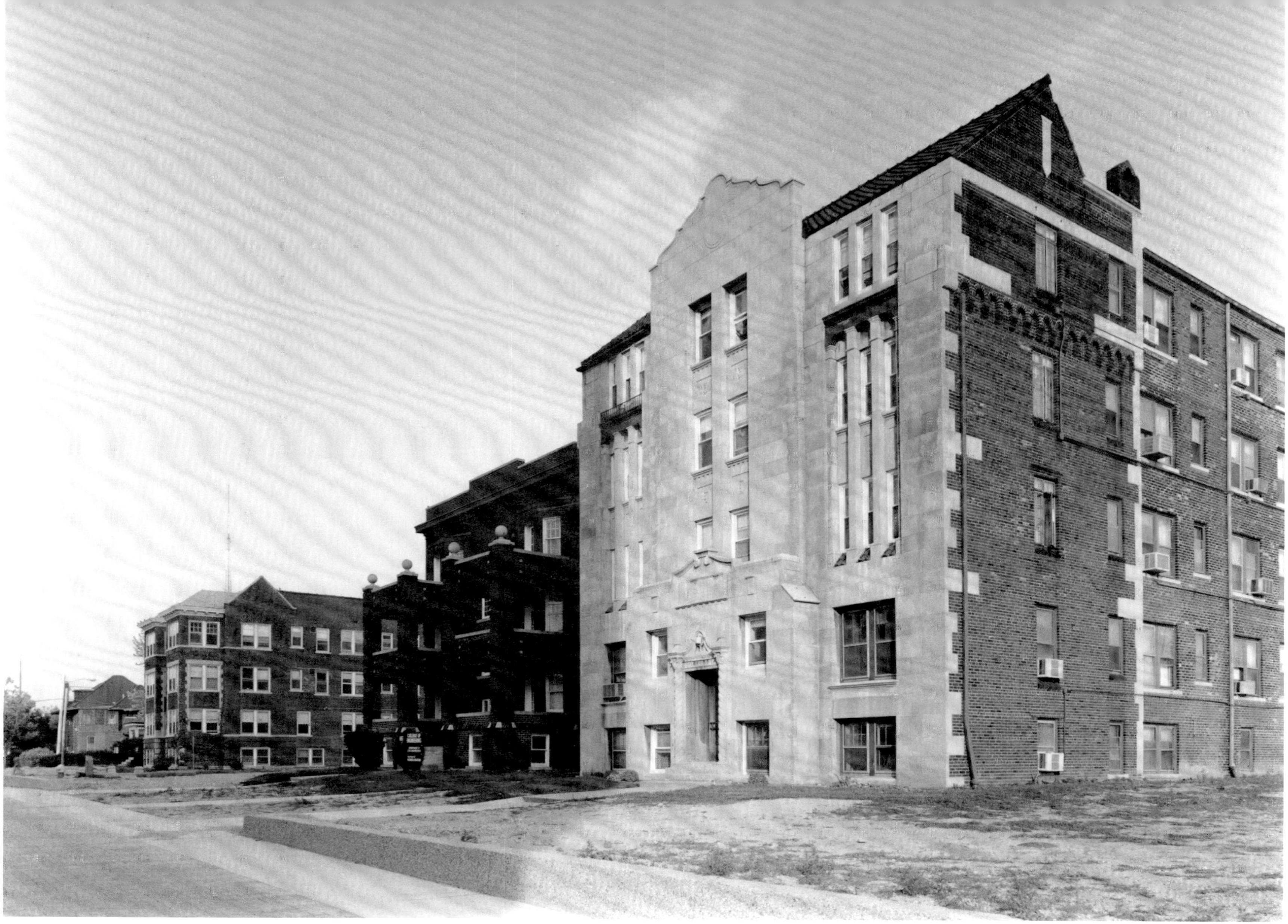

Santa Fe Apartments, 691 Merrick Street, late 1970s. The Santa Fe Apartments, the first building on the right, were located down the street from the Chatsworth Tower and Annex. The sign in front of the building to the left of the Santa Fe reads "College of Engineering/Department of Civil Engineering." The Santa Fe, along with the Katherine Faville Residence Hall and the Library Court apartments, also located on Merrick, were owned by the university and used for campus housing. In 1996, both the Santa Fe and the Faville Residence Hall were demolished for the construction of the Undergraduate Library. (Walter P. Reuther Library, Archives of Labor and Urban Affairs, Wayne State University.)

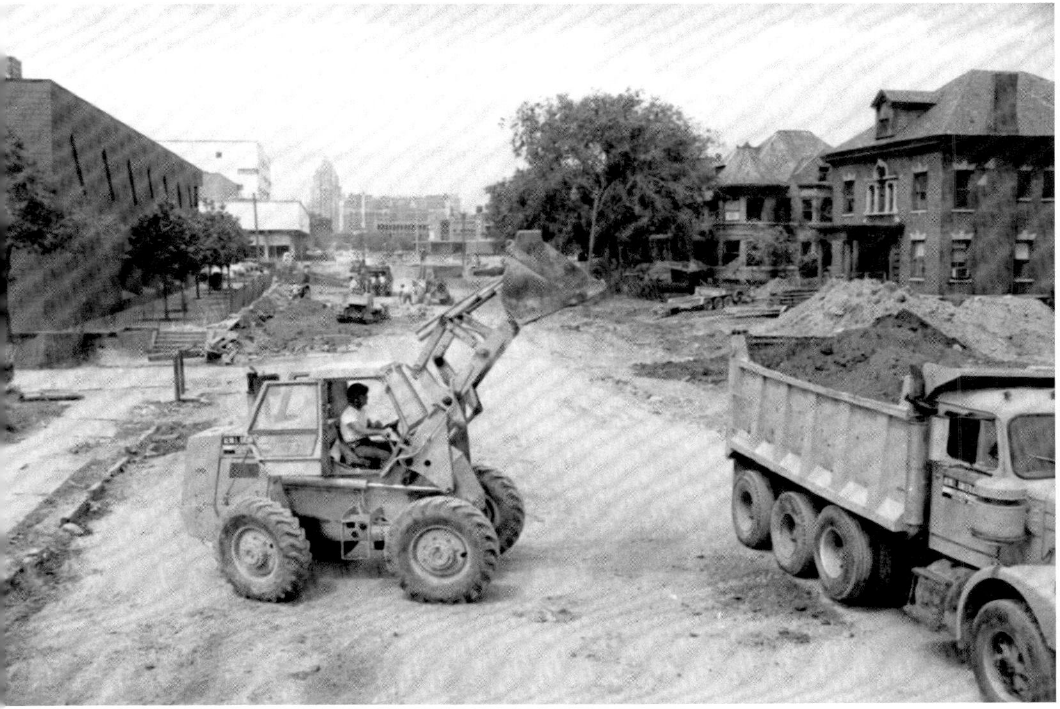

Construction on Gullen Mall, 1979. This photograph looks north down Second Avenue, soon after it was renamed Gullen Mall. Landscaping for the mall is in progress. The campus bookstore can be seen on the far left, and the Linsell House is the first home on the right. The hazy Fisher Building can be seen in the distance. (Walter P. Reuther Library, Archives of Labor and Urban Affairs, Wayne State University.)

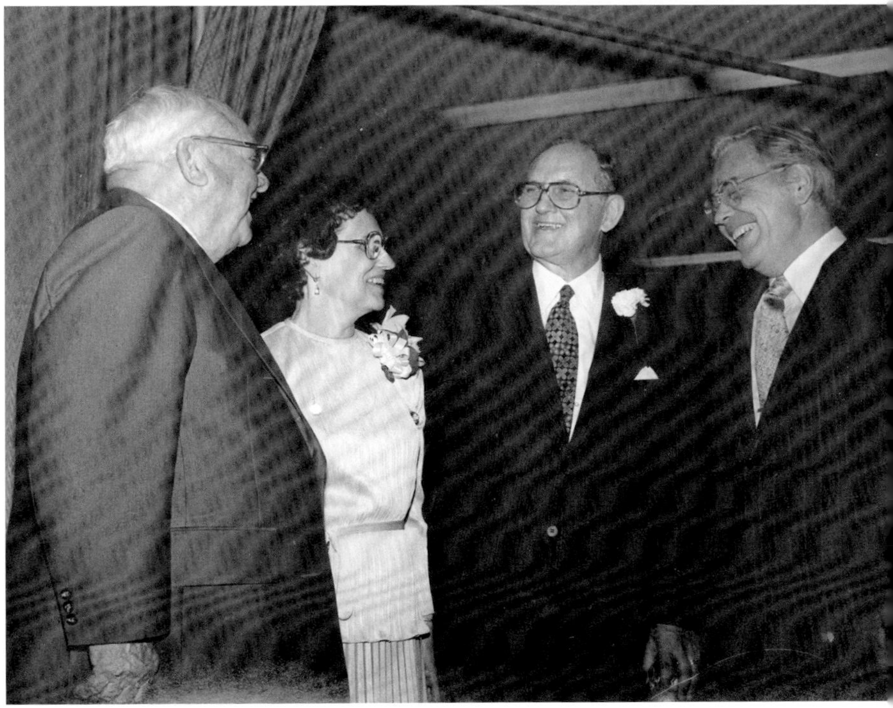

Two Wayne State University presidents, 1978. The incoming and outgoing university presidents are pictured at a tribute dinner. George Gullen, second from the right, was the outgoing president and the first university president who was also a Wayne State alumnus. During his tenure, Gullen oversaw the construction of more student housing on campus and increased emphasis on graduate programs. Wayne State University's affirmative action program was also implemented during his watch. On the far right is the incoming president, Thomas Bonner, a distinguished historian. Bonner forged relations with several international universities and oversaw the reorganization of the President's Commission on the Status of Women, which advises the president on issues concerning Wayne State University's female faculty, professors, and students. (Walter P. Reuther Library, Archives of Labor and Urban Affairs, Wayne State University.)

CHAPTER 6

THE PATH TO RENEWAL, 1980–97

During the early 1980s, Detroit was in crisis. The city was devastated by an economic recession; unemployment and crime skyrocketed, while Detroit continued to lose population to the suburbs. As the city suffered, so did the university. The university became associated with the city's problems, and Wayne State faced serious financial losses as student enrollment dropped. During this period, Wayne State officials concentrated on maintaining the university's existing buildings rather than on new construction. By the early 1990s, student enrollment began to rise again, and the university experienced a building boom after a nearly ten-year lapse in construction. In 1991, Wayne State received a Carnegie I rating, cementing its reputation as a quality research institution, while it sought to maintain affordable tuition.

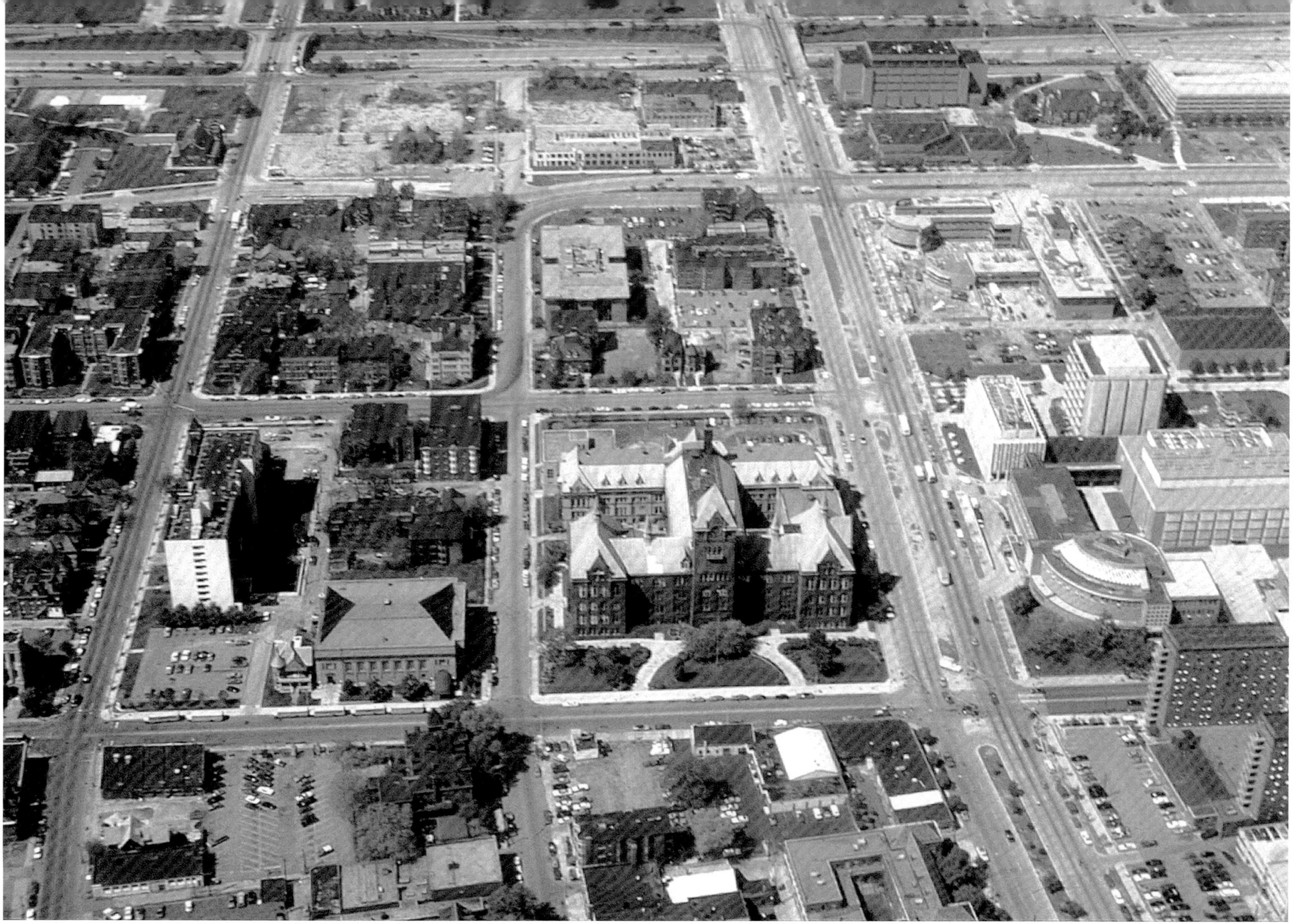

Aerial view of campus, looking west, 1986. Old Main sits in the center of the picture, and Mackenzie Hall and Science Hall are visible in the lower right corner. The upper right quadrant of the photograph shows increased development on the west end of the campus: the low, dark General Lectures Building and the taller Manoogian Hall are seen on the right, and across Anthony Wayne Drive, to the east, the curved addition to the Engineering Building. Neither the Undergraduate Library nor the Biological Sciences Building has been constructed yet. (Walter P. Reuther Library, Archives of Labor and Urban Affairs, Wayne State University.)

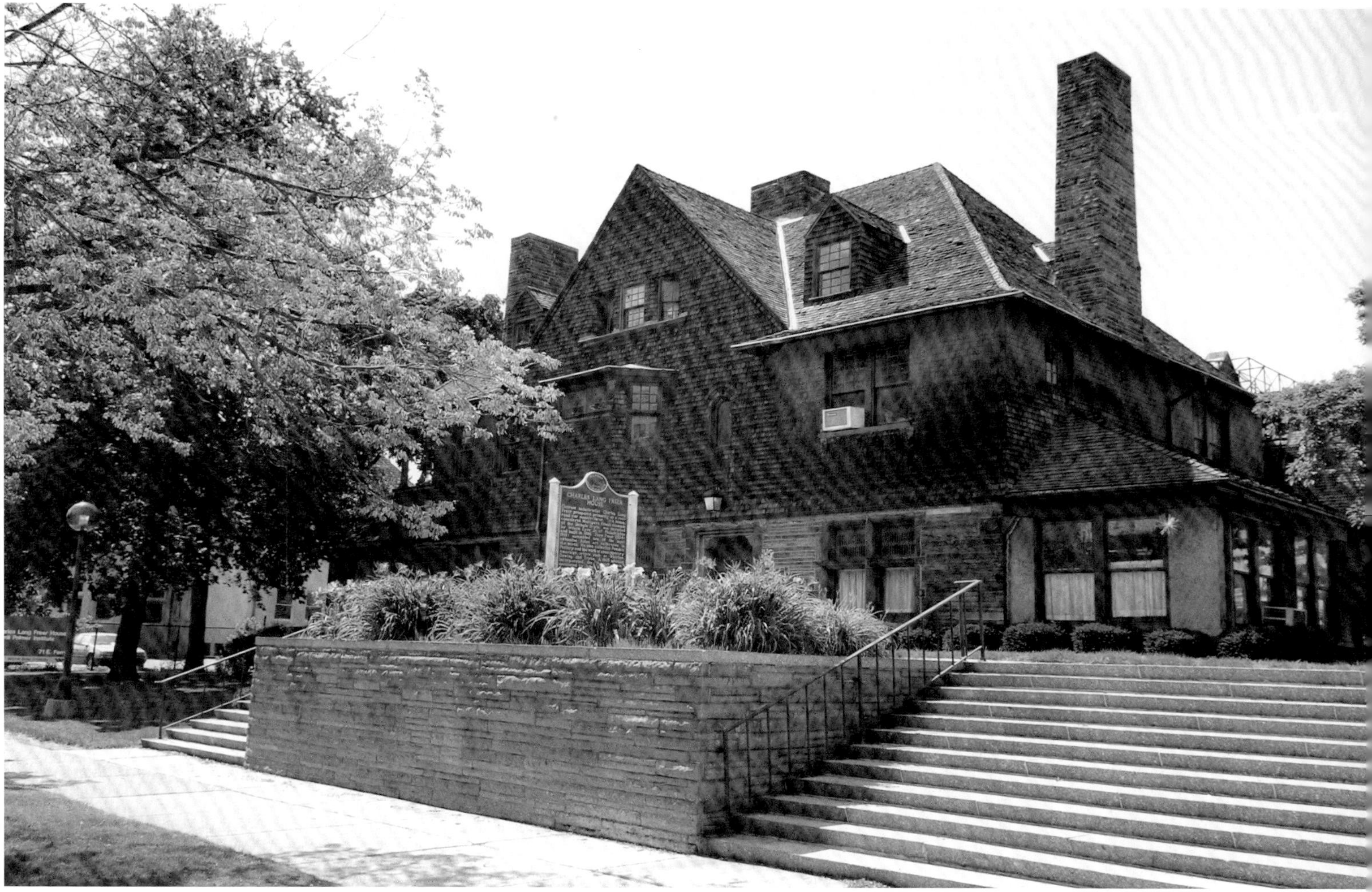

Merrill-Palmer Institute, 71 E. Ferry Street. Founded in 1920 as a center for the study of families and human development, the Merrill-Palmer Institute developed close ties to Wayne State University over the years. Those ties were made stronger in 1981, when Wayne State acquired the financially troubled institute in order to prevent it from closing its doors. The institute's headquarters have been located in the historic Charles Freer House, pictured here, since 1921. The Freer House was built in 1892. Both the Pauline Knapp Building at 87 E. Ferry, which houses the institute's child development laboratory, and the Freer House are located near the East Ferry Avenue Historic District. In 2005, Merrill Palmer merged with Wayne State's Skillman Center for Children and Families to form the current Merrill Palmer Skillman Institute for Child and Family Development. (Courtesy of Wayne State University Photographic Services.)

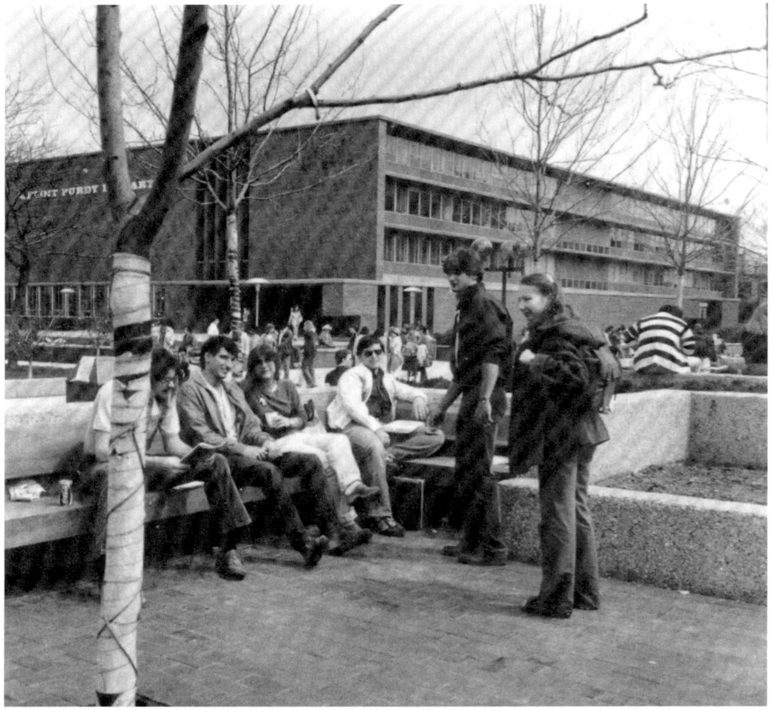

Students on campus, 1980. Students gather in front of the Purdy/Kresge Library. One result of Wayne State's emphasis on graduate programs was a decline in undergraduate enrollments, those students most likely to participate in campus activities. While Wayne State still remained an important destination for undergraduates, the university did not emphasize traditional college social activities and athletics. (Walter P. Reuther Library, Archives of Labor and Urban Affairs, Wayne State University.)

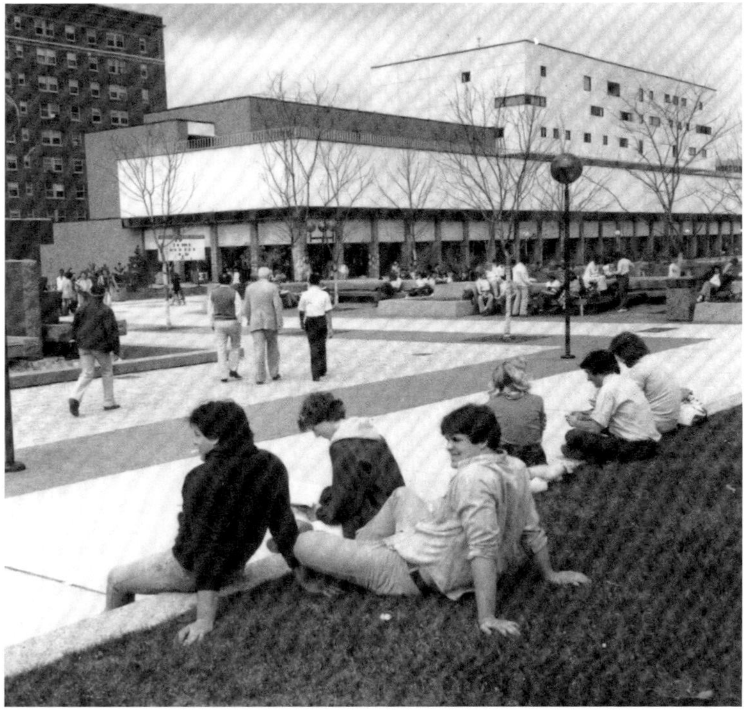

Students on campus, 1980. After hitting a peak in 1976, Wayne State's student enrollment began to decline until the mid-1980s. However, Wayne State University officials worked hard to change that trend, and by the end of the 1980s more students were again enrolling in the university. The Student Center is the main building pictured here, with the Chatsworth Tower visible behind it, to the left. The fountain, partially visible at the far left, is located in the center of Wayne's campus and was constructed during the late 1970s, when Gullen Mall was relandscaped. (Walter P. Reuther Library, Archives of Labor and Urban Affairs, Wayne State University.)

View of campus, looking northwest, 1984. Throughout the 1980s, most of the neighborhood houses that had surrounded Old Main were demolished, such as the house seen here in front of the Chatsworth Tower Apartments. Four of the old homes, however—including the Linsell House, in the foreground on the right—were preserved. The University Bookstore, since replaced by the Undergraduate Library, is on the left. DeRoy is the tall apartment building visible behind the bookstore, and the Student Center is the white building in the distance on the right. (Walter P. Reuther Library, Archives of Labor and Urban Affairs, Wayne State University.)

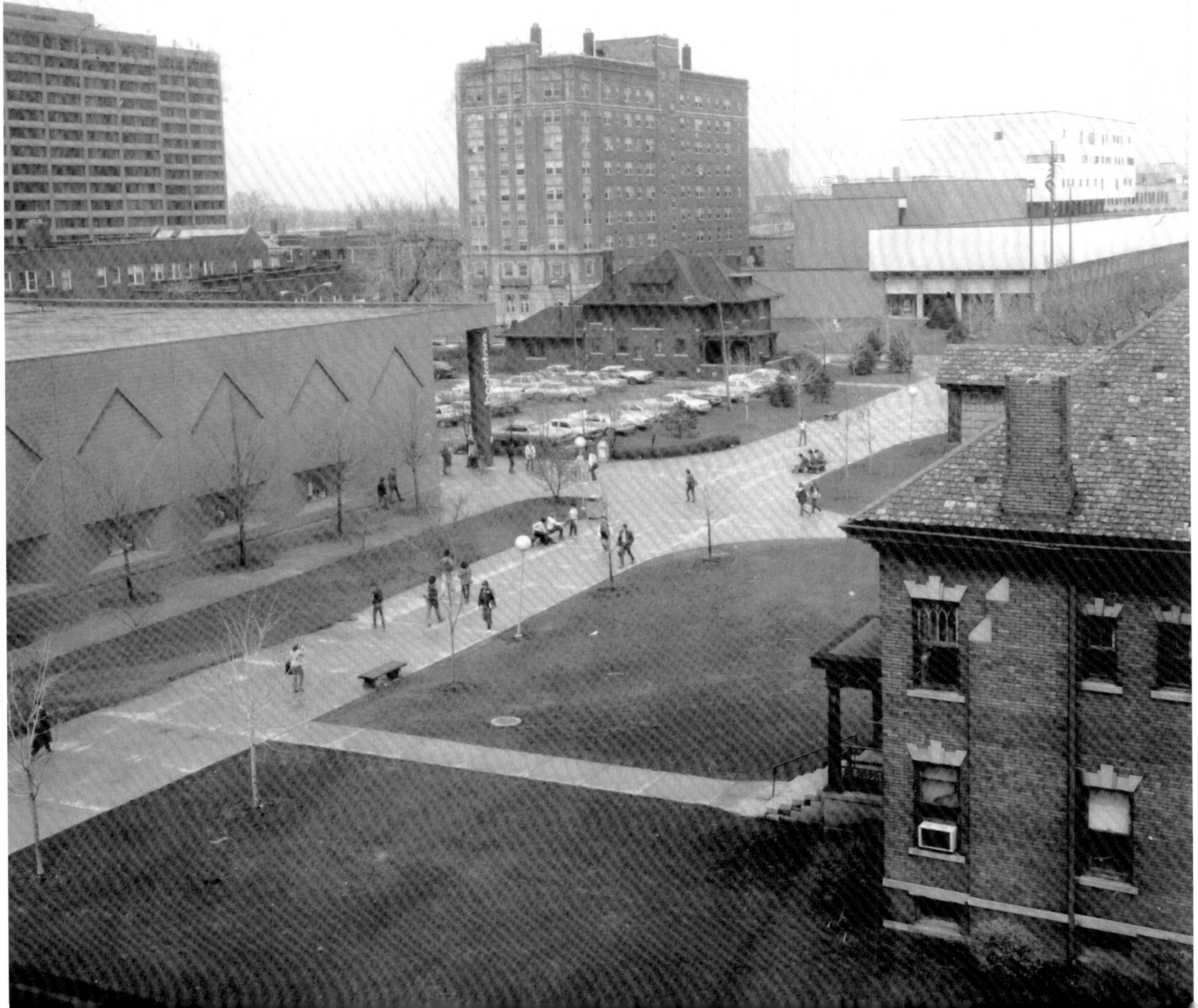

View of houses on Putnam Street, looking northeast, 1985. Demolition of old houses to clear space for Science Hall began in 1947 and continued until the 1980s. This image shows the last row of houses on campus before they were torn down. The site is approximately where the David Adamany Undergraduate library stands today. The Chatsworth Tower Apartments rise in the distance on the left. (Walter P. Reuther Library, Archives of Labor and Urban Affairs, Wayne State University.)

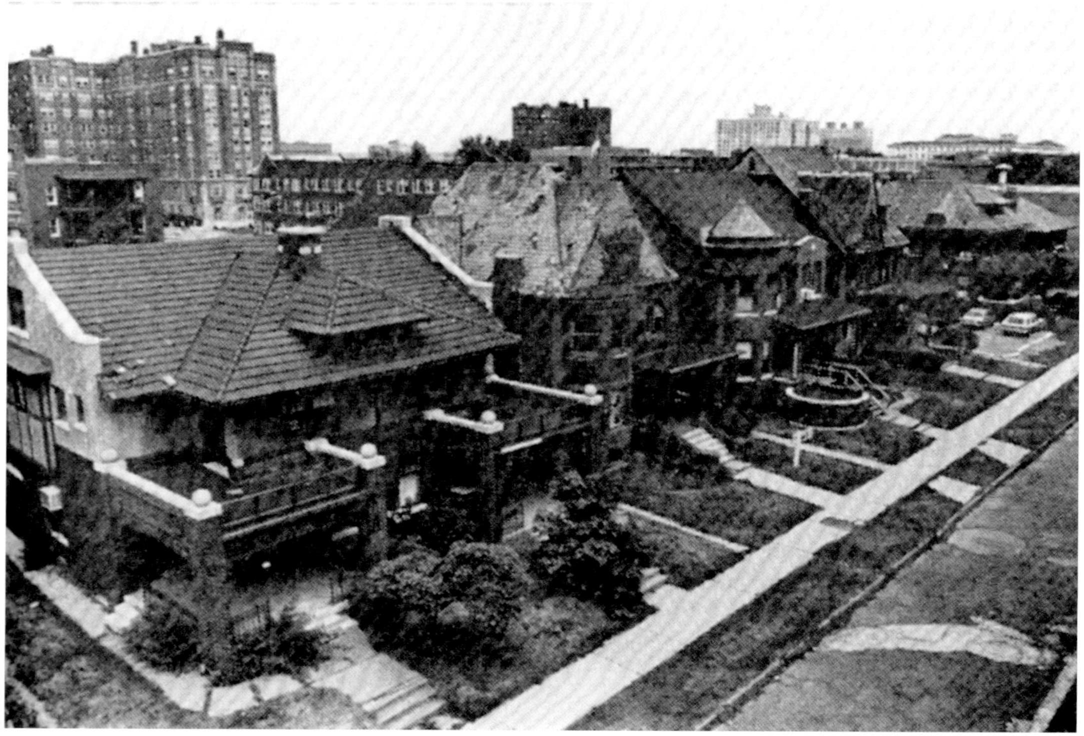

Interior of the Student Center, 1980s. A close look at the ceiling reveals many paper airplanes hanging from the tiles above the food commons. It is unclear how this intriguing tradition first started, but it does take a certain skill to construct and launch a paper airplane so that it lodges in the ceiling. Since the building's renovation in 2017, the tradition has, unfortunately, stopped. (Walter P. Reuther Library, Archives of Labor and Urban Affairs, Wayne State University.)

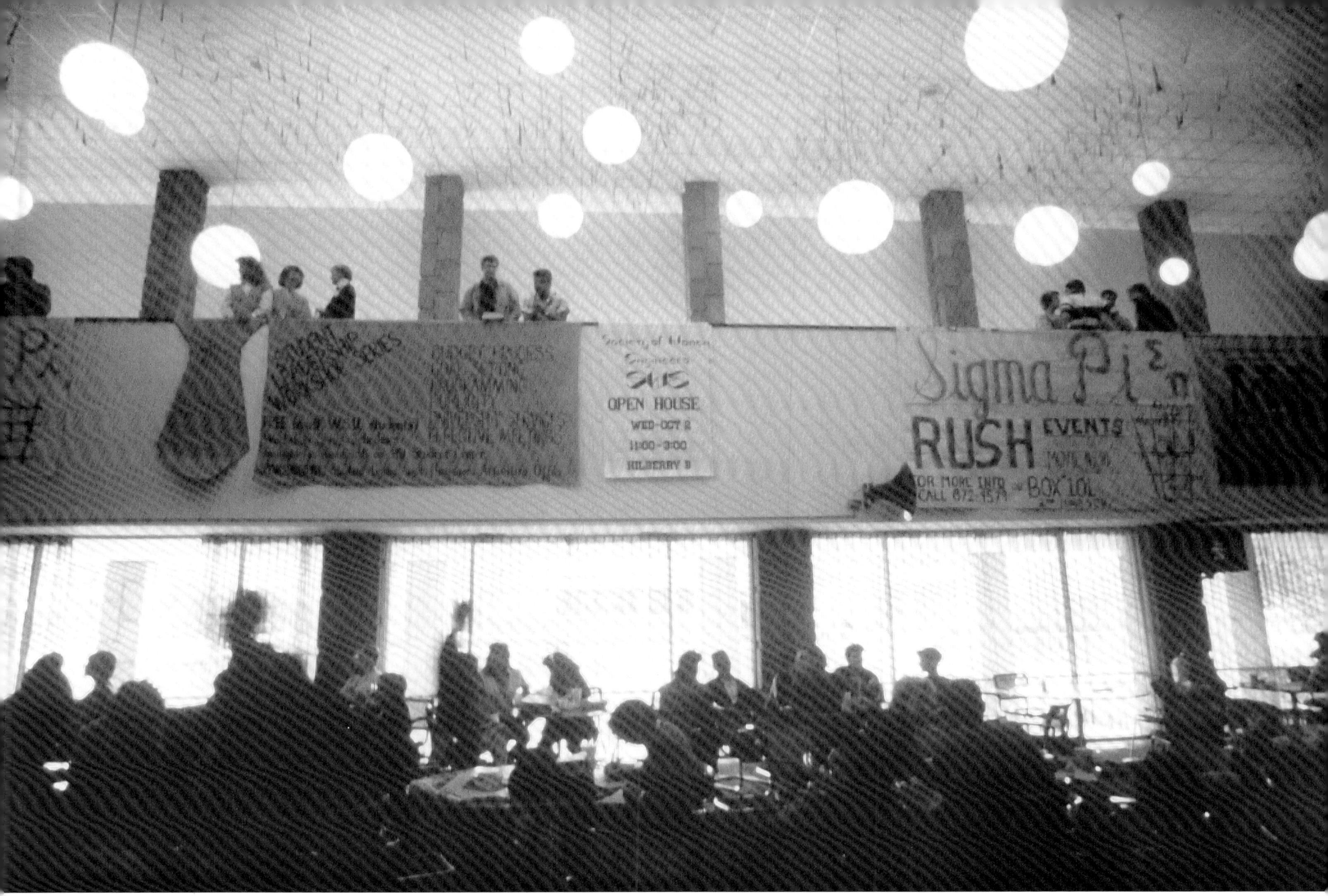
OPEN HOUSE
Sigma Pi
RUSH
EVENTS

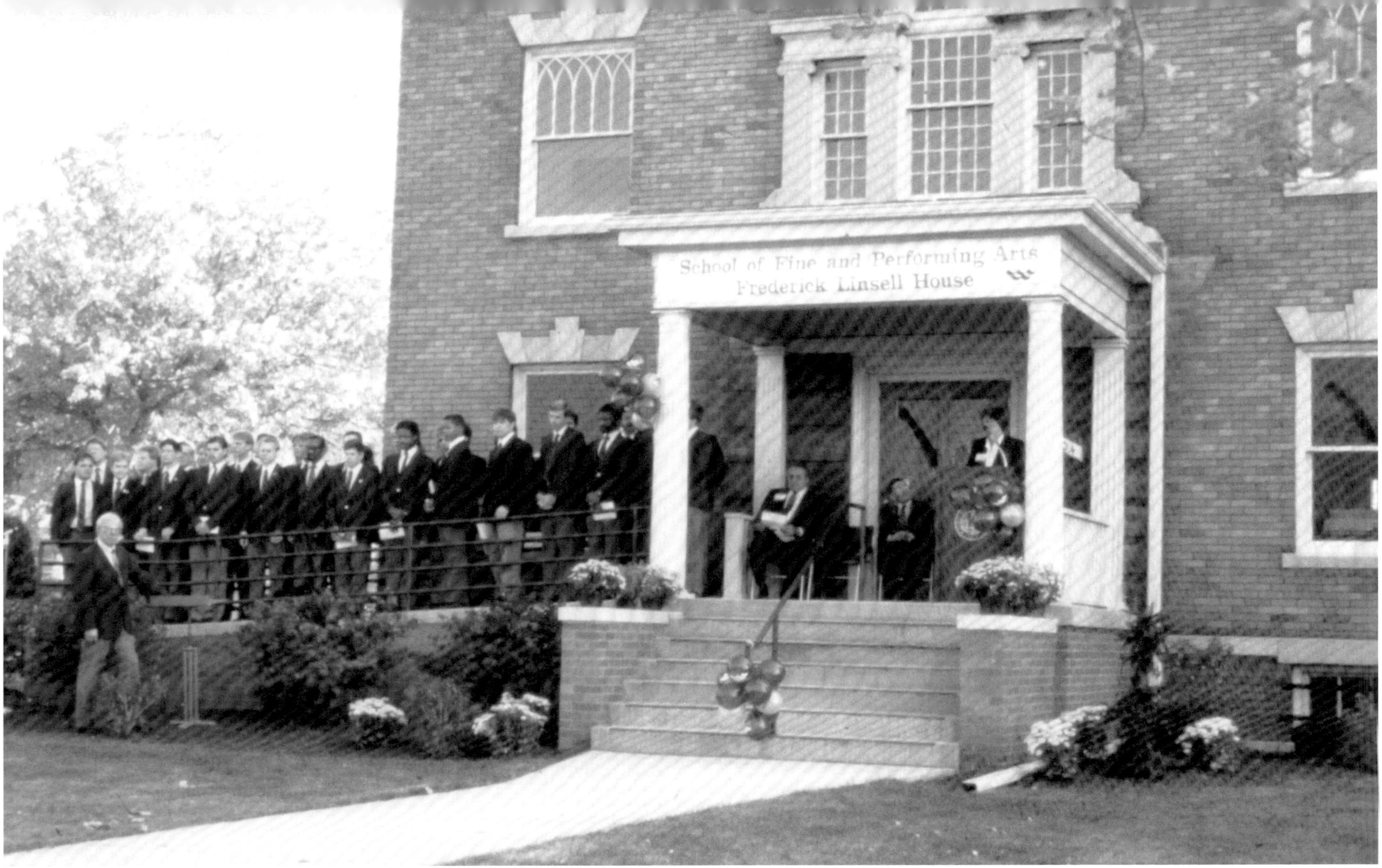

Frederick Linsell House, October 16, 1987. The Wayne State University Men's Glee Club is lined up to take part in the dedication of the Linsell House as the home of the recently established College of Fine and Performing Arts. The day also marked significant moments in several other construction projects: the dedication of the G. Mennen Williams Mall (formerly Merrick Street); the dedication of the new addition to the Engineering Building; the reopening of Helen Newberry Joy Residence for Women as the Student Services Center; and groundbreaking for the Faculty/Administration Building. (Walter P. Reuther Library, Archives of Labor and Urban Affairs, Wayne State University.)

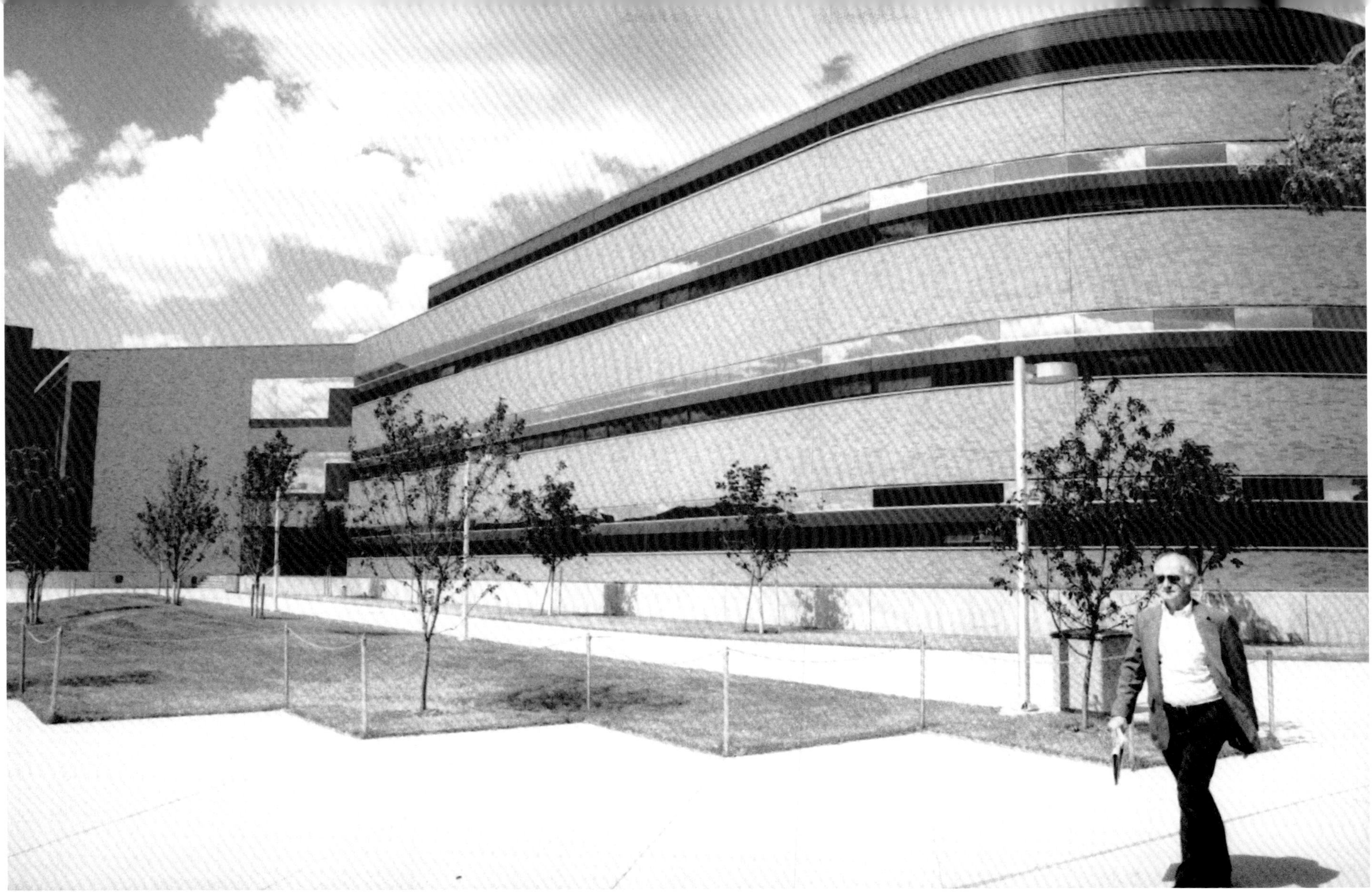

Engineering Building addition, 1987. The university's long moratorium on new construction was broken with this addition to the Engineering Building. Before the completion of the addition, the last new building constructed on Wayne State's campus had been the Forest Apartments, completed in 1976. The new engineering wing extended the building south, to the corner of Warren Avenue and Anthony Wayne Drive. It housed a laboratory and a new office wing—so all of the engineering faculty, who had been scattered across campus, could be under the same roof. The addition, together with several other campus construction projects, was dedicated in October 1987. (Walter P. Reuther Library, Archives of Labor and Urban Affairs, Wayne State University.)

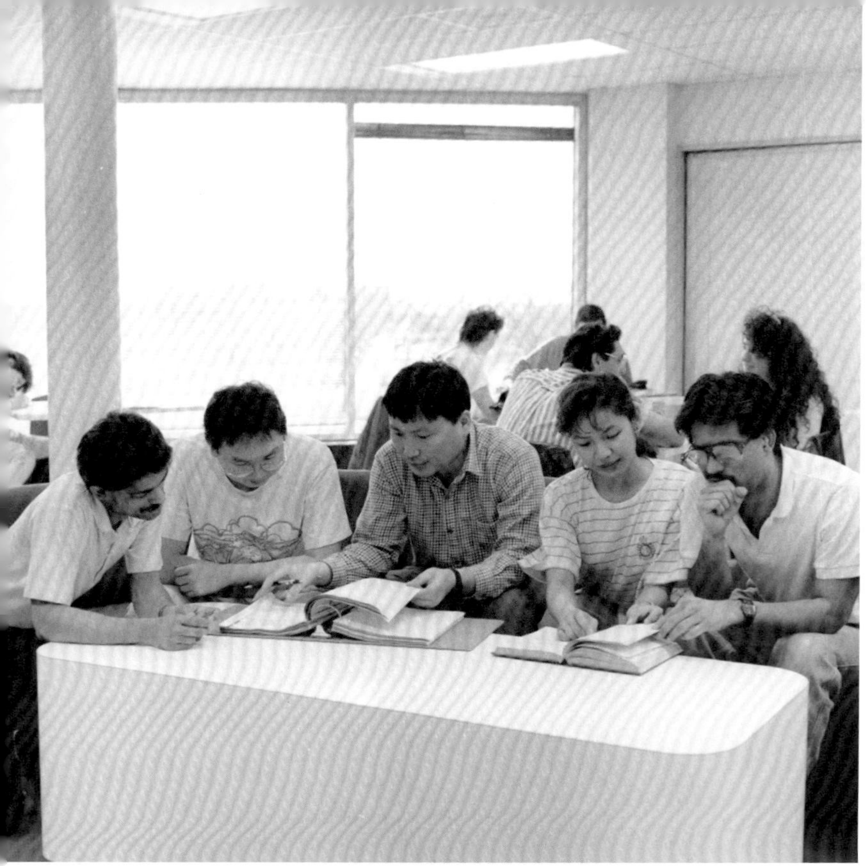

Engineering students studying, 1981. (Walter P. Reuther Library, Archives of Labor and Urban Affairs, Wayne State University.)

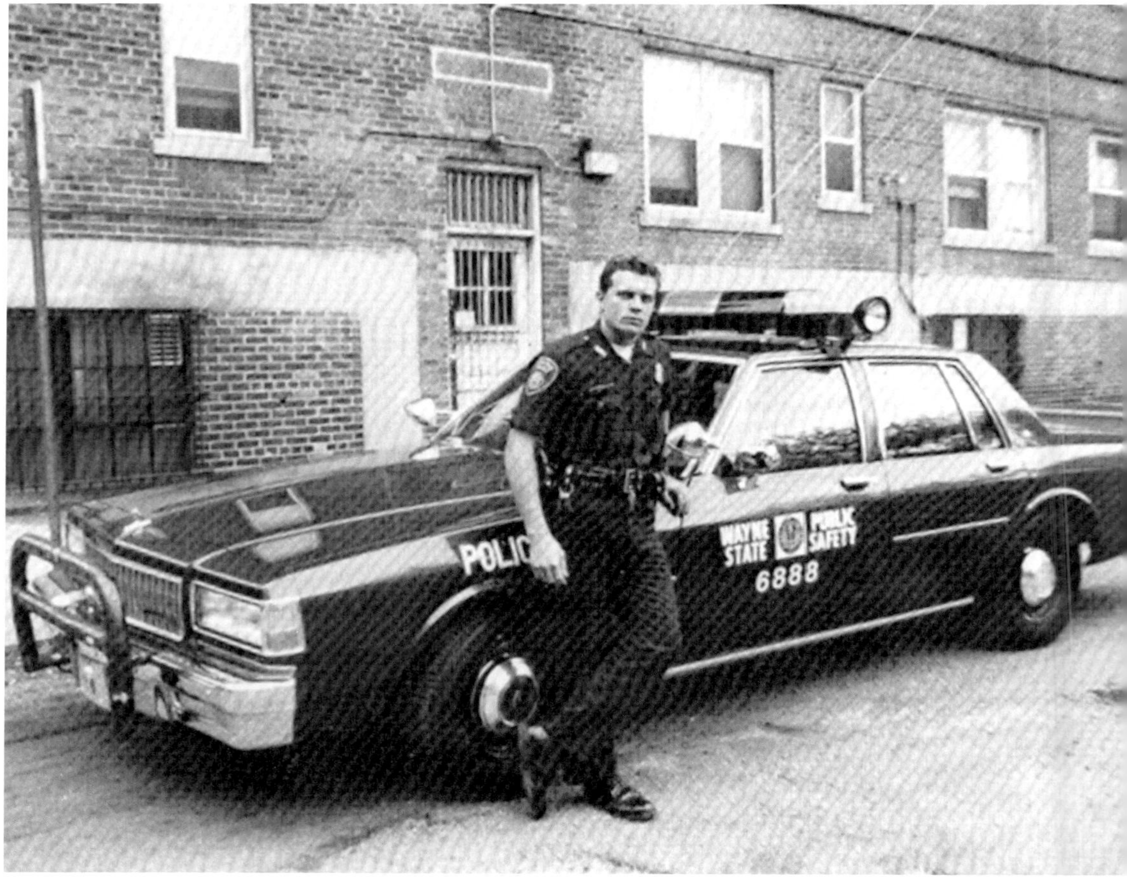

Wayne State University police officer, 1989. After the Wayne State University Department of Public Safety was established in 1966, Wayne State police officers became a familiar sight on campus. Later, the name of the division was changed to the Wayne State University Police Department. (Walter P. Reuther Library, Archives of Labor and Urban Affairs, Wayne State University.)

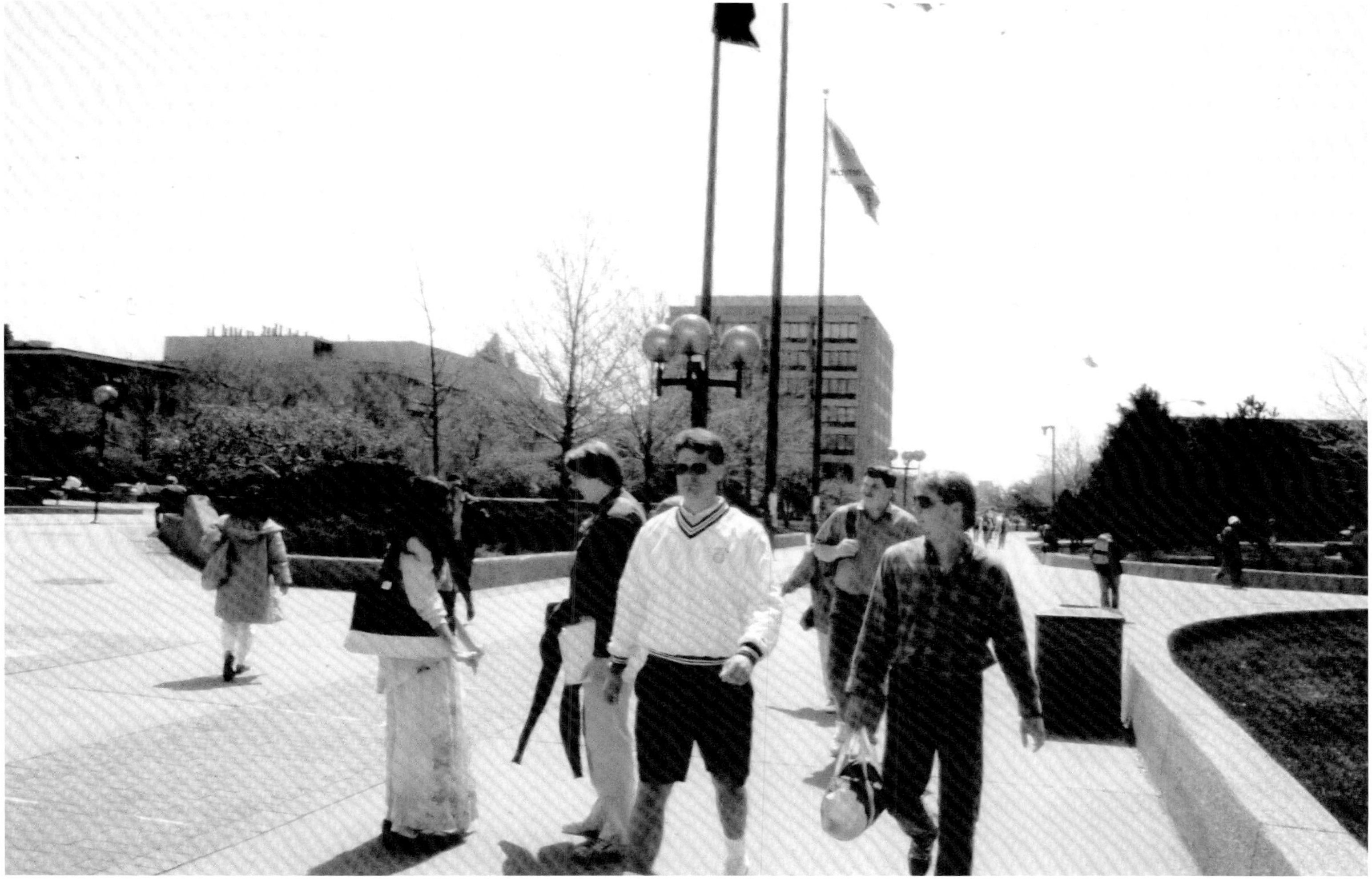

View from central campus, facing south, 1989. Looking down Gullen Mall toward Warren Avenue. The Science and Engineering Library is the tall building in the background, behind the flagpoles. The University Bookstore is the low, dark building on the right, and part of State Hall is visible behind the trees on the left. (Walter P. Reuther Library, Archives of Labor and Urban Affairs, Wayne State University.)

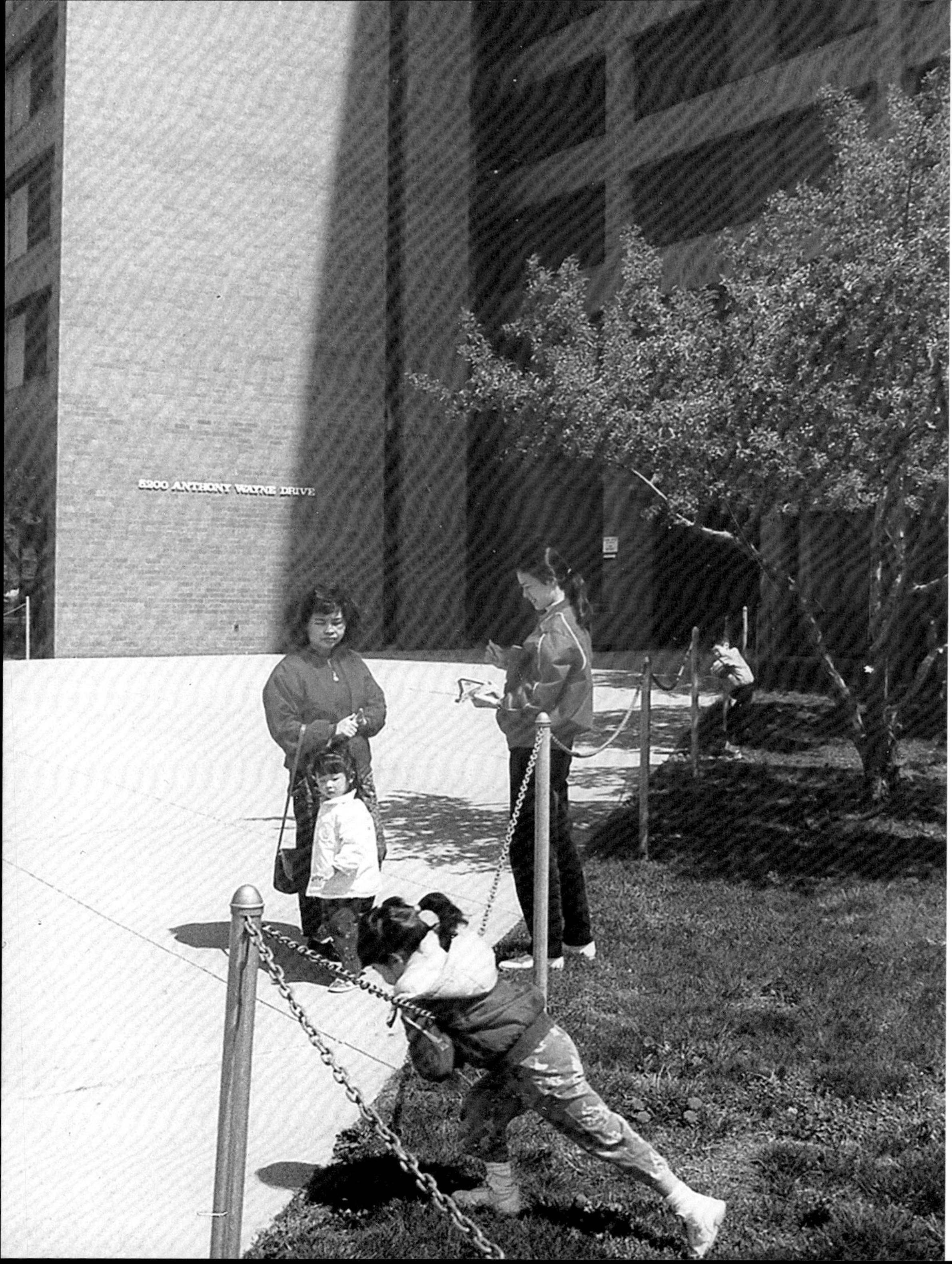

Outside the Helen L. DeRoy Apartments, spring 1989. Wayne State's housing facilities have never been reserved exclusively for students. The apartment buildings that the university has built and purchased over the years have also housed faculty members and their families. (Walter P. Reuther Library, Archives of Labor and Urban Affairs, Wayne State University.)

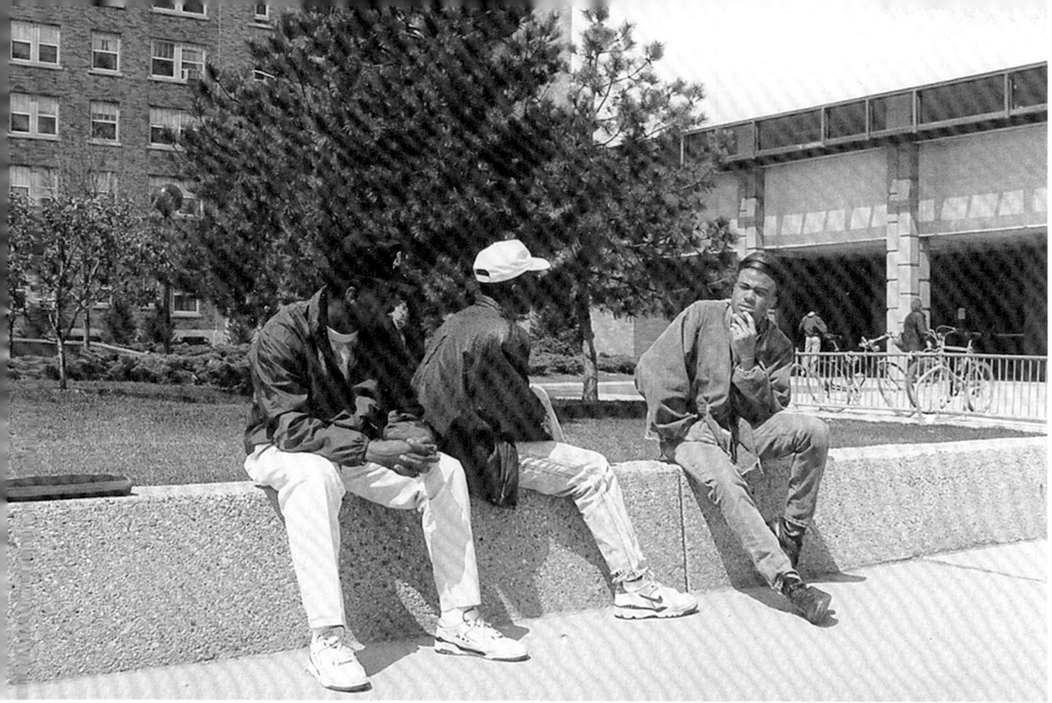

Students outside the Student Center, spring 1989. (Walter P. Reuther Library, Archives of Labor and Urban Affairs, Wayne State University.)

Interior of the Purdy Library, 1989. Computers have become ubiquitous on college campuses, both in classrooms and in libraries—for research, for class registration, or for searching for books and articles, as seen in this picture. (Walter P. Reuther Library, Archives of Labor and Urban Affairs, Wayne State University.)

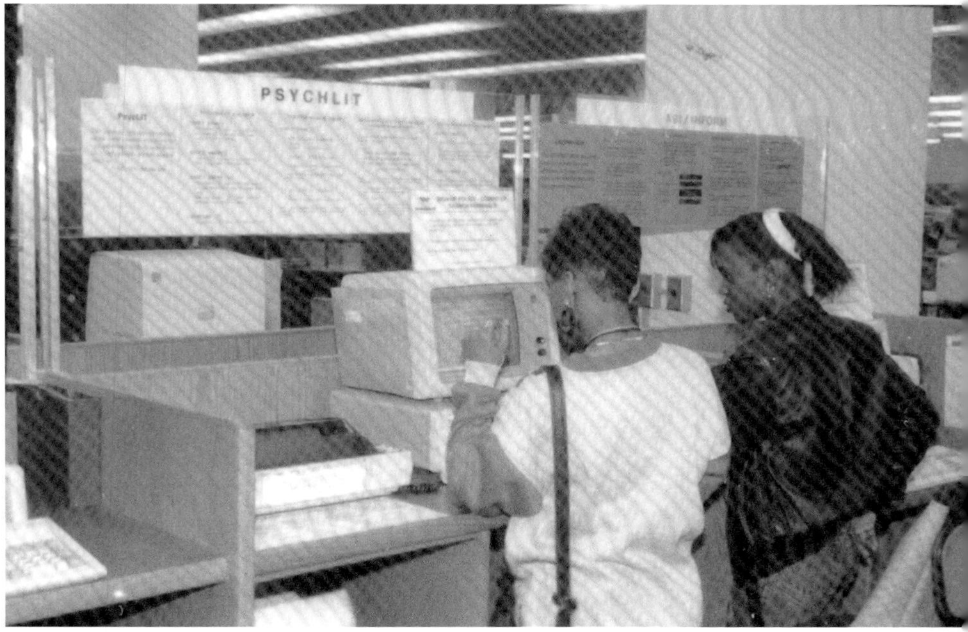

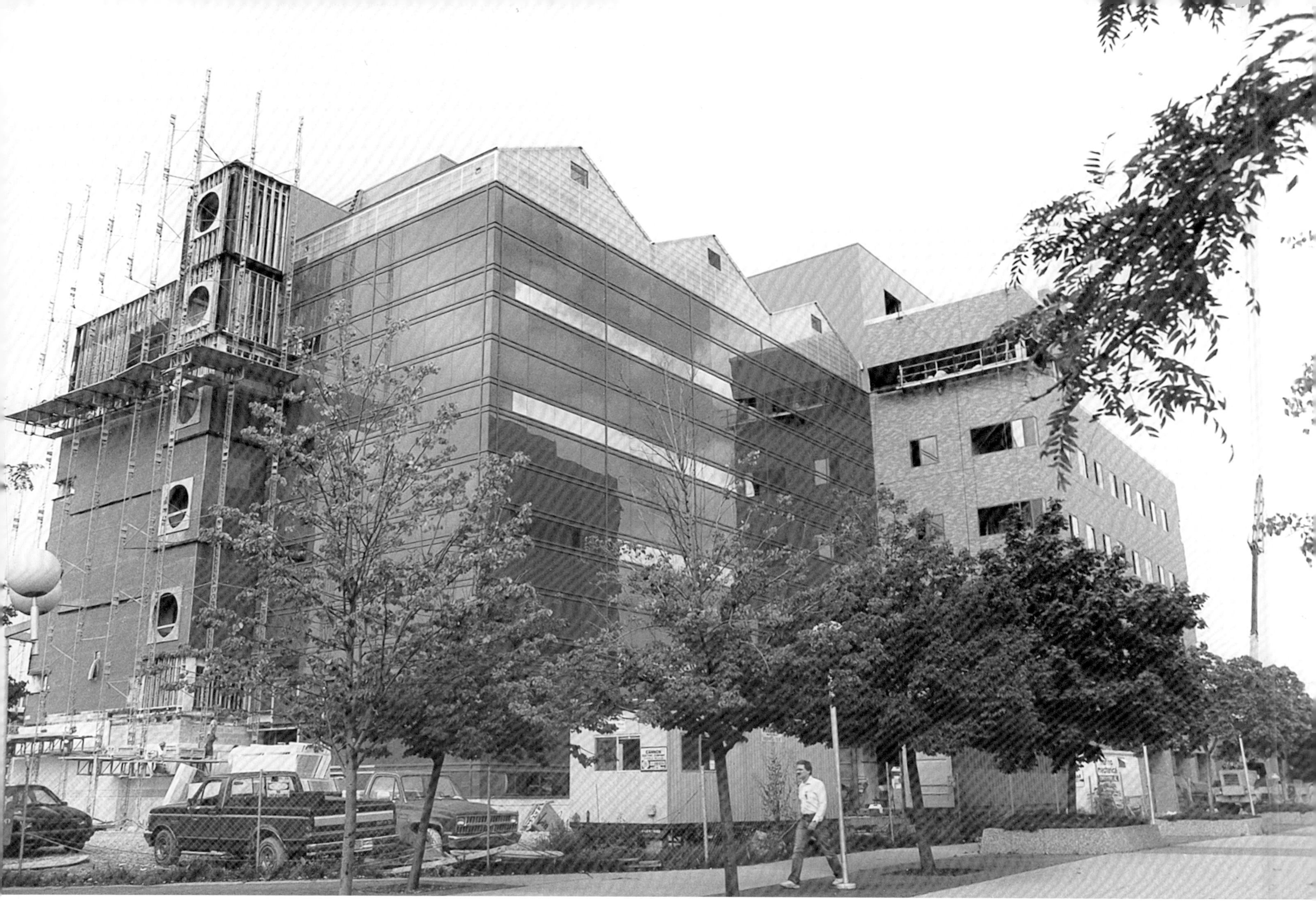

Biological Sciences Building under construction, 5047 Gullen Mall at Warren, southeast facade, 1989. Before the Biological Sciences Building was constructed, the biology department was spread out over seven buildings, including Old Main, the Natural Science Building, the Chemistry Building, and the Science and Engineering Library. The new building provided space for laboratories for faculty members and graduate students, a sixth-floor greenhouse, and faculty offices. (Walter P. Reuther Library, Archives of Labor and Urban Affairs, Wayne State University.)

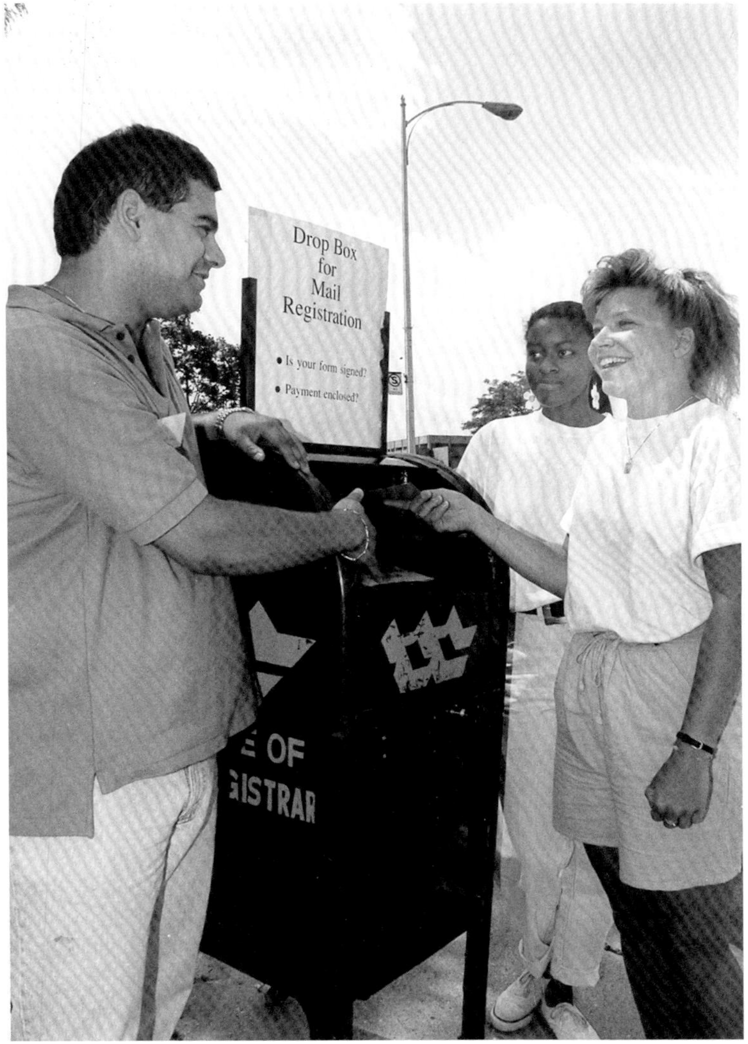

Registration, 1991. In 1986, the punch-card registration system was replaced by a mail-in system. Since the last days of registration are naturally very busy, the registrar's office provided a mailbox on Anthony Wayne Drive so that students like these could drop off their registration forms without having to park. (Walter P. Reuther Library, Archives of Labor and Urban Affairs, Wayne State University.)

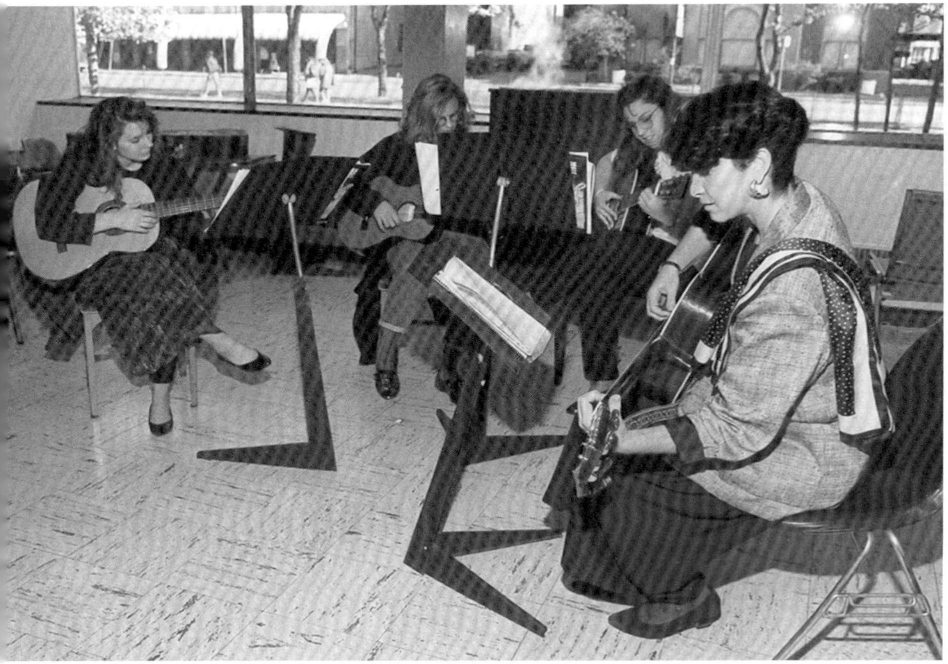

Music therapy students practicing, early 1990s. The students are, from the left, Carlotta Scott, Mari Freudl, and Caroly Parravano. In the foreground is Sammi Liebman, director of the music therapy program. The windows of the practice room look out onto Cass Avenue. The white awning visible through the window on the left marks the front of the Facilities, Planning and Management Building, the Campus Restaurant, and the Circa 1890 Saloon, a favorite campus hangout. It closed in 2017. (Walter P. Reuther Library, Archives of Labor and Urban Affairs, Wayne State University.)

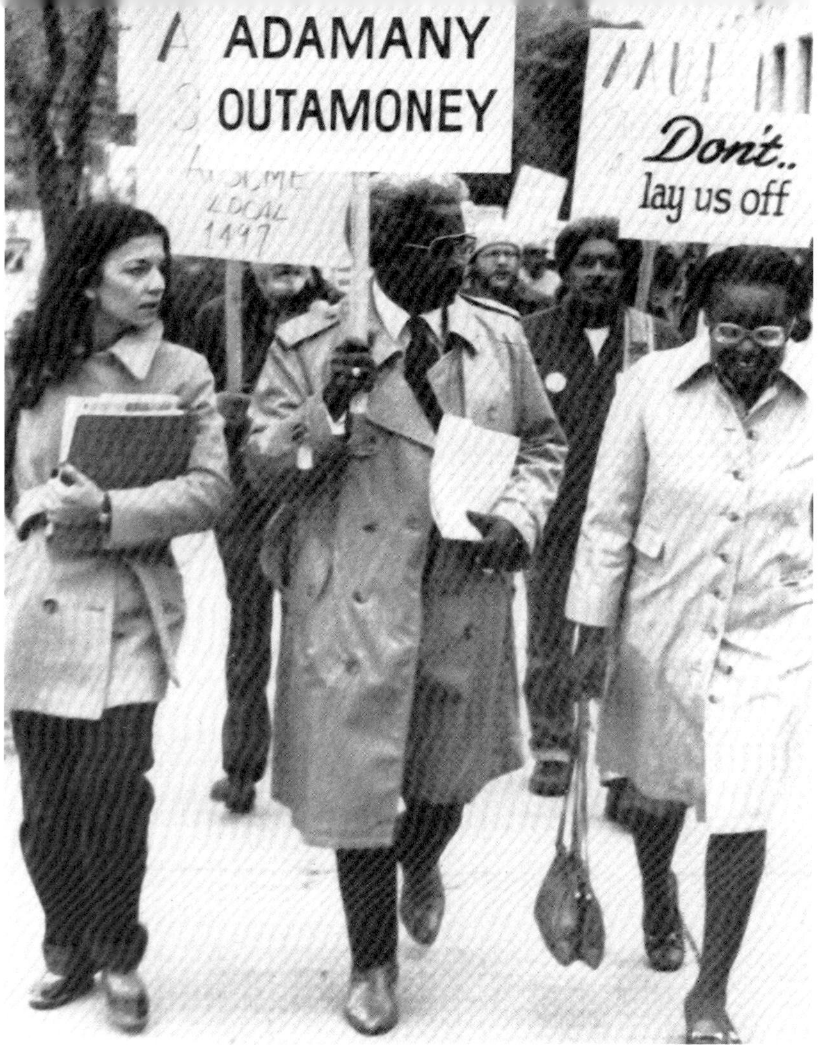

Members of campus unions marching in support of striking faculty, September 1990. In the 1980s, relations between Wayne State University's president and professors were often adversarial. During President David Adamany's tenure, professors went on strike several times. The strikers pictured are members of the Local 2071, AFSCME, and the Local 1497. (Walter P. Reuther Library, Archives of Labor and Urban Affairs, Wayne State University.)

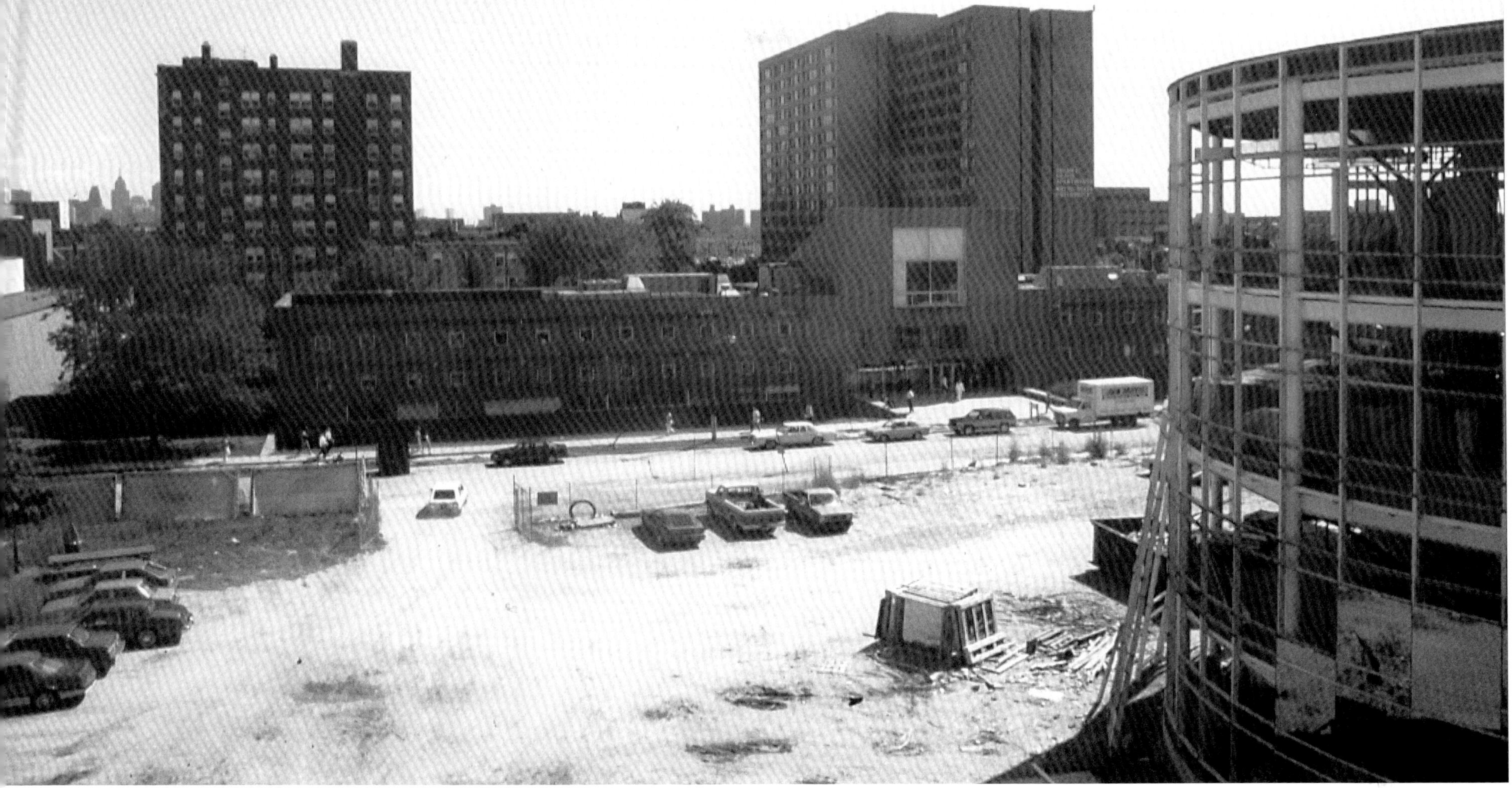

Faculty/Administration Building construction, south side, late 1980s. Groundbreaking for the Faculty/Administration Building (FAB) took place in October 1987, the same period during which several other campus construction projects were begun. The frame of the FAB can be seen at the far right of the photograph. In the distance are the Chatsworth Tower Apartments on the left and the DeRoy Apartments on the right. Helen Newberry Joy Residence Hall is the shorter building in front of the two apartment buildings. The Joy Residence Hall was the first dorm that WSU constructed, and it was later converted into office space. (Walter P. Reuther Library, Archives of Labor and Urban Affairs, Wayne State University.)

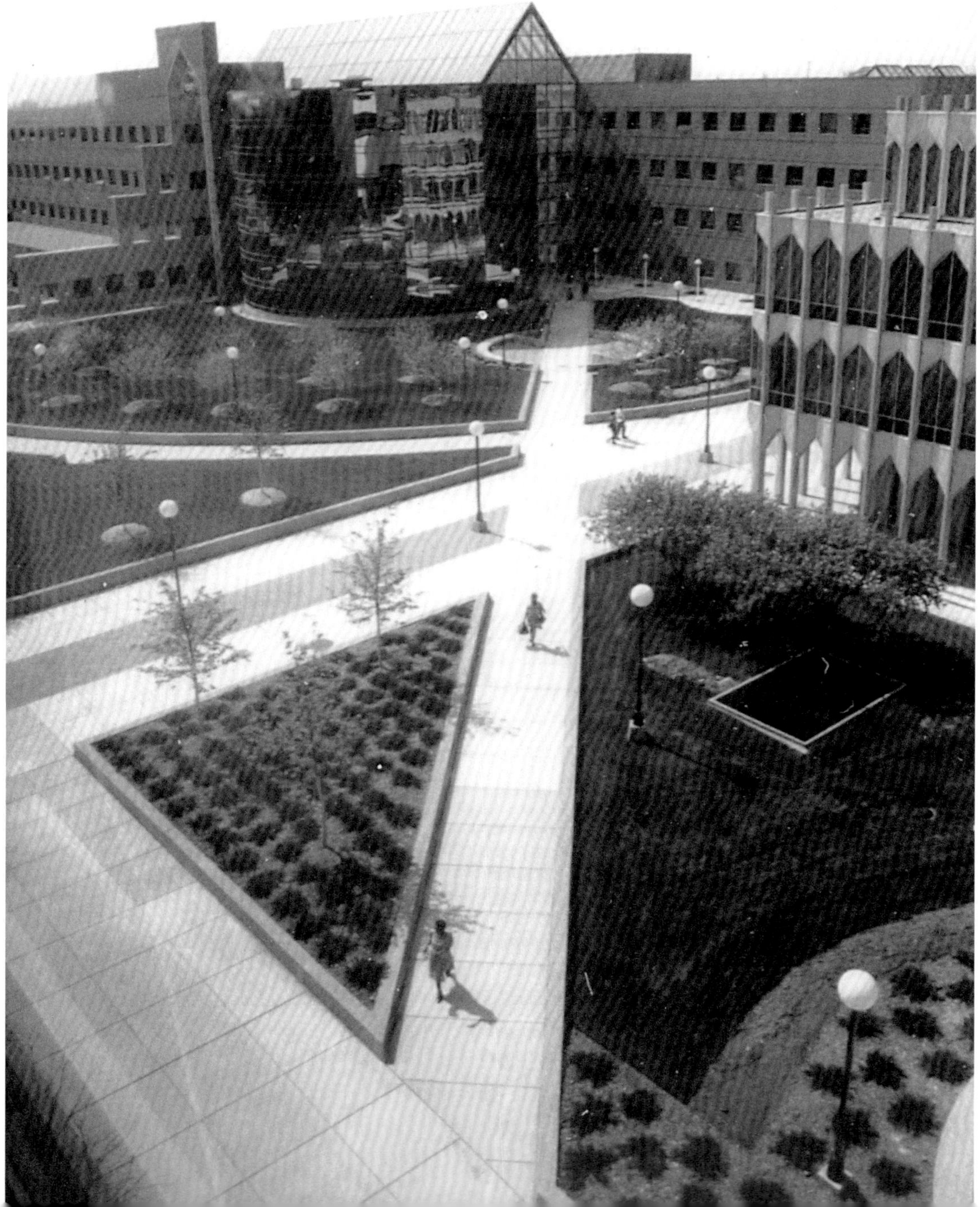

Faculty/Administration Building, 656 Reuther Mall southeast facade, 1992. This glass-walled, four-story faculty office building, completed in 1990, would house faculty whose offices had been in Mackenzie Hall, which was slated for demolition. The building's most distinctive feature is an atrium in the center, lit by a skylight. The College of Education Building is seen on the right. (Walter P. Reuther Library, Archives of Labor and Urban Affairs, Wayne State University.)

Mackenzie Hall implosion, February 17, 1991. At 10:15 on that Sunday morning, a thousand dynamite charges reduced Mackenzie Hall to a pile of rubble. The center of Wayne State's student life since the late 1940s, the former Student Center Building (Webster Hall) had been vacated after the construction of the Faculty/Administration Building. Mackenzie was imploded because the aging structure required extensive renovations, and construction of a replacement building was deemed less costly. (Courtesy of Kirt Dozier, *The Detroit News*.)

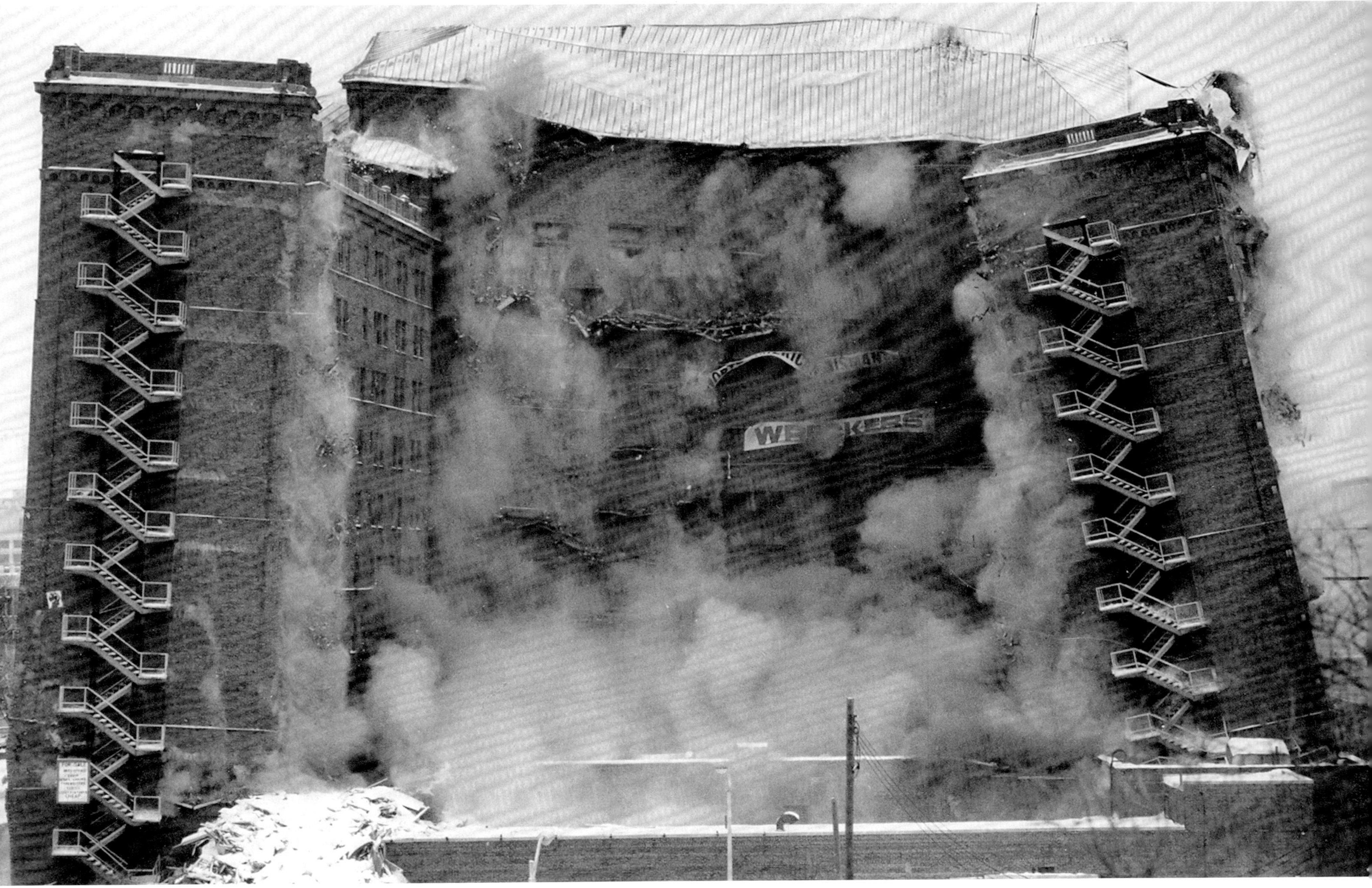

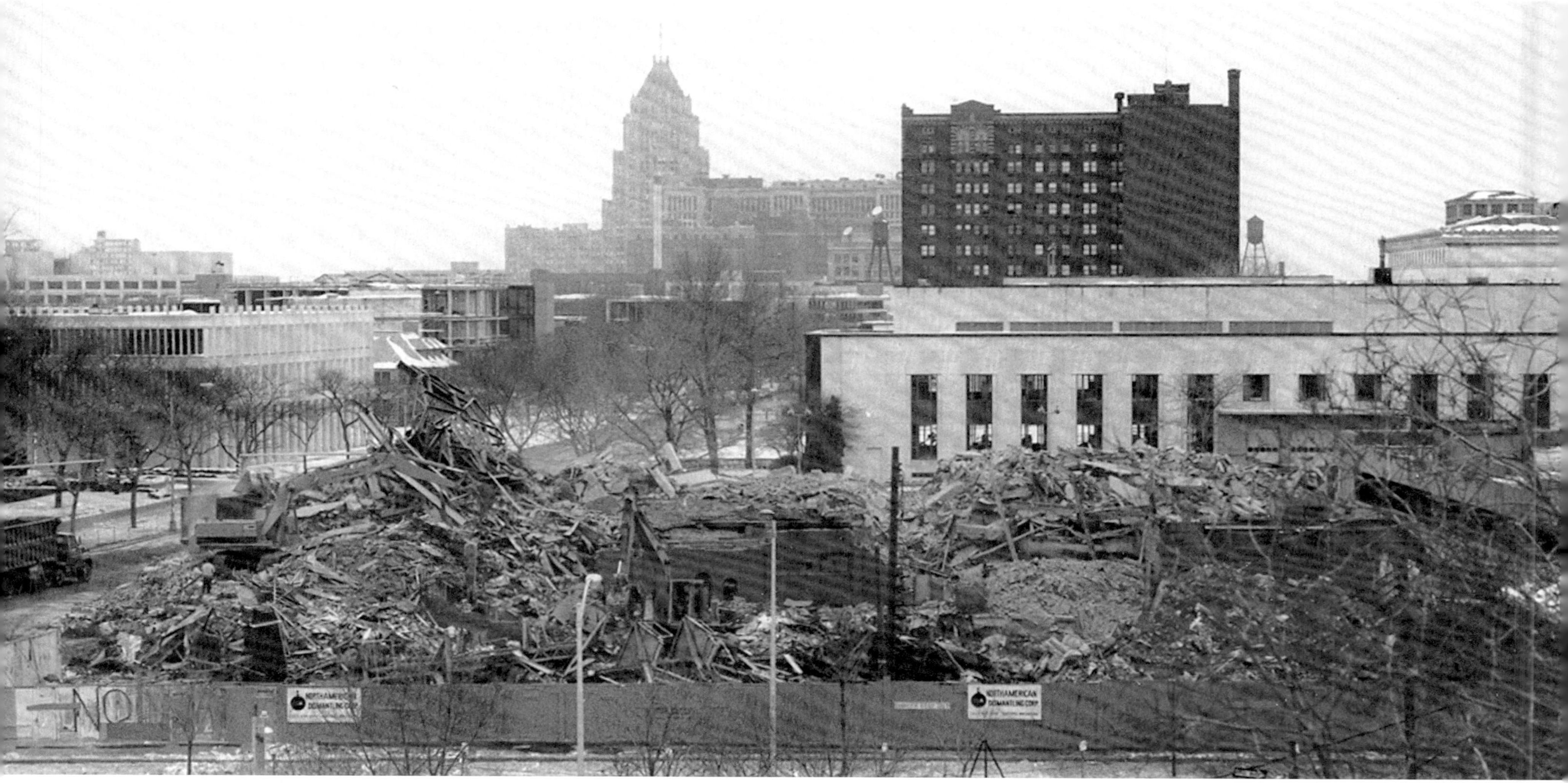

Former site of Mackenzie Hall, as seen looking north, February 17, 1991. Rubble is all that remains of the historic hotel. Dynamite caused Mackenzie Hall to implode and drop into its own basement. After the demolition, the site was turned into a parking lot and later a parking structure. The top of the Fisher Building can be seen in the distance. (Courtesy of Kirt Dozier, *The Detroit News*.)

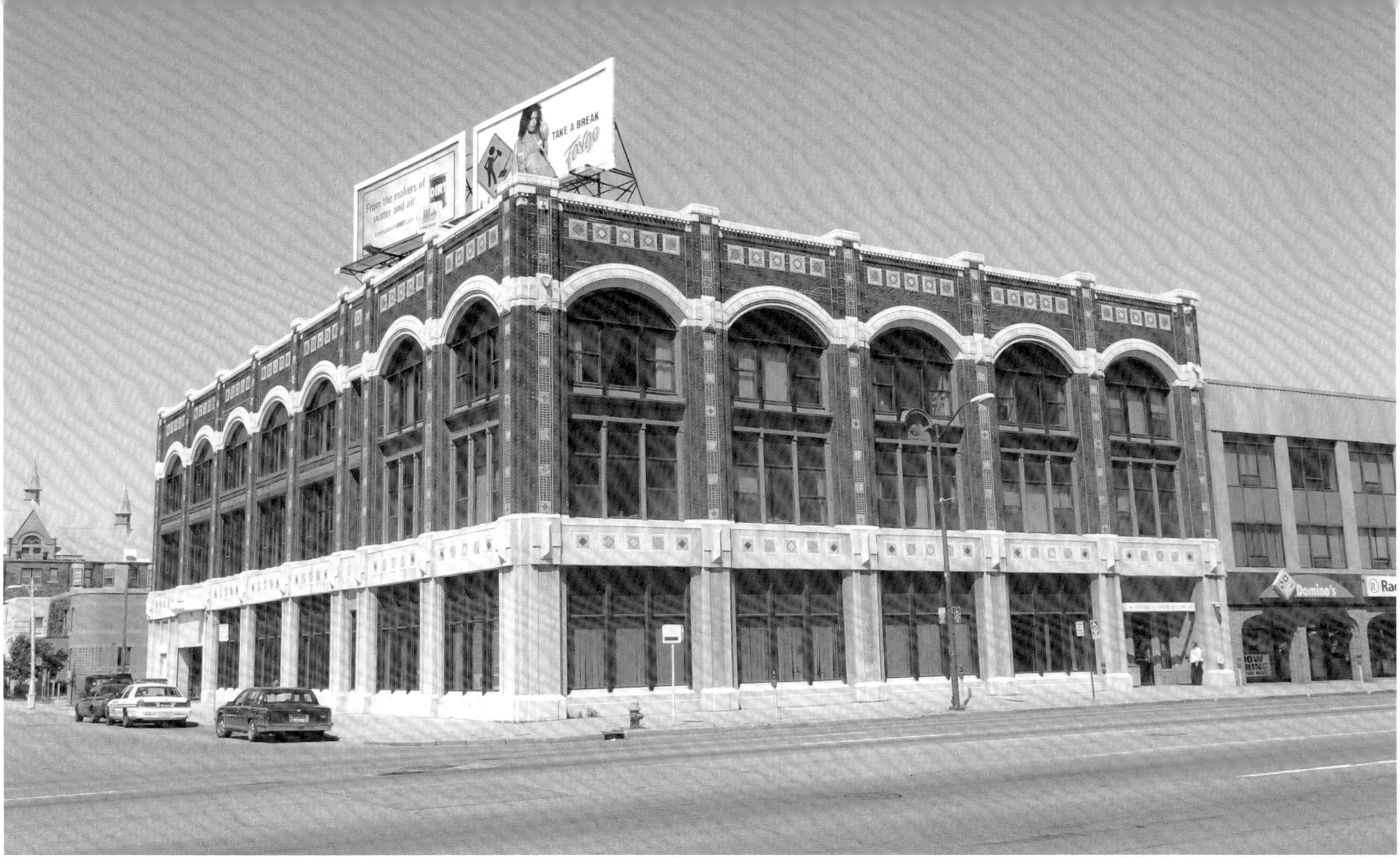

Wayne State University Press, Leonard N. Simons Building, 4809 Woodward Avenue at Hancock Street. Wayne State University Press has published scholarly books since 1941, specializing in books devoted to Jewish studies, African American studies, film and media studies, folklore and fairy-tale studies, and regional history and culture, with an emphasis on the City of Detroit. The Press moved into this building in 1994, the second campus building named for Leonard N. Simons. Simons helped found the Press, served as the first president of the Press's Board of Advisors, and was its staunch supporter and benefactor for forty years. The building, originally designed by Albert Kahn in 1913 for the B. F. Goodrich Tire Company, was subsequently occupied by the Fisher Wallpaper and Paint Company before Wayne State purchased it. (Courtesy of Wayne State University Photographic Services.)

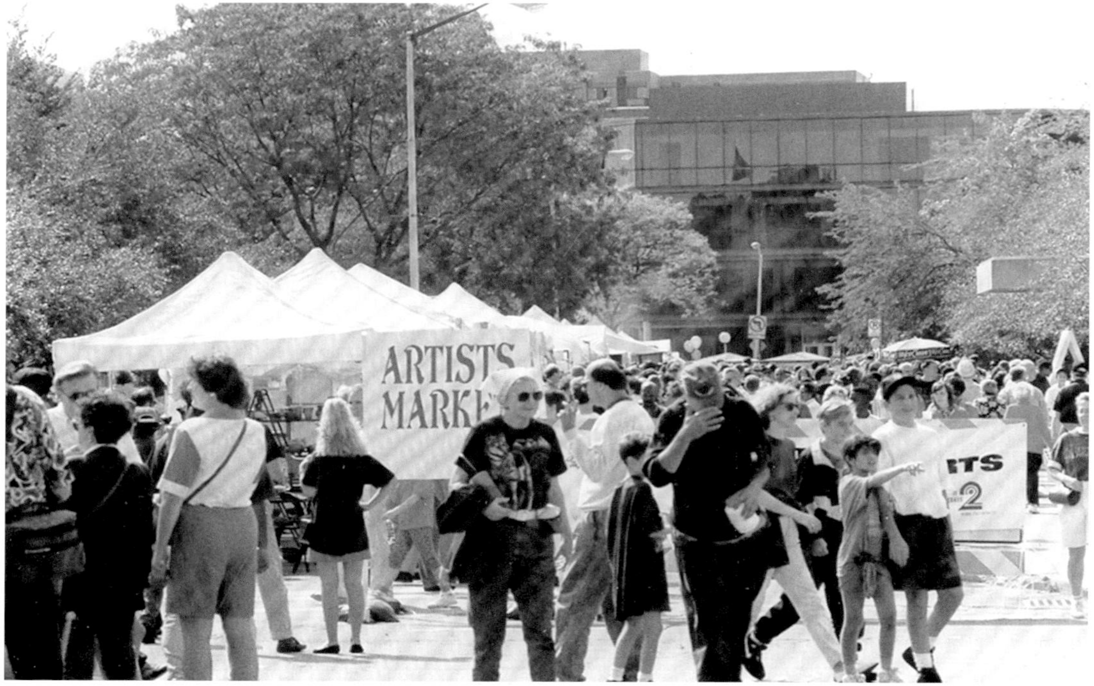

Detroit Festival of the Arts, 1992. An outdoor event celebrating Detroit's creative energies, the Festival of the Arts has been held annually since 1986 in the Cultural Center, near Wayne State's campus. Featuring visual artists, musicians, and dance and theater performers, the three-day festival is entering its fourth decade. In 2009, due to budget constraints because of a struggling economy, it was replaced by an event called "Midsummer Nights in Midtown," which only lasted a year. The Walter P. Reuther Library can be seen in the background. (Walter P. Reuther Library, Archives of Labor and Urban Affairs, Wayne State University.)

Horace H. Rackham Building, 60 Farnsworth. While Horace Rackham is better known as a supporter of the University of Michigan, his legacy also continues in Detroit's Cultural Center. In 1933, his widow provided funds for a building for U-M and the Engineering Society of Michigan, and it was completed in 1941. The Harley, Ellington and Day firm designed the structure in a neo-classical style. Marshall Fredericks, who is known for designing the Spirit of Detroit, has sculptures decorating the entryway facing the Detroit Institute of Arts. In October 1993, WSU agreed to lease the building from U-M, as U-M was only using a small amount of space in it. Wayne State needed the space for classrooms, as Old Main was being renovated, and classes were held there during 1995–96. The Rackham building currently houses academic and support services for Wayne State. When the twenty-five-year lease expires in 2019, WSU plans to buy the building from U-M for $8 million. (Courtesy of Wayne State University Photographic Services.)

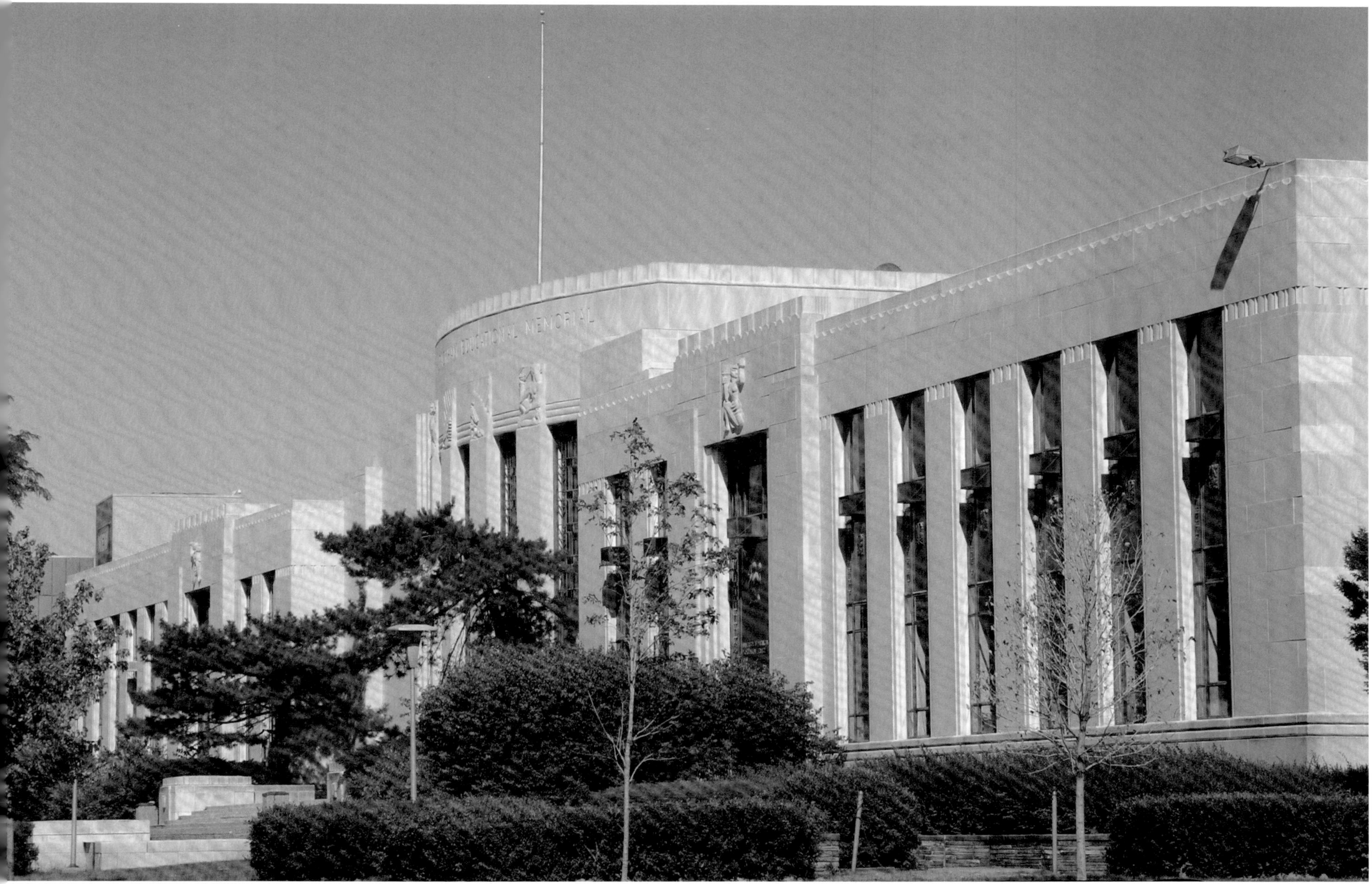
EDUCATIONAL MEMORIAL

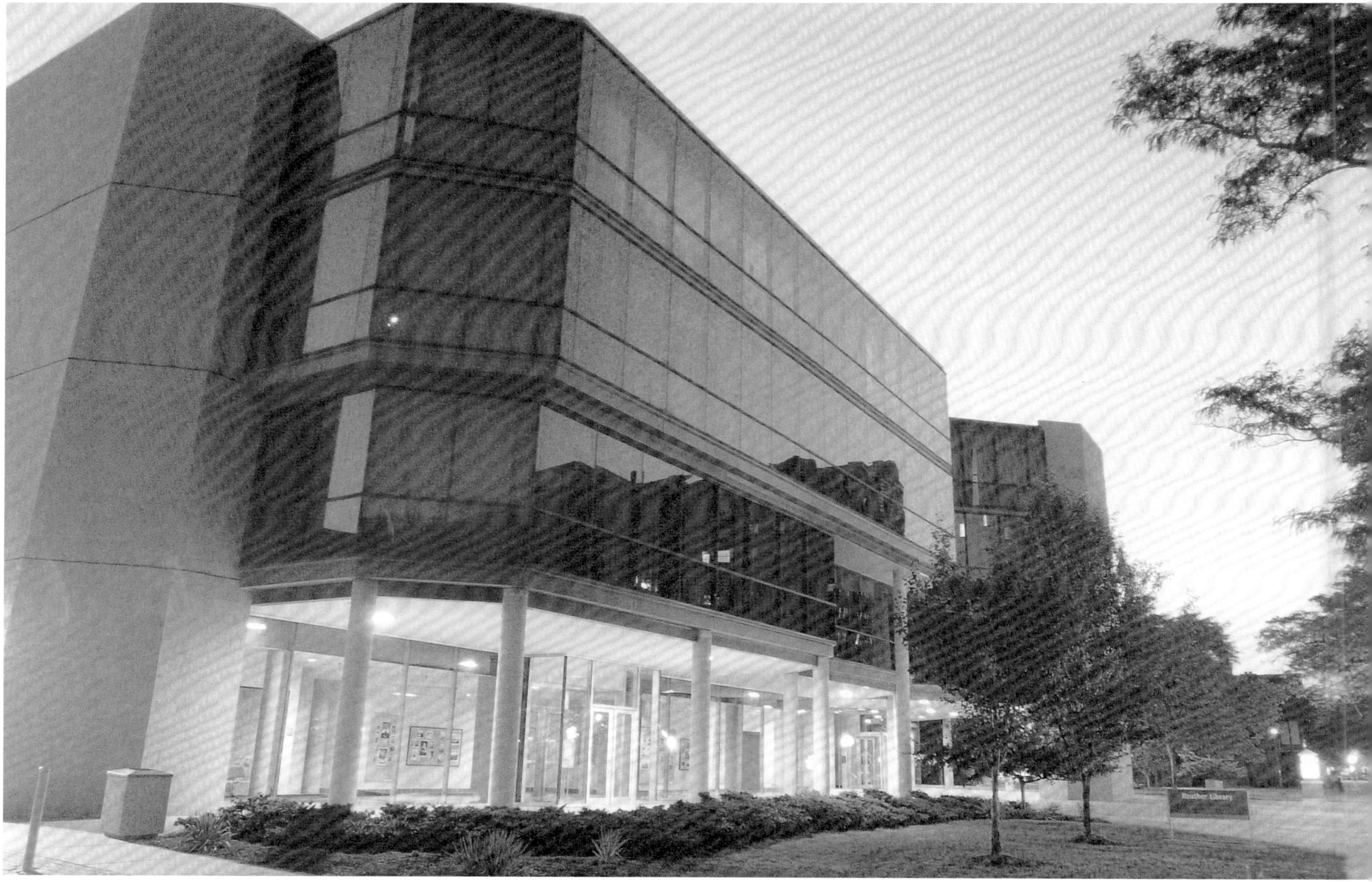

The Walter P. Reuther Library, Archives of Labor and Urban Affairs, 5401 Cass Avenue, at night. Constructed in 1975, the Reuther Library is devoted to collecting and preserving material related to the history of the labor movement. Indeed, it serves as the official repository for the records of a number of labor unions. The library's collection includes historical documents, recordings, and photographs that trace Detroit history and labor history. The photographic archives of the *Detroit News*, as well as those of renowned *Detroit Free Press* photographer Tony Spina, are housed in the Reuther, as are Wayne State's official records. The library is named for Walter Reuther, a giant in the labor movement. Reuther served as president of the United Auto Workers (UAW) and made the union a major force in politics as well as in the auto industry. The Leonard Woodcock Wing, an addition to the library, was completed in 1991. Woodcock was president of the UAW from 1970 to 1977 and served as a member of Wayne State's Board of Governors for eleven years. (Courtesy of Wayne State University Photographic Services.)

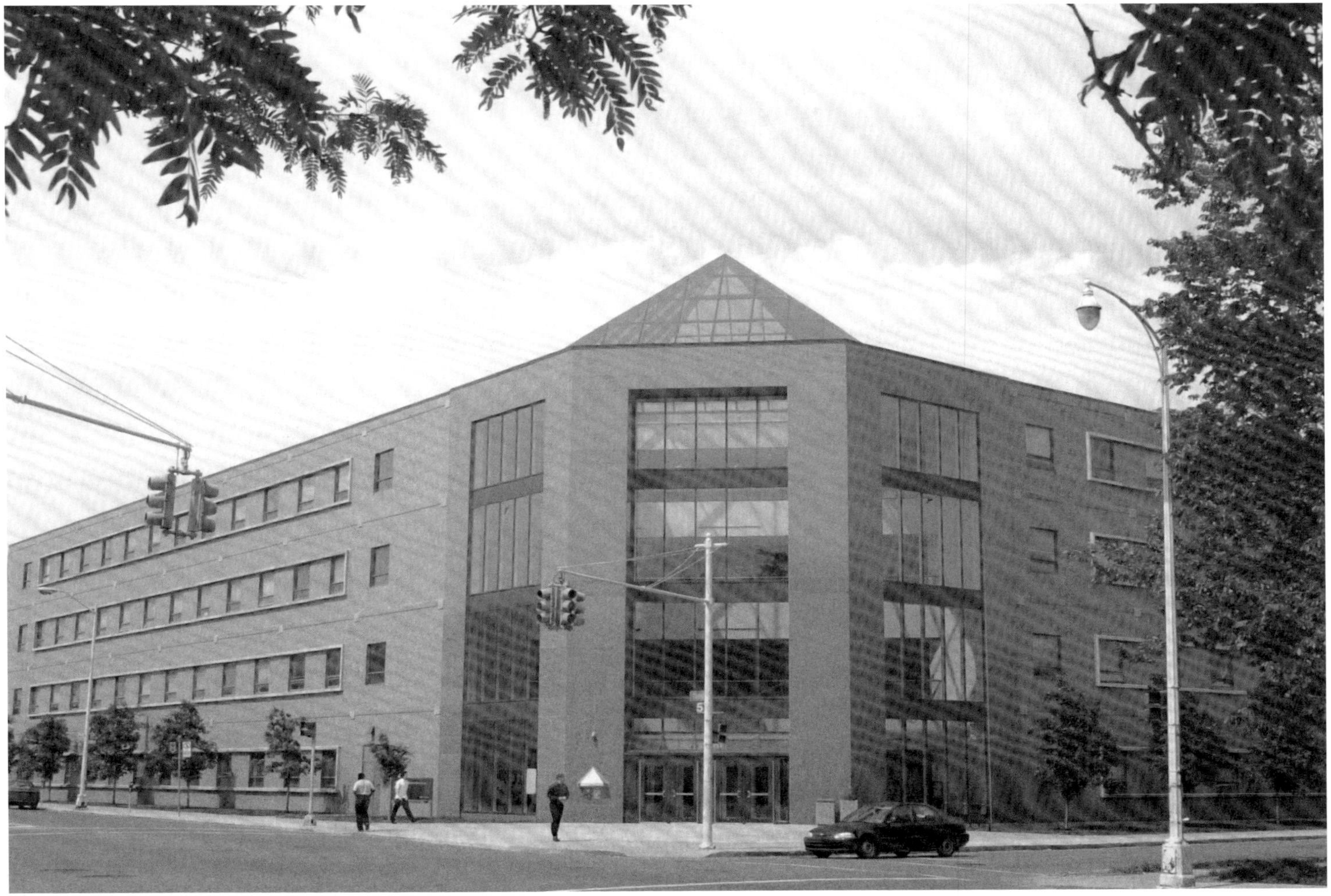

Academic/Administrative Building, 5700 Cass Avenue at Palmer Street, looking northeast. Located kitty-corner across Cass from the Cohn Building, the Academic/Administrative Building was completed in 1995. It houses office space for many university services and largely replaced the Administrative Services Building formerly located at Cass and Antoinette avenues. (Courtesy of Wayne State University Photographic Services.)

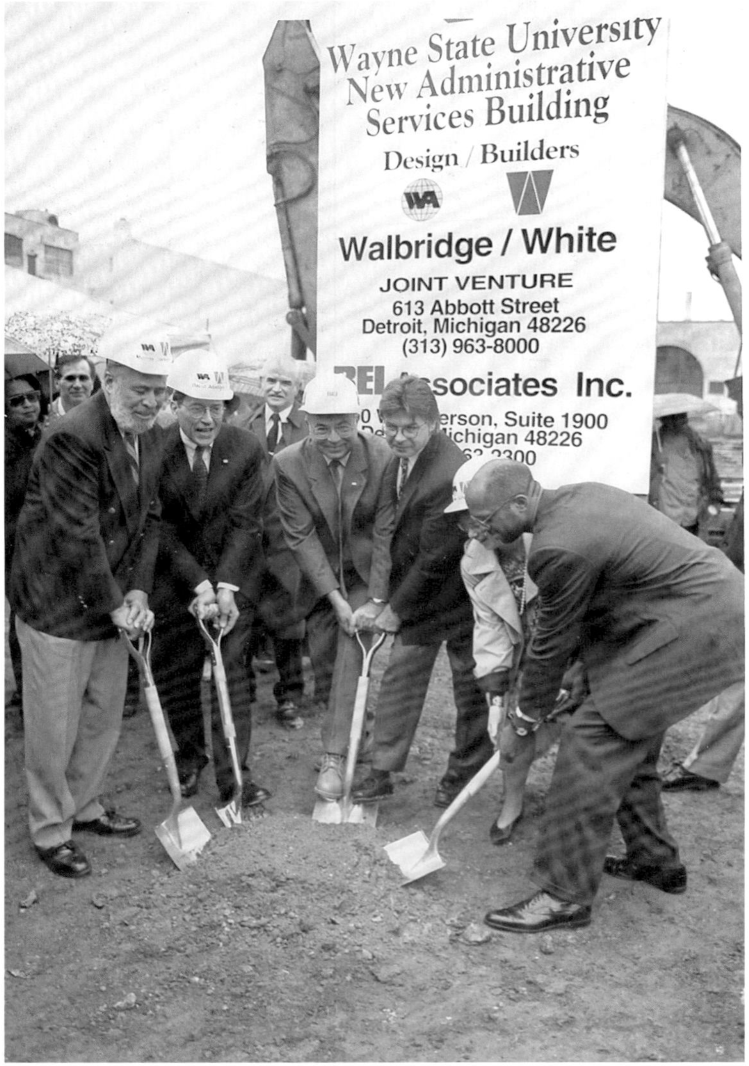

Academic/Administrative Building groundbreaking, 1994. David Adamany, second from the left, was Wayne State University's longest-serving and perhaps most contentious president. While he clashed with the professors' union repeatedly, he also saw the university through an economic recession. On the far left is Murray Jackson, chair of the Wayne State University Board of Governors. Third from the left is Coleman A. Young, former mayor of Detroit. (Walter P. Reuther Library, Archives of Labor and Urban Affairs, Wayne State University.)

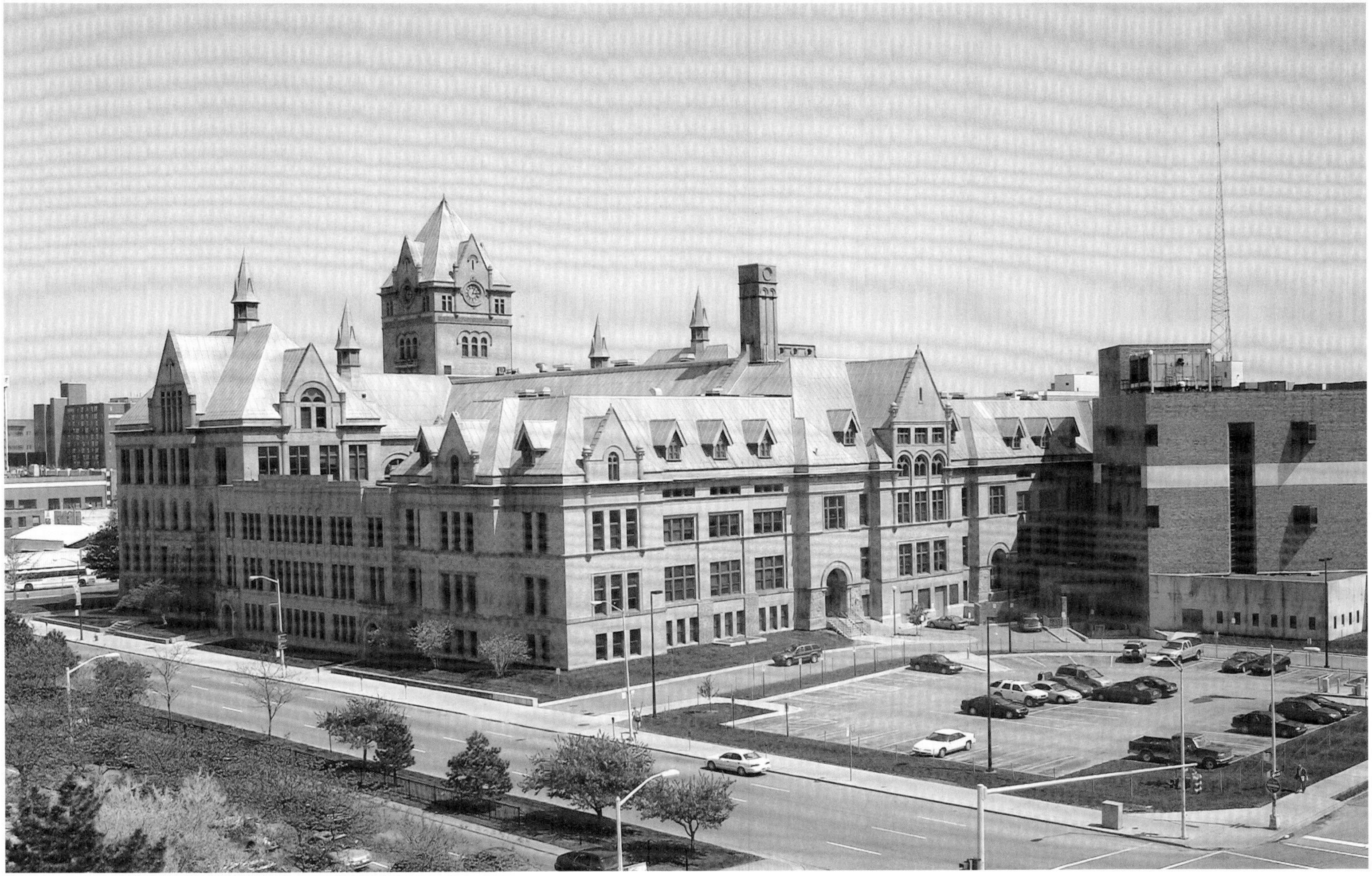

Old Main, northern and western facades, 1990s. To commemorate Old Main's centennial, work on its restoration began in the fall of 1994. A new wing, the Elaine L. Jacob Gallery, which can be seen on the right, was added to the back of the building, on the northeast corner of Hancock Street and Second Avenue. The new wing houses a planetarium, recital space, and art galleries. The restoration project updated and replaced Old Main's one-hundred-year-old electrical and mechanical systems. New windows and air conditioning were also installed. The project was completed in 1997. (Courtesy of Wayne State University Photographic Services.)

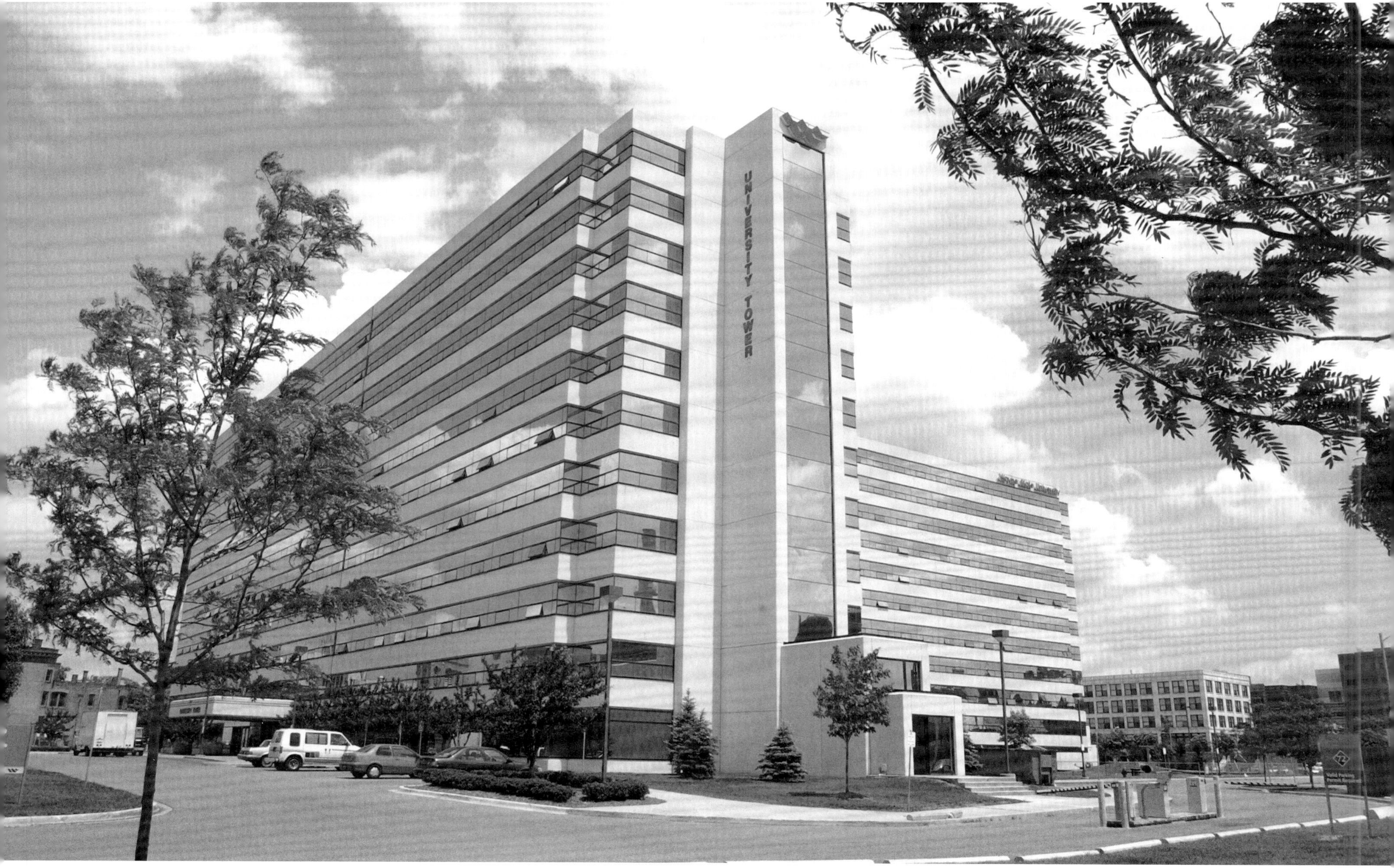
UNIVERSITY TOWER

University Tower Apartments, 4500 Cass Avenue, as seen looking west. The first student housing constructed since the 1970s, University Tower Apartments building was completed in 1995. This eleven-story building was constructed on the site of a former Vernors soda plant. University Tower also houses WDET-FM, the public radio station owned by Wayne State. (Courtesy of Wayne State University Photographic Services.)

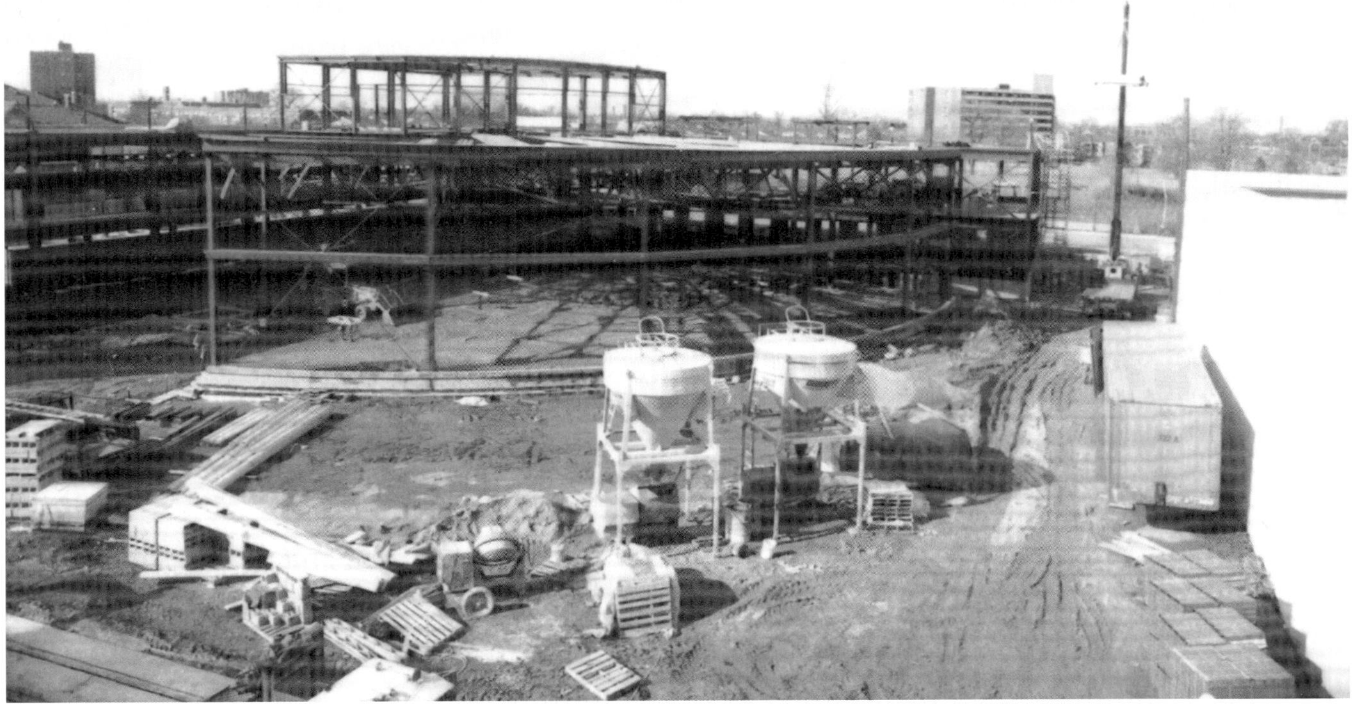

Manufacturing Engineering Building construction, 4815 Fourth Street, looking southwest, 1996. Located on the south side of Warren Avenue, across from Manoogian Hall, this building opened in November 1996. The rounded glass front of the building houses laboratory space for the Manufacturing Engineering Department. The tall apartment building in the distance to the left is part of the Jeffries Housing Projects. (Walter P. Reuther Library, Archives of Labor and Urban Affairs, Wayne State University.)

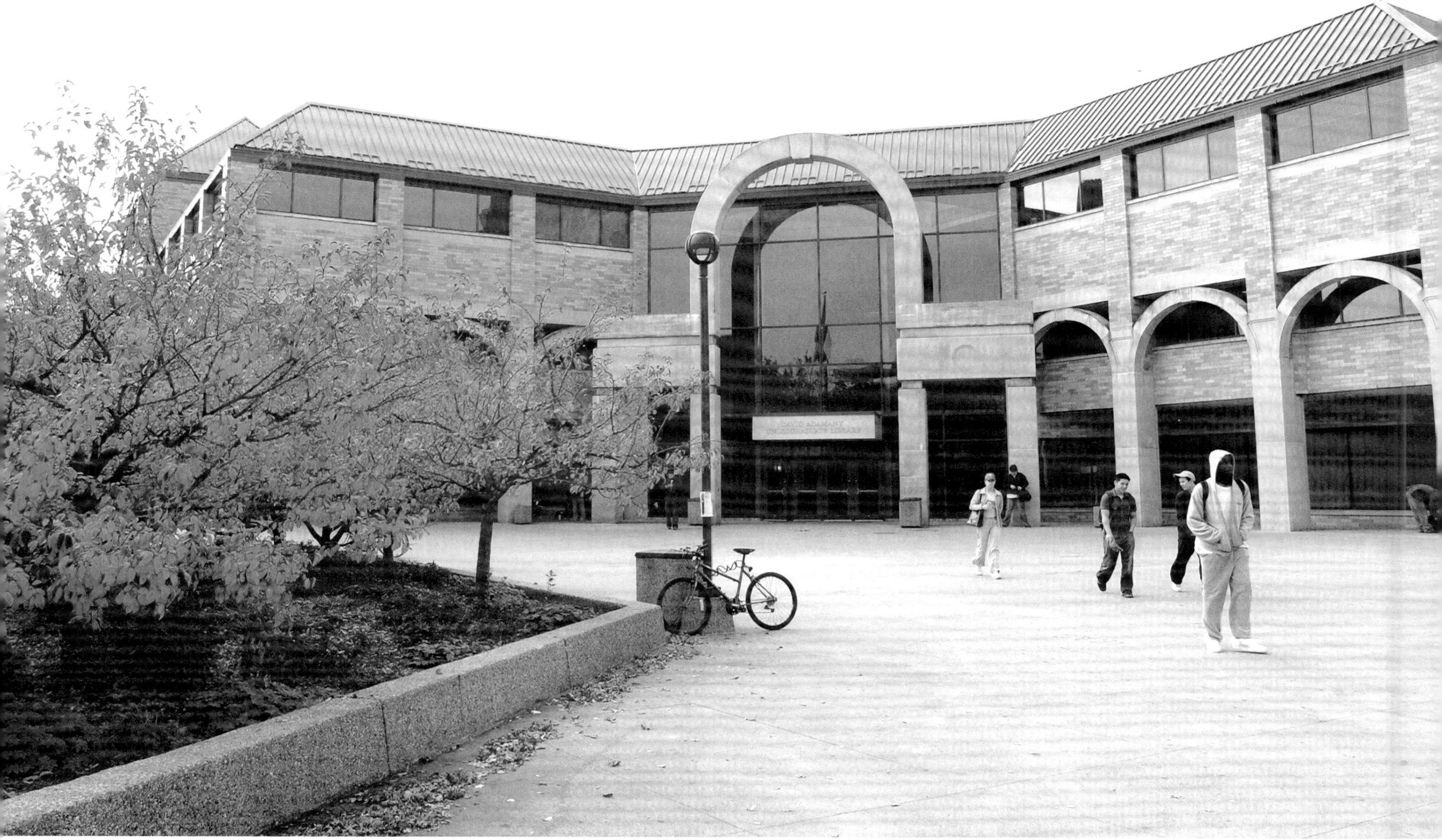
DAVID ADAMANY

David Adamany Undergraduate Library, 5155 Gullen Mall. Construction for the Undergraduate Library began in the fall of 1996 on the former site of the University Bookstore. It opened in the fall of 1997 and was named for President David Adamany by the Board of Governors. (Courtesy of Wayne State University Photographic Services.)

Interior of the Undergraduate Library, 1997. The library houses an auditorium, a room for exhibits, a community meeting room, twenty-four-hour study space, and computers. Until 2002, it also housed the University Bookstore, which then moved to a new building at Cass and Warren avenues. (Walter P. Reuther Library, Archives of Labor and Urban Affairs, Wayne State University.)

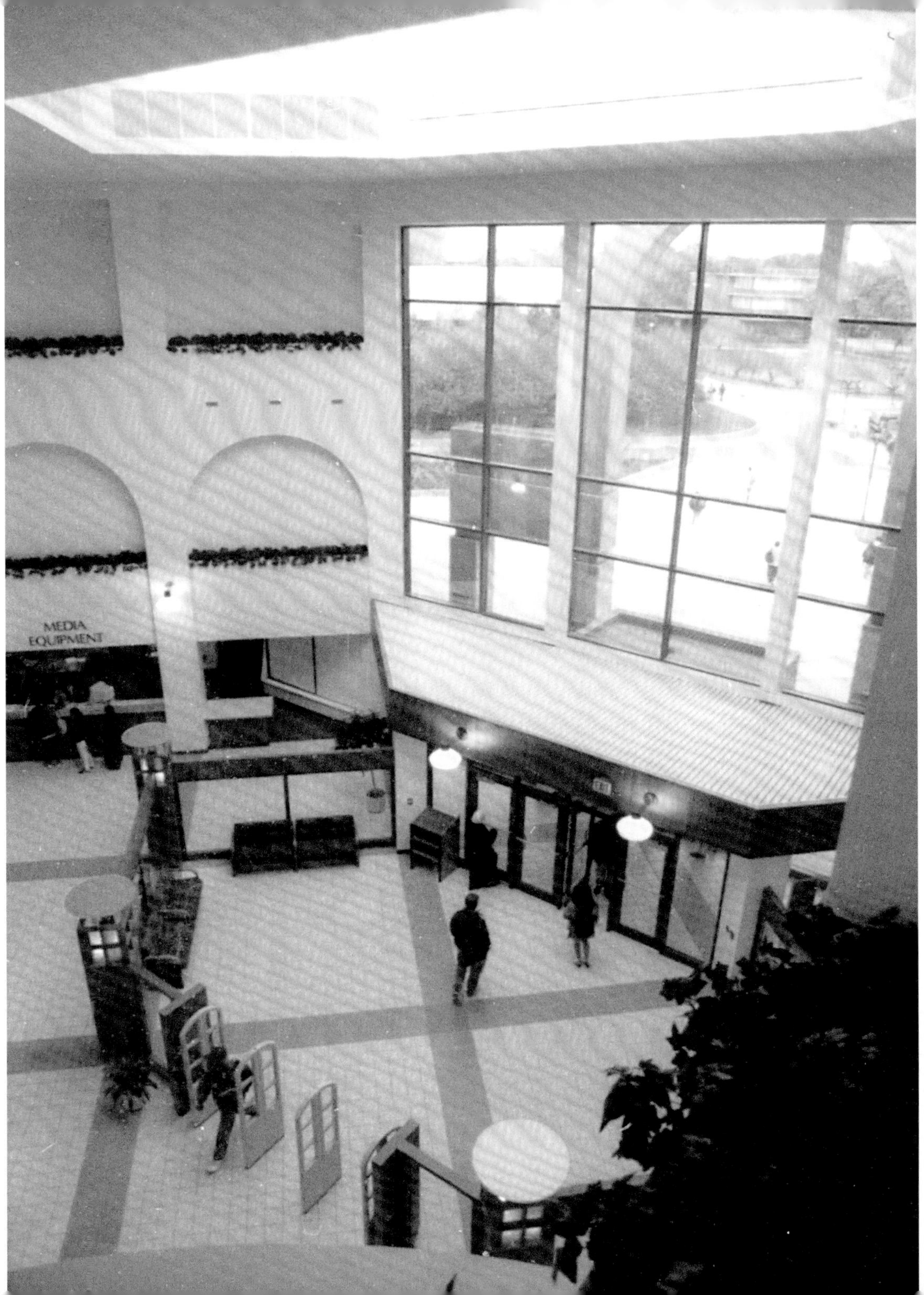

The four "survivors." Only four houses located in the neighborhood destined to become Wayne State University's central campus remain standing today. Most of these homes were constructed between 1904 and 1920 for Detroit's growing middle class. For example, Ty Cobb owned a house (1910–23) located on the south side of Merrick Street (now Williams Mall) next to the house in which G. Mennen Williams was born. Although groups such as Preservation Wayne were instrumental in helping slow the demolition of the neighborhood, the university ultimately prevailed and succeeded in replacing the majority of old homes with new buildings. Over the years, however, many of these stately structures served a variety of educational purposes, acting as classrooms, laboratories, office space, art studios, and meeting spaces for student groups. Today, only the four survivors remain, all of which have been gracefully restored and successfully converted for university use. All four houses are now listed on the National Register of Historic Places.

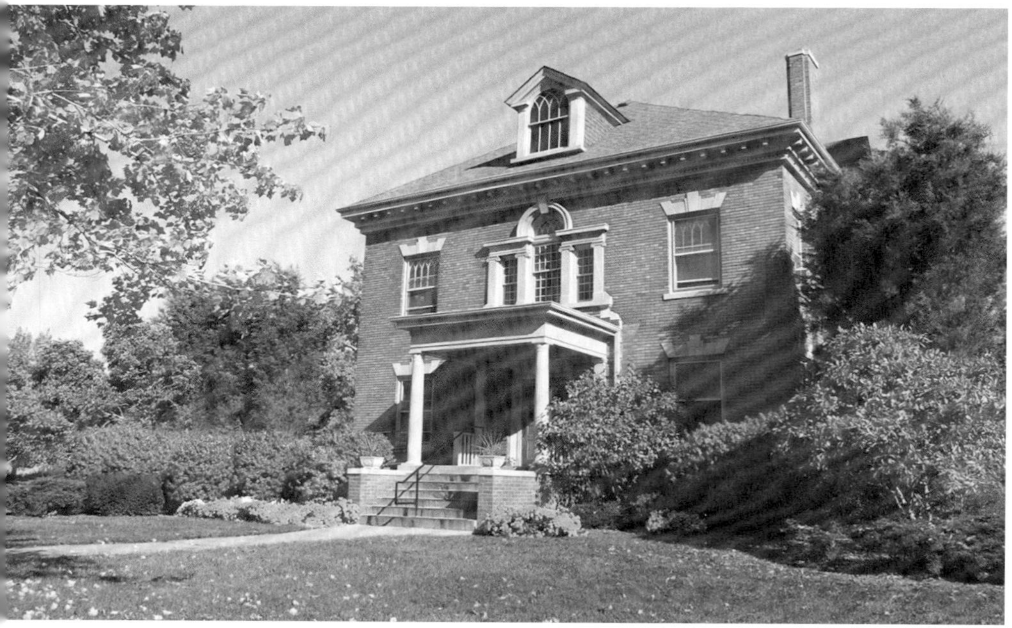

Frederick Linsell House in the fall, 5104 Gullen Avenue, ca. late 1990s. Built in 1904, the Frederick Linsell House was designed by John Clarence Stahl Jr. Linsell was the secretary of the treasury for the William Wright Company, a decorating and specialty furniture manufacturing firm. The Linsell House, located on the corner of what was originally Second Avenue and Putnam Street, was one of the first residences purchased by the university when Wayne began to acquire property in the neighborhood around Old Main. In 1987, the Linsell House was formally dedicated as the administrative headquarters for the College of Fine, Performing and Communication Arts. (Courtesy of Wayne State University Photographic Services.)

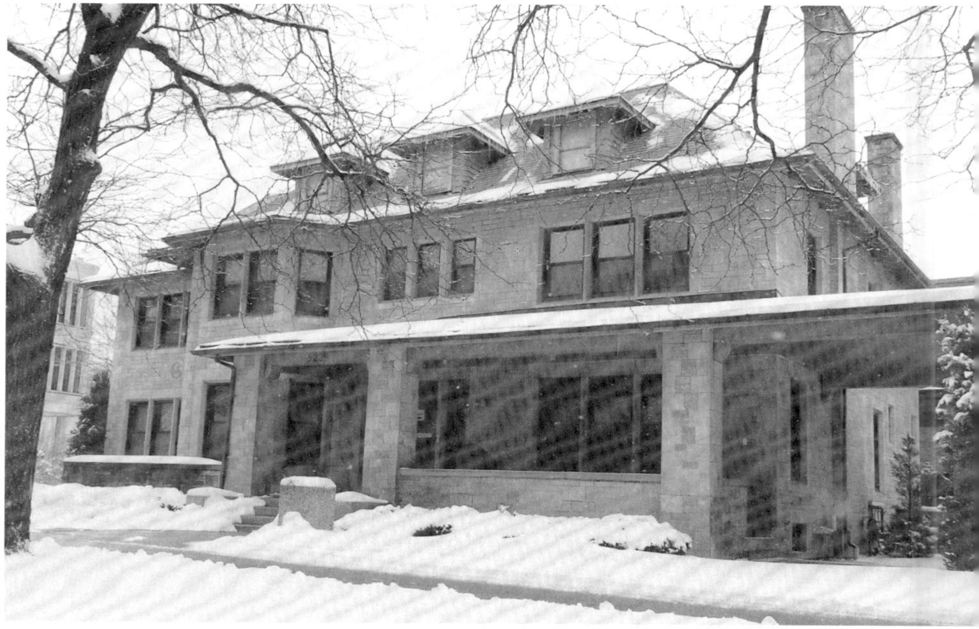

William C. Rands House in winter, 5229 Cass Avenue, ca. late 1990s. William C. Rands, who began in the bicycle business and then moved into auto-parts manufacturing—supplying parts for cars like the Ford Model T—had this house constructed in 1913. In 1944, the Detroit Board of Education purchased the block on which the Rands House was located. In 1946, the house was converted into offices and classrooms. For some years it served as the Law School. In the late 1990s, it was renovated and linked to a new office building. It was officially dedicated as the School of Business Administration Annex in 1991. (Courtesy of Wayne State University Photographic Services.)

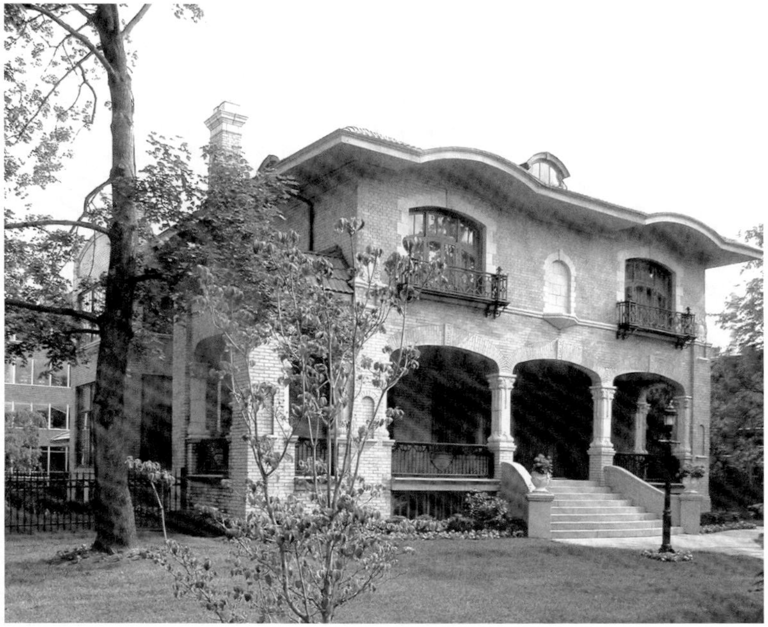

Max Jacob House in spring, 451 W. Kirby, ca. late 1990s. Max Jacob was a Lithuanian immigrant who founded M. Jacob and Sons, a Detroit bottle-distribution company. The Jacob family lived in this house, built in 1915, until 1924. In November 1944, the Detroit Board of Education acquired the house—along with the Rands House—as part of a three-block expansion plan for Wayne University. The home, reconfigured in 1977 as classroom and office space, was used principally by the Department of Art and Art History. In 1999, the Jacob House was again remodeled and became the official residence of Wayne State's president. (Courtesy of Wayne State University Photographic Services.)

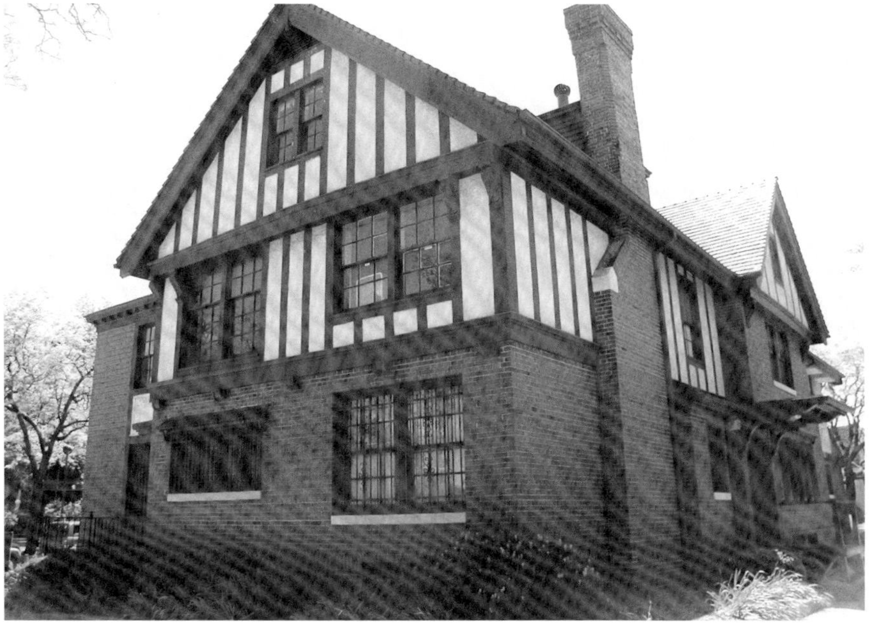

Herman Strasburg House in summer, 5415 Cass, 2006. The Strasburg House has a long-standing connection to the performing arts. The Strasburg family, who were dance teachers, built the house in 1915 and lived in it until 1925. From 1931 to 1944, it was occupied by a private music school. When the Community Arts Center was under construction in the mid-1950s, this house, adjacent to the center, became the Wayne University Choral Studio. Today it serves as an annex to the music department. (Photo courtesy of Thomas Featherstone.)

CHAPTER 7

BUILDING THE FUTURE, 1998–2018

The future is here and Wayne State University is helping build it. As the city moves forward with energy and promise, the university finds itself, after 150 years, at the very center of Detroit's revitalization. Things that seemed impossible only a few years ago in the Cass Corridor are now commonplace in Midtown. Campus and the surrounding area are dotted with bicycle lanes and bike-share stations, trendy apartments, eclectic restaurants, and boutique shops.

University officials have transformed Wayne State from a university that serves primarily local commuters into an institution that attracts students from across the state and from around the globe. New and renovated residence halls and a campus vibrant with athletics and activities welcome students from around the world to Detroit.

A thriving and respected urban research university, Wayne State continues to offer affordable tuition and boasts Michigan's most diverse student body. Situated between the museums of the Detroit Cultural Center and the businesses of Detroit's New Center, the university stands poised to encourage, develop, and support new industries, especially through TechTown, its business incubator. Since its founding as the Detroit Medical College in 1868, Wayne State University has worked to meet the practical needs of the people of Detroit; 150 years later, its legacy of serving the professional and academic needs of the Detroit metro area continues. The university has become integral to the city as a place of learning, inclusion, and progress and is playing a vital role in shaping Detroit's future.

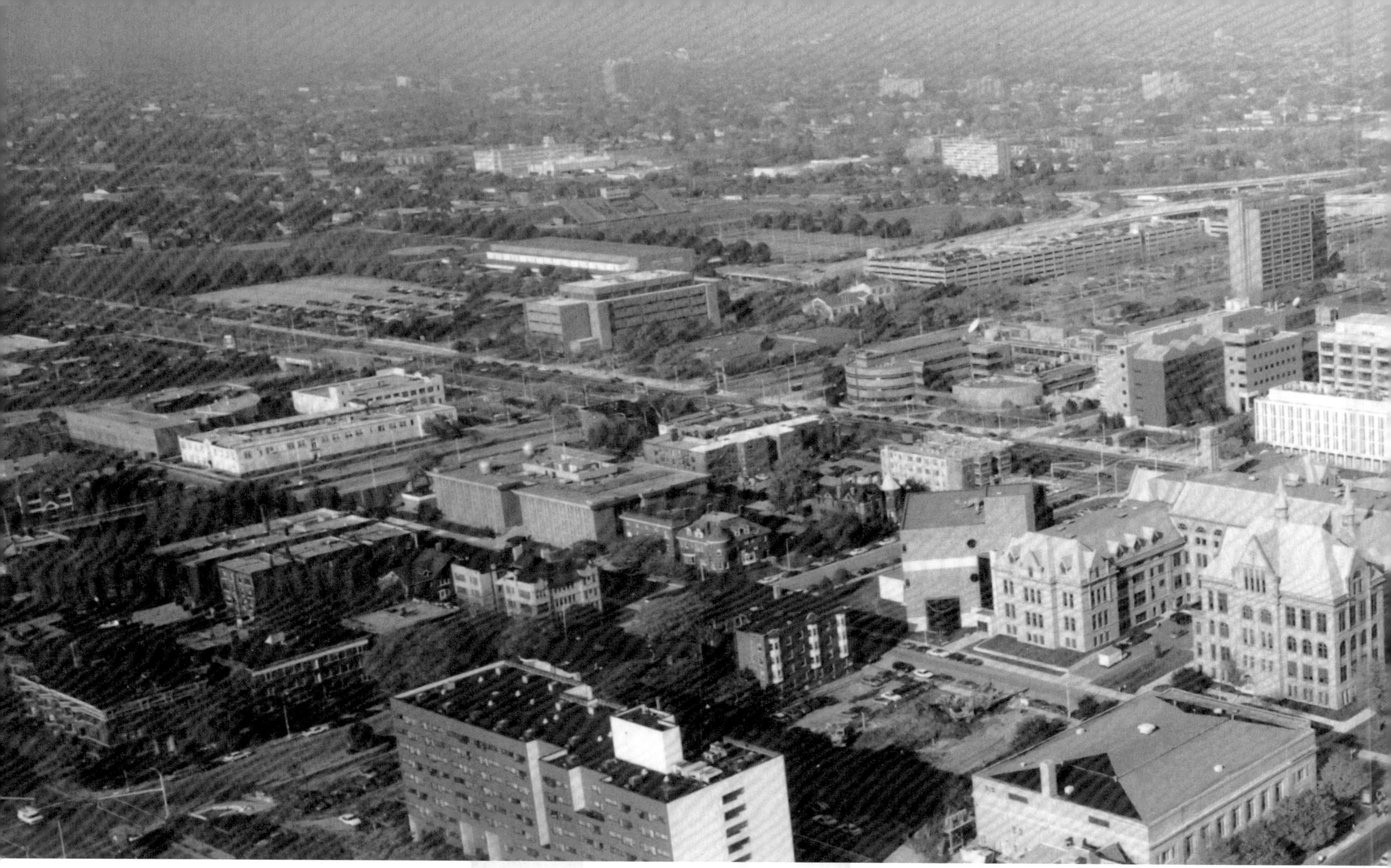

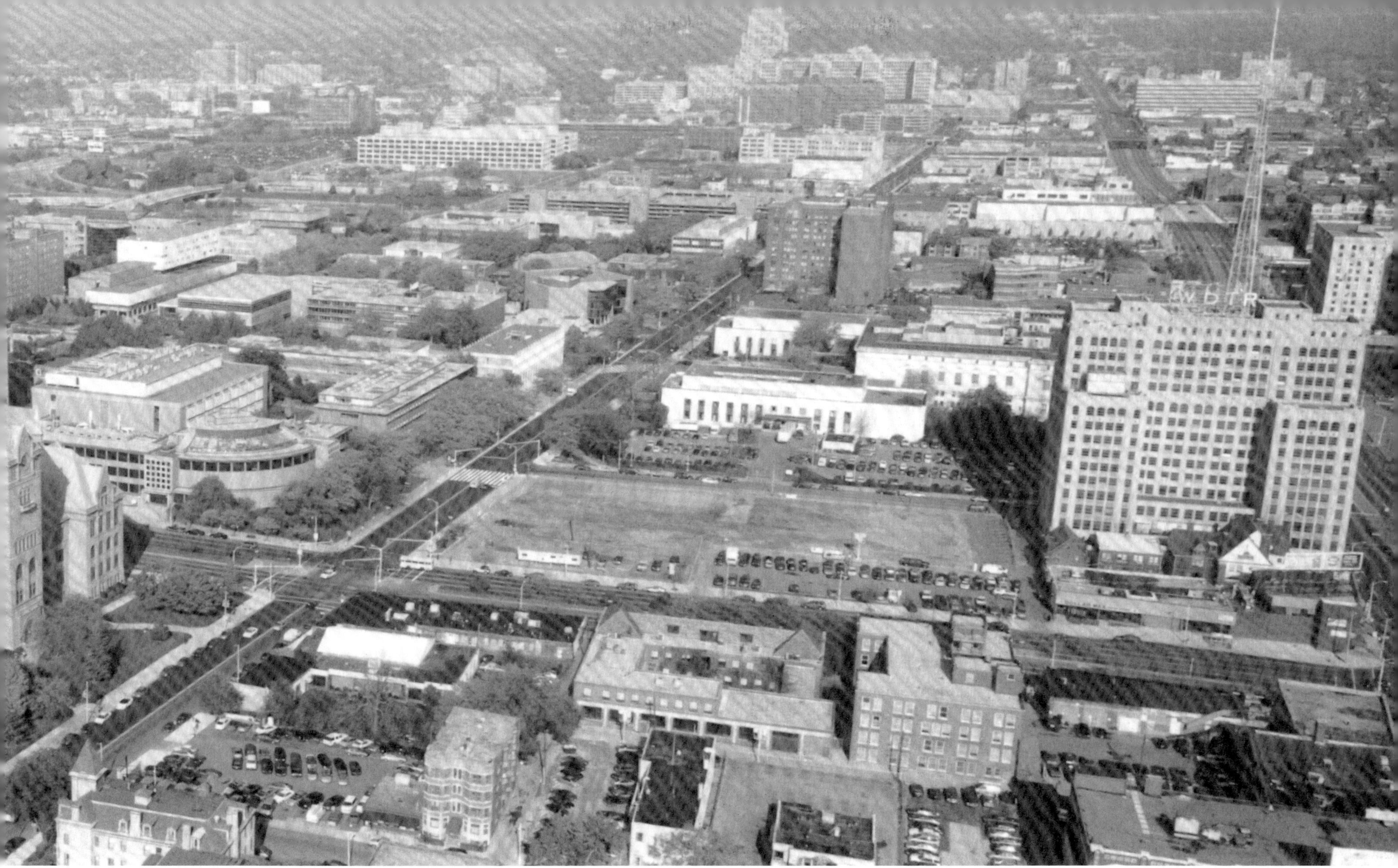

Aerial view of campus, looking northwest, 2001. Old Main is located to the far left in the photograph, with Cass Avenue running in front of it, diagonally to the right. Demonstrating the pace of campus construction over the last two decades, numerous buildings have been added since the photograph was taken, including new student housing, new laboratory and entrepreneurial spaces, and facilities for a number of schools and colleges. (Courtesy of Wayne State University Photographic Services.)

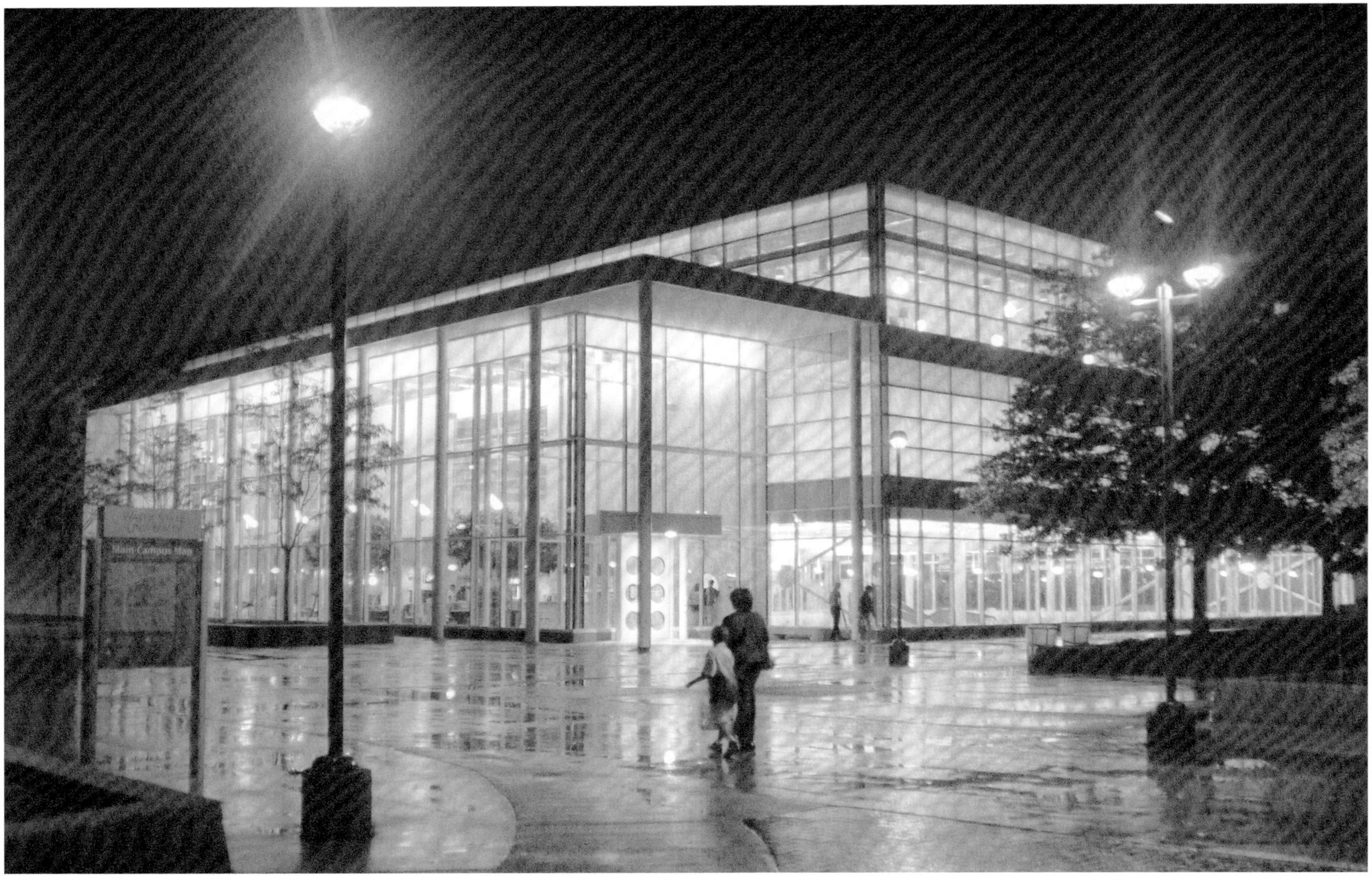

The Mort Harris Recreation and Fitness Center at night, 5210 Gullen Mall, as seen from the southwest. Built in 2000, the fitness center was the first of many building projects that aimed to provide amenities for students and faculty members on campus. Adjacent to the Purdy/Kresge Library, the center features a rock climbing wall, weights and fitness equipment, basketball courts, and a walking track. (Courtesy of Wayne State University Photographic Services.)

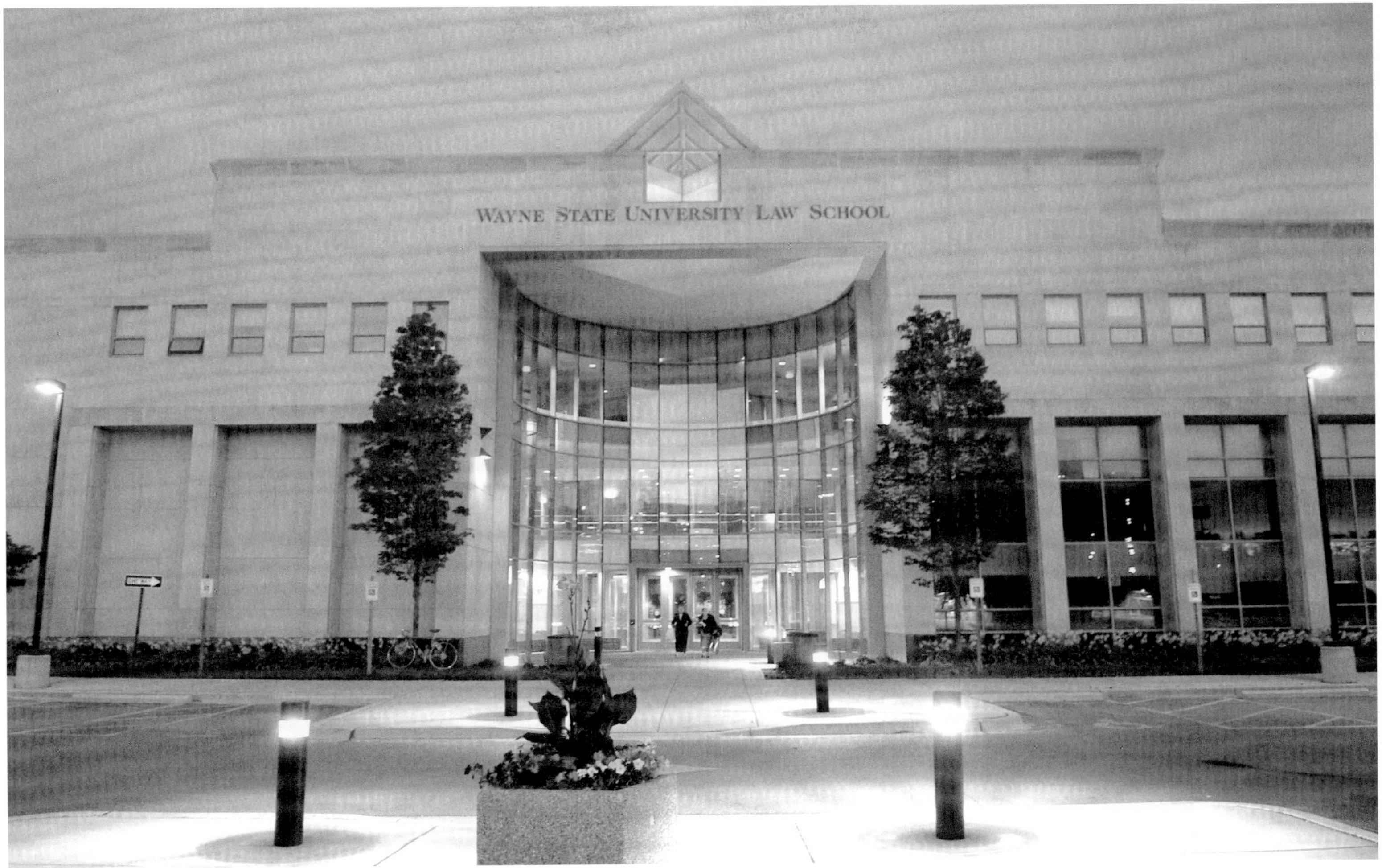

Addition to Wayne Law on Palmer Street at night, northern facade. In 2000, the Law School was renovated and a 54,000-square-foot wing completed, which includes the glass front of this building and the Spencer M. Partrich Auditorium. The Law School addition replaced the existing Law School Annex, which was constructed in 1971 as a temporary structure. (Courtesy of Wayne State University Photographic Services.)

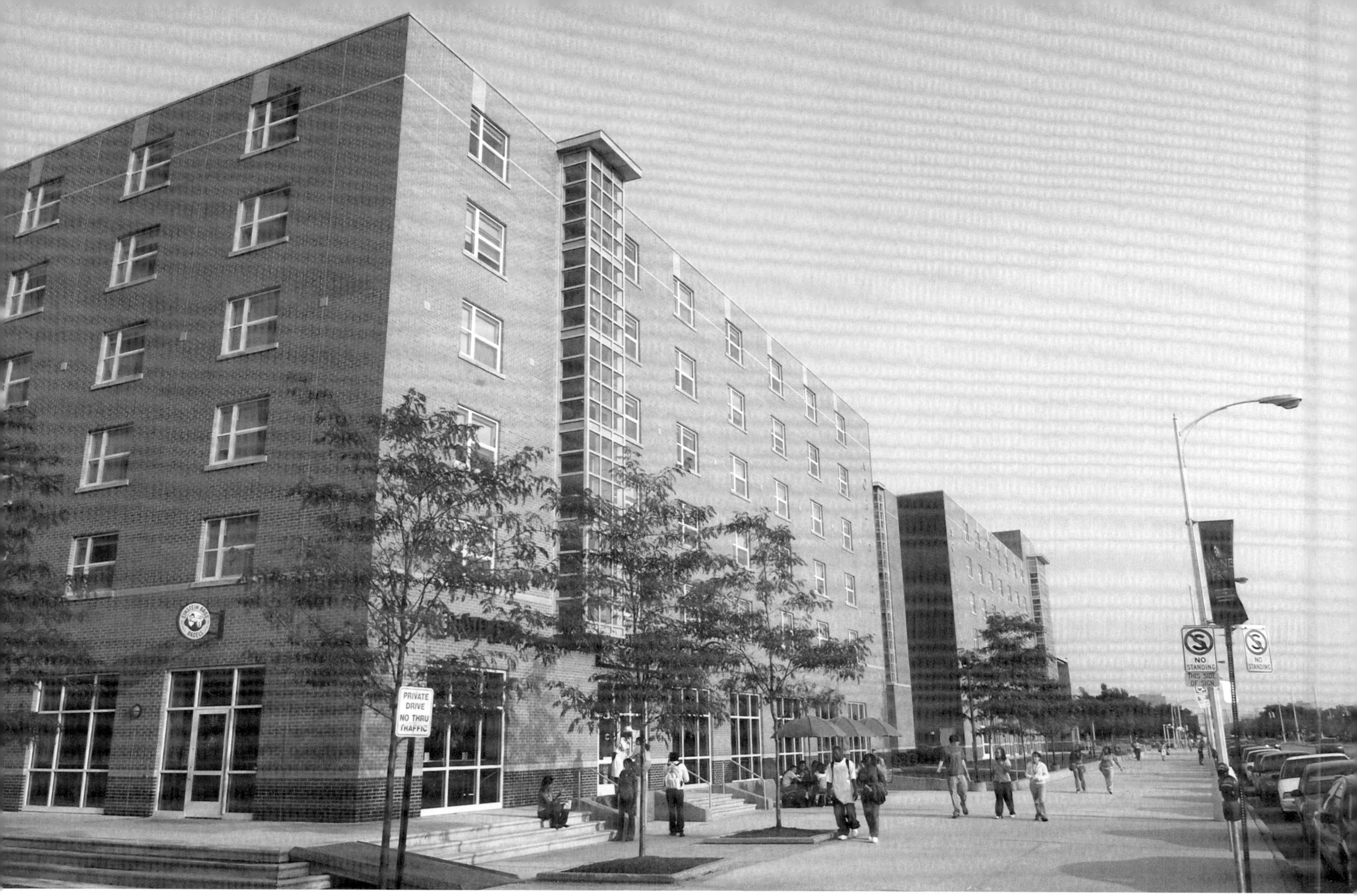
PRIVATE DRIVE NO THRU TRAFFIC
NO STANDING THIS SIDE OF SIGN
NO STANDING

Wayne State University residence halls, as seen looking southeast along Anthony Wayne Drive. In the foreground is North Hall, completed in 2002, the first of three residential halls built to further Wayne State's goal of encouraging more residential students. South Hall, to the right of North Hall, was completed the following year. Both North Hall and South Hall are traditional student housing—dormitories—rather than apartment buildings like the University Tower Apartments. North Hall was renamed Ghafari Hall in 2005, in honor of Yousif Ghafari, an architect and Wayne State University alumnus who donated $9 million to Wayne State's fund-raising campaign in 2005. In 2008, South Hall was renamed Leon H. Atchison Hall, after the longest-serving Board of Governors member. In 2017, construction began on an additional residence hall—the Anthony Wayne Drive Apartments—across the street. (Courtesy of Wayne State University Photographic Services.)

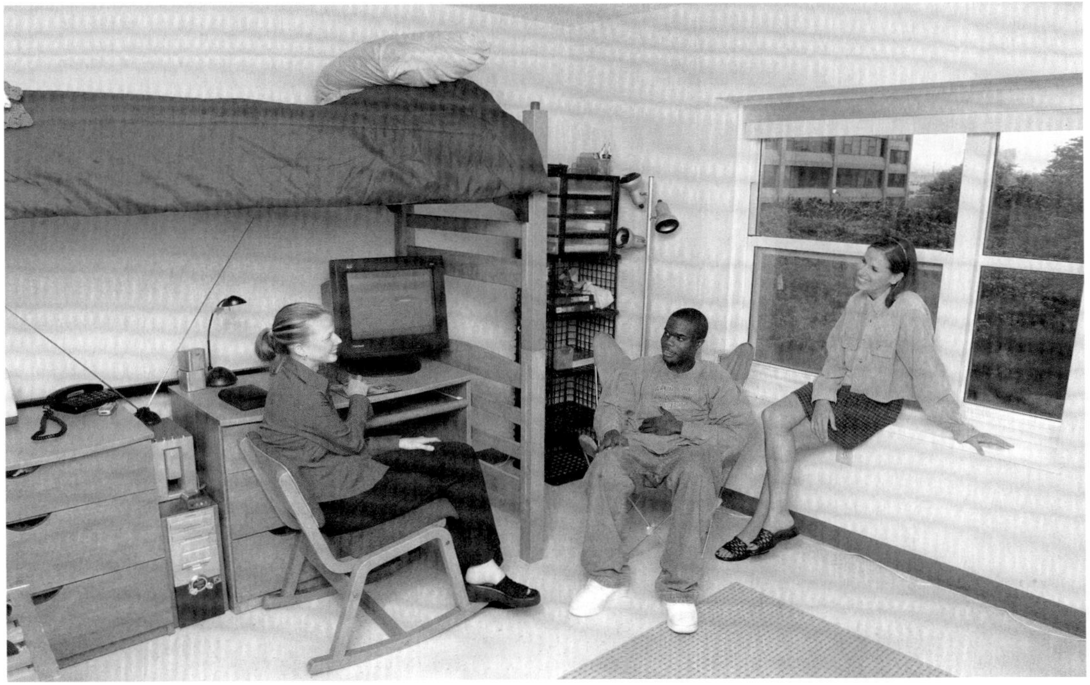

Interior of a residence hall. Since computers and Internet access have become essential to college work, residence halls are equipped with both. The DeRoy Apartments are visible through the window. (Courtesy of Wayne State University Photographic Services.)

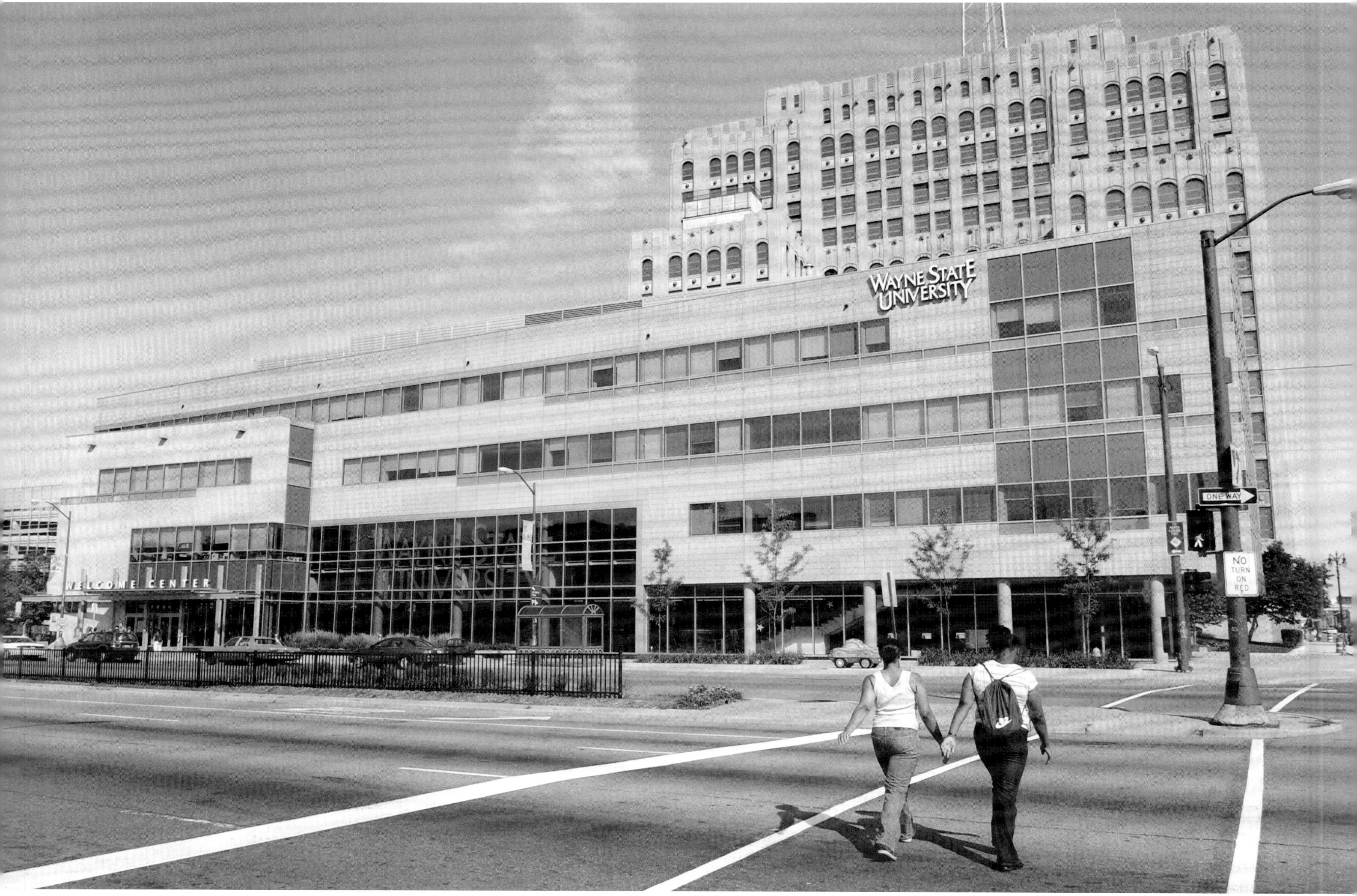
WAYNE STATE UNIVERSITY
WELCOME CENTER
ONE WAY
NO TURN ON RED

Welcome Center, 42 W. Warren Avenue, as seen looking north. Constructed on the corner of Woodward and Warren avenues, the Welcome Center provides Wayne State University with a permanent presence on Woodward, Detroit's main thoroughfare. Completed in 2002, the Welcome Center consolidated student services such as admissions, financial aid, cashier services, and housing under one roof. The Maccabees Building, purchased by the university the same year, is seen behind the Welcome Center. (Courtesy of Wayne State University Photographic Services.)

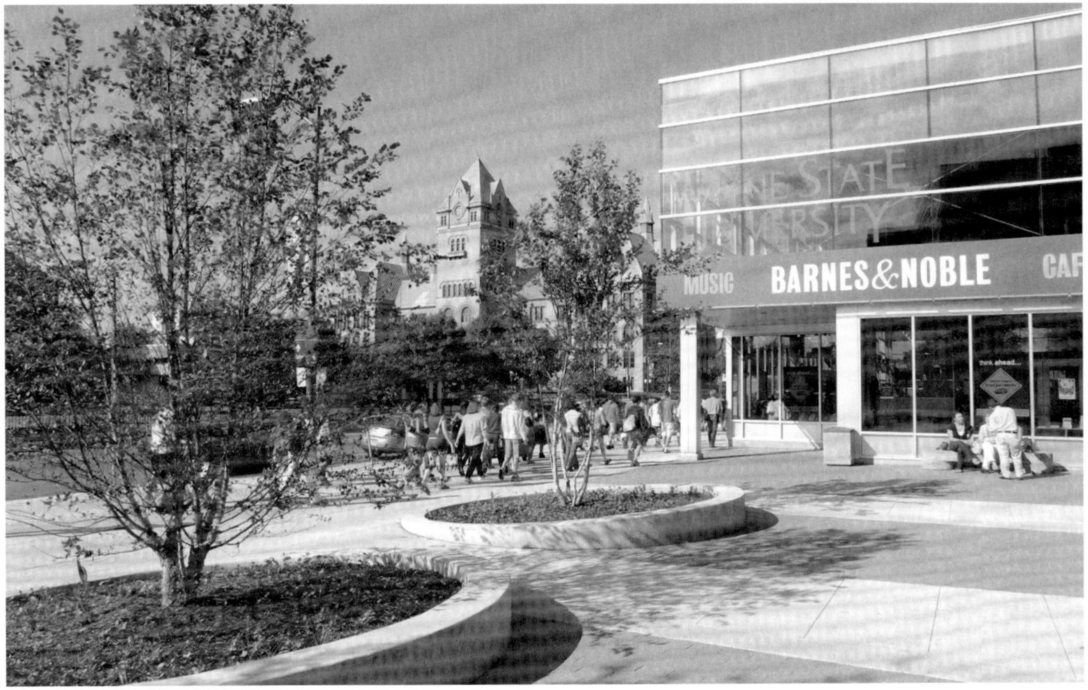

University Bookstore, 82 W. Warren Avenue at Cass Avenue, eastern facade. Along with the Welcome Center, the university's new bookstore was completed in 2002. Old Main is visible in the distance. (Courtesy of Wayne State University Photographic Services.)

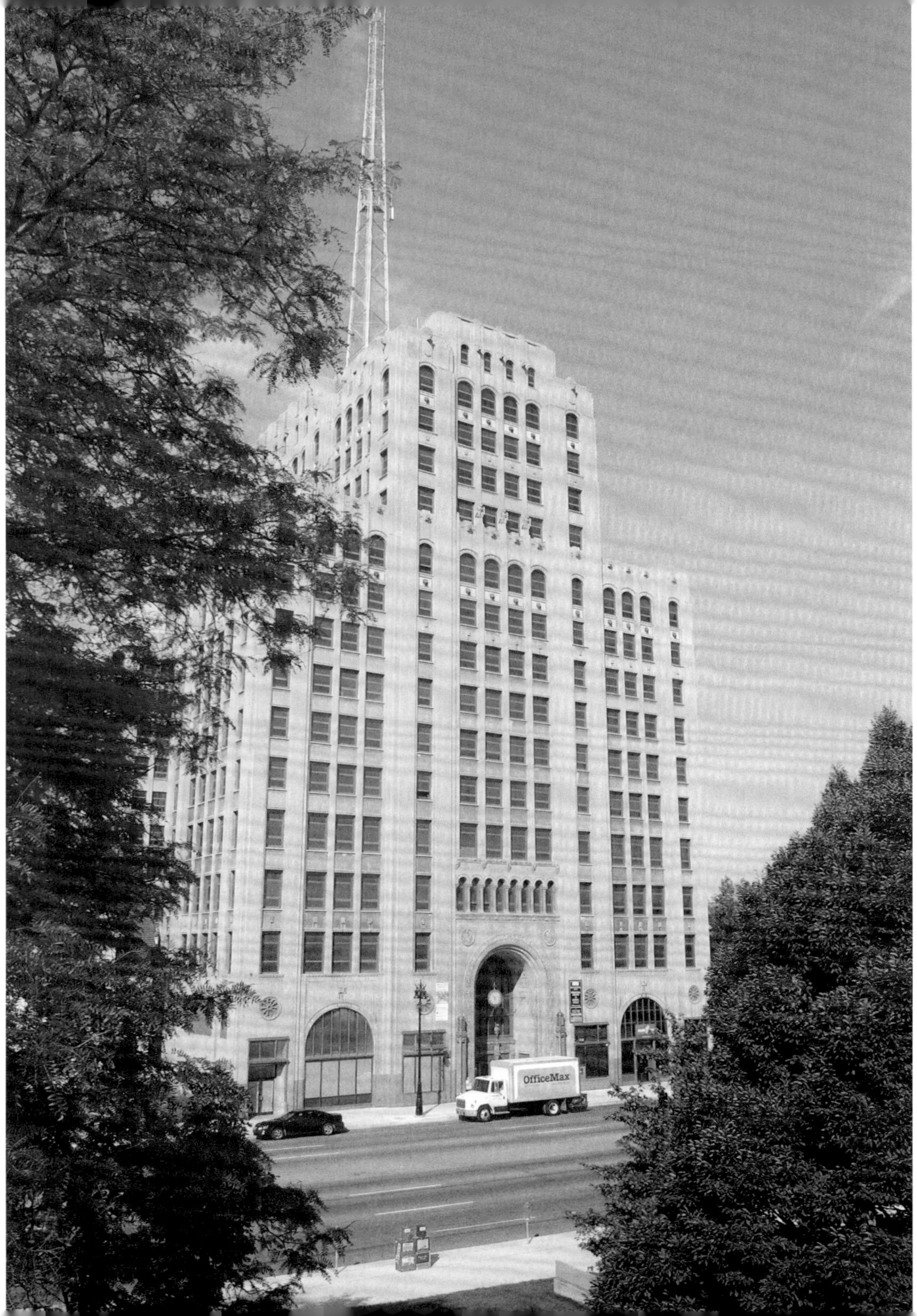

The Maccabees Building, 5057 Woodward Avenue at Putnam Street, as seen looking west. Designed by renowned architect Albert Kahn, the Maccabees Building was built in 1927. From 1960 until 2002, the building was owned by the Detroit Public Schools and was known as the School Center Building. Purchased by Wayne State in 2002 to increase the school's presence on Woodward Avenue, it currently houses the Departments of African American Studies, English, Philosophy, and Psychology, as well as the Office of the Registrar. (Courtesy of Wayne State University Photographic Services.)

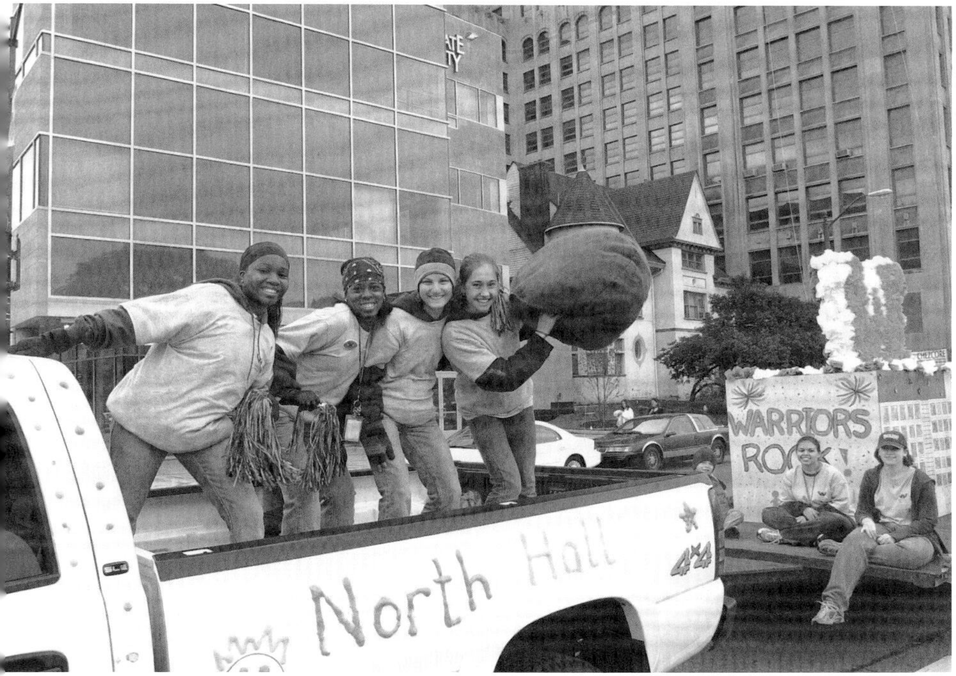

Homecoming parade, student float. The parade, an activity revived at Wayne State in 2002, takes place along Woodward Avenue. The Welcome Center and the Maccabees Building are visible behind the float. While Homecoming has been held at Wayne State since the 1930s, parades were not held consistently over the years because the majority of students commuted to their classes instead of living on campus. (Courtesy of Wayne State University Photographic Services.)

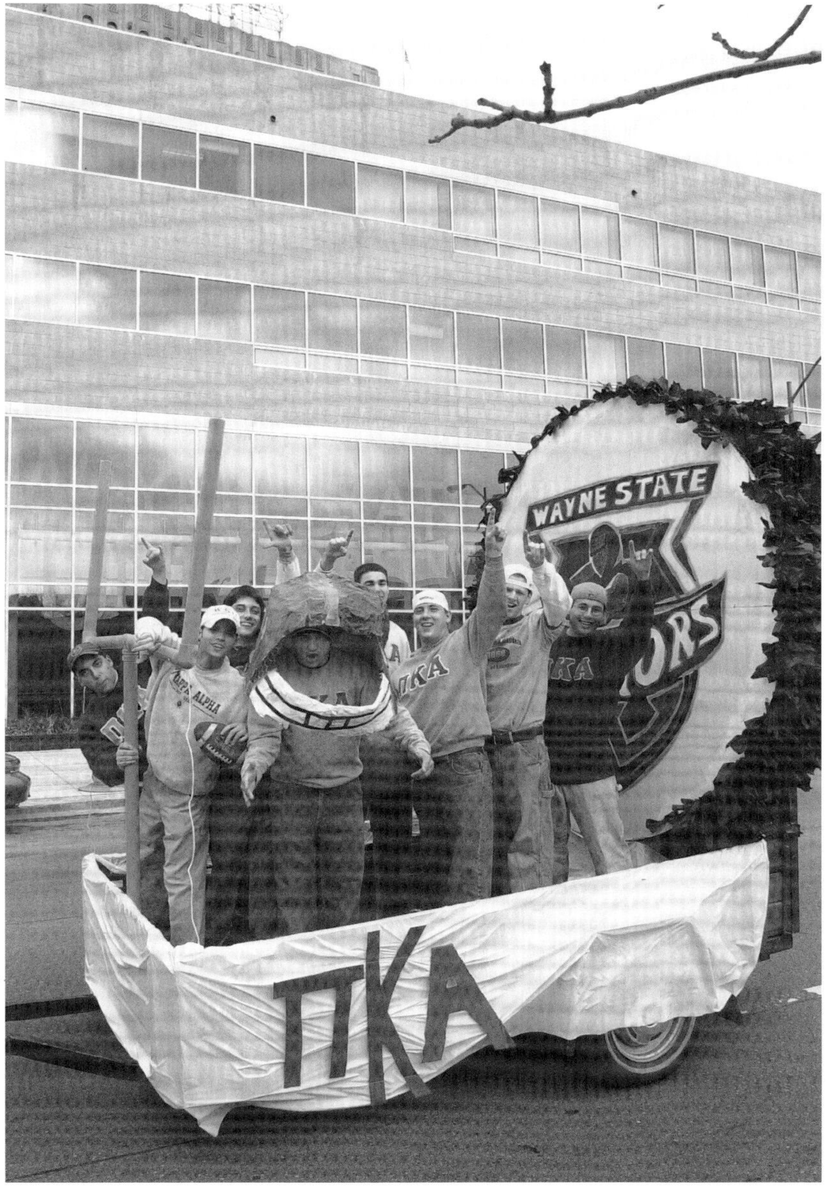

Homecoming parade, student float. A renewed interest in Homecoming activities is clearly tied to the increased number of undergraduates living on campus. The Welcome Center can be seen behind the students. (Courtesy of Wayne State University Photographic Services.)

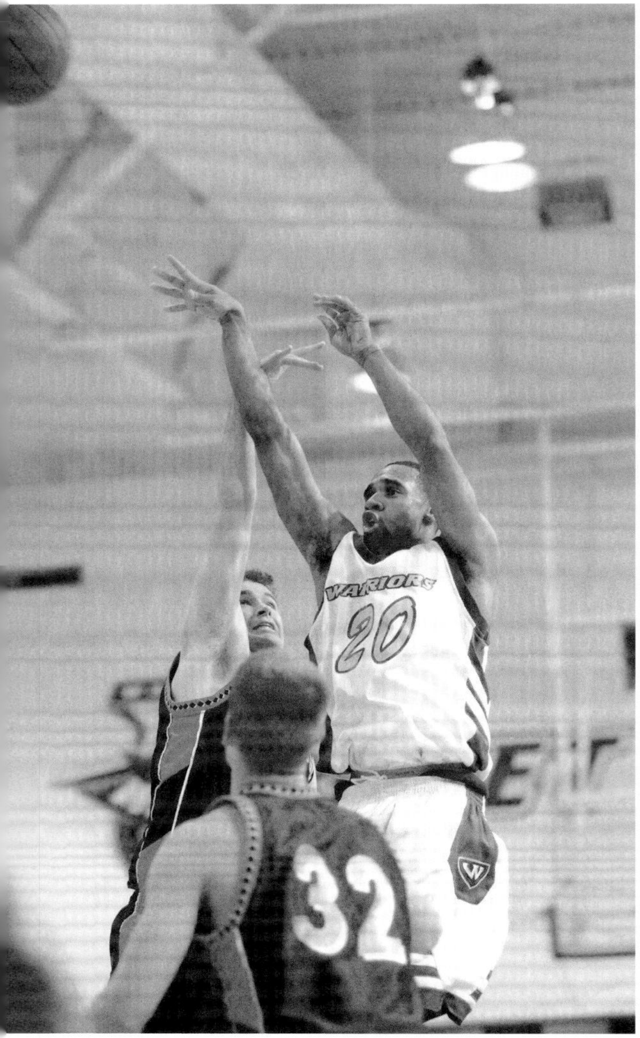

Basketball game, 2003. While in the past Wayne State placed a limited emphasis on athletics, current university officials encourage student interest in intercollegiate sports. (Courtesy of Wayne State University Photographic Services.)

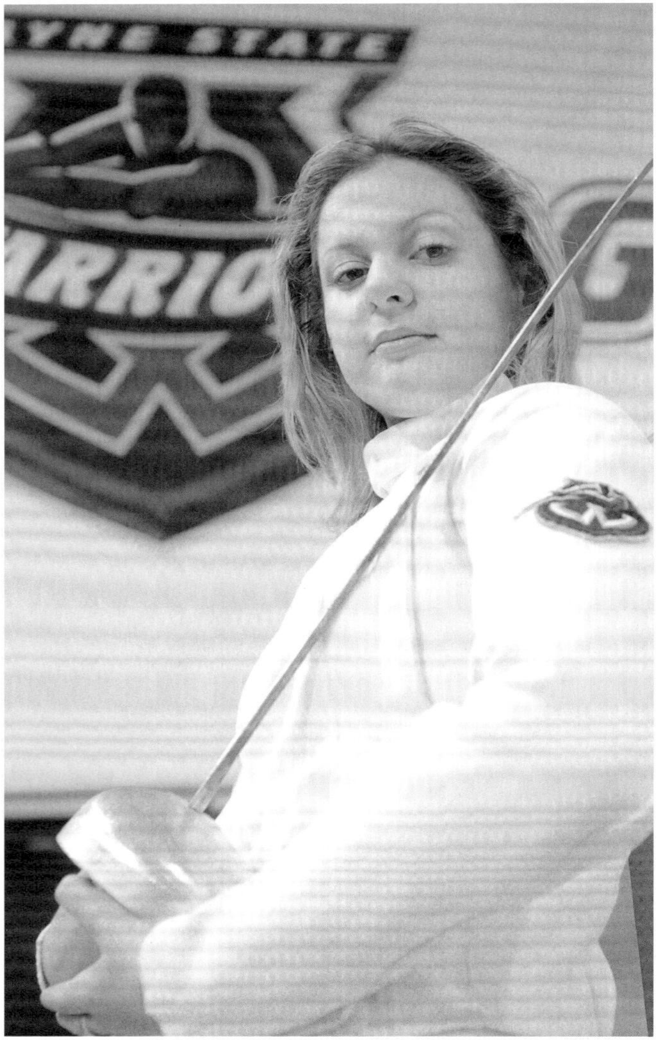

Fencer with foil. Wayne State's fencing team still ranks high in the National Collegiate Athletic Association (NCAA). (Courtesy of Wayne State University Photographic Services.)

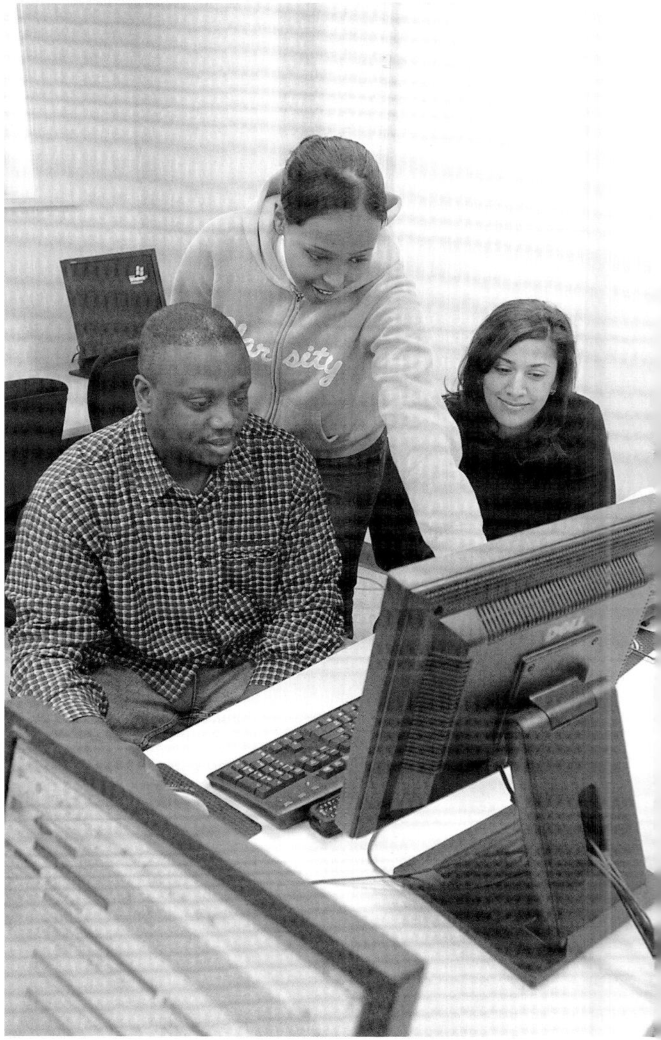

Wayne State students in a computer lab. By the time class registration went online in the fall of 2002, computers were an essential part of life at Wayne State. Grades, transcripts, and course materials—syllabi, assignments, and quizzes—are now available online. (Courtesy of Wayne State University Photographic Services.)

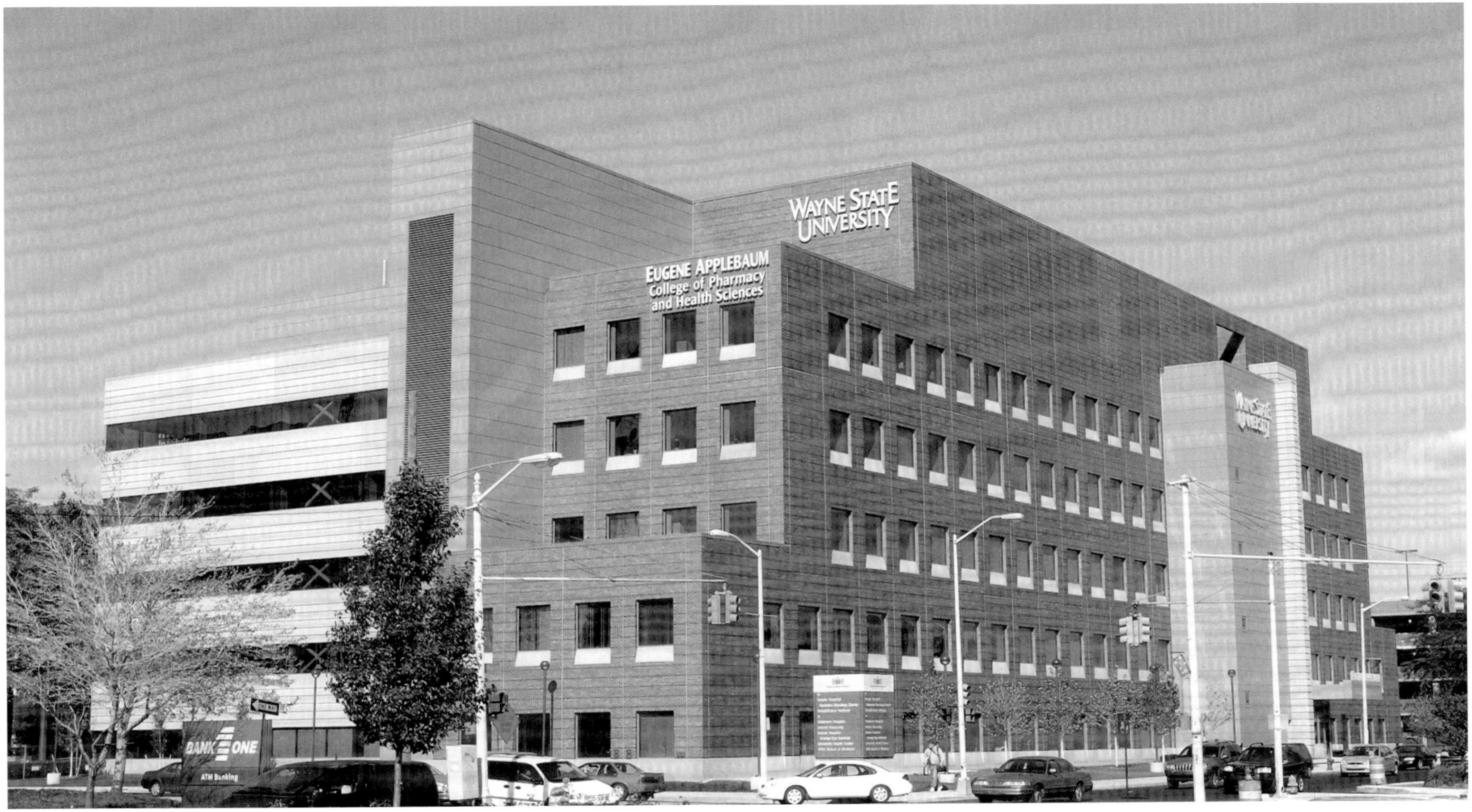

Eugene Applebaum College of Pharmacy and Health Sciences, 259 Mack at John R Avenue. Constructed in the Detroit Medical Center in 2002, this state-of-the-art facility permitted pharmacy students to move out of the old building at 1400 Chrysler Drive. (Courtesy of Wayne State University Photographic Services.)

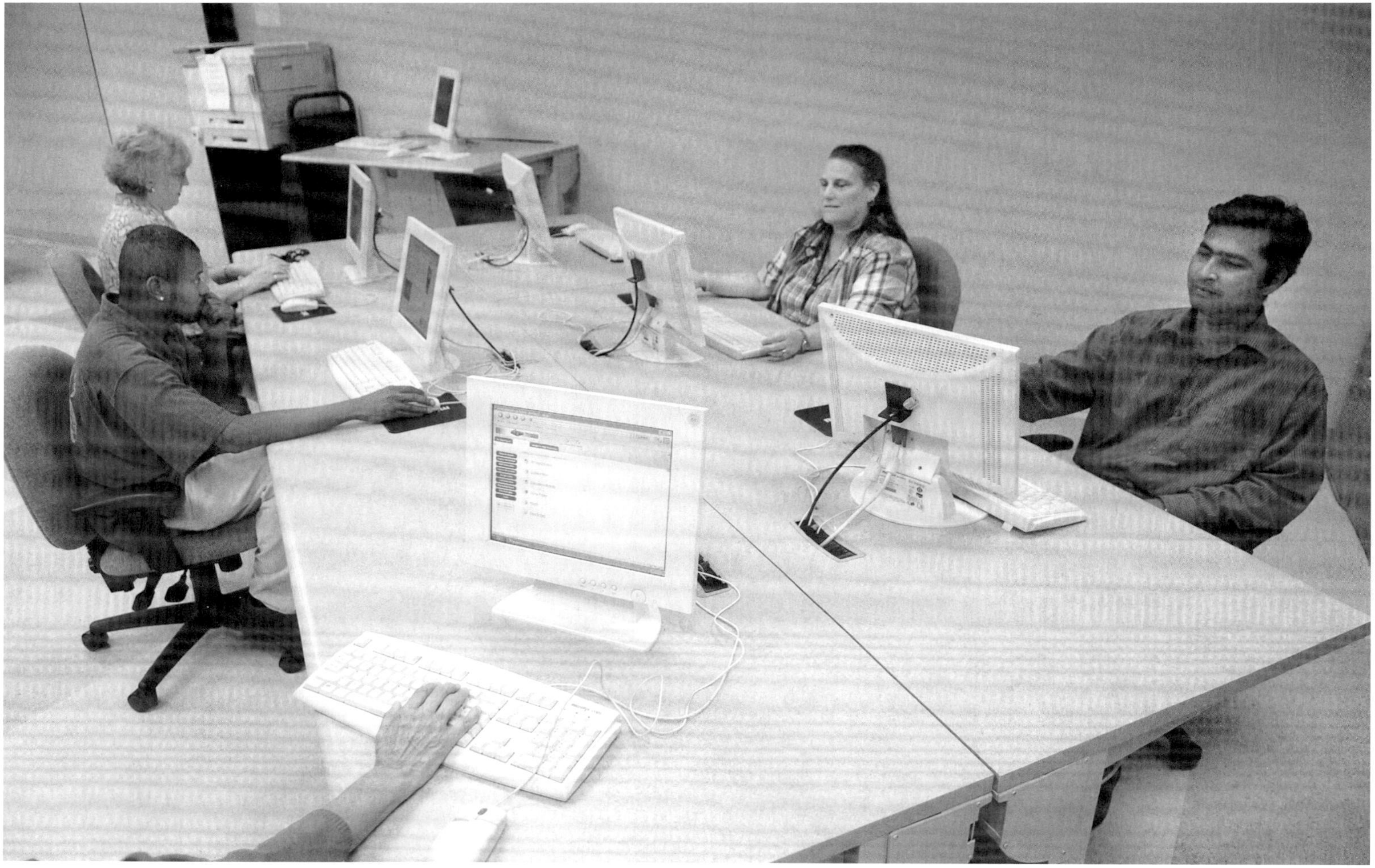

College of Pharmacy computer lab. (Courtesy of Wayne State University Photographic Services.)

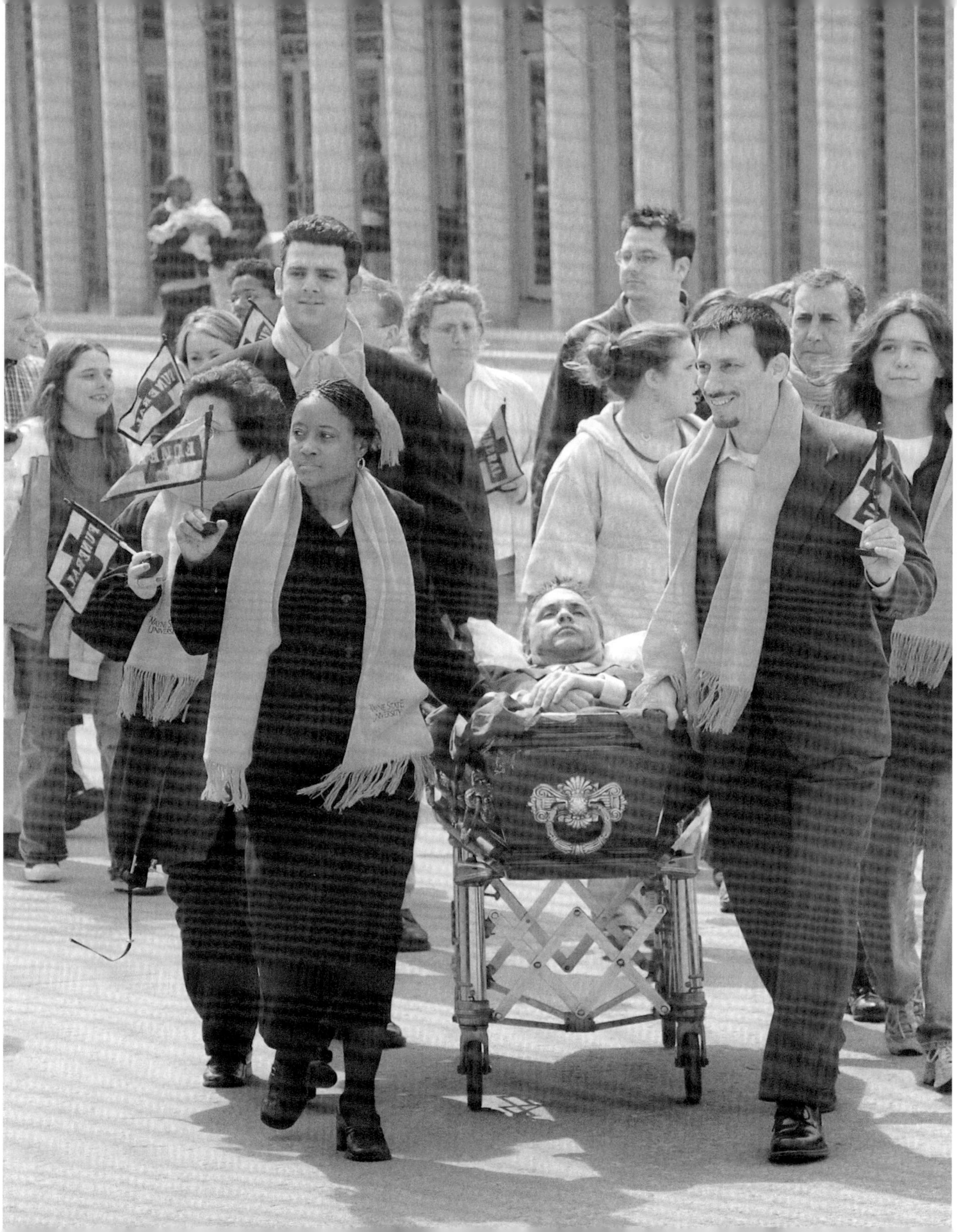

Funeral for Old Man Winter, 2003. From the 1980s until the early 2000s, Wayne State students staged a mock New Orleans–style funeral for Old Man Winter to celebrate the coming of spring. Students acted as "pallbearers" and "mourners," and the procession marched across campus to the Circa 1890 Saloon, a favorite campus hangout. Wayne State's jazz band performed as a student playing the role of "Spring" threw flowers on a coffin supplied by the mortuary science department. Traditionally, the owner of Circa 1890 donated the saloon's proceeds from the day to various departments at Wayne State. Originally held April 16, the event was started by the owners of the Circa 1890 Saloon. (Courtesy of Wayne State University Photographic Services.)

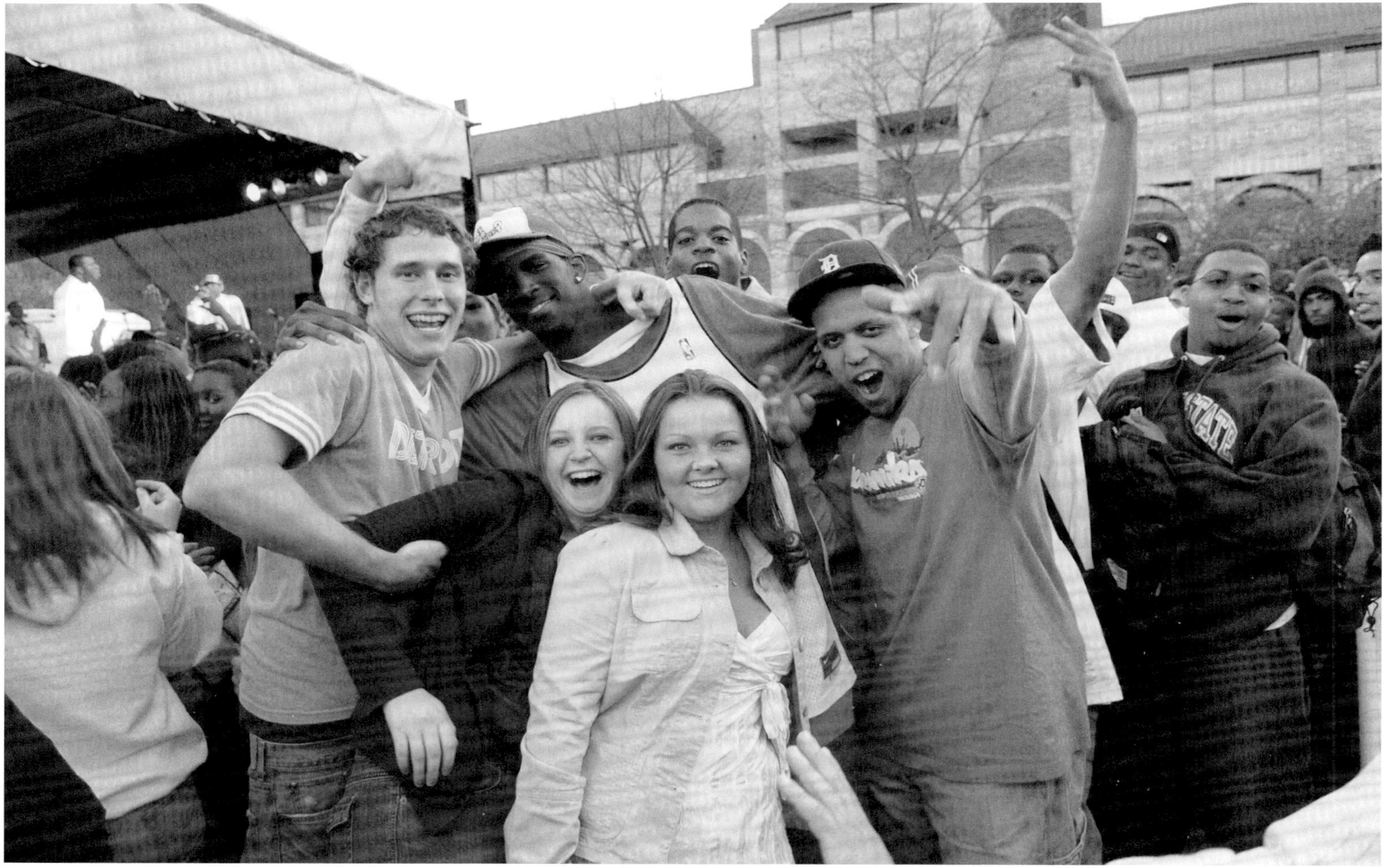

Bold and risky war tactics performed by the university's namesake, General Anthony Wayne, earned him the nickname "Mad Anthony." Students took that name and created a fun music event called the Mad Anthony Wayne concert. The first Mad Anthony Wayne concert was held in 2000. The concert brought together nationally known artists, like Run-DMC and Uncle Kracker, along with local artists, for a free outdoor event in the center of Wayne State's campus. The event was organized by various student groups and sponsored by the student council. The students are pictured on the central campus. The Undergraduate Library is visible behind them. The last concert was held in 2008. (Courtesy of Wayne State University Photographic Services.)

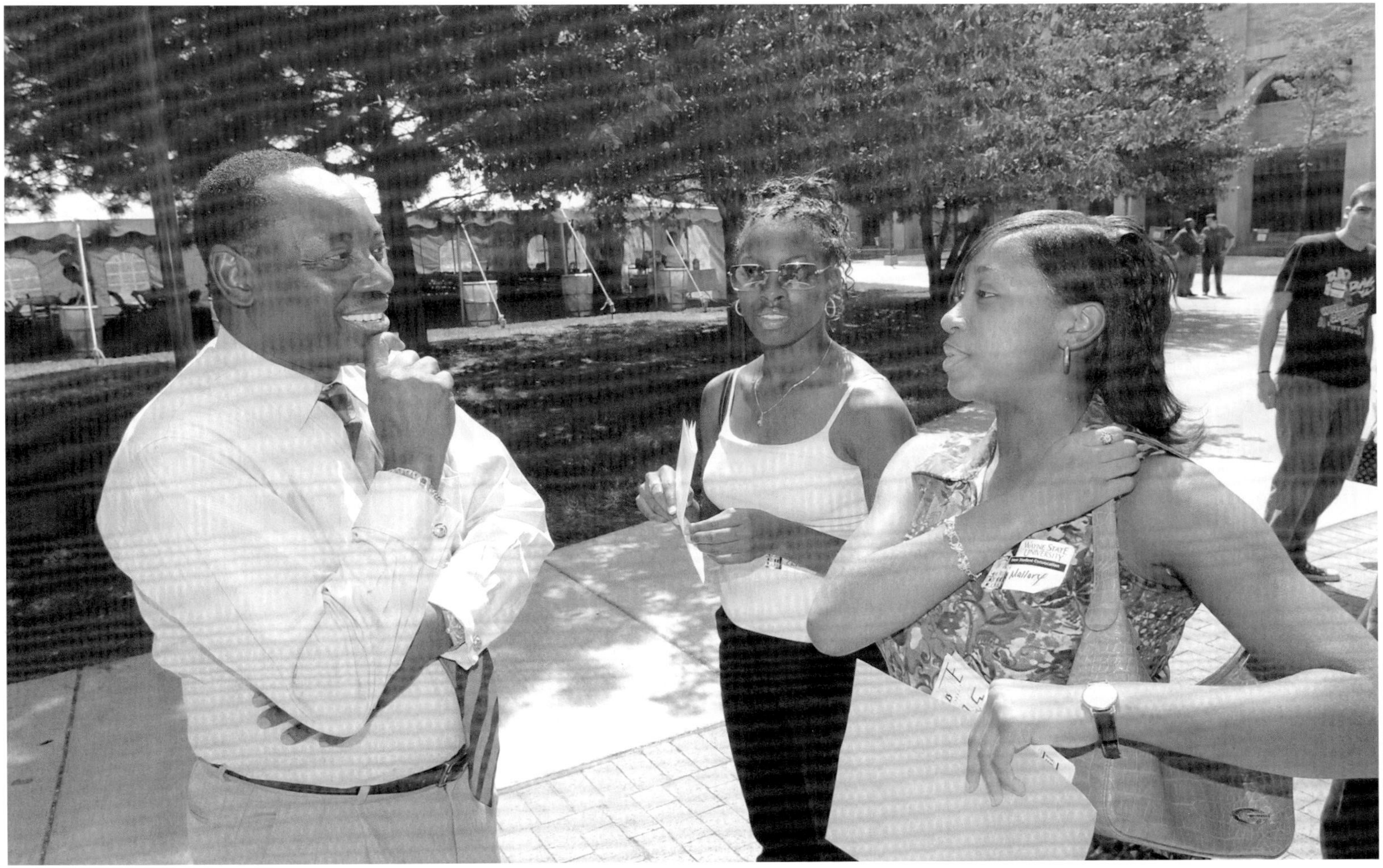

Wayne State University president Irvin D. Reid with students on campus. Reid succeeded David Adamany as president in 1997. During Reid's administration, several new residence halls were built to further his goal of attracting more undergraduates and creating a residential campus. Reid's administration also oversaw the planning and creation of a research and technology park, TechTown, to encourage economic growth in the area. (Courtesy of Wayne State University Photographic Services.)

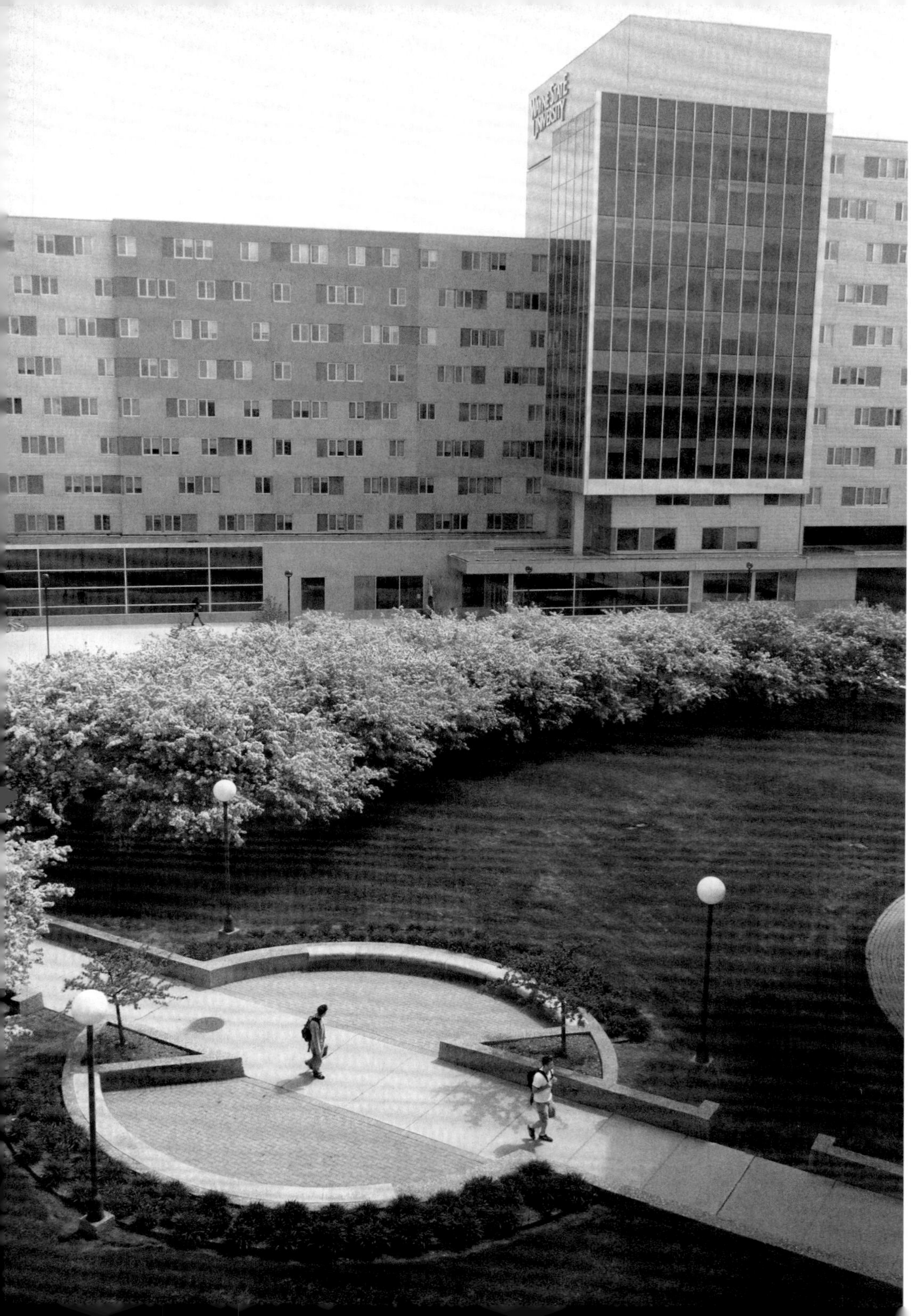

Towers Residence Hall, 655 W. Kirby Street. The northern facade of the newest residence hall. Completed in 2005, the nine-story building was constructed on the former site of the Helen Newberry Joy Residence for Women. The landscaped walkway in the foreground of the photo leads to the front of the Faculty/Administration Building. (Courtesy of Wayne State University Photographic Services.)

Marvin I. Danto Engineering Development Center, 5050 Anthony Wayne Drive, facing east, 2016. Construction on the three-story Engineering Building addition began in spring 2007. The addition provides the college—including the alternative energy technology program—with more research space for areas like bioengineering, nanotechnology, and fuel cells. Danto is the third addition to the College of Engineering's buildings. In this photo, the second addition is on the left, the dramatic silver spire of the *Helios Trail* rises in the middle, and Old Main is on the far right. Alumnus Yousif Ghafari's architecture and design firm, Ghafari and Associates, designed the engineering addition, as well as aspects for the renovations of Old Main and St. Andrew's Hall. Danto was a Wayne State engineering alum and Detroit philanthropist who donated $3 million toward the overall construction cost of $27.3 million. (Courtesy of Wayne State University Photographic Services.)

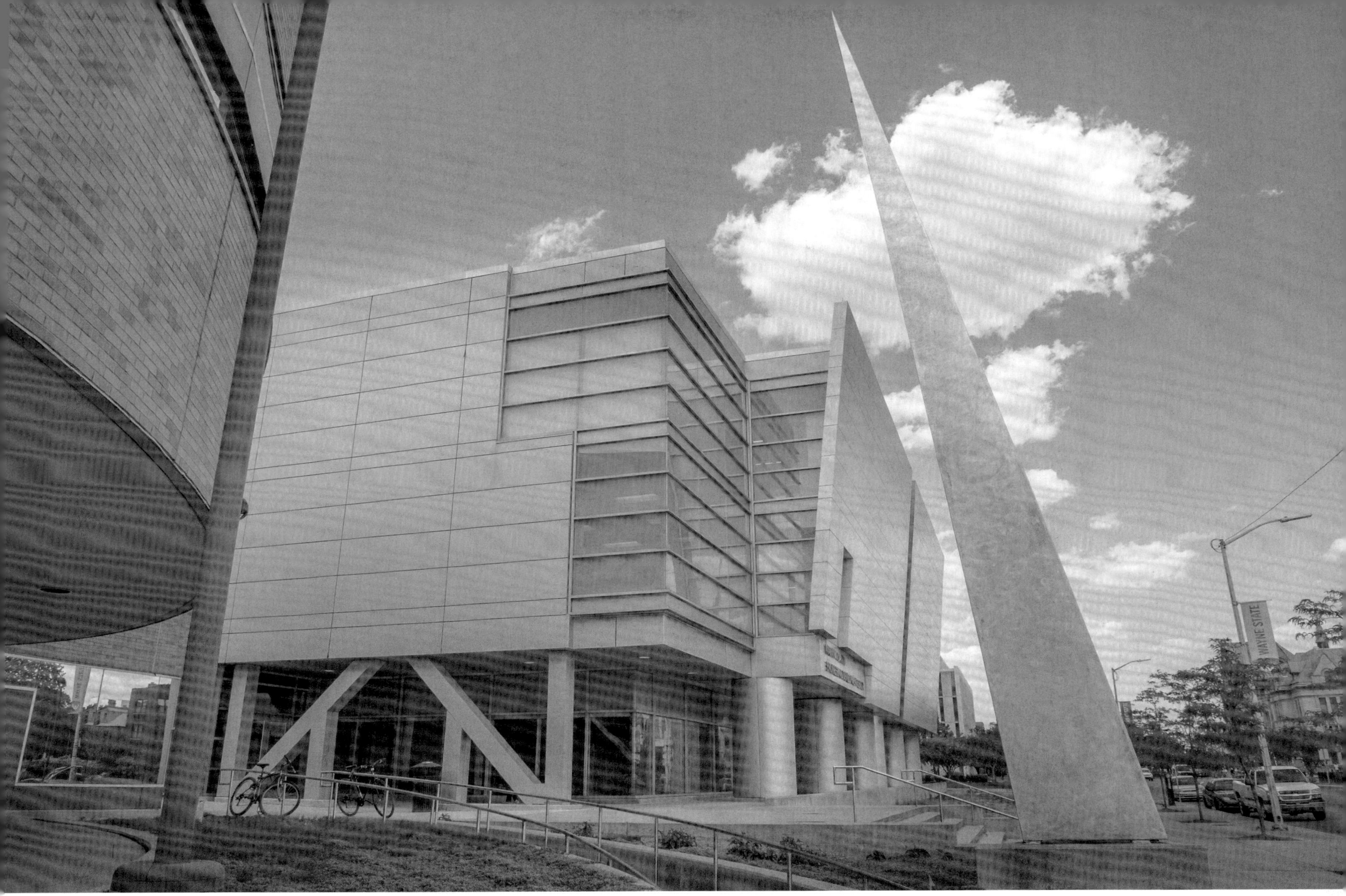
WAYNE STATE

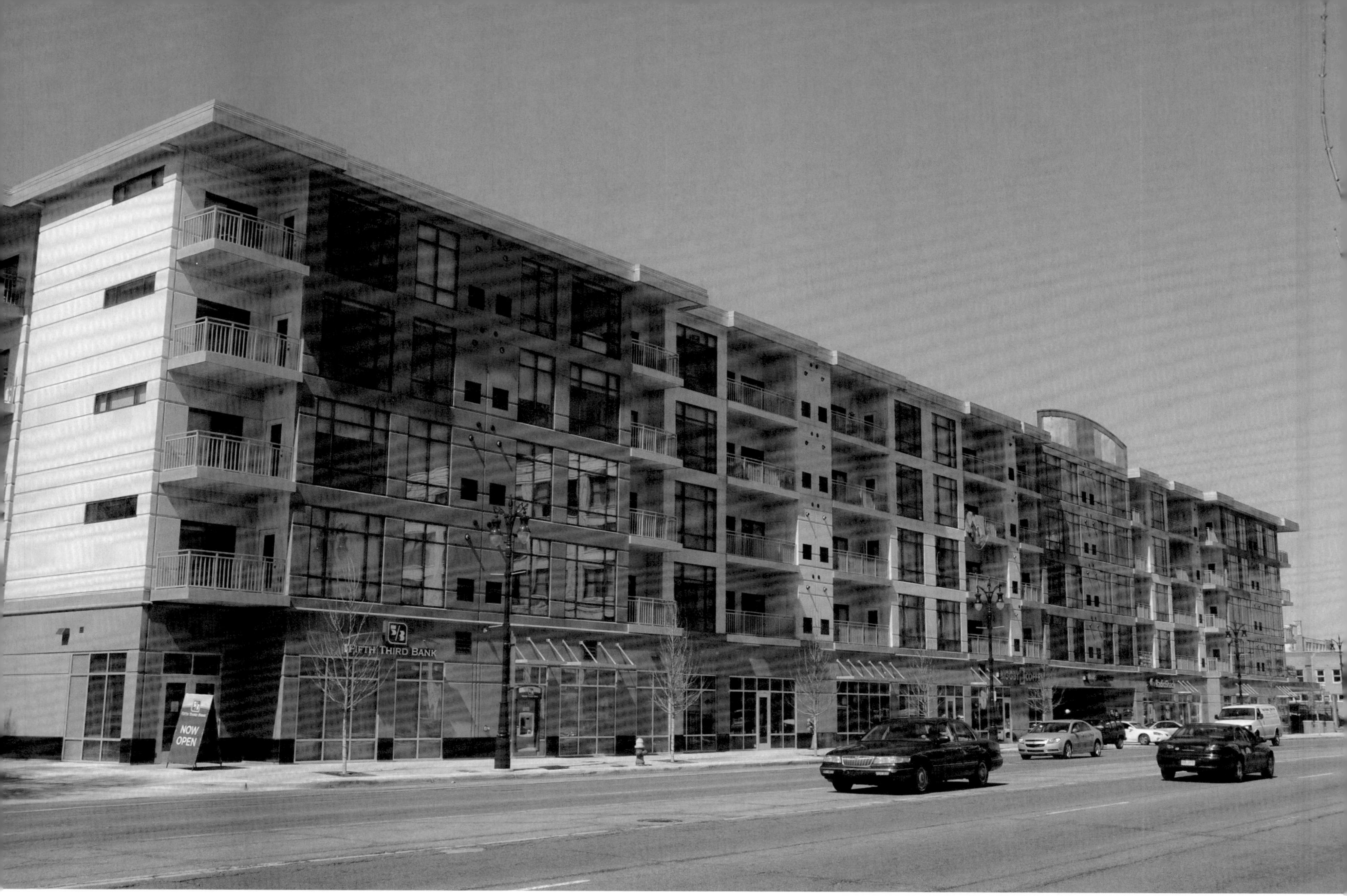
FIFTH THIRD BANK
NOW
OPEN

South University Village, 4501 Woodward. Located on a major thoroughfare in Detroit, this project aims to bring new business and residents to Midtown by constructing more residential buildings and storefronts in the neighborhood. Phase 1 of the project was the Studio One Apartments, which included retail space on the first floor. Construction began in 2007 on the old Vernors plant site, between Forest and Cass avenues, and was completed the following year. The first phase was named Development of the Year by *Crain's Detroit Business* when the apartments opened in 2008. Designed by Prime Developer, there are two more phases of the project planned. Phase 2 bids began in 2013, and the slated completion date is 2020. (Courtesy of Wayne State University Photographic Services.)

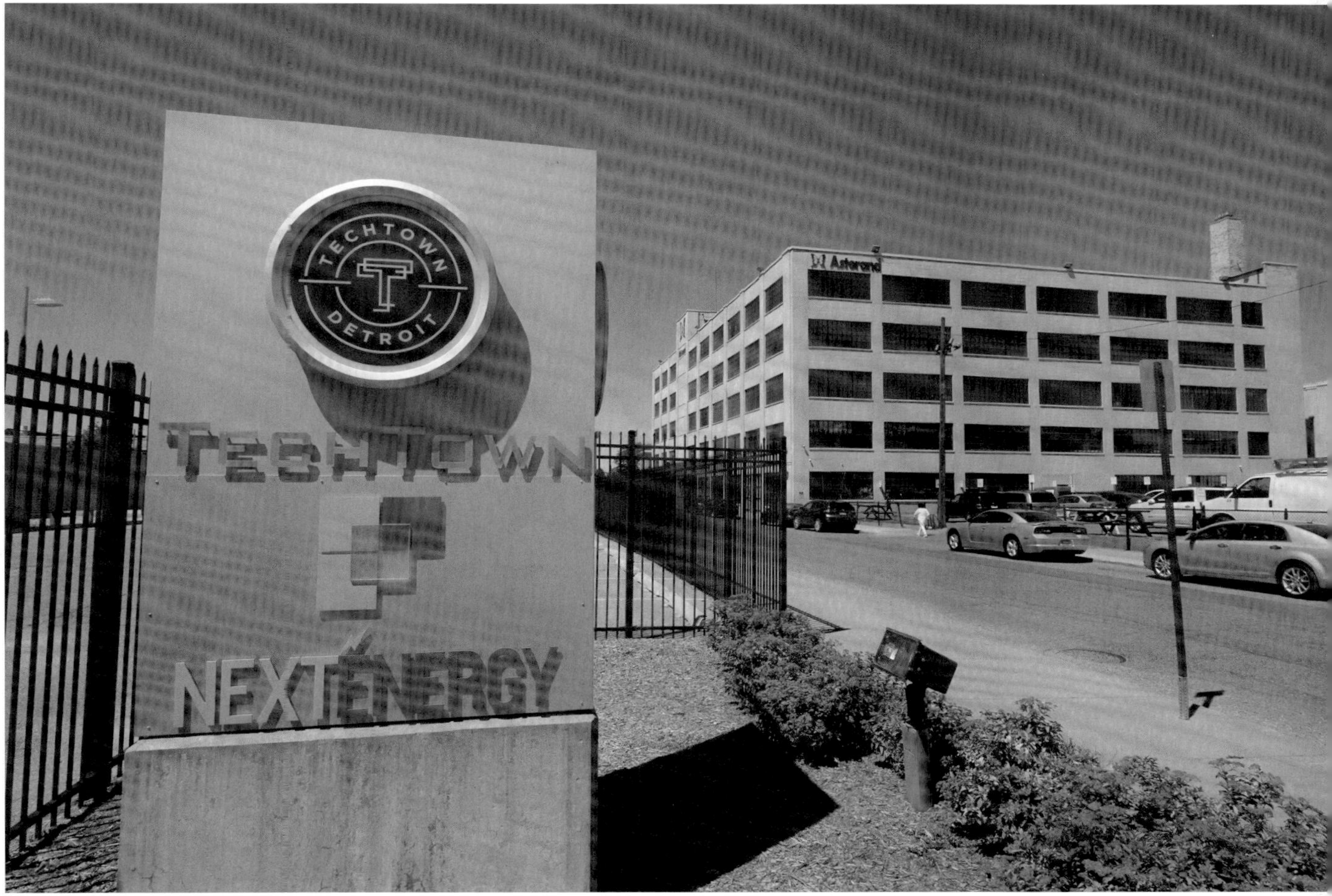

TechTown, 440 Burroughs Street at Cass Avenue. TechTown was developed as a collaboration between the university, Henry Ford Health System, General Motors, and numerous private research companies to foster technological research and business development. Today, TechTown partners with Wayne State's Office of Economic Development, the university's hub for catalyzing business activity in Midtown and across the region. It's only appropriate that buildings that once housed the businesses that fueled Detroit's economy are being reborn as incubators for new enterprise. (Courtesy of Wayne State University Photographic Services.)

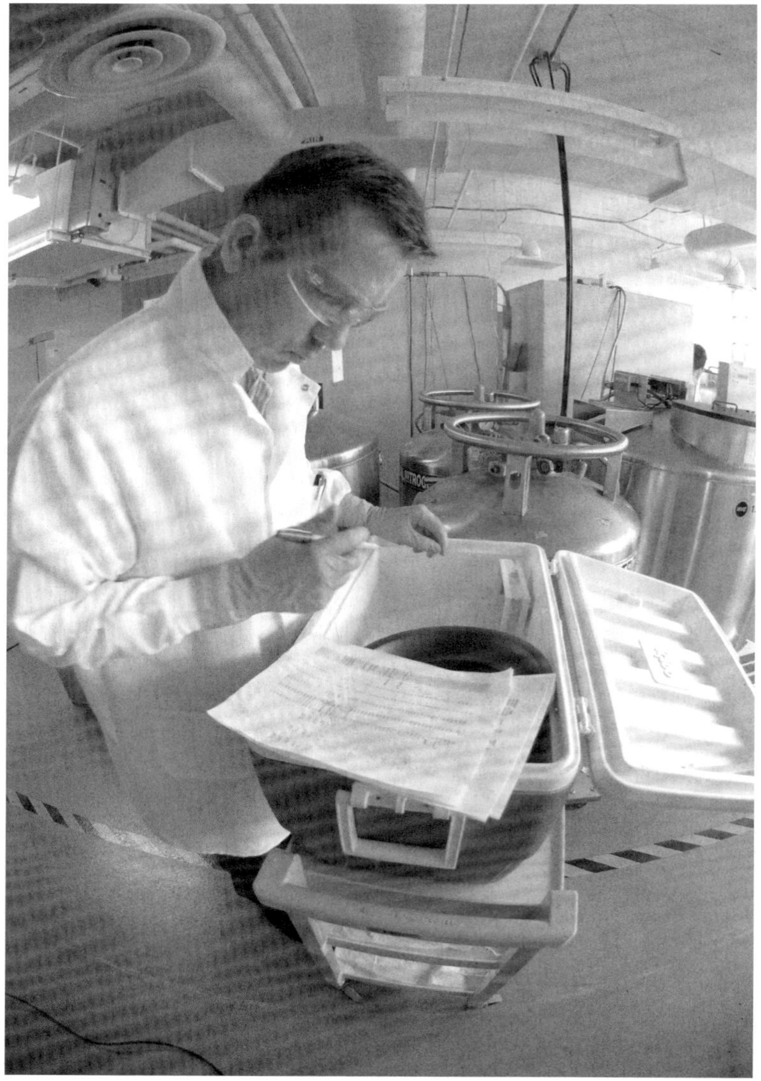

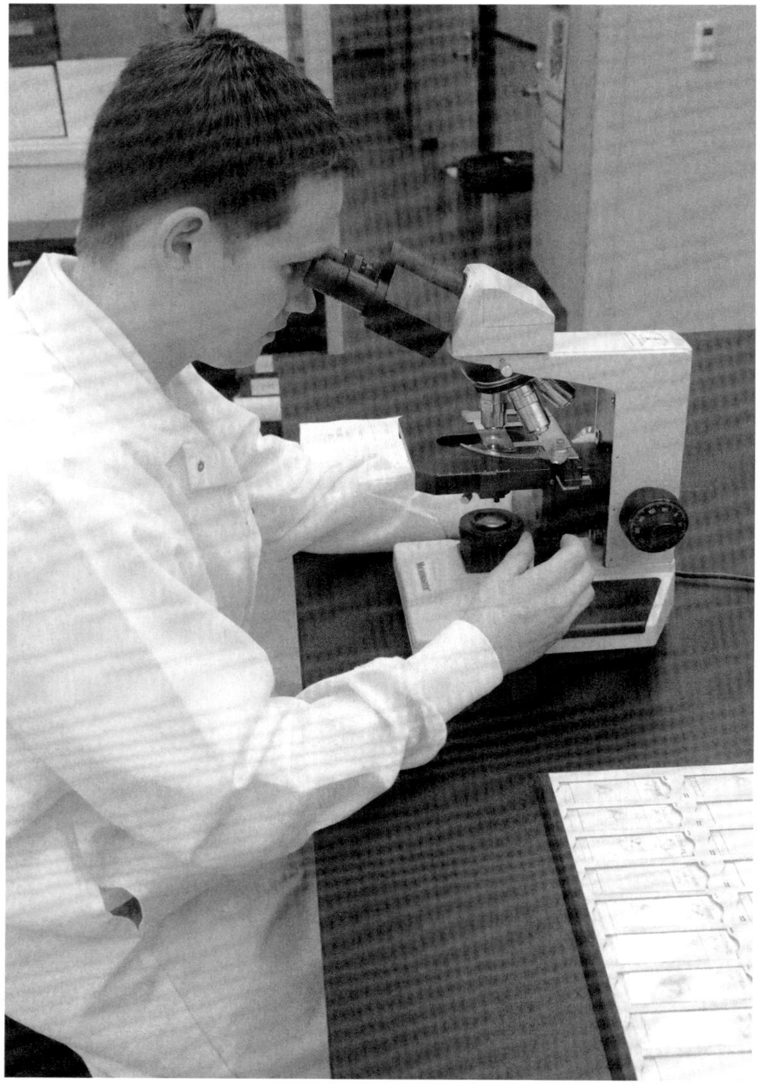

Scientists conducting research in TechTown. As Wayne State University's professional schools in medicine, teaching, and engineering were created out of student demand, so was TechTown created to further economic development while encouraging cutting-edge research and the pursuit of knowledge. (Courtesy of Wayne State University Photographic Services.)

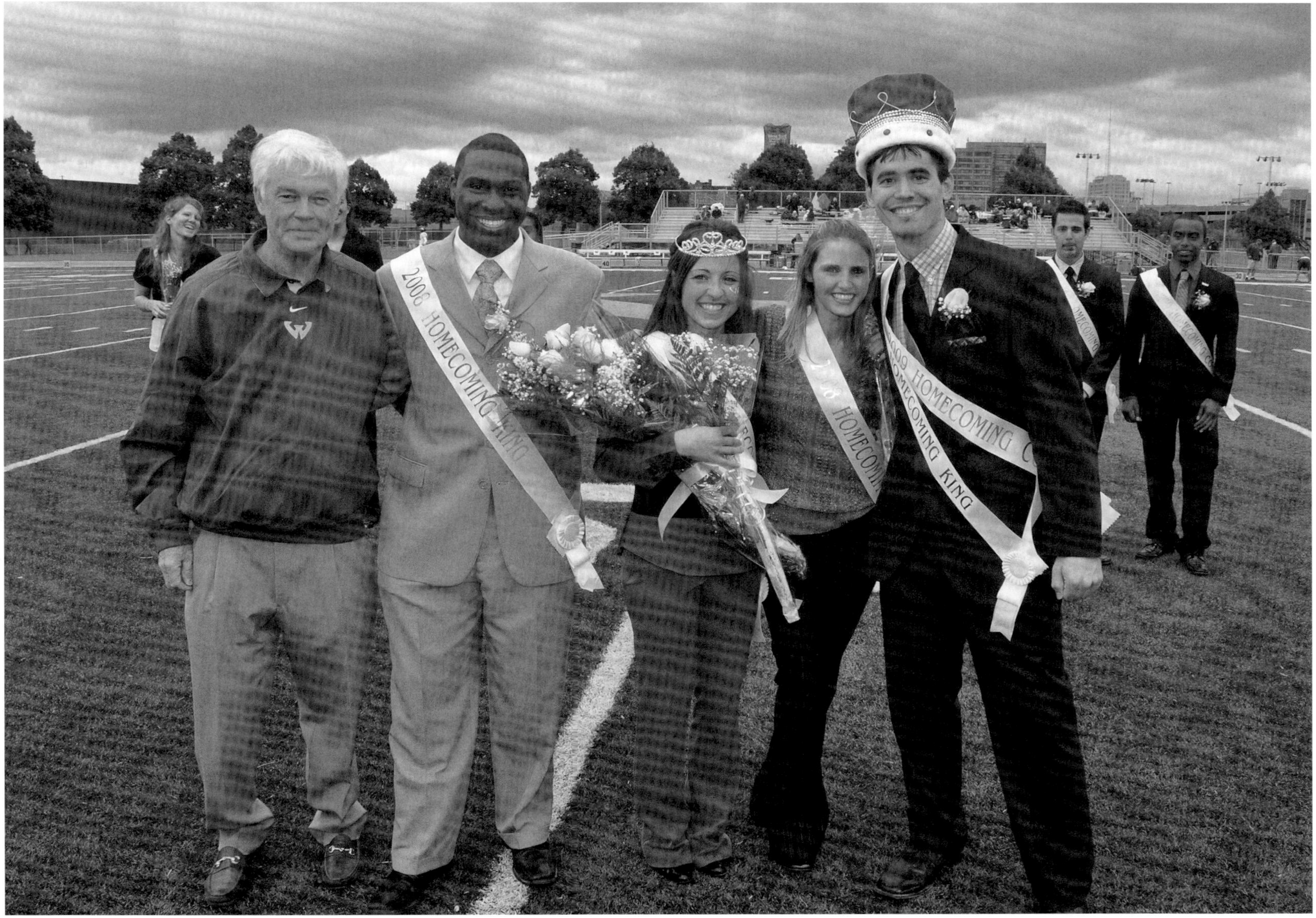

Wayne State's tenth president, Jay Noren, halftime at a football game with the Wayne State Homecoming court. Noren helped strengthen relationships between the university and the Detroit Medical Center. (Courtesy of Wayne State University Photographic Services.)

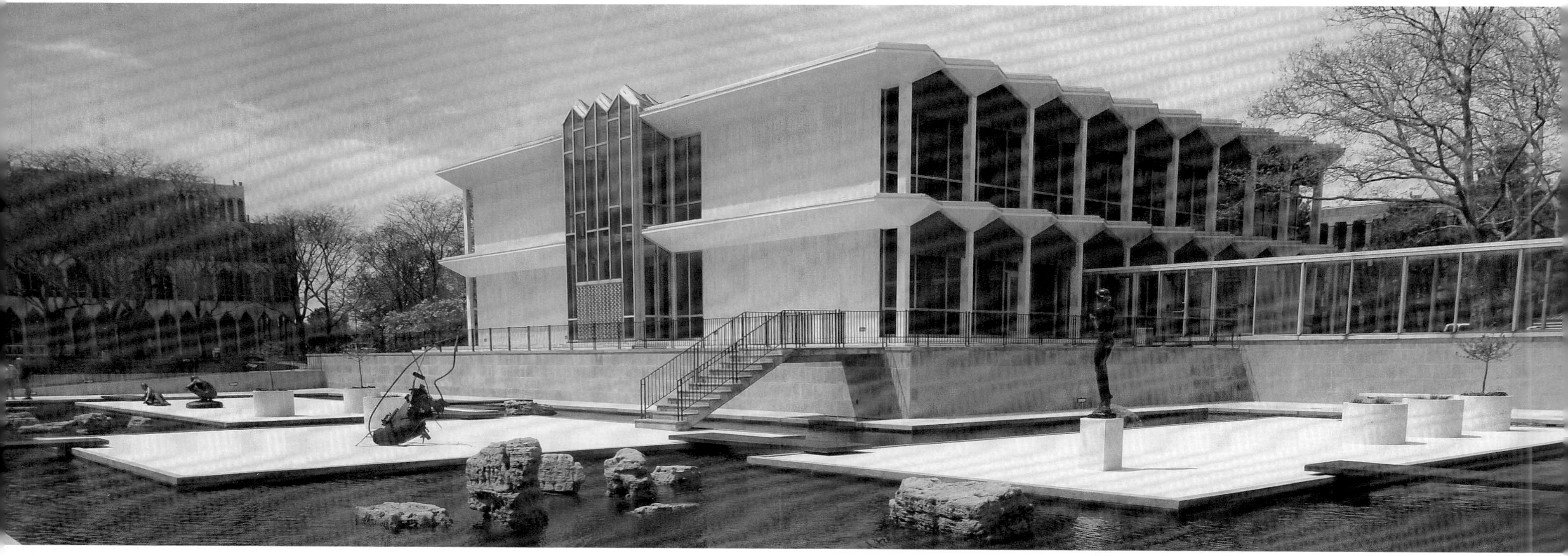

Renovated McGregor Memorial Conference Center. Designed by American architect Minoru Yamasaki, who designed several of Wayne State's buildings as well as a campus plan, the McGregor Center is one of the architectural jewels of the campus. Originally built in 1958, a renovation project was completed in 2013, restoring the reflecting pools to their former glory. (Courtesy of Wayne State University Photographic Services.)

Reflecting pool, Belcrest in the background. (Courtesy of Wayne State University Photographic Services.)

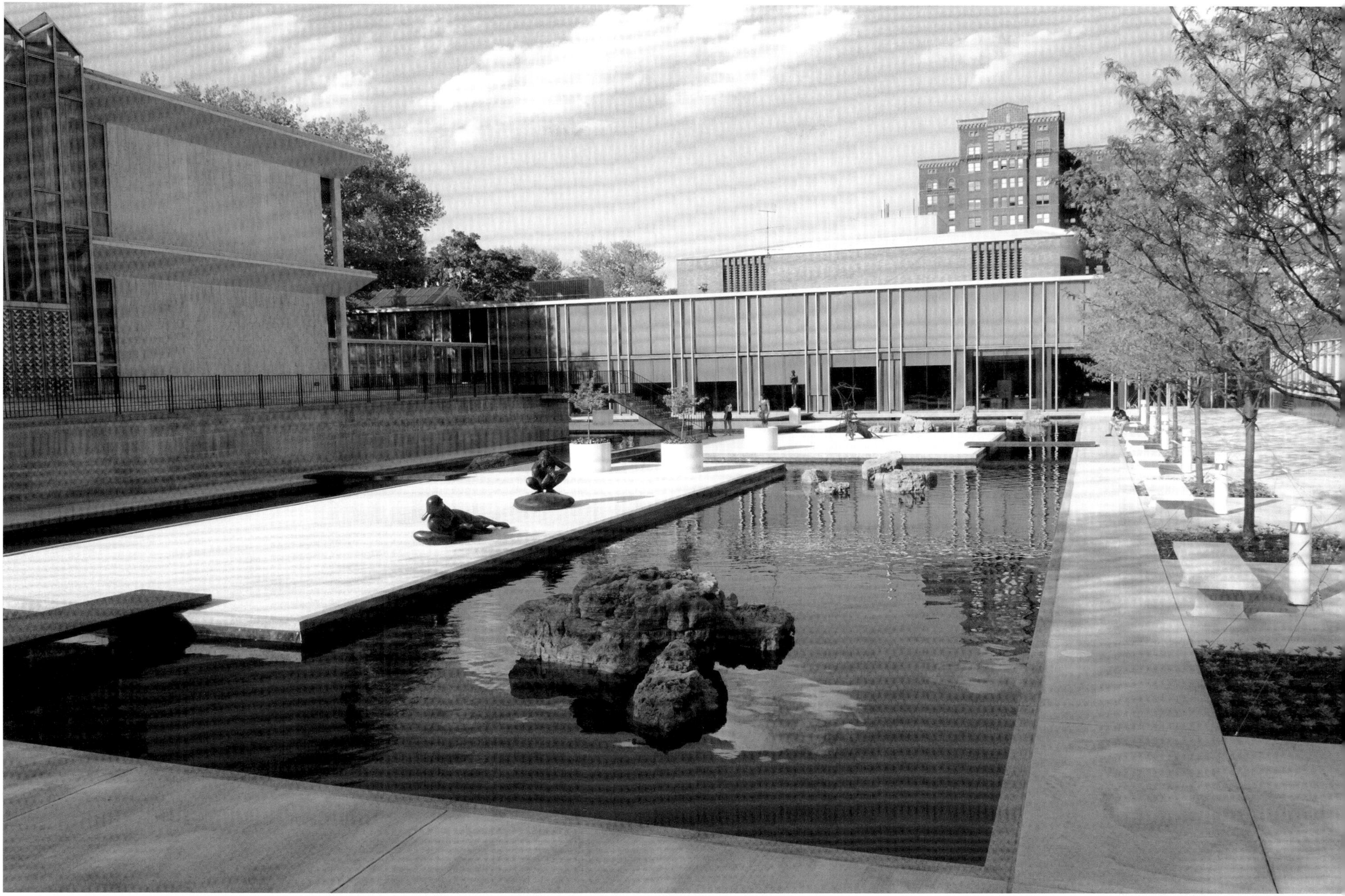

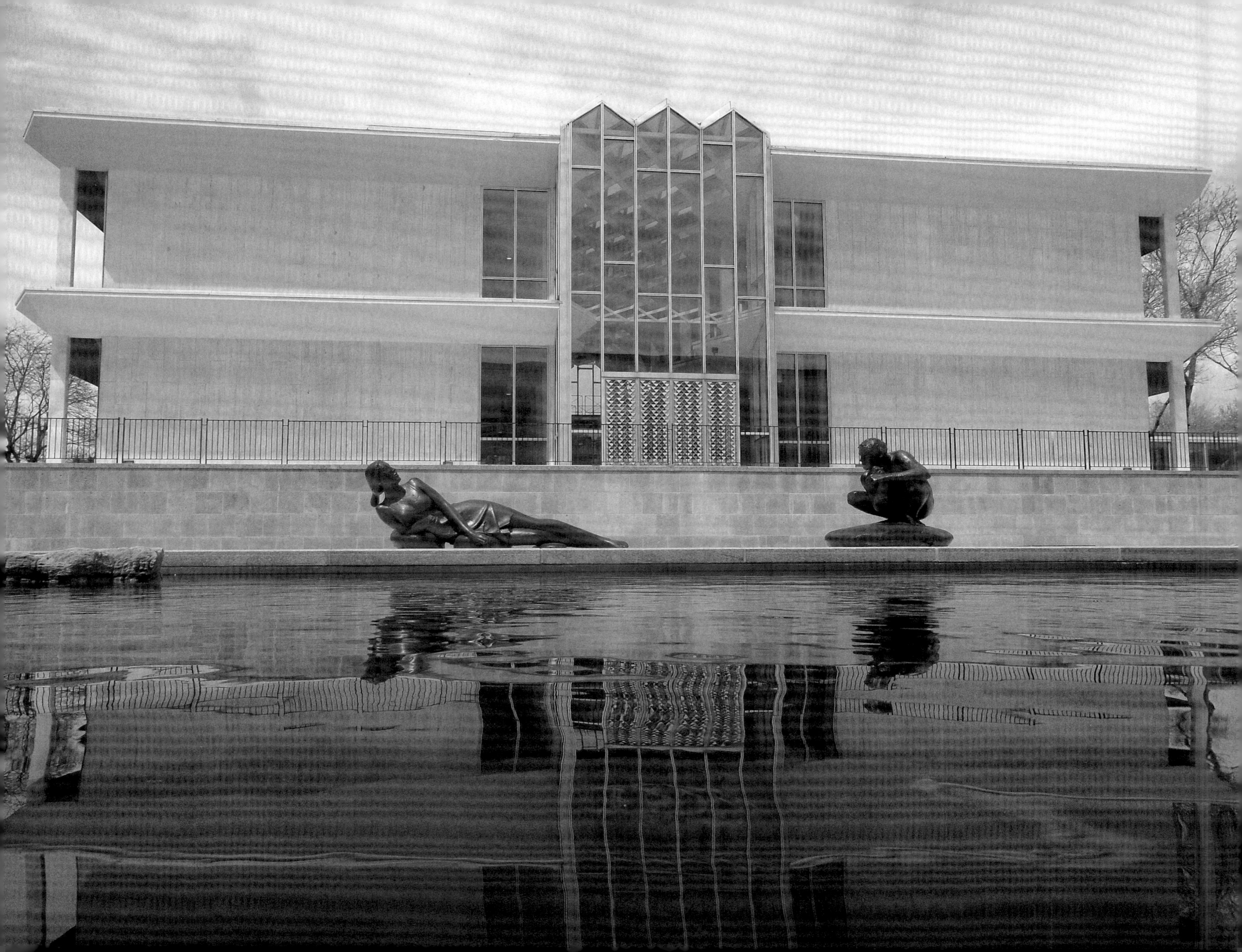

Statues, McGregor in background. (Courtesy of Wayne State University Photographic Services.)

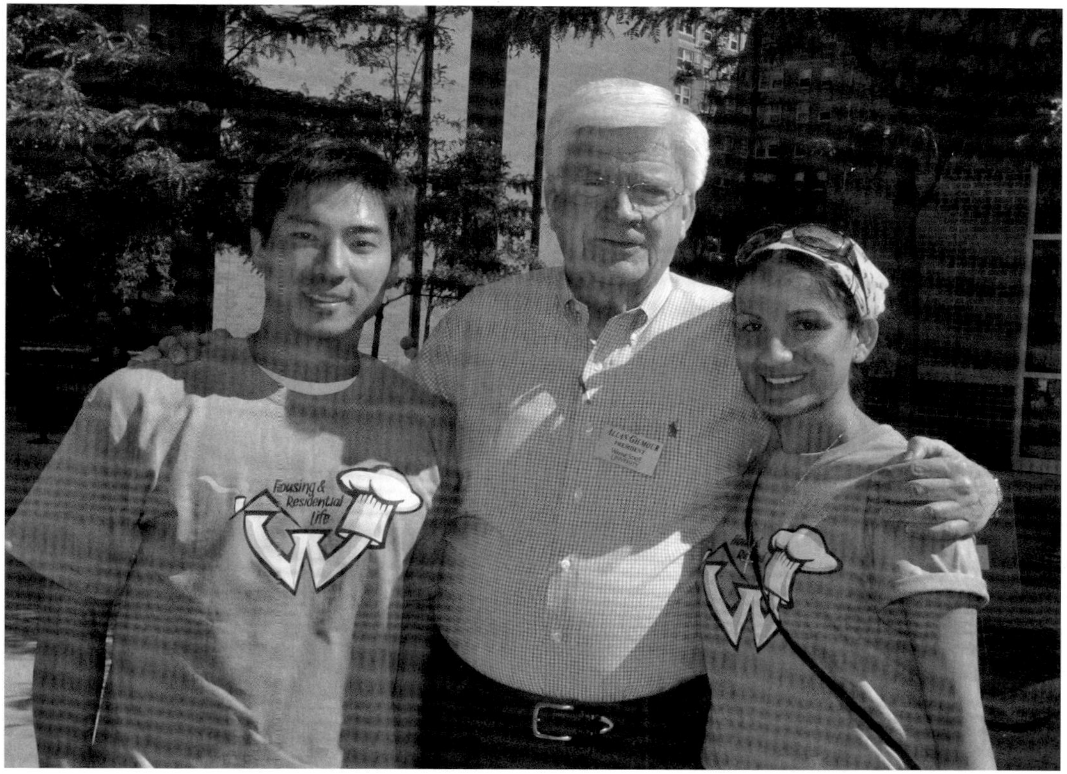

Wayne State's eleventh president, Allan Gilmour, in front of student housing. Gilmour, a former Ford Motor Company executive, continued to help grow the university's research reputation, as the Integrative Biosciences Center building construction near TechTown began during his tenure. Gilmour is pictured with two WSU students on freshman move-in day, and DeRoy and Chatsworth are behind him. (Courtesy of Wayne State University Photographic Services.)

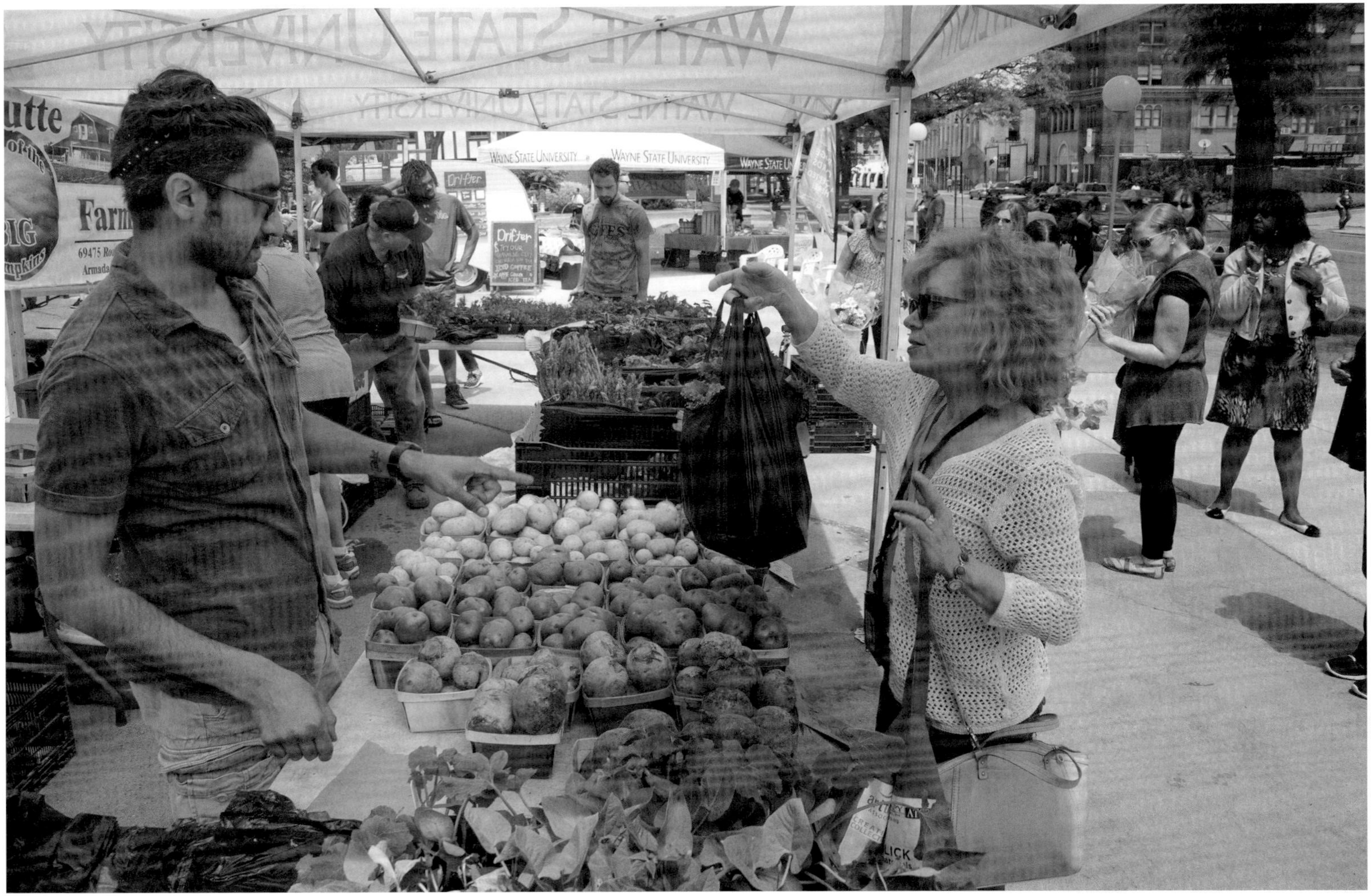

Wayne State Farmers Market, near the Reuther Library. Along with Detroit, Wayne State has embraced community gardens. The project was piloted in 2008 and began its first full season in 2009. Part of the local and slow food movement, area gardens sell their produce alongside food from local restaurants during the summer months. (Courtesy of Wayne State University Photographic Services.)

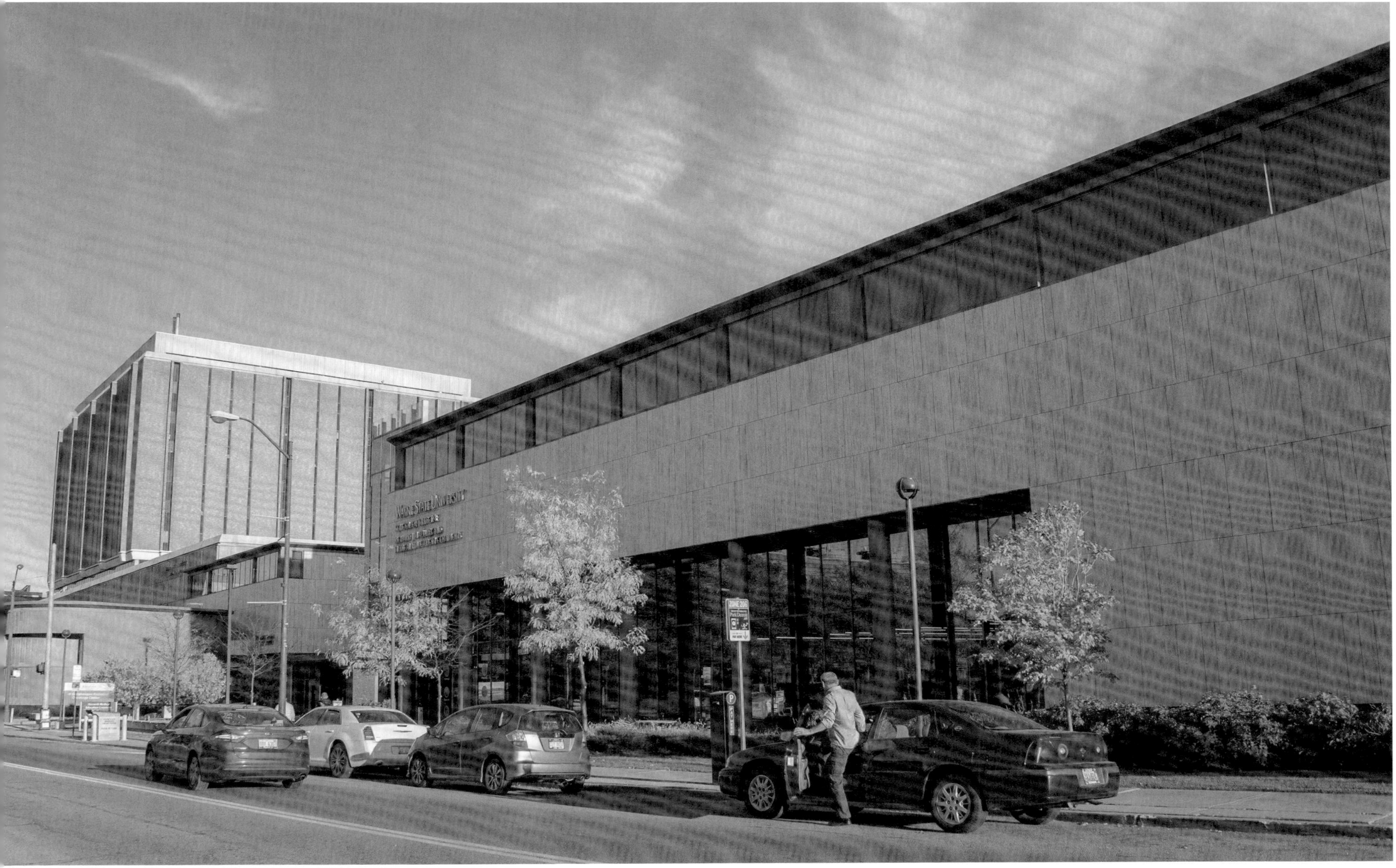

Richard J. Mazurek Medical Education Commons, 320 E. Canfield. Connected to Scott Hall, this building doubled the size of the medical school. It includes practice exams rooms and places all medical student services, including administration and support, under one roof. Costing $35 million, construction began in 2007 and the building opened in 2009. Dr. Mazurek was a 1961 graduate of the School of Medicine. (Courtesy of Wayne State University Photographic Services.)

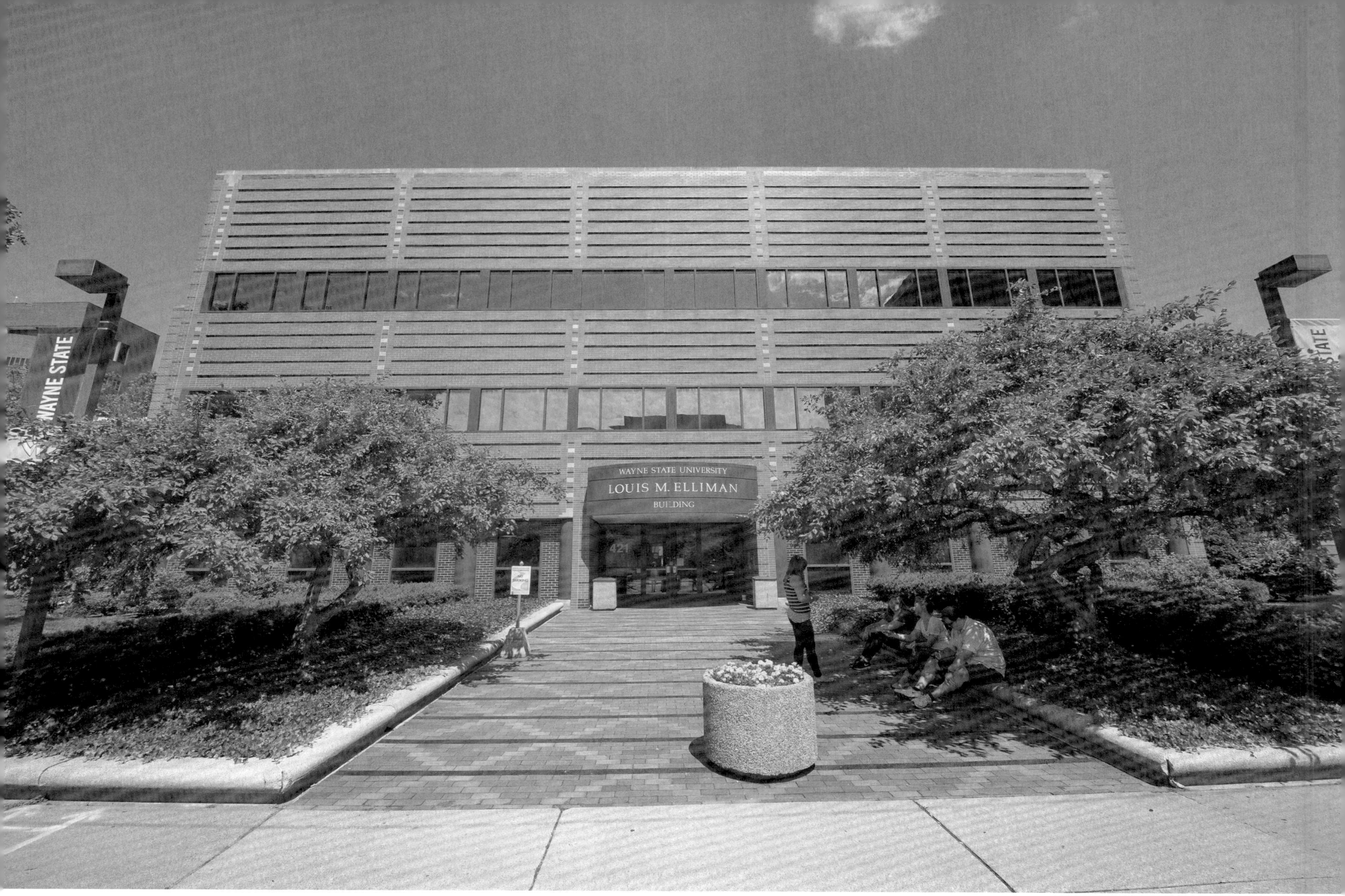
WAYNE STATE
WAYNE STATE UNIVERSITY
LOUIS M. ELLIMAN
BUILDING
421

The Louis M. Elliman Clinical Research Building, 421 E. Canfield Avenue. Built in 1989, this building provides laboratory and office space for the School of Medicine. Renovations to modernize it were completed in 2015, the same year that the Integrative Biosciences Center (IBio) opened. Several research teams and programs were then moved to IBio or Scott Hall. (Courtesy of Wayne State University Photographic Services.)

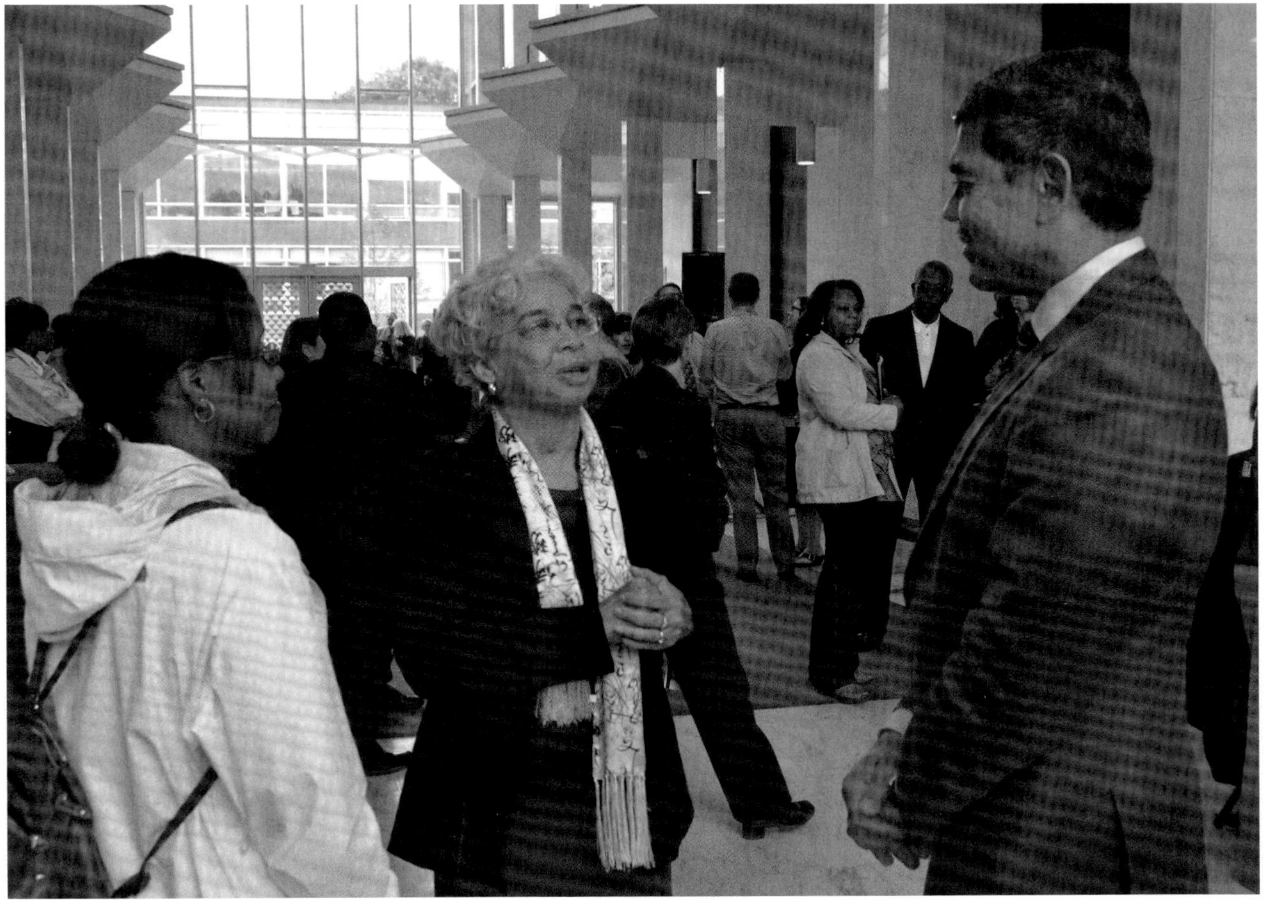

Wayne State's twelfth president, M. Roy Wilson, campus reception, McGregor Conference Memorial Center. Wilson, who has a background in medicine and health, has overseen the first jump in enrollment in seven years, a new contract for the management of Wayne State's student housing, and construction for a new home for the Mike Ilitch School of Business. (Courtesy of Wayne State University Photographic Services.)

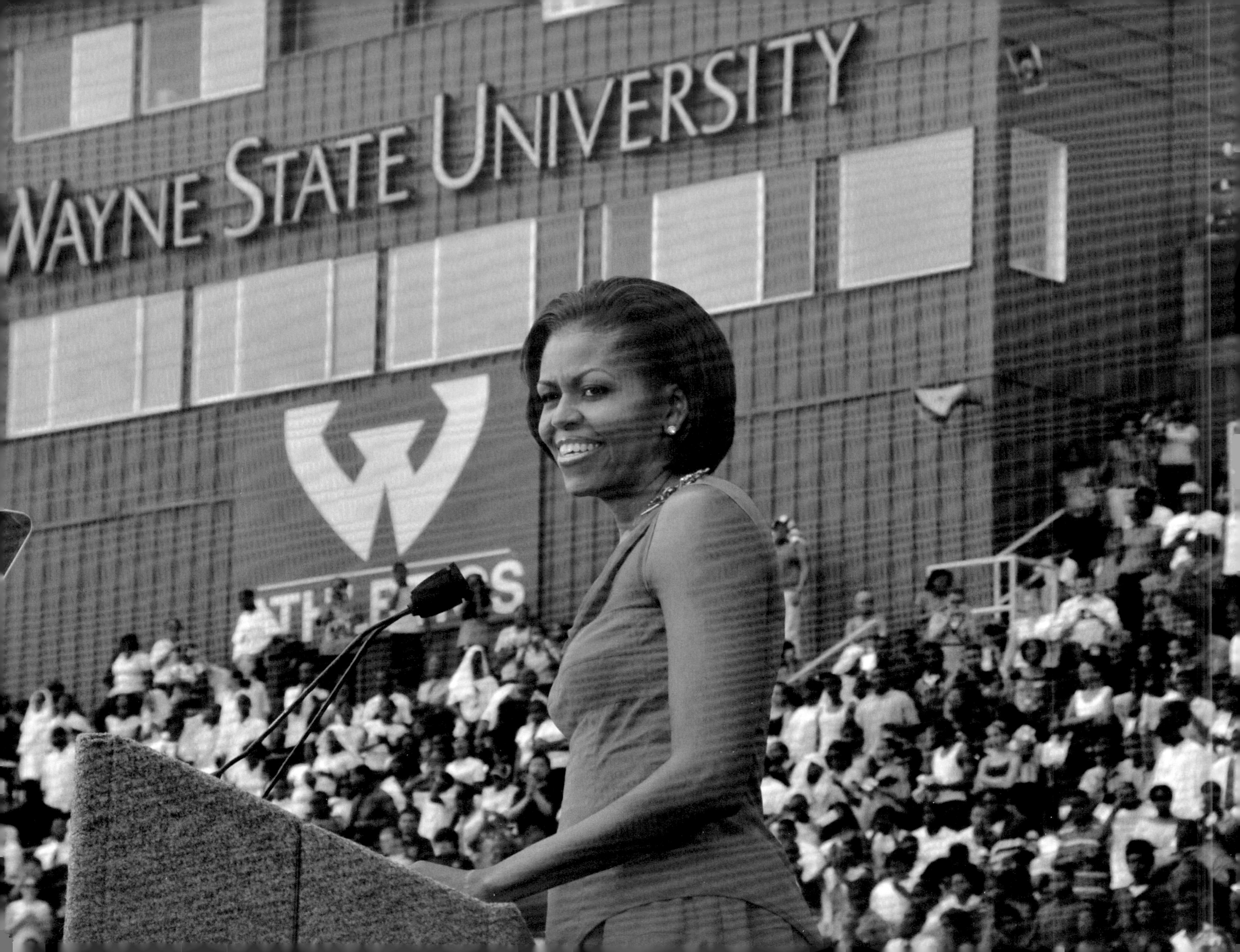
WAYNE STATE UNIVERSITY

First Lady Michelle Obama speaking at Wayne State. Michelle Obama visited Wayne State University in May 2015 to address more than 2,000 Detroit high school students at the city's first college signing day, sponsored by the Detroit College Access Network. (Courtesy of Wayne State University Photographic Services.)

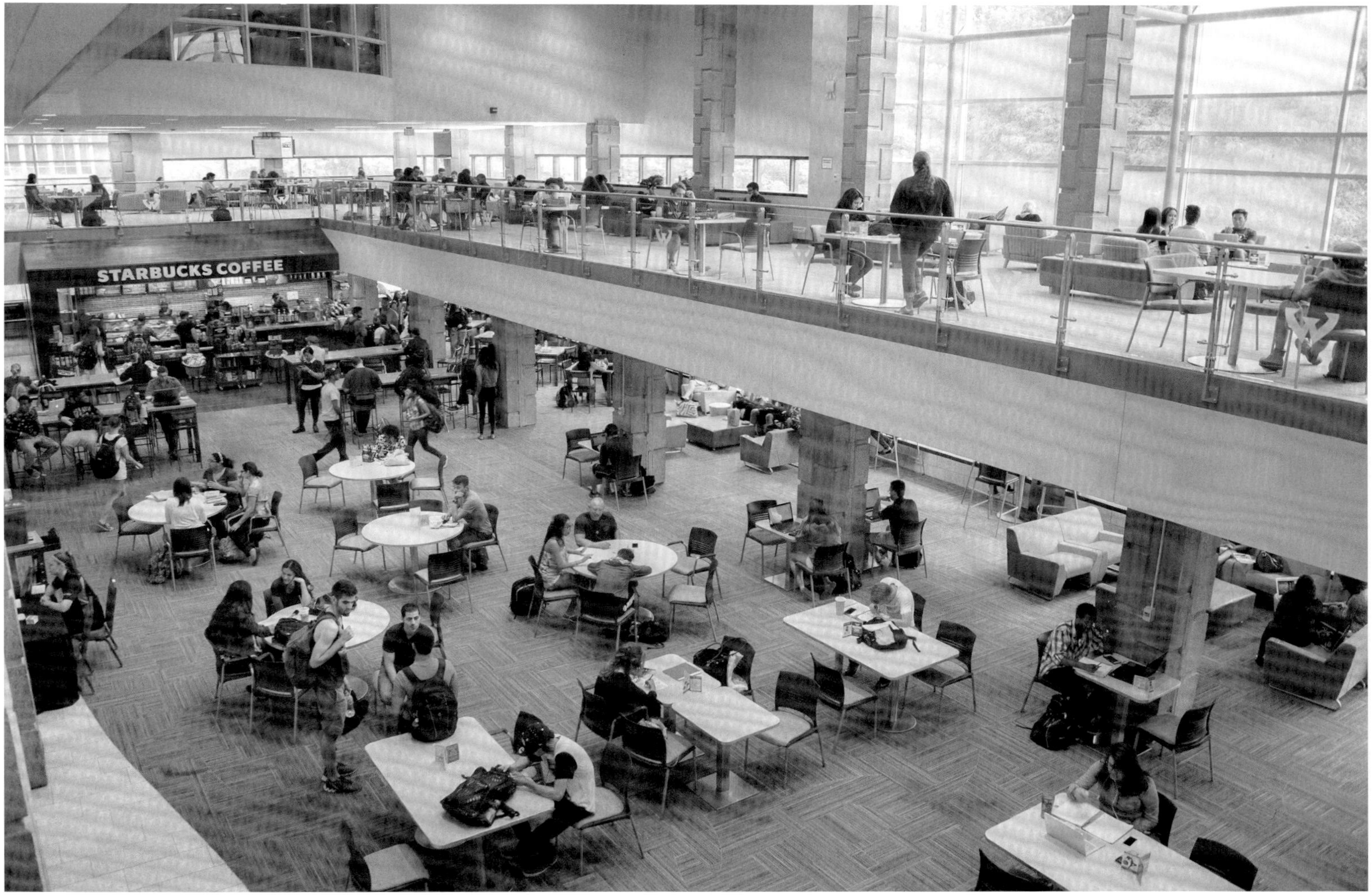

Student Center Building, interior. Since its construction in 1969, the Student Center Building hadn't undergone any major improvements—until 2013, when a complete renovation and refurbishment of the building began. Costing about $23 million, there were two significant phases to the project. Phase one was sprucing up: new carpet, new furniture, more natural light on the first floor, and new entrances. Phase two included renovated recreation space in the basement, for ping-pong and pool, as well as a new ballroom, auditorium, and meeting spaces on the second floor. Both phases were completed in 2015. The upper floors, from the fourth to the seventh, underwent renovations as well. (Courtesy of Wayne State University Photographic Services.)

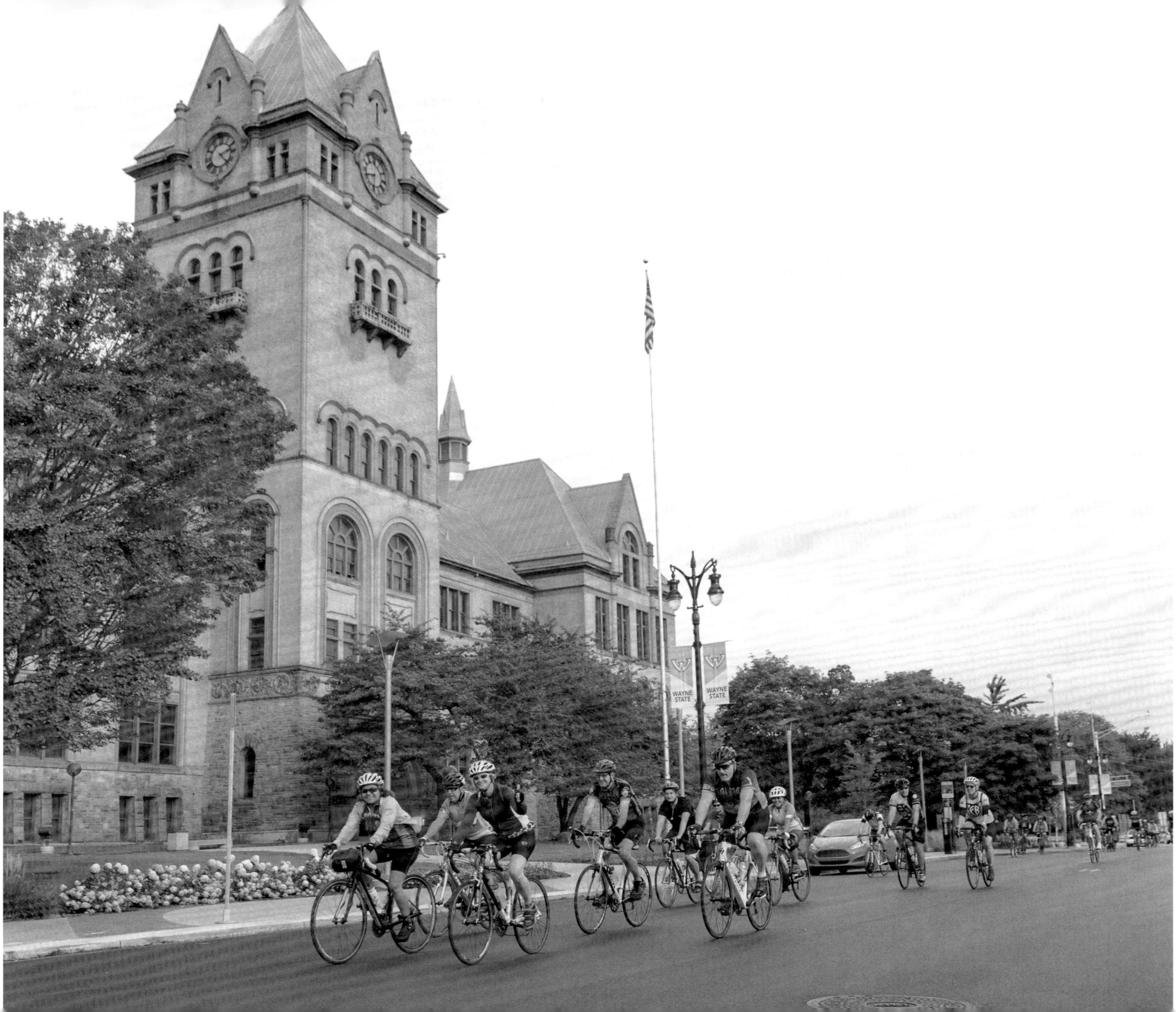
WAYNE STATE
WAYNE STATE

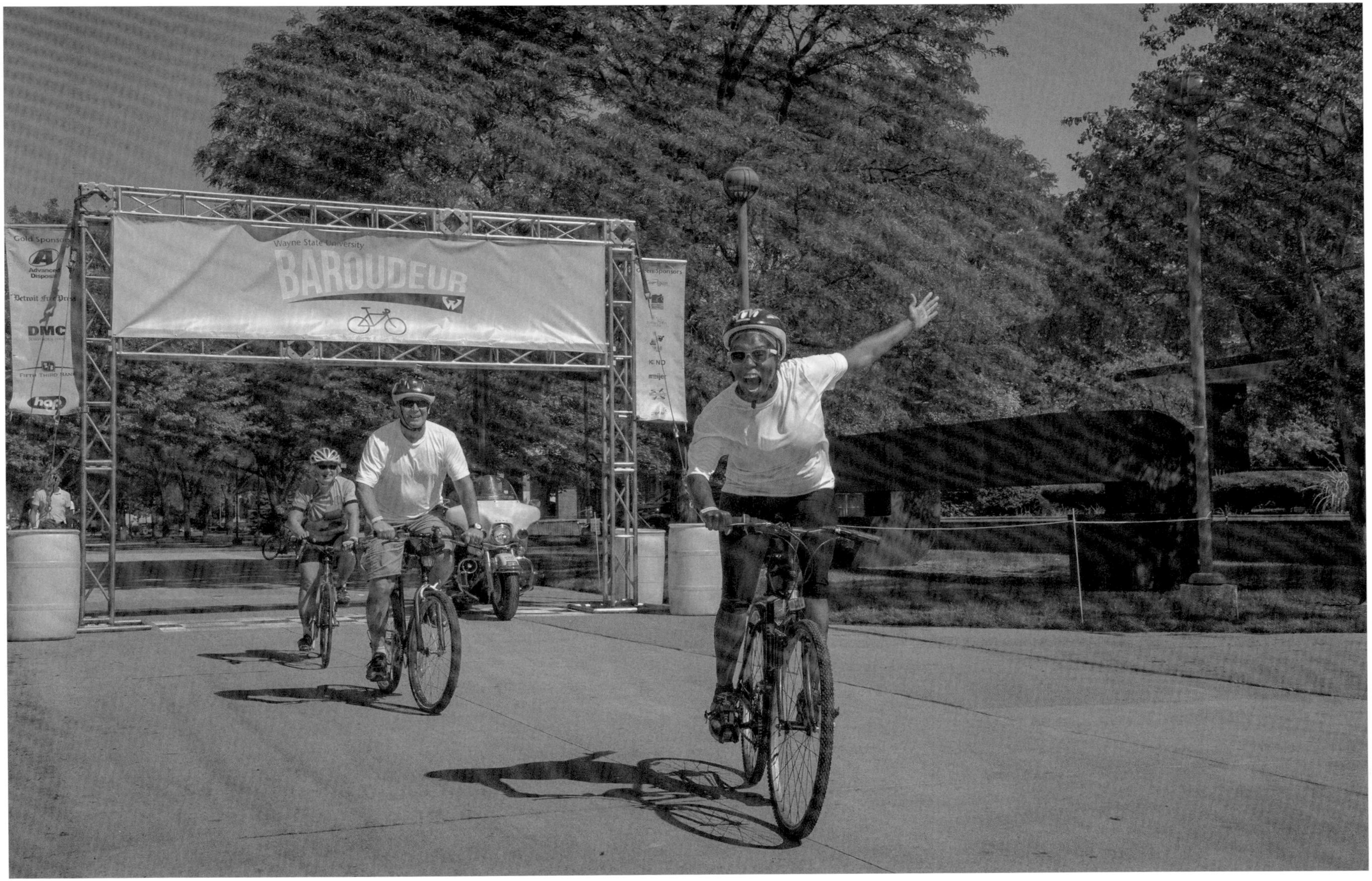

Cyclists riding in the Baroudeur. Participants in Wayne State's annual cycling event help raise funds for student scholarships. The Baroudeur began in 2015 by President M. Roy Wilson, an avid cyclist, and is a noncompetitive event that starts and ends on the Wayne State campus, with routes ranging from twenty to one hundred miles through the city. (Courtesy of Wayne State University Photographic Services.)

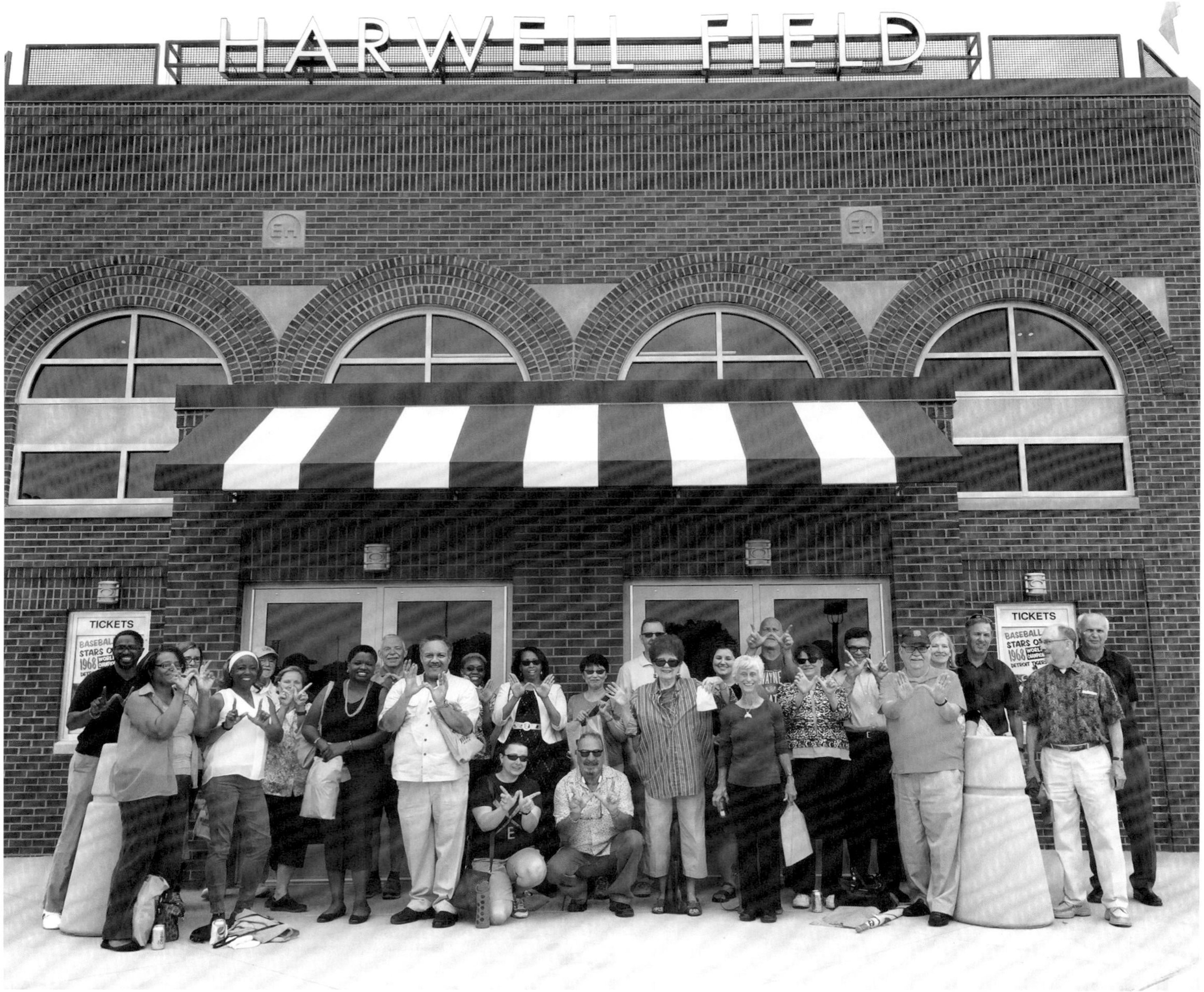
HARWELL FIELD
TICKETS
TICKETS

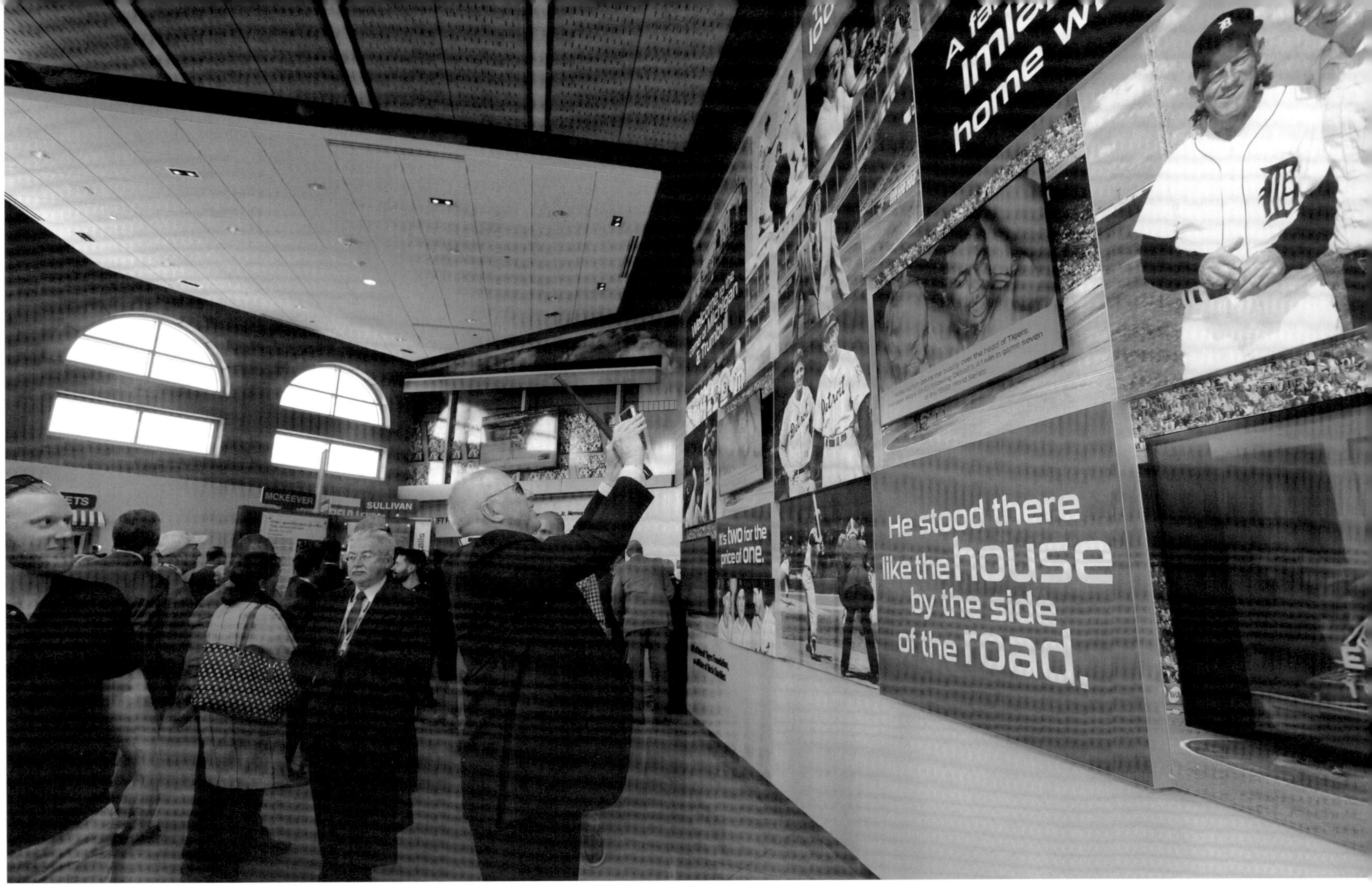

Interior of Harwell Baseball Field Building. (Courtesy of Wayne State University Photographic Services.)

Harwell Baseball Field Building, Matthaei Center. One of Wayne State's newest projects, this building showcases baseball memorabilia collected by the Harwell Foundation and the Detroit Historical Society. It also commemorates popular Detroit Tigers sportscaster Ernie Harwell. Located adjacent to the backstop of the men's baseball field, on the Matthaei athletic campus, the building was financed by funds from the athletic department. (Courtesy of Wayne State University Photographic Services.)

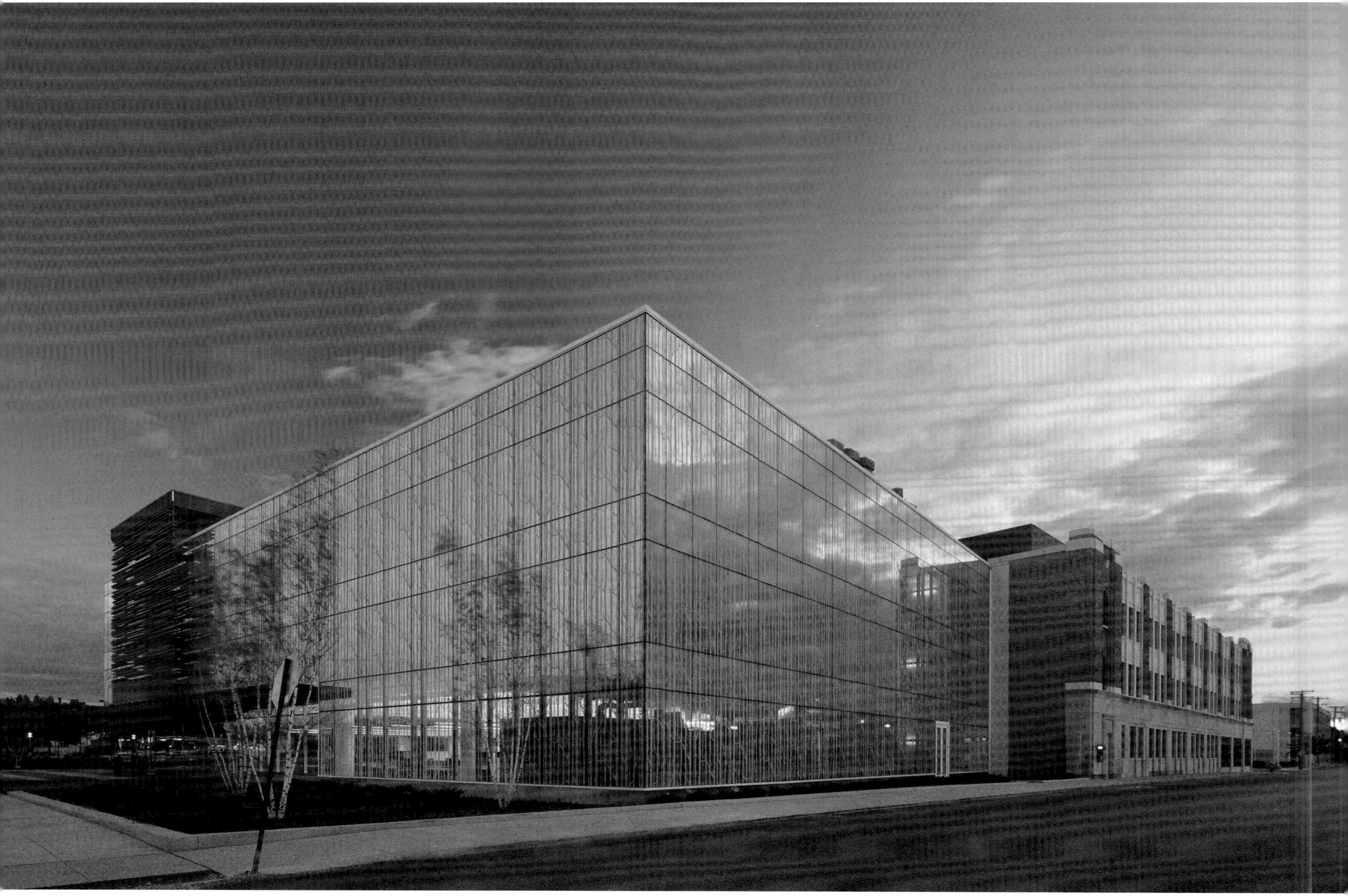

Integrative Biosciences Center, 6135 Woodward. IBio was designed to provide space for science, engineering, and technology, with laboratory space for physics, computer science, nutrition and food science, and biological science. Located adjacent to TechTown in the New Center area, the former Dalgleish Cadillac dealership building was renovated for its use, with new Woodward frontage added. IBio opened in October 2015 and is dedicated to fostering research that addresses the health disparities affecting Detroit's residents. (Courtesy of Wayne State University Photographic Services.)

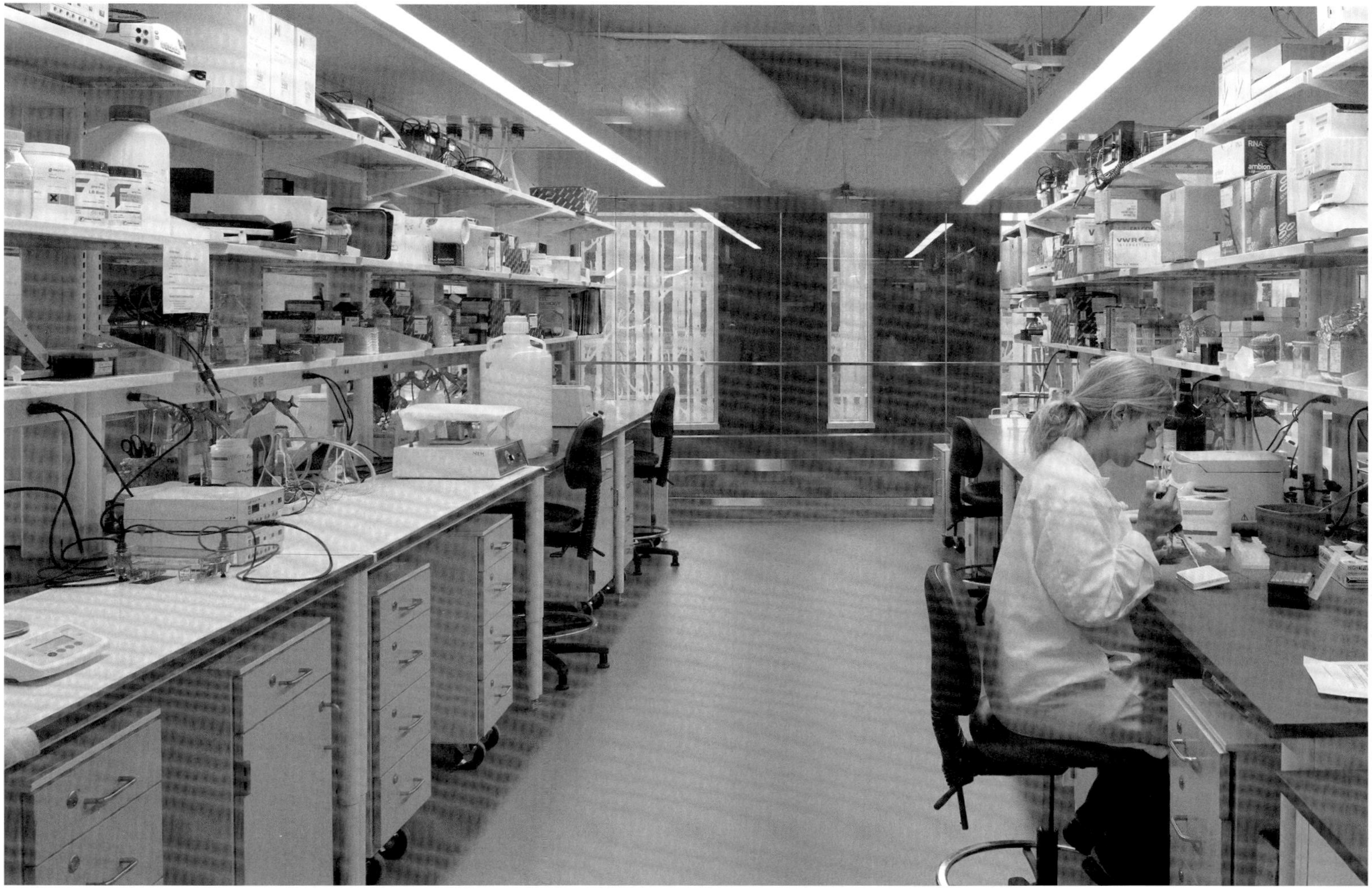

Interior of IBio, researcher working. (Courtesy of Wayne State University Photographic Services.)

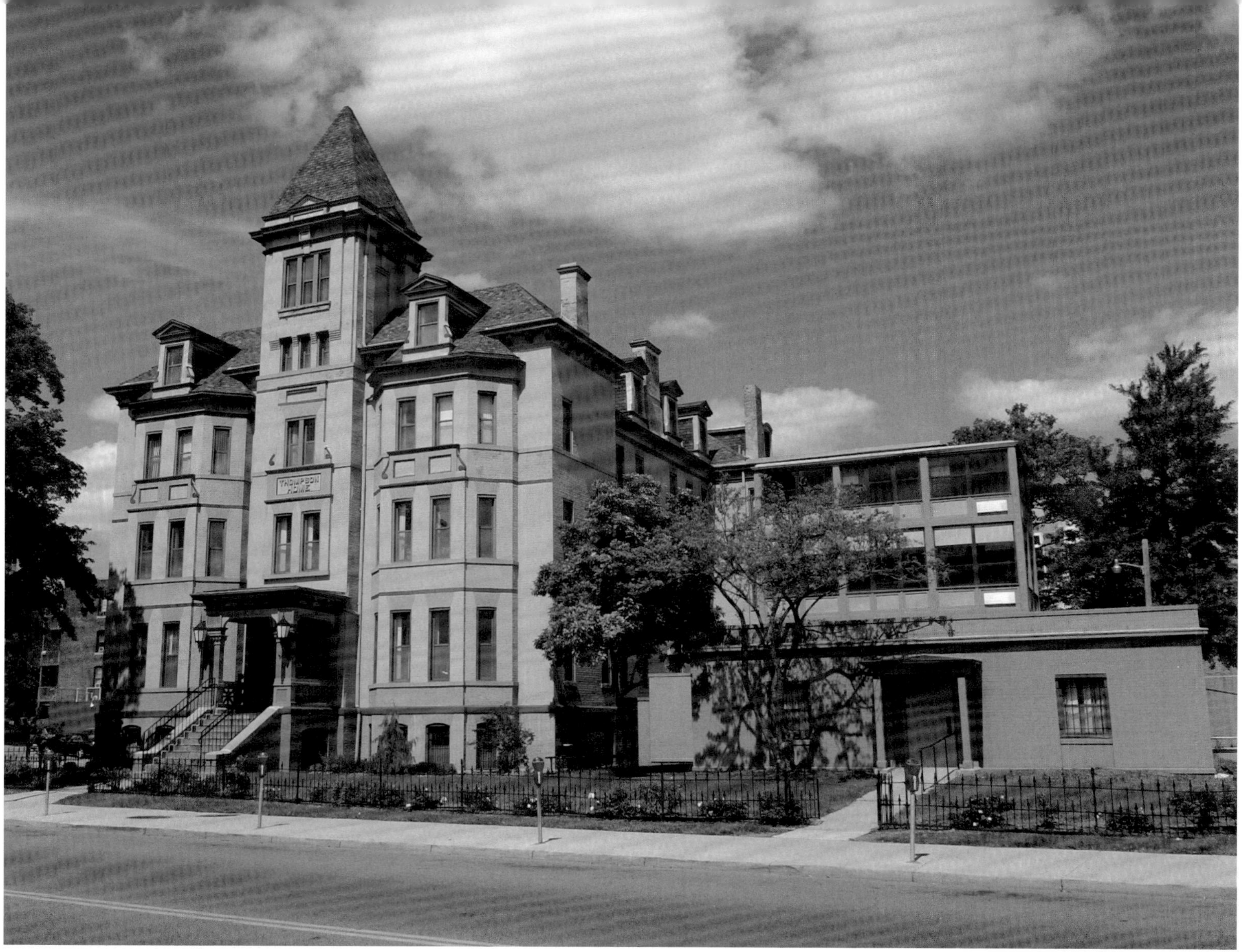

Thompson Home, 4756 Cass at Hancock. Originally opened in 1884, this stately Victorian home has been a fixture of WSU's campus for years. Built as a retirement home, then later home to the Faculty Club and then the School of Social Work, the Thompson Home is getting new life. In 2016, the Wayne State Board of Governors granted $350,000 for the building to be converted to accommodate sixty-five residents. The home reopened in fall 2017 as student housing for the College of Fine, Performing and Communication Arts. (Courtesy of Wayne State University Photographic Services.)

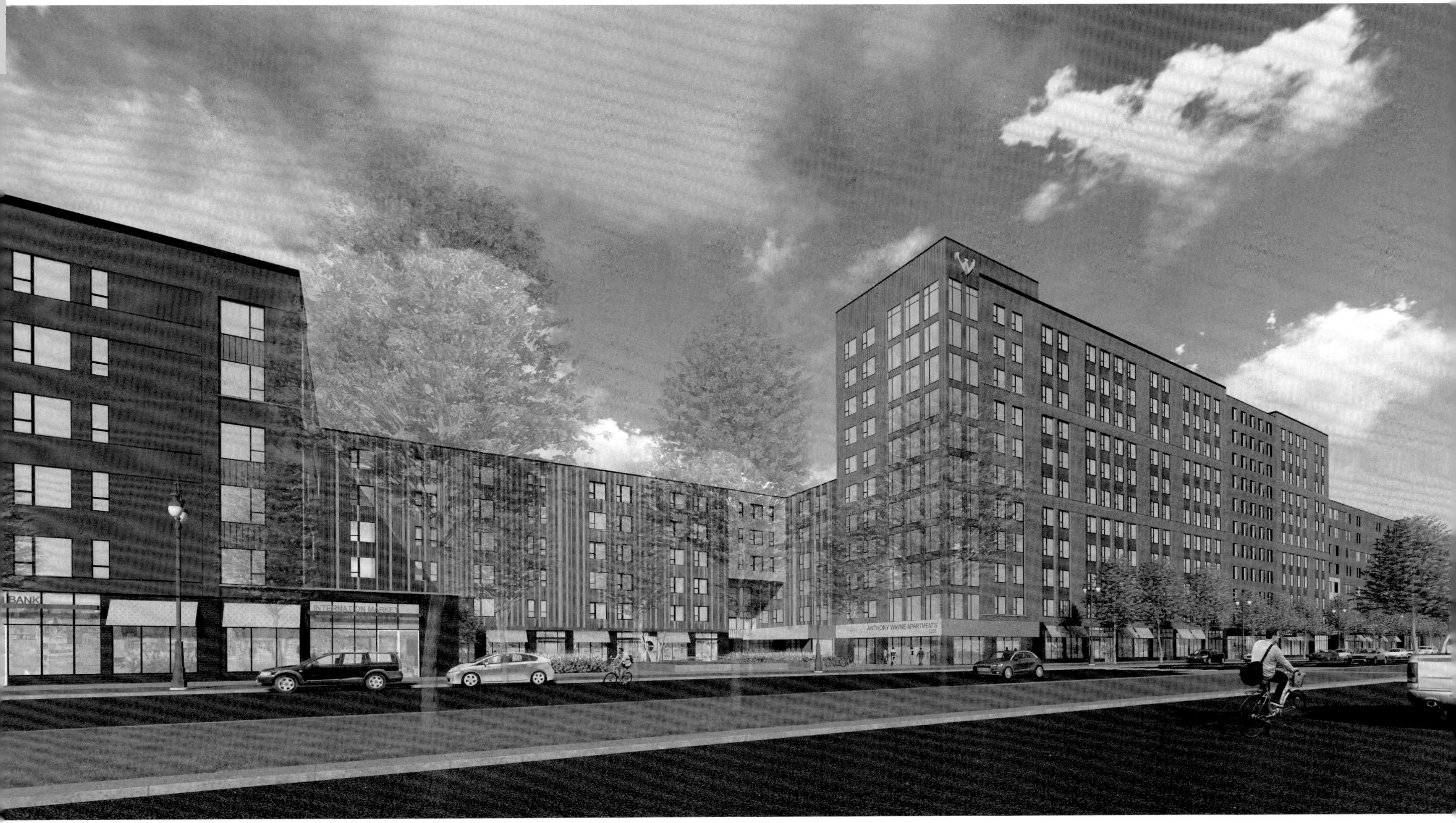

Anthony Wayne Drive Apartments at Warren Avenue. Part of a master plan to increase the amount of student housing available on campus, these two apartments will be built over surface parking lots. In addition, there are plans to demolish the Helen DeRoy Apartments and renovate the Chatsworth Apartments. The university partnered with Corvias Campus Living for the project, and the new apartments are designed by Hamilton Anderson. In addition, Corvias will be in charge of running student housing for the university.

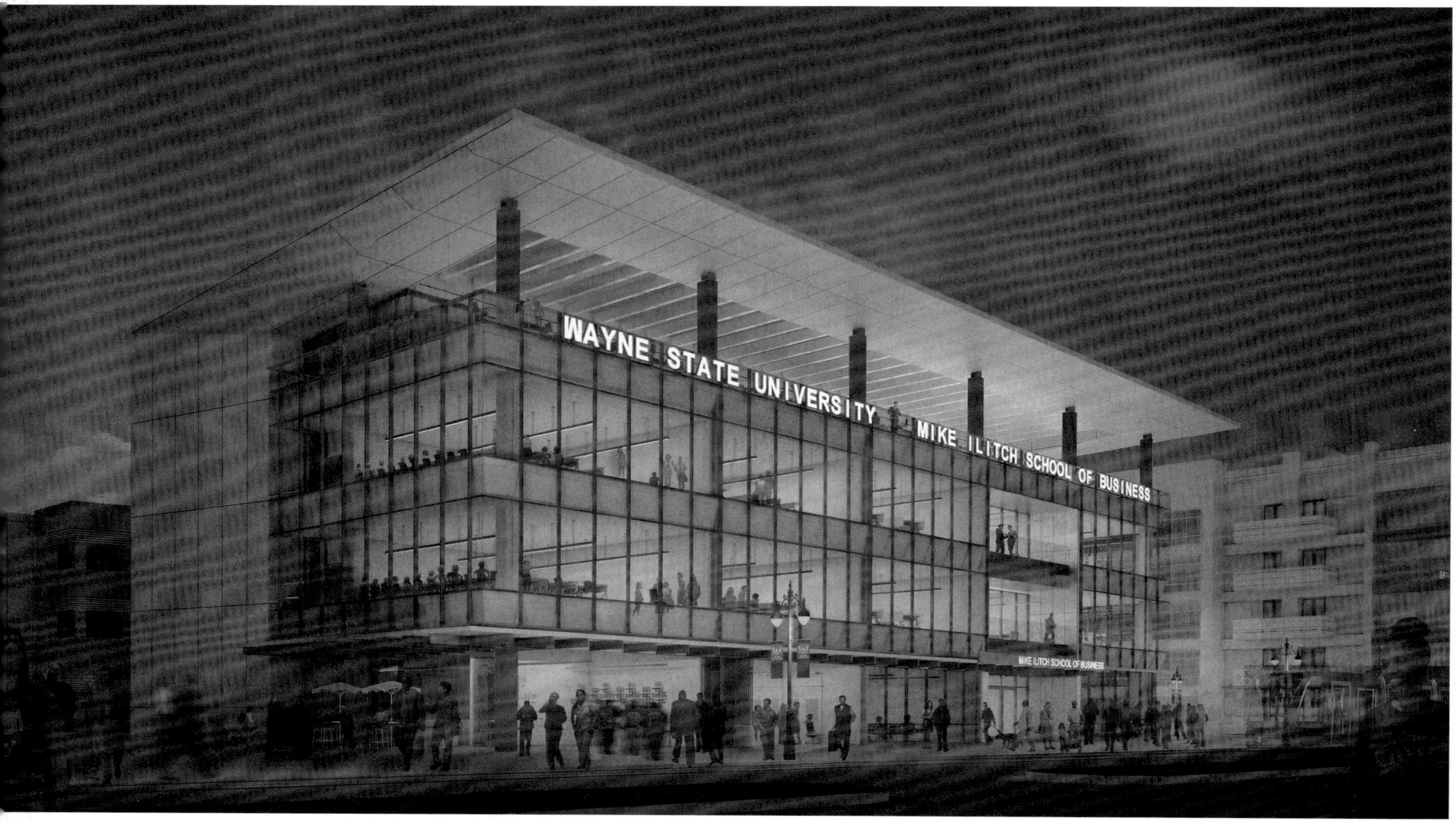

Mike Ilitch School of Business on Woodward Avenue. This new project will mean a new home for the business school on Woodward at Temple, near the Ilitches' District Detroit near downtown. The cost will be about $50 million, and the Ilitch family has contributed $35 million to the project. Ground was broken in July 2016, and the steelworks was completed in 2017. The building is set to open in 2018. (Rendering courtesy of Wayne State University and SmithGroupJJR.)

Students from the College of Fine, Performing and Communication Arts take part in the kickoff event for Wayne State's Sesquicentennial, January 26, 2018. (Courtesy Wayne State University Photographic Services.)

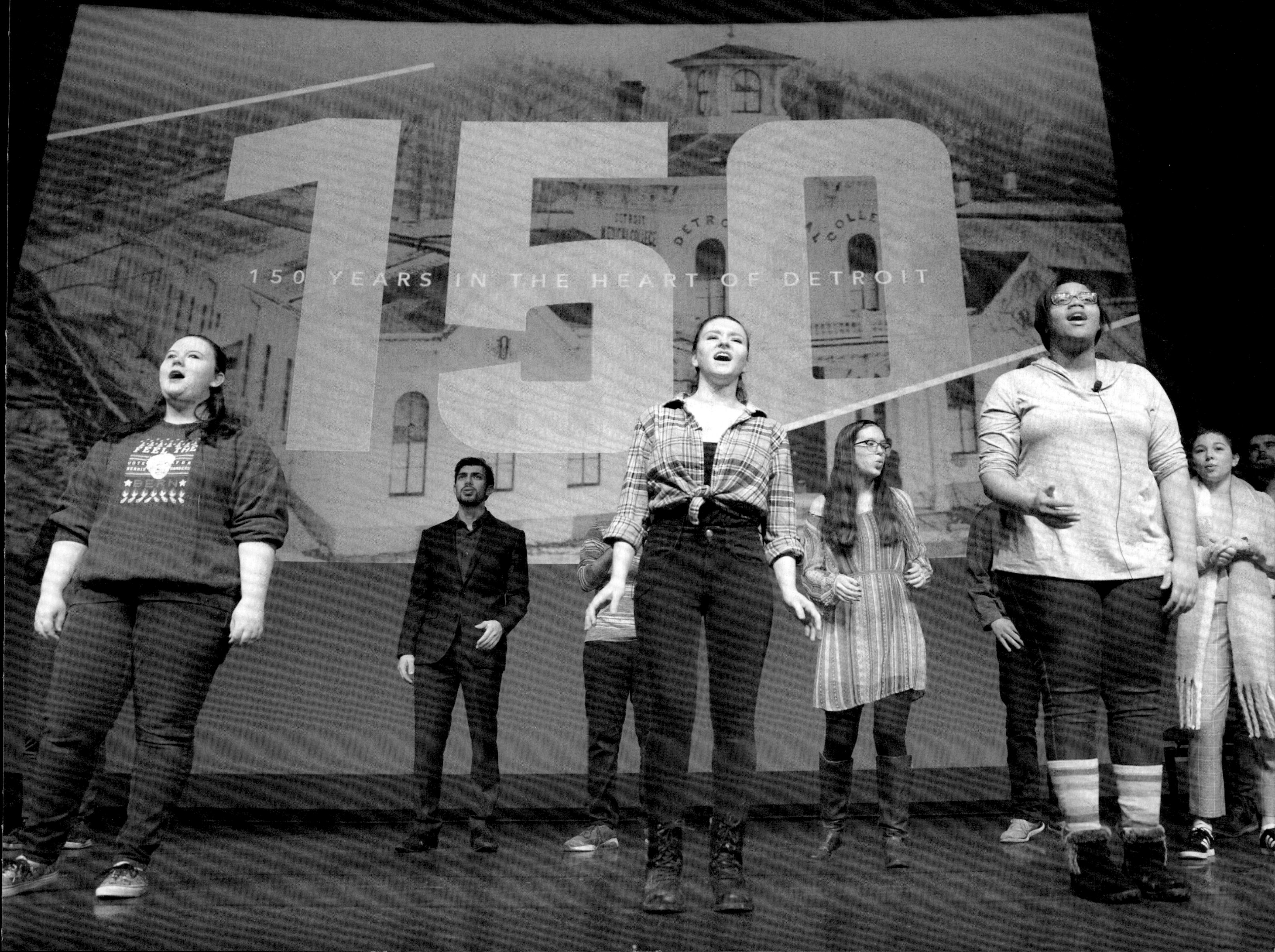
150
150 YEARS IN THE HEART OF DETROIT

APPENDIX A

WAYNE STATE UNIVERSITY PRESIDENTS

Frank Cody, superintendent of Detroit public schools, 1933–42

Warren Edward Bow, superintendent of Detroit public schools, 1942–45

David Dodds Henry, 1945–52

Clarence Beverly Hilberry, 1952–65

William Rea Keast, 1965–71

George Edgar Gullen Jr., 1971–78

Thomas Neville Bonner, 1978–82

David W. Adamany, 1982–97

Irvin D. Reid, 1997–2008

Jay Noren, 2008–11

Allan Gilmour, 2011–13

M. Roy Wilson, 2013–Present

APPENDIX B

TIMELINE OF MAJOR EVENTS AT WAYNE STATE UNIVERSITY

1868	Detroit Medical College founded
1875	Medical Alumni Association formed
1881	Detroit Normal Training School (predecessor to College of Education) founded
1883	Detroit Medical College moved to old YMCA building on Farmer Street
1885	Detroit Medical College and the Michigan College of Medicine merge to form the Detroit College of Medicine
1888	Normal Training School moved to Russell School
1889	Detroit College of Medicine building at St. Antoine and Mullett completed
1890	Normal Training School moved to Miami School, 1354 Broadway
1894	*The Leucocyte*, Detroit College of Medicine student magazine, first published
1895	Normal Training School moved to Washington Normal at Beaubien and St. Harriet
1896	Central High School building (later renamed the Main Building and then Old Main), 4841 Cass at Warren, completed

1904 David Mackenzie named principal of Central High School

1907 Major addition to Central High School completed

1913 First college classes held at Central High School

Detroit College of Medicine reorganized; renamed the Detroit College of Medicine and Surgery

1914 Normal Training School moved to Northwestern High School on West Grand Boulevard

1915 College classes at Central High School accredited by North Central Association

1917 Detroit Junior College authorized by state legislature, two-year course

Detroit College of Medicine admits first female students

Detroit Normal Training School admits first married women

1918 First edition of *The Collegian*, the Detroit Junior College student newspaper, published

Junior College Student Council formed; Old Gold and Kelly Green adopted as school colors

First evening classes and first summer session held at Detroit Normal Training School

First male students admitted to Detroit Normal Training School

Control of Detroit College of Medicine and Surgery transferred to Detroit Board of Education

1920 Detroit Normal Training School upgraded to a four-year school, renamed the Detroit Teachers College

1921 Detroit Public Library, Main Branch, 5201 Woodward, completed

1923 Detroit Junior College upgraded to a four-year institution, renamed the College of the City of Detroit, also known as City College

David Mackenzie appointed dean of the College of the City of Detroit

1924 Webster Hall Hotel, 5050 Cass, completed

Detroit Teachers College: first bachelor's degrees awarded

1925 College of the City of Detroit: first graduating class

1926 High school classes moved from Central High School to the new building at Roosevelt Field

Central High School building designated the Main Building of the College of the City of Detroit

1927 Tartars adopted as City College school mascot

Detroit City Law School founded

Detroit Institute of Arts, 5200 Woodward Avenue, completed

1928 College of Pharmacy founded

1929 Department of Engineering established

1930 Department of Nursing established

Detroit Teachers College moved to Main Building

1933 Detroit Board of Education combines six of its colleges—liberal arts, education, pharmacy, engineering, medicine, and a graduate school—into one university

1934 Name Wayne University adopted

1935 School of Social Affairs established; renamed School of Public Affairs and Social Work in 1936

First Homecoming Day

1936 Frank Cody, superintendent of Detroit public schools, appoints a committee to study the needs of Wayne University

Resident fee for tuition expanded from Detroit to all of Wayne County

1937 Warren Avenue wing to Main Building completed

Citizens' Committee recommends that the university acquire the three blocks north of Main Building for campus expansion

Detroit City Law School accredited by the American Bar Association and incorporated into Wayne University as the Law School

1939 Department of Business Administration established

1941 Engineering wing of Main Building completed

Wayne University Press formed (later renamed Wayne State University Press)

1942 Architect Suren Pilafian wins competition for developing a campus master plan

First block of real estate (Warren to Putnam, west of Cass) purchased for the Wayne University campus

College of Medicine staffs 36th General Hospital in Europe, which operates throughout the war in Algiers, Naples, and three cities in southern France

Horace H. Rackham Building, 106 Farnsworth Street, completed, the first new building in the Cultural Center of Detroit since 1927

1943 Michigan College of Mortuary Science purchased and renamed Department of Mortuary Science

1944 Second block (Putnam to Merrick) purchased for the Wayne University campus

1945 College of Nursing founded

Third block (Merrick to Kirby) purchased for the Wayne University campus

1946 Webster Hall Hotel (later renamed Mackenzie Hall) purchased, renamed the Student Center Building

Resident fee for tuition made statewide

1947 Peak of veteran enrollment: 7,685 in fall semester

1948 State Hall, 5143 Cass, completed

First doctoral degree, in biochemistry, awarded

1949 Science Hall, 5045 Cass, completed

Peak of postwar enrollment: 18,612 in calendar year

1950 Main Building officially renamed Old Main

First wing of the Engineering Building at 5050 Third Avenue occupied

School of Social Work given separate status from the School of Public Affairs

Edsel Ford Expressway (I-94) opened to traffic

1951 Detroit Historical Museum, 5401 Woodward at Kirby, completed

1952 Third and final wing of the Engineering Building, 5050 Third Avenue, completed

Radio station WDET-FM given to university by UAW-CIO

1953 General Library at 5244 Second Avenue and Science Library at 5294 Second Avenue completed

First section of John C. Lodge Freeway (M-10) opened to traffic

1954 Medical Science Building at 1401 Rivard Street completed; parts of Rivard, including this stretch, later become the Chrysler Service Drive running alongside the Chrysler Freeway

Tartar Field north of the Ford Expressway opens, replaces Kelsey Field

1955 Music Building of Community Arts Center, 5451 Cass, completed

1956 Governor G. Mennen Williams signs Public Act 183, providing for state control and support of Wayne University, which becomes Wayne State University; transition to state control begins July 1

Art Building of Community Arts Center, 5400 Second Avenue (Gullen Mall), completed

War Memorial Mall dedicated

Bonstelle Playhouse at 3424 Woodward purchased, renamed the Wayne University Theatre and later the Bonstelle Theatre

1957 State Hall addition (Cass wing) completed

1958 University Archives formed

Nonmatriculated category of students closed

Graduate division established; name "graduate school" dropped

Minoru Yamasaki presents master plan for campus

McGregor Memorial Conference Center, 495 Ferry, completed

1959 First six-member Wayne State University Board of Governors elected in statewide election; completion of transfer to state control

Monteith College founded

Community Arts Auditorium, 450 Kirby, completed

Alumni House/President's home, 441 Ferry, completed

Richard Cohn Memorial Building (College of Nursing), 5557 Cass, completed

Administrative Services Building (Bliss Building), 5946 Cass, purchased

Last of temporary barrack classrooms demolished

1960 College of Education Building, 5425 Second Avenue, completed

Life Science Building, 5000 Second Avenue (Gullen Mall), completed

1961 Student Center Building (Webster Hall) renamed David Mackenzie Hall

Chatsworth Tower and Chatsworth Annex, 630 and 650 Merrick, purchased

First Church of Christ, Scientist, 4743 Cass at Hancock, purchased; renamed Hilberry Theatre

Planning for University City urban renewal project begins

1962 Quarter system of scheduling the academic year instituted

1963 Helen Newberry Joy Residence for Women, 655 Kirby (now Reuther Mall), completed

Major additions to Detroit Public Library completed

Chrysler Freeway (I-75) opened to traffic

1964 Closing of Second Avenue north of Warren

Helen L. DeRoy Auditorium, 5203 Cass, completed

Meyer and Anna Prentis Building (School of Business Administration), 5201 Cass, completed

Division of Urban Extension established

1965 Shapero Hall of Pharmacy, 5501 Second Avenue Mall, completed

Physics Research Building, 666 Hancock, completed

Medical Research Building, 550 E. Canfield, completed

West Central Organization (WCO) emerges as a major opponent to the University City project

1966 Law School Building on Ferry Mall completed (including Law Library and Classroom Building)

Palmer Parking Structure (Parking Structure #1) completed

Wayne State University Department of Public Safety formed

1967 Detroit riots

The *Daily Collegian* replaced by the first edition of the *South End* student newspaper

Frederick C. Matthaei Physical Education and Recreation Building completed

Center for Urban Studies established

College of Education's library science program fully accredited by the American Library Association

1968 Vera Parshall Shiffman Medical Library, 4325 Brush, completed

Wayne State University Centennial Week, June 9–15

Glenn Manor Apartments (purchased in 1959), 645 Merrick, renamed Katherine Faville Residence Hall

Third Avenue renamed Anthony Wayne Drive

1969 University Center, 5221 Second Avenue Mall, completed; name changed to the Student Center in 1974

University Bookstore moved to first floor of Mackenzie Hall

1970 Speech and Languages Building, 906 W. Warren, completed

Chemistry Building, 5101 Cass, completed

Science Library, 5048 Second Avenue Mall, completed

PhD program in pharmacy offered

1971 General Lectures Building, 5045 Anthony Wayne Drive, completed

Blue Light Phone System—direct telephone lines to campus police—installed

1972 Gordon H. Scott Hall of Basic Medical Sciences, 540 E. Canfield, completed

Center for Chicano-Boricua Studies in Monteith College established

General Motors gives Wayne State University a six-story building at 6001 Cass and York; becomes Criminal Justice Building

American Association of University Professors (AAUP) certified as faculty bargaining agent

Affirmative Action policy adopted by Wayne State University Board of Governors

Parking Structure #2 on Anthony Wayne Drive completed

General Library renamed G. Flint Purdy Library; along with Kresge Library, becomes known as Purdy/Kresge Library

1973 The College of Lifelong Learning founded; successor to the Division of Urban Extension

Bachelor's degree offered by School of Social Work

Old Main's sixty-year-old powerhouse demolished

1974 Helen L. DeRoy Apartments, 5200 Anthony Wayne, completed

Wayne State joins Great Lakes Intercollegiate Conference

Reuther Mall, formerly Kirby Mall, dedicated

Ludington Plaza dedicated

Medical Science Building at 1400 Chrysler Drive renamed Health Sciences Building

College of Pharmacy and Division of Allied Health Programs merge; renamed College of Pharmacy and Allied Health Professions

1975 Walter P. Reuther Library, 5401 Cass, completed

University Bookstore, 5125 Second Avenue Mall, completed

PhD program in nursing offered

Preservation Wayne formed

Board of Governors votes to end Monteith College; phaseout to be completed by 1981

Speech and Languages Building renamed Alex Manoogian Hall

1976 Forest Apartments, 460 W. Forest, completed

Warren Avenue widening finished

Medical Research Building renamed Helen Vera Prentis Lande Medical Research Building

1977 Campaign by Preservation Wayne to preserve the David Mackenzie House begins

1978 Thompson Home, 4756 Cass, purchased

1979 Second Avenue Mall renamed Gullen Mall

Detroit Science Center, 5020 John R Avenue, completed

1980 Semester system of scheduling the academic year reinstated, replacing quarter system

1981 Merrill-Palmer Institute acquired by the university

1984 Health Sciences Building, 1400 Chrysler, renamed Shapero Hall

Barnes and Noble begins operating University Bookstore

1985 College of Urban, Labor and Metropolitan Affairs founded

College of Fine and Performing Arts founded

Bachelor's degree offered by Mortuary Science

Shapero Hall, 5501 Gullen Mall, renamed Natural Science Building

Science Library renamed Science and Engineering Library

1986 Mail-in system for class registration introduced

Building at 818 W. Hancock purchased for use by bioengineering department

1987 Expansion of Engineering Building completed

Parking Structure #5 on Anthony Wayne Drive completed

Community Services Building at 51 W. Warren purchased for use by Psychology Department

Helen Newberry Joy Residence reopened as Student Services Center

Williams Mall (formerly Merrick Street) dedicated

Linsell House dedicated as the College of Fine and Performing Arts

1988 Programs in Speech and Rhetorical Processes, Journalism, and Radio-TV-Film transferred from the College of Liberal Arts to the College of Fine and Performing Arts

1989 Africana Studies Department established

St. Andrew's Memorial Episcopal Church (1902), 918 Ludington Mall, purchased

College of Fine and Performing Arts renamed College of Fine, Performing and Communication Arts

Louis M. Elliman Clinical Research Building, medical school, completed

1990 Wayne State University and the University of Windsor sign reciprocity agreement; Canadian Studies minor offered

Faculty/Administration Building, 656 Reuther Mall, completed

Historic William Rands House (1913) rehabilitated to serve as the School of Business Administration Annex

1991 Mackenzie Hall demolished by implosion

Leonard Woodcock Wing of the Walter P. Reuther Library completed

Biological Sciences Building, 5047 Gullen Mall, completed

1992 College of Science founded

1993 Division of Library Science renamed the Library and Information Science Program

Horace H. Rackham Building, 60 Farnsworth Street, leased by the university

1994 Wayne State University classified as a Research I university by Carnegie Foundation

Major renovation of Old Main begins

Wayne State University Press moves to newly renovated Leonard Simons Building (formerly Fisher Wallpaper and Paint), 4809 Woodward

Refurbishment of St. Andrew's Memorial Episcopal Church

1995 Academic/Administration Building, 5700 Cass at Palmer, completed

University Tower Apartments, 4500 Cass, completed

1996 Manufacturing Engineering Building, 4815 Fourth, completed

Santa Fe and Katherine Faville apartment buildings demolished

1997 Elaine L. Jacob Gallery addition to Old Main completed

Major renovation of Old Main completed

David Adamany Undergraduate Library, 5155 Gullen Mall, completed

Charles H. Wright Museum of African American History, 315 E. Warren at Brush, completed

1998 Telephone system for class registration introduced

1999 Warriors replace Tartars as school mascot

Max Jacob House, 451 Reuther, becomes President's House

2000 Mort Harris Recreation and Fitness Center, 5210 Gullen Mall, completed

Addition to Law School completed

2001 College of Pharmacy and Allied Health Professions renamed College of Pharmacy and Health Sciences

2002 North Residence Hall, 695 Williams Mall, completed

Welcome Center, 42 W. Warren, completed

University Bookstore, 82 W. Warren, completed

Eugene Applebaum College of Pharmacy and Health Sciences, 259 Mack, completed

Maccabees Building, 5057 Woodward at Putnam, purchased

Online system for class registration introduced

2003 South Residence Hall, 5110 Anthony Wayne Drive, completed

College of Lifelong Learning transferred to the College of Urban, Labor and Metropolitan Affairs

2004 TechOne, 440 Burroughs at Cass, first phase of TechTown project, completed

Helen Newberry Joy Residence demolished

2005 Towers Residence Hall, 655 W. Kirby, completed

College of Science and College of Liberal Arts merge; renamed College of Liberal Arts and Sciences

College of Urban, Labor and Metropolitan Affairs dissolved; all degree programs transferred to other colleges

North Hall renamed Ghafari Hall

Chatsworth Annex demolished

2006 Planning for South University Village begins

2007 Construction for South University Village, Woodward between Forest and Canfield, begins

Construction begins on Engineering Building addition, Marvin I. Danto Engineering Development Center

Detroit Institute of Arts renovations completed

Forest Apartments demolished

2008 Wayne State University Board of Governors establishes the Irvin D. Reid Honors College

South University Village completed

South Hall renamed Leon H. Atchison Hall

Marvin I. Danto Engineering Development Center completed

2009 Richard J. Mazurek Medical Education Commons

2011 The Warrior football team plays its first NCAA Division II game

2012 Construction begins on Integrative Biosciences Center

2013 McGregor Conference Memorial Center renovated

2015 Student Center Building renovations completed

The School of Business Administration renamed the Mike Ilitch School of Business

Integrative Biosciences Center completed

2016 Construction begins on Mike Ilitch School of Business

Police department celebrates its fifty-year anniversary

2017 Harwell Baseball Field Building completed